# NEGOTIATION THEORY AND STRATEGY

# NEGOTIATION THEORY AND STRATEGY

**Russell Korobkin**
*Professor of Law*
*University of California, Los Angeles*

**ASPEN LAW & BUSINESS**
A Division of Aspen Publishers, Inc.
New York          Gaithersburg

Printed in the United States of America.

1 2 3 4 5 6 7 8 9 0

**Library of Congress Cataloging-in-Publication Data**

Negotiation theory and strategy / Russell Korobkin
    p. cm.
  Includes bibliographical references and index.
  ISBN 0-7355-2770-9
    1. Negotiation in business. 2. Negotiation. 3. Dispute resolution (Law)
  4. Strategic planning. I. Korobkin, Russell.
HD58.6 .N468 2000
658.4'052 — dc21

                                  2001053827

# About Aspen Law & Business
# Legal Education Division

With a dedication to preserving and strengthening the long-standing tradition of publishing excellence in legal education, Aspen Law & Business continues to provide the highest quality teaching and learning resources for today's law school community. Careful development, meticulous editing, and an unmatched responsiveness to the evolving needs of today's discerning educators combine in the creation of our outstanding casebooks, coursebooks, textbooks, and study aids.

**ASPEN LAW & BUSINESS**
A Division of Aspen Publishers, Inc.
A Wolters Kluwer Company
*www.aspenpublishers.com*

To my parents, who taught me love of learning and pride in accomplishment

# SUMMARY OF CONTENTS

# CONTENTS

# PREFACE

Negotiating is a routine part of the professional life of virtually all lawyers, regardless of their area of specialty. With the possible exception of writing, no subject is as important for lawyers to understand thoroughly and practice competently. In the 21st century, law school curriculums are reflecting this reality more and more. Most law schools offer a course devoted entirely to the study of negotiation, many schools offer multiple courses, and a few have even developed special programs in the field of negotiation and dispute resolution. This book was written with the goal of providing an in-depth, intellectually rigorous yet practically useful introduction to the study of negotiation for law students, as merited by the importance of negotiation to the practice of law.

The design of the book reflects, of course, my personal views about the study of negotiation. The following four themes, I believe, are reinforced throughout the volume, and give the book its unique character:

First, negotiation is an inherently interdisciplinary subject. The reprinted excerpts, narrative sections, and note material in this book draw heavily on insights from a variety of social sciences (particularly economics, psychology, and sociology), as well as more traditional legal sources such as judicial opinions and law review articles.

Second, lawyers and other professional negotiators are best served by developing a thorough understanding of the structure of negotiation rather than merely mastering the execution of a list of tactics. The book attempts first to provide a conceptual framework for understanding negotiation, and then to consider how tactics that negotiators use and issues that arise at the bargaining table fit into that framework. By leaving the classroom with such a framework, students will have the tools to teach themselves to be successful negotiators throughout their lives as they continually face the need to adapt their skills to new contexts and changing situations.

Third, the basic structure of negotiation is the same regardless of the particular bargaining context. Many of the examples provided in the book come from contexts in which lawyers often find themselves. And some of the concepts covered, i.e., challenges and opportunities created by the relationship of a principal party and his agent, are of particular relevance to lawyers, given the context in which they work. Nonetheless, the core concepts taught in the book can be applied to all negotiation situations, not just legal ones. Students should benefit from this approach whatever their career goals. Similarly, although the book is written for law students, it can be successfully used for a course taught to graduate students in other fields, or even advanced undergraduate students.

Fourth, the goal of equipping students with the ability to implement what they have learned in their daily personal and professional dealings is best served by the following three pedagogical steps:

1) Communicate intellectually challenging concepts.
2) Reinforce those concepts by challenging students to apply them to new situations and to their life experiences.
3) Provide an opportunity for students to tailor the concepts for their own use in an interactive setting.

Each chapter of the book exposes students to challenging theoretical concepts through a combination of narrative material, excerpts of published books and articles, and note material that further explains and builds on points made in the narrative and excerpted sections. The "discussion questions and problems" that end each chapter provide an opportunity for students to explore and apply the reading material in a class discussion format. Finally, a recommended negotiation simulation accompanies each chapter. These exercises, provided in the teacher's manual that accompanies this book, were selected or designed to reinforce the concepts emphasized in the relevant chapter.

The book contains 15 chapters — or approximately one chapter per week for a one-semester law school course — divided into five parts. Each part adds a new layer of complexity to the core concepts of the course. Although the book has a conscious progression and is designed to be taught in its entirety in one semester, it was also designed to be flexible in order to accommodate instructors with different approaches to teaching negotiation and/or particular areas of interest. No supplementary materials are needed, but instructors who wish to assign supplementary reading materials or additional simulation exercises can easily combine two chapters into a week of study or skip some chapters altogether (especially after Part II) in order to free up additional time. Instructors can also choose to assign the chapters in a different order to better suit their conception of the course without creating undue confusion on the part of students.

---

Many people have influenced my approach to thinking about and teaching negotiation, so a number of grateful acknowledgements are in order. As a law student at Stanford University in the early 1990s, I studied negotiation with Professor Robert Mnookin (now at Harvard), and then became a graduate student research fellow at the Stanford Center on Conflict and Negotiation (SCCN). Although my views on negotiation are constantly evolving, I owe my interest in negotiation theory and the interdisciplinary perspective with which I approach the subject to these experiences generally and to Bob Mnookin in particular.

A large number of faculty associated with the SCCN at that time and students associated with the SCCN who have gone on to teach and study negotiation have influenced and continue to influence my thinking on the subject, including Janet Cooper Alexander, Paul Brest, Lee Ross, and the late Amos Tversky of Stanford, Ian Ayres (now at Yale), Richard Birke (now at Willamette), Craig Fox (now at Duke), Jeff Rachlinski (now at Cornell), Andrea Kupfer Schneider (now at Marquette), Eric Talley (now at the University of Southern California), and especially Chris Guthrie (now at the University of Missouri), with whom I have collaborated on a number of articles. In addition to this group, thanks are due to many other colleagues who have generously given me their advice and/or comments on some portions or all of this book at its various stages, including Linda Babcock, David Binder, Jennifer Gerarda Brown, Rachel Croson, John Fleming, Don Gifford, Ken Klee, Al Korobkin, Michael Meurer, Janice Nadler, Alan Rau, Ed Sherman, and Tom Ulen.

Finally, this book could not have been completed — at least not this decade — without the excellent research assistance provided by Leib Lerner and Paul Foust and the support of the UCLA School of Law administration and library staff. And, of course, my greatest appreciation is due to my wife, Sarah, for her support, encouragement, and relentless good humor throughout this project.

Russell Korobkin

February 2002

# ACKNOWLEDGMENTS

Axelrod, Robert, The Evolution of Cooperation. Copyright © 1984 by Robert Axelrod. Reprinted by permission of Basic Books, a member of Perseus Books, L.L.C.

Brett, Jeanne M., Culture and Negotiation, 35 International Journal of Psychology 97 (2000). Copyright © 2000. Reprinted by permission of The International Union of Psychological Science and of the author.

Cialdini, Robert B., Influence: Science and Practice. Copyright © 1993 by Allyn & Bacon. Reprinted/adapted by permission.

Craver, Charles B., & David W. Barnes, Gender, Risk Taking, and Negotiation Performance, 5 Mich. J. Gender & L. 299 (1999). Copyright © 1999 by Charles B. Craver and David W. Barnes. Reprinted with permission.

Craver, Charles B., Negotiation Ethics: How to be Deceptive Without Being Dishonest/How to be Assertive Without Being Offensive, 38 S. Tex. L. Rev. 713 (1997). Copyright © 1997 by South Texas Law Review, Inc. Reprinted with permission.

Fisher, Roger, William Ury & Bruce Patton, Getting to Yes 2/e. Copyright © 1981, 1991 by Roger Fisher and William Ury. Reprinted by permission of Houghton Mifflin Company. All rights reserved.

Gelfand, Michelle J., & Sophia Christakopoulou, Culture and Negotiator Cognition: Judgment Accuracy and Negotiation Processes in Individualistic and Collectivistic Cultures, in Organizational Behavior and Human Decision Processes, Volume 79, 248-269. Copyright © 1999 by Academic Press. Reprinted by permission of the publisher.

Gifford, Donald G., Legal Negotiation: Theory and Applications. Copyright © 1989 by West Publishing Co. Reprinted with permission of West Group.

abridged with the permission of The Free Press, a division of Simon & Schuster, Inc. Copyright © 1986 by David A. Lax and James K. Sebenius.

Loder, Reed Elizabeth, Moral Truthseeking and the Virtuous Negotiator, 8 Geo. J. Legal Ethics 45 (1994). Copyright © 1994 by the Georgetown Journal of Legal Ethics. Reprinted with permission.

Loewenstein, George, Samuel Issacharoff, Colin Camerer & Linda Babcock, Self-Serving Assessments of Fairness and Pretrial Bargaining, 22 J. Legal Stud. 135 (1993). Published by The Journal of Legal Studies, the University of Chicago. Copyright © 1993 by the University of Chicago. All rights reserved. Reprinted by permission of the authors and the publisher.

Lubet, Steven, Notes on the Bedouin Horse Trade or "Why Won't the Market Clear, Daddy?", 74 Tex. L. Rev. 1039 (1996). Copyright © 1996 the Texas Law Review Association. Reprinted by permission.

Menkel-Meadow, Carrie, Toward Another View of Legal Negotiation: The Structure of Problem-Solving, 31 UCLA L. Rev. 754 (1984). Originally published in 31 UCLA L. Rev. 754. Copyright © 1984 The Regents of the University of California. All rights reserved. Reprinted by permission of the author, the publisher and William S. Hein & Co., Inc.

Mnookin, Robert H., Why Negotiations Fail: An Exploration of Barriers to the Resolution of Conflict, 8 Ohio St. J. Disp. Res. 235 (1993). Copyright © 1993 by the Ohio State Journal on Dispute Resolution. Reprinted with permission.

Mnookin, Robert H., Scott R. Peppet & Andrew S. Tulumello, The Tension Between Empathy and Assertiveness, 12 Negotiation J. 217 (1996). Copyright © 1996 by Kluwer Academic/Plenum Publisher. Reprinted with permission.

Moore, Christopher W., The Caucus: Private Meetings that Promote Settlement, 16 Mediation Quarterly 87 (1987). Copyright © 1987 by Jossey-Bass Inc., Publishers and Jossey-Bass Limited. Reprinted by permission of Jossey-Bass, Inc., a subsidiary of John Wiley & Sons, Inc.

Rachlinski, Jeffrey J., Gains, Losses, and the Psychology of Litigation, 70 S. Cal. L. Rev. 113 (1996). Copyright © 1996 by the Southern California Law Review. Reprinted with permission.

# NEGOTIATION THEORY AND STRATEGY

# PART I

# INTRODUCTION

Negotiation is an interactive communication process by which two or more parties who lack identical interests attempt to find a way to coordinate their behavior or allocate scarce resources in a way that will make them better off than they could be if they were to act alone. This broad definition suggests that negotiation is nearly as ubiquitous as human interaction itself. Nearly every person negotiates over small matters, if not large ones, on a daily basis: with friends, family members, colleagues, merchants, or customers.

Given the prevalence of negotiation in daily life, it is unsurprising to observe that most lawyers negotiate on a regular basis as part of their professional responsibilities. Litigators invoke the negotiation process in virtually every case, while invoking the adjudication process relatively rarely. Fewer than 5 percent of all civil litigation matters are tried to judgment. A significant percentage are resolved by judges on the pleadings or following dispositive motions, but most are resolved by the parties themselves rather than by the judicial system. Criminal trials are likewise rare events, at least compared to plea bargains, by which prosecutors and defense attorneys resolve the vast majority of criminal prosecutions through negotiation. Transactional lawyers are principally engaged in the business of negotiating deals or other business relationships on behalf of their clients. Regulatory lawyers of various types attempt to conform the behavior of their clients to the relevant legal regimes, but even here disputes must be resolved and uncertain areas clarified, and this is accomplished largely through the negotiation process. Thus, although there are many important differences between various types of law practice, an understanding of and facility with the negotiation process is useful for all lawyers and critical to the success of most. Whatever your law-practice interest, this book aims to provide you with such an understanding and facility.

In light of the centrality of negotiation to the practice of law, the question at the forefront of the minds of most lawyers and law students studying the subject is "how should I negotiate?" Some negotiation texts designed for legal audiences, as well as many designed for more general audiences, attempt to respond to this question by providing what amount to instruction manuals, promising success to negotiators who complete a series of discrete activities in a specified order. Other texts provide laundry lists of tactical tricks, the usefulness of which is demonstrated through various anecdotes about how the author used the recommended tactics advantageously in his or her particular line of work or personal life.

This book, in contrast, is based on the premise that "one-size-fits-all," "how-to" approaches to the subject of negotiation are misguided. The reason is not that all approaches to negotiation are equally valid, or that tactics have no effect on bargaining outcomes. The reason is that negotiation is too context-dependent an activity for any particular approach or set of tactics to be universally effective. The answer to the question, "how should I negotiate?," depends on the specific situation and the approach of the other negotiator, as well as on your goals and your personality.

Rather than focusing on the question of "how should I negotiate?," this book is organized around the questions "what occurs during a negotiation?" and "why?" Put another way, the primary focus of the book is on *understanding* negotiation, rather than on *doing* negotiation. The reason for this is simple. Negotiation success requires the negotiator to adapt her approach and tactics to particular negotiating environments rather than following a standard script. And to be adaptive, the negotiator must be equipped with an understanding of the fundamental elements of the negotiation process. Armed with such an understanding, the negotiator can continually develop situation-specific tactical approaches throughout her career. To help you develop a thorough understanding of the negotiation process, this book combines cutting edge insights from economics, psychology, and sociology, as well as from legal texts and the most sophisticated works aimed specifically at lawyers.

Although this book is geared toward helping you develop an *un-*

*derstanding* of negotiation rather than attempting to tell you how to negotiate, it also challenges you to use your insights into the process of negotiation to begin the life-long task of developing situation-specific approaches to negotiating. First, narrative material, excerpted readings, and notes included in each chapter raise and discuss tactical negotiating issues and particular negotiation skills. Second, each chapter ends with a series of "discussion questions and problems" that require you to consider how you might apply what you have learned about the negotiation process to specific negotiating situations. Third, negotiation exercises and simulations that your instructor will assign to complement the materials in this book will give you an opportunity to apply what you learn in highly contextual, actual negotiating settings. Throughout this course, then, you should focus on achieving two objectives: developing a thorough understanding of negotiation theory and translating your theoretical understanding into a practical approach to negotiating in your professional and personal life.

Understanding a complex process like negotiation requires the development of conceptual models. As this book addresses various negotiation issues, it will continually attempt to provide structures to organize the complex features of negotiation into manageable categories. The challenge for you is to begin to view various features of negotiation in a structured way that can help you make sense out of the various negotiating situations you observe and find yourself in throughout your career. Part I of the book introduces you to this process and provides an overview in two ways. First, it describes the tasks that are common to negotiations in the order they most often occur. Second, it presents a series of different conceptual structures for viewing and understanding negotiation as a coherent activity rather than as a series of only loosely related tactics and activities.

Part II of the book, Chapters 2-6, presents a conceptual structure for understanding the strategic dynamics of all negotiating situations. The fundamental concept of this structure is the "bargaining zone," defined as the distance between the maximum amount that the buyer is willing to pay for the subject of the negotiation and the minimum amount that the seller is willing to accept to give up the subject of the negotiation. All negotiating activities and tactics can be understood as attempts to (a) identify whether there is in fact a bargaining zone (otherwise a negotiated agreement is impossible),

(b) expand the bargaining zone so that a resulting agreement is more valuable to both negotiators, (c) capture most or all of the value represented by the bargaining zone, or (d) find a method of agreeing on a deal at a specific point within the bargaining zone. Mastering these concepts will help you to understand why negotiators do what they do in bargaining situations as well as guide your actions in negotiating situations.

Part III of the book, Chapters 7-9, shifts focus from the underlying strategic structure of the negotiation process to how the identity of and basic choices made by the negotiators affect bargaining. This Part considers the effect on bargaining of negotiators' propensity to reveal or conceal private information known only to them, the interpersonal and communication styles that negotiators adopt in conflict situations, and the gender and cultural backgrounds of negotiators.

Parts I through III implicitly assume a simple two-party model of negotiation, in which one principal party negotiates against one other principal party with conflicting interests. Many negotiations — and most legal negotiations in particular — have a more complex structure. When lawyers negotiate, they usually do so as agents acting on behalf of clients, such that what appears to be a two-party negotiation situation really involves a minimum of four individuals (two principal parties and their two lawyers). In addition, many bargaining situations are multilateral rather than bilateral, meaning that there are more than two principal parties at the negotiating table. And the increasing use of mediation in negotiation settings can bring at least one additional individual to the bargaining process — the mediator — who is neither a principal party nor an agent for a principal. Part IV, Chapters 10-12, considers the extent to which negotiation dynamics change, and the extent to which they do not change, when negotiations involve more than two parties.

The first four Parts of the book treat negotiation as a purely private process, in which negotiator behavior is dependent only on the personal desires of the negotiators, rules that the negotiators themselves might implicitly or explicitly agree to, and perhaps social norms. Although negotiation is largely a private process, it is governed by some publicly prescribed rules that can affect the course of bargaining and negotiation outcomes. Part V, Chapters 13-15, takes account of this fact by considering the law of negotiation, including rules proscribing misrepresentation and requiring good faith that apply to all negotiation contexts and the more complex legal regime governing litigation settlement negotiations specifically.

**Chapter 1**

# Toward a Conceptual Approach to Negotiation

## A. THE STEPS OF NEGOTIATION: AN OVERVIEW

Because specific negotiation dynamics vary so considerably across contexts, it is impossible to provide a single "script" to advise negotiators on how to navigate through the process. It is possible, however, to provide an overview by describing a small number of negotiation tasks common to most negotiations at a general level of detail. This section describes these tasks in the order in which they most commonly take place. Even if you lack formal negotiating experience in legal or business contexts, you have obtained a great deal of informal negotiating experience throughout your lifetime; consequently, the steps of the negotiating process described in this section should seem familiar to you. Throughout the remainder of this book, the tasks described in this section will be analyzed in considerable depth, with attention paid in particular to the questions of precisely what negotiators attempt to accomplish through these tasks, and what the strategic decisions are that negotiators must make as they decide how to pursue these tasks. At this introductory stage of the course, however, it is important only that you gain a basic appreciation of what the tasks are.

First, all negotiations begin with some amount of pre-bargaining preparation. Later, when opposing negotiators communicate, they generally exchange information, and then make offers and counteroffers. Finally, the bargaining interaction eventually concludes with the negotiators either reaching an agreement or declaring an impasse and accepting that they will not reach agreement. Although these basic negotiation tasks, or steps, are presented here in an order that is roughly chronological, you should not take the chronology too literally. Negotiators often undertake these tasks concurrently rather than strictly sequentially, or they undertake them in a different order entirely. For example, a negotiator might make an offer before any information is exchanged, and it is common for offers and counteroffers to be intertwined with an ongoing exchange of information. In some cases, analysis that would ideally be conducted as part of pre-bargaining preparation is undertaken by negotiators after some preliminary exchange of information or even after the presentation of initial offers.

## 1.  Preparation

Pre-bargaining preparation can be understood as three related activities: the negotiator must clearly understand his own situation and interests, understand the situation and interests of his opponent, and synthesize the competing interests in order to conceive of a strategy for reconciling them.

### a.   "Internal" Preparation

The first of these tasks can be labeled "internal" preparation. This involves the negotiator critically assessing (a) what he desires to achieve from the negotiation, (b) what is the relative importance of his various desires, and (c) what would be a minimally acceptable agreement (which in turn requires the negotiator to identify what the consequences would be of failing to reach an agreement). The appropriate extent of this analysis will, of course, depend on the specific negotiating context.

Consider, first, a relatively uncomplicated and routine type of negotiation, similar to negotiations we all engage in on a daily basis. Husband, preparing to telephone his wife in the afternoon, might conduct his "preparation" in a few seconds without much conscious thought about what he is doing by (1) identifying that he would like to make evening plans with Wife that include going out to a nice restaurant for dinner and then seeing an action movie, (2) noting that he cares more about going to a nice restaurant than attending any particular type of movie, or any movie at all, and (3) determining that if Wife has very definite ideas that are contrary to his he is ultimately willing to agree to any set of evening plans rather than have an argument, so long as the plan does not require him to both go to the grocery store and cook dinner.

More complex negotiations, of course, will often indicate a considerably more complex approach to internal preparation. Corporation, considering entering into a major joint venture with another business, will more likely spend a great deal of effort in pre-bargaining preparation, evaluating the desirability of a range of organizational structures, contract terms, and the alternative business possibilities that would exist if no agreement is reached. Whether a negotiation is a simple personal interaction or a complex business or legal interaction, internal preparation requires the negotiator to evaluate and understand his preferences.

A well-prepared negotiator will also consider what information he lacks that the opposing negotiator might provide that could change his evaluation. Husband, for example, might determine that his preference for seeing an action movie might be altered if Wife has read a positive film review of a comedy or a romance. Corporation might determine that the optimal organizational structure for the joint venture could change depending on what it learns about the particular capabilities of its joint venture partner, or that it might be willing to accept a less desirable set of contract terms if it can verify that the partner has more to offer than Corporation initially thought.

When a lawyer negotiates, of course, it is usually on behalf of a client. In this situation, the negotiator needs to understand the client's preferences rather than his own. Thus, internal preparation is a collaborative rather than a solitary task, in which interviewing the client takes on a central role.

### b.  "External" Preparation

External preparation requires the negotiator to assess the likely desires, requirements, and alternatives of the opposing negotiator. As is true for internal preparation, the amount and complexity of external preparation depends a great deal on the negotiation's context. Husband preparing to telephone Wife might briefly consider whether Wife enjoys action movies or prefers some other form of entertainment, and whether if the two do not agree on a preferred evening plan Wife is likely to consent to his proposal, argue strenuously for what she would prefer, or make separate plans. Defendant preparing to negotiate over a lawsuit recently filed against her by Plaintiff will want to assess whether Plaintiff desires money, an apology for past actions, a promise to refrain from future actions, or some other form of redress. Defendant will also want to assess what steps Plaintiff is likely to take if no negotiated agreement is reached and how valuable those options are to Plaintiff. If, for example, Plaintiff has a strong legal position and sufficient funds to wage a litigation battle, then Plaintiff is likely to bring his case to trial if he is unable to fulfill his goals through the negotiation process. If his legal claim is weak, in contrast, he might either be willing to dismiss his suit in return for a minimal payment from Defendant, or he might dismiss the suit even in the event that the litigants fail to reach agreement.

As part of external preparation, negotiators will also often consider what information might alter the opponent's positions. This usually means considering what information might change the opponent's preferences or convince the opponent that his alternatives to reaching a negotiated agreement are less desirable than he previously believed. For example, if Defendant is more willing to refrain from future activity than provide monetary compensation for past activity, she might consider how she might persuade Plaintiff to place a higher value on such future restraint and a lower value on compensation for past actions. If Defendant believes that Plaintiff's willingness to accept a negotiated settlement depends on Plaintiff's evaluation of the strength of his legal claim, Defendant will consider what facts and legal arguments might undermine Plaintiff's confidence in his case.

Because it is easier to know one's own mind and options than to know someone else's mind and options, external preparation usually will be less complete than internal preparation. Introspection usually will enable Husband to determine what type of movie he would prefer to see. In contrast, he might have a good prediction about what type of movie Wife would prefer to see based on the preferences she has expressed in the past, but he cannot know her preference with certainty prior to their negotiation. Defendant can determine prior to bargaining what she is willing to offer Plaintiff to dismiss his lawsuit, subject to some later adjustment. Based on her analysis of the strength of Plaintiff's case, she can estimate what Plaintiff would be willing to accept for dismissing the lawsuit, but her estimate is unlikely to be precise.

### c.   Synthesis

Finally, as part of preparation, negotiators often consider how to find a common ground between the desires of the negotiator and the desires of his opponent, such that a mutual agreement is possible. There is often both a substantive and procedural aspect to this strategizing. As to substance, negotiators will usually try to predict what possible agreement terms would be acceptable to both sides. Husband might try to determine, for example, whether dinner at an Italian restaurant followed by a foreign film would be acceptable to both he and Wife. Defendant might attempt to determine whether an apology for past actions and a promise not to continue those actions (but no cash payment) would be sufficiently beneficial to both she and Plaintiff in order for the two to reach an out-of-court settlement agreement. As to procedure, negotiators will often consider how they will try to steer the bargaining to arrive at a mutually acceptable agreement. Husband may plan to list a number of alternative evening plans and gauge Wife's reaction; Defendant may plan to offer Plaintiff nothing at first, and then reluctantly make some concessions.

## 2. Information Exchange

When negotiators begin the bargaining process, they usually exchange a range of information. From one perspective, the need for information exchange is a direct consequence of the fact that limited information at the pre-bargaining stage usually makes thorough external preparation impossible and sometimes places limits on the thoroughness of internal preparation as well. When negotiators begin the actual bargaining process, they need to reveal information about their desires and needs and garner such information about their opponents. Thus, information exchange can be seen as two separate sub-tasks: acquiring information and disclosing information.

### a. Acquiring Information

Good negotiators prepare for bargaining by trying to anticipate the desires, requirements, and alternatives to agreement of the opposing party but, as mentioned above, this process is unlikely to be complete without obtaining some information directly from the opposing party. Even when the negotiator has much in common with her opponent, the opponent will almost certainly have some differences in values and preferences, have access to different information, and interpret that information differently than the negotiator.

To begin with, thorough negotiators seek direct information about their opponent's absolute and relative goals in the bargaining process. In the context of litigation, the negotiator might seek to discover whether the opposing litigant wants only money or is really more concerned with gaining respect or assurances about the future. If money is the opponent's primary proximate goal, what does he ultimately want the money for, and can his ultimate goals be satisfied by something other than a cash payment? In the context of a negotiation between Husband and Wife over evening plans, does the other spouse want excitement or relaxation? Does he or she care about the specific form of entertainment? Does he or she just want to have a role in making the decision?

Negotiators also seek to directly acquire information about the opponent's alternatives to reaching a negotiated agreement and how the opponent perceives the value of these alternatives. Corporation A will want to learn whether, if Corporations A and B fail to reach a joint venture agreement, Corporation B would ally with competing Firm C. How desirable would such an alliance be for B relative to a successful alliance with A? Defendant will try to determine whether, if Plaintiff and Defendant fail to reach an out-of-court settlement agreement, Plaintiff will proceed with the lawsuit. If so, Defendant will want to know how strong a case Plaintiff believes he has, as this will influence how large an out-of-court settlement he will demand.

Finally, the negotiator will often seek information from the opponent that will help the negotiator better assess the value to her of reaching an agreement. For example, Corporation A might seek to acquire information from B concerning B's capabilities in order to assess how desirable a joint venture agreement would be. Defendant might seek to acquire from Plaintiff facts relevant to the lawsuit in order to determine how strongly he would prefer reaching a settlement agreement relative to not reaching agreement and proceeding to trial instead.

Acquiring information is a skill that requires the negotiator to be facile with the use of open-ended questions and probing follow-up questions, as well as an ability to listen carefully and interpret nonverbal communication. Rarely will simply asking the opponent "what do you want from this negotiation?" uncover the information necessary for the negotiator to determine what agreements would be possible, much less what agreements would be optimal.

### b.   Disclosing Information

Just as negotiators need to acquire information in order to attempt to identify possible agreements, they must disclose a certain amount of information as well. To take an extreme example, when Husband telephones Wife, no agreement is likely to be reached unless Husband discloses that he would like to make plans for the evening, and that he is interested in dining out and seeing a movie. But the act of disclosing information also requires the negotiator to consider what information not to disclose as well, as disclosing too much information might disadvantage the negotiator in the bargaining process. Corporation A might have to determine, for example, whether revealing that it desires a joint venture with Corporation B because A's capabilities are much weaker than B's will help or hinder its attempts to negotiate an agreement. Alternatively, it might have to determine whether disclosing that it is strongly considering a joint venture with Firm C will help or hinder its efforts to create a partnership with Corporation B.

In addition to disclosing information to inform the opponent of their needs and desires, negotiators often disclose information to persuade the opponent to revise his or her position. For example, Husband might tell Wife that the movie he would like to see received excellent reviews in the local media to persuade her to reevaluate her preferences. Defendant might disclose her opinion that recent case law is hostile to Plaintiff's position in an effort to persuade Plaintiff to accept a lower out-of-court settlement amount.

## 3.   Agreement Proposals

Broadly defined, negotiators engage in two basic activities when in direct communication with each other. The first, described above, is information exchange. In addition to exchanging information, of course, negotiators exchange proposed agreements. This activity may be divided into two categories: making the initial, or "first offer," and making subsequent proposals, or "counteroffers."

### a.   The First Offer

At some point in the bargaining encounter one of the negotiators must make the first offer — that is, create a proposed set of terms for an agreement. When the subject of the negotiation is simple, the first offer will usually be the complete set of terms necessary for an agreement, should the opposing party accept the terms. For example, Husband may propose to Wife that they dine at Restaurant X and then attend Movie Y. In a more complex negotiation, the first offer might be a complete proposal of all necessary terms, or it might be a proposal that specifies only some of the necessary terms for an actual agreement. For example, Corporation A might propose that it and Corporation B form a joint venture to produce and market a new style of running shoe, with A responsible for the manufacturing, B responsible for the marketing, and the two sharing profits 60 percent/40 percent, without specifying the various other contract terms that would have to be specified before the venture were to proceed. Often the first offer will follow a substantial amount of information exchange between the negotiators, but on some occasions a first offer might precede information exchange or follow only a minimal amount of information exchange.

By making the first offer, the negotiator reveals some information about what would be acceptable to her. Thus, the decision as to whether to make an offer is similar to the decision as to whether to disclose information. Negotiators often hesitate to make the first offer, because an offer that is aggressive might convince the opponent that there is no possibility of reaching a negotiated agreement, or that the negotiator is not bargaining in good faith, whereas an offer that is too generous might give the opponent more than is necessary to reach agreement. On the other hand, negotiators often choose to make the first offer because doing so can shape the opponent's expectations about the range of potentially possible agreements in a way that is beneficial to the negotiator.

### b.   Counteroffers

In some negotiation contexts, first offers are generally either accepted or rejected and no further offers are made. Consider, for example, your most recent trip to the grocery store. The price tag on a half gallon of milk can be understood as a first offer that is not subject to further negotiation. You either accept the offer by purchasing the milk or decline the offer by not purchasing the milk, but any effort to propose a different price to the store clerk would be considered highly unusual. In many negotiation contexts, and most negotiation contexts involving lawyers, however, the first offer is generally not the last proposal made. The offeree is likely to make a counteroffer, and both parties may make several further counteroffers.

When negotiators propose a counteroffer, they must consider the same factors that they consider when making an offer — a counteroffer can shape the expectations of the other party, but an offer that is either too aggressive or too generous can be problematic. Negotiators making a counteroffer also must consider whether the terms of their proposal should mirror the terms of the offer, or whether they should use the counteroffer to reframe the subject matter of the negotiation. For example, if Defendant offers to pay Plaintiff $20,000 in return for Plaintiff dismissing his lawsuit, a counteroffer by Plaintiff might either offer the same consideration (dropping the suit) in return for a higher price (perhaps $30,000), or it might redefine the subject of the negotiation, perhaps by asking for an apology and a promise by Defendant to take certain actions in the future to avoid conflict, in addition to a cash payment.

## 4.  Resolution

Finally (and fortunately!), all negotiations eventually come to a conclusion. Two results are possible. The parties can either reach an agreement that satisfies the interests of both or resolves their conflict, or they can recognize an impasse and leave negotiations with no agreement.

### a.   Agreement

When negotiators are able to reach agreement, this fact strongly suggests that the agreement leaves both parties better off than they would have been had they failed to reach agreement and instead pursued other alternatives (i.e., contracting with other parties, seeking to resolve a dispute through trial, etc.). Although this logically should always be the case — and it usually is — agreements can occasionally leave at least one party worse off than he would have been had he pursued other alternatives. This is especially likely to happen when a negotiator becomes so invested in reaching agreement that he loses sight of his alternative courses of action and becomes willing to make almost any concession in order to achieve agreement.

While it is usually a necessary precondition of agreement that a set of deal terms make both parties better off than they would be if they were to pursue alternative courses of action, identifying this set of terms is not a sufficient condition for an agreement to be struck. In addition to a mutually advantageous set of terms, the parties must both determine that the benefits of agreeing to that set of terms outweigh the expected benefits of continuing to negotiate for an even more desirable outcome. This can occur when both parties decide that any additional advantage they might obtain from further negotiation will not be worth the time investment, or when both parties decide that no benefit from continued bargaining is likely because the other party is unlikely to yield further no matter how long negotiations continue, or when an external time constraint (such as a trial date or the passing of a business opportunity) forces the parties to settle on agreement terms on threat of losing any possibility of reaching an agreement.

When negotiators do reach an agreement, the terms of the agreement are often memorialized in writing. This is especially likely to be the case when lawyers are involved in the negotiation, both because the presence of lawyers suggests that the stakes of the negotiation are sufficiently high to warrant the time and effort required for memorialization, and because lawyers are trained to be precise and cautious. When an agreement is relatively uncomplicated, or the negotiators have an ongoing relationship with each other such that a misunderstanding or attempt to renege on terms is unlikely, the terms of the agreement might not be memorialized in writing.

### b.  Impasse

Impasse can occur for several reasons. The most common reason is that no possible set of terms exists that make both parties believe that reaching an agreement will make them better off than they would be if they pursued an alternative. If Plaintiff and Defendant both are highly confident that they would prevail in a trial, for example, Plaintiff is likely to believe that pursuing a trial is a superior alternative to accepting an out-of-court settlement unless Defendant offers to pay a very large sum of money, and Defendant is likely to believe that pursuing a trial is a superior alternative to reaching an out-of-court settlement unless Plaintiff will accept a very small sum of money, or nothing at all. In such a situation, there is no imaginable agreement that would make both parties believe settlement is preferable to the alternative (i.e., trial), and impasse will occur.

Even if a mutually desirable agreement is theoretically available, the parties might reach impasse if they determine that the costs of identifying such a set of terms are greater than the marginal benefit that would come from reaching an agreement rather than pursuing alternatives, if an external time constraint eliminates the value of any agreement before the parties can arrive at one, or if one party has staked out a position on the issues that is incompatible with any mutually desirable agreement and that party refuses to accept less because doing so would mean "losing face."

## B.  CONCEPTUAL MODELS OF NEGOTIATION

The previous section described negotiation in terms of the activities in which the bargaining parties engage, in the order in which they generally occur. Viewing negotiation as a set of tasks arrayed on a timeline is a relatively simple way to develop a basic level of understanding of negotiation, but you will ultimately develop a deeper understanding of negotiation if you focus on the underlying strategic issues involved in bargaining rather than the physical activities of which the process consists. For example, knowing that negotiators prepare, exchange information, and make offers and counteroffers, provides some insight into the negotiating process, but you will develop a much more sophisticated knowledge of negotiation by investigating what goals the parties are attempting to achieve by engaging in these activities. This book will refer to its focus on underlying strategic issues rather than activities as a "conceptual approach" to the study of negotiation.

The following three articles attempt to develop simple conceptual frameworks for understanding the negotiation process. Although the three articles differ substantively, they share the goal of making it manageable to understand the rich array of activities in which negotiators engage by creating a small number of analytical categories and assigning negotiating activities to one of those categories. None of the conceptual structures is the "right" or "wrong" way to think about negotiation, and the three are not mutually exclusive ways of organizing the subject. They are best considered as alternative frameworks for simplifying and understanding a complicated process.

In the first article, Carrie Menkel-Meadow creates two categories of negotiations — "problem-solving" and "adversarial" — and classifies negotiations as falling within one of these two categories depending on whether the negotiators attempt to use bargaining to make both parties better off or to capture gains at the expense of their opponent. In this framework, negotiations are defined by the fundamental goal of the negotiating parties.

In the second article, Russell Korobkin also suggests that negotiations can be understood in a two-category framework, but he defines the categories as "zone definition" and "surplus allocation." In this approach, the elements that are categorized are not the overall tenor of the negotiations, but negotiating *tactics*. Tactics are defined fundamentally by whether they help the negotiators to understand the parameters of the bargaining zone or whether they help the parties to allocate the cooperative surplus produced when the parties agree to a transaction that makes both better off than they were previously. According to this framework, some tactics that are characteristic of what Menkel-Meadow calls "adversarial" negotiations fit into the "zone definition" category, while others fit into the "surplus allocation category," whereas tactics characteristic of Menkel-Meadow's "problem-solving negotiations" would all be identified as "zone definition" tactics.

In the third article, Robert Mnookin presents a different conceptual structure for understanding negotiation. Rather than organizing the negotiation process according to the orientation of the negotiation generally or the strategic purpose of particular tactics, this article suggests that negotiation be understood by focusing on the factors that can impede the parties' ability to reach mutually advantageous bargains. In the excerpt, Mnookin suggests three such factors — strategic barriers, the principal-agent problem, and cognitive barriers — but in theory the list could be expanded (unlike the Menkel-Meadow and Korobkin frameworks which are meant to be complete descriptions of the negotiation system).

As you read these articles, consider the extent to which each framework, through its attempt to simplify and organize the fundamental elements of bargaining, improves your understanding of the complicated negotiation process.

■ **Carrie Menkel-Meadow, Toward Another View of**
**Legal Negotiation: The Structure of Problem-Solving\***
31 UCLA L. Rev. 754, 765-772, 780, 800-805 (1984)

. . .

## I. Assumptions of the Traditional Model: Adversarial Negotiation

Much of the legal negotiation literature emphasizes an adversarial model, implying an orientation or approach that focuses on "maximizing victory." This approach is based on the assumption that the parties desire the same goals, items, or values. It is assumed that the parties must be in conflict and since they are presumed to be bargaining for the same "scarce" items, negotiators assume that any solution is predicated upon division of the goods. In the language of game theorists, economists, and psychologists, such negotiations become "zerosum" or "constant-sum" games and the bargaining engaged in is "distributive" bargaining. Simply put, in the pure adversarial case, each party wants as much as he can get of the thing bargained for, and the more one party receives, the less the other party receives. There is a "winner" in the negotiation, determined by which party got more.

Legal negotiations, at least in dispute resolution cases, are marked by another adversarial assumption. Because litigation negotiations are conducted in the "shadow of the law," that is, in the shadow of the courts, the negotiators assume that what is bargained for are the identical, but limited, items a court would award in deciding the case. Typically, it is assumed that all that is bargained for is who will get the most money and who can be compelled to do or not to do something. Indeed, it may be because litigation negotiations are so often conducted in the shadow of the court that they are assumed to be zerosum games.

In transactional negotiation, the "common business practice" or "form provision" may serve the same limiting function. If the parties cannot resolve a particular point but still prefer to consummate the transaction, they may permit a form provision or common business practice to decide the issue. This may be true even where an unusual provision would more closely meet the parties' needs. Clauses which assign or allocate risks routinely to one side of a transaction are one example. Although transactional negotiations differ from dispute negotiations because in the former no court can force a solution, the two types of negotiation may be analogous where the shadow of the court or the "shadow of the form contract" encourage a habit of mind in the negotiators to rely on common solutions, rather than to pursue solutions which may be more tailored to the parties' particular needs.

These basic adversarial assumptions affect not only the conceptions of negotiations that their proponents assert, but the behaviors that are recommended for successful negotiation. . . .

### A.   THE STRUCTURE AND PROCESS OF ADVERSARIAL
### NEGOTIATION

The literature of negotiation presents a stylized linear ritual of struggle — planned concessions after high first offers, leading to a compromise point along a linear field of pre-established "commitment and resistance" points. In such legal negotiations the compromise settlement point is legitimized by comparing it to the polarized demands of plaintiff and defendant and the relatively improved "joint gain" of the compromise point in comparison to the "winner take all" result achieved in court. In the most reductionist form of this adversarial model, analysts predict that the final outcome of any distributive bargaining problem will be at the "focal point" midway between the first offers of each party. . . .

Although such a model encourages compromise at some midway point, it frequently fails to provide a satisfactory solution for the parties. Consider the example of two children arguing over a piece of chocolate cake. The parental compromise solution, cutting the piece in half, will not be satisfactory to either child if one prefers the cake and the other the icing. Compromises may be highly dysfunctional in cases where one needs a pair, rather than a single shoe, to do the necessary walking.

A linear negotiation structure might work in those few cases where there is really only one issue, but it is clearly insufficient when the issues in a negotiation are many and varied. For instance, in negotiating a personal injury case one party may seek an apology, as well as lost earnings, rehabilitation costs, and pain and suffering damages. The "concession" of an apology from the other side may or may not reduce the amount of money to be negotiated as compensation for the other things. Similarly, in the formation of a partnership a "concession" on one issue of control does not necessarily move the "result" away from or toward one of the parties, especially if unaccompanied by an equivalent "trade" or contribution. Indeed, it may be impossible to represent graphically the negotiation of a complex, multi-issue transaction as a two dimensional structure, without imagining a many-planed axis with hundreds of potential coordinates. . . .

What is astounding about the conventional literature on tactics and strategies is the assumption of universal applicability. Strategic exhortations are offered without reference to how negotiations might vary in different contexts or under different circumstances, such as under the influence of various clients' desires. . . .

The literature is replete with advice to overpower and take advantage of the other side. But as one of the popular guides to negotiation has so wisely stated, "a tactic perceived is no tactic." If two competitive negotiators read the same literature it is difficult to see how these strategies will be employed to maximize individual gain. Who will win when both sides know all the same tricks?

The one strategic exhortation that seems to dominate most descriptions of adversarial negotiation is the admonition that the negotiator should never reveal what is really desired. Thus, the process of exaggerated offers is designed to cloak real preferences so that one negotiator cannot obtain unfair advantage over another by knowing what the other really wants. . . .

## II.  TOWARD A MODEL OF PROBLEM SOLVING NEGOTIATION: A THEORY OF NEEDS

Problem solving is an orientation to negotiation which focuses on finding solutions to the parties' sets of underlying needs and objectives. The problem-solving conception subordinates strategies and tactics to the process of identifying possible solutions and therefore allows a broader range of outcomes to negotiation problems. . . .

### A.   THE UNDERLYING PRINCIPLES OF PROBLEM SOLVING: MEETING VARIED AND COMPLEMENTARY NEEDS

Parties to a negotiation typically have underlying needs or objectives — what they hope to achieve, accomplish, and/or be compensated for as a result of the dispute or transaction. Although litigants typically ask for relief in the form of damages, this relief is actually a proxy for more basic needs or objectives. By attempting to uncover those underlying needs, the problem-solving model presents opportunities for discovering greater numbers of and better quality solutions. It offers the possibility of meeting a greater variety of needs both directly and by trading off different needs, rather than forcing a zero-sum battle over a single item. . . .

. . . Suppose that a husband and wife have two weeks in which to take their vacation. The husband prefers the mountains and the wife prefers the seaside. If vacation time is limited and thus a scarce resource, the couple may engage in adversarial negotiation about where they should go. The simple compromise situation, if they engage in distributive bargaining, would be to split the two weeks of vacation time spending one week in the mountains and one week at the ocean. This solution is not likely to be satisfying, however, because of the lost time and money in moving from place to place and in getting used to a new hotel room and locale. In addition to being happy only half of the time, each party to the negotiation has incurred transaction costs associated with this solution. Other "compromise" solutions might include alternating preferences on a year to year basis, taking separate vacations, or taking a longer vacation at a loss of pay. Assuming that husband and wife want to vacation together, all of these solutions may leave something to be desired by at least one of the parties.

By examining their underlying preferences, however, the parties might find additional solutions that could make both happy at less cost. Perhaps the husband prefers the mountains because he likes to hike and engage in stream fishing. Perhaps the wife enjoys swimming, sunbathing and seafood. By exploring these underlying preferences the couple might find vacation spots that permit all of these activities: a mountain resort on a large lake, or a seaside resort at the foot of mountains. By examining their underlying needs the parties can see solutions that satisfy many more of their preferences, and the "sum of the utilities" to the couple as a whole is greater than what they would have achieved by compromising. . . .

. . . [I]n a personal injury case the injured plaintiff may have economic needs for compensation and rehabilitation costs that extend into the future. In such cases, structured settlements, paid over time, and according to a variety of formulas, may more closely meet the needs of the parties than a single lump sum payment. Conversely, given the difficulty of enforcement of spousal support the parties to a dissolution might prefer a single payment, if it can be afforded, in order to avoid the transaction costs of enforcement proceedings. The failure of conventional court solutions to return the parties to the status quo ante demonstrates how negotiated solutions may meet other needs of the parties. In some recent products liability cases, for example, plaintiffs who could not be fully returned to their previously uninjured selves have requested that the defendants rewrite their warnings in order, at least, to prevent similar injuries to others. These plaintiffs have altruistic objectives in addition to their needs to be compensated, which likely would be unattended to in a court-decided solution. . . .                                                           ■

## ■ Russell Korobkin, A Positive Theory of Legal Negotiation*

**88 Geo. L.J.** 1789, 1791-1792, 1799-1812, 1816-1831 (2000)

. . .

This article presents a new dichotomy that creates a clear theoretical structure for viewing the legal negotiation process. This "zone definition/surplus allocation" dichotomy provides a complete description of the negotiating process: every action taken by negotiators in preparation for negotiations or at the bargaining table fits into one of these categories.

First, negotiators attempt to define the bargaining zone — the distance between the reservation points (or "walkaway" points) of the two parties — in the manner most advantageous to their respective clients. I call this activity "zone definition." Exploring alternatives to agreement, questioning, persuading, misleading, committing to positions, and redefining the negotiation's subject matter are all tactical tools used in zone definition. Because transactions are economically rational — in the sense that reaching agreement is better than not reaching agreement for both parties — only at points within the bargaining zone, zone definition can be understood as an inherently economic activity.

Second, negotiators attempt to convince their opponent to agree to a single "deal point" within the bargaining zone. I call this activity "surplus allocation." Surplus allocation effectively divides the cooperative surplus that the parties create by reaching an agreement. For both parties, transacting at any point within the bargaining zone is more desirable than not reaching agreement, but each knows that the same is true for the other. Once the bargaining zone is established, there is no economically obvious way for the parties to select a deal point. As a result, surplus allocation usually requires that negotiators appeal to community norms of either procedural or substantive fairness. Consequently, surplus allocation can be understood as an inherently social activity.

## I.   ZONE DEFINITION

. . . Perhaps the most common activity negotiators engage in at the bargaining table is attempting to persuade their opponent of the value of the negotiation's subject matter or of other alternatives. The arguments advanced often appear remarkably similar to those that litigating parties might make to a judge or jury. David is likely to present a detailed argument for why he is not liable for battery, claiming that the facts of his conflict with Goliath are analogous to the facts of precedential cases in which courts found no liability. Goliath will likely respond by disputing David's characterization of the facts of the dispute and/or claiming that other precedent is more "on point." Both parties' arguments superficially seem difficult to understand, given that there is little possibility that either will suddenly concede the superiority of the other's position. . . .

Efforts at persuasion in negotiation are best understood as attempts to satisfy one or both of two goals: (1) to shift the bargaining zone to the advantage of the negotiator, either by convincing the opponent that his RP [reservation price] is worse than he believed before beginning negotiations or that the negotiator's RP is better than previously believed; and (2) to establish an objective — and therefore "fair" —

method of agreeing on a sale price that falls within the bargaining zone. The first point is considered here; the second is discussed in Part II. In either case, the importance of persuasion demonstrates that both zone definition and surplus allocation are dynamic activities, dependent not only on negotiators' individual prebargaining analysis but also on their interaction.

Negotiators often attempt to shift the bargaining zone advantageously by making their RPs appear to their opponents to be better than they actually are. Assume that [plaintiff] Goliath's RP for a litigation settlement is $60,000. . . . Assume also that Goliath estimates [defendant] David's RP to be $90,000. . . . If David can convince Goliath that David has set his RP lower than $90,000, he can shift the bargaining zone in his favor. . . .

Good negotiators do as much or more "asking" as they do "telling." Significant negotiating time is spent with one party asking the other questions, seeking information. Negotiators do this primarily to generate more accurate estimates of their own and the opponent's RP — and therefore of the bargaining zone — than they can generate from prenegotiation preparation alone.

Questioning the opponent directly can help to better estimate the opponent's RP for two reasons. First, the negotiator's opponent is likely to have private information relevant to his RP, which cannot be discovered through prenegotiation external preparation. Second, as discussed above, the opponent's RP depends on his subjective evaluation of even public information. When the opponent has private information relevant to the negotiation's subject matter or his quality as a trading partner, information-seeking at the bargaining table can also help negotiators to redefine their own RPs. When being questioned, negotiators respond with varying degrees of candor, depending, of course, on whether they perceive that the benefits to themselves or their clients of doing so outweigh the risks entailed. . . .

Negotiators often threaten to break off negotiations if the other side will not offer a specified minimum value. . . . With this tactic, [the negotiator] attempts to gain an advantage in zone definition by replacing his RP with a "commitment point" (CP), thus truncating the bargaining zone. . . .

. . . Expanding the bargaining zone . . . can also benefit the negotiator by increasing the distance between his RP and the bulk of the possible deal points within the zone. This is because the greater the distance between the eventual deal point and the negotiator's RP, the greater the benefit he derives from reaching a negotiated agreement. . . . Tactics that enable negotiators to define a larger bargaining zone than would otherwise exist are collectively termed "integrative" bargaining. . . .

. . . [I]ntegrative bargaining requires the parties to redefine the negotiation's subject matter in a way that benefits one party more than it costs the other. When Esau and Jacob sit down for their first negotiating session, the subject matter of the negotiation is Jacob's business, which is worth $200,000 to Esau and $150,000 to Jacob. Suppose, however, that Esau would value Jacob's consulting services for one year after the sale at $50,000, but Jacob, interested in staying involved with the business, would be willing to provide those services for as little as $10,000. By redefining the subject matter of the negotiation as "Jacob's business + consulting," Esau's RP will increase $50,000 to $250,000, while Jacob's will increase only $10,000, to $160,000. Consequently, the bargaining zone will be $90,000 ($250,000 − $160,000) — $40,000 larger than it would have been had they merely negotiated a price for the business. Assuming for the moment that the parties will ultimately select a deal point midway between their RPs, the use of such integrative bargaining techniques translates into $20,000 worth of additional benefit for each. . . .

## II.   Surplus Allocation

Through zone definition, negotiators establish a bounded set of possible negotiated outcomes, or "deal points." If the bargaining zone consists of only a single point, it is the only possible deal point. Unless the parties mistakenly believe that there is no bargaining zone at all, they should reach a deal at precisely that point. But in many, and perhaps most, cases in which a bargaining zone exists, the zone will include a range of potential deal points. In this situation, agreement at each possible deal point is superior for both parties to not reaching agreement, or, put in economic terms, every deal point is Pareto superior to no deal. The problem is that, in this situation, no potential deal point is obviously superior to any other. . . .

How do negotiators solve this dilemma and agree on a single deal point? This part argues that bargainers usually rely on socially constructed norms of reaching agreement that are based implicitly on notions of fair dealing. Failure to agree on how to fairly allocate the cooperative surplus can, perversely, cause negotiators to fail to consummate a deal even when both would be better off striking a deal. . . . This is because negotiators often will refuse to agree to a distribution of assets they consider unfair even if the proposed deal point exceeds their RP. . . .

Many common negotiating tactics are best understood as attempts to establish a procedure that the other party will view as "fair" for agreeing on a deal point within the bargaining zone. In employing such tactics, the negotiator may have either of two motives. He might believe that the procedure is equitable to both parties, and the resulting deal point will thus create a mutually beneficial transaction in which neither side gets the better of the other. Alternatively, he might attempt to establish a procedure that will lead to an agreement that benefits him or his client substantially more than it benefits the other negotiator. Whether the negotiator's motives are communitarian or individualistic, however, the procedures must have the appearance of equity in order to win acceptance. . . .

Singling out a deal point requires the parties to agree on what is fair. In many negotiations, agreement is achieved by the parties acting consistently with procedural norms of bargaining behavior such as reciprocity, splitting the difference, and the selection of prominent focal points. The deal point that emerges from a procedurally fair process is accepted by the parties as itself fair, assuming it lies within the bargaining zone. In other negotiations, the parties instead negotiate over what specific deal point would be most substantively fair.

In the best-selling book, Getting to Yes, Fisher and his coauthors urge negotiators to "insist on using objective criteria,"[130] which might include such benchmarks as market price, historic price, historic profit level, or some conception of merit. In other words, the authors present a normative case for agreeing on a deal point via negotiations over the most substantively fair way to divide the cooperative surplus, which they can create by reaching an agreement. Calling such criteria "objective" is a misnomer because (1) any such criteria will benefit one party over the other as compared to a different criteria and (2) none can be conclusively established by logical argument to be justifiable ways to divide the cooperative surplus. Nonetheless, they are critical concepts in legal negotiation because they facilitate the parties' agreement on a single deal point that both can perceive as fair. . . .

At the level of tactics, negotiation is a complicated endeavor. Reaching a beneficial agreement requires not only a plethora of analytical and communication skills, but also the ability to deploy them in different ways depending on the context of the negotiation and the personality of the opposite party. But legal negotiation can appear less inscrutable when the process is systematically organized according to its critical strategic imperatives. This article has provided a new, yet simple structure for systematically thinking about negotiation. Negotiators seek the most desirable outcomes possible for themselves or their clients by pursuing only two goals: zone definition and surplus allocation. Everything negotiators do can be assimilated into this construct. . . .                                                                   ■

130. Roger Fisher, et al., Getting to Yes 81-94 (2d ed. 1991).

# ■ Robert H. Mnookin, Why Negotiations Fail: An Exploration of Barriers to the Resolution of Conflict*

8 Ohio St. J. Disp. Res. 235-245 (1993)

. . . In our everyday personal and professional lives, we have all witnessed disputes where the absence of a resolution imposes substantial and avoidable costs on all parties. . . .

My first example involves a divorcing family in California who were part of a longitudinal study carried out by Stanford psychologist Eleanor Maccoby and me. Mary and Paul Templeton spent three years fighting over the custody of their seven-year-old daughter Tracy after Mary filed for divorce in 1985. Mary wanted sole custody; Paul wanted joint physical custody. This middle-income family spent over $37,000 on lawyers and experts. In the process, they traumatized Tracy and inflicted great emotional pain on each other. More to the point, the conflict over who would best care for their daughter damaged each parent's relationship with Tracy, who has suffered terribly by being caught in the middle of her parents' conflict. Ultimately the divorce decree provided that Mary would have primary physical custody of Tracy, and Paul would be entitled to reasonable weekend visitation. The parents' inability to negotiate with one another led to a result in which mother, father, and daughter were all losers.

A conflict between Eastern Airlines and its unions represents another conspicuous example of a lose-lose outcome. In 1986, Frank Lorenzo took over Eastern, then the eighth largest American airline, with over 42,000 employees and about 1,000 daily flights to seventy cities. For the next three years, Lorenzo, considered a union buster by organized labor, pressed the airline's unions for various concessions, and laid off workers to reduce costs. The unions retaliated in a variety of ways, including a public relations campaign suggesting Eastern's airplanes were being improperly maintained because Lorenzo was inappropriately cutting costs. In March 1989, labor-management skirmishes turned into all-out war. Eastern's machinists went on strike, and the pilots and flight attendants initially joined in. The ensuing "no holds barred" battle between Lorenzo and the machinists led to losses on both sides. [Eastern filed for bankruptcy in 1990 and permanently shut down operations in 1991.]

The titanic struggle between Texaco and Pennzoil over Getty Oil provides another example of a bargaining failure, although of a somewhat more subtle sort. Here, both corporations survived, with a clear winner and loser; Texaco paid Pennzoil $3 billion in cash to end the dispute in 1988. The parties reached settlement, however, only after a year-long bankruptcy proceeding for Texaco and protracted legal wrangling in various courts. While the dispute dragged on, the combined equity value of the two companies was reduced by some $3.4 billion. A settlement *before* Texaco filed for bankruptcy would have used up fewer social resources and would have been more valuable to the shareholders of both companies than the resolution created by the bankruptcy court about a year later. . . .

. . . Examples like these, and I am sure you could add many more of your own, suggest a central question for those of us concerned with dispute resolution: Why is it that under circumstances where there are resolutions that better serve disputants, negotiations often fail to achieve efficient resolutions? In other words, what are the barriers to the negotiated resolution of conflict? . . .

## A.  STRATEGIC BARRIERS

[The author first discusses how "informational asymmetry" — the possession by each negotiator of some information that the other does not have — can be a strategic barrier to reaching a negotiated agreement, because the parties might bluff and lie about their interests and preferences in an effort to get more from the other side.]

Even when both parties know all the relevant information, and that potential gains may result from a negotiated deal, strategic bargaining over how to divide the pie can still lead to deadlock (with no deal at all) or protracted and expensive bargaining, thus shrinking the pie. For example, suppose Nancy has a house for sale for which she has a reservation price of $245,000. I am willing to pay up to $295,000 for the house. Any deal within a bargaining range from $245,000 to $295,000 would make both of us better off than no sale at all. Suppose we each know the other's reservation price. Will there be a deal? Not necessarily. If we disagree about how the $50,000 "surplus" should be divided (each wanting all or most of it), our negotiation may end in a deadlock. . . .

Strategic behavior — which may be rational for a self-interested party concerned with maximizing the size of his or her own slice — can often lead to inefficient outcomes. Those subjected to claiming tactics often respond in kind, and the net result typically is to push up the cost of the dispute resolution process. . . . Parties may be tempted to engage in strategic behavior, hoping to get more. Often all they do is shrink the size of the pie. Those experienced in the civil litigation process see this all the time. One or both sides often attempt to use pre-trial discovery as leverage to force the other side into agreeing to a more favorable settlement. Often the net result, however, is simply that both sides spend unnecessary money on the dispute resolution process.

### B.   THE PRINCIPAL/AGENT PROBLEM

The second barrier is suggested by recent work relating to transaction cost economics, and is sometimes called the "principal/agent" problem. . . . The basic problem is that the incentives for an agent (whether it be a lawyer, employee, or officer) negotiating on behalf of a party to a dispute may induce behavior that fails to serve the interests of the principal itself. The relevant research suggests that it is no simple matter — whether by contract or custom — to align perfectly the incentives for an agent with the interests of the principal. This divergence may act as a barrier to efficient resolution of conflict.

The Texaco/Pennzoil dispute may have involved a principal/agent problem of a different sort. My colleague Bob Wilson and I have argued that the interests of the Texaco officers and directors diverged from those of the Texaco shareholders in ways that may well have affected the conduct of that litigation. Although the shareholders would have benefited from an earlier settlement, the litigation was controlled by the directors, officers, and lawyers whose interests differed in important respects. . . .

[An initial trial verdict for Pennzoil created a basis for collateral lawsuits against the Texaco directors and officers for failure to fulfill their duty of care to the corporation.] Because they faced the risk of personal liability, the directors and officers of Texaco acted in such a way as to suggest they would prefer to risk pursuing the case to the bitter end (with some slight chance of complete exoneration) rather than accept a negotiated resolution, even though in so doing they risked subjecting the corporation to a ten billion dollar judgment. The case ultimately did settle, but only through a bankruptcy proceeding in which the bankruptcy court eliminated the risk of personal liability for Texaco's officers and directors.

### C.   COGNITIVE BARRIERS

. . . Suppose everyone attending this evening's lecture is offered the following happy choice: At the end of my lecture you can exit at the north end of the hall or the south end. If you choose the north exit, you will be handed an envelope in which there will be a crisp new twenty dollar bill. Instead, if you choose the south exit, you will be given a sealed envelope randomly pulled from a bin. One quarter of these envelopes contain a $100 bill, but three quarters are empty. In other words, you can have a sure gain of $20 if you go out the north door, or you can instead gamble by choosing the south door where you will have a 25% chance of winning $100 and a 75% chance of winning nothing. Which would you choose? A great deal of experimental work suggests that the overwhelming majority of you would choose the sure gain of $20, even though the "expected value" of the second alternative, $25, is slightly more. This is a well known phenomenon called "risk aversion." The principle is that most people will take a sure thing over a gamble, even where the gamble may have a somewhat higher "expected" payoff.

Daniel Kahneman and Amos Tversky have advanced our understanding of behavior under uncertainty with a remarkable discovery. They suggest that, in order to avoid what would otherwise be a sure loss, many people will gamble, even if the expected loss from the gamble is larger. Their basic idea can be illustrated by changing my hypothetical. Although you didn't know this when you were invited to this lecture, it is not free. At the end of the lecture, the doors are going to be locked. If you go out the north door, you'll be required to pay $20 as an exit fee. If you go out the south door, you'll participate in a lottery by drawing an envelope. Three quarters of the time you're going to be let out for free, but one quarter of the time you're going to be required to pay $100. Rest assured all the money is going to the Dean's fund — a very good cause. What do you choose? There's a great deal of empirical research, based on the initial work of Kahneman and Tversky, suggesting that the majority of this audience would choose the south exit — i.e., most of you would gamble to avoid having to lose $20 for sure. Kahneman and Tversky call this "loss aversion."

Now think of these two examples together. Risk aversion suggests that most of you would not gamble for a gain, even though the expected value of $25 exceeds the sure thing of $20. On the other hand, most of you would gamble to avoid a sure loss, even though, on the average, the loss of going out the south door is higher. Experimental evidence suggests that the proportion of people who will gamble to avoid a loss is much greater than those who would gamble to realize a gain.

Loss aversion can act as a cognitive barrier to the negotiated resolution of conflict for a variety of reasons. For example, both sides may fight on in a dispute in the hope that they may avoid any losses, even though the continuation of the dispute involves a gamble in which the loss may end up being far greater. Loss aversion may explain Lyndon Johnson's decision, in 1965, to commit additional troops to Vietnam as an attempt to avoid the sure loss attendant to withdrawal, and as a gamble that there might be some way in the future to avoid any loss at all. ◾

## DISCUSSION QUESTIONS AND PROBLEMS

*1. The Steps of Negotiation.*   Section A divides the negotiation process into the steps of preparation, information exchange, agreement proposals, and resolution. You are no doubt familiar with all these steps, having been through all of them in your personal and professional lives many times. Which of these steps do you think you do well in your daily life, and which of the steps do you think you need to provide more attention to in future negotiating situations? What lessons were you able to draw from the brief overview provided in Section A about how you can improve your negotiating ability?

*2. A New Deck.*   Nora Naturalist has just purchased a home that backs onto a lovely, wooded area of town. She would like to build a redwood deck behind her house suitable for a table and chairs, where she can sit and enjoy her nice view of the forest. She has talked with a number of friends who have built similar outdoor decks in the last few years. Two strongly recommended the work of Carlton Contractor, a local tradesman specializing in carpentry projects, but they have warned that Carlton is "not cheap." Nora has set up an appointment with Carlton for next week to discuss the possibility of her hiring him to build a deck.

Nora has $4,000 that she has saved for home improvements. The deck is her top priority, but she also hopes to do some landscaping soon and perhaps renovate one of her bathrooms. She would like a deck that is 20 feet long by 15 feet deep, but it is not absolutely critical that it be that big. Carlton has an excellent reputation in the community, his time is usually booked months in advance, and as a result he is able to charge somewhat more than other contractors for his work. For a 20' × 15' redwood deck, materials would cost him $1,500. His standard practice would be to add on $2,000 for labor and therefore charge $3,500 in total to build such a deck. Recently, however, the home improvement business has been slow, and he has only had enough work to keep him busy about 75 percent of the time. To keep himself busier, he has started to expand his business to include some landscaping work as well as carpentry.

Using the steps of negotiation described in Section A as a guide, consider how you would expect both Nora and Carlton to approach the upcoming negotiation. First, what would you expect each to do to prepare for the negotiation? Second, what information would you expect each to attempt to acquire and to disclose during bargaining? Third, what type of offers and counteroffers would you expect the two parties to make? Fourth, what type of resolution do you think they will reach?

*3. Viewing Negotiation as a Set of Conceptual Categories.* Think back to a recent negotiation in which you were involved, whether it was a business or legal negotiation, or a negotiation with a friend or family member, and try to recall specific statements made by you or the other party. Can you describe some aspects of the negotiation in terms of the categories proposed by Menkel-Meadow? That is, can you identify some aspects of the negotiation as examples of either "problem-solving" or of "adversarial" bargaining? Can you characterize the same or different parts of the negotiation in terms of Korobkin's categories of "zone definition" or "surplus allocation"? Can you explain why the negotiation succeeded or why it failed in terms of overcoming or failing to overcome one or more of Mnookin's categories of "barriers" to conflict resolution?

*4. What Approaches Dominate in Negotiation?* Menkel-Meadow describes negotiations as being "adversarial" or "problem-solving" in nature. Which term do you think best describes most negotiations? If your answer would depend on the particular context of the negotiation, which term do you think best describes most legal negotiations? Korobkin describes negotiation tactics as being geared either to defining the bargaining zone or allocating the cooperative surplus. Which of these activities do you think dominates the time or attention of negotiators in most bargaining situations? Again, do you think that legal negotiations are different in this respect than other types of negotiations?

*5. A New Deck, Revisited.* Reconsider the bargaining scenario described above in Note 2 using the conceptual frameworks provided by Menkel-Meadow, Korobkin, and Mnookin. Using the Menkel-Meadow approach, describe how the negotiation might unfold if both Nora and Carlton take a "problem-solving" approach compared to if they both take an "adversarial" approach to the negotiation. Using the Korobkin approach, describe what tactics the two negotiators might use to (a) define the bargaining zone and (b) allocate the cooperative surplus. Using the Mnookin approach, describe what types of barriers might prevent the parties from reaching a mutually beneficial agreement.

*6. Comparing the Conceptual Approaches.* Which of the three approaches, Menkel-Meadow's, Korobkin's, or Mnookin's, is most helpful to you in gaining an overall understanding of the negotiation process? Why?

# PART II

# THE STRUCTURE OF NEGOTIATION

Because negotiation is an interactive process, success depends on the negotiator's ability to understand and respond to the approaches adopted by the opposing negotiator or negotiators. For this reason, mastering the art of negotiation — if it can ever be truly mastered — requires careful observation of human behavior, years of practice, and much trial and error. But, this said, the basic structure of negotiation is relatively simple to understand. Even the novice attorney can understand its structure and master its core principles and consequently approach any negotiating situation in an analytically coherent way that offers the highest possible probability of success.

This Part attempts to provide the lawyer-negotiator with a complete yet manageable analytical framework for thinking about the negotiation process by describing all negotiating interactions as designed to serve one of four basic strategic goals or, sometimes, more than one of the goals simultaneously:

1. Determining whether a bargaining zone exists — that is, whether a mutually beneficial agreement is possible — and identifying the range of possible agreements.
2. Changing the scope or emphasis of the negotiation in a way that makes a transaction mutually beneficial when otherwise there would be no possibility of finding a mutually beneficial agreement, or in a way that makes an agreement even more mutually beneficial than it would otherwise be.
3. Exercising negotiating power to capture some or all of the benefit that the parties will create by reaching an agreement at the expense of the other party.

4. Appealing to procedural or substantive social norms to reach
   agreement on how to divide the benefits that the parties create
   by entering into a transaction.

By understanding these four categories of strategic goals, lawyer-
negotiators can make sense of what is transpiring structurally when
negotiators interact, whether they are participants in the negotiation or observers, and regardless of the range of tactical approaches
that are employed. This understanding, in turn, can enable negotiators to teach themselves to become more effective bargainers
throughout their careers by assessing whether or not each tactical
decision they make at the bargaining table helps to satisfy one or
more strategic goals.

Chapters 2 and 3 focus on the first strategic goal — determining
whether a bargaining zone exists and, if it does, estimating the
range of possible agreements that fall within that zone. Temporally,
negotiators attempt to make such estimates *prior* to the onset of
bargaining, but they continually update their estimates as they learn
new information during the negotiation process. Chapter 2 describes this strategic goal and ways in which negotiators satisfy it
from the perspective of economics-based decision theory, while
Chapter 3 considers important psychological factors that can affect
the contours of the bargaining zone that the economic approach
overlooks.

Chapter 4 considers the second strategic goal of shaping a negotiation such that an agreement creates more joint value for the
negotiators than it otherwise would. Tactics that satisfy this goal are
often called "integrative" or "problem-solving" approaches to bargaining, because they aim to identify agreements that satisfy the
interests of both parties, rather than satisfying the interests of one
at the expense of the other.

Chapter 5 and 6 discuss negotiation approaches — often labeled
"distributive" — by which the negotiator gains advantage by claiming resources that the opponent also wishes to claim. Chapter 5
considers one distinct class of distributive strategies: those in which
the negotiator gains advantage through the exercise of power; specifically, by threatening to not agree or to impose unacceptable
costs on the other party if the negotiator does not get what she
wants. Chapter 6 considers a very different class of distributive strategies: those in which the negotiator appeals to conceptions of fair-

ness, objectivity, or other neutral principles in an effort to convince her opponent to agree to a proposed division of the cooperative surplus. Negotiating approaches in the latter category are less confrontational than the former, but they serve the same purpose of dividing between the parties a fixed cooperative surplus.

## Chapter 2

# Estimating the Bargaining Zone

## A. BATNAS AND RESERVATION PRICES

### ■ Russell Korobkin, A Positive Theory of Legal Negotiation*

88 Geo. L.J. 1789, 1792-1798 (2000)

In any negotiation, the maximum amount that a buyer will pay for a good, service, or other legal entitlement is called his "reservation point" or, if the deal being negotiated is a monetary transaction, his "reservation price" (RP). The minimum amount that a seller would accept for that item is her RP. If the buyer's RP is higher than the seller's, the distance between the two points is called the "bargaining zone." Reaching agreement for any amount that lies within the bargaining zone is superior to not reaching an agreement for both parties, at least if they are concerned only with the transaction in question.

For example, suppose Esau, looking to get into business for himself, is willing to pay up to $200,000 for Jacob's catering business, while Jacob, interested in retiring, is willing to sell the business for any amount over $150,000. This difference between Esau's and Jacob's RPs creates a $50,000 bargaining zone. At any price between $150,000 and $200,000, both parties are better off agreeing to the sale of the business than they are reaching no agreement and going their separate ways.

The same structure used to describe a transactional negotiation can be used to describe a dispute resolution negotiation. Suppose that Goliath has filed suit against David for battery. David is willing to pay up to $90,000 to settle the case out of court — essentially, to buy Goliath's legal right to bring suit — while Goliath will "sell" his right for any amount over $60,000. These RPs create a $30,000 bargaining zone be-

---

*Reprinted with permission of the publisher, Georgetown Law Journal © 2000.

tween $60,000 and $90,000. Any settlement in this range would leave both parties better off than they would be without a settlement.

In contrast, if the seller's RP is higher than the buyer's RP, there is no bargaining zone. In this circumstance, there is no sale price that would make both parties better off than they would be by not reaching a negotiated agreement. Put another way, the parties would be better off not reaching a negotiated agreement. If Jacob will not part with his business for less than $150,000 and Esau will not pay more than $100,000 for it, there is no bargaining zone. If David will pay up to $50,000 to settle Goliath's claim, but Goliath will not accept any amount less than $60,000, again there is no bargaining zone. An agreement in either case would leave at least one party, and possibly both parties, worse off than if they were to decide not to make a deal. . . .

### 1.   INTERNAL PREPARATION: ALTERNATIVES AND BATNAS

A negotiator cannot determine his RP without first understanding his substitutes for and the opportunity costs of reaching a negotiated agreement. This, of course, requires research. Esau cannot determine how much he is willing to pay for Jacob's business without investigating his other options. Most obviously, Esau will want to investigate what other catering companies are for sale in his area, their asking prices, and how they compare in quality and earning potential to Jacob's. He also might consider other types of businesses that are for sale. And he will likely consider the possibility of investing his money passively and working for someone else, rather than investing in a business.

Alternatives to reaching an agreement can be nearly limitless in transactional negotiations, and creativity in generating the list of alternatives is a critical skill to the negotiator. The panoply of alternatives is generally more circumscribed in dispute resolution negotiations. If Goliath fails to reach a settlement of some sort with David, he has the alternative of seeking an adjudicated outcome of the dispute and the alternative of dropping the suit. Most likely, he does not have the choice of suing someone else instead of David, in the same way that Esau has the choice of buying a business other than Jacob's.

After identifying the various alternatives to reaching a negotiated agreement, the negotiator needs to determine which alternative is most desirable. Fisher and his coauthors coined the appropriate term "BATNA" — "best alternative to a negotiated agreement" — to identify this choice.[28] The identity and quality of a negotiator's BATNA is the primary input into his RP.

If the negotiator's BATNA and the subject of the negotiation are perfectly interchangeable, determining the reservation price is quite

28. Roger Fisher, et al., Getting to Yes 100 (2d ed. 1991).

simple: the reservation price is merely the value of the BATNA. For example, if Esau's BATNA is buying another catering business for $190,000 that is identical to Jacob's in terms of quality, earnings potential, and all other factors that are important to Esau, then his RP is $190,000. If Jacob will sell for some amount less than that, Esau will be better off buying Jacob's company than he would be pursuing his best alternative. If Jacob demands more than $190,000, Esau is better off buying the alternative company and not reaching an agreement with Jacob.

In most circumstances, however, the subject of a negotiation and the negotiator's BATNA are not perfect substitutes. If Jacob's business is of higher quality, has a higher earnings potential, or is located closer to Esau's home, he would probably be willing to pay a premium for it over what he would pay for the alternative choice. For example, if the alternative business is selling for $190,000, Esau might determine he would be willing to pay up to a $10,000 premium over the alternative for Jacob's business and thus set his RP at $200,000. On the other hand, if Esau's BATNA is more desirable to him than Jacob's business, Esau will discount the value of his BATNA by the amount necessary to make the two alternatives equally desirable values for the money; perhaps he will set his RP at $180,000 in recognition that his BATNA is $10,000 more desirable than Jacob's business, and Jacob's business would be equally desirable only at a $10,000 discount.

Assume Goliath determines that his BATNA is proceeding to trial. He will attempt to place a value on his BATNA by researching the facts of the case, the relevant legal precedent, and jury awards in similar cases, all as a means of estimating the expected value of litigating to a jury verdict. If Goliath's research leads to an estimate that he has a 75% chance of winning a jury verdict, and the likely verdict if he does prevail is $100,000, then using a simple expected value calculation ($100,000 $\times$ .75) would lead him to value his BATNA at $75,000.

For most plaintiffs, however, a settlement of a specified amount is preferable to a jury verdict with the same expected value, both because litigation entails additional costs and because most individuals are risk averse and therefore prefer a certain payment to a risky probability of payment with the same expected value. Goliath might determine, for example, that a $50,000 settlement would have the equivalent value to him of a jury verdict with an expected value of $75,000, because pursuing a jury verdict would entail greater tangible and intangible costs such as attorneys' fees, emotional strain, inconvenience, and the risk of losing the case altogether. If so, Goliath would set his RP at $50,000. On the other hand, it is possible that Goliath would find a $75,000 verdict more desirable than a $75,000 pretrial settlement. For example, perhaps Goliath would find additional value in having a jury of his peers publicly recognize the validity of his grievance against David. If Goliath believes that such psychic benefits of a jury verdict would make a verdict worth $10,000 more to him than a settlement of the same amount (after taking into account the added risks and costs of litigation), he would set his RP at $85,000.

The relationship between a party's BATNA and his RP can be generalized in the following way. A party's RP has two components: (1) the market value of his BATNA; and (2) the difference *to him* between the value of his BATNA and the value of the subject of the negotiation. A seller sets his RP by calculating (1) and either *subtracting* (2) if the subject of the negotiation is more valuable than his BATNA (and therefore he is willing to accept less to reach an agreement) or *adding* (2) if the BATNA is more valuable than the subject of the negotiation (and therefore, he would demand more to reach an agreement and give up his BATNA). A buyer sets his RP by calculating (1) and either *adding* (2) if the subject of the negotiation is more valuable than his BATNA (and therefore he would pay a premium to reach an agreement) or *subtracting* (2) if his BATNA is more valuable than the subject of the negotiation (and therefore he would demand a discount to give up the BATNA).

Internal preparation serves two related purposes. By considering the value of obvious alternatives to reaching a negotiated agreement, the negotiator can accurately estimate his RP. This is of critical importance because without a precise and accurate estimation of his RP the negotiator cannot be sure to avoid the most basic negotiating mistake — agreeing to a deal when he would have been better off walking away from the table with no agreement.

By investigating an even wider range of alternatives to reaching agreement, and by more thoroughly investigating the value of obvious alternatives, the negotiator can alter his RP in a way that will shift the bargaining zone to his advantage. Rather than just considering the asking price of other catering companies listed for sale in his town, Esau might contact catering companies that are not for sale to find out if their owners might consider selling under the right conditions. This could lead to the identification of a company similar to Jacob's that could be purchased for $175,000, which would have the effect of reducing Esau's RP to $175,000 and therefore shifting the bargaining zone lower. Goliath's attorney might conduct additional legal research, perhaps exploring other, more novel, theories of liability. If he determines that one or more alternative legal theories has a reasonable chance of success in court, Goliath might adjust upward his estimate of prevailing at trial — and therefore the value of his BATNA of trial — allowing him to adjust upward his RP.

### 2.  External Preparation: The Opponent's Alternatives and BATNA

Internal preparation enables the negotiator to estimate his RP accurately and favorably. Of course, the bargaining zone is fixed by *both* parties' RPs. External preparation allows the negotiator to estimate his opponent's RP. If Esau is savvy, he will attempt to research Jacob's alternatives to a negotiated agreement as well as his own alternatives. For example, other caterers might know whether Jacob has had other offers for his business, how much the business might bring on the open market, or how anxious Jacob is to sell — all factors that will help Esau to accurately predict Jacob's RP and therefore pinpoint the low end of the bargaining zone. This information will also prepare Esau to attempt to persuade Jacob during the course of negotiations to lower his RP. . . .

It is worth noting that in the litigation context both parties often have the same alternatives and the same BATNA. If plaintiff Goliath determines that his BATNA is going to trial, then defendant David's only alternative — and therefore his BATNA by default — is going to trial as well. In this circumstance, internal preparation and external preparation merge. For example, when Goliath's lawyer conducts legal research, he is attempting to simultaneously estimate the value of both parties' BATNAs. Of course, just because the parties have the same BATNA, they will not necessarily estimate the market value of it identically, much less arrive at identical RPs. . . .                               ∎

## Notes

*Critical Definitions.*  The above excerpt defines a number of terms of art that are critical to understanding the basic dynamics of negotiation:

*(a) Reservation Price.*  A party's "reservation price" is the most she will pay to obtain a valuable item through negotiation or the least that she will accept to give up a valuable item. Depending on the context of the negotiation, a party's reservation price might be measured in currency other than money. Because it is not always convenient to think about a reservation price in monetary terms, the more general term "reservation point" is sometimes used instead. If a negotiator is offering or demanding time, praise, labor, or any other commodity besides money, the party's reservation price, or reservation point, is the most he will give or the least he will accept of whatever the relevant commodity is. In complex negotiation settings, negotiators' reservation prices might be measured in packages of goods, services, or other valuable items. For example, if Farmer Andrews is attempting to bargain for a cow belonging to Farmer Brown, the former might be

willing to offer a maximum of four hogs, ten chickens, three hogs plus three chickens, $500, or $100 plus two hogs. In this example, all of these packages represent reservation prices, as they are each individually the most that Farmer Andrews will give up for the cow.

Because a reservation price is simply a point that divides potential deals that a negotiator would accept from potential deals that he would not accept, every negotiator has a reservation price, whether he has consciously thought about the concept or not. As the next section discusses, however, careful negotiators thoroughly analyze the negotiating situation and consciously determine their reservation price in order to be sure that any potential agreement that they would accept would make them better off than not reaching an agreement, and that any potential agreement that they would not accept would not leave them worse off than they would be not reaching agreement.

*(b) Bargaining Zone.* The bargaining zone is defined as the space below a buyer's reservation price but above the seller's reservation price. The concept is critical in negotiation because, as long as negotiators are free to walk away from a negotiation without reaching agreement (as is usually the case), only potential agreements that lie within the bargaining zone are possible as a practical matter. Potential agreements lying outside of the bargaining zone cannot be reached because they would make at least one party worse off than he thinks he would be if no agreement is reached. If there is no bargaining zone, then by definition no agreement is possible.

*(c) Cooperative Surplus.* The breadth of the bargaining zone — that is, the distance between the two parties' reservation prices — is the "cooperative surplus" or "joint value" that the parties can create by reaching agreement. For example, if Esau is willing to pay $200,000 for Jacob's catering business, and Jacob is willing to accept $150,000, then by agreeing to a sale at any point between those two numbers Esau and Jacob create a cooperative surplus of $50,000. How that $50,000 of cooperative surplus — or joint value — is divided between the two negotiators depends on what price is agreed upon. If the negotiators agree to a sales price of $160,000, Jacob will be $10,000 better off than he would have been had no deal been reached (having received $10,000 more than his reservation price), and Esau will be $40,000 better off than he would have been had no deal been reached (having obtained a valuable asset for $40,000 less than his reservation price), for a total joint profit of $50,000. If the sales price were $175,000, each party would capture $25,000 of the cooperative surplus.

# B.  CALCULATING RESERVATION PRICES: A PRESCRIPTIVE APPROACH

All negotiators have a reservation price, whether or not they arrive at it in an analytically sophisticated way. By definition, any proposed agreement that the negotiator favors over not reaching an agreement is superior to his reservation price, and any proposed agreement that the negotiator does not prefer to not reaching agreement is inferior to his reservation price. Good negotiators, however, take great care in determining their reservation price in an analytically sophisticated way. Doing so insures that the negotiator will not make the most devastating of possible negotiation mistakes: reaching agreement when she would be better off not reaching agreement, or failing to reach agreement when a deal that would make her better off than not reaching agreement is possible.

Determining an accurate reservation price — one that correctly divides potential deals that are superior to "no agreement" from those that are not — often requires substantial research and analysis. Much of this analysis can and should be done prior to any negotiating sessions, but the analysis should be updated if new and relevant information becomes available during the bargaining process or outside of the bargaining process but after negotiations have commenced.

Seven factors affect a negotiator's reservation price: his alternatives to agreement, his preferences for reaching agreement, his estimates of the probability of future events, his tolerance for risk, the value he places on time, transaction costs, and the effect on future relationships or opportunities of reaching agreement. Carefully considering each of these factors will guarantee that a negotiator will determine his reservation price as accurately as possible.

## 1.  Alternatives

A negotiator's reservation price is intimately related to his no-agreement alternatives; specifically, to his BATNA. Assume that B is considering buying a juicy pear from A. C is selling pears for $1 each, D for $2 each, and E for $3 each. B therefore has alternatives of buying a pear from C, D, or E, or of not buying a pear at all. Assuming that C, D, and E are selling identical pears, and that B enjoys pears enough to pay at least $1 for one, his BATNA is buying a pear from C. (If B liked pears only enough to pay 50 cents for one, his BATNA would have been not buying a pear at all.) B must, therefore, calculate his reservation price on the basis of the difference in value he would receive if he were to buy a pear from A than from C.

## 2. Preferences

The most obvious factor that should affect B's reservation price other than the fact that he could buy a pear from C for $1 is whether he prefers A's pears to C's pears, and by how much. If A's pears taste twice as good as C's, B might set his reservation price at $2 — he would be willing to pay $2 for the right to eat one of A's pears, but if A demanded any amount more than this B would be happier buying a pear from C than paying A's price. On the other hand, if B believes that C's pears are a slightly higher quality than A's, he might set his reservation price at 75 cents. If A's price is higher than $.75, B would rather pay $1 for one of C's better pears. If A's price is less than or equal to $.75, however, he would prefer to pay that price for A's pears rather than the significantly higher price for C's pears.

## 3. Probabilities of Future Events

In many circumstances, reaching agreement will result in a certain state of affairs for the negotiator, whereas pursuing his BATNA could result in two or more different states of affairs, each with some probability of occurring that is less than 100 percent. Suppose that B is negotiating with A for a contract to purchase a pear in one week's time. B knows that one week from now C will be selling identical pears, but he does not know with certainty what price C will be charging. Thus, to set a reservation price B must compare the certain price he will pay A if the two reach agreement with an uncertain range of prices that he might have to pay C if he and A do not reach agreement and he is thus forced to pursue his BATNA. To do so requires an "expected value" calculation. An expected value calculation converts a range of probabilistic possibilities to a single weighted average of those possibilities. The calculation allows B to compare a probabilistic alternative to a certain alternative, or to compare two probabilistic alternatives with different probabilities to each other.

To calculate the expected value of B's BATNA, he must multiply the possible future states of the world by his best estimate of the probability that they will come to pass, and then add the products. Assume that there is a 25 percent probability that C will be charging $1 per pear one week from now, a 25 percent probability that C will be charging $2 per pear, and a 50 percent probability that C will be charging $3 per pear. The expected value (in this case, the expected cost) to B of his BATNA of buying his pear from C is ($1 × .25) + ($2 × .25) + ($3 × .50) = $2.25. Consequently, if a pear is worth at least that much to B, and the quality of A's and C's pears are identical, his reservation price in his negotiation with A might be $2.25.

## 4. Risk Preference

In the previous example, B's reservation price will be $2.25 if he is "risk neutral," meaning that he would be indifferent between paying a certain price of $2.25 or an uncertain price that might be either higher or lower than $2.25 but has an expected value of $2.25.

Economic theory predicts that rational individuals will usually be "risk averse," meaning that they prefer a certain cost (or benefit) to a probabilistic cost (or benefit) with the same expected value. This prediction is derived from the observation that individuals experience a declining marginal utility of money, meaning that we derive more benefit from one dollar than a second, more benefit from a second dollar than a third, etc. To see why, imagine that you had a choice between working one year for a salary of $10,000 or working for one year for a 50 percent chance of receiving a salary of $20,000 and a 50 percent chance of receiving a salary of $0. Which would you choose? Most people would prefer the certain $10,000, even though the two options have the same expected value. The reason is that with the first $10,000 you earn you can purchase the goods and services that are most valuable to you: for example, food, clothing, shelter. With the second $10,000 you would purchase items that are somewhat less important to you than what you would purchase with the first $10,000 (if the items were more important, you would have allocated part of the first $10,000 to purchase them). Consequently, it would be undesirable to risk the first $10,000 for a 50 percent chance of getting the second $10,000, as the probabilistic salary option requires.

If a negotiator is risk averse, a probabilistic BATNA is less valuable than a certain agreement with the same expected value. Consequently, if B is risk averse, his reservation price in his negotiations with A would be somewhat higher than the $2.25 expected cost of pursuing his BATNA of purchasing from C. Another way of looking at this is to say that B would be willing to pay some premium over the expected cost of buying from C to avoid the uncertainty associated with that option. B would be willing to pay some amount of money over the $2.25 expected cost of purchasing the pear next week to lock in the price today.

For the same reason, plaintiffs in lawsuits are usually willing to accept a settlement offer of somewhat less money than the expected value of pursuing their case through the litigation process, because a settlement payment is certain whereas a litigation result is uncertain. Litigation could result in a large judgment, but it could also result in a small judgment or no judgment at all. If a plaintiff estimates that litigation has an expected value of $50,000, she will likely establish a reservation price in settlement negotiations somewhat lower than $50,000 because, all other things being equal, she would prefer the certain payment to the uncertainties of the trial process. How much lower than $50,000 the plaintiff would set her reservation price depends on how risk averse she is. If she is only slightly risk averse, she will only be willing to give up a small amount of the expected value of litigation in return for the certainty of settlement, so she might set her reservation price at $45,000. If she is very risk averse — perhaps, for example, because she is in desperate need of money to pay the medical bills associated with the injury that gave rise to the litigation and cannot risk even a small possibility of a trial verdict for the defense — she might set her reservation price well below $50,000.

Although it seems rational for individuals to exhibit risk aversion in many situations, individuals or businesses that participate in many similar transactions are more likely to exhibit risk neutrality. Assume that B purchases pears each week, either for his own consumption or because he operates a retail pear stand. If C's prices fluctuate between $1 and $3 for pears but average out to $2.25 over time, B might feel confident that the price he pays C for pears will average out to $2.25 per pear over the many months or years in which he maintains a relationship with C, even though next week he might pay as much as $3 per pear or as little as $1. In this case, B will probably exhibit risk neutrality by setting his reservation price for his negotiation with A at $2.25. Because B can essentially spread the risk of potentially having to pay C a higher price over many similar transactions over time, he would be unwilling to pay A any premium over $2.25 to avoid the uncertainty associated with C's prices.

Similarly, when a party to a lawsuit is a "repeat player" — that is, participates in many similar litigation matters — it is likely to be risk neutral rather than risk averse. Automobile insurance companies, for example, find themselves as defendants in negligence suits repeatedly. In the settlement negotiations for any given case, an insurance company is likely to be risk neutral. Holding all other factors equal, the company is likely to be willing to pay only the expected value of the plaintiff's lawsuit to settle. If settlement negotiations fail and the company is forced to pursue its BATNA of trial, it will sometimes lose more than the expected value of the case, and it will sometimes lose less than the expected value of the case. Over a long period of time, however, it will probably lose, on average, exactly the expected value of its cases. Consequently, it will refuse to pay any more than that amount to settle out of court.

## 5.  Transaction Costs

Taking advantage of an opportunity — whether through agreement with the opposite negotiator or the pursuit of a BATNA — can often require a variety of indirect costs, referred to here broadly as transaction costs. To set an accurate reservation price, the negotiator must take into account not only the relative desirability of the subject of the negotiation and his BATNA, but also the relative transaction costs associated with pursuing a negotiated agreement and pursuing his BATNA.

Suppose that B is negotiating to buy 100 pears from A, and his BATNA is to purchase 100 pears from C for $100 ($1 each). Suppose also that A's orchard is next door to B's fruit stand, and that C's orchard is a 30 minute drive away. If B fails to reach agreement with A, he will have to send an employee earning $10/hour on a one-hour roundtrip errand to C's orchard to pick up C's pears. The errand will also require $2 worth of gasoline. What should B's reservation price be in his negotiation with A? Even if the quality of A's and C's pears is identical, B's reservation price should not be the same as the nominal cost of purchasing from C, because the transaction costs of contracting with C are $12 higher than the transaction costs of contracting with A. Consequently, B's reservation price should be $112, to take account of the fact that contracting with C will cost him $100 in direct costs (payment to C) plus $10 in labor plus $2 in gasoline.

In the dispute resolution setting, the transaction costs associated with out-of-court settlement are usually different than the transaction costs associated with adjudication. Even risk neutral plaintiffs will usually set a reservation price lower than the expected value of adjudicating their claim, because the attorneys' fees and other costs associated with adjudication are usually much higher than the costs associated with reaching an out-of-court settlement. The degree of disparity, however, often changes over the course of the discovery and pretrial preparation process. Before any discovery takes place, a plaintiff is likely to set his reservation price relatively far below the expected value of adjudication, because reaching settlement will entail very few transaction costs compared to adjudication. In contrast, the plaintiff's reservation price for settlement after discovery is completed and his attorney has prepared for trial might be only marginally less than the expected value of adjudication because the marginal transaction costs of adjudication compared to settlement once her attorney has prepared for trial is relatively small.

## 6.  Value of Time

Because time usually has opportunity costs, two alternatives that will
take place at different times have different values. Consider a plaintiff
who has filed a lawsuit with an expected value of $50,000, who is risk
neutral, and who is represented by a friend pro bono, thus obviating
the need to consider the cost of attorneys' fees. Assume that the defendant will pay a negotiated settlement immediately, but a trial verdict
will take two years to secure and prejudgment interest is not available.
Under these circumstances, the plaintiff's reservation price should be
less than $50,000 because adjudication entails a cost that can be
avoided through settlement: the lost use of the expected $50,000 for
one year.

This is a specific application of the more general point that income
from different time periods must be discounted to its present value to
be compared. The basic formula for calculating the present value of
future income is Future Income $\times (1/(1 + I)^n)$, where "I" equals the
risk-free rate of return and "n" equals the number of years in the future
that the income will be received. In our example, we assume that income from a negotiated settlement will occur two years earlier than
income from an adjudicated outcome, and that the plaintiff can earn
an 8 percent return on his investments without risk, such as U.S. Treasury Bills. His reservation price in settlement negotiations should be
$50,000 $\times (1/1.08^2) = $42,867$.

To understand this intuitively, assume that the plaintiff accepted a
settlement payment today of $42,867 and invested the money in a risk-
free treasury bill earning 8 percent simple interest annually. After one
year, that amount would grow to $46,296. After a second year, it would
grow to $50,000 — precisely the same amount the plaintiff would ex-
pect to receive after a lengthy trial. Of course, if prejudgment interest
at the market rate is available, the plaintiff's reservation price in settlement negotiations would be $50,000, because his BATNA of trial would
have an expected value of $50,000 *plus interest* two years into the future.

Many commodities other than money are also more valuable the
sooner they are obtained. The purchaser of a car is likely to place a
higher value on a car that is available today than on the same model
that isn't available until tomorrow. If he obtains the car right away, he
can begin enjoying it immediately and get to work more easily.

In some unusual circumstances, negotiators might place a higher
value on a transaction that can be consummated in the future than
one that must be consummated immediately. Consider a home buyer
choosing between two houses that are identical except that the sellers
of the first house want to close the transaction immediately and the
sellers of the second house are not willing to close the transaction for
two months. If the buyer is moving to town from another city in two

months, he might place a higher value on the second house because he would not be forced to pay the mortgage on it for two months in which he would not be able to live in it.

## 7. Effect on Future Opportunities

To this point, we have assumed that in establishing their reservation prices negotiators are concerned only with the transaction at hand. That is, we have assumed that whether a negotiation results in agreement or impasse (thus leaving the negotiators to pursue their BATNAs) has no relevant effect on the party's future opportunities and/or relationships. In fact, the success or failure of a negotiation can affect the negotiator's opportunities to transact business with his opponent in the future. It can also affect the negotiator's reputation in the community, which can, in turn, affect his opportunities to transact business with others in the future. Either of these factors can and should affect a negotiator's calculation of his reservation price.

Assume, for example, that B's BATNA is to buy pears for his fruit stand from C for $2 each, and that B is negotiating to purchase pears from A. C grows only pears. A, however, grows a limited quantity of high-quality apples and peaches in addition to pears. B has been considering expanding his inventory to include apples and peaches, but he has yet to find a reliable source of those fruits at the consistently high quality that his customers demand. What reservation price should B establish? Ordinarily, B should probably establish a reservation price of $2. But if contracting with A will help B to establish himself as a reliable and valued customer of A, which might in turn enable B to establish additional profitable contracts in the future with A for apples and peaches, perhaps B would establish a higher reservation price. B would be unlikely to pay A $10 per year just to establish a relationship, but perhaps the chance to establish a relationship with A would justify a 25- or 50-cent premium over $2 per year.

To understand the possibility of using the reservation price to establish a valuable general reputation in the community, imagine that you are the lawyer representing a toaster manufacturer that is being sued by a customer who was severely burned by one of your client's toasters and suffered $500,000 in damages. You believe that the evidence clearly demonstrates there is no design or manufacturing defect, and that the injuries resulted entirely from the plaintiff's negligence in operating the toaster. You estimate that the plaintiff has only a 5-percent chance of winning a verdict, but that litigating the case will cost your client $20,000 more than settling the case.

You might calculate that the expected value of a verdict is $500,000 $\times 5\% = \$25,000$ and that this plus the transaction costs of litigation suggest that your client's reservation price should be $45,000. The problem is that if your client pays a settlement of $45,000 (or even $40,000 or $35,000), this might send the signal that your client is an easy target for nuisance suits, which could encourage plaintiffs' attorneys to bring similar suits on behalf of anyone who is ever burned by a toaster. Suppose that instead you set your client's reservation price at $5,000. If the plaintiff would be willing to settle out-of-court for $10,000 but not $5,000, the low reservation price would prevent agreement, and subject your client to a trial with direct and indirect expected costs of $45,000. On the other hand, the tough posture might discourage additional customers with marginal claims from filing lawsuits, thus saving your client a substantial sum.

## Notes

*1. Adjusting the Reservation Price During Bargaining.* A well-prepared negotiator thoroughly investigates his alternatives to a negotiated agreement and estimates his reservation price, at least preliminarily, before beginning negotiations. An important purpose of negotiating, however, is to acquire relevant information about the proposed transaction that might affect the negotiator's own reservation price but could not be discovered through pre-bargaining research. For example, if Esau is interested in buying Jacob's business, Esau should have a preliminary reservation price before beginning negotiations based on how strongly he desires to own a catering business relative to other opportunities he might have and the attributes of Jacob's business that Esau can learn through his own investigation. But it is extremely likely that Jacob will have information about his business that is otherwise unavailable to Esau — i.e., "private information" — that is quite relevant to the amount Esau would be willing to pay for it. For example, if Esau is a thorough negotiator, he will use the bargaining process in part to ask Jacob specific questions about his business's services, customers, products, financial situation, etc. — all information likely to cause Esau to update his reservation price.

Reservation prices, then, are not static points. They must be continually revised by negotiators in light of new information that arises during the negotiating process, and thorough negotiators will actively seek to discover such information by asking questions and carefully listening to the information their opponent provides. The negotiator must keep in mind, however, that his opponent has an interest in how information is presented. It is to Jacob's advantage to convince Esau that the business is very valuable so that Esau will be willing to pay more for it. It is also to Jacob's advantage to convince Esau that many other eager buyers wish to buy the business at a high price, in part to convince

Esau that he has undervalued the business' quality, and also in part to convince Esau that Jacob has a high reservation price. Consequently, Esau needs to view Jacob's representations with cautious skepticism, and, when possible, demand that Esau's claims are backed up with objective data — i.e., independently audited financial statements, names of other potential buyers who have expressed interest, etc.

Establishing an accurate reservation price, then, can be viewed as a three-step process: (1) acquiring and analyzing all relevant information that is available from sources other than the opposing negotiator before the bargaining begins; (2) actively seeking to discover information relevant to one's reservation price known only to the opposing negotiator (or which the opposing negotiator can access more readily) at the bargaining table; and (3) viewing information provided by the opposing negotiator with cautious skepticism as the situation warrants and verifying the information whenever possible.

***2. Estimating the Opponent's Reservation Price.*** One's negotiating opponent will often have private information relevant to the negotiator's reservation price, but the opponent will always have information about his own reservation price and options. Although "external preparation" can help the negotiator estimate his opponent's reservation price prior to bargaining, the negotiation itself presents a crucial opportunity for the negotiator to gather information about the opponent's reservation price. For example, Esau might use the bargaining process to improve his understanding not only of facts concerning the business relevant to how much Esau would be willing to pay to buy it, but also facts relevant to how much Jacob will demand to sell it.

In some circumstances, information will serve both purposes. For example, if Jacob's business has a solid base of customers, Jacob will demand a higher price and Esau will be willing to pay a higher price than if the business has few customers. In other circumstances, Esau will seek to acquire information that affects Jacob's reservation price but not his own. For example, Esau might have developed his own predictions about the future of the local business climate, but he would still want to learn what Jacob's predictions were about the business climate because Jacob's predictions will affect Jacob's reservation price. Esau might find Jacob's predictions unrealistically optimistic, but the information will still be useful because it will suggest that Jacob will not be willing to sell for anything less than a high price. Esau might also seek to discover whether Esau has a reason he needs to sell the business quickly, as this will affect Jacob's reservation price even if it does not affect Esau's own reservation price.

***3. Methods of Information Gathering: Active Questioning and Silence.*** How can (and how do) negotiators acquire relevant information during the course of bargaining? The most straightforward approach is to consider prior to negotiations what information the opponent might have that is relevant to one's own reservation price and the opponent's reservation price, to prepare questions designed to discover this information, to listen carefully and critically to the opponent's responses, to ask follow-up questions when answers are incomplete or not forthcoming, and to demand verification of self-serving claims made by the opponent. A less obvious — but often equally valuable — tool of information acquisition is silence. Most people are uncomfortable with silence, and they will seek to eliminate it by talking. In the process, more often than not they will reveal information. Consequently, effective negotiators often gather information just by becoming comfortable with silence. Consider the following advice:

> Needless to say, one who is naturally responsive and gregarious cannot be made closemouthed and inscrutable simply by wishing to be so. On the other hand all negotiators can exercise some control over their reactions and considerable control over the amount of talking they do. Again and again in the observation of student negotiating tapes we see opponents attempting to talk simultaneously. In that circumstance neither is convincing the other but more important, neither is learning what he can about the opponent's position by allowing the opponent to talk.
>
> . . . In most cases [the negotiator should] restrain his natural desire to speak when a silence of any length in the negotiation occurs. One of the impediments that the Institute for Survey Research at Michigan has found to training interviewers is the interviewer's desire to talk. The Institute's experience reveals that silence in the presence of other people causes considerable and rising anxiety and that in response to that anxiety the inexperienced interviewer will not wait for an answer from the respondent but will offer the answer himself. The same anxiety will operate on the untrained negotiator and it must be resisted by conscious effort.

Harry Edwards and James J. White, The Lawyer as a Negotiator 114-115 (1977).

***4. Using Decision Trees to Evaluate Alternatives.*** When alternatives to agreement are few and the consequences of reaching agreement or pursuing an alternative are relatively simple, it is often possible for the negotiator to determine his reservation price in his head or with the type of simple arithmetic used in the preceding examples. For more complex analyses, however, a decision tree can be a useful tool in evaluating and comparing the expected value of reaching agreement to the expected value of not reaching agreement and instead pursuing an alternative course of action. A decision tree is nothing more complicated than a diagram that displays the negotiator's options, the various potential consequences of those options, and the monetary or utility consequences of each potential outcome.

As an example, consider the following hypothetical dispute, which creates a more complicated decision problem than the simple examples discussed above, but one that is only moderately complicated relative to real-world business disputes:

Hesperian Inc. manufactures and sells condiments nationwide. For many years, it has marketed its brand of ketchup in a unique, cylindrical shaped bottle with a light blue label. Kelly Corp. is a regional manufacturer of barbecue sauce that operates only in New England. It recently began marketing a line of ketchup, which it has packaged in a cylindrical bottle identical to the type used by Hesperian with a dark blue label. Hesperian's attorneys filed suit against Kelly claiming violation of trade dress. Hesperian claims that its style of bottle has acquired a secondary meaning in the marketplace, such that it is associated by consumers with Hesperian's brand of ketchup, that Kelly's use of the same bottle has created confusion, and that Hesperian is entitled to recover its lost profits and the amount Kelly has been unjustly enriched by the confusion it has created. Attorneys for the two parties are set to meet to try to negotiate a settlement.

Hesperian's attorneys have considered their alternatives should the negotiations fail. It could choose to dismiss its lawsuit. If it were to do so, there is a 40 percent chance that Kelly will stop using the cylindrical bottles because it does not want to risk future legal actions by Hesperian. If this happens, the value to Hesperian is $0. There is also a 60 percent chance that Kelly will continue to use the bottles. If this happens, the attorneys estimate Hesperian will suffer lost sales in the northeast. The value to Hesperian of this outcome (in present dollars) is *negative* $100,000. If Kelly continues to use the bottles, there is a 50 percent chance that no one else will learn of the suit and its dismissal; therefore, Hesperian will suffer no reputational cost. But there is a 50 percent chance that word will get out, and other small companies will believe they can infringe on Hesperian's trade dress with impunity. Hesperian's lawyers estimate this would cost the company an additional $180,000 (present value) in future lost profits.

Alternatively, Hesperian could pursue its lawsuit. If it does, Kelly will file a motion to dismiss, and there is a 5 percent chance that such a motion would be successful, thus ending the case and allowing Kelly to continue to use the bottles. It will cost Hesperian $5,000 to defend the motion to dismiss. If Kelly loses such a motion, it will file a motion for summary judgment, which would have a 30 percent chance of success, thus ending the litigation. Defending against this motion would cost Hesperian $10,000. If Hesperian survives motions to dismiss and motions for summary judgment, the case would go to a jury. A jury trial would cost Hesperian $20,000. There is a 40 percent chance that Kelly would prevail, arguing that because the bottles have different labels there is no confusion, and a 60 percent chance Hesperian would prevail. If Hesperian prevails, there is a 90 percent chance the court would award lost profits and enjoin Kelly from further use of the bottle. There is a 50 percent chance lost profits would be assessed at $80,000, and a 50 percent chance they would be assessed at $60,000, based on the jury's view of the expert testimony concerning Hesperian's actual losses. There is a 10 percent chance that the court would award restitution damages, with a 50 percent chance of these being set at $50,000 and a 50 percent chance of these being set at $60,000.

Given these assumptions, Hesperian's attorneys might find it advantageous to use a decision tree to identify their BATNA and establish a reservation price for their settlement negotiations with Kelly. Such a decision tree, Figure 2-1, would display graphically Hesperian's alternatives to settlement, the range of possible outcomes that could result from each alternative, and the probability of each possible outcome. Hesperian's attorneys can then identify the expected value of each alternative by multiplying the value of each possible outcome by the likelihood of that outcome occurring, and then summing the products.

By mapping out their alternatives and all the possible results of each alternative, Hesperian's lawyers will learn two important pieces of information. First, litigating is clearly preferable to dismissing. Dismissing the case would have an expected net cost of $114,000, while litigating will have an expected net cost of $465. Second, their BATNA of litigating has a negative expected value, albeit a very small one. (Notice that one of the reasons for this is that, as the plaintiff, Hesperian must prevail on Kelly's motion to dismiss, on Kelly's summary judgment motion, and at trial, in order to recover. If Kelly prevails at any one of these stages in the litigation, Hesperian will suffer litigation costs but not recover.) Thus, Hesperian should probably prefer a settlement in which Kelly agrees to cease using the cylindrical bottles in the future but pays no damages to not reaching a settlement. If Hesperian is risk averse, it might even prefer a settlement in which it pays Kelly to stop using the cylindrical bottles to pursuing its BATNA of litigation.

The decision tree is also a useful tool for identifying how the value of alternatives change as events occur and the outcomes of probabilistic events become known with certainty. For example, assume that, in light of learning that litigation has a small expected net cost rather than benefit, Hesperian offers to settle the case for $0 if Kelly agrees to stop using the cylindrical bottles, but Kelly refuses so the litigation process begins. Subsequently, Kelly fails on its motion to dismiss and motion for summary judgment. On the eve of trial, Kelly approaches Hesperian and suggests that it would now be willing to stop using the cylindrical bottles if Hesperian will still settle for no cash payment. Should Hesperian accept? At this point, Hesperian needs to adjust the probabilities in the decision tree (see Figure 2-2) to take into account that it prevailed in the first two stages of litigation. Effectively, the "chance"

# HESPERIAN INC. DECISION TREE

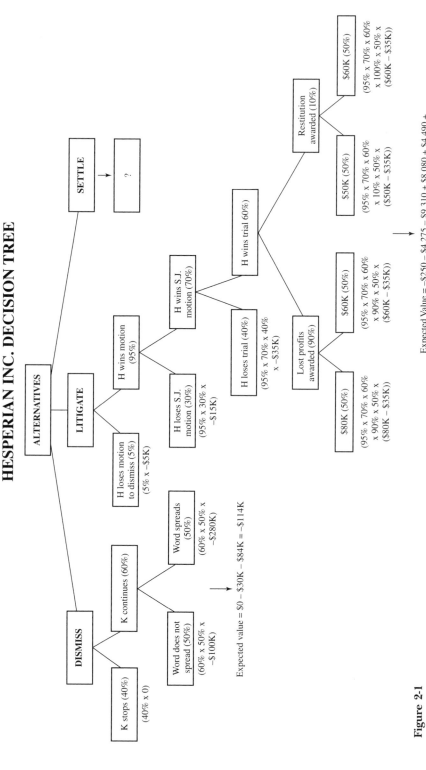

**Figure 2-1**
**Hesperian Decision Tree Prelitigation**

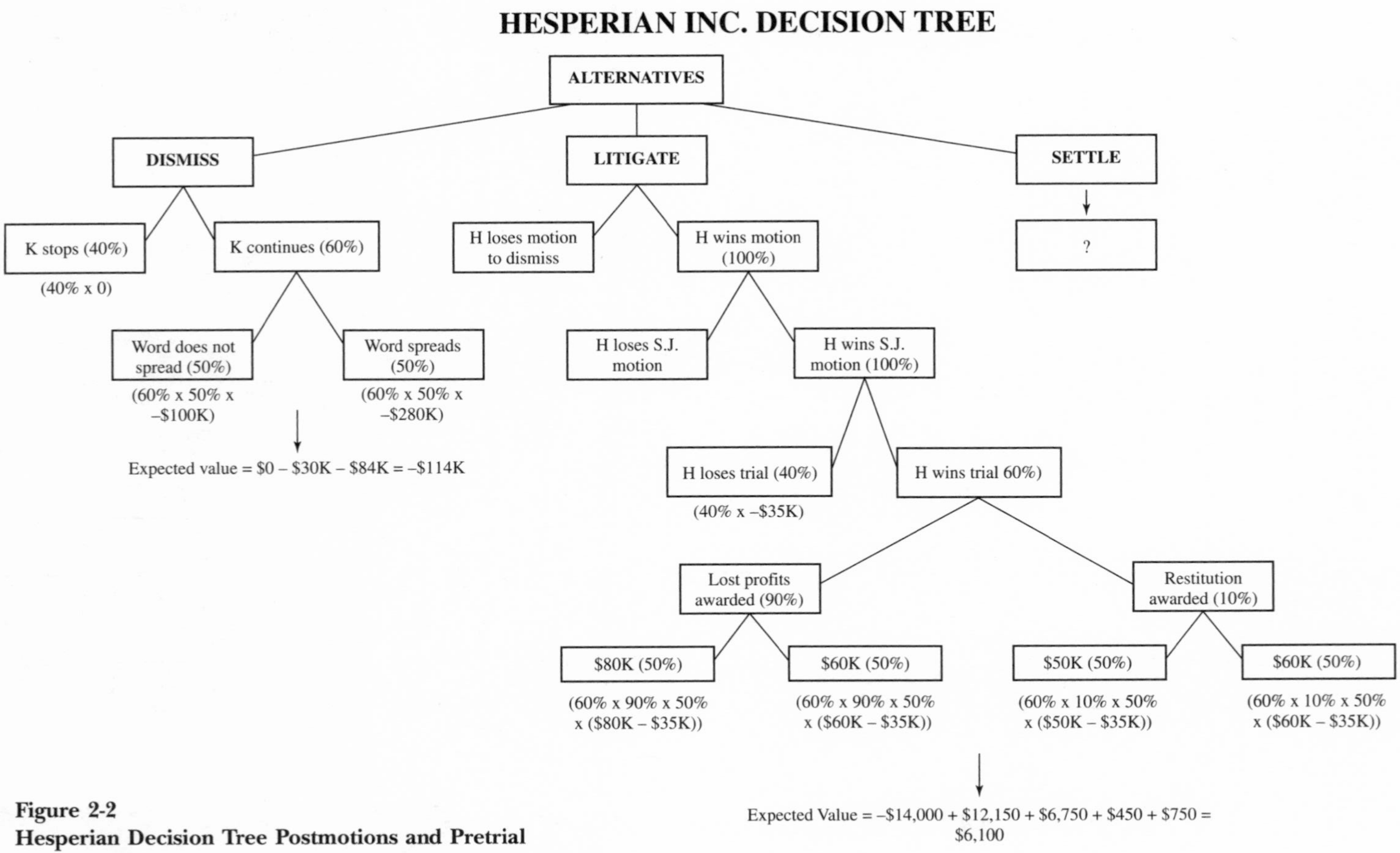

# HESPERIAN INC. DECISION TREE

**Figure 2-2**
**Hesperian Decision Tree Postmotions and Pretrial**

of Hesperian prevailing in those two stages becomes 100 percent, and the various possible trial recoveries do not have to be discounted for the possibility that Hesperian would be defeated by a motion to dismiss or a motion for summary judgment. As a result, litigation now has a positive expected value of $6,100.

Therefore, if Hesperian is not risk averse, it should not accept a settlement offer unless Kelly pays that amount in addition to promising to cease production of the cylindrical bottles.

## C.  ASPIRATIONS

When a negotiator sits down at the bargaining table, awareness of his reservation price places a minimum constraint on what terms of agreement he will accept. While negotiators usually will accept a deal at their reservation price rather than reach a bargaining impasse, they most often hope to negotiate an agreement that leaves them better off than would a minimally acceptable agreement. The terms of an agreement that the negotiator hopes to achieve — as distinguished from his reservation point — can be called the negotiator's "goal" or "aspiration."

This raises the question of what type of aspirations negotiators should and do set for themselves prior to bargaining. One approach is for negotiators to bargain with the goal of obtaining an agreement as favorable as possible subject to the condition that the agreement is superior to their reservation point. This can be called a "do your best" approach. It is fully consistent with the view of negotiators as rational utility maximizers: the negotiator strives for the best possible deal, but at the end of the day he settles for any agreement superior to his reservation point.

Behavioral research in a wide variety of contexts (including but not limited to bargaining) suggests, however, that individuals usually obtain better bargaining outcomes if they begin an endeavor with a specific, concrete aspiration rather than a more ambiguous "do your best" aspiration. See Edwin A. Locke & Gary P. Latham, A Theory of Goal Setting and Task Performance (1990). The following excerpt contends that negotiators who arm themselves with and concentrate on achieving specific aspirations will achieve superior results to negotiators who focus only on their "bottom line," as defined by their reservation point.

## ■ G. Richard Shell, Bargaining for Advantage: Negotiation Strategies for Reasonable People*

24-32 (1999)

In Lewis Carroll's *Alice's Adventures in Wonderland,* Alice finds herself at a crossroads where a Cheshire Cat materializes. Alice asks the Cat, "Would you tell me please, which way I ought to go from here?" The Cat replies, "That depends a good deal on where you want to get to." "I don't much care where — " says Alice. "Then it doesn't matter which way you go," the Cat replies, cutting her off.

To become an effective negotiator, you must find out where you want to go — and why. That means committing yourself to specific, justifiable goals. It also means taking the time to transform your goals from simple   targets   into   genuine — and   appropriately   high — *expectations. . . .*

Setting goals is useful advice for many activities in life, not just negotiations. An entire field, sports psychology, has grown up to help athletes perform at peak capacity. One recent article in the *Journal of Sport and Exercise Psychology* summarized thirty-six different studies on setting goals, concluding that the use of specific, challenging goals significantly improves performance for athletes regardless of what sport is involved. . . .

Negotiations are no different from other areas of achievement. What you aim for often determines what you get. Why? The first reason is obvious: Your goals set the upper limit of what you will ask for. You mentally concede everything beyond your goal, so you seldom do better than that benchmark.

Second, research on goals reveals that they trigger powerful psychological "striving" mechanisms. Sports psychologists and educators alike confirm that setting specific goals motivates people, focusing and concentrating their attention and psychological powers.

Third, we are more persuasive when we are committed to achieving some specific purpose, in contrast to the occasions when we ask for things half-heartedly or merely react to initiatives proposed by others. Our commitment is infectious. People around us feel drawn toward our goals. Early in the American Civil War, when General Robert E. Lee took over as head of the Confederate Army, he needed generals to lead his soldiers in the field. One man Lee chose was Thomas J. Jackson, nicknamed "Stonewall" by his men for the stand his troops had made in the Civil War's first battle at Manassas. Why did Lee pick Jackson? "He is true, honest and brave," wrote Lee in his letter recommending Jackson's promotion. "He has a single eye to the good of the service and spares no exertion to accomplish his object." Jackson went on to become a legendary general, garnering respect from people on both sides of the conflict because he had the power to focus on his goals with a "single eye," sparing "no exertion to accomplish his object."

President Lyndon Johnson once said, "What convinces is conviction." And H. Wayne Huizenga, an energetic American entrepreneur, maintains that one of the secrets of success in business negotiations is having a passionate commitment to ambitious goals. This trait enables effective negotiators to communicate enthusiasm and direction at the bargaining table. . . .

I have personally observed this "goal effect" in watching some of the best negotiators in the business both at the bargaining table and in executive training sessions. Negotiators striving to achieve concrete goals are more animated, committed, prepared, and persistent. Nor is this effect limited to experienced deal makers. Everyone gains a significant psychological edge when he or she is working to achieve a specific target in bargaining.

### GOALS VERSUS "BOTTOM LINES"

Most negotiation books and experts emphasize the importance of having a "bottom line," "walkaway," or "reservation price" for negotiation. Indeed, the bottom line is a fundamental bargaining concept on which much of modern negotiation theory is built. It is the *minimum acceptable level* you require to say "yes" in a negotiation. . . .

A well-framed goal is quite different from a bottom line. As I use the word, "goal" is your *highest legitimate expectation* of what you should achieve. For example, in the case of [a] used CD player . . . , the seller has a bottom line of getting at least $100, but the seller might set a *goal* of $130 based on the prices paid for similar CD players in used equipment stores. Bottom lines are vitally important to negotiation theory, but I think that focusing on goals is more important in negotiation practice. Let me explain why.

Researchers have discovered that humans have a limited capacity for maintaining focus in complex, stressful situations such as negotiations. Consequently, once a negotiation is under way, we gravitate toward the single focal point that has the most psychological significance for us. Once most people set a firm bottom line in a negotiation, that becomes their dominant reference point as discussions proceed. They measure success or failure with reference to their bottom line, and it is very difficult to psychologically reorient themselves toward a more ambitious bargaining goal.

Thus, if you are selling your used CD player and have focused on getting at least $100 in order to buy some other item that costs about that much, you will tend to relax once the buyer makes an offer above $100. You can now end your search for a buyer and begin mentally possessing the other item you want. If the buyer is alert (and most are when it comes to money), he will sense your relaxation and stop the bidding. If, instead of focusing on your bottom line, you orient toward your goal of getting $130 based on comparable store prices, you don't relax quite so soon. And if the buyer is focused on *his* bottom line of $150, chances are you will end up with a higher price than you otherwise would receive.

What is the practical effect of having your bottom line become your dominant reference point in a negotiation? Over a lifetime of negotiating, your results will tend to hover at a point just above this minimum acceptable level. For most reasonable people, the bottom line is the most natural focal point. Disappointment arises if we cannot get the other side to agree to meet our minimum requirements (usually established by our available alternatives or our needs away from the table), and satisfaction arises just above that level. Meanwhile, someone else who is more skilled at orienting himself toward ambitious goals will do much better. Not surprisingly, research shows that parties with higher (but still realistic) goals outperform those with more modest ones, all else being equal.

If setting goals is so vital to effective preparation, how should you do it? Use the following simple steps:

1. Think carefully about what you really want — and remember that money is often a means, not an end.
2. Set an optimistic — but justifiable — target.
3. Be specific.
4. Get committed. Write down your goal and, if possible, discuss the goal with someone else.
5. Carry your goal with you into the negotiation.

### Set an Optimistic, Justifiable Target

When you set goals, think boldly and optimistically about what you would like to see happen. Research has repeatedly shown that people who have higher aspirations in negotiations perform better and get more than people who have modest or "I'll do my best" goals, provided they really believe in their targets.

In one classic study, psychologists Sydney Siegel and Lawrence Fouraker set up a simple buy-sell negotiation experiment. They allowed the negotiators to keep all the profits they achieved but told the subjects they could qualify for a second, "double-their-money" round if they met or exceeded certain specified bargaining goals. In other words, Siegel and Fouraker gave their subjects both concrete *incentives* for hitting a certain specified level of performance and, perhaps unintentionally, a hint that the assigned target levels were realistically attainable (why else would subjects be told about the bonus round?). One set of negotiators was told they would have to hit a modest $2.10 target to qualify for the bonus round. Another set of negotiators was told they would have to hit a much more ambitious target of $6.10. Both sides had the same bottom line: They could not accept any deal that involved a loss. The negotiators with the more ambitious $6.10 goal achieved a mean profit of $6.25, far outperforming the median profit of $3.35 achieved by those with the modest $2.10 goal.

My own research has confirmed Siegel's and Fouraker's findings. In our experiment, unlike the one Siegel and Fouraker conducted, negotiation subjects set their own bargaining goals. And instead of letting everyone keep whatever profits they earned, we gave separate $100 prizes to the buyer and the seller with the best individual outcomes. The result was the same, however. Negotiators who reported higher prenegotiation expectations achieved more than those who entered the negotiation with more modest goals. . . .                               ■

## Notes

*1. The Power of Aspirations.*   As Shell notes, impressive laboratory evidence demonstrates that negotiators with high aspirations obtain more desirable outcomes than negotiators with more modest aspirations. In one experiment, White and Neale had subjects negotiate the price of a house. Buyers were told that their reservation price was $235,000, and sellers were told their reservation price was $225,000. Some buyer subjects were then told that their aspiration price was $220,000 (low aspiration) and others were told their aspiration price was $200,000 (high aspiration). Some seller subjects were given the aspiration price of $240,000 (low aspiration), and others $260,000 (high aspiration). In dyads where the buyer had a low aspiration and the seller had a high aspiration, the average agreement was $232,664. In dyads where the buyer had a high aspiration and the seller a low aspiration, the average agreement was for $227,921. When both subjects had either high aspirations or low aspirations, the average agreement was between these two figures. Sally Blount White & Margaret A. Neale, The Role of Negotiator Aspirations and Settlement Expectancies in Bargaining Outcomes, 57 Org. Behav. & Human Decision Proc. 303 (1994).

*2. Why Should Aspirations Affect Outcomes?*   Despite the evidence that aspirations do matter to negotiation outcomes, it is difficult to explain why this is so. If a buyer's reservation price is $235,000 and a seller's reservation price is $225,000, we know that they will reach agreement, if at all, in the $10,000 bargaining zone that exists between those two figures. Why should whether one or both parties have aggressive goals affect what deal point in that range is reached?

Jennifer Brown suggests one interesting hypothesis. Perhaps negotiators achieve more satisfaction, or "utility," from each dollar they receive up to their aspiration level than each dollar they receive beyond their aspiration level, causing them to bargain harder to satisfy their aspiration than to exceed their aspiration. Jennifer Gerarda Brown, The Role of Hope in Negotiation, 44 UCLA L. Rev. 1661, 1672-1673 (1997). This explanation suggests that aspirations might matter for either of two reasons, or perhaps both. (1) Negotiators set their aspiration levels at the point where their marginal utility of achieving more from the bargain peaks. Thus, a specific aspiration level serves as a marker for the point at which fighting for more of a cooperative surplus is less valuable to the negotiator. (2) Negotiators can create such a peak in the marginal utility they enjoy as a result of achieving more by setting an aspiration level. Thus, aspiration levels do not respond to peaks in the negotiator's marginal utility curve, they create the peak by establishing a target.

Explanation (2) can be viewed as consistent with "prospect theory," discussed in detail in the next chapter. Prospect theory posits that individuals view the possible outcomes of making a particular choice not in absolute terms, but relative to some reference point, and that they care more about avoiding "losses" relative to that point than achieving "gains" of the same amount from that point. The power of aspirations might be understood as the result of negotiators viewing their target goals as reference points. Falling short of that point would then be perceived as a "loss" relative to expectations — something to be avoided if at all possible — while exceeding it would be perceived as a "gain" — nice to have, but less critical.

**3. The Risks of High Aspirations.** Shell argues that negotiators should enter bargaining encounters with specific, high aspirations, and focus their attention on those aspirations. It is hard to criticize this advice as long as the negotiator always remembers that his aspiration is not his reservation point, and that ultimately an agreement at any point superior to his reservation point is more desirable than no agreement, even if this means accepting less than his aspiration.

The problem with Shell's advice is that negotiators often fail to determine a precise reservation point prior to bargaining because calculating a reservation point is quite difficult and often requires making probability estimates based on a number of uncertain possible results of not reaching agreement. In contrast, it is cognitively very easy to set an aspiration. Negotiators with a fixed aspiration and only a hazy estimation of their reservation point will be tempted to treat their aspiration as though it were their reservation point, even though the aspiration will usually be more aggressive. The consequence of this can be an unfortunate bargaining mistake: the negotiator ends up walking away from a possible deal that would be superior to pursuing his BATNA just because the deal terms fail to meet his aspiration. If both negotiators set high aspirations and fix their attention on those aspirations, it is easy to imagine how impasse can result even where there is a potential mutually beneficial agreement. By aspiring only to achieve a deal at his reservation point, the negotiator might sometimes settle for less than he could have achieved, but at the same time he will minimize the risk of causing an impasse when a possible deal exists that would be in his best interest.

*4. How Should Negotiators Determine Their Aspirations?* There is no single rule of thumb of how negotiators should set their aspiration levels, but one sensible approach is for the negotiator to set her aspiration at her estimate of the opponent's reservation point. Thus, to borrow one of Shell's examples, if the seller of a used CD player has a reservation price of $100 but estimates that the buyer's reservation price is $150, the seller might establish a prenegotiation aspiration of receiving $150. Because the buyer's reservation price is the maximum the seller can ever receive, setting an aspiration any higher than $150 would only invite bargaining impasse or, at a minimum, disappointment on the part of the seller. Setting an aspiration any lower than $150 might result in the seller accepting less for the CD player than he might have received.

Note, however, that there are a number of problems with this approach. First, negotiators usually are uncertain about their opponent's precise reservation price. If the seller sets his aspiration at what he thinks is the buyer's reservation price, but the buyer's reservation price is actually lower, impasse or disappointment could result. Second, if two negotiators both attempt this strategy, it will be impossible for both to satisfy their aspiration: one or the other, or both, will fall short, or else impasse will result. Third, if the negotiators anticipate repeat dealings with each other, it might not be in either's long-term interest to aspire to capture all of the cooperative surplus, as the benefit achieved in the current negotiation must be weighed against the risk that the opponent who accepts a deal at his reservation point and thus walks away only minimally satisfied might look for other trading partners in the future.

## DISCUSSION QUESTIONS AND PROBLEMS

*1. The Associate.* Ben, a third-year law student, has a meeting this afternoon with the small law firm of Chasome & Wretch to discuss the possibility of him joining the firm as an associate. He currently has two job offers: one from Firm A for $58,000 per year, one from Firm B for $61,000 per year. He considers jobs with all three firms equally attractive, and all would provide roughly the same fringe benefits. Chasome & Wretch needs to hire only one new associate this year. They are indifferent between Ben and Beelzebub, a student from another school. The firm knows that Beelzebub has an offer of $85,000 from firm C, and would be unlikely to accept an offer from C&W for less money than this. The firm's third choice is a student named Todd who is bright but abrasive and might offend clients. Todd has indicated he would work for C&W for $75,000 per year.

Going into the negotiations, what are Ben's alternatives to a negotiated agreement? What is his BATNA? What is his reservation price? What is Chasome & Wretch's BATNA? What is its reservation price? What is the bargaining zone?

**2. The Slippery Banana.**    Amy slipped on a banana at the local supermarket ("Herefords") and suffered a broken leg. She has since filed a lawsuit against Herefords' corporate owner. She would like to be compensated for her injuries, but is very fearful of Herefords accusing her of being clumsy should the case go to trial. Amy's attorney and Herefords' attorney agree on the following possible outcomes if the case goes to trial:

50% chance: Jury finds Herefords not negligent, Amy recovers $0.
25% chance: Jury finds Herefords negligent, Amy recovers $20,000.
25% chance: Jury finds Herefords negligent, Amy recovers $40,000.

Amy's attorney, a sole practitioner, would charge $5,000 for taking the case to trial. Herefords' more expensive corporate law firm would charge $10,000 in fees for taking the case to trial.

Amy and Herefords, along with their attorneys, plan to meet to discuss settlement. What are Amy's alternatives, BATNA, and reservation price? What are Herefords' alternatives, BATNA, and reservation price? What is the bargaining zone?

**3. The Venture Capitalist.**    Gil Bates represents a venture capitalist firm that invests in biotech startup companies. When he evaluates potential investments, he is equally interested in two features: the expected profit of the investment, and the amount of control his firm will have over the startup company (i.e., representation on the startup company's board of directors). Currently, he is in the process of evaluating ten companies, and he has $1 million to invest in a single one of the ten. To date, he has met with two companies:

"Genetico," which seeks to patent new gene therapies, is a gamble. If things go well, the shares of stock Genetico would give Gil in return for a $1 million investment will return $5 million (in current dollars), but the company might never secure a patent, in which case all the shares will be worthless. (Gil thinks the chances of each outcome are roughly 50/50.) Genetico has offered Gil three of five seats on its board of directors if Gil will fund it.

"Olympia Products" already has a patent for a hair replacement drug, and FDA approval is imminent. Consequently, it is somewhat less risky. The number of shares it is offering in return for a $1 million investment will return between $2 million and $3 million (in current dollars), depending on how popular the drug becomes. Olympia will give Gil only two of five seats on its board of directors in return for funding.

Today Gil has a meeting with "Cardiotech," which hopes to market a new type of artificial heart valve. The valve is promising, but it has yet to be considered for FDA approval. Cardiotech has told Gil that if no deal is reached today, it will accept venture financing from another company and will no longer be interested in making a deal with Gil's company.

Gil has not had time to evaluate the other seven companies yet. One or more might provide better opportunities than Genetico, Olympia Products, or Cardiotech. Then again, they might not.

What "reservation prices" do you recommend Gil establish before going into today's negotiations with Cardiotech? How do you justify your recommendation?

**4. Malpractice.** Lawyer represents Patient in a medical malpractice lawsuit filed against Doctor and Hospital in Chicago. Patient consented to routine arthroscopic knee surgery to relieve discomfort that he felt while exercising. Following the surgery, his knee was considerably worse, causing Patient to walk with a limp. Lawyer has identified two respected orthopedic surgeons in Chicago who will testify that Patient's injuries are a result of malpractice and that the limp is probably permanent. Lawyer has also researched Illinois jury verdicts for the last few years in cases with injuries similar to this one. He has identified five such verdicts: two in Chicago for $100,000 and $80,000, and three in rural Illinois for $80,000, $65,000, and $20,000. In preparing for settlement negotiations with the insurance companies representing Doctor and Hospital, Lawyer established the averaged of the five jury verdicts — $69,000 — as his reservation price. Do you agree with his methodology? What reservation price would you establish for Patient given these facts?

**5. The Shoplifting Charge.** You represent a client who has been charged by the district attorney with shoplifting. On the day of the alleged crime, your client visited a local drug store. She was arrested minutes after she left the store by police who were called by the store clerk. The police found a moderately expensive bottle of perfume in your client's purse that came from the store. The prosecution's case rests on the testimony of the store clerk, who claims that your client did not pay for the perfume. Your client claims that she paid for it with cash, and then browsed in the store for 15 more minutes before walking out, and that the clerk simply forgot that she had paid. Your client has no receipt for the perfume. If the case goes to trial, it will be your client's word against the clerk's. If your client is found guilty, the applicable sentencing guidelines provide that she can be sentenced to probation, or up to two years of incarceration in the county jail, at the judge's discretion. It is your client's first offense, but the judge assigned to the case has a reputation of being very tough on crime. You are meeting with the deputy district attorney today to discuss the possibility of a plea bargain. What will your reservation point be, and why?

**6. Structured Settlements and the Time Value of Money.** You represent a plaintiff in a personal injury lawsuit. You estimate that the expected value of trying the case is $50,000. Assume for the moment that your client is risk neutral, the costs of litigation are not an issue, it will take one year to secure a trial verdict, and there is no prejudgment interest available. The defendant is interested in negotiating a settlement, but it wants to pay the settlement award in equal installments over a ten-year period, beginning in year one. What should your client's reservation price be in settlement negotiations? How would your answer change if your client needed a substantial amount of money immediately and, as a consequence, were extremely risk averse?

**7. The Role of Aspirations.** What does Shell's discussion imply about why he thinks aspirations have an effect on negotiation outcomes? Does Shell's discussion of the role of aspirations differ from Jennifer Brown's hypothesis about why aspirations matter in negotiation, or is it consistent? Given a set reservation price, do you think you would achieve better results in negotiation by having an aggressive aspiration as opposed to (a) a modest aspiration, or (b) a simple "do your best" aspiration? Why or why not?

**8. Costs of Aspirations.** Are there any reasons that a negotiator might not want to establish a specific aspiration before entering into negotiations? If so, what are those reasons? Are there situations in which, on balance, a firm aspiration might be undesirable, or will the benefits of setting an aspiration always outweigh the costs?

**9. Setting Aspiration Prices.** Review the problems described above in Notes 1 through 5. For each of those problems, what aspiration levels would you recommend for the relevant parties? How did you go about establishing your aspiration level recommendations?

# Chapter 3

# Psychological Factors in Evaluating Alternatives

By estimating a reservation price prior to bargaining, the negotiator essentially compares a range of possible negotiated agreements to her BATNA. The negotiator's reservation price then divides the possible agreements that would be more desirable than pursuing her BATNA from those that would be less desirable than pursuing her BATNA. For example, if a plaintiff would prefer a fixed payment of $25,000 to going to trial, but would prefer going to trial to a fixed payment of $24,999, her reservation price would be $25,000. A reservation price, then, can be understood as the sum total of a series of discrete comparisons between alternatives. As we have seen, the value of some alternatives might be known with precision by the negotiator, whereas the value of other alternatives might be probabilistic.

To this point, we have made implicit assumptions about how decision makers such as negotiators — at least those who are suitably prepared prior to bargaining — will go about making these comparisons. These assumptions are derived from a set of postulates that social scientists often refer to as "rational choice theory." When negotiators behave according to the predictions of rational choice theory, they evaluate the value of alternatives objectively given their preference structure and the information available to them, they reach identical choices between available alternatives regardless of how the choice is presented to them, and their choices exhibit either risk aversion or risk neutrality.

There is considerable empirical evidence, however, that individuals who make comparisons between alternatives often violate these assumptions (and others) of rational choice theory. This is highly relevant to negotiation, because it suggests negotiators will not always set their reservation points in precisely the way that the previous chapter describes. The following set of materials presents experimental evidence that negotiators often establish reservation prices in manners that are at odds with rational choice theory. As you read these excerpts, ask yourself whether the observed violations of rational choice theory would likely cause the decision makers to enter into undesirable agreements or to fail to enter into desirable agreements. In other words, are the deviations from so-called "rational" behavior ones that you as a negotiator would want to avoid, or are they acceptable?

## A. RISK PREFERENCE AND THE FRAMING EFFECT

As Chapter 2 described, economic theory predicts that rational negotiators will be risk averse due to the declining marginal utility of money. This means that negotiators are expected to prefer a negotiated agreement with a certain value to a BATNA with a probabilistic value when the two have the same expected value (or a BATNA with a certain value to a negotiated agreement with a probabilistic payoff that has the same expected value). When negotiators are repeat players in a particular type of bargaining situation, such that they can spread over many transactions the risk inherent in selecting risky alternatives, economic theory predicts that negotiators will be risk neutral when comparing a possible negotiated agreement to a BATNA and determining a reservation price.

Through the experimental investigation of the choices that individuals actually make when presented with different alternatives, psychologists Daniel Kahneman and Amos Tversky discovered that, in fact, the risk preference exhibited by decision makers often depends on whether they perceive the alternatives under consideration to be "gains" or "losses" in relation to their original situation. From their data, Kahneman and Tversky derived "prospect theory," which predicts individuals' preferences for certain vs. risky alternatives in different situations. See Daniel Kahneman and Amos Tversky, Prospect Theory: An Analysis of Decision Under Risk, 47 Econometrica 263 (1979). Consistent with economic theory, prospect theory predicts that in the usual case decision makers choosing between a certain gain and a probabilistic gain will indeed be risk averse — that is, they will prefer the alternative that promises a certain gain to an alternative that has the same expected value but promises a probabilistic gain. Unlike economic theory, prospect theory predicts that in the usual case decision makers will exhibit risk seeking tendencies when choosing between certain and probabilistic losses — that is, they will prefer a probabilistic loss to a certain loss when the two have the same expected value. This prediction of prospect theory — that individuals will prefer certain alternatives to risky ones in the realm of gains but will prefer risky alternatives to certain ones in the realm of losses — is often known as the "framing" effect.

The framing effect has significant implications for understanding negotiating behavior, because it implies that when a negotiated agreement would lead to a certain outcome but the negotiator's BATNA will lead to a probabilistic outcome (or vice versa), the negotiator's reservation price will depend on whether he views the alternatives as "gains" or as "losses." Whether alternatives appear to be gains or losses depends, in turn, on the reference point the negotiator relies on when evaluating his alternatives. The following passage explores how the framing effect can affect negotiators' reservation prices in litigation bargaining situations.

## ■ Jeffrey J. Rachlinski, Gains, Losses, and the Psychology of Litigation*
### 70 S. Cal. L. Rev. 113, 116-117, 128-129, 136-139 (1996)

. . . The economic model predicts that litigants will make choices that lead to the greatest expected returns. For example, assuming the plaintiff is risk-neutral, he should accept a settlement offer of $10,000 in lieu of a trial where he has a 50% chance of winning $20,000 at a cost of $5,000 in litigation expenses (the expected value of trial in this case equals $20,000 × .5 − 5,000, or $5,000, while the expected value of the settlement equals $10,000). As a general matter, a litigant should accept a settlement only when its value exceeds the expected value of continued litigation. Litigants should also make similar calculations when evaluating other choices in litigation. For example, a defendant who has had a judgment for $20,000 entered against her should appeal if the likelihood of success on appeal multiplied by $20,000 exceeds the costs of the appeal. Models of litigation also allow for risk-averse decisionmaking, since litigants are assumed to maximize utility and not merely wealth. Many scholars in the field also note that other factors, such as a desire for justice, process, fairness, or one's day in court may influence decisionmaking as well, but either hold these factors aside, or incorporate them into the economic costs and benefits of litigation. . . .

Behavioral decision theory suggests that plaintiffs and defendants face markedly different decisions in litigation. For example, consider the issue of settlement. Plaintiffs typically choose between accepting a sure gain by settling a case, and accepting an uncertain but potentially more rewarding outcome by litigating further. In contrast, defendants choose between accepting a sure loss by settling, and accepting an uncertain but potentially worse outcome by litigating further. Research by Daniel Kahneman and Amos Tversky has demonstrated that when people choose among gains, they tend to make risk-averse choices, preferring sure gains over larger but riskier gains. Conversely, when people choose among losses, they tend to make risk-seeking choices, preferring riskier outcomes over sure losses. Characterizing a decision as a loss or a gain, which Kahneman and Tversky refer to as a decision's "frame," determines the risk preferences of the decisionmaker. The law and economics literature asserts that litigants will make either risk-neutral or risk-averse decisions, depending upon their wealth; behavioral decision theory suggests that regardless of their wealth, litigants' risk preferences will vary systematically, depending upon whether they are in the role of plaintiff or defendant. . . .

## B.   FRAMING OF DECISIONS IN LITIGATION

Most decisions concerning the course of litigation involve risk. As a result, litigation decisions are influenced by the risk preferences of the parties, which, in turn, are determined by the character of the decision as a gain or as a loss. Predicting the behavior of litigants therefore requires an understanding of whether a party views their decision from the perspective of a gain or loss.

Settlement choices seem particularly vulnerable to framing effects. Consider the litigation setting as a rough analog to Kahneman and Tversky's public health hypothetical described earlier:

### VERSION 1

Imagine you are the plaintiff in a copyright infringement lawsuit. You are suing for the $400,000 that the defendant allegedly earned by violating the copyright. Trial is in two days and the defendant has offered to pay $200,000 as a final settlement. If you turn it down, you believe that you will face a trial where you have a 50% chance of winning a $400,000 award.

Do you agree to accept the settlement?

### VERSION 2

Imagine you are the defendant in a copyright infringement lawsuit. You are being sued for the $400,000 that the you allegedly earned by violating the copyright. Trial is in two days and the plaintiff has offered to accept $200,000 as a final settlement. If you turn it down, you believe that you will face a trial where you have a 50% chance of losing a $400,000 award.

Do you agree to pay the settlement?

. . . [B]oth versions represent economically identical outcomes. Both parties in the problem above choose between keeping $200,000 for sure and a gamble with a 50% chance of winning $400,000 or $0. The context of litigation, however, sets up the defendant as the stakeholder, making it appear that the defendant chooses among losses while the plaintiff chooses among gains.

As a simple demonstration that framing influences risk preferences in litigation, I presented this hypothetical to first-year law school students at Cornell Law School. Of the 13 students evaluating the plaintiff's perspective, 10, or 77%, chose to settle, while only 4 of the 13, or 31%, of the students evaluating the defendant's perspective chose to settle. Despite the small sample size, the difference in settlement rates was both striking and statistically significant.

Litigation appears to supply a natural frame. When deciding whether to settle a case, plaintiffs consistently choose between a sure gain by settling and the prospect of winning more at trial. This closely resembles a gains frame, although losing at trial may entail the loss of one's attorney's fees and may therefore be a mixed loss/gain prospect. Conversely, defendants choose between a sure loss by settling and the prospect of losing more at trial. This is a choice made in a loss frame. Hence, cross-claims aside, litigation presents a fairly consistent frame. . . .

### a. Methods

To provide this demonstration, subjects (undergraduates at Stanford University) evaluated the merits of a risk-neutral settlement offer in a factually richer hypothetical. In the hypothetical, the plaintiff, a wealthy Silicon Valley executive who owned vacation property in Oregon, sued the bed and breakfast inn adjacent to that property. On a recent vacation, the plaintiff discovered that the neighboring inn had been expanded onto a corner of his property. After efforts to contact the owners failed, the plaintiff filed a lawsuit seeking an injunction ordering the defendant to remove the encroachment. At trial a judge would either issue an injunction with some probability or would order the plaintiff to sell the land to the defendant for its true value ($50). If the court issued an injunction, the defendant would offer to purchase the property for a fixed amount that the plaintiff would be willing to accept ($100,000). Thus, the trial represented a gamble in which the plaintiff stood to win $100,000 or $50. In each version of the case, the questionnaire stated that a partner in the law firm knew the judge personally, and the partner predicted the outcome with a specific probability which varied in different conditions. Attorney's fees were not mentioned in the questionnaire.

Eight different versions of the materials filled the eight cells of the factorial design. The facts of each version were identical except that they were described from the perspective of either the plaintiff or the defendant. In each of these two perspectives, the plaintiff had either a 70% chance of winning $100,000, a 30% chance of winning $100,000, a 70% chance of winning $200,000, or a 30% chance of winning $200,000. In these four versions, the settlement offers were $70,000, $30,000, $140,000, and $60,000, respectively. All probabilities were given as the chance that the plaintiff would prevail at trial, even in the defendant's materials. Consequently, the comparison of the settlement rates between the plaintiff and defendant subjects within a probability level required comparing the settlement rate for the plaintiff subjects at that probability level with the rate for defendant subjects at the other level. For example, plaintiff subjects who had a 30% chance of a plaintiff's verdict were analyzed with defendant subjects who had a 70% chance of a plaintiff's verdict (and thus had a 30% chance of winning the case themselves).

The top of each questionnaire listed the name of the case followed by a description of the facts. The first line of the facts asked the subject to "imagine that you are an attorney. . . ." The text that followed varied little between the plaintiff's and defendant's versions. The final lines in the materials stated, "It is one day before trial. The plaintiff/defendant has contacted you and informed you that he will be willing to settle for $X. The plaintiff/defendant proposes this as a nonnegotiable, final offer."

### b.   Results

. . . Overall, 81.3% of the subjects who evaluated the case from the perspective of plaintiff chose to accept the settlement while only 45.5% of the defendant subjects did so. At each combination of probability and stakes, the plaintiff subjects preferred settlement relative to the defendant subjects. Only one condition failed to produce a statistically significant difference — $100,000 stakes and a 30% chance of winning. But the trend in this condition, which approached significance, suggests that plaintiffs preferred settlement to their defendant counterparts. When subjects had a 30% chance of prevailing at trial, 79.2% of the plaintiff subjects accepted the settlement as compared to 51.7% of the defendant subjects. At the 70% level, 83.6% of the plaintiff subjects chose to settle as compared to 38.2% of defendant subjects.

The data support the hypothesis that subjects reviewing a case from the plaintiff's perspective settle more readily than do subjects reviewing that case from the defendant's perspective. At every level of probability and stakes, a higher percentage of plaintiff subjects than defendant subjects accepted the settlement offer. Across all conditions, plaintiff subjects were thirty-six percentage points more likely to settle. The vast majority of the plaintiff subjects accepted the offer while less than half of the defendant subjects accepted. Plaintiff subjects' greater tendency to accept risk-neutral settlement offers suggests that they were more risk-averse than defendant subjects.

The effect was apparent at the high and low stakes and at both levels of probability. When the subjects faced a 30% chance of winning at trial, 79.2% of the plaintiffs accepted the offer whereas only 51.7% of the defendant subjects did so. When winning was 70% likely, the plaintiff subjects settled at a rate of 83.6%, whereas defendant subjects settled at a rate of only 38.2%. Furthermore, within each level of probability, plaintiff subjects at both high and low stakes settled more often than their defendant counterparts. Although this effect was marginal at the 30% level in the $100,000 stakes, where settlement rates differed by only fifteen percentage points, the trend supported the hypothesis. In the other three cells, the effect was quite potent and ran as high as an approximate fifty percentage-point difference in two of the cells.

### c.  Discussion

The fact that the difference in settlement rates occurred in all four combinations of probability and award size suggests that it cannot be explained by any unique reaction to these variables. In theory, the tendency to accept or reject the awards could have been driven by over-weighing or under-weighing the probability of winning. However, for this phenomenon to explain these data, this bias would have to have affected the plaintiff subjects differently than the defendant subjects, and would have to have occurred in an identical fashion at both levels of probability. This seems somewhat unlikely.

Similarly, the settlement offers at any one level could have seemed unfairly high or low to the subjects. Rejecting or accepting an offer might simply have reflected the subjects' estimated value of the case, rather than their risk preferences. Such an explanation, however, could not account for these data because the effect occurred at two different award levels. The tendency in all four cells of this study for plaintiff subjects to accept the offers more frequently than defendant subjects indicates that the explanation for the effect lies in some feature of being a plaintiff or defendant rather than in a reaction to a probability or award size.

When defendant and plaintiff subjects are considered separately, it becomes clear that the results differ in terms of their conformity to predictions. The overall settlement rate for defendant subjects was 45.5%, meaning that as a class they neither consistently rejected nor consistently accepted the risk-neutral settlement offer. If they were truly risk-seeking, the dominant response should have been to litigate. By contrast, the plaintiff subjects, as predicted, exhibited an over-whelming tendency to accept the offer, which fully supports the theory that they were risk-averse.

This pattern of results may reflect some consideration of trial ex-penses. If some of the defendant subjects considered the cost of attorney's fees to their hypothetical clients, then even an ambivalent reaction to the settlement offers would reflect some risk-seeking. The sure cost of further attorney's fees for more litigation makes the deci-sion to reject the settlement offer a relatively risk-seeking choice. Con-versely, the consideration of attorney's fees augmented the reluctance of the already risk-averse plaintiff subjects to gamble on a trial. In any case, the higher settlement rate among plaintiffs as compared to de-fendants shows that whatever the underlying preference structure may be, plaintiff subjects in this study were more risk-averse than their de-fendant counterparts. . . .

## Notes

*1. Plaintiffs, Defendants, and Framing.*   In the above excerpt, Rach-linski claims that defendants will frame litigation decisions as choices among losses, while plaintiffs will frame litigation decisions as choices among gains. Although it may be that these are the most likely frames, Korobkin and Guthrie have demonstrated that plaintiffs can also frame settlement as a loss if settling would leave them worse off than they were prior to the event that gave rise to the litigation.

In one experiment, subjects were asked to play the role of the plain-tiff in a lawsuit in which their car had been totaled in an accident caused by the defendant. The defendant's insurance company admitted that the defendant was liable for the accident and that the plaintiff suffered $28,000 in damages, but claimed its policy with the defendant limited its liability to $10,000. The subjects were then asked whether they would prefer a $21,000 settlement or a trial with roughly a 50 percent chance of recovering $28,000 and a 50 percent chance of re-covering $10,000. Half of the subjects were told they had been driving a $14,000 Toyota at the time of the accident (the remainder of their $28,000 in damages were made up of medical expenses that had been reimbursed), while the other half were told they had been driving a $24,000 BMW at the time of the accident (with the remainder of their

$28,000 in damages being reimbursed medical expenses). Although the type of car they drove did not affect the subjects' legal rights, "BMW Drivers" were far more likely to reject the settlement offer and risk a trial than the "Toyota Drivers." Russell Korobkin & Chris Guthrie, Psychological Barriers to Litigation Settlement: An Experimental Approach, 93 Mich. L. Rev. 107, 133 (1994).

The experimenters hypothesized that the higher reservation prices exhibited on average by "BMW Drivers" was due to the fact that they could perceive settlement to be a "loss," since it would not provide enough money to replace their car, whereas "Toyota Drivers" could only view settlement as a "gain." Id. at 133.

***2. Plaintiffs, Defendants, and Low Probability Cases.***   While prospect theory predicts that individuals will usually exhibit risk averse preferences when evaluating "gains" and risk seeking preferences when evaluating "losses," it predicts that the *exact opposite* will be the case when certain alternatives are compared to very low probability alternatives with the same expected value. For example, prospect theory predicts an individual will prefer a certain gain of $50 to a 50 percent chance to gain $100 (exhibiting risk-averse preferences), but that an individual will prefer a 1 percent chance to gain $100 to a certain gain of $1 (exhibiting risk seeking preferences). Conversely, prospect theory predicts an individual will prefer a 50 percent chance of losing $100 to a certain loss of $50 (risk seeking), but a certain loss of $1 to a 1 percent chance of losing $100. See Amos Tversky & Daniel Kahneman, Advances in Prospect Theory: Cumulative Representation of Uncertainty, 5 J. Risk & Uncertainty 297 (1992).

Based on this aspect of prospect theory, Chris Guthrie has suggested a modification to Rachlinski's predictions about the usual risk preferences of plaintiffs and defendants. Guthrie predicts that in lawsuits in which the plaintiff's chance of prevailing is very low — lawsuits that are often thought of as "frivolous" — plaintiffs will have relatively high reservation prices (relative to the expected value of the case) and defendants relatively low reservation prices. Guthrie provides some support for his theory by demonstrating experimentally that a majority of research subjects asked to play the role of plaintiff in a lawsuit report that they would prefer trial over settlement when the two alternatives have the same expected value but the trial prospect is described as having a very low probability of success (combined with a relatively high damage award if the plaintiff prevails) while a majority of subjects asked to play the role of defendant in the same lawsuit favor the certain settlement over the risky trial. Chris Guthrie, Framing Frivolous Litigation: A Psychological Theory, 67 U. Chi. L. Rev. 163 (2000).

## B.  THE ENDOWMENT EFFECT AND THE STATUS QUO BIAS

A second prediction of prospect theory, known as "loss aversion," is that individuals will exhibit a stronger preference for avoiding something they perceive to be a "loss" than for achieving something that appears to be a "gain" of the equivalent magnitude. A consequence of loss aversion is that individuals will usually prefer to keep an item they possess (and thus avoid a "loss") than trade that item for one of objectively identical value (and thus achieve a "gain"). This consequence, known as the "status quo bias" or the "endowment effect," suggests that, holding constant differences in preferences between two negotiators, the negotiator who possesses property or a legal entitlement (the seller) is likely to have a higher reservation price than a negotiator who does not possess the property or entitlement (the buyer). Put another way, all other things being equal, an individual is likely to exhibit a higher reservation price for an item if she owns it than if she does not own it. As the experiments described in the following article demonstrate, the result of this phenomenon is smaller bargaining zones and fewer successful transactions than rational choice theory would predict.

■ Daniel Kahneman, Jack L. Knetsch & Richard H. Thaler, **Experimental Tests of the Endowment Effect and the Coase Theorem***

**98 J. Pol. Econ.** 1325, 1325-1332, 1338-1339, 1342-1344 (1990)

The standard assumptions of economic theory imply that when income effects are small, differences between an individual's maximum willingness to pay (WTP) for a good and minimum compensation demanded for the same entitlement (willingness to accept [WTA]) should be negligible (Willig 1976). Thus . . . there is wide acceptance of the Coase theorem assertion that, subject to income effects, the allocation of resources will be independent of the assignment of property rights when costless trades are possible.

The assumption that entitlements do not affect value contrasts sharply with empirical observations of significantly higher selling than buying prices. . . .

The hypothesis of interest here is that many discrepancies between WTA and WTP, far from being a mistake, reflect a genuine effect of reference positions on preferences. Thaler (1980) labeled the increased value of a good to an individual when the good becomes part of the individual's endowment the "endowment effect." This effect is a manifestation of "loss aversion," the generalization that losses are weighted substantially more than objectively commensurate gains in the evaluation of prospects and trades (Kahneman and Tversky 1979; Tversky and Kahneman, in press). An implication of this asymmetry is that if a good is evaluated as a loss when it is given up and as a gain when it is acquired, loss aversion will, on average, induce a higher dollar value for owners than for potential buyers, reducing the set of mutually acceptable trades. . . .

The results from a series of experiments involving real exchanges of tokens and of various consumption goods are reported in this paper. In each case, a random allocation design was used to test for the presence of an endowment effect. Half of the subjects were endowed with a good and became potential sellers in each market; the other half of the subjects were potential buyers. Conventional economic analysis yields the simple prediction that one-half of the goods should be traded in voluntary exchanges. If value is unaffected by ownership, then the distribution of values in the two groups should be the same except for sampling variation. . . . The null hypothesis is, therefore, that half of the goods provided should change hands. Label this predicted volume V\*. If there is an endowment effect, the value of the good will be higher for sellers than for buyers, and observed volume V will be less than V\*. The ratio V/V\* provides a unit-free measure of the undertrading that is produced by the effect of ownership on value. To test the hypothesis that market experience eliminates undertrading, the markets were repeated several times. . . .

## II. Repeated Market Experiments

In experiment 1, 44 students in an advanced undergraduate law and economics class at Cornell University received a packet of general instructions plus 11 forms, one for each of the markets that were conducted in the experiment.

. . . [S]ubjects on alternating seats were given Cornell coffee mugs, which sell for $6.00 each at the bookstore. The experimenter asked all participants to examine a mug, either their own or their neighbor's. The experimenter then informed the subjects that four markets for mugs would be conducted using the same procedures as the prior induced markets with two exceptions: (1) One of the four market trials would subsequently be selected at random, and only the trades made on this trial would be executed. (2) In the binding market trial, all trades would be implemented, unlike the subset implemented in the induced-value markets. The initial assignment of buyer and seller roles was maintained for all four trading periods. The clearing price and the number of trades were announced after each period. The market that "counted" was indicated after the fourth period, and transactions were executed immediately. All sellers who had indicated that they would give up their mugs for a sum at the market-clearing price exchanged their mugs for cash, and successful buyers paid this same price and received their mugs. This design was used to permit learning to take place over successive trials and yet make each trial potentially binding. The same procedure was then followed for four more successive markets using boxed ballpoint pens with a visible bookstore price tag of $3.98, which were distributed to the subjects who had been buyers in the mug markets.

For each goods market, subjects completed a form . . . with the following instructions:

> You now own the object in your possession. [You do not own the object that you see in the possession of some of your neighbors.] You have the option of selling it [buying one] if a price, which will be determined later, is acceptable to you. For each of the possible prices below indicate whether you wish to: (1) Sell your object and receive this price [Pay this price and receive an object to take home with you] or (2) Keep your object and take it home with you. [Not buy an object at this price.] For each price indicate your decision by marking an X in the appropriate column.

> [Part of the response form for sellers follows:

> At a price of $8.75 1 will sell _____ I will not sell _____.
> At a price of $8.25 1 will sell _____ I will not sell _____.

> The same rectangular distribution of values — ranging from $0.25 to $8.75 in steps of $0.50 — was prepared for both buyers and sellers.]
> . . . Buyers maximized their potential gain by agreeing to buy at all prices below the value they ascribed to the good, and sellers maximized their welfare by agreeing to sell at all prices above the good's worth to them. . . .

As shown in Table 2, . . . the median selling prices in the mug and pen markets were more than twice the median buying prices, and the V/V* ratio was only .20 for mugs and .41 for pens. Observed volume did not increase over successive periods in either the mug or the pen markets, providing no indication that subjects learned to adopt equal buying and selling prices.

**Table 2**
**Results of Experiment 1**

| | | | Consumption Goods Markets | |
|---|---|---|---|---|
| Trial | Trades | Price | Median Buyer Reservation Price | Median Seller Reservation Price |
| | | *Mugs (Expected Trades = 11)* | | |
| 4 | 4 | 4.25 | 2.75 | 5.25 |
| 5 | 1 | 4.75 | 2.25 | 5.25 |
| 6 | 2 | 4.50 | 2.25 | 5.25 |
| 7 | 2 | 4.25 | 2.25 | 5.25 |
| | | *Pens (Expected Trades = 11)* | | |
| 8 | 4 | 1.25 | .75 | 2.50 |
| 9 | 5 | 1.25 | .75 | 1.75 |
| 10 | 4 | 1.25 | .75 | 2.25 |
| 11 | 5 | 1.25 | .75 | 1.75 |

## IV.   Reluctance to Buy versus Reluctance to Sell

Exchanges of money and a good (or between two goods) offer the possibilities of four comparisons: a choice of gaining either the good or money, a choice of losing one or the other, buying (giving up money for the good), and selling (giving up the good for money) (Tversky and Kahneman, in press). The endowment effect results from a difference between the relative preferences for the good and money. The comparison of buying and selling to simple choices between gains permits an analysis of the discrepancy between WTA and WTP into two components: reluctance to sell (exchanging the good for money) and reluctance to buy (exchanging money for the good).

Experiments 6 and 7 were carried out to assess the weight of reluctance to buy and reluctance to sell in undertrading of a good similar to the goods used in the earlier experiments. The subjects in experiment 6 were 77 Simon Fraser students, randomly assigned to three groups. Members of one group, designated sellers, were given a coffee mug and were asked to indicate whether or not they would sell the mug at a series of prices ranging from $0.00 to $9.25. A group of buyers indicated whether they were willing to buy a mug at each of these prices. Finally, choosers were asked to choose, for each of the possible prices, between a mug and cash.

The results again reveal substantial undertrading: While 12.5 trades were expected between buyers and sellers, only three trades took place (V/V* = .24). The median valuations were $7.12 for sellers, $3.12 for choosers, and $2.87 for buyers. The close similarity of results for buyers and choosers indicates that there was relatively little reluctance to pay for the mug. . . .

The evidence presented in this paper supports what may be called an instant endowment effect: the value that an individual assigns to such objects as mugs, pens, binoculars, and chocolate bars appears to increase substantially as soon as that individual is given the object. The apparently instantaneous nature of the reference point shift and consequent value change induced by giving a person possession of a good goes beyond previous discussions of the endowment effect, which focused on goods that have been in the individual's possession for some time. While long-term endowment effects could be explained by sentimental attachment or by an improved technology of consumption in the Stigler-Becker (1977) sense, the differences in preference or taste demonstrated by more than 700 participants in the experiments reported in this paper cannot be explained in this fashion. . . .

The results of the experimental demonstrations of the endowment effect have direct implications for economic theory and economic predictions. Contrary to the assumptions of standard economic theory that preferences are independent of entitlements, the evidence presented here indicates that people's preferences depend on their reference positions. Consequently, preference orderings are not defined independently of endowments: good A may be preferred to B when A is part of an original endowment, but the reverse may be true when initial reference positions are changed. . . .

The existence of endowment effects reduces the gains from trade. In comparison with a world in which preferences are independent of endowment, the existence of loss aversion produces an inertia in the economy because potential traders are more reluctant to trade than is conventionally assumed. This is not to say that Pareto-optimal trades will not take place. Rather, there are simply fewer mutually advantageous exchanges possible, and so the volume of trade is lower than it otherwise would be.                                                                                  ■

---

When transactional lawyers negotiate contracts, they often fail to negotiate all of the terms necessary to describe the parties' rights and responsibilities in the case of every imaginable contingency, no matter how unlikely. When contingencies arise that are not provided for in contracts, courts must fill the "gaps" left by the negotiators with default terms. The following article suggests that a psychological preference for the status quo will bias negotiators' preferences such that they will prefer a term — i.e., have a higher reservation price for the term — if it is a law-supplied default rather than the opposite of a law-supplied default, or if it is the term prescribed by a commonly used form contract rather than the opposite of a term prescribed by the form contract. This becomes important when negotiators bargain over whether to include in their contract a term that mirrors the default term or instead to "contract around" the default by specifying a different term. The party benefited by the default term or the form contract term can be viewed as the "seller" of the term, since she will demand compensation in return for contracting around the default term that benefits her. The party disadvantaged by the default term can be viewed as the "buyer" of the term, because he will have to offer compensation to the other party in return for her agreement to add a more desirable term to the contract and thus avoid the law-provided default.

The data presented in the following study suggests, as is the case for tangible consumer goods like mugs and pens, the seller of a contract term will set a high reservation price (relative to what rational choice theory would predict), and that the buyer will set a relatively low reservation price. This could reduce the size of the bargaining zone relative to the predictions of rational choice theory or eliminate it altogether.

## ■ Russell Korobkin, Inertia and Preference in Contract Negotiation: The Psychological Power of Default Rules and Form Terms*

**51 Vand. L. Rev.** 1583, 1588-1590, 1605-1508 (1998)

. . . [L]aw students who had completed a contracts course were asked to play the role of an attorney in a series of hypothetical negotiation scenarios. In each scenario, subjects were provided with written fact patterns describing negotiations between their client, a company called "NextDay" that specializes in overnight package delivery, and a customer of NextDay's called "Gifts, Inc.," a catalog operator ready to enter into a contract with NextDay for the shipment of its packages around the country. After being presented with the relevant information, subjects were asked to provide advice to their client on how to proceed in the negotiations. The advice was solicited by asking the subjects to place a monetary value on contract terms that were the subject of negotiations.

For each negotiation scenario, subjects were randomly given one of two or more experimental conditions that differed from each other in only one way: the information provided about whether the contract term at issue was the default term (that would govern the parties unless they agreed otherwise) or an alternative to the default term. The importance of a term's status as the "default" was measured by comparing the value placed upon the term by subjects who were told that it was the default with the value assigned it by those who were told that it was an alternative to the default.

The first experiment ("Consequential Damages") dealt with a contract term delineating the amount of damages for which the subject's client, NextDay, could be held liable if it failed to deliver a Gifts, Inc. package on time. The experiment tested whether the subjects' preference for a favorable contract term depended on whether the term was the default or an alternative to the default. All of the subjects participating in this experiment were told that Gifts, Inc. would prefer a contract term that would hold NextDay liable for all damages caused by its failure to meet its delivery obligations. They were also told that NextDay, in contrast, would prefer a contract term limiting its potential liability to damages that were "reasonably foreseeable" at the time that NextDay took possession of the package in question. Subjects were advised that NextDay's accountants had estimated that there was a ninety-five percent chance that a contract including the broader "full liability" damages clause would cost NextDay, on average, $0-$10 more per package than would a contract with the narrower "limited liability" damages clause.

Subjects randomly assigned to condition 1 ("Limited Liability") of the experiment were told that the limited "reasonably foreseeable" damages term was the legal default in their state. They were asked how much money per package Gifts, Inc. would have to agree to pay NextDay above what the contract price would otherwise be before they would recommend that NextDay contract around the limited liability default in favor of a full liability term. In contrast, subjects assigned to condition 2 ("Full Liability") of the experiment were informed that the default term was one of full liability. They were asked how much of a per-package reduction in the contract price (below what it would otherwise be) they would recommend NextDay be willing to accept for shipping if, in return, Gifts, Inc. would agree to include a limited liability term in the contract.

The transaction costs associated with contracting around the default term in the experiment were negligible, if they existed at all. Contracting around the default did not require more mental effort than accepting the default, as all subjects were required to value the difference between the default term and its alternative. And there were no marginal drafting costs associated with contracting around the default, as both conditions of the experiment provided the subjects with the precise language that would be inserted into the contract if the parties agreed to contract around the default. Additionally, there were no strategic reasons for subjects to decline to contract around the default terms (it was clear to both parties prior to negotiating that NextDay would prefer limited liability, and that Gifts, Inc. would prefer full liability) or to be less than truthful in revealing the value they placed on contracting around the default (subjects were asked to provide their valuation to their client in order to determine a negotiating strategy, not to suggest a value that would actually be used in bargaining). Consequently, [rational choice theory] would predict that valuations would not differ, on average, between subjects assigned to condition 1 and those assigned to condition 2.

The mean valuations were, however, significantly affected by condition. Subjects in condition 1 ("Limited Liability") (N=26) recommended, on average, that NextDay demand a minimum of $6.96 per package before agreeing to include a full liability term in the contract. Condition 2 ("Full Liability") subjects (N=28), on the other hand, recommended, on average, that NextDay be willing to offer a maximum discount of $4.46 per package for Gifts, Inc.'s agreement to include a limited liability term in the contract. The difference between the mean responses of subjects in the two conditions can best be understood as one measure of the strength of the substantive bias for terms that are identified as the default over those identified as alternatives to the default. . . .

## C.  Form Contracts and the Power of Inertia

. . . Parties sometimes begin contract negotiations with a standardized form contract drafted by a private entity such as a law firm or an industry trade association, rather than with a blank sheet of paper backstopped by a set of legally defined default rules which will be operative except where the parties affirmatively contract around its terms. . . .

Like subjects in the original Consequential Damages scenario, subjects in the new manipulation (conditions 3 and 4) were asked to value the difference between a contract that would hold NextDay liable to Gifts, Inc. for all consequential damages caused by NextDay's failure to meet its delivery obligations, and a contract that would limit NextDay's liability to damages that were reasonably foreseeable at the time that Gifts, Inc. delivered any particular package to NextDay for shipment. Unlike subjects in the original experimental groups, the new subjects were told that the two companies had "agreed to adopt, as a starting point in negotiations, a standard form contract prepared by attorneys for the Overnight Delivery Trade Association ("ODTA"), to which both parties are members." The form contract, the subjects were informed, "is typically used as a basis for negotiations in this type of transaction, with contracting parties making changes to the form provisions where necessary."

Condition 3 subjects were informed that the industry form contract included a term that provided damages would be limited to those "reasonably foreseeable when Carrier accepted merchandise from shipper," whereas the default rule that would govern the parties in the absence of any explicit term was one of full liability. They were asked to state the minimum amount, per package, that they would demand Gifts, Inc. offer NextDay, over and above what the contract rate would otherwise be, before they would recommend that NextDay agree to remove the favorable "limited liability" consequential damages term from the form contract, thus allowing the less favorable "full liability" default term to govern. Condition 4 subjects were told that the industry form contract provided for full liability, whereas the legal default was one of limited liability. They were asked to reveal the maximum amount of money NextDay should be willing to offer Gifts, Inc. (in the form of a per-package discount below what the contract price would otherwise be) in return for Gifts, Inc. agreeing to eliminate the form contract term providing "full liability," thus permitting the "limited liability" default to govern.

If inertia were driving the subjects' bias in favor of the legal default term over a contrary industry norm in the previous experimental ma-nipulation, subjects responding to condition 3 of the Consequential Damages scenario should have provided larger responses than condi-tion 4 subjects. Notice that from a [rational choice] perspective both groups of subjects were asked to perform the same task: place a value on the difference between a contract with a limited liability term and one with a full liability term. If parties do prefer inaction over action, however, condition 3 subjects should have placed a higher value on the limited liability term than condition 4 subjects, because limited liability would result from inaction for condition 3 subjects but not for condition 4 subjects.

The experimental results bear out the inertia hypothesis. Condition 3 subjects (N=33) revealed that they would demand, on average, a minimum of $7.24 per package before recommending NextDay agree to remove the limited liability term from the industry form contract (leaving a full liability default to govern the contract). Condition 4 subjects (N=25), in contrast, would recommend, on average, that NextDay offer Gifts, Inc. a maximum discount of $4.08 per package in return for Gifts, Inc. agreeing to remove a full liability term from the industry form contract (leaving a limited liability default). The differ-ence between the condition 3 and 4 Consequential Damages subjects is statistically significant, and the gap between condition 3 and 4 sub-jects is not significantly different than the gap between condition 1 and 2 Consequential Damages subjects. In other words, the experimental subjects showed a bias in favor of whatever consequential damages term would govern as a result of inertia (requiring no action at all on the part of the negotiating parties). Whether the term associated with inaction was derived from a legal default rule or an industry form contract serving as the basis for contract negotiations had no statisti-cally significant effect on subjects' average responses. . . .

The psychological power of inertia . . . suggests that the reference point for contract negotiations will affect the preferences of bargaining parties. Negotiators will prefer an advantageous term more strongly (or oppose a disadvantageous term less strongly) if the term is perceived to result from inaction rather than from action. . . .                    ■

## Notes

*1. How Widespread Are the Endowment Effect and Status Quo Bias?* Research has demonstrated that the endowment effect exists in a wide range of circumstances. Early studies often focused on the preservation of environmental resources and found that individuals who possessed an entitlement to protect such resources reported reservation prices for selling the entitlement that were far greater than the reservation prices for buying the same entitlement reported by individuals without it. For example, one study found that duck hunters would pay up to $247 each to protect a wetland from development that would make hunting there impossible, but hunters who were told they had the right to enjoin the development said they would demand a minimum of $1,044 each to permit the development. Judd Hammack & Gardner Mallard Brown, Jr., Waterfowl and Wetlands: Toward Bioeconomic Analysis 26 (1974).

The mug and pen experiments by Kahneman et al. demonstrate the endowment effect for personal property. There is no endowment effect for money — i.e., people seem to place the same value on a dollar whether they own it or not — but there is evidence of an endowment effect for financial instruments. Experiments have shown that people demand more money to sell a chip with an uncertain monetary exchange value than they would be willing to pay for the same chip, Eric van Dijk & Daan van Knippenberg, Buying and Selling Exchange Goods: Loss Aversion and the Endowment Effect, 17 J. Econ. Psych. 517 (1996), and that they are reluctant to part with lottery tickets given to them even when they would not be interested in buying the same tickets. Jack L. Knetsch & J. A. Sinden, Willingness to Pay and Compensation Demanded: Experimental Evidence of an Unexpected Disparity in Measures of Value, 99 Q. J. Econ. 507 (1984).

As the experiments by Korobkin suggest, people are often reluctant to part with the status quo, even when there is no property right or definitive legal entitlement at stake. Studies have shown that customers used to a given level of service from a vendor would demand much more compensation to voluntarily accept a lower level of service than customers accustomed to that lower level of service would pay to receive the higher level. Raymond S. Hartman et al., Consumer Rationality and the Status Quo, 106 Q. J. Econ. 141, 143 (1991). In another study, subjects asked to compare two hypothetical jobs with somewhat different qualities tended to prefer the first job if they were told to imagine they currently held that job but the second job if they were told to imagine that job was their current employment. Daniel Kahneman & Amos Tversky, Choices, Values, and Frames, 39 Am. Psychologist 341, 348 (1984).

Some studies suggest that the endowment effect is relatively greater when there is no close market substitute for the item at issue. For example, one study found that the difference between the reservation price of buyers and sellers for tickets to a National Hockey League playoff game was smaller if the game would be broadcast live on television and radio than if it would not be broadcast. Viktor L. Adamowicz et al., Experiments on the Difference Between Willingness to Pay and Willingness to Accept, 69 Land Econ. 416, 421-424 (1993). Consequently, negotiators might expect on average that a bargaining zone will be less likely (and, when it exists, smaller) when negotiations concern items without close substitutes than when they concern items commonly traded or with substitutes that are commonly traded.

*2. Causes of the Endowment Effect.*   There is no clear, widely agreed-upon cause of the endowment effect. While most commentators assume that the effect is the result of "loss aversion," this only begs the question of why people seem to abhor losses more than they desire equivalent gains.

Korobkin argues that negotiators are biased in favor of the "status quo" because this minimizes the likelihood of experiencing future regret as a result of their decisions:

> In most situations, contracting for terms that deviate from default rules or form contracts carries the risk of suboptimal results from the ex post perspective. That is, a negotiator knows when she contracts around a baseline or reference contract term that she is taking a gamble of sorts, which may or may not be profitable, depending upon unknown future circumstances. If a negotiator anticipates that an unprofitable ex post outcome would cause her to regret having chosen the gamble ex ante, she might demand a premium above the expected value of the gamble before she would be willing to choose the gamble. Put another way, when deciding whether to take an action with uncertain consequences, the decision maker may determine that the expected utility of choosing the action is lower than the inherent expected utility of the action itself.

Russell Korobkin, Inertia and Preference in Contract Negotiation, The Psychological Power of Default Rules and Form Terms, 51 Vand. L. Rev. 1583, 1610-1611 (1998).

For this explanation to be persuasive, it would have to be the case that negotiators suffer more regret if they enter an agreement that turns out in retrospect to have been undesirable than if they fail to enter into an agreement and in retrospect it turns out that the agreement would have been desirable.

To use an example, imagine that A sets his reservation price for purchasing a used car at $5,000, based in part on his estimation that there is a 50 percent chance that the car will require significant repairs. A ultimately purchases the car for $5,000, and the next month it requires significant repairs. Compare that situation to B, who also sets his reservation price for a used car at $5,000 based on the same probability estimate concerning repair needs. B is unable to purchase the used car because it turns out that his reservation price is slightly below the seller's. B subsequently purchases a new car for substantially more money, and his new car requires substantial repairs. Both A's and B's negotiating outcomes look bad in hindsight, and both might feel the emotion of regret. But is A more likely to suffer regret than B? Some theoretical and empirical literature suggests that the answer is "yes." "Norm theory" contends that people suffer more regret when they act affirmatively than when they are passive, because action is more conducive to imagining steps that could have been taken that would have led to more desirable results. See Daniel Kahneman & Dale T. Miller, Norm Theory: Comparing Reality to Its Alternatives, 93 Psychology Rev. 136 (1986).

## C.  ANCHORING

When people are required to place a value on something — be it a good, a service, or a set of terms embodied in a negotiated agreement — they often determine that value cognitively by beginning with a pre-existing reference point and then adjusting from that point. For example, if Algernon is considering purchasing Benno's business and must determine the value of the business to him for purposes of establishing his reservation price, he might begin his analysis by noticing that Cameron's similar business recently sold for $25,000, and then adjust his valuation of Benno's business from that price based on how much more or less valuable than Cameron's business he believes Benno's business is. Thus, the sales price of Cameron's business might "anchor" the value that Algernon places on Benno's business, although Algernon will make relevant adjustments to that anchor value.

This mental approach is consistent with the negotiator's goal of setting a reservation price precisely such that any offer better than the reservation point is more desirable than not reaching an agreement, and any offer worse than the reservation point is less desirable than not reaching an agreement, so long as the reference value, or "anchor," is relevant to his reservation price. In our example, the sales price of Cameron's business is relevant to Algernon's reservation price if his BATNA is to buy a similar business at the market price and he assumes that other similar businesses will be available at market prices in the future. On the other hand, people are routinely exposed to valuations that are logically irrelevant to the value of the subject of a negotiation. For example, perhaps Algernon is spending the afternoon attempting to assess the value of Benno's business after spending the morning shopping for a new car. If this is the case, his evaluation of the business logically should not depend on whether he spent the morning looking at a $50,000 Jaguar or a $10,000 Hyundai.

Although we would not expect Algernon's car search to affect the value he places on Benno's business, there is a great deal of information that first appears related to a valuation question that, on closer examination, might not be relevant at all to the valuation issue, or might only be marginally relevant. In negotiation, an offer or a demand can often fit this profile. For example, if a buyer makes a very low offer for a seller's wares, the offer appears relevant to the seller's reservation price because the buyer might have information about the quality of the wares that informs that offer. The problem is that a low offer can be made equally as easily by buyers who think that the wares are of high quality as buyers who think the wares are of low quality. A low offer might be relevant to the seller's determination of her reservation price, but it might be completely irrelevant as well. Research has shown, however, that this type of information can anchor parties' evaluations and, thus, indirectly impact reservation prices. The following excerpt further describes the concept of anchoring and demonstrates the anchoring effect that offers can have indirectly on negotiators' reservation prices.

### ■ Russell Korobkin & Chris Guthrie, Psychological Barriers to Litigation Settlement: An Experimental Approach*

**93 Mich. L. Rev.** 107, 138-142 (1994)

. . . Cognitive psychologists have shown that people make estimates by starting at an initial "anchor" position, which they adjust to yield a final estimate. Different anchors create different expectations and yield different estimates, and these estimates tend to be biased toward the original anchor. Thus, anchors, like frames, serve to impede rational problem solving and decisionmaking.

In one anchoring study, Edward Joyce and Gary Biddle divided professional auditors into two groups. The experimenters anchored the groups as follows: The study asked members of Group A whether they thought significant executive-level management fraud occurred in more than ten of each 1000 companies audited by Big Eight accounting firms. The members of Group B were asked to indicate whether they thought significant executive-level management fraud occurred in more than 200 of each 1000 companies audited by Big Eight accounting firms. The experimenters tested whether these anchors — 10 in Group A and 200 in Group B — would influence the answer to the second question they asked the members of both groups: "What is your estimate of the number of Big Eight clients per 1,000 that have significant executive-level management fraud?" Consistent with anchoring and adjustment theory, Group A and B responses varied systematically. Group A subjects estimated an average of 16.52 incidents of fraud per 1000, while Group B subjects estimated an average of 43.11 incidents of fraud per 1000. Thus, the rational judgments of these professional auditors were influenced by the initial anchors to which they were exposed. . . .

Dispute resolution scholars have noted that anchoring effects may impede rational decisionmaking in the negotiation context, particularly with respect to opening offers. That is, opening offers may anchor the opposing side's expectations in negotiation and impede rational decisionmaking behavior. We explored the effect of an opening offer anchor on subjects' expectations and willingness to accept a final settlement offer. Specifically, we hypothesized that different opening settlement offers would anchor subjects' expectations regarding the value of the lawsuit in different ways and would affect the likelihood of out-of-court settlement.

To test this hypothesis, we asked two groups of subjects to assume the role of plaintiff in a hypothetical lawsuit involving a customer unhappy with a new car. All the plaintiffs had recently purchased a new BMW 318 automobile from a local car dealer for $24,000. Shortly after purchasing the car, the subjects discovered that the car had a major problem they had not detected during the test drive: "[I]t occasionally stall[ed] at stop lights and stop signs and [was] extremely difficult to start in the morning." Subjects took the car to the BMW mechanics twice. Both times the mechanics claimed the car was not defective and that they could not do anything to fix it. Their own mechanic agreed that the car's condition could not be improved.

As a result, subjects approached the BMW dealer and asked for a refund of their money. The dealer refused. Accordingly, subjects retained a lawyer and filed a lawsuit against the dealer seeking a refund.

The subjects' attorney advised them that the only legal issue in the case was whether the car was in fact "defective." If so, a court would require the dealer to refund the subjects' money. If not, the subjects would have to keep the car. The instructions informed the subjects, "Your lawyer thinks this is a very close case, and could easily go either way." Prior to trial, the BMW dealer offered the subjects a final settlement offer of $12,000 in cash to drop the lawsuit; the subjects could either accept the offer or reject it and proceed to trial.

We assigned subjects randomly to either Group A (Low-Ball Initial Offer) or Group B (Reasonable Initial Offer). The subjects in the two groups received identical versions of the scenario except for a single difference: the subjects were exposed to different anchors. The BMW dealer had initially offered the Low-Ball Initial Offer subjects $2,000 to settle the case — an offer subjects were told that they had rejected. Reasonable Initial Offer subjects, on the other hand, received an offer of $10,000, which they had rejected. The instructions asked subjects in both groups to indicate their willingness to accept the dealer's final settlement offer of $12,000 by selecting one of our five answer choices.

Although the legal endowments of both subject groups were identical — both faced a choice between a certain cash settlement of $12,000 or an uncertain trial in which they could receive a complete refund or no compensation — the opening offer anchor significantly affected the likelihood of the subjects to accept the offer or to reject it and proceed to trial. Low-Ball Initial Offer subjects responded favorably to the final offer: their mean response was 3.54. Reasonable Initial Offer subjects were slightly more likely, on average, to reject the offer than to accept it: their mean response was only 2.97. This difference is statistically significant. Sixty-three percent of the Low-Ball Initial Offer subjects said they would "definitely accept" or "probably accept" the $12,000 settlement offer, while only 34% of the Reasonable Initial Offer subjects would "definitely accept" or "probably accept" the final offer.

These results support our basic anchor-as-frame hypothesis. The initial anchor influenced subjects' expectations — subjects in Group A, who received the low-ball initial offer of $2,000, expected to settle for less, so the final offer of $12,000 looked very good by comparison. Subjects in Group B, who received a reasonable initial offer of $10,000, expected to settle for more, so the final offer of $12,000 seemed less appealing by comparison. The objective information that subjects should have used to determine the expected value of going to trial was identical for subjects in both groups. Thus, there appears to be no economically rational explanation for the differential in how the groups evaluated the $12,000 settlement offer.

The anchoring and framing experiments both tend to demonstrate that rational actor models cannot account for the full range of settle-

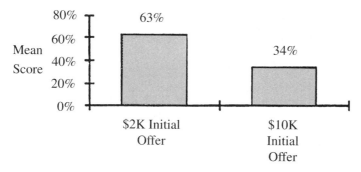

**The Weight of an Anchor:**
**Percentage Definitely or Probably Accepting**

ment breakdown. When choosing between a concrete settlement offer and an uncertain trial result, our subjects faced cognitive biases that prevented at least some of them from acting in what decision theorists would consider a rational manner. The framing experiments illustrate that people use a reference point to code options as gains or losses and that this coding systematically influences settlement behavior. The anchoring experiment demonstrates that an opponent's opening offer may unduly influence people's expectations and, hence, their decisions about whether to settle. Together, the results suggest that litigants — who are not always rational actors — may fail to reach settlement on some occasions when settlement makes good economic sense.    ■

## Notes

*1. The Effect of Offers on Reservation Prices.*    The experiment described above indirectly demonstrates that subjects who received the low opening offer ($2,000) on average had a lower reservation price for settlement than subjects who received the reasonable opening offer ($10,000). Because subjects had to decide whether to accept a $12,000 final settlement offer or proceed to trial, the subjects were effectively asked whether their reservation price for selling their right to a trial was higher or lower than $12,000. More subjects who received the $10,000 opening offer declined the final offer than did subjects who received the $2,000 opening offer. Consequently, more subjects in the latter group had reservation prices at or below $12,000 than did subjects in the former group.

*2. Should the Defendant's Offer Affect the Plaintiff's Reservation Price?*
As suggested at the beginning of this section, an offer can communicate information that would be relevant to the opposing negotiator's

reservation price. A plaintiff's reservation price for settlement depends significantly on her chances of prevailing at trial. The plaintiff and her lawyer estimate this based on their knowledge of the facts of the dispute, the law, and jury verdicts in similar cases, but such predictions are far from scientific. The predictions of likely litigation outcomes made by the defendant's lawyer are relevant to the plaintiff's reservation price, as this provides another perspective on a very uncertain event. If the defendant's lawyer is particularly experienced or knowledgeable, his litigation prediction might be extremely relevant to the plaintiff's reservation price. If the defendant offers $2,000 to settle the case, this might suggest that the defendant's lawyer thinks the plaintiff's case is relatively weak; if the defendant offers $10,000, this might suggest that the plaintiff's case is relatively strong.

There are two problems with the plaintiff basing her reservation price in part on the defendant's offer, one general and one specifically related to the facts of the hypothetical dispute over the BMW that did not operate properly. The general problem is that there is not necessarily a relationship between the defendant's initial offer and his lawyer's evaluation of the merits of the plaintiff's case. By making a low offer, the defendant no doubt *wishes to suggest* that his lawyer believes the plaintiff has a weak case and therefore should have a low reservation price — this is an example of an attempt to use negotiating power, described in detail in Chapter 5. But the defendant can make a low offer and thus imply a low opinion of the plaintiff's case whether he actually believes the plaintiff has a strong case or a weak case. Economists would thus refer to a low initial offer as "cheap talk" because it does not necessarily convey any information about the defendant's actual beliefs. Thus, plaintiffs are well advised to be careful in what information they infer from a defendant's offer (and vice versa, of course). At the same time, however, it is not illogical for a plaintiff to adjust her reservation price to some extent based on the defendant's offer, *if* the plaintiff believes that the defendant's offer does in fact convey that the defendant's lawyer thinks the plaintiff has a weak case and is not merely a strategic ploy.

The second and more serious problem is relevant to the psychological mechanism of anchoring. Although the defendant's initial offer, standing alone, might cause a rational plaintiff to adjust her reservation price, once the defendant has replaced the initial offer with a final offer, any relevant information about the defendant's view of the merits of the case is logically included in the final offer. In other words, once the defendant increases his offer to $12,000, the initial offer ceases to have any logical relevance for the plaintiff's reservation price. To the extent that the defendant's view of the merits affects his offer, his view of the merits suggests that a $12,000 settlement is preferable to trial for him. At this point, whether he initially offered $10,000 or $2,000 conveys no information about his view of the case. Thus, although it might be reasonable for the plaintiff to base her reservation price in part on the defendant's offer, the offer that is relevant is the $12,000 final offer — and all of the subjects received this offer. Thus, it appears that the experiment demonstrates that subjects' reservation prices were affected by a seemingly relevant but actually irrelevant anchor — namely, the defendant's initial offer.

*3. Another Example — Real Estate Listing Prices.*  In another experiment, Max Bazerman and Margaret Neale asked real estate agents to determine a reasonable price for a buyer to pay for a particular house and the minimum amount the seller should be willing to accept for the same house (roughly speaking, a reservation price both for a buyer and a seller). The experimenters then gave real estate agent subjects all the information that agents said they would need in order to place a value on the house, including a great deal of information about the characteristics of the house itself and information about sales prices of other houses in the neighborhood over the previous six-month period. The experimenters also told the subjects the listing price of the house (which is effectively the seller's initial offer), but they varied the amount of the purported listing price. On average, subjects who were provided with higher listing prices reported higher valuations of the house, both in terms of the price that a buyer should pay and the minimum that a seller should accept, thus suggesting that the subjects' valuations were anchored by the listing price information. The experimenters concluded that "the anchoring effect is not only present, it is pronounced." Max H. Bazerman & Margaret A. Neale, Negotiating Rationally (1992).

*4. Strategy: Anchoring and Initial Offers.*  The anchoring phenomenon, standing alone, suggests that an extreme opening offer can benefit the negotiator by favorably shifting the opponent's reservation price, thus enlarging the bargaining zone, see Russell Korobkin & Chris Guthrie, Opening Offers and Out-of-Court Settlement: A Little Moderation May Not Go a Long Way, 10 Ohio St. J. Disp. Res. 1, 21 (1994), so long as the offer is not so extreme that the opponent will not even consider it as a starting point for negotiations. See also Max H. Bazerman & Margaret A. Neale, Negotiating Rationally 29 (1992). It is very important to realize, however, that a negotiator needs to consider many issues other than the anchoring value of an offer when deciding whether to make an aggressive, one-sided offer or a more moderate or "reasonable" offer. An extreme offer might send a signal that the negotiator has a strong BATNA and reservation price or a great deal of patience, issues considered in Chapter 5, or high aspirations, an issue considered in Chapter 2. An extreme offer also might position the negotiator to engage in a pattern of reciprocal concessions that result in a desirable final agreement, an issue considered in Chapter 6. On the other hand, an extreme offer might have the negative effects of sending a signal that there is no bargaining zone, reducing the potential for integrative bargaining (Chapter 4), or reducing the level of trust among the negotiators (Chapter 7).

# D.   OVERCONFIDENCE AND THE SELF-SERVING BIAS

For negotiators to establish reservation prices that will help them to reach desirable agreements and avoid undesirable agreements, they need to be able to accurately assess the value to them of reaching a negotiated agreement, and to accurately assess the value of their BATNA. When the value of either is uncertain, rational choice theory implicitly assumes that negotiators will be able to accurately estimate the *probability* of various possible values. For example, if Algernon is going to bargain to buy Benno's business, Algernon is probably concerned with the income that the business will generate in the future. The future income probably cannot be known with certainty, but the best information available might enable Algernon to estimate that there is a 20 percent chance that the business will earn $75,000 in profits over each of the next five years, a 70 percent chance that it will earn $100,000 for each of the next five years, and a 10 percent chance that it will earn $200,000 for each of the next five years. He can then use these estimates to calculate an expected value of the business' future income stream, which would undoubtedly be a primary input in determining his reservation price.

It is possible, of course, that Algernon will not make the best predictions possible of the business's future income because he is not skilled as a business appraiser. If this is the case, however, it would be difficult to predict whether Algernon's predictions would be too high or too low. It is also possible that Algernon's predictions will not be as accurate as possible because he lacks information that would be relevant to estimating an expected value. Perhaps Algernon lacks complete knowledge of Benno's operations, products, profit history, or competitors, or of economic trends that could affect the business. If this is the case, not only would it be impossible to predict whether Algernon's estimates are too high or too low, rational choice theory would predict that Algernon's estimates would get better and better the more relevant information he collected and included in his analysis.

The following excerpt challenges these assumptions by arguing that negotiators' estimates of value can be systematically biased in predictable directions because of a psychological tendency to view uncertain evidence in the best possible light. As the experiment described in the excerpt demonstrates, the "self-serving bias" can result in buyers setting relatively low and sellers setting relatively high reservation prices, thus reducing the size of a bargaining zone or eliminating a bargaining zone that might have existed in the absence of this bias.

■ **George Loewenstein, Samuel Issacharoff, Colin Camerer, & Linda Babcock, Self-Serving Assessments of Fairness and Pretrial Bargaining***
22 J. Legal Stud. 135, 135-141, 144-153 (1993)

A persistently troubling question in the legal-economic literature is why cases proceed to trial. . . . Although civil litigation is resolved by settlement in an estimated 95 percent of all disputes, what accounts for the failure of the remaining 5 percent to settle prior to trial?

The standard economic model of legal disputes posits that settlement occurs when there exists a positively valued *settlement zone* — a range of transfer amounts from defendant to plaintiff that leave both parties better off than they would be if they went to trial. The location of the settlement zone depends on three factors: the parties' probability distributions of award amounts, the litigation costs they face, and their risk preferences.

According to this model, so long as the parties share a common assessment of the potential risks and rewards from continuing litigation, they will assign a jointly held expected value to the litigation. At that point, any settlement above the expected value *minus* anticipated costs is desirable for a plaintiff, and any settlement below the expected value *plus* anticipated costs is desirable for a defendant. Therefore, risk-neutral or risk-averse parties with similar expectations regarding the award amount contingent on nonsettlement have an incentive to settle that increases with the magnitude of the settlement zone.

. . . [T]here exists substantial psychological research documenting the prevalence of "egocentric" biases in estimation. When people estimate quantities that are relevant to their own self-image — for example, the fraction of credit that they deserve for a collaborative task, how well they drive (compared to others), the esteem in which others hold them, or how well they have performed a task — their estimates tend to be biased in a self-serving fashion. This raises the question of whether parties to a lawsuit in fact can make an unbiased estimate of the value of a case. . . . [P]laintiffs are likely to systematically overestimate the value of their claims, and defendants are likely to under-estimate the value of claims brought against them. . . .

. . . In an experimental simulation of pretrial negotiations in a dispute arising from a motor-vehicle accident, we monitored the perceptions of parties regarding the judgment they anticipate if they were to go to trial. We then examined the relationship between these perceptions and bargaining behavior and settlement. We presented subject pairs with identical case materials, designated one defendant and the other plaintiff, endowed the defendant with a fixed fund from which any settlement or judgment would have to be paid, and allowed the parties to attempt to negotiate a settlement. Absent a settlement, funds were distributed according to a preexisting independent "trial" judgment, and litigation costs (that were manipulated in the experiment) were levied.

Our findings demonstrate the importance of [the] psychological considerations discussed above. Contrary to the explicit assumption [of economic theory], predictions of the value of the claim [were] biased in a self-serving manner. Moreover, the magnitude of the bias is a strong predictor of nonsettlement. . . .

## II.   Psychological Factors in Bargaining

### A.   SELF-SERVING BIASES

Whereas the common assumption in economics is that errors of judgment will not be systematically biased, such biases have been the active focus of recent research in psychology. Studies have documented biases in probability judgments that are not eliminated by incentives for accuracy or feedback. Such biases include overweighting of vivid information, revision of probability estimates more radically in some situations and less radically in others than is called for by Bayes's theorem, failure to expect regression to the mean (and misattribution when it occurs), misapplication of the law of large numbers to small samples, and a tendency to think that the plausible conjunction of two events is more probable than is either event alone. These biases are widely believed to result from the use of judgmental *heuristics* — cognitive rules of thumb that are naturally adapted to limited human information-processing capabilities instead of optimal statistical rules.

Most relevant to the current endeavor are "egocentric" or "self-serving" estimation biases. Seminar participants overestimate the amount of time they speak relative to estimates by other participants. In two-person discussions, both people typically believe they spoke more than half the time. When asked to guess the fraction of various household tasks they are responsible for, married couples give estimates that add up to more than 100 percent. . . .

Egocentric biases have also been observed in dispute settings. A classic study measured student perceptions of a contentious football game between Princeton and Dartmouth.[17] Students from both schools watched a film of the game and rated the number of penalties committed by both teams. On the one hand, Princeton students saw the Dartmouth team commit twice as many flagrant penalties and three times as many mild penalties as their own team. On the other hand, Dartmouth students recorded an approximately equal number of penalties by both teams. Team allegiance influenced the students' perceptions of penalties. . . .

In the bargaining experiment discussed below, we test for the existence of a pervasive self-serving bias by asking subjects to predict the case's value. The experimental setting measures bias in expectations by providing adversarial parties with identical information, assuring them that the other party has no additional information, and introducing financial incentives for reporting expectations accurately. . . .

### III.   THE EXPERIMENT

Eighty undergraduates from the University of Chicago and eighty students at the University of Texas at Austin School of Law participated in our study. We assigned pairs of subjects the roles of plaintiff and defendant, and then they attempted to negotiate the settlement of a tort case arising from the collision of an automobile and a motorcycle. The injured plaintiff (the motorcyclist) was suing the driver of the automobile for $100,000. We gave both subjects precisely the same case materials and informed them that the information they were given was identical. The subjects received twenty-seven pages of actual testimony abstracted from a real case in Texas, including witness testimony, police reports, maps, and the testimony of the parties. Subjects were informed that, after editing the case materials, we had given them to a judge in Texas who had reached a decision regarding whether there would be compensation to the plaintiff and, if so, the amount.

Before negotiating, we asked the subjects to write down their guess of what the judge would award. We told them they would receive a $1 bonus at the end of the session if their prediction was within $5,000 (plus or minus) of the actual judge's award. We also asked what they considered a *fair* amount for the plaintiff to receive in an out-of-court settlement from the vantage point of a neutral third party.

We paid each subject a fixed fee ($3 at Chicago and $4 at Texas) for participating and gave the defendant an extra $10. The two parties then attempted to negotiate a settlement orally. If they settled, the defendant paid the plaintiff an amount of money that depended on

17. Albert H. Hastorf & Hadley Cantril, They Saw a Game: A Case Study, 49 J. Abnormal & Soc. Psychology 129 (1954).

the value of the settlement. Every $10,000 from the case was equivalent
to $1 for the subjects. For example, given a $60,000 settlement, the
defendant kept $4 and gave $6 to the plaintiff. If the parties failed to
settle, the defendant had to pay the plaintiff an amount that depended
on the judge's decision in the case. Since the actual judgment was
$30,560, this meant the defendant paid the plaintiff $3.06. In addition,
costs for not settling were levied and systematically manipulated. Finally, after the negotiation ended, we asked both parties to recall and
rate the importance of arguments favoring both the plaintiff and the
defendant.

. . . We gave the subjects identical testimony and information about
the rules of the game, so that any systematic differences in estimates
between defendant and plaintiff could not be attributed to differences
in information. Even though there was uncertainty about what the
judge would do if the parties could not settle, no private information
was held by either party. In addition, we guaranteed both parties that
the information was the complete set of facts discoverable as to the
controversy: that the judge ruled on the case based on the same case
materials. We also chose a fact-intensive scenario in which witness credibility and coherence of testimony would predominate; there were no
unclear legal issues that might prompt uncertainty as to arbitrator conduct.

First, all subjects were paired off and assigned the role of plaintiff
or defendant. . . . After reading the case materials, subjects made a prediction of the judge's settlement. . . . They were then allowed to negotiate for thirty minutes. If they failed to reach a voluntary settlement
within that period, the judge's decision determined the plaintiff's payment to the defendant, and legal costs were levied on the parties. . . .

In the final stage of the experiment after negotiating, all subjects
were asked to list all the arguments they could think of that favored
each side and to rate the importance of these arguments on a four-
point scale that consisted of "very important," "moderately important,"
"minor," and "trivial." The page eliciting arguments favorable to the
plaintiff instructed the subject, "List all of the arguments you can think
of that support a large settlement for [plaintiff] Jones. When you finish
listing the arguments, rate each argument in terms of how important
you think it is. How much do you think the argument would influence
a judge or jury who tried the case?"

## IV.  RESULTS

. . . Plaintiffs' predictions of the judge's award, on average, were
$14,527 higher than defendants'.

. . . To determine whether there was a relationship between the
magnitude of the self-serving bias and the settlement rates . . . we ex-

amine the differences in the parties' assessments. The differences are broken down by the pairs who settled and those who did not. The evidence for such a relationship is strong. . . . For the fifty-nine pairs who settled, the mean difference between the plaintiffs' and defendants' predictions of the judge's settlement . . . was $9,050; for the twenty-one pairs who did not settle, the average difference was $29,917. . . . The probability of settling decreases with the difference between the parties' assessments of . . . what a judge will award. . . .

Our experiment provides strong evidence for the existence of a self-serving bias. . . . Thus, the central assumption of the [economic] model — that errors in the estimation of potential award amounts are random — is rejected.

Moreover, the statistical link between the bias and nonsettlement is strong. The magnitude of the bias, although also present among pairs who settled, is over three times greater for pairs who did not. The strong correlation between the magnitude of the bias in a particular bargaining pair and nonsettlement supports the self-serving bias explanation for nonsettlement. . . .                                               ■

## Notes

*1. Explanations of the Self-Serving Bias.* What explains the finding that plaintiffs tend to interpret uncertain and conflicting litigation facts as supporting their position while defendants tend to view the same facts as supporting their position? One theory is that people are selective in the attention they pay to various facts, focusing more on the facts that support their position than those that undermine their position. Loewenstein and colleagues tested to see whether this theory could account for the self-serving bias exhibited in their experiments by comparing their subjects' predictions about the judge's settlement to the arguments presented in the litigation materials that they recalled after participating in the experiment. This analysis strongly supported the theory. The authors found that plaintiffs in their experiments recalled significantly more of the arguments presented in the litigation materials that favored themselves than those that favored the defendant, and that the recall of defendants in their study was biased in the opposite direction. The authors also weighted the arguments presented in the litigation materials by their importance and found that subjects' recall of the more important arguments was even more subject to a self-serving bias. George Loewenstein et al., at 150-151.

Another factor that might lead to the self-serving bias is systematic overconfidence on the part of negotiators. The overconfidence bias comes in two varieties. First, there is evidence that individuals often act as though they can control situations over which they logically have no control. For example, experiments have demonstrated that subjects demand more money to sell a lottery ticket if they picked the number than if the number was assigned randomly. See Ellen J. Langer, The Illusion of Control, 32 J. Pers. & Soc. Psychol. 311 (1975). Second, there is evidence that individuals systematically exhibit more confidence in their ability than is warranted when ability does matter. Most negotiators, for example, believe they are more competent than their opponents, although logically this can only be true for 50 percent of negotiators at most. See Roderick M. Kramer et al., Self-Enhancement Biases and Negotiator Judgment: Effects of Self-Esteem and Mood, 56 Org. Behav. & Human Decision Proc. 110 (1993). These and a wealth of similar findings led one pair of commentators to hypothesize that "lawyers at all skill levels are very likely to overestimate their abilities relative to those of their peers." Richard Birke & Craig R. Fox, Psychological Principles in Negotiating Civil Settlements, 4 Harv. Negotiation L. Rev. 1, 16 (1999).

If negotiators are systematically overconfident in their abilities, this could lead them to overvalue alternatives with probabilistic outcomes relative to those with certain outcomes, on the theory that they can exert more control over the probabilistic outcome than is realistically practical. Thus, plaintiffs and defendants might each interpret identical facts as favoring their position because they assume they could use those facts to convince a judge or jury to side with them.

*2. Ambiguity Aversion.* There is some experimental evidence that the effect of the self-serving bias might depend on how confident negotiators are in their evaluations. In one study, experimenters had subjects playing the roles of plaintiff and defendant attempt to negotiate an out-of-court settlement of a lawsuit. Plaintiff and defendant subjects were each given the same estimate of the amount of damages that would be awarded if the plaintiff prevailed, but plaintiffs were advised by their hypothetical lawyers that they stood an 80 percent chance of prevailing, while defendants were advised that the plaintiff stood only a 20 percent chance of prevailing — a discrepancy that might result from a strong case of self-serving bias on the part of one or both litigants. Some of the subject pairs were told that their lawyers had "extreme confidence" in their estimated probabilities, while other pairs were told that their lawyers had "little confidence" in their estimated probabilities. Few of the "extreme confidence" pairs reached a settlement agreement, consistent with the large disparity in predictions, but more than 50 percent of the "little confidence" pairs reached an agreement. The experimenters concluded that increasing ambiguity of probability estimates increases risk aversion and serves to encourage settlements. Cynthia S. Fobia & Jay J. Christensen-Szalanski, Ambiguity and Liability Negotiations: The Effects of the Negotiators' Role and the Sensitivity Zone, 54 Org. Behav. & Human Decision Proc. 277 (1993).

***3. Information and Settlement.*** Traditional economic analysis of litigation settlement predicts that most lawsuits will settle out of court because litigant risk aversion and the high costs of litigation will cause plaintiffs to set their reservation prices below the expected value of a court-determined resolution of the dispute and defendants to set their reservation prices above the expected value of court-determined resolution. Disputes will fail to settle when the plaintiff's estimation of the expected value of trial is (1) higher than the defendant's estimation and (2) the magnitude of the difference in estimations is large enough to swamp the effects of risk aversion and transaction costs. See George Priest & Benjamin Klein, The Selection of Disputes for Litigation, 13 J. Legal Stud. 1, 12-13 (1984).

For example, assume Bonnie is suing Clyde, both parties are sufficiently risk averse that they would pay a $5,000 premium for the certainty of settlement rather than the risk of trial, and staging a trial would cost both parties $10,000 more than settling out of court. Given these facts, a bargaining zone would exist for an out-of-court settlement unless Bonnie's estimate of the expected value of trial were at least $30,000 higher than Clyde's. If Bonnie and Clyde both estimated that the expected value of a trial verdict would be $100,000 for Bonnie, Bonnie's reservation price would be $85,000 ($100,000 − $10,000 − $5,000) and Clyde's would be approximately $115,000 ($100,000 + $10,000 + $5,000), creating a $30,000 bargaining zone. If Bonnie estimated the expected value of trial to be $110,000 while Clyde expected it to be only $90,000, there would still be a bargaining zone, albeit a smaller one, because Bonnie's reservation price would be $95,000 ($110,000 − $10,000 − $5,000) and Clyde's would be $105,000 ($90,000 + $10,000 + $5,000).

Economic theory assumes that Bonnie and Clyde will evaluate the expected value of the case in an unbiased manner, but that the quality of their evaluations will depend on the extent to which relevant information is available to them. If they know very few of the legally relevant facts, their evaluations might vary substantially. Bonnie's estimate of the expected value of trial will sometimes be higher and sometimes be lower than Clyde's. When Bonnie's estimate is higher than Clyde's, and the difference between their respective evaluations is great, settlement negotiations will fail. The more information about legally relevant facts that the parties have, the less likely that the parties' evaluations of trial will be different by an amount so great that a bargaining zone will not exist.

In litigation, parties obtain a substantial portion of the information they need to estimate the expected value of an adjudicated outcome from the discovery process, by which the litigants may depose witnesses and request relevant documents in control of the opposing party. The liberal amount of discovery available under the federal rules of civil procedure as well as most state and local rules is rooted in part on the theory that more information will lead to more similar evaluations of cases by the parties and thus more out-of-court settlements. The experimental results of Loewenstein and his colleagues call into question the assumption that more discovery will necessarily lead to higher rates of settlement and suggest that other interventions might better promote settlement. The authors conclude:

> As structured, civil litigation attempts to promote settlement by isolating genuine uncertainty about the law and by providing the parties with liberal access to each other's information. . . .
> This study reveals the shakiness of the assumption that the parties will integrate the information revealed through these processes in an unbiased fashion in order to settle. Rather, our study shows that, even with perfectly shared information and a complete absence of disputed legal issues, self-serving biases can cause inefficient impasses. . . .
> If nonsettlement is driven by systematic bias instead of random error or a lack of information, the practical ramifications are numerous. First, it indicates that exchanges of information are not in themselves necessarily conducive to settlement but must be analyzed in terms of how they interact with preexisting biases. Second, it suggests that effective alternative dispute-resolution mechanisms, at least in part, should be directed at "debiasing" parties rather than simply facilitating the exchange of information.

George Loewenstein et al., Self-Serving Assessments of Fairness and Pre-Trial Bargaining, 22 J. Legal Stud. 135 (1993).

## E.  REACTIVE DEVALUATION

Rational choice theory predicts that the negotiator will set his reservation point by identifying his BATNA and then determine what offer he would have to obtain from his opponent in order to be indifferent between reaching agreement and pursuing the BATNA. From this perspective, the value of a proposed agreement is effectively evaluated before it is even made. There is some evidence, however, that a negotiated agreement may be of less value to a negotiator than it would otherwise be merely because his opponent proposed it. This phenomenon — "reactive devaluation" — suggests that in some circumstances transactions that would ordinarily be judged by a negotiator to be more desirable than pursuing his BATNA may be judged less desirable than pursuing his BATNA when proposed by the opponent.

## ■ Lee Ross, Reactive Devaluation in Negotiation and Conflict Resolution*

**Barriers to Conflict Resolution** 27-42 (Kenneth J. Arrow et al. eds., 1995)

. . . [E]ven when . . . a "mutually-acceptable-in-principle" proposal can be formulated, there may be an additional barrier to be overcome, one that arises, at least in large part, from the dynamics of the negotiation process. This barrier has been termed *reactive devaluation* (Ross and Stillinger 1991; Ross and Ward 1995; Stillinger, Epelbaum, Keltner, and Ross 1990). It refers to the fact that the very offer of a particular proposal or concession — especially if the offer comes from an adversary — may diminish its apparent value or attractiveness in the eyes of the recipient. . . .

### SUMMARY OF EMPIRICAL RESEARCH

Initial evidence for the reactive devaluation barrier was provided in a 1986 sidewalk survey of opinions regarding possible arms reductions by the U.S. and the U.S.S.R. (Stillinger et al. 1991). Respondents were asked to evaluate the terms of a simple but sweeping nuclear disarmament proposal — one calling for an immediate 50 percent reduction of long-range strategic weapons, to be followed over the next decade and a half by further reduction in both strategic and short-range tactical weapons until, very early in the next century, all such weapons would have disappeared from the two nations' arsenals. As a matter of history, this proposal had actually been made slightly earlier, with little fanfare or impact, by the Soviet leader Gorbachev. In the Stillinger et al. survey, however, the proposal's putative source was manipulated — that is, depending on experimental condition, it was ascribed by the survey instrument either to the Soviet leader, to President Reagan, or to a group of unknown strategy analysts — and only the responses of subjects who claimed to be hearing of the proposal for the first time were included in subsequent analyses.

The results of this survey showed, as predicted, that the proposal's putative authorship determined its attractiveness. When the proposal was attributed to the U.S. leader, 90 percent of respondents thought it either favorable to the U.S. or evenhanded; and when it was attributed to the (presumably neutral) third party, 80 percent thought it either favorable to the U.S. or evenhanded; but when the same proposal was attributed to the Soviet leader, only 44 percent of respondents expressed a similarly positive reaction. . . .

Although this initial reactive devaluation study provided positive results, the findings are unlikely to seem particularly surprising or provocative to negotiation theorists or practitioners. The reason for this is clear. While the tendency to devalue the adversary's concessions and proposals undeniably is a barrier to dispute resolution, such a tendency can readily be defended on normative grounds. Certainly there is nothing counternormative about treating a proposal's authorship as informative with respect to the balance of advantages and disadvantages that would accrue to its author. ("They wouldn't have offered those terms if those terms didn't advance their interests.") And, where the author in question is presumed to be a foe who seeks to dominate the proposal's recipients, there may be nothing counternormative about also treating such authorship as potentially informative about the proposal's prospects for the recipient. ("They wouldn't have offered those terms if those terms strengthened our position relative to theirs.")

It was such normative considerations, at least in part, that dictated the design and procedural details of the next set of reactive devaluation studies conducted by Stillinger et al. In these studies the responses contrasted were not ones made to proposals from hostile versus non-hostile sources. In fact, the responses examined were made in reaction to compromise measures offered by a source who was perceived by most recipients as not opposed to their own interests, but merely acting in that source's interests. The context of this research was a campus-wide controversy at Stanford about the university's investment policy. Students generally favored a policy calling for total and immediate divestment by the university of all stock holdings in companies doing business in South Africa. The university, claiming to share the students' opposition to apartheid, but to be constrained by its responsibilities to maximize the value of its portfolio and earnings, set up a committee to study the problem and devise a divestment policy that would be both financially prudent and socially responsible. Once again using a real-world issue, and once again relying upon the use of an experimental manipulation within the context of a survey, Stillinger et al. seized this opportunity to study further the phenomenon of reactive devaluation.

In the first such study, students simply were asked to read a booklet describing the divestment controversy, then to evaluate two potential compromise proposals. One of these proposals, which was termed the "Specific Divestment" plan, entailed immediate divestment from corporations doing business with the South African military or police. The other alternative, termed the "Deadline" plan, proposed to create a committee of students and trustees to monitor "investment responsibility," with the promise of total divestment two years down the road if the committee was not satisfied with the rate of progress shown in dismantling the apartheid system in South Africa. Subjects were randomly assigned to three experimental conditions, identical in all respects except for the particular program that the university was purported to be on the verge of enacting. One group read that the university planned to undertake Specific Divestment; another group read that the university planned to undertake the Deadline plan; and the remainder were given no reason to believe that the university was considering the immediate adoption of either alternative. The experimental hypothesis, of course, was simply that the "offered" concession plan would be devalued relative to the "non-offered" one.

The results obtained in this study seemed once again to offer straightforward evidence for the predicted reactive devaluation phenomenon. That is, students tended to rate whichever of the two proposals the trustees had ostensibly offered as a smaller and less significant compromise than the alternative, non-offered, proposal. Thus, when Stanford purportedly was ready to implement the Deadline plan, 85 percent of the respondents ranked Specific Divestment as a bigger concession than the Deadline. By contrast, when the university purportedly was ready to pursue Specific Divestment, only 40 percent rated Specific Divestment as the more consequential of the two compromise plans. Not surprisingly, when neither concession plan was purported to be imminent, the percentage of students rating Specific Divestment as a bigger and more significant concession than the Deadline plan was between the extremes in the two experimental conditions — i.e., 69 percent. Clearly, the "offered" versus "non-offered" status of the relevant divestment plans influenced the student respondents' evaluation of their apparent significance and attractiveness. . . .

### MECHANISMS UNDERLYING REACTIVE DEVALUATION

Research on reactive devaluation initially was undertaken to show that biased construal of an adversary's concession or compromise proposal could lead to devaluation — and hence could launch a downward spiral of misunderstanding and mistrust, whereby dismissal and lack of reciprocation by the recipient of a proposal discouraged further initiatives. As that research program evolved, however, it became increasingly clear that a number of different psychological processes might underlie reactive devaluation-processes that differ considerably both in their normative status and in their implications for negotiation theory and practice. Two specific processes, or rather types of processes, merit consideration in more depth.

One set of underlying processes involves changes in *perception, inter-*

*pretation, or inference,* either about individual elements in a proposal or about the overall valence of that proposal. To the extent that the other side's initiative seems inconsistent with our understanding of their interests and/or past negotiation behavior, we are apt, perhaps even logically obliged, to scrutinize their offer rather carefully. That is, we are inclined to look for ambiguities, omissions, or "fine print" that might render the terms of that proposal more advantageous to the other side, and perhaps less advantageous to our side, than we had assumed them to be (or would have assumed them to be, had the question been asked) prior to their being offered. The results of such skeptical scrutiny — especially if the terms in question are unclear, complex, or imperfectly specified, and especially if trust vis-à-vis implementation of these terms is called for — are apt to be a revised assessment of what we stand to gain, both in absolute terms and relative to what we believe the other side stands to gain, from acceptance of the relevant proposal. . . .

The second type of underlying process or mechanism, suggested by demonstrations of the devaluation phenomenon in the Stanford divestment studies in which the source of the devalued proposal was not really an enemy of the recipient, is very different. This mechanism involves neither mindful nor mindless changes in interpretation, but rather changes in underlying *preferences.* Human beings, at least in some circumstances, may be inclined to reject or devalue whatever is freely available to them, and to covet and strive for whatever is denied them. Moreover, they may be inclined to do so even when no hostility is perceived on the part of the individual or institution determining what will or will not be made available. (See Brehm 1966; Brehm and Brehm 1981; also Wicklund 1974, for theoretical accounts of such "psychological reactance"). The familiar aphorism that "the grass is always greener on the other side of the fence" captures this source of human unhappiness and frustration very well, and it is easy to think of anecdotal examples in which children or adults, rather than "counting their blessings," seem to place inordinately high value on whatever commodity or opportunity is denied them.

A simple role-play study by Lepper, Ross, Tsai, and Ward (1994) documents this "change of preference" process quite clearly. At the same time, this study provides further evidence that the reactive devaluation phenomenon depends neither on an adversarial relationship nor on ambiguity in proposed terms. The subjects in the study, all social science majors, were asked to imagine that they had undertaken a summer job with a distinguished professor, one which entailed low pay and unrewarding and difficult library research. They further were asked to imagine that they later discovered that the professor was on the verge of publishing, and receiving a hefty royalty for, a chapter based heavily on their work. The fictional professor, however, offered them neither additional money nor a coauthorship in recognition of their efforts (two rewards that had been vaguely alluded to as "further possibilities" if the students' efforts led to a publishable article). Next, they were asked to imagine that, after writing a polite but firm note to the professor complaining about the lack of fair recognition or compensation and reminding the professor of the vague assurances offered them at the outset of the project, they had received one of two possible concessions — either a "third authorship" (with their name following that of a second author who to their knowledge had contributed little to the project) or a sum of $750. Finally the students were asked to assess, among other things, the attractiveness and value of the two relevant concessions — the one that they had been granted by the professor and the alternative concession that had not been granted.

Reactive devaluation was found, just as predicted. That is, it was the students who had been granted the money who found the third authorship to be the most attractive and of greater interest to them, and the students who had been offered the third authorship who found the money most attractive and valuable. These students, it is worth noting, gave no evidence of having reinterpreted the meaning or reassessed the objective worth of the two relatively unambiguous compromises in question. They simply expressed preferences and values that seemed to be tilted in the direction of whichever one of the two compromises had proven "unavailable" or been "withheld." ∎

## Notes

***The Causes of Reactive Devaluation.***   As Ross notes, there are a number of plausible explanations for the observed phenomenon of reactive devaluation. In what might be called "true reactive devaluation," the phenomenon might be caused by the human desire to have what is out of our reach. When a particular agreement comes within a negotiator's grasp, that agreement might seem less desirable because it is available.

In contrast to this psychological explanation, some experimental results showing reactive devaluation might be explained as a rational updating of preferences when new relevant information becomes available (an explanation that might be labeled "private information"). If an opponent has private information about the quality of the negotiation's subject matter, the negotiator might reasonably reassess that quality if the opponent is suddenly willing to part with the subject matter. If an American has incomplete information about the value of a particular arms control agreement but judges that it is *probably* superior to a BATNA of no agreement, he might rationally revisit that judgment after he learns that agreement is championed by the leader of the Soviet Union.

Another possible explanation not suggested by Ross, which can be called "spite," is that if the negotiator dislikes his opponent, he may have a preference that the opponent not get what she wants. Consequently, when the opponent reveals what she wants by proposing an agreement, the value to the negotiator of reaching an agreement as opposed to pursuing his BATNA declines. For an experimental test of these different explanations in the context of evaluating an offer of settlement in litigation, see Russell Korobkin & Chris Guthrie, Psychological Barriers to Litigation Settlement: An Experimental Approach, 93 Mich. L. Rev. 107, 150-160 (1994).

## DISCUSSION QUESTIONS AND PROBLEMS

*1. The Puzzle of Settlement.* The studies of the psychology of decision making excerpted in this section present a dim view of the likelihood of settling lawsuits out of court. The self-serving bias suggests opposing lawyers might both view their trial odds in a more favorable light than is warranted. Prospect theory suggests some types of litigants might exhibit risk seeking tendencies, preferring the risks of trial to a certain settlement with the same expected value. The status quo bias suggests negotiators might be reluctant to make deals because doing so changes the status quo. Yet, in spite of all of this, the vast majority of lawsuits do settle out of court, suggesting that there is a bargaining zone between litigants' reservation prices most of the time. What factors do you think account for this?

*2. External Validity.* Like many social science experiments, all of the experiments presented in this chapter used student subjects — either undergraduates or law students. The use of student subjects raises "external validity" concerns — that is, whether the effects demonstrated in the experiments would also be found in equivalent situations in the real world — because students are not representative of the class of litigants or contracting parties. Even when studies employ law students as subjects and ask them to play the role of lawyer-negotiators, the subject pool will fail to reflect some characteristics of lawyer-negotiators in ways that could potentially skew the experimental results. What is perhaps most problematic about the use of students as subjects is that they lack experience in legal negotiation. When this is combined with an experimental design that has the subjects participate in only a single experiment, it becomes a concern that the subjects have had little or no opportunity to learn from past experiences before providing data for the studies. To what extent do you think that litigants, contracting parties, and practicing lawyers are subject to the framing effect, the status quo bias, the self-serving bias, and reactive devaluation described in the experiments?

Loewenstein and colleagues offer the following observations:

> Our experiment is different from earlier empirical investigations in that it is a one-shot negotiation. . . . On the one hand, if given multiple opportunities to participate in the experiment, subjects might exhibit less bias and greater tendencies to settle. On the other hand, the feedback provided by repeated play could conceivably inflame self-serving assessments and make impasse more frequent if subjects selectively encode feedback or ignore disconfirming feedback instead of learning from it.
>
> In any case, it is unclear whether one-shot experiments or those in which subjects repeatedly confront the same situation more closely approximate conditions prevailing in actual litigation. Most people participate in only a small number of serious disputes, each of which typically differs in important respects from those that come before. Differences between suits experienced in the past and the present controversy complicate the task of drawing insights from the former and applying them to the latter.

George Loewenstein et al., Self-Serving Assessments of Fairness and Pre-Trial Bargaining, 22 J. Legal Stud. 135, 155-156 (1993).

*3. Which Psychological Processes Are Undesirable?* Negotiators determine their reservation prices differently from what rational choice theory predicts in a number of ways: evaluations of potential outcomes may be affected by the self-serving bias, risk preference may be affected by whether alternatives are framed as losses or gains from a reference point, reservation prices may depend on perceptions of the status quo, and valuations of proposals may depend on who initiates them. Assuming that negotiators wish to establish their reservation points such that they enter into negotiated agreements when agreement is superior to pursuing their BATNAs and do not enter into agreements when doing so would be inferior to pursuing their BATNAs, which of these observed psychological phenomena are desirable and which are undesirable? If any or all of the phenomena are undesirable, what steps might you take to try to avoid them or to help your clients to avoid them?

*4. Countering Psychological Processes.* What steps might you take in negotiation to reduce the likelihood that the psychological processes discussed in this section will not cause your negotiating opponent to reject a proposed agreement that she would have accepted if she evaluated the situation in a way strictly consistent with rational choice theory. That is, how might you counter the effects of the framing effect, the status quo bias, anchoring, the self-serving bias, and reactive devaluation on your opponent? Do you think it would be easier to counter the effects of some of these processes than others?

**5. Psychological Factors and Opening Offers.**   An important tactical question in negotiation is whether the negotiator should make the first offer or try to persuade the opponent to make the first offer. The question is difficult because a number of tactical arguments exist both for and against making the first offer. This difficult question is made even harder to resolve, however, by the fact that even some of the psychological processes discussed in this chapter can cut both ways. For example, the anchoring effect suggests a negotiator might be better off making the first offer, because that offer can anchor the opponent's judgment of his reservation price. On the other hand, the reactive devaluation effect suggests the negotiator is better off not making the first offer, because even a generous first offer is likely to be devalued by the opponent. From a psychological viewpoint, which of these competing arguments seem stronger to you? Are you inclined to make a first offer to try to anchor the other party's expectations, or invite the opponent to make the first offer to avoid the devaluation of your initial proposal?

**6. Predicting and Confronting Psychological Factors.**   Broadcast America, Inc., which owns a nationwide network of television and radio stations, wishes to purchase KSQD, a midsized radio station in Colorado that has been owned and operated by Fran Chrismark for the last ten years. During Fran's ownership, the station has been modestly profitable overall, but profits have fluctuated from year to year, ranging from substantial to meager. Fran is willing to sell the station, but only if the price is right. There are no other potential buyers at this time. How would you predict that the psychological phenomena discussed in this section will affect Fran's reservation price relative to what it would be if she were a completely "rational" decision maker? Will the psychological phenomena make an agreement more or less likely? If you were representing Broadcast America in the negotiations, what might you do to attempt to mitigate the psychological phenomena that could make Fran's reservation price higher than it otherwise would be?

# Chapter 4

# Integrative Bargaining

## A. EXPANDING THE BARGAINING ZONE

When negotiators sit down to bargain with an opponent, they often make the mistake of assuming that a gain for one party necessarily means an equivalent loss for the other party. Economists refer to negotiations with this characteristic as "zero-sum," and negotiation theorists often call them purely "distributive" negotiations. When there is only one issue on the table and parties' interests are in direct opposition, negotiations can fit this description. For example, if Mutt and Jeff find a dollar bill on the street and wish to bargain over how to divide it, their negotiation can be described as zero sum. The only subject matter of the negotiation is a single item of currency, and both prefer more money to less. Consequently, every penny that Jeff gets means a penny less for Mutt, and vice versa.

Most human interactions are complex enough, however, that they are not purely zero-sum. One party values some aspect of the negotiation relatively more and the other party values a different aspect of the negotiation relatively more. In other words, there are potential ways to structure a deal that will benefit the parties more than merely dividing a single asset. Negotiations that take advantage of this potential are often referred to as "integrative," "value creating," or "problem solving."

In an ideal world, negotiated agreements would benefit both parties without burdening either with any countervailing costs. In this situation, the parties are sometimes said to have "shared" or "common" interests. See David A. Lax & James K. Sebenius, The Manager as Negotiator 88-116 (1986). A nursery rhyme nicely illustrates this situation: you might recall that Jack Spratt could eat no fat, and his wife could eat no lean. If the two wish to negotiate the division of a roast, all the meat could be allocated to Jack, and all the fat could be allocated to Jack's wife, and neither would envy any part of what the other received. To use a more standard negotiation example, consider a home seller who wishes to avoid the costs of dismantling and moving a chandelier he has installed in his house and a buyer who loves the chandelier. By agreeing to include the chandelier in the sale, both parties benefit from a shared interest in allocating the chandelier to the buyer. Notice that the parties don't merely each enjoy a *net* benefit. Neither gives up anything of value to him.

When parties are able to identify a common interest in negotiation, they can expand the cooperative surplus that an agreement would create because both their reservation prices shift in directions that make reaching agreement more valuable. As an illustration, imagine that the home buyer's reservation price is $100,000, and the seller's reservation price is $95,000. Because the buyer likes the chandelier so much, he would be willing to pay up to an extra $1,000 for the house if the chandelier is included, making his new reservation price $101,000. Because the seller dreads moving the chandelier, he would be willing to accept up to $1,000 less for the house if he is relieved of that responsibility that he assumed would go along with the sale, making his new reservation price $94,000. By identifying their common interest in including the chandelier with the sale of the house, the parties can create $2,000 of joint value by replacing a transaction that would have created $5,000 of cooperative surplus with a new transaction that will create $7,000 of cooperative surplus. If the buyer's reservation price was below the seller's by less than $2,000 prior to identifying their common interest in transferring the chandelier, identifying this opportunity for integrative bargaining would mean transforming a negotiation that could not succeed because the buyer's reservation price was lower than the seller's into a negotiation with the possibility of a mutually beneficial transaction.

Many negotiators assume without investigation that their interests will conflict with their opponent's, and they consequently fail to capitalize on opportunities to exploit the potential of common interests. A buyer who wants the chandelier will often assume that the seller wants the chandelier as well without even considering the possibility that the seller might be better off without it. By investigating these assumptions, negotiators will often realize that common interests exist.

In the real world, however, common interests will not always exist, especially in the types of negotiations involving lawyers. In many negotiations, the parties' interests are adverse: the buyer and seller both want the chandelier, a plaintiff wants a larger settlement while the defendant wants a smaller settlement, both divorcing parents want custody of the children, and so on. In other words, negotiators will often find that their interests are opposed on every issue. Fortunately, *integrative bargaining is usually possible even when the parties have opposing interests.* That is, the bargaining zone can usually be expanded even if the parties want the same things. This important point is extremely counterintuitive, which is why most negotiators routinely fail to identify opportunities for integrative bargaining.

Integrative negotiation requires only that the parties have different preference structures such that they place a differential value on items that are the subject of the negotiation, even if they want all of the same things. Suppose Horace is negotiating with a used car dealer, Slick Sally, over a somewhat dilapidated Studebaker. Sally says she wants a high price for the car, while Horace says he wants to pay a low price. At first glance, this looks like a purely distributive negotiation. Because both parties clearly prefer more money to less, every additional penny that Horace agrees to pay for the car benefits Sally 1 cent and costs him 1 cent. To make matters worse, Horace says he wants the car to come with a warranty, but Sally prefers not to provide a warranty because to do so would cost her money. Both parties want the car, both want every possible dollar, and Horace wants a warranty whereas Sally does not want to provide one.

Although the parties have opposing interests, there is a potential for integrative bargaining in this situation so long as the benefits to Horace of a warranty would exceed the costs to Sally of providing one. Perhaps Horace is very concerned with the uncertainties associated with purchasing a used car and would place a very high value on a warranty that would cover the car if it breaks down. And perhaps Sally can provide a warranty relatively cheaply (i.e., at a cost to her lower than the value of the warranty to Horace) because her dealership maintains a garage that repairs cars. If so, including a warranty with the car will create value by expanding the bargaining zone. Unlike circumstances of common interests where the buyer's reservation price can be increased and the seller's decreased simultaneously, because the parties have opposing interests in the warranty their reservation prices will move in the same direction. But because Horace values the warranty more than it will cost Sally to provide, his reservation price will increase more than Sally's.

Imagine that Horace's reservation price for the Studebaker was $6,000 and Sally's reservation price was $2,000. Any agreement would create $4,000 in cooperative surplus for the parties — at any price between $2,000 and $6,000 both parties would be better off reaching an agreement than pursuing their BATNAs — but how the joint gains are divided would depend on the final price to which the negotiators agreed. See Figure 4-1 (next page). Now assume that Horace values a warranty at $1,000, but it will only cost Sally $500 to provide the warranty (this is the expected cost of servicing the car, taking into account the probability that it will break down and the probability that it will not). By including the warranty in the deal, Horace's reservation price would now be $7,000, and Sally's would be $2,500. Any deal between those two points would create a total of $4,500 in cooperative surplus,

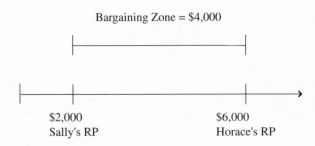

Figure 4-1
**Original Bargaining Zone**

$500 more than would have existed before the parties realized that Horace and Sally had differential values for a warranty and incorporated this observation into their negotiation. See Figure 4-2 below.

The value of integrative bargaining can be further illuminated by changing a few of the assumptions in the example. Suppose that Horace's reservation price for the Studebaker was $4,000 (perhaps he could purchase a used Edsel for $3,000, but he likes Studebakers more than Edsels enough to pay an additional $1,000), and that Sally's reservation price was $4,200 (perhaps she predicts someone will buy the car for $5,000 within the next six months, but the time value of money makes it worth $800 to her to have the cash immediately). In this case, there will be no deal between the two, and both are prepared to walk away from negotiations and pursue their BATNAs. By adding the warranty to the Studebaker, Horace's reservation price will increase by $1,000 to $5,000. Sally's will increase also, but only by $500 to $4,700, making a mutually advantageous agreement possible where one was impossible before.

The example involving Horace and Sally illustrates the critical insights about the potential of integrative bargaining: different relative

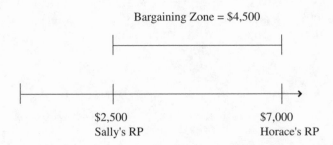

Figure 4-2
**Bargaining Zone after Value Creation**

preferences often form the basis for expanding the bargaining zone and thus creating value. Here, even though Horace and Sally had opposing interests, the difference in the relative value they placed on a warranty allowed them to expand the bargaining zone.

In the following excerpt, David Lax and James Sebenius examine in detail the range of differences between parties that can serve as the cornerstone of integrative bargaining. Gerald Wetlaufer then offers two important caveats to the notion that differences can form the basis of integrative bargains.                                                                 ■

## ■ David A. Lax & James K. Sebenius, The Manager as Negotiator*

90-102 (1986)

. . . There would be little point to this chapter if all negotiating possibilities were fully known in advance. But this would be to assume away a crucial part of the problem. . . . The parties must explore — imperfectly — the arrangements they may jointly be able to create. In practice many gains go unrealized. Inferior agreements are made. Impasse results and conflict escalates when cooperative action might have been far better for all. . . .

### CREATING PRIVATE VALUE: THE KEY ROLE OF DIFFERENCES

Gain from negotiation often exists because negotiators *differ* from one another. Since they are not identical — in tastes, forecasts, endowments, capabilities, or in other ways — they each have something to offer that is relatively less valuable to them than to those with whom they are bargaining. . . .

That differences lie at the heart of many joint gains follows readily from the fact that two utterly identical individuals may have no basis for any negotiation: neither has or wants anything that the other does not. If differences are admitted among many dimensions, however, negotiation opens up the prospect of joint gains. For example, gains may arise from differences in interests, in possessions, in forecasts, in aversion to risk, in attitudes toward the passage of time, in capabilities, in access to technology, and in other areas.

Since joint gains often derive from such differences, a primary orientation of managers, negotiators, and mediators should be toward

*Reprinted and abridged with the permission of The Free Press, a division of Simon & Schuster, Inc., from The Manager as Negotiator: Bargaining for Cooperation and Competitive Gain by David A. Lax and James K. Sebenius. Copyright © 1986 by David A. Lax and James K. Sebenius.

discovering and dovetailing them. In line with this observation, this section will argue on behalf of two broad prescriptions:

1. When contemplating the potential gains from agreement, begin with a careful inventory of all the ways that the parties differ from one another — not how they are alike.
2. The basic principle underlying the realization of joint gains from differences is to match what one side finds or expects to be relatively costless with what the other finds or expects to be most valuable, and vice versa.

. . . The remainder of this section seeks to give form, precision, and prominence to the means of using common differences to create value.

DIFFERENCES OF INTEREST IMPLY EXCHANGES

If a vegetarian with some meat bargains with a carnivore who owns some vegetables, it is precisely the *difference* in their known preferences that can facilitate reaching an agreement. No one would counsel the vegetarian to persuade the carnivore of the zucchini's succulent taste. More complicated negotiations may concern several items. Although the parties may have opposing preferences on the settlement of each issue, they may feel most strongly about different issues. An overall agreement can reflect these different preferences by resolving the issues of relatively greater importance to one side more in favor of that side. A package or "horse trade" can be constructed this way so that, as a whole, all prefer it to no agreement.

. . . This theory applies not only to trading discrete things but also to constructing agreements that respond to different underlying interests. One party may primarily fear the precedential effects of a settlement; another may care about the particulars of the current question; thus, both might profit by contriving a unique-looking agreement on the immediate issue. One side may be keen on a political "victory"; the other may want quiet accommodation for a particular constituency. Whether the differences are between vegetables and meat, form and substance, ideology and practice, reputation and results, or the intrinsic versus the instrumental qualities of a settlement, cleverly crafted agreements can often dovetail differences into joint gains. . . .

### Unbundling Differences of Interest

It is an obvious enough prescription to "seek and dovetail asymmetries of interest." But frequently what appear to be zero-sum or purely distributive negotiations may conceal underlying differences that can be unbundled for joint gain.

Consider the homey story of two sisters arguing over the division of one orange, each claiming an absolute need for three-quarters of it. If however, their discussion reveals that one is hungry and the other wants the peel for a recipe, the negotiation could shift from where to cut the fruit to how to separate its different components.

In a more significant example, recall the midwestern utility that wanted to build a dam. The company had become embroiled in a dispute with farmers about downstream water flow and with conservationists worried about the effects of water diversion on the downstream habitat of the endangered whooping crane. After years of wrangling, the utility offered to guarantee downstream waterflow and to pay $7.5 million to purchase additional water rights or otherwise to protect the whooping crane habitat. Although both the utility and the conservationists saw the offer on the issue of financial compensation as generous, the utility was surprised that the conservationists rejected it.

After much more discussion, the utility came to understand that the conservationists' personal control over the money might make it appear as if they were being paid off and reduce their credibility with conservationist groups. An acceptable settlement had to unbundle the issue of financial compensation in a way that separated compensation and control. So, the parties created a $7.5 million trust fund to protect the whooping crane with a strict covenant that limited its trustees' control over the fund. To reach agreement, the parties needed to learn a great deal about the others' real interests. They had to identify differentially valued interests that were unnecessarily bundled. Then, they needed to invent ways to modify the issues and unbundle the interests to permit joint gains.

In short, where different interests are bundled into a negotiating issue, a good strategy can be to unbundle and seek creative ways to dovetail them. Many other differences beyond those of interest, however, also provide opportunities for joint gains. The next sections consider differences in probability assessments, time preference, and capability as means to create value.

### PROBABILITY DIFFERENCES SUGGEST CONTINGENT AGREEMENTS

At the heart of the sale of an investment property may be the buyer's belief that its price will rise and the seller's conviction that it will drop. The deal is facilitated by differences in belief about what will happen. . . . Probability assessments of uncertain events derive from the combination of prior beliefs and observed evidence; discrepancies in either of these factors may form the basis for contingent agreements.

### Issues Subject to Different Odds

In the first case, outcomes of the event under discussion may be uncertain and subject to different probability estimates. . . . For example, an engineering firm had completed plans for a plant designed to burn garbage, to produce steam, and to convert it into electricity. The firm was negotiating with a medium-sized southern city over the sale of this electricity to the city. The city wanted to pay a lower price; the company insisted on a much higher one. As the discussions proceeded and then stalled, it became clear that the city representatives expected an oil glut and hence a drop in the price of the fuel most important to its electrical generation. The company believed that an oil price rise was much more likely. After protracted talks, the two sides could not agree on a set price for the sale of the plant's electricity to the city. Finally, however, they agreed to tie that price to the future cost of oil. Thus, the city expected to pay a lower price while the company expected to receive a higher price. When they also negotiated an upper and lower cap on the range of acceptable fluctuations, both sides could live with either outcome, and the plant went forward. . . .

### Different Assessments of the Attractiveness of Proposed Procedures

Contingent agreements may be employed in a second common class of situations where the parties believe that they can positively affect the chances for favorable outcome of the uncertain event. Consider the voluntary submission of a dispute to arbitration. Firmly believing the persuasiveness of its position and highly confident in the quality of its representation before the tribunal, each side may feel that its chances of obtaining the desired outcome are very good. Their beliefs may, in fact, be incompatibly optimistic. For this reason, the two parties may have been unable to negotiate their way to one or another specific proposed outcomes. With both sides nonetheless perceiving the value of a settlement, the parties might agree to arbitration, which is in effect, a contingent settlement. From each disputant's standpoint, the uncertain event is the arbitrator's decision. Other third party procedures may also be thought of as contingent agreements where the underlying probabilities differ. . . .

### DIFFERENCES IN RISK AVERSION LEAD TO RISK-SHARING SCHEMES

Suppose that two people agree on the probabilities of an uncertain prospect. Even so, they may still react differently to taking the risks involved. In such cases, they may devise a variety of ways to share the risk. In general, such mechanisms should shift more of the risk to the party who is less risk-averse than the other. For example, suppose that Mr. Broussard, a single, fairly wealthy, middle-aged accountant, and Ms. Armitage, a younger, less-well-off lawyer with significant family responsibilities, are planning to buy and operate a business together. The younger, more risk-averse Ms. Armitage may prefer to take a larger but fixed salary while Mr. Broussard may prefer a smaller set salary but much larger share of any profits. Though they may expect the same total amount of money to be paid in compensation, both parties are better off than had they, say, both chosen either fixed salaries or large contingent payments. . . .

Consider an example. Different tax or contract terms — fixed fees, royalties, and profit shares — shift risk very differently. Suppose that the investment costs, operating costs, and revenues of an advanced plastics-forming plant are uncertain. Further, say that the investor undertaking it and the owner of the major patent critical to the process share the same beliefs about how these uncertainties are likely to turn out. If the investor agrees to pay the patent holder a large fixed fee, the investor bears the risk that returns will end up lower than expected while enjoying the prospect that higher profits may result. If the patent holder received a share of revenues (a royalty), his returns would be low when revenues were low and high when they were high, but the investor would fully bear the cost risks. If the two men agreed to share profits, all cost and revenue risks would be shared.

If the economic scenario that both parties expect in fact occurs, all three different combinations of fees, royalties, and profit shares could have been set to yield the same payment to the patent holder. Yet, since the actual outcome is uncertain and each type of contract has a different "upside potential" and "downside risk," a more risk-averse patent holder would prefer to receive a fee while a greater risk taker would prefer the profit-share. . . .

### DIFFERENCES IN TIME PREFERENCES SUGGEST ALTERED PAYMENT PATTERNS

People may value the same event quite differently, depending on when it occurs. If one side is relatively less impatient than the other, mechanisms for optimally sharing the consequences over time may be devised.

A particularly simple form of time preference difference may be reflected in discount rates. Consider a highly stylized example. Suppose that Ms. Kanwate has a 10 percent discount rate, that Mr. Hurree's rate is 20 percent, and that each party cares about the present value of income. Ms. Kanwate will receive $100 next year; Mr. Hurree is slated to receive $100 the year afterward. Thus the present value of her income is about $91 and his is $69. The two could engineer a variety of profitable trades to dovetail this difference. Because Mr. Hurree values early income relatively more than does Ms. Kanwate, though, he should get the first year's $100. If, in the second year, Ms. Kanwate gets $100 plus $20 from him, the present value of her income rises from $91 in the original division to $99. The present value of Mr. Hurree's income stream ( + $100 in a year, − $20 in two years) remains at about $69. If he gave $10 to Ms. Kanwate in the second period, she could have the same present value as in the original division ($91), while the present value of his income would be $76 instead of the original $69. Any outcome in which he gets the first $100 and she gets between $110 and $120 in the second period is as good as or better than the original division for both parties.

Whenever time preference differences exist, the principle that future consequences can be beneficially rearranged in a way that gives earlier amounts to the more impatient party may be useful to negotiators and mediators. As with risk aversion, such characteristics occur in a variety of circumstances. Apart from ad hoc, individual differences, time attitudes may vary in cross-cultural dealings. Where the parties are of quite different ages or their opportunities to use money, say, are not the same, joint gains may be possible. People at different organizational levels or at different career stages can hold quite different time horizons for valuing the results of a negotiation. Time preference differences may be particularly important in some public/private negotiations over projects with future ramifications; governments or public entities may weight benefits or costs to future generations more heavily than do their private counterparts. This state of affairs offers room for mutually advantageous sharing over time that enhances the possibilities of agreement.

### COMPLEMENTARY CAPABILITIES CAN BE COMBINED

. . . Differences in capabilities can take many forms. Individuals may have differing access to technology, to the rights to use it, or to the physical, financial, or human capital needed to implement it. They may face differing costs of investment — for example, large organizations often have lower transactions costs in financial markets, may face lower costs of borrowing, or may have access to investment opportunities that yield higher rates of return. At any given moment, some individuals and organizations will have their assets in a more liquid form than others and will therefore be in a better position to take advantage of transient opportunities. One party may have access to better diversification possibilities. From the perspective of individual parties, differences in corporate and personal income tax status can generate opportunities for arrangements that produce higher after-tax income. Differences in legal, accounting, engineering, and sale talents can combine at the group, department, or organizational level to form the basis of productive agreements. Any such capability differences can form the basis for mutually profitable arrangements.                    ■

## ■ Gerald B. Wetlaufer, The Limits of Integrative Bargaining*

85 Geo. L.J. 369, 1370, 1374-1187 (1996)

. . . It is now conventional wisdom that opportunities for integrative bargaining are widely available, that they are often unrecognized and unexploited, and that as a result both the parties to negotiations and society as a whole are worse off than would otherwise have been the case. . . .

[But a] good deal of confusion arises from the assertion that opportunities for "integrative" or "win-win" bargaining are distinguishable from opportunities for "distributive" or "win-lose" bargaining in that the former can "create value" and "expand the pie" while the latter cannot. Characterizing the distinction in this way causes confusion because, in fact, all opportunities for bargaining, including opportunities that are solely win-lose or zero-sum games, present opportunities to "create value" and to "expand the pie."

For purposes of clarification, I will distinguish three forms of value creation. . . . The first of these forms is found where the pie can be made larger only in the sense that is true of all bargaining including all bargaining that is merely distributive. In such circumstances, there is a zone of agreement (i.e., a range of possible agreement) within which both parties will be better off than they would have been in the absence of the agreement. Thus, in this minimal sense, purely distributive bargaining can be said to "create value" or "expand the pie." . . . Though it involves the "creation" of value [this type of transaction], does not involve integrative bargaining and is not a situation in which the more open tactics associated with integrative bargaining will promote the immediate pecuniary self-interest of a party.

The same can also be said of opportunities for "Form II" value creation. Form II value creation is possible when there is one issue (e.g., the amount of money to be paid for some product), and one party cares more about that issue than does the other. This is a situation in which, assuming there is a range of possible agreements that would leave both parties better off, there is an opportunity for Form I value creation in that the aggregate benefits to the parties will vary depending on whether or not they can reach agreement. Also, and this is what distinguishes Form II value creation, this is a situation in which the aggregate benefits to the parties, the size of the pie, will vary across the range of possible agreements. Thus, the total value created by the agreement will be relatively large if most of that over which the parties are negotiating (e.g., surplus as measured in dollars) is captured by the party who cares more about that issue. Similarly, the total value created by the agreement will be relatively small if most of the surplus is captured by the party who cares less about that issue. . . .

Only what I shall call "Form III" value creation offers an opportunity for integrative or win-win bargaining. Unlike Forms I and II, Form III value creation involves that kind of pie-expansion or value creation in which the parties can reach a range of different agreements, in which the size of the pie will vary across the range of possible agreements (also true of Form II), but in which some of those agreements leave both parties better off than do others. If there are some possible agreements that both parties would regard as better than others, then the size of the pie created by the agreement depends both upon the parties' ability to reach some agreement (Form I value creation) and upon their wit and ability to arrive at one of the better agreements. It is in this sense that a situation presenting an opportunity for Form III value creation is a non-zero-sum game and an opportunity for integrative or win-win bargaining. . . .

## A. Differing Interests, Including Multiple Issues Differently Valued

We might begin with the situation in which the parties have differing interests and with the question whether, under all or some such circumstances, those differences in interests create opportunities for integrative bargaining. While I shall argue that opportunities for integrative bargaining do not exist in all such circumstances, they do appear to exist in some. Imagine, for instance, that a corporate plaintiff sues an airline, that the parties have been exploring the possibility of settlement, and that they have reached a tentative agreement on $80,000. Next assume that the defendant, just back from a seminar on win-win negotiation, proposes an in-kind settlement in which the defendant would provide the plaintiff with $120,000 worth of air travel. Because of the airline's high fixed costs and the frequency with which it carries empty seats, the cost to the airline will be only $30,000. Both parties find the in-kind settlement to be highly preferable to the cash agreement they had tentatively reached. In this sense, the parties have found themselves in a situation where there is a range of possible agreements and some of those agreements are better than others for both parties. Thus there is an opportunity for Form III value creation and for integrative bargaining. . . .

[Consider a situation where multiple issues that are valued differently by the parties creates] an opportunity for integrative bargaining. . . . [A]ssume, stereotypically, that one party is a work-at-home mom who cares more about custody and the other is a workaholic husband who barely knows his children but cares desperately about the things that money can buy. Then consider three possible agreements. In the first, the money is split down the middle and custody is shared on a true 50-50 basis. In the second, the wife gets full and exclusive custody of the children and the husband gets all of the money. And in the third, the wife gets all the money (which she doesn't want) and the husband gets custody of the children (whom he doesn't know). There is a Form III relationship among these three possible agreements. Under the first agreement, the parties reach a split-the-difference compromise on each of the two issues. Both parties will be better off than they would have been in the absence of an agreement, and thus we have Form I value creation. But as one moves from the first agreement (compromise on both issues) to the second agreement (wife gets the children, husband gets the money), both parties will regard themselves as better off than they would have been under the first agreement. And as one moves from the first agreement to the third agreement (wife gets the money, husband gets the children), both parties will see themselves as worse off than they had been under the first agreement. Accordingly, this is an opportunity for Form III value creation in that the size of the pie varies across a range of possible agreements and in which, for both parties, some of those agreements may be better than others. . . .

### B.  Differing Assessments as to Future Events: Differing Probabilistic Assessments of the Likelihood of Some Future Event or the Likely Future Value of Some Variable

[Others] assert that differences in probabilistic assessments create opportunities for integrative bargaining.[24] It would be more accurate, however, to say that these circumstances will sometimes present opportunities for a particular kind of integrative bargaining if, but only if, the parties are both willing to bet on their differing assessments. The differences being exploited here are differences in the parties' predictions concerning future events. More specifically, they are either differing probabilistic assessments of the likelihood of some future event or differing assessments of the likely future value of some variable.

---

24. David A. Lax & James E. Sebenius, The Manager as Negotiator 94-98 (1986).

Negotiators may exploit these opportunities for integrative bargaining only through a contingent agreement. Differing probabilistic assessments of the likelihood of some future event create opportunities for contingent agreements in the form "if X, then A; if not X, then B." Differing assessments of the likely future value of some variable afford opportunities for contingent agreements in which some aspect of the agreement, probably price, is tied to the now-indeterminate future variable. These agreements take the form "we agree that A will be determined in accordance with some future value of X." This opportunity for integrative bargaining may be illustrated through three examples. First, the parties may have different assessments of the likelihood that some thing — in our example it will be a used car — will work. Second, they may have different assessments of the likely future price of a commodity. And third, they may have different assessments of the number of seats that will be sold for a recital. Notice that although all of these differing assessments involve matters directly relevant to the agreement the parties are seeking to make (the car, the commodity, and the recital), a contingent agreement could be reached that turned on different assessments unrelated to the transaction. Thus, an agreement concerning the sale of land could carry a price that was contingent on whether the Chicago Cubs win next year's World Series.

. . . A common example of an opportunity for integrative bargaining involves a situation in which the parties have, and then exploit, different assessments of the likelihood that some tangible device (e.g., a used car or a new technology) will work. Assume that Mr. Used Car Seller is trying to sell the car he has been driving for several years and that his reservation price is $2200. He is willing to sell the car for $2200 or more, but not for less than that amount. To state the matter more fully, he is willing to sell the car if and only if he receives in exchange either $2200 or more or something that he currently believes is worth such an amount. At the same time, Ms. Used Car Buyer has looked at Mr. Seller's car and concluded that, although it would suit her purposes, she can pay up to, but no more than, $2000. Because she can only pay $2000 and he must receive at least $2200, there is no simple dollar amount that is acceptable to both parties. There is no zone of agreement and, as things now stand, no possibility of agreement.

It turns out, however, that there is a difference between the parties' expectations concerning the likelihood that the car will require major repairs. Mr. Seller believes the car is in great shape mechanically and he is perfectly certain it will not require major repairs over the next two years. Ms. Buyer, for her part, has some reservations. Specifically, on the basis of a detailed mechanical inspection, she believes there is a 60% probability the car will need no major repairs but a 40% probability the cost of such repairs will be $1000. Indeed, the $2000 that Ms. Buyer is prepared to pay for the car already reflects the 40% probability that she will be paying $1000 in major repairs. If that probability could be eliminated, she would be willing to pay $2400 for the car.

This additional information presents the possibility of a contingent agreement in which Ms. Buyer pays $2300 for the car and Mr. Seller guarantees her against any major repair costs during the first two years. To Mr. Seller, the value of this transaction is $2300 because he receives the purchase price ($2300) and, in his mind, there is a zero percent probability that he will have to pay anything on his guarantee. Thus, taking everything into account, he still values this agreement at $2300, which is $100 better than (higher than) his $2200 reservation price. To Ms. Buyer, the expected total cost of this transaction is $2300. That is $100 better than (lower than) what would have been her $2400 reservation price if she were not required to bear what she believes to be the significant risk that the car will require major repairs. Absent a contingent agreement, there was no possibility of agreement at all. But once the parties identified and exploited the opportunity for a contingent agreement, a mutually advantageous transaction became possible. The possibility of a contingent agreement allows the parties to transform their situation from one presenting no zone of agreement to one presenting a sizable zone of agreement, thereby expanding the size of the pie. . . .

Certain differences of this kind do not, at least as a practical matter, give rise to opportunities for integrative bargaining. For instance, if I am selling a car and the buyer believes the car will run fine, but I (the seller who ought to know) believe it will need major repairs, then the parties differ in their probabilistic assessment of the likelihood of some future event, yet no opportunity for integrative bargaining exists. In the normal course, the buyer will bear the risk of repair. If in this case we were to shift that risk to the seller through a guarantee, it would make the pie smaller, not larger. And if the buyer were to learn of the seller's differing assessment of the likelihood that major repairs would be required, she (the buyer) likely would revise her assessment and, accordingly, lower her reservation price. This difference does not create an opportunity to expand the pie, but rather only an opportunity to reduce its size. And if it is discovered, it will not enhance, but instead diminish, the possibility of agreement. . . .

## C.  DIFFERENT PREFERENCES REGARDING RISK

Differences in risk aversion may also create opportunities for integrative bargaining. I begin, however, by drawing a distinction between two parties' potentially dissimilar assessments of particular risks and two parties' potentially dissimilar aversions to risk. The previous Section deals with the former, and we are here concerned with the latter.

If the parties to a negotiation have different aversions to risk, and if the negotiation involves something that carries a risk, then there may (but also may not) be an opportunity for integrative bargaining in the sense that an agreement, reached without regard to the allocation of risk, may be modified so as to leave both parties better off. Such an opportunity will exist when, and only when, the preliminary agreement leaves the risk in the wrong hands. Under those circumstances, the party who is not left bearing the risk can be given the risk, the party who will thus get rid of the risk will be better off in more than the amount by which the party acquiring the risk will be worse off, and the party getting rid of the risk will be in a position to compensate the party acquiring the risk in an amount that will leave both parties better off than they were before the compensated shifting of the risk.

One can think of this as a special case of multiple issues differently valued. The object of the negotiation appears to be unitary but, on closer examination, it can be unbundled into, on the one hand, the concrete object of the negotiation (e.g., the car) and, on the other, a risk that someone must bear (e.g., the potential costs of repair). This may present an opportunity for what amounts to an insurance transaction. As usual, the solution is to arrange matters so that the concrete object of the negotiation goes to the party who values it more and the risk goes to the party who assigns to that risk the lower negative value. He who avoids the risk is then in a position to compensate she who accepts the risk, and to do so in a way that leaves both better off than they would have been in the absence of its transfer.

There is then the question of whether all such differences constitute opportunities for integrative bargaining. They do not. Thus, if in the normal course of the negotiation the risk ends up with the party who assigns to it the lower negative value, the risk is already where it ought to be and transferring it to the other party would not increase the aggregate value arising from the transaction but would, instead, decrease it. Such a transfer would not cause the pie to expand, but rather to contract.                                                                               ■

## Notes

*1. An "Integrative Agreement" Is Relative.*   An agreement can only be "integrative" relative to something else. That is, an agreement is integrative if it creates a larger cooperative surplus than the parties would enjoy in some other state of the world. As Wetlaufer points out, any time there is a bargaining zone a subsequent agreement creates value in the trivial sense that the parties are better off than if they had pursued their BATNAs. When students of negotiation use the term "integrative" to describe an agreement, however, they usually mean that the bargain created joint value relative to a different but still mutually advantageous possible agreement, or that a bargain created enough value to establish a bargaining zone when one otherwise would not have existed. Or, in other words, integrative agreements are those that *expand* a bargaining zone, not those that merely *identify* that a bargaining zone exists between two parties for an obvious transaction.

**2. Economies of Scale.** Although the role of differences in creating opportunities for integrative bargaining can hardly be overstated, it is important to note that another avenue for creating value in negotiation is through capitalizing on economies of scale. Suppose that Mutt and Jeff, who each manufacture guns and butter for themselves, are negotiating a trade agreement. If Mutt could build guns more cheaply than Jeff, and Jeff can make butter more cheaply than Mutt, there is an obvious opportunity for a profitable trade of Mutt's guns for Jeff's butter. The same would be true if Mutt enjoyed making guns, while Jeff's passion was churning butter.

But what if Mutt and Jeff can produce both guns and butter at exactly the same cost and with exactly the same amount of enjoyment? Is there no way for the two to create value through integrative bargaining? It is likely that the production of both guns and butter will be subject to economies of scale, meaning that the per-unit cost of production decreases as production increases. Suppose that it costs $10 to produce one gun or one stick of butter, but only $5 for a producer to produce a second gun or stick of butter. If this is the case, Mutt and Jeff might be able to create a large cooperative surplus if one produces only guns and the other only butter, even though it does not matter which person produces which good. Both parties have a BATNA of producing their own gun and butter at a cost of $20. Since each can produce two guns or two sticks of butter for $15, each should be willing to pay up to $5 for a contract that permits him to produce both guns or both sticks of butter and then trade their excess item for one of the other. Economies of scale thus create $10 of surplus for the parties jointly.

**3. Integrative versus Distributive Bargaining.** Integrative bargaining creates value for the parties jointly, establishing a bargaining zone where none would have otherwise existed or expanding a bargaining zone that would have existed anyway. The value created by integrative bargaining is sometimes divided equally among the parties, but often one negotiator or the other captures most or all of it. How the negotiators divide the cooperative surplus is a matter of distributive bargaining, which will be discussed in Chapters 5 and 6, not integrative bargaining.

It would be tempting to assume that, in the previous example, if Mutt and Jeff are successful integrative bargainers they will agree that one will produce two guns and the other two sticks of butter, and they will then trade one gun for one stick of butter in an even trade. This could happen, but it need not for the integrative aspect of their negotiation to be successful. The $10 of cooperative surplus might be divided equally, but it might be divided in some other way. That is, Jeff might agree to make a side payment to Mutt of up to $5 to consummate the deal, and Mutt might agree to make a side payment of up to $5 to Jeff to consummate the deal. It is important to realize that how the $10 of surplus will be divided is a question of distribution not of value creation. The full integrative potential of the situation is reached if Mutt and Jeff agree to each produce two units of one item and then trade, regardless of whether Mutt makes a side payment to Jeff, Jeff makes a side payment to Mutt, or neither makes a side payment.

Similarly, consider the example in which Sally sells a used Studebaker with a warranty to Horace. As the example was originally described, Horace's reservation price for the Studebaker alone was $6,000, and Sally's reservation price was $2,000. For simplicity, assume that had they made a deal at that point without considering a warranty, they would have agreed on a price of $3,000. The bargaining zone can be expanded if the parties include a warranty in the deal, because Horace values a warranty at $1,000 but it will only cost Sally $500 to provide the warranty, and therefore Horace's reservation price increases to $7,000 and Sally's increases only to $2,500. How that additional $500 in cooperative surplus is allocated, however, is a question of distribution bargaining. Perhaps Horace will end up paying $4,000 for the car and warranty, in which case Sally would capture all the cooperative surplus created from identifying the integrative potential of the warranty. Perhaps Horace will end up paying $3,500, in which case he would capture the entire added surplus created by the warranty. Perhaps Horace will pay $3,750. In any event, these are distributive questions logically separate from the question at the heart of integrative bargaining: how can negotiators structure a transaction so as to create the largest possible cooperative surplus to be gained by reaching an agreement?

*4. Depicting Integrative Bargaining Graphically.*   This chapter has described integrative bargaining as a process by which the parties expand a one dimensional bargaining zone, by increasing the distance between the two parties' reservation prices. Integrative bargaining can also be depicted visually as moving in a northeasterly direction on a two dimensional graph, where the value enjoyed by one negotiator is represented by the X axis and the value enjoyed by the other negotiator is represented by the Y axis. You should think about the impact of integrative bargaining in whichever way is more intuitively appealing to you — both types of graphs depict the same result.

Suppose Fred and Barney are negotiating how to divide a Brontosaurus burger. If Fred received the whole burger, the result in value, or "utility" can be represented by point "a": Fred enjoys a great deal of value, while Barney enjoys no value. If Barney received the whole burger, the result is represented by point "b": Barney enjoys a great deal of value, and Fred enjoys none. Fred and Barney might decide to cut the burger in half, in which case each will receive one-half of the value they would receive from receiving the entire burger, a result graphically depicted by point "c." An integrative solution is one in which the parties *jointly* enjoy more than 100% of the value that one would enjoy from receiving the entire burger. Perhaps Barney prefers the more well-done portion of the burger around the edges, while Fred prefers the more rare portion of the burger near the center. By giving the middle of the burger to Fred and the edges to Barney, the parties find themselves at point "d." Neither one receives as much value as he would have had he received the entire burger, but their joint value exceeds the joint value they would have enjoyed at points a, b, or c.

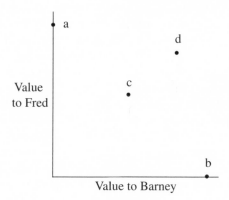

## B.   STRATEGIES FOR REACHING INTEGRATIVE AGREEMENTS

As section A demonstrated, integrative agreements are possible when the negotiating parties have different interests or different priorities of interests, even when their stated interests initially appear to be in direct contrast. Because no two negotiators are exactly the same, differences are present and some opportunity thus exists to expand the bargaining zone in the vast majority of negotiating situations. Identifying the integrative potential of a negotiation, however, is difficult work. It requires both creative thinking about how to solve problems and superb communication skills. This section describes a variety of techniques that can improve the negotiator's ability to expand the bargaining zone and thus to create value through the negotiation process, rather than just dividing an obvious cooperative surplus.

## 1. Adding to and Subtracting Issues from the Negotiation "Package"

Many negotiators enter a bargaining situation believing the subject of the negotiation is fixed. When Horace discusses with Sally the possibility of buying a Studebaker, both parties are likely to identify the subject of the negotiation as "Studebaker," with the only issue being how much money Horace will pay for it. When a plaintiff and defendant sit down to discuss settlement, both might define the subject of the negotiation as a release from liability issued by the plaintiff, with the only issue being how much the defendant will pay for this item. Negotiators with such a narrow view will miss out on opportunities to identify integrative solutions, because they fail to consider that the subject of the negotiation — or the "package" of items that will be transferred from seller to buyer if the negotiation succeeds — can be altered to the parties' mutual advantage.

Negotiators expand the bargaining zone by adding or subtracting issues from what they initially perceive to be the negotiation package. In the case of Horace and Sally, the bargaining zone was expanded when the negotiators added the issue of a warranty to what began as a negotiation over the issue of a Studebaker. Horace and Sally had opposing interests. Horace wanted to pay less money for the car, Sally wanted Horace to pay more money. Horace wanted a warranty, Sally preferred not to provide a warranty. But, importantly, Horace placed a relatively higher value on the warranty than did Sally, so adding the issue of the warranty to the negotiation package expanded the bargaining zone (and thus the cooperative surplus that could be created by the two ultimately striking a bargain) by increasing Horace's reservation price more than Sally's. If Sally and Horace had limited their view of what was included in the negotiation package to the Studebaker, they may have been able to divide the cooperative surplus that existed because Horace valued the car more than Sally did, but they would have missed out on the opportunity to expand the bargaining zone and increase the cooperative surplus created by their agreement.

Three additional points bear mentioning. First, as Wetlaufer's examples of integrative bargaining in Section A of this chapter illustrate, adding an issue will only expand the bargaining zone when that issue is valued more by the buyer than by the seller. If Horace valued the warranty at only $100, and it would cost Sally $300 to provide the warranty, adding the issue of the warranty to the negotiation package would have had the opposite effect of reducing the bargaining zone.

Second, adding issues is an effective strategy when the parties have common interests, just as it is when the parties have opposing interests but differences in their preference structure. Recall the example of the home buyer who wanted the lovely chandelier and the seller who wanted to leave the chandelier with the house so as not to have to transport it. Assuming that the usual house transaction does not include chandeliers, by adding the chandelier to the negotiation package the parties could increase the bargaining zone by raising the buyer's reservation price and lowering the seller's.

Third, it is often the case that even more value can be created when the negotiators add more than one issue to a negotiation. Perhaps in addition to valuing a warranty more than it would cost Sally to provide one, Horace would find it extremely convenient to have the car delivered to his residence in the next town, and doing so would be only marginally inconvenient to Sally. By adding both issues to the negotiation, Horace's reservation price would increase by a much larger amount than it would if only one of the issues were added, while Sally's reservation price would increase by less than Horace's, making the bargaining zone larger than it otherwise would be. By merely taking time to consider what issues could be added to the negotiation package that the buyer would value more than the seller, negotiators can substantially improve their ability to find integrative solutions to bargaining problems.

It is reasonably intuitive for negotiators to think about adding issues of differential value to the parties as a way of creating value. It is less intuitive, but equally useful, for negotiators to think about how they can create value by subtracting issues. In general, subtracting issues creates value for the negotiators when a component of the package being negotiated is more valuable to the party that currently possesses it than to the other party. For example, perhaps Sally had advertised the Studebaker for sale with a car cover to protect it from the elements. If Horace has a garage for the car and Sally has other customers who would purchase the cover from her, it is possible that the cover is worth more to Sally than to Horace. In this case, the parties can create value by subtracting the cover from the bargain. With the cover subtracted, Horace's reservation price will decrease less than Sally's, thus increasing the size of the bargaining zone.

Successful integrative negotiators can envision how apparently indivisible items can in fact be divided and unbundled so that value can be created by subtracting issues. To slightly alter the famous story recounted by Lax & Sebenius, suppose that Sister A is negotiating to purchase an orange from Sister B. Both place approximately the same value on the orange, so it is uncertain whether any bargain will be possible. Because the only issue under consideration is a single orange, it initially appears that there is nothing to subtract from the negotiation package without leaving the package completely empty. On further investigation, however, this analysis proves to be false. Suppose that Sister A wants the orange only to eat the fruit. Sister B is somewhat less enamored with the fruit, but she also wishes to use the peel to bake a cake. If the sisters redefine the subject of their bargain from "the orange" to "the fruit from the orange," Sister B's reservation price will fall while Sister A's remains approximately the same, insuring that a bargaining zone exists. In other words, value is created by dividing the issue of "orange" into two issues, "fruit" and "peel," and then subtracting the issue of "peel," which the seller values more than does the buyer, from the negotiation package.

To use another example, if Bonnie sues Clyde, a settlement need not necessarily be viewed as a single, indivisible item. Bonnie might have two or more causes of action. If she believes she is likely to prevail on the first, but not on the second, while Clyde thinks she might prevail on the second, but not on the first, their different predictions might form the basis of a negotiated agreement of the second cause of action. Essentially, value can be created by unbundling the claims and subtracting the first from the negotiation package.

## 2.  Logrolling

"Logrolling" is a term often used to describe the practice of two or more legislators trading votes on bills that are of little importance to them in return for votes on bills that are very important to them. For example, a legislator from a rural district might agree to vote for a public transportation bill in return for a legislator from an urban district agreeing to vote for a farm subsidy bill. Logrolling creates value, because both legislators are much better off if both bills pass than if neither passes. The rural legislator strongly favors the farm bill and only moderately opposes the transportation bill, while the urban legislator strongly favors the transportation bill and only moderately opposes the farm bill. The concept is useful in thinking about how to create value in all types of bargaining situations, not just in negotiations between politicians.

Conceptually, logrolling is just a slightly different perspective on the strategy of adding and subtracting issues. Many examples of successful integrative bargaining can be viewed through either conceptual framework. The negotiation between Sally and Horace can be understood as adding an issue (the warranty) that the buyer valued more than the seller, thus expanding the bargaining zone. Alternatively, it could be understood as an example of logrolling, in which Sally traded the item of relatively more value to Horace (warranty) for something of relatively more value to Sally (a higher price for the car).

In practice, it is probably useful to think in terms of adding and subtracting issues when the negotiation package is open ended and malleable, and to think in terms of logrolling when the negotiation package contains multiple items that appear fairly well fixed. For example, if you are negotiating to buy a car, it is more useful to enter the negotiations thinking about how you might add issues of more value to the buyer and subtract issues of more value to the seller. If you are negotiating a property settlement between divorcing spouses who own a well-identified collection of assets, it might be more useful to think in terms of logrolling. For example, the wife gives the husband the motorcycle, which he loves to race, and the husband gives the wife the boat, because she loves to water ski. This trade would likely create more value than if the husband and wife randomly divided their possessions or used some other method of splitting them that did not take into account their different preferences.

Even when logrolling is a useful conceptual framework, however, it is important to remember that the set of relevant issues is rarely fixed and to consider carefully whether an even more integrative agreement could be designed by adding issues to or subtracting issues from the negotiation package. For example, we can conceptualize the divorce as the wife "buying" a divorce agreement from the husband (or vice versa) in return for relinquishing her claim to some jointly held assets. If the husband is handy and can maintain the boat with little trouble, and this would provide more value to the wife than would keeping the motorcycle, value can be created by adding the issue of "boat maintenance" to the package of goods the wife is bargaining to buy from the husband and subtracting the issue of "motorcycle."

## 3. Avoiding the Fixed-Sum Error

Negotiators often enter negotiations assuming that the other party's preferences and interests are in complete opposition to their own. If Sister A prefers oranges to apples, and values oranges for their fruit, she is likely to project these preferences onto Sister B, although in reality Sister B might prefer apples to oranges, or might value oranges for the peel rather than the fruit. The tendency to see a complete clash of preferences and priorities when there is actually an opportunity for integrative bargaining has been called the "fixed-sum error." Leigh Thompson & Reid Hastie, Social Perception in Negotiation, 47 Org. Beh. & Human Dec. Processes 98, 101 (1990). Research has demonstrated that negotiators more susceptible to the fixed-sum error achieve poorer results in bargaining exercises than negotiators who accurately perceive or identify during bargaining interactions that the opponent has a different preference structure. See id. at 108-109. To be successful at integrative bargaining, then, it is important for negotiators to enter bargaining situations with precisely the opposite assumption: that the opponent probably has either somewhat different preferences or, at a minimum, the same preferences but in a different order of priority.

## 4.  Focusing on Ultimate Interests Rather Than Superficial Positions

Once you develop the outlook that any negotiating situation is likely to present the opportunity for integrative bargaining, how can you go about identifying the specific means by which the bargaining zone can be expanded? One important tactic is to look past superficial demands advanced at the bargaining table by both parties, and investigate the more general, or core interests that underlie those demands. While the parties' demands will often appear to be in complete conflict, there are often methods of satisfying the core interests of one party at a relatively low cost to another, thus creating value. The following excerpt from the book that popularized the concept of integrative bargaining for a general audience describes the bargaining benefits of focusing on core interests.

### ■ Roger Fisher, William Ury & Bruce Patton, Getting to Yes*

40-51 (2d ed. 1991)

Consider the story of two men quarreling in a library. One wants the window open and the other wants it closed. They bicker back and forth about how much to leave it open: a crack, halfway, three quarters of the way. No solution satisfies them both.

Enter the librarian. She asks one why he wants the window open: "To get some fresh air." She asks the other why he wants it closed: "To avoid the draft." After thinking a minute, she opens wide a window in the next room, bringing in fresh air without a draft.

## FOR A WISE SOLUTION RECONCILE INTERESTS, NOT POSITIONS

This story is typical of many negotiations. Since the parties' problem appears to be a conflict of positions, and since their goal is to agree on a position, they naturally tend to think and talk about positions — and in the process often reach an impasse.

The librarian could not have invented the solution she did if she had focused only on the two men's stated positions of wanting the window open or closed. Instead she looked to their underlying interests of fresh air and no draft. This difference between positions and interests is crucial.

### INTERESTS DEFINE THE PROBLEM

The basic problem in a negotiation lies not in conflicting positions, but in the conflict between each side's needs, desires, concerns, and fears. The parties may say:

> "I am trying to get him to stop that real estate development next door."
> Or
> "We disagree. He wants $100,000 for the house. I won't pay a penny more than $95,000."

But on a more basic level the problem is:

> "He needs the cash; I want peace and quiet."
> Or
> "He needs at least $100,000 to settle with his ex-wife. I told my family that I wouldn't pay more than $95,000 for a house."

Such desires and concerns are *interests*. Interests motivate people; they are the silent movers behind the hubbub of positions. Your position is something you have decided upon. Your interests are what caused you to so decide.

The Egyptian-Israeli peace treaty blocked out at Camp David in 1978 demonstrates the usefulness of looking behind positions. Israel had occupied the Egyptian Sinai Peninsula since the Six-Day War of 1967. When Egypt and Israel sat down together in 1978 to negotiate a peace, their positions were incompatible. Israel insisted on keeping some of the Sinai. Egypt, on the other hand, insisted that every inch of the Sinai be returned to Egyptian sovereignty. Time and again, people drew maps showing possible boundary lines that would divide the Sinai between Egypt and Israel. Compromising in this way was wholly unacceptable to Egypt. To go back to the situation as it was in 1967 was equally unacceptable to Israel.

Looking to their interests instead of their positions made it possible to develop a solution. Israel's interest lay in security; they did not want Egyptian tanks poised on their border ready to roll across at any time. Egypt's interest lay in sovereignty; the Sinai had been part of Egypt since the time of the Pharaohs. After centuries of domination by Greeks, Romans, Turks, French, and British, Egypt had only recently regained full sovereignty and was not about to cede territory to another foreign conqueror.

At Camp David, President Sadat of Egypt and Prime Minister Begin of Israel agreed to a plan that would return the Sinai to complete Egyptian sovereignty and, by demilitarizing large areas, would still assure Israeli security. The Egyptian flag would fly everywhere, but Egyptian tanks would be nowhere near Israel.

Reconciling interests rather than positions works for two reasons. First, for every interest there usually exists several possible positions that could satisfy it. All too often people simply adopt the most obvious position, as Israel did, for example, in announcing that they intended to keep part of the Sinai. When you do look behind opposed positions for the motivating interests, you can often find an alternative position which meets not only your interests but theirs as well. In the Sinai, demilitarization was one such alternative.

Reconciling interests rather than compromising between positions also works because behind opposed positions lie many more interests than conflicting ones.

### BEHIND OPPOSED POSITIONS LIE SHARED AND COMPATIBLE INTERESTS, AS WELL AS CONFLICTING ONES

We tend to assume that because the other side's positions are opposed to ours, their interests must also be opposed. If we have an interest in defending ourselves, then they must want to attack us. If we have an interest in minimizing the rent, then their interest must be to maximize it. In many negotiations, however, a close examination of the underlying interests will reveal the existence of many more interests that are shared or compatible than ones that are opposed.

*For example, look at the interests a tenant shares with a prospective landlord:*

Both want stability. The landlord wants a stable tenant; the tenant
    wants a permanent address.
Both would like to see the apartment well maintained. The tenant

is going to live there; the landlord wants to increase the value of the apartment as well as the reputation of the building.

Both are interested in a good relationship with each other. The landlord wants a tenant who pays the rent regularly; the tenant wants a responsive landlord who will carry out the necessary repairs.

*They may have interests that do not conflict but simply differ. For example:*

The tenant may not want to deal with fresh paint, to which he is allergic. The landlord will not want to pay the costs of repainting all the other apartments.

The landlord would like the security of a down payment of the first month's rent, and he may want it by tomorrow. The tenant, knowing that this is a good apartment, may be indifferent on the question of paying tomorrow or later.

When weighed against these shared and divergent interests, the opposed interests in minimizing the rent and maximizing the return seem more manageable. The shared interests will likely result in a long lease, an agreement to share the cost of improving the apartment, and efforts by both parties to accommodate each other in the interest of a good relationship. The divergent interests may perhaps be reconciled by a down payment tomorrow and an agreement by the landlord to paint the apartment provided the tenant buys the paint. The precise amount of the rent is all that remains to be settled, and the market for rental apartments may define that fairly well. . . .

### THE MOST POWERFUL INTERESTS ARE BASIC HUMAN NEEDS

In searching for the basic interests behind a declared position, look particularly for those bedrock concerns which motivate all people. If you can take care of such basic needs, you increase the chance both of reaching agreement and, if an agreement is reached, of the other side's keeping to it. Basic human needs include:

* security
* economic well-being
* a sense of belonging
* recognition
* control over one's life

As fundamental as they are, basic human needs are easy to overlook. In many negotiations, we tend to think that the only interest involved is money. Yet even in a negotiation over a monetary figure, such as the amount of alimony to be specified in a separation agreement, much more can be involved. What does a wife really want in asking for $500 a week in alimony? Certainly she is interested in her economic well-being, but what else? Possibly she wants the money in order to feel psychologically secure. She may also want it for recognition: to feel that she is treated fairly and as an equal. Perhaps the husband can ill afford to pay $500 a week, and perhaps his wife does not need that much, yet she will likely accept less only if her needs for security and recognition are met in other ways. . . .                                     ■

## 5.  Confronting Adverse Selection and Moral Hazard Problems

Negotiators can increase the value of an agreement, and thus expand the bargaining zone, by focusing on mitigating two common risks of contracting: "adverse selection" and "moral hazard." The problem of adverse selection stems from the fact that sellers usually have more information about the quality of their wares than do potential buyers. Because buyers know that sellers will have a lower reservation price for a low-quality item than a high-quality item, if a seller is willing to part with his goods for $X the buyer will rationally fear that the item is of relatively low quality. This will cause a rational buyer to lower his reservation price for the item. If the goods are high-quality, value can be created by the seller insuring the quality of the goods in some way, often by providing a warranty. This expands the bargaining zone by adding an issue that typically will have great value to the buyer, because it limits the buyer's adverse selection risk, but will usually have only a minimal cost to the seller, because she knows the goods are high quality (assuming that they are!) and the warranty will not likely be invoked.

The problem of moral hazard arises when the seller's actions after an agreement has been reached can affect the value of the subject of the negotiation. For example, suppose Alan, who owns a pizza parlor, wants to hire Betsy to paint pictures of pizzas on his fleet of delivery vans. Alan knows Betsy is an excellent painter when she works slowly and carefully. If he could be sure that she would do her best work, Alan would have a reservation price of $1,000 for the job. The problem is that once Alan has paid Betsy (or even agreed to pay her $1,000 for the job), Betsy might lack the incentive to do her best, most careful work. Because of this moral hazard, Alan might reasonably decide his reservation price is only $600, the value he would place on the work assuming it were to be done sloppily. If the parties were to structure the transaction so that Betsy's compensation were dependent on an evaluation of quality by an independent third party, the moral hazard problem might be eliminated. Such a device will expand the bargaining zone by adding an issue (here, third-party evaluation) that Alan will value highly, thus causing him to raise his reservation price substantially, and will be relatively less costly to Betsy, thus raising her reservation price only slightly.

The ability to structure contracts to minimize the risks of adverse selection and moral hazard is an integrative bargaining skill that scholars have identified as one hallmark of superior transactional lawyers. See Ronald J. Gilson, Value Creation by Business Lawyers: Legal Skills and Asset Pricing, 94 Yale L.J. 239 (1984) (excerpted in Chapter 11); Robert H. Mnookin et al., Beyond Winning, Negotiating to Create Value in Deals and Disputes 129-144 (2000). Understanding that these problems are common and focusing on how to address them in bargaining situations can greatly improve a negotiator's ability to create integrative agreements.

## 6. Exploring the Opponent's Interests and Preferences: Asking Questions

Skill in integrative bargaining requires crafting proposals to take advantage of differences in interests and preferences between the negotiators. Bargaining should therefore be seen as an opportunity to develop the knowledge about the opposing negotiator that can make such proposals possible. Research suggests that negotiators spend most of their time during bargaining making arguments in an attempt to persuade the opponent. Integrative bargaining requires negotiators to place a greater emphasis on developing an understanding of the opposing party.

An obvious place to begin is by using bargaining sessions to ask questions about the other party's preferences. Asking "what" questions, such as "what is it that you want to obtain from this negotiation?" is a good place to start, but unless the negotiators have common interests these questions are likely to yield statements of positions that may seem irreconcilable with the negotiator's interests and may not even contemplate all the issues that might add value to the negotiation. Horace the car buyer might tell Sally he wants a low price and a warranty, which initially seems irreconcilable with Sally's desire to obtain a high price and not offer a warranty. And Horace might not have even considered whether he would value other related items Sally might provide.

After understanding the opponent's positions, it is important to search for the interests that underlie those positions and the relative value that the opponent places on each of those interests, as it is differences in interests and in priorities that form the basis for integrative agreements. Interests can be probed by following up "what" questions with "why" questions, such as, "why are a low price and a warranty important to you?" Horace might respond that a change in jobs has left him with limited resources at the moment and that it is very important to him to know that his investment is protected, prompting Sally to investigate whether adding the issue of a car alarm or a credit payment plan might expand the bargaining zone.

Priorities can be probed directly by asking which of the many interests expressed by the opponent are most important, or what relative value the opponent places on his various interests. Although this will sometimes be helpful, the opponent will not always have thought through his priorities carefully or feel comfortable revealing what is of lesser importance. One way to gain insight into the relative value that the opponent places on various features of the negotiation package is to ask a series of "what if" questions designed to elicit the opponent's opinions about a variety of potential tradeoffs. For example, to better understand the value Sally places on various issues that could be added to the negotiation package, Horace might first ask Sally to quote him a price for the Studebaker alone, and then ask "what if I wanted an extended warranty," or "what if I gave you my current car in trade," or "what if I took the car you had on the lot rather than waiting for a car in the color of my choice." A defendant in an employment discrimination case might ask the plaintiff's lawyer "what if my client gave your client his job back," or "what if my client wrote your client a letter of apology," or "what if my client agreed to send its employees to a seminar on discrimination law." The "what if approach," when used skillfully, can help understand the opponent's unexpressed values and preferences as a means of identifying the mix of issues that creates the largest bargaining zone.

A variation on asking "what if" questions is making multiple alternative proposals for agreements, varying the issues included in the negotiation package in each. For example, Sally might offer Horace his choice of the Studebaker for $3,000, the Studebaker with a three-year warranty for $3,500, or the Studebaker with a warranty and a car alarm for $3,900. To respond to these multiple offers, Horace will have to think carefully about the value to him of the potential additional issues of the warranty and the car alarm, and his response will provide Sally with an indication of whether or not adding these issues would expand the bargaining zone. Making proposals in the alternative is a useful strategy for another reason as well: by doing so, Sally provides information to Horace about the relative value she places on the additional issues. Horace can incorporate this information in future integrative proposals that he must make.

## 7.  Revealing Interests and Preferences

Finally, consider a point that seems obvious but is often overlooked by negotiators: as integrative bargaining requires building on the differences in interests between the negotiators, it is helpful to explicitly describe your underlying interests, and how you value and prioritize potential elements of the negotiation package. Being clear about what you want, why you want it, how you prioritize issues, and the relative value you place on different aspects of the negotiation can encourage your opponent to avoid falling prey to the fixed-sum error and help him to identify the integrative potential of a negotiation.

Fisher et al. provide the common-sense observation that "The purpose of negotiating is to serve your interests. The chance of that happening increases when you communicate them." Roger Fisher, William Ury & Bruce Patton, Getting to Yes 51 (2d ed. 1991). Your clarity in expressing your desires is especially important when your opponent is unwilling to reveal his interests or preference structure, thus making it difficult for you to develop integrative proposals. Backing up offers with an explanation of how they fulfill your specific interests can reduce reactive devaluation as well: if your opponent understands that your interests or priorities are different and not in complete conflict, she will be more likely to see that satisfying your interests is not necessarily contrary to her interests.

## 8.  Post-Settlement Settlements

Negotiators often assume that when the terms of an agreement desirable to both parties are identified, bargaining necessarily ends. But the search for integrative agreements need not stop at this point. One useful tactic is to explicitly search for integrative potential after a tentative agreement is reached. Howard Raiffa has called the resulting agreements "post-settlement settlements." Howard Raiffa, Post-Settlement Settlements, 1 Negotiation J. 9 (1985). The idea is as follows: once negotiators have agreed on a specific transaction, they continue to brainstorm various other agreements that would adjust the initial agreement or add or subtract issues. The parties agree to abide by the terms of the original agreement, however, unless both agree to revise the agreement based on their further discussions. Thus, the parties can speak and brainstorm freely, knowing that they have a mutually acceptable agreement. If they uncover a deal that is better for both parties, however, they can take advantage of it.

## Notes

*1. Is Adding Issues Really Integrative Bargaining?*   Recall that in Section A, Gerald Wetlaufer observed that when the parties enter into a transaction for a single item because the buyer has a higher reservation price than does the seller, the transaction "creates value" relative to no agreement, but we would tend not to call this an "integrative bargain" because it only identifies a bargaining zone rather than increasing the size of the bargaining zone. To call such a transaction "integrative" would mean that every negotiated agreement would be "integrative."

Now suppose that Horace has a reservation price of $6,000 for the Studebaker and Sally's reservation price is $2,000. There is a bargaining zone, and a sale of the car would create value, but it would not properly be called "integrative." Wetlaufer contends that if Horace has a reservation price of $1,000 for a warranty and Sally's reservation price is only $500, by adding the issue of warranty to the subject matter of the negotiation, the parties similarly are not doing anything "integrative," they are just combining two ordinary transactions that create value for the parties by identifying that a bargaining zone exists. See Gerald B. Wetlaufer, The Limits of Integrative Bargaining, 85 Geo. L.J. 369, 378-379 (1996).

On one hand, Wetlaufer's argument has appeal. Imagine that a customer goes to a supermarket and buys a roll of paper towels that she values at $2 on sale for $1 and also purchases a bunch of bananas priced at $2 for which she would have been willing to pay $5. This would hardly be an "integrative bargain" just because the supermarket processes both transactions simultaneously at the same cash register. On the other hand, however, adding the issue of a warranty to Horace's and Sally's Studebaker negotiation bundles together two logically related items in a way that creates more value than would have been created had the two contracted just for the purchase of the car. If an integrative bargain is defined as one that creates a larger cooperative surplus than an alternative transaction with a different negotiation package would have created, adding the issue of the warranty appears to satisfy this definition.

*2. Potential Inefficiencies of Adding Issues.*   An important limitation on the value of adding issues to a negotiation is that doing so often can expand the bargaining zone but still be undesirable to one or both parties. Most scholarship on integrative bargaining focuses entirely on the negotiations between the negotiators in question. In so doing, it fails to take into account other opportunities that the negotiators might have to satisfy their interests. For example, suppose again that Horace's reservation price for the purchase of the Studebaker is $6,000, and Sally's reservation price for its sale is $2,000. Assume also that Horace's reservation price for a warranty would be $1,000, and Sally's is $500. If the parties add the issue of the warranty to the negotiation, Horace's reservation price will increase to $7,000 and Sally's will increase only to $2,500. By adding the new issue to the basic issue in the negotiation, the parties can create $500 of additional surplus value. Integrative bargaining theory suggests that it is therefore desirable for the parties to add the issue of the warranty to the bargaining.

But this conclusion implicitly assumes that Sally will be the most efficient provider of the warranty. This might or might not be the case. Assume that there is a third party insurance company that sells warranties and has a reservation price of $300 for selling a warranty on the Studebaker to Horace. In this case, adding the issue of the warranty to the negotiation between Horace and Sally would be inefficient, because a $700 cooperative surplus could be created if Horace buys the warranty from the insurance company whereas purchasing it from Sally would create only $500 in additional surplus value. More to the point, adding the issue to the negotiation with Sally would be undesirable for Horace (assuming that the transaction costs associated with bargaining with Sally over the car and the insurance company over the warranty would not be $200 greater than bargaining only with Sally). It might or might not be undesirable for Sally, depending on whether she is able to sell only a limited quantity of warranties and whether there are other potential purchasers of her warranties that have a higher reservation price than Horace. The conclusion to be drawn is that for adding issues to be a desirable tactic for a given negotiator, the additional issues must not only create value by expanding the bargaining zone in question, they must also create *more* value than if the negotiator were to bargain over that issue with a third party.

It is worth observing that in many negotiating contexts the parties are locked into a bilateral monopoly situation, meaning that they can only negotiate over the issues in question with the other party, so this caution does not apply. For example, suppose a plaintiff and defendant are attempting to negotiate an out-of-court settlement, the defendant places a high value on the plaintiff agreeing to a nondisclosure agreement, and the plaintiff's opposition to a nondisclosure agreement is only minor. An integrative solution can be reached by the parties if they redefine the subject of the negotiation from "settlement" to "settlement with nondisclosure agreement." There is no possibility that such an agreement would be inefficient, because the defendant cannot possibly buy a nondisclosure agreement from anyone other than the plaintiff.

**3. The Camp David Peace Agreement Revisited.** The Israeli-Egyptian Camp David peace agreement, described above by Fisher et al., is a commonly used example of the power of integrative bargaining, and it can be explored from many perspectives. Fisher et al. use the example to illuminate the value of focusing on the parties' core interests (which were not in direct opposition) rather than their superficial and directly opposing positions — in this case, each side's demand for control of the Sinai Peninsula. Another useful way to view the example, however, is to see that by understanding each other's core interests, the two countries were able to subtract an issue from the negotiation package and create a bargaining zone where none previously existed.

In the transaction, Israel could be viewed as being, in effect, a potential "seller" of land (the Sinai Peninsula), which Egypt offered to "buy" using a peace treaty as currency. Initially, there was no bargaining zone, because Israel's reservation point for the land was higher than Egypt's. In other words, Egypt's highest possible offer of a peace treaty was insufficient to convince Israel to part with the land. A bargaining zone was created, however, when the parties divided the land into two sub-issues, which can be labeled "political control" and "military potential." Egypt wanted complete control over the Sinai, of course, but it cared relatively more about exercising political sovereignty over the territory than being able to use the land to station its military forces. Israel, on the other hand, placed a high value on the land because it feared the consequences of Egypt using it as a forward military base. In the Camp David agreement, Egypt agreed to demilitarize the Sinai upon its return, thus effectively subtracting the issue of "military potential" from the negotiation package and leaving only the issue of "political sovereignty." Israel had a much lower reservation point for parting with this newly defined negotiation package, such that Egypt's offer of a peace treaty was sufficient to create a bargaining zone.

## DISCUSSION QUESTIONS AND PROBLEMS

*1. The Enzytec Negotiation.* Sam Scientist, a chemistry professor at a local university, has isolated an enzyme that he hopes can one day be used to improve the quality of medications designed to control high blood pressure. Recently, he took out a patent on his discovery. Sam's position at the university makes it possible for him to spend about 25 percent of his time working on this project, and his university laboratory equipment has made his research possible to this point. In order to make his idea commercially viable, however, Sam knows he will need to hire a staff of full time scientists to assist him and also purchase a good deal of expensive equipment that the university cannot afford.

One possibility is for Sam to sell his patent to a major pharmaceutical company and let it expend the resources necessary to bring his idea to market, but for personal reasons (i.e., wanting to leave his mark in the world) as well as financial reasons, Sam would prefer to continue to work on developing the commercial applications of the enzyme himself. He believes that with appropriate staffing and funding, the product might be ready to be marketed in five years. Sam has contacted a number of individuals and firms who invest in biotechnology start-up companies in search of an investor. Sam has proposed that an interested investor become a silent partner in his new company, Enzytec, investing $5 million in cash (what Sam estimates he will need for employees and supplies for the next five years) receiving in return a 40 percent equity stake in the company.

After a long career as an executive in the biotech and pharmaceutical industries, Gil Bates started a venture capital fund that invests in companies like Enzytec. Gil believes that Sam's discovery might someday turn out to be important and profitable if developed and marketed correctly, although he thinks there is also a strong possibility Enzytec will ultimately fail. Gil is seriously considering Sam's proposal that Gil's fund invest $5 million in Enzytec in return for a 40 percent equity stake, but he is still uncertain as to whether the expected return on the investment would satisfy his fund's investment goals.

Sam and Gil have arranged a meeting to discuss a possible deal between the two. They are both interested in identifying creative ways to find integrative opportunities that will expand the size of the bargaining zone so that an agreement between the two will create a large cooperative surplus. What procedural and substantive advice would you give Sam and Gil on how they might best achieve this objective?

**2. The Integrative Potential of Common Disputes.**   Many lawyers assume that in most litigation matters the parties' only interest is money — plaintiffs want more, defendants want to pay less — and thus there is no potential for finding integrative agreements. Even when dollars are the issue of predominant interest to both sides, however, it is rare that there are no relevant differences between them that can be the basis for creating joint value. Consider how the interests of the parties might differ in the following typical disputes, and how agreements might be structured in an integrative way:

*(a) Breach of Contract:*   Buyer contracted to purchase 100 widgets from Seller for use in Buyer's manufacturing process. Seller delivered the widgets. Buyer claims the widgets failed to meet the specifications, causing defects in Buyer's product and resulting in damages of $10,000. Seller claims the widgets did meet specifications, and it is not liable for any damages.

*(b) Personal Injury:*   Customer suffered a severe cut on his foot while using a lawnmower sold by Manufacturer. Despite multiple sur-

geries, Customer still suffers from intermittent pain that prevents him from working as a construction worker and playing sports with his children. He has been forced to accept a clerical job that pays significantly less than construction work. Customer seeks a high damage award; Manufacturer concedes liability but believes a far lower damage award is appropriate.

(c) *Criminal Prosecution:*   Suspect is charged with armed robbery after holding up a convenience store. Prosecutor wants Suspect to serve the maximum sentence for armed robbery. Three eyewitnesses identified Suspect, but only one will testify that Suspect had a gun with him at the time of the robbery. Suspect claims that he did not use a weapon during the robbery. He is willing to plead guilty to the less serious charge of larceny, which carries a much lighter sentence.

**3. *Integrative Bargaining in a Divorce Settlement.***   Howard and Wendy have been married for 15 years, and they have decided to seek a divorce. The two are on friendly terms, and wish to agree to an amicable settlement agreement quickly to avoid litigation or any additional emotional hardship on their two children, ten-year-old Grace and eight-year-old Ben.

Wendy earns $40,000 a year working for an insurance company. She works full-time, but keeps very regular hours, always leaving the office by 5 P.M. Howard works in sales, and his salary is largely based on commissions. His average income is about $40,000 per year, but it can fluctuate a great deal from year to year. He is frequently out of town for one or two days at a time when he visits nearby cities, but he has a large amount of flexibility concerning his hours when he does not have to be out of town. Howard and Wendy own a house. It is worth approximately $150,000. They still owe $100,000 on the mortgage, so they have $50,000 of equity in the house. They also own a portfolio of stocks split evenly between high-tech and blue chip companies. The portfolio's current market value is $70,000.

Howard and Wendy have suggested that they would both be willing to agree to a settlement that equally divides custody of their children and their financial assets. Their tentative agreement is to sell the house and split the $50,000 in equity, divide each stock holding equally, and alternate physical custody of the children each month. Each would keep his or her own salary, and neither would pay the other alimony or child support. What possibilities can you see for a more integrative agreement that would expand the cooperative surplus of Howard's and Wendy's settlement, thus potentially increasing the benefit to both? How would you go about exploring with them the possibility of reaching a more integrative agreement?

**4. *Predictions About the Future.***   Different predictions about the future effects of an action can create a basis for integrative agreements, but crafting such agreements is not always easy. Consider a manufacturing firm and its union negotiating wages for the coming year.* The manufacturer claims wage reductions are necessary for the company to maintain its market share in the face of global competition, while the union believes that a raise for union workers would not hurt the company's competitiveness. One obvious approach would be a straight compromise: both sides would agree to freeze next year's wages at the current level. How might the two sides craft a more integrative agreement?

If you were the union's negotiator, how would you respond to a proposal by management that the union receive a raise from current levels next year, but if the company's market share declined the union would agree to accept a steep cut from current levels in year two? Is this a mutually beneficial approach that allows both sides to essentially "put its money where its mouth is"? Is there anything problematic with this integrative approach? Would you prefer a similar proposal with the outcome based on the price of the company's products relative to foreign competitors rather than on the company's market share?

**5. Relationships and Integrative Bargaining.**   One study of students in a negotiation class found that the students were able to achieve more integrative agreements in class exercises when they were negotiating against friends rather than mere acquaintances. See Max H. Bazerman & Margaret A. Neale, The Role of Fairness Considerations and Relationships in a Judgmental Perspective of Negotiation, in Barriers to Conflict Resolution 87, 105 (Kenneth J. Arrow et al., eds. 1995). Do you think that you are able to reach more integrative agreements with friends than with others? If so, why do you think this is?

**6. Dealing with Adversarial Negotiators.**   As this chapter has described, integrative bargaining requires the parties to approach a negotiation with a joint problem solving mindset, to think about both parties' underlying interests, and to think creatively about how to alter the context of the negotiation in ways that can be mutually beneficial. When you attempt to bargain integratively, however, many bargaining opponents will fail to respond in kind. They will come to the table with a set of positions, demand that those positions be satisfied, and resist attempts to think creatively or to jointly problem solve. What tactics might you use to attempt to increase the size of the bargaining zone when you confront such an adversarial negotiator who is focused entirely on distributive issues?

---

*This example is based on a discussion by Lax & Sebenius. David A. Lax & James E. Lax & Sebenius, The Manager as Negotiator 94-98 (1986).

## Chapter 5

# Power

Negotiation, of course, is not only about identifying opportunities for mutually beneficial transactions and finding ways to make them even more beneficial by increasing the cooperative surplus. In most negotiating contexts, the parties must divide the cooperative surplus created by a transaction. The bargaining zone defines the set of deals that are theoretically possible because they would leave both sides better off than if they were to pursue their BATNAs. When a bargaining zone is evident, however, negotiators must agree on a single "deal point" within that zone in order to consummate an agreement. This necessary component of the negotiation process is often referred to as "distributive bargaining." Whereas integrative bargaining is about enlarging the cooperative surplus that the negotiators can create by reaching an agreement, distributive bargaining is about dividing that cooperative surplus. This chapter and the next consider the concepts and tools that negotiators can draw on to divide that cooperative surplus.

Before exploring distributive bargaining tactics, two initial observations are worth making concerning when distributive bargaining is and is not necessary:

First, distributive bargaining is necessary in any bargaining situation in which the bargaining zone is wider than a single point. If Conglomerate Inc.'s reservation price for purchasing Local Co. is $1 million, and Local Co.'s reservation price for selling to Conglomerate Inc. is $600,000, an agreement between the parties will create $400,000 of joint value, or cooperative surplus (over what the parties would enjoy by pursuing their BATNAs). In order to conclude a deal, the parties must agree on a selling price somewhere between $600,000 and $1 million, effectively dividing the $400,000 of surplus between them. Thus, distributive bargaining is necessary.

There are a surprising number of situations, however, in which the negotiators' bargaining zone will be only a single point, or such a small number of points that as a practical matter distributive bargaining is unnecessary. The usual circumstance in which this is the case is where there is a competitive and liquid market for the item in question. For example, suppose that you wanted to buy 100 shares of Conglomerate Inc. stock — traded on the New York Stock Exchange — and your neighbor wished to sell 100 shares of Conglomerate stock that he owns. Because there is an active market in the stock, your BATNA would be to buy 100 shares through the stock exchange at the market price. Your reservation price would therefore be the market price (or perhaps just slightly more to account for the transaction cost of purchasing stock on the exchange). Your neighbor would have a BATNA of selling his stock through the exchange, also at the market price. His reservation price would consequently be the market price (or perhaps just slightly lower to account for transaction costs of selling on the exchange). In this situation, you and your neighbor will reach a negotiated agreement at the market price or not at all.

Second, distributive and integrative bargaining are complementary rather than mutually exclusive approaches. Integrative bargaining is non-zero sum: it concerns finding ways to increase the parties' joint benefits from contracting. Distributive bargaining is zero sum: each benefit to one party entails an equivalent cost to the other. As a result, integrative and distributive bargaining are often portrayed as tactical alternatives, with "cooperative" or "problem solving" negotiators engaging in the "nicer" integrative tactics and "competitive" negotiators engaging in the more ruthless distributive tactics. Such characterizations are extremely misleading. Integrative bargaining only obviates the need for distributive bargaining in the special circumstance in which a negotiation with no bargaining zone is transformed into a negotiation with a bargaining zone of a single point. Ironically, the more successful negotiators are at integrative bargaining the more necessary distributive bargaining will be, because they will have created a larger cooperative surplus that then must be divided.

For example, suppose that Plaintiff's reservation price for settling her lawsuit is $100,000, and Defendant's reservation price is $110,000. Suppose further that Defendant fears settling for a large sum will encourage others similarly situated to Plaintiff to file lawsuits, so that including a nondisclosure agreement with the settlement would raise Defendant's reservation price to $130,000, but the inclusion of a nondisclosure agreement would increase Plaintiff's reservation price only to $105,000. If the negotiators successfully discover that adding a nondisclosure agreement to the settlement talks will create joint value, they will effectively increase the cooperative surplus that reaching agreement would create from $10,000 to $25,000, thus increasing the stakes of the distributive aspect of the negotiation.

Even when integrative bargaining takes place in a nonmonetary setting, the possibility of side payments means that there is always a distributive aspect to the negotiation. Consider the well-known story of conflict between two library patrons, recounted by Roger Fisher et al. in Chapter 4, one of whom wanted the window open and the other of whom wanted the window closed. By focusing on their underlying interests, the patrons discovered they could both be made happy by opening a window in the next room, giving one patron the fresh air he wanted without the draft that the other wished to avoid. This was an integrative solution relative to the alternatives (ranging all the way from opening the window half-way to fist-fighting) because it made both much better off. Still, the parties had to divide all that extra utility that they created. Implicitly, the parties decided to allocate the surplus utility where it fell: one patron kept all the pleasure he received from having fresh air, the other kept all the pleasure he received from avoiding a draft. Recognize, though, that this is a particular distribution of the cooperative surplus, and not the only possible one. Patron A could have made a side payment (in cash or in kind) to Patron B and still found himself better off with the integrative solution minus the side payment than he would have been with a less efficient resolution of the problem. The same can be said of Patron B.

There are two basic methods for dividing the cooperative surplus created through negotiation. First, negotiators can use power to force their opponents to concede to their demands by explicitly or implicitly threatening to break off negotiations without reaching agreement if the opponent does not yield. Second, negotiators can rely on social norms that govern what constitutes a fair division of a cooperative surplus. This chapter addresses the use of power, while Chapter 6 considers the use of social norms.

Negotiating "power" can be defined as the ability of the negotiator to convince the opposing party to give her what she wants even when doing so is incompatible with the opponent's interests. Put another way, power is the ability to bend the opponent to your will. The basis of power is the threat that you will not give the opponent what she wants — specifically, a negotiated agreement — if she will not agree to the terms that you demand. The successful exercise of power, however, requires more than merely the threat of impasse. That threat must be *credible.* That is, the opponent must believe that the negotiator who threatens impasse in fact will walk away from the bargaining table without a deal if her demands are not met. Such a threat is credible when the opponent believes that the negotiator has less to lose from failing to reach agreement than does the opponent.

This chapter considers four tactics by which negotiators can successfully exercise negotiating power: improving their BATNA or reducing their opponent's BATNA and thus actually shifting the bargaining zone; manipulating the opponent's perceptions of the bargaining zone; making a commitment not to agree to anything less than a particular agreement, even if a less favorable agreement would be superior to impasse; and demonstrating the ability to wait longer for concessions than the opponent is willing to wait.

---

## A.   CHANGING THE BARGAINING ZONE

Because the negotiator who can most credibly threaten to walk away from the bargaining table has the power to impose his will on his opponent, negotiating power emanates directly from the parameters of the bargaining zone.

Consider, for example, a man enjoying a day at the beach who is interested in purchasing lunch from a beach-side hamburger stand. The buyer wants to pay a low price for a hamburger — let's say $2. The seller wants a high price — let's say $5. Assume for the moment that there is no possibility of using integrative bargaining to expand the bargaining zone by adding or subtracting issues (such as including french fries in the bargain, which the buyer desires and the seller can make cheaply, or subtracting the fancy wrapping paper which is expensive for the seller and of no interest to the buyer).

Which negotiator has negotiating power that he can use to obtain his desired price? The answer depends on who has better alternatives and thus a stronger reservation price. If there is only one hamburger stand on the beach, the buyer is extremely hungry, and there are 50 customers all holding $5 bills in their hands in line behind the buyer, the seller has an excellent BATNA (sell the hamburger to the next customer for $5) and a strong reservation price of $5, while the buyer has a weak BATNA (go without lunch?) and thus probably a weak reservation price. In this example, the seller has negotiating power and will probably be able to demand — and get — his desired price, on threat of ending negotiations and entering into a transaction with the next customer in line. The seller does not value reaching agreement with the buyer very much relative to his BATNA of selling the hamburger for $5 to the next person in line, while the buyer values reaching an agreement much more than pursuing his BATNA. Alternatively, if there are 20 hamburger stands on the beach, all of which have burgers that have been prepared and are getting cold, and there are no other buyers in sight, the buyer's BATNA (buy from another stand) is stronger relative to reaching an agreement than the seller's BATNA (allow the hamburger to go to waste). In this circumstance, the buyer will probably have a stronger reservation price than the seller and should be able to obtain a lower price by making the credible threat to walk away from the stand and buy his lunch elsewhere.

This analysis can be placed squarely in the context of what you learned in Chapter 2 about the central importance of the bargaining zone in negotiation. If a seller — in this case the hamburger stand — has a strong BATNA and thus a high reservation price (i.e., $5), and a buyer — in this case the beachgoer — has a weak BATNA and thus a high reservation price (let's say, for example, $8), the resulting bargaining zone between $5 and $8 gives a great deal of power to the seller. The seller can credibly threaten to pursue his BATNA unless the buyer agrees to his $5 demand. If the seller has a weak BATNA (throwing away the burger) and thus a low reservation price (let's say $1), while the buyer has a strong BATNA (buying from any of numerous other stands) and thus a low reservation price (let's say $2), then the resulting bargaining zone between $1 and $2 gives the buyer a good deal of negotiating power. In this case, the buyer can credibly threaten to pursue his BATNA if the seller won't concede to his demand to sell the hamburger for $2.

The basic insight that power results from a strong BATNA, while quite intuitive, has also been demonstrated empirically through negotiation experiments. In one study, the experimenters had subjects playing the role of job recruiter or job candidate negotiate with each other over an employment contract containing salary and fringe benefits. Subjects in both roles could earn up to 13,200 total points, depending on how beneficial their final agreement was to them. Some of the subjects were told that they had a BATNA that would earn them 4,500 points ("high BATNA"), while others were told that they had a BATNA that would earn them 2,200 points ("low BATNA"). As one would expect, recruiter subjects with high BATNAs negotiated more favorable contracts than recruiter subjects with low BATNAs, and candidate subjects with high BATNAs negotiated more favorable contracts than candidate subjects with low BATNAs. Robin L. Pinkley et al., The Impact of Alternatives to Settlement in Dyadic Negotiation, 57 Org. Behav. & Human Decision Proc. 97, 108 tbl. 3 (1994).

It is often assumed that negotiators who possess general indicia of social power, such as wealth, strength, political clout, intelligence, or good looks, also enjoy power in negotiations. This is not true, at least not directly. Notice that in the hamburger stand example, which party has negotiating power does not depend on whether the buyer is an extremely rich and clever man — Microsoft Corporation chairman Bill Gates, for example — or an ordinary beachgoer of modest means. Neither does it depend on whether the hamburger stand is owned by its sole attendant who is struggling to make a living or by the McDonald's Corporation. What matters is which party has the better BATNA.

This is not to say that wealth and political clout are irrelevant to bargaining power. The rich and strong often have access to more and better alternatives than the poor and weak. For example, if there are no other hamburger stands on the beach, the poor buyer's BATNA might be to go hungry, while Bill Gates' BATNA might be to send an aide across town in a limousine to procure lunch from another source. If there are no other potential buyers, the BATNA of throwing out an uneaten burger might create a hardship for the sole proprietor of the hamburger stand, but very little hardship to McDonald's. Thus, holding all other factors equal, Bill Gates and the McDonald's Corporation are likely to have more bargaining power than buyers and sellers of more modest means. But it is the presence of relatively good alternatives to reaching an agreement, not their wealth or social status per se, that provides the negotiating power.

Because negotiating power depends first and foremost on the parameters of the bargaining zone, negotiators can affect their relative power by taking steps away from the bargaining table to improve their BATNA (thus improving their reservation point) or by worsening their opponent's BATNA (thus worsening the opponent's reservation point).

First, consider the former tactic. Although it is not always the case, in most circumstances negotiators have at least some control over their BATNA — at least if they are willing to work hard prior to the commencement of negotiations. Consider the case of Graduate, who recently finished law school and passed the bar examination and has received an offer to join Firm as an associate. Firm has offered a starting salary of $50,000, and Graduate has asked for a salary of $70,000. Which side can exercise more power in the negotiation?

Assume that Firm has a BATNA of hiring a classmate of Graduate's with slightly less impressive credentials for $50,000. If Graduate has no other job prospects, his BATNA will likely be to continue searching for a job — a relatively unattractive option. With such a weak BATNA, Graduate will probably have a relatively low reservation price for his salary, and the firm will be able to prevail on the graduate to accept the $50,000 offer. On the other hand, if Graduate invests the time and effort necessary to improve his BATNA by acquiring job offers at other firms — even if those firms are not quite as desirable to him — he can reduce the power differential between his negotiating position and Firm's. If Firm lacks a strong BATNA (e.g., it has not interviewed other graduates, or it has but has been unable to identify any with strong credentials), the greater difference between the value Firm will receive by reaching an agreement with Graduate and by pursuing its BATNA, relative to the difference in value to Graduate between reaching agreement with Firm and pursuing his BATNA, will result in Graduate enjoying a significant power advantage.

In the context of litigation, because the parties' alternative to out-of-court settlement is usually formal adjudication, power usually resides with the party with the stronger legal case. Litigants invest time and resources in developing the factual basis for their case and conducting legal research in order to improve the value of their BATNA of adjudication and thus their reservation price. Investigating the facts surrounding the dispute, deposing witnesses, and conducting legal research to identify helpful precedent, enables litigants to increase their power by enhancing the credibility of the threat that they will proceed to adjudication if the opponent refuses to agree to the settlement they demand.

On some occasions, negotiators can also increase their bargaining power by weakening their opponent's BATNA, thus increasing the relative importance to the opponent of reaching a negotiated agreement. Assume again that Firm is negotiating with Graduate, and that Firm has a BATNA of hiring one of Graduate's classmates at a salary of $50,000 per year. Assuming that the classmates are well qualified for the position, Firm will probably value hiring Graduate only slightly more than it would value pursuing its BATNA, giving it a powerful negotiating position. But what if Graduate could convince his classmates to reject all job offers from Firm? This would effectively enhance Graduate's relative negotiating power by weakening Firm's position. At this point, a threat by Graduate to break off negotiations and pursue his BATNA would be much more troubling to Firm, and Firm would be more likely to concede to Graduate's demand for a higher salary.

Since a stronger BATNA can help a party to exercise bargaining power and claim a larger share of the cooperative surplus, it would be easy to conclude that seeking a better BATNA is always a good negotiation tactic. Easy, but wrong. When developing a better BATNA is costly, negotiators must balance those costs against the potential benefits of increased bargaining leverage.

Consider again the hypothetical situation involving the beachgoer in search of a hamburger. Assume that the beachgoer is hungry for lunch, and there is a single hamburger stand on the beach advertising burgers for $5. With no other lunch options in view, the beachgoer determines that his BATNA is going without lunch, and accordingly determines that his reservation price is $10. Now assume that the beachgoer picks up his cellular phone and calls 10 restaurants in town, finding one that will deliver a burger to him on the beach for $4. Having identified this option and thus improved his BATNA, the beachgoer might determine his new reservation price for buying lunch from the beachside stand is $4. If the hamburger stand has a lower reservation price than $4, the beachgoer might exercise his new-found negotiation power to negotiate the price down from $5 to $4, or maybe even a bit lower. Was his tactic successful? It depends on the cost. If he had to pay $10 in cellular phone charges to improve his reservation price by $6 and ultimately save $1-$2 on lunch, then his pursuit of negotiation power was ill advised.

Lawyer-negotiators must balance the costs and benefits of seeking to improve their BATNAs all the time. Consider a common scenario in litigation: Plaintiff has suffered $100,000 in damages, and believes she has a 50 percent chance of prevailing at trial. She thus determines the expected value of her BATNA (trial) is $50,000, and, discounting for the costs of a trial, she fixes her reservation price for an out-of-court settlement at $40,000. Plaintiff believes she could increase her likelihood of prevailing at trial — thus improving her BATNA and her bargaining power — by hiring an expert witness to testify at trial at a cost of $15,000. Should she retain the expert? Plaintiff should try to determine whether hiring the expert would increase her expected value of trial by at least $15,000. If not, it is not cost-effective to improve her BATNA. The problem is made more complex by the fact that the negotiator will usually not know whether expending additional resources on improving the quality of her case will be cost effective until after she has expended the resources — in this case, until after she has hired, prepared, deposed, and watched the opposing lawyer cross-examine the expert!

## B.  MANIPULATING PERCEPTIONS OF THE BARGAINING ZONE

Section A claimed that negotiating power emanates from a strong BATNA relative to the opponent and the resulting favorable bargaining zone. This description of power, however, glosses over one important subtlety: the success of a negotiator's attempt to exercise power by threatening impasse will actually depend on the opponent's *perception* of the bargaining zone, rather than the *actual* parameters of the bargaining zone. An implication of this is that negotiators can gain power by changing their opponents' perceptions of the bargaining zone, even if they do not change the actual bargaining zone. Perceptions of the bargaining zone are subject to manipulation because even the most diligently prepared negotiators are usually unable to precisely identify the zone's parameters. Two sources of uncertainty make this the case.

The most obvious of the two sources is that a negotiator can rarely know her opponent's reservation price with certainty. Negotiators are usually reluctant to reveal their reservation price voluntarily out of fear that opponents will offer just exactly that much and no more. Often, the negotiator will not know for certain what her opponent's BATNA is, making even a prediction concerning the opponent's reservation price difficult. Even if the negotiator can identify her opponent's BATNA, she is unlikely to know for certain how the opponent subjectively evaluates the quality of his BATNA relative to the possibility of reaching a negotiated agreement.

Less obviously, the negotiator often does not know her own precise reservation price with certainty. The opponent might possess private information about the subject of the negotiation that is relevant to the negotiator's reservation price. For example, if Horace is purchasing a used car from Sally, his reservation price will depend in large part on the quality of the car. If Sally has more information about the car, Horace might not know prior to negotiating with Sally the exact maximum amount he is willing to pay. In some cases, the opponent might possess relevant information about the negotiator's BATNA. In litigation settlement negotiations, the defendant might have information relevant to evaluating the strength of the negotiator's BATNA of going to trial.

Because all negotiators can have only uncertain estimates of the bargaining zone, the negotiator can capture some or all of the cooperative surplus created by reaching agreement by convincing the opponent to revise her estimates of the size and location of the bargaining zone. The following excerpt explains how the negotiator can capture a larger portion of the cooperative surplus by shaping his opponent's perceptions of one or both parties' reservation prices to his advantage.

## ■ Russell Korobkin, A Positive Theory of Legal Negotiation*

88 Geo. L.J. 1789, 1799-1804 (2000)

. . . Perhaps the most common activity negotiators engage in at the bargaining table is attempting to persuade their opponent of the value of the negotiation's subject matter or of other alternatives. The arguments advanced often appear remarkably similar to those that litigating parties might make to a judge or jury. David is likely to present a detailed argument for why he is not liable for battery, claiming that the facts of his conflict with Goliath are analogous to the facts of precedential cases in which courts found no liability. Goliath will likely respond by disputing David's characterization of the facts of the dispute and/or claiming that other precedent is more "on point." Both parties' arguments superficially seem difficult to understand, given that there is little possibility that either will suddenly concede the superiority of the other's position.

Similarly, Esau would be likely to claim that Jacob's business is worth substantially less than $150,000, citing facts and figures in support of

*Reprinted with permission of the publisher, Georgetown Law Journal © 2000.

his position. Jacob would most likely respond with an argument that the business is worth substantially more than $150,000, citing different facts and figures or citing different interpretations of the same facts and figures; neither party is likely to concede or compromise on the value. . . .

## 1. REDUCING THE OPPONENT'S RP

When Esau argues that Jacob's catering business is worth only $120,000, he hopes to persuade Jacob that other buyers are unlikely to offer more than this amount. That is, Esau's true goal is to convince Jacob that Jacob has overestimated the value of an alternative likely to be Jacob's BATNA — in this case, waiting for another suitor's offer.

If Jacob's BATNA is to wait for another potential purchaser to make an offer, he might have estimated the value of that BATNA at $160,000 and set his RP at $150,000 (based on a $10,000 value of selling the business sooner rather than later). If Esau's argument reduces Jacob's confidence in Jacob's initial estimate, Esau's efforts will have succeeded. Esau's arguments might, for example, cause Jacob to reduce his estimate of his BATNA's value to $140,000, and consequently his RP to $130,000, thus shifting the bargaining zone to Esau's advantage. Of course, if waiting for another offer is not Jacob's BATNA, Esau's attempts at persuasion are likely to fail. For example, Jacob might have another offer in hand for $150,000, in which case Esau's arguments for the low market value of the business will have no impact on Jacob's RP and no impact on the bargaining zone.

David's legal arguments offered to Goliath can be understood in the same way. Assume that Goliath has determined that his BATNA is pursuing a jury verdict and has estimated that he stands a 75% chance of winning a $100,000 verdict if settlement negotiations fail. Although David's arguments are unlikely to convince Goliath and

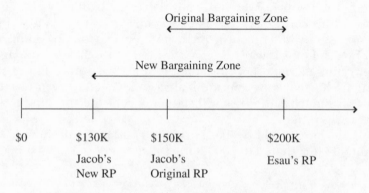

**Using Persuasion to Reduce the Opponent's RP**

cause him to apologize for bringing suit, they might cause Goliath to reassess his estimate of a 75% chance of victory. If Goliath downgrades his success estimate from 75% to 50%, his BATNA valuation will drop from $75,000 to $50,000, causing him to reduce his RP accordingly. David will have succeeded in shifting the bargaining zone to his advantage.

Jacob and Goliath are unlikely to sit idly while their negotiating opponents attempt to convince them to decrease their RPs. If they are typical negotiators, they will respond with rebuttal arguments of their own. Jacob will attempt to justify a higher value for his business; Goliath will muster factual and legal arguments to support his battery claim. But why should they bother? Each negotiating party determines his own RP — the setting of one party's RP is not a matter that requires a consensus of all participants in the negotiation. If Esau's or David's arguments are unpersuasive, why should Jacob and Goliath not sit quietly, content to let their opponents' arguments fall on deaf ears and have no substantive effect on the bargaining?

Rebuttal arguments can serve three purposes. First, to the extent that Esau's arguments caused Jacob to question his RP, making rebuttal arguments can help Jacob to test the persuasiveness of Esau's points. In other words, Jacob might well be arguing for his own benefit, not for Esau's. Second, by rebutting, Jacob tries to convince Esau that Esau's efforts at reducing Jacob's RP have failed and, consequently, the bargaining zone has not been shifted to Esau's advantage. Finally, a rebuttal gives Jacob an opportunity to turn the tables on Esau: that is, he attempts to shift Esau's RP. If Jacob can convince Esau that the latter's valuation of the business is too low, purchasing Jacob's business will look better relative to Esau's BATNA — perhaps of purchasing a competing business — causing Esau to raise his RP. Success in this endeavor, of course, may be necessary to create a bargaining zone (if Esau's RP would otherwise be below Jacob's), and at the very least it will shift the bargaining zone to Jacob's advantage.

### 2.   IMPROVING THE NEGOTIATOR'S OWN "APPARENT" RP

Negotiators often attempt to shift the bargaining zone advantageously by making their RPs appear to their opponents to be better than they actually are. Assume that Goliath's RP for a litigation settlement is $60,000, based on an estimate of a $75,000 expected value of a jury verdict (a 75% chance of prevailing at trial, and an estimated verdict of $100,000) discounted by $15,000 to account for risk aversion and costs of litigation that will be saved if the case is settled out of court. Assume also that Goliath estimates *David's* RP to be $90,000, based on the *same* estimates of the value of a jury verdict and the costs of litigation (David has a 75% chance of losing a $100,000 verdict, and would pay a $15,000 premium at settlement to avoid the risks and costs of litigation). If David can convince Goliath that David has set his RP lower than $90,000, he can shift the bargaining zone in his favor.

Two types of arguments might serve this purpose. Recall that there are two components to David's RP: the value of his BATNA (in this case, a trial) and the difference in value between his BATNA and the subject of the negotiation (in this case, settlement). Consequently, David might try to convince his adversary either that he believes his BATNA is more valuable than Goliath estimates or that the difference in value to him between trial and settlement is smaller than Goliath estimates.

First, David is likely to present a detailed legal argument to Goliath documenting why he believes he has, for example, a 50% chance of prevailing at trial. If Goliath does not accept David's analysis and still believes that he has a 75% chance of prevailing, Goliath will not reduce his own RP of $60,000. But David need not be so convincing to gain an upper hand in the negotiation — *he need only convince Goliath that he (David) believes the argument he is advancing.* If David does this, Goliath will adjust downward his estimate of David's RP to $65,000. By convincing Goliath of his own *subjective* belief in the strength of his BATNA, David can shift the range of possible settlements from $60,000-$90,000 down to $60,000-$65,000.

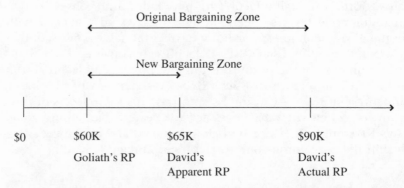

**Using Persuasion to Improve One's Own "Apparent" RP**

Alternately, David might tell Goliath that he is not risk averse and that his brother-in-law will be representing him in court at no charge. The purpose of these statements would be to reduce Goliath's estimate of his RP by convincing Goliath that David values trial and settlement equivalently. If David convinces Goliath that he speaks the truth, Goliath will reduce his estimate of David's RP by $15,000, from $90,000 to $75,000, even if David agrees with Goliath's estimates concerning his likelihood of prevailing at trial and the likely size of a jury verdict.

In the two preceding examples, nothing depends on whether David actually believes the arguments he makes — all that matters is David's ability to persuade Goliath that he believes the arguments he advances and, thus, has set his RP accordingly. In the first example, if David actually believes that Goliath has only a 50% chance of prevailing at trial, his RP *is* $65,000. If David secretly believes that Goliath has a 75% chance of prevailing at trial, his RP is $90,000, but his RP appears to Goliath to be $65,000. In either case, Goliath believes that the possible points of settlement lie between $60,000 and $65,000, which improves David's strategic position substantially compared to what it was when Goliath believed a settlement up to $90,000 was possible. The same analysis holds for the second example.

Changing the facts slightly, however, demonstrates the significance of David's state of mind. Suppose that David convinces Goliath that he (David) believes Goliath has only a 50% chance of prevailing at trial *and* that David values a trial and a settlement equivalently. This would cause Goliath to estimate David's RP at $50,000 (50% × $100,000 + $0), placing it below Goliath's RP of $60,000. Goliath would then conclude that no agreement is possible. If David accurately represented his position to Goliath, then his RP *is* $50,000 and there is no bargaining zone. The parties are best served by ending negotiations and preparing for trial. But if David misrepresented his position — perhaps estimating that Goliath's RP is somewhat lower than $50,000 — and has an actual RP of $90,000, his persuasiveness is likely to backfire. Goliath might end negotiations because he thinks no agreement is possible when, in fact, there is a $30,000 bargaining zone between the parties' RPs. An opportunity for an agreement superior to both party's BATNAs — and significantly so — will be lost.

This insight accounts for two observable features of negotiating behavior: parties do not always misrepresent their valuations, and when they do misrepresent they often leave a path over which they can later retreat if necessary. If misrepresenting one's BATNA could never make an actual bargaining zone apparently disappear, negotiating parties would have no reason not to always attempt to misrepresent — and grossly so — save personal ethical principles and, perhaps, the fear of developing a reputation as an overreacher should the misrepresentations not be believed. However, misrepresentations of the value the negotiator places on the subject of the negotiation or his BATNA, while commonplace, are not universal. With misrepresentation comes risk. The negotiator must balance the possible benefits of improving his bargaining position by misrepresenting his valuations against the possible cost of causing impasse when a beneficial transaction was possible.

The fear of creating the perception that no bargaining zone exists when one actually does can cause negotiators to assert misrepresentations of value softly or hesitantly. For example, David might attempt to give the impression that he *tentatively* has concluded that Goliath is only 50% likely to prevail at trial, rather than that he is firm in this belief. This tactic can give him latitude to backtrack — perhaps conceding that Goliath's chances are closer to 60% or even higher — should he sense from the course of the bargaining that Goliath's RP is higher than what David has implied about his own.                    ■

## Notes

*1. Manipulating Perceptions: An Historical Example.*  As Theodore Roosevelt was campaigning for the presidency in 1912, his campaign staff prepared and printed 3 million brochures featuring a stern photograph of Roosevelt and the text of a campaign speech, which were to be distributed on a whistle-stop tour of the country. Just before the tour began, the staff realized that they had failed to secure permission to reprint the photograph from its copyright holder, a Chicago photography studio.

With only the poor alternatives of not using the brochures at all, reprinting all 3 million brochures without the photograph, or risking a lawsuit for copyright infringement, the staff knew it would have to reach an agreement with the studio to use the photograph. Roosevelt's campaign manager sent a message to the studio offering to distribute a campaign pamphlet with their photograph of the candidate on the cover, pointing out the excellent publicity that the studio would enjoy, and asking how much *the studio* would be willing to pay for the privilege. The studio responded with an offer of $250, which the campaign graciously accepted. See Lawrence Bakow & Michael Wheeler, Environmental Dispute Resolution 73-74 (1984).

*2. The Use of Power and the Problem of Common Knowledge.*  When negotiators attempt to manipulate their opponents' perceptions of the bargaining zone, the implications are often threatening, insulting, or both. If a buyer attempts to convince a seller that the former's reservation price is very low, he is effectively claiming that the seller's product is not very valuable and threatening to break off negotiations if the seller refuses to lower her price. If the buyer attempts to convince the seller that the seller's reservation price should be lower than the seller maintains that it is, he might be implicitly claiming that the seller is lying about having better options. The problem is that by making these types of statements, even implicitly, the buyer might make it more difficult for him and the seller to maintain an ongoing cooperative relationship. The seller might be reticent to do business with a buyer who has threatened him, called him a liar, or deemed his wares chintzy. The buyer, in turn, might be reluctant to do business with a seller who knows he has been treated this way because he assumes that the seller will not trust him. Thus, although the buyer might succeed in reducing the seller's reservation price, he might poison the relationship in the process. See Ian Ayres & Barry J. Nalebuff, Common Knowledge as a Barrier to Negotiation, 44 UCLA L. Rev. 1631 (1997).

Whether this is particularly problematic depends on the nature of the negotiation. A poisoned relationship between opposing litigants who will never meet again might not be troublesome, whereas a poisoned relationship between negotiators bargaining over the terms of a joint venture that would require them to work together probably would be.

***3. The Status Quo Bias Revisited.*** A negotiator's reservation price depends on how he compares the value of a negotiated agreement to the value of his BATNA. Evidence of the status quo bias, discussed above, suggests that this comparison is likely to be biased in favor of whichever of the two options (agreement or BATNA) the negotiator perceives as consistent with the status quo state of the world. Consider the following prescriptive advice for negotiators:

> The psychological power of inertia suggests that negotiators who are able to define the status quo position, against which all proposed terms are judged, are likely to enjoy an important bargaining advantage. Before negotiating terms of a contract, a strategic negotiator should evaluate which of many plausible reference points for negotiations is most advantageous to her client's interests. Initial efforts to convince the opposing negotiator that the advantageous reference point is the most natural or reasonable from which to begin negotiations may have a large impact on the outcome of those negotiations. The initial terms are likely to be perceived as the terms that will govern the parties' relationship if no further action takes place, and thus as the status quo.

Russell Korobkin, Inertia and Preference in Contract Negotiation: The Psychological Power of Default Rules and Form Terms, 51 Vand. L. Rev. 1583, 1608 (1998).

## C. COMMITMENTS

It is relatively easy for a negotiator to threaten impasse if his demands are not met; the challenge is to make such a threat *credible*. A threat is at best worthless, and at worst positively dangerous, unless the threatened party believes that the party making the threat will actually carry it out if his demands are not met. The difficulty in establishing the credibility of the threat of impasse is that if a bargaining zone exists, impasse is harmful to the party who makes the threat as well as to the party who receives it. Suppose Catherine is negotiating with Donald to buy widgets to construct air conditioning units, and Donald is asking for a price of $7 per widget. Catherine might demand that Donald reduce his price to $5 per widget and threaten to end negotiations unless he reduces his price. But if Donald believes that Catherine's reservation price is $8 per widget, he won't believe her threat, reasoning that Catherine will not really walk away from his $7 per-widget offer because doing so would hurt herself as well as him.

The previous two sections suggest that Catherine is likely to try to improve her BATNA and thus her reservation price, or to try to persuade Donald that her reservation price is better than it actually is. Assume that Ethan also sells widgets of equivalent quality to Donald's. Catherine might try to obtain an offer from Ethan to sell her widgets for $5 each. If she is unsuccessful, she might attempt to convince Donald (falsely) that she believes Ethan's $8 widgets are much superior to Donald's. Through either tactic, Catherine would essentially be trying to convince Donald that her impasse threat is credible because she does not value Donald's widgets at more than $5, and therefore that she would not harm herself by walking away from an offer that is any higher than $5.

But what if Donald does not believe that Catherine's reservation price is only $5? Assume, for example, that Donald knows (1) that widgets are a critical component to Catherine's air conditioning units, (2) that his and Ethan's widgets are identical in quality, and (3) that Ethan will not sell his widgets for less than $8. Does Catherine have any other hope of making her threat credible, such that Donald will fear that an impasse will result unless he meets Catherine's demand to reduce his price to $5? The answer is that Catherine's threat can be effective if she has a means of making a binding commitment to refuse to pay any more than $5 before Donald can bind himself not to accept less than $7. If Catherine can bind herself first, she will force Donald to choose between impasse and lowering his price to $5. Assuming Donald's reservation price is below $5, his only rational choice would be to lower his price to $5 in order to avoid losing out on a profitable deal. In the following seminal work, Thomas Schelling explores how negotiators can make commitments to courses of action not in their best interests in order to force concessions from their opponents.

## ■ Thomas Schelling, The Strategy of Conflict*

21-37 (1960)

. . . Our concern will not be with the part of bargaining that consists of exploring for mutually profitable adjustments, and that might be called the "efficiency" aspect of bargaining. . . . Instead, we shall be concerned with what might be called the "distributional" aspect of bargaining: the situations in which a better bargain for one means less for the other. . . .

These are situations that ultimately involve an element of pure bargaining — bargaining in which each party is guided mainly by his expectations of what the other will accept. . . . Why does he concede? Because he thinks the other will not. "I must concede because he won't. He won't because he thinks I will. He thinks I will because he thinks I think he thinks so. . . ." There is some range of alternative outcomes in which any point is better for both sides than no agreement at all. To insist on any such point is pure bargaining, since one always would take less rather than reach no agreement at all, and since one always *can* recede if retreat proves necessary to agreement. Yet if both parties are aware of the limits to this range, *any* outcome is a point from which at least one party would have been willing to retreat and the other knows it! There is no resting place. . . . The purpose of this chapter is to call attention to an important class of tactics, of a kind that is peculiarly appropriate to the logic of indeterminate situations. The essence of these tactics is some voluntary but irreversible sacrifice of freedom of choice. They rest on the paradox that the power to constrain an adversary may depend on the power to bind oneself; that, in bargaining, weakness is often strength, freedom may be freedom to capitulate, and to burn bridges behind one may suffice to undo an opponent. . . .

The sophisticated negotiator may find it difficult to seem as obstinate as a truly obstinate man. If a man knocks at a door and says that he will stab himself on the porch unless given $10, he is more likely to get the $10 if his eyes are bloodshot. The threat of mutual destruction cannot be used to deter an adversary who is too unintelligent to comprehend it or too weak to enforce his will on those he represents. . . .

When one wishes to persuade someone that he would not pay more than $16,000 for a house that is really worth $20,000 to him, what can he do to take advantage of the usually superior credibility of the truth over a false assertion? Answer: make it true. How can a buyer make it true? If he likes the house because it is near his business, he might move his business, persuading the seller that the house is really now worth only $16,000 to him. This would be unprofitable; but he is no better off than if he had paid the higher price.

But suppose the buyer could make an irrevocable and enforceable bet with some third party, duly recorded and certified, according to which he would pay for the house no more than $16,000, or forfeit $5,000. The seller has lost; the buyer need simply present the truth. Unless the seller is enraged and withholds the house in sheer spite, the situation has been rigged against him; the "objective" situation — the buyer's true incentive — [has] been voluntarily, conspicuously, and irreversibly changed. The seller can take it or leave it. This example demonstrates that if the buyer can accept an irrevocable *commitment*, in a way that is unambiguously visible to the seller, he can squeeze the range of indeterminacy down to the point most favorable to him. . . .

The most interesting parts of our topic concern whether and how commitments can be taken; but it is worth while to consider briefly a model in which practical problems are absent — a world in which absolute commitments are freely available. Consider a culture in which "cross my heart" is universally recognized as absolutely binding. Any offer accompanied by this invocation is a final offer, and is so recognized. If each party knows the other's true reservation price, the object is to be first with a firm offer. Complete responsibility for the outcome then rests with the other, who can take it or leave it as he chooses (and who chooses to take it). Bargaining is all over; the commitment (that is, the first offer) wins. . . .

[I]t has not been uncommon for union officials to stir up excitement and determination on the part of the membership during or prior to a wage negotiation. If the union is going to insist on $2 and expects the management to counter with $1.60, an effort is made to persuade the membership not only that the management could pay $2 but even perhaps that the negotiators themselves are incompetent if they fail to obtain close to $2. The purpose — or, rather, a plausible purpose suggested by our analysis — is to make clear to the management that the negotiators could not accept less than $2 *even if they wished to* because they no longer control the members or because they would lose their own positions if they tried. In other words, the negotiators reduce the scope of their own authority and confront the management with the threat of a strike that the union itself cannot avert, even though it was the union's own action that eliminated its power to prevent the strike.

When national representatives go to international negotiations knowing that there is a wide range of potential agreement within which the outcome will depend on bargaining, they seem often to create a bargaining position by public statements, statements calculated to arouse a public opinion that permits no concessions to be made. If a binding public opinion can be cultivated and made evident to the other side, the initial position can thereby be made visibly "final." . . .

*Secrecy vs. Publicity.* A potent means of commitment, and sometimes the only means, is the pledge of one's reputation. If national representatives can arrange to be charged with appeasement for every small concession, they place concession visibly beyond their own reach. If a union with other plants to deal with can arrange to make any retreat dramatically visible, it places its bargaining reputation in jeopardy and thereby becomes visibly incapable of serious compromise. (The same convenient jeopardy is the basis for the universally exploited defense, "If I did it for you I'd have to do it for everyone else.") . . .

*Intersecting Negotiations.* If a union is simultaneously engaged, or will shortly be engaged, in many negotiations while the management has no other plants and deals with no other unions, the management cannot convincingly stake its bargaining reputation while the union can. The advantage goes to the party that can persuasively point to an array of other negotiations in which its own position would be prejudiced if it made a concession in this one. (The "reputation value" of the bargain may be less related to the outcome than to the firmness with which some initial bargaining position is adhered to.) . . .

*Continuous Negotiations.* A special case of interrelated negotiations occurs when the same two parties are to negotiate other topics, simultaneously or in the future. The logic of this case is more subtle; to persuade the other that one cannot afford to recede, one says in effect, "If I conceded to you here, you would revise your estimate of me in our other negotiations; to protect reputation with you I must stand firm." The second party is simultaneously the "third party" to whom one's bargaining reputation can be pledged. . . .

*Principles and Precedents.* To be convincing, commitments usually have to be qualitative rather than quantitative, and to rest on some rationale. It may be difficult to conceive of a really firm commitment to $2.07½; why not $2.02¼? The numerical scale is too continuous to provide good resting places, except at nice round numbers like $2.00. But a commitment to the *principle* of "profit sharing," "cost-of-living increases," or any other basis for a numerical calculation that comes out at $2.07½, may provide a foothold for a commitment. . . .

The commitment problem is nicely illustrated by the legal doctrine of the "last clear chance" which recognizes that, in the events that led up to an accident, there was some point at which the accident became inevitable as a result of prior actions, and that the abilities of the two parties to prevent it may not have expired at the same time. In bargaining, the commitment is a device to leave the last clear chance to decide the outcome with the other party, in a manner that he fully appreciates; it is to relinquish further initiative, having rigged the incentives so that the other party must choose in one's favor. If one driver speeds up so that he cannot stop, and the other realizes it, the latter has to yield. A legislative rider at the end of a session leaves the President the last clear chance to pass the bill. This doctrine helps to understand some of those cases in which bargaining "strength" inheres in what is weakness by other standards. When a person — or a country — has lost the power to help himself, or the power to avert mutual damage, the other interested party has no choice but to assume the cost or responsibility. . . .                                              ■

## Notes

*1. The Last Clear Chance.*   According to Schelling, commitments work by leaving the "last clear chance" to avoid a bargaining breakdown to the other negotiator. Ironically, negotiators gain power through commitments by voluntarily giving up power over their own actions. Consider the game of "chicken," in which two drivers steer their cars directly at the other and the first car to swerve to avoid a collision is the loser. A driver able to give up control over his car gains power by doing so because he provides the other driver with the last clear chance to avoid a crash. For example, if a driver can remove his steering wheel while accelerating toward the other car and then, in full view of the other driver, throw the steering wheel out the window, his resulting helplessness will win the contest for him. At that point, the other driver has the choice of swerving (the equivalent of conceding the cooperative surplus in negotiation) or accepting a certain accident (the equivalent of allowing a negotiation to end with no agreement).

In the chicken scenario, both parties initially have the ability to avoid a mutually undesirable result until one takes action that eliminates his ability to do so. In some circumstances, however, a negotiator does not have to affirmatively act in order to render himself helpless and thus gain a negotiating advantage . . . the negotiator might actually be helpless from the beginning. Consider the following negotiation, reported to have been conducted over radios at sea*:

*Negotiator #1:*   We are on a collision course. You are instructed to change your course 10 degrees starboard.

*Negotiator #2:*   We instruct you to change your course 10 degrees port.

*Negotiator #1:*   We reiterate: change your course 10 degrees starboard immediately.

*Negotiator #2:*   We will not change course. You must immediately change your course 10 degrees port.

---

*This example, shared with the author by Professor Craig Fox, is quite possibly an urban legend.

*Negotiator #1:*   This is a fully armed navy vessel — change course now.
*Negotiator #2:*   This is a lighthouse — your move.

**2. Preemptive and Reactive Commitments.**   Jack Hirshleifer suggests that commitments can be usefully divided into two categories: "preemptive" commitments and "reactive" commitments. When a negotiator makes a preemptive commitment, he takes an irrevocable action, such that no response to the opponent's subsequent action is possible. Throwing the steering wheel out of the window in chicken would constitute a preemptive commitment not to swerve. When a negotiator makes a reactive commitment, in contrast, he retains the physical ability to respond to the opponent's subsequent action, but he pledges that the character of his response will be contingent on the opponent's action. Jack Hirshleifer, Game-Theoretic Interpretations of Commitment, in Evolution and the Capacity for Commitment (Randoph M. Nesse ed. 2001).

Preemptive commitments are desirable because they are by definition credible. The problem is that in most negotiating situations true preemptive commitments are impossible. It is difficult for negotiators to make it physically impossible to make last-minute concessions if it would be in their best interests to do so. In contrast, it is easy for negotiators to make reactive commitments, but the problem of convincing the opponent that the commitment is credible remains.

**3. Increasing the Cost of Concessions.**   Given the difficulty of making true preemptive commitments, the more common tactic is for negotiators to take an action that increases the cost of accepting anything less than what they demand to the point that making a concession would be less desirable than reaching impasse. To understand the structure of this approach, consider the following stylized example: Defendant's reservation price for settling her lawsuit out of court is $80,000, but she believes Plaintiff's reservation price is below $50,000. Defendant offers to pay Plaintiff $50,000 to settle the case. She also makes a legally enforceable pledge to donate $30,000 to a political party with whom she disagrees on all issues if and only if she settles her lawsuit for any amount greater than $50,000. Finally, she conveys to Plaintiff that she has made this pledge. At this point, if Plaintiff refuses to accept the $50,000 offer, Defendant could theoretically agree to pay more — nothing makes it physically impossible for her to pay $60,000 or $70,000 — but doing so would impose on her net costs of more than her $80,000 reservation price. Thus, the pledge makes her commitment to pay Plaintiff no more than $50,000 credible. Through the use of a commitment tactic, Defendant has created the same settlement incentive that she would have if her reservation price were $50,000 rather than $80,000.

Although pledging a side payment to a third party would be an unusual negotiating gambit, negotiators routinely attempt to make credible commitments by creating negative reputational consequences to accepting less than what they demand. For example, Defendant might announce at a televised press conference that she will never pay more than $50,000 to settle the lawsuit, guaranteeing that she would suffer a reputational cost were she ever to agree to pay more than that amount. If Plaintiff believes that this reputational cost would be significant, the commitment not to make bargaining concessions can be credible, just as a promised side payment in cash would be.

*4. Irrationality.* This chapter has emphasized that the fundamental roadblock to exercising negotiation power is convincing the other party that you will walk away from the negotiating table if your demands are not met. Because a rational negotiator will not turn his back on possible agreements that would leave him better off than not reaching agreement, this section, as well as the previous two sections, have focused on ways in which negotiators can convince their opponents that they would be better off with an impasse than with an agreement that does not fully satisfy their demands.

Negotiators can also render the threat of impasse credible, however, by convincing their opponents that they are not rational. Consider a mugger who tells his victim, "if you don't give me all of your money, I will kill you." If the mugger were rational, this threat would not be credible, because the money that the victim is likely to be carrying certainly would not be worth the risk that the mugger would incur by carrying out his threat and likely spending many years in prison for murder! Victims are wise to relinquish their wallets, however, because muggers are apt to not rationally weigh the benefits of a wallet against the costs of years of incarceration. In more routine bargaining situations, as well, a negotiator can exercise power by threatening an impasse that will harm both parties if the opponent believes that the negotiator will not take adequate account of the harm that the negotiator would be doing to himself by forcing the impasse. Appearing emotional or otherwise out of control can often have this effect.

*5. Responding to Commitments.* An effective way for a negotiator to respond to a commitment is to undo it — that is, to take actions that put the committing party in the same position he was in before making the commitment. To understand the concept, think about how you would respond in a game of chicken if the other driver threw his steering wheel out of his car, thus making an extremely credible commitment not to swerve. If time would allow, you likely would pick up the steering wheel and reconnect it to the shaft from which it was torn. By physically undoing your opponent's action, you would have rendered his commitment not to swerve not credible, just as it would have been before he threw the steering wheel out the window.

In less extreme situations, commitments are often made merely by a negotiator taking a firm position and pledging not to budge from that position. If the negotiator taking the firm position has a great deal of pride and his adversary knows this, the fact that the negotiator would "lose face" by backing down might make the commitment credible. In this situation, the opposing negotiator can only undo the commitment by creatively finding a way for the first negotiator to accept less than he has demanded without losing face. William Ury advises that a negotiator can help his opponent save face by conceding that the opponent's position would have been justified at an earlier time but arguing that circumstances have changed, or by bringing in a neutral third-party to recommend a resolution of the dispute. William Ury, Getting Past No: Negotiating Your Way From Confrontation to Cooperation 120-122 (1993).

Another way to respond to a commitment is to make a concession that is trivial to you but allows the opponent to claim he received a concession equal to him giving up his commitment. For example, to give Soviet Premier Nikita Khrushchev a face-saving way to remove his country's nuclear missiles from Cuba during the Cuban missile crisis, President Kennedy promised Krushchev that the United States would not invade Cuba — a promise of little cost to Kennedy but of great benefit to Krushchev when explaining why he backed down. See Ury at 122-124.

## D. PATIENCE

A negotiator can make a threat to reject any offer below a certain value credible by convincing her adversary that her demand is her reservation price, or that because she has taken steps to make it so costly to accept less, her demand has effectively become her new reservation price. But what if both negotiators make firm demands that are higher than their respective reservation prices, what we can term adopting an "aggressive" strategy? Who will prevail in the ensuing battle of the wills?

To give the question some content, suppose that Bonnie is suing Clyde. After estimating the expected value of pursuing her case to trial, and discounting for the high costs of litigating, she sets her reservation price at $80,000. Clyde's reservation price is $100,000. In real life, litigants can only estimate each other's reservation prices, but for simplicity assume here that Bonnie knows Clyde's reservation price and

Clyde knows Bonnie's. Consequently, Bonnie demands a settlement of $100,000 (Clyde's reservation price), and Clyde insists he will pay only $80,000 (Bonnie's reservation price). Neither side is willing to make a concession. How will the negotiation end?

The party that is more impatient to reach an agreement will likely lose this zero-sum battle of the wills. Intuitively, this proposition should seem plausible. As Bonnie and Clyde glare at each other across the metaphorical bargaining table, with Bonnie insisting on $100,000 and Clyde insisting on $80,000, the first party to tire of the stand-off will concede to the other's demand. Because both parties know the more impatient one will concede first, the negotiator who is able to convince the other that he or she would be more patient in such a stand-off can exercise bargaining power before such a stand-off occurs. If Bonnie knows she is less patient than Clyde, she can reason that she would lose any extended stand-off, so she might as well concede most of the cooperative surplus to Clyde before such a stand-off begins.

The source of Clyde's power in such a situation is similar to, but slightly different than, the sources of power discussed in Sections A-C of this chapter. As is true in the previous sections, Clyde's power comes from being able to threaten to refuse to reach an agreement if Bonnie does not give him what he demands. The difference is the precise nature of Clyde's threat. Instead of threatening to pursue his (real or perceived) BATNA if Bonnie refuses to accede to his demand, Clyde threatens to delay reaching an agreement. Because nearly all negotiators are somewhat impatient — that is, they would prefer reaching an agreement now to reaching an agreement later — delay will be somewhat painful to Clyde. But his threat can still be credible if both parties know that delay will be more painful to Bonnie than to Clyde. Because Bonnie will suffer more from delay, Clyde can logically reason that the costs of delaying an agreement will be more than compensated for by the benefits of capturing more of the cooperative surplus.

As the previous paragraph suggests, the power of patience is best understood by thinking of patience as a measure of how costly it is for a party to delay in reaching an agreement. A negotiator is patient if the costs to her of continuing negotiations rather than reaching an immediate agreement are relatively low; a negotiator is impatient if the costs to her of continuing negotiations are relatively high.

Because patience provides bargaining power, negotiators often go to great lengths not only to convince the opponent that their BATNA is good and their reservation point is high, but also that they can afford to be more patient than the opponent at the bargaining table. In other words, a negotiator might try to communicate implicitly the message that "I can bargain indefinitely and suffer few costs, whereas you will find protracted negotiations so costly that you will have to concede the

majority of the cooperative surplus to me before the costs ruin you."
In labor negotiations, for example, it is common for both union and
management to try to convince each other that their side would suffer
lower costs in the case of a strike and the other would be forced to
concede first. In litigation, the party with more resources might
threaten to deliberately increase the costs of ongoing discovery because
it is better able to bear these costs than the party with fewer resources,
thus increasing the relative burden of protracted negotiations on the
weaker party.

When the parties have different estimates of the relative costs to the
parties of continued negotiations, they can easily fail to reach agreement and continue bargaining until one party exhausts its ability to
continue (i.e., the union strike fund is depleted) or the cooperative
surplus originally available is completely destroyed (i.e., the company
loses so many customers that its future prospects become so dim it
cannot afford to offer union members any wage superior to the union
members' BATNA of finding another job).

Because patience is an important factor in a negotiator's ability to
exercise bargaining power, it is important to understand what causes a
party to be impatient. Put another way, why is delay more costly to
some negotiators than to others? Two factors are the primary drivers
of impatience: costs of time, and costs of negotiating. The remainder
of this section describes these two types of costs and investigates how
they can reduce a negotiator's ability to exercise power.

## 1.  Costs of Lost Time

One or both parties to a negotiation may suffer costs by not being able
to make use of whatever they would otherwise gain from the negotiation during the time that bargaining is deadlocked. In our hypothetical, a protracted negotiation is costly to Bonnie, because for every day
settlement is delayed, she will lose a day's use of the settlement money.
Exactly how costly this will be depends on Bonnie's circumstances. If
Bonnie does not plan to use the money immediately, delay costs her
the interest she would earn on the settlement amount. If prejudgment
interest is available *and* it is set at the market rate, Bonnie might suffer
little or no cost of delay. If Bonnie needs the settlement money immediately for food, rent, health care, etc., her cost of delay might be
extremely high, weakening her ability to hold out for her demand and
making it more likely that she will accept Clyde's offer (so long as it is
higher than her reservation price).

If prejudgment interest is available to Bonnie, Clyde suffers a cost
of lost time in that amount less the return he can earn on the settlement money before turning it over to Bonnie. Depending on whether

the prejudgment interest rate is higher, lower, or the same as the investment return that Clyde can earn, his cost of lost time might be high, low, or even negative (that is, delay could actually benefit him). If Bonnie cannot collect prejudgment interest, Clyde will benefit from a time delay, at least financially. In either case, Clyde might suffer nonfinancial costs of protracted negotiations. What he stands to gain from settlement is a release from Bonnie's claims against him. If the threat of litigation is emotionally burdensome to him, the cost to him of each day that passes without an agreement might be extremely high, and he might be very impatient to reach a settlement. If Clyde is a corporation rather than an individual, the threat of litigation might not burden him personally, but it could potentially entail significant costs nonetheless. For example, investors might be leery of investing in a company facing an uncertain litigation outcome, and suppliers might be hesitant to enter into long-term contracts with such a company. Each day that passes without an agreement therefore might impose additional opportunity costs on the corporation.

## 2.  Costs of Negotiating

Negotiation deadlock means more negotiation is necessary. This can create both financial and nonfinancial costs. Financial costs are greatest when a party negotiates through an agent. In legal negotiating situations where parties bargain through lawyers, a drawn-out negotiating process means higher attorneys' fees (assuming the lawyers charge by the hour) than would a quick settlement. Even if a principal party negotiates on his own behalf, more negotiation often means higher transportation costs and time away from other profitable opportunities.

In litigation situations, negotiations often proceed in parallel with the discovery process by which the parties prepare for the possibility of adjudication. As settlement negotiations drag on, the litigants often suffer high costs of preparing their own cases and responding to the discovery requests of the other party. If these costs are significantly higher for one party, or if the costs are nominally equivalent but relatively more burdensome for one given a disparity of resources, the party facing the relatively higher costs will often be more anxious to reach agreement, thus conferring substantial bargaining power on his opponent.

Ongoing negotiations can also have nonfinancial costs that make negotiators impatient to reach agreement. Bargaining can be an unpleasant activity, especially if the negotiations turn acrimonious or the opposing negotiator is personally aggressive, obnoxious, or disrespectful. Even negotiators who find the bargaining process stimulating and challenging can also find it unpleasant if it lasts for an extended period of time. At the margin, if lengthy negotiations do not cut into other profit-making opportunities, they probably cut into leisure opportunities that the negotiator would prefer to pursue rather than spending more time at the bargaining table.

## Notes

*1. Personality.* Impatience is not only an externally created phenomenon. Many negotiators' impatience stems from their personality — emotionally, they desire a quick resolution to problems even if the visible costs of delay are minor. Because impatience is a disadvantage in bargaining, negotiators who visibly remain patient even when they are feeling extremely impatient will likely achieve better results, holding all other factors equal. Cultivating a reputation for patience can also pay large dividends. If a negotiator believes that his opponent is patient in bargaining, he is less likely to hold firm to demands for agreements that are better than his reservation price, and he is more likely to yield to demands made by the opponent, knowing that engaging in a battle of the wills is likely to yield delay and negotiating costs without a more favorable agreement.

*2. Miscalculation and Negotiation Breakdown.* When negotiators adopt aggressive strategies, a common outcome is negotiation breakdown. When there is no bargaining zone, this is a desirable result, since no possible agreement would leave both parties better off than they would be pursuing their BATNAs. But when parties adopt aggressive strategies, it is quite possible for an impasse to occur even in circumstances in which there is a bargaining zone. This can happen for one of two reasons: one negotiator (or both) misestimates the other's reservation price; or one negotiator (or both) misestimates the other's patience.

To illustrate the first situation, assume that Bonnie's reservation price is $70,000 and Clyde's is $120,000, and that Bonnie adopts an aggressive strategy by threatening not to settle for any amount less than $125,000 and sticking to this position. Because this amount exceeds Clyde's reservation price (and therefore he would prefer to go to trial than to pay that amount), negotiations will fail, and an opportunity for a mutually desirable agreement will be lost.

To illustrate the second situation, now assume that Bonnie adopts an aggressive, but somewhat less aggressive strategy, and threatens not to settle for any amount less than $100,000. Meanwhile, Clyde also adopts an aggressive strategy, threatening not to settle for any amount greater than $80,000. Both parties hold firm to their demands, believing that the other will be more impatient and will ultimately concede. In this case, obviously one party is mistaken about the other's level of patience, and unless that party revises his or her estimate, an impasse will result. The reason is that either (1) the costs of delay and negotiation will eat away at the cooperative surplus that the parties could capture by reaching agreement such that there is no longer a bargaining zone, or (2) an external constraint will render agreement impossible.

Assume that Bonnie estimates the expected value of trial is $100,000, but she sets her reservation price at $70,000 because she estimates a trial will cost $30,000 in attorneys' fees. As settlement negotiations drag on and the trial date approaches, Bonnie's lawyer prepares for trial at a cost of $20,000. At this point — now that trial preparation is done — actually staging the trial will only cost $10,000 more than settlement, so Bonnie revises her reservation price to $90,000. Now Bonnie's reservation price is higher than Clyde's demand, making settlement impossible. At this point, this situation looks like the first situation.

Alternatively, assume that on the morning of the trial Bonnie's reservation price remains lower than Clyde's demand, and Clyde's reservation price remains higher than Bonnie's demand, such that a settlement at the amount demanded by either would still be mutually desirable relative to no agreement. Both parties know that they would be better off accepting the other's demand than going to trial, but both believe the other's patience is about to run out. If both are wrong, the trial will take place, rendering settlement impossible.*

**3. Rational Breakdown.**    Is refusing to concede to an opponent's aggressive strategy even though conceding would give you an outcome superior to your reservation price ever a rational approach to negotiation? The answer is yes. As one analysis puts the point, a litigant "computes his optimal demand by balancing the gain from settling on more favorable terms against the risk of trial." Robert Cooter et al., Bargaining in the Shadow of the Law: A Testable Model of Strategic Behavior, 11 J. Legal Stud. 225, 237 (1982). Thus, the negotiator's best strategy depends on his analysis of the expected value of conceding and of not conceding.

If Clyde has offered an $80,000 settlement — $10,000 more than Bonnie's reservation price of $70,000 — should Bonnie accept or adopt an aggressive strategy by demanding $100,000 and refuse to yield? The answer depends on Bonnie's *estimate* of the likelihood that her aggres-

*Reality is a bit more complicated than this example. Bonnie and Clyde could still settle the case right up to the moment the jury announces its verdict. Even after the verdict, a settlement might be possible with one or both parties giving up their rights to appeal. The important insight is that at some point events will occur that make even a mutually desirable negotiated agreement moot.

sive strategy will succeed and Clyde will agree to her demand. Remember that Bonnie cannot know precisely Clyde's reservation price or his level of patience. Let us assume that Bonnie estimates that there is an 80 percent chance that Clyde's reservation price is lower than $100,000, and a 20 percent chance his reservation price is higher than $100,000. This means that there is a 20 percent chance that Bonnie's demand will be outside the bargaining zone and a trial will result, which she values at $70,000. Let us assume also that Bonnie estimates that, if her demand is within the bargaining zone, there is a 75 percent chance that Clyde will accept it and a 25 percent chance that he will hold out for $80,000 because he believes Bonnie will ultimately agree to that amount. This means that, with regards to this 80 percent probability, there is a 75 percent chance that Bonnie will receive a $100,000 settlement and a 25 percent chance that a trial will result, which she values at $70,000. By combining these probabilities, we can find out the expected value to Bonnie of making a firm $100,000 demand: (20% × $70,000) + (80% × 25% × $70,000) + (80% × 75% × $100,000) = $88,000. Should Bonnie accept Clyde's offer of $80,000 or adopt an aggressive strategy with an expected payoff of $88,000?

At this point, Bonnie's calculation is identical to the approach she used (or should have!) when she calculated her reservation price. Bonnie's best alternative to reaching an immediate agreement with Clyde is adopting an aggressive strategy. She needs to determine what her reservation price would be for an immediate settlement. If Clyde's $80,000 offer exceeds that reservation price, Bonnie should accept it; if it does not, Bonnie should reject it. Relative to an immediate settlement, adopting the aggressive strategy will entail accepting delay costs (it will take longer to get her money), transaction costs (more negotiation), and the risk associated with an uncertain outcome. If Bonnie is risk neutral, is paying her lawyer on a straight contingency basis rather than hourly, and has no immediate need for the settlement money, her reservation price for an immediate settlement is probably higher than $80,000. If she is extremely risk averse, is paying her lawyer a high hourly fee, and/or has immediate and important uses for the settlement money, her reservation price might be substantially below $80,000, making Clyde's offer attractive.

**4. Problems with Power Tactics.**   When effectively used by a skilled negotiator, power tactics can be extremely effective. Power tactics have their pitfalls, however. Among them are the following:

*(a) The Negotiator's Claims or Threats May Not Be Credible.*   A well-prepared opponent will have a clear idea of his own reservation price and a good estimate of the negotiator's, making it quite difficult for the negotiator to manipulate the opponent's perceptions of the bargaining zone. The negotiator's commitments not to agree to accept

anything less than the lion's share of the cooperative surplus may not be credible. The negotiator may not be able to be more patient than his opponent or, even if he has the ability to be more patient, he might not be able to convince the opponent of this.

(b) *Negotiators Can Misestimate the Bargaining Zone.*   Power tactics can only succeed if the negotiator's stated reservation price and his opponent's actual reservation price create a bargaining zone. The problem is that negotiators rarely know their opponents' reservation prices with certainty. Suppose a defendant estimates a plaintiff's reservation price is $100,000 and claims his reservation is $100,000 or threatens to pay no less than that amount. If the plaintiff's reservation price is actually $110,000, there can be no agreement, even if the plaintiff believes the defendant's claims are credible.

(c) *Power Tactics Can Produce an Emotional Response.*   Power tactics rely on the expectation that the opponent will react rationally and unemotionally to them. For example, if a buyer credibly claims he will pay no more than $50,000 for the seller's business, he assumes that the seller will agree to accept $50,000 if the seller's reservation price is in fact less than that amount. The seller, however, may react emotionally to this tactic, vowing to never do business with the buyer, even if this inflicts damage to his own interest. This is especially likely if the opponent believes that the commitment tactic is unfair or contrary to relevant norms of acceptable negotiating tactics (a point developed in detail in Chapter 6). No one likes to be on the receiving end of power tactics, and no one wants to cultivate a reputation as a patsy!

(d) *Power Tactics Can Affect Reputations.*   The use of power tactics can cultivate a reputation of being an uncooperative negotiator and/or one who takes advantage of his adversaries. Some negotiators wish to cultivate such a reputation. Many others, however, wish to avoid developing such a reputation either because they believe it will cause others to avoid doing business with them in the future, or merely because they do not want others, especially colleagues in a profession, to think of them this way.

## DISCUSSION QUESTIONS AND PROBLEMS

### 1. *Revealing BATNAs and Reservation Prices.*

(a) You are moving to a new city and you are looking to buy a house. On your real estate agent's advice, you have been preapproved for a loan by a local bank. The bank has issued you a letter that states it has approved you for a loan on any house with a purchase price of up to but not exceeding $200,000. After touring many houses, you have identified the perfect home for you, which has an asking price of $211,000. When you sit down to negotiate with the seller, will you reveal your $200,000 reservation price and show the seller the letter from the bank to verify it? Why or why not?

(b) You are looking to buy a new car. After looking at many models, you have decided that you would most like to buy a Honda Accord — if the price is right, of course. Having done your homework, you know you can purchase a similar Toyota Camry (with the same options) for $18,000. The Honda dealer is asking $19,200 for the Accord that you want. Will you tell him that your BATNA is to purchase the Camry for $18,000? Why or why not? Would it matter to your answer if the dealer was asking $17,500 for the Accord?

(c) Based on your understanding of the determinants of negotiation power and your answers to the previous two questions, what generalizations can you make about when you should reveal your BATNA and/or reservation price and when you should keep that information confidential?

**2. The Vanishing Demand.**   One practicing attorney proposes the following negotiation tactic for plaintiffs' attorneys: some time after making a settlement demand that the defense has refused to accept, send the defense attorney a letter referring to that demand and stating, without providing further information, that the "demand is hereby withdrawn effective immediately." Richard G. Halpern, Settlement Negotiations: Taking Control, 34 Trial 64, 66 (Feb. 1998). How might this tactic benefit the negotiator who makes use of it?

**3. The Roosevelt Photo Deconstructed.**   Using your knowledge of the concepts of BATNAs, reservation prices, and bargaining zones, describe exactly how the Roosevelt presidential campaign's negotiating technique with the Chicago photography studio, described in Section B, Note 1 of this chapter, helped the campaign to receive such a favorable negotiation result. To what extent were the successful tactics completely honest, and to what extent were they misleading? Would you feel ethically comfortable adopting the tactic used by the Roosevelt campaign?

**4. Credible Commitments.**
(a) In an extensive study of settlement behavior in various types of lawsuits, Samuel Gross & Kent Syverud observe that "insurance companies systematically offer only a fraction of the expected value of personal injury judgments in cases with substantial damages. . . ." Samuel Gross & Kent Syverud, Getting to No: A Study of Settlement Negotiations and the Selection of Cases for Trial, 90 Mich. L. Rev. 319, 353 (1991). Can such low offers be credible? Why or why not?

(b) You have been offered a position as an associate at a large law firm at a salary of $70,000. You graduated #1 in your class, and feel you are far more qualified than most of the other associates to whom the firm has made offers. Nonetheless, the firm says that it will not offer you a higher salary. Is the firm's position credible? Why or why not?

(c) The President of the United States and leaders of Congress are attempting to enact legislation to fund transportation infrastructure. Both President and Congress strongly support new funding for transportation and would prefer any legislation to no legislation at all, but the President wants most of the money to go for public transportation (i.e., subways and light rail) subsidies while Congress prefers building more interstate highways. You are advising the President on negotiation strategy. Can you conceive of a commitment strategy to recommend to the President? Does your recommendation call for a "preemptive" or "reactive" commitment? How successful do you think your strategy would be in achieving the President's objective, and how would you anticipate Congress would respond to it?

**5. Responding to a Commitment.**   You represent the defendant in a personal injury lawsuit. The plaintiff was injured by your client's product. Medical care cost her $5,000, and she suffered $10,000 in lost wages when she was recuperating from the injuries. She has filed suit against your client for negligent design, claiming $200,000 in damages. You believe that there is nothing wrong with the product's design, that the injury was caused solely by the negligence of the plaintiff, and that the chances of the plaintiff prevailing in court are extremely small. You are willing to pay a small amount of money to settle the case to avoid the cost and the negative publicity that would accompany a trial. Last week, the plaintiff's attorney held a news conference and stated that his client would accept no settlement for less than the $200,000 necessary to fully compensate her for her injuries — a figure far higher than your reservation price. What negotiating approaches might you employ to try to undo or reduce the force of that commitment and avoid a trial?

**6. Irrationality and Power.**   It is often suggested that irrationality or emotional instability can be an asset in negotiations. One analysis of emotion in negotiation puts the point this way: "Obviously, if a negotiator can convince the opponent that he is crazy, this can be an effective strategy." Leigh L. Thompson et al., Some Like It Hot: The Case for the Emotional Negotiator, in Shared Cognition in Organizations: The Management of Knowledge 139, 155 (Leigh L. Thompson et al. eds. 1999). In light of your understanding of negotiating power, why do you think convincing an adversary that you are irrational can be useful? Is it also useful to *actually be* irrational? How might a display of anger work in the same way or differently from a display of irrationality?

**7. *The Release Tactic.*** Consider a bargaining tactic often used in litigation by defense attorneys: mailing the plaintiff's lawyer a check for an amount of money less than the plaintiff's demand along with a release form for the plaintiff to sign (if the plaintiff signs the release, he can cash the check). Do you think this is a useful tactic? Why or why not? Consider what you have learned both about power and the psychology of negotiation.

**8. *Reputation.*** Negotiators who routinely attempt to get what they want by overtly employing power tactics can develop a reputation as being unfair, being a bully, and being unpleasant to deal with. In what types of negotiating contexts might such a reputation be harmful to a negotiator generally or a lawyer-negotiator specifically? Might such a reputation ever be desirable?

# Chapter 6

# Fair Division and Related Social Norms

When negotiators are unable or unwilling to divide the cooperative surplus created by an agreement with power tactics, the basic problem of distribution remains. Consequently, negotiators often reach agreements by appealing to substantive or procedural norms of fairness.

Why is fairness an important concept in negotiation? Consider the results of an experiment known as the "ultimatum game," which consists of two players, the "proposer" and the "responder." The experimenter gives the proposer a certain amount of money (the "stake"). The proposer must then propose a division of the stake to the responder. The responder may either accept the proposed division, in which case the money is divided according to the proposal, or the responder may reject the proposed division, in which case the stake goes back to the experimenter and both parties get nothing. In this game, the rational responder's reservation price should be 1 cent. After all, his BATNA is receiving nothing, so any non-zero offer is superior to not reaching an agreement.

It turns out, however, across many iterations of the experiment in a variety of settings, that most responders will reject a proposal of less than 20-30 percent of the stake, even though doing so leaves them worse off than they would be had they accepted. See Ernst Fehr & Simon Gachter, Fairness and Retaliation: The Economics of Reciprocity, 14 J. Econ. Persp. 159 (2000); Richard H. Thaler, Anomalies: The Ultimatum Game, 2 J. Econ. Persp. 195 (1988). In one study, if the responder rejected the offer, he was permitted to present the proposer with a proposed division of a much smaller stake. The researchers found that a large majority of rejected offers were followed by a proposed division that would provide the original responder with a lesser payoff than if he had accepted the original proposal! Jack Ochs & Alvin E. Roth, An Experimental Study of Sequential Bargaining, 79 Am. Econ. Rev. 335 (1989). The conclusion most often drawn from these results is that players will reject offers they view as "unfair," even when doing so is costly to them.

Negotiators, like players of the ultimatum game, will often reject even profitable offers if they perceive them as being unfair. Consequently, concluding an agreement often requires negotiators not only to believe that the deal point lies within the bargaining zone, and therefore is mutually beneficial, but also that the division of the co-operative surplus is a fair one. Stating this thesis, however, merely begs the question of what types of divisions will negotiators perceive as being fair. "Fairness," after all, has no established definition. It is a socially constructed concept that depends on context and the negotiators' world views. In many negotiation settings, what deal point is most fair will be heatedly contested.

While it is unsurprising that negotiators want to be treated fairly, there is also evidence that many negotiators also place a high value on treating the opponent fairly, at least in some types of situations. Consider experimental results of the "dictator game," which differs from the ultimatum game in an important way: the responder must accept the proposer's suggested division of the stakes. This is to say the dictator game is not a "game" at all. One subject unilaterally decides how to divide the money at issue. Even under these circumstances, the majority of proposers offer a non-zero portion of the stakes to the completely helpless responder. See, e.g., Max H. Bazerman & Margaret A. Neale, The Role of Fairness Considerations and Relationships in a Judgmental Perspective of Negotiation 87, 91 in Barriers to Conflict Resolution (Kenneth Arrow et al. eds. 1995).

## A.  THE RECIPROCITY NORM

When people picture a negotiation in their minds, they often conjure up visions of offers and counteroffers flying back and forth like a ping-pong ball: the buyer makes a low offer, the seller responds with a high demand; the buyer raises his offer, the seller in turn lowers his demand; and so forth until the positions of the parties converge. Howard Raiffa has called this "the negotiation dance." Howard Raiffa, The Art and Science of Negotiation 47 (1982). Many negotiations, although certainly not all, include such a dance. Why doesn't a buyer usually begin negotiations by stating his best offer? Why doesn't a seller usually begin by stating his lowest demand?

Social convention demands reciprocity. If one person gives something of value to another, we usually expect that the recipient will reciprocate in some way. When people demonstrate reciprocity, they satisfy social convention. The next excerpt describes a host of social science research on the power of the reciprocity norm. When you read the excerpt, think about how it helps to explain the negotiation dance.

## ■ Robert B. Cialdini, Influence: Science and Practice*
19-49 (1993)

A few years ago, a university professor tried a little experiment. He sent Christmas cards to a sample of perfect strangers. Although he expected some reaction, the response he received was amazing — holiday cards addressed to him came pouring back from people who had never met nor heard of him. The great majority of those who returned cards never inquired into the identity of the unknown professor. . . .

While small in scope, this study shows the action of one of the most potent of the weapons of influence around us — the rule of reciprocation. The rule says that we should try to repay, in kind, what another person has provided us. If a woman does us a favor, we should do her one in return; if a man sends us a birthday present, we should remember his birthday with a gift of our own; if a couple invites us to a party, we should be sure to invite them to one of ours. By virtue of the reciprocity rule, then, we are *obligated* to the future repayment of favors, gifts, invitations, and the like. So typical is it for indebtedness to accompany the receipt of such things that a phrase like "much obliged" has become a synonym for "thank you," not only in the English language but in others as well.

The impressive aspect of reciprocation with its accompanying sense of obligation is its pervasiveness in human culture. It is so widespread that, after intensive study, Alvin Gouldner (1960), along with other sociologists, report that all human societies subscribe to the rule. Within each society it seems pervasive also; it permeates exchanges of every kind. Indeed, it may well be that a developed system of indebtedness flowing from the rule of reciprocation is a unique property of human culture. The noted archaeologist Richard Leakey ascribes the essence of what makes us human to the reciprocity system. He claims that we are human because our ancestors learned to share food and skills "in an honored network of obligation" (Leakey & Lewin, 1978). Cultural anthropologists Lionel Tiger and Robin Fox (1971) view this "web of indebtedness" as a unique adaptive mechanism of human beings, allowing for the division of labor, the exchange of diverse forms of goods and different services, and the creation of interdependencies that bind individuals together into highly efficient units. . . .

*Robert B. Cialdini, Influence: Science and Practice. Copyright © 1993 by Allyn & Bacon. Reprinted/adapted by permission.

To understand how the rule of reciprocation can be exploited by one who recognizes it as the weapon of influence it certainly is, we might closely examine an experiment conducted by psychologist Dennis Regan (1971). A subject who participated in the study rated, along with another subject, the quality of some paintings as part of an experiment on "art appreciation." The other rater — we can call him Joe — was only posing as a fellow subject and was actually Dr. Regan's assistant. For our purposes, the experiment took place under two different conditions. In some cases, Joe did a small, unsolicited favor for the true subject. During a short rest period, Joe left the room for a couple of minutes and returned with two bottles of Coca-Cola, one for the subject and one for himself, saying "I asked him [the experimenter] if I could get myself a Coke, and he said it was OK, so I bought one for you, too." In other cases, Joe did not provide the subject with a favor; he simply returned from the two minute break empty-handed. In all other respects, however, Joe behaved identically.

Later on, after the paintings had all been rated and the experimenter had momentarily left the room, Joe asked the subject to do him a favor. He indicated that he was selling raffle tickets for a new car and that if he sold the most tickets, he would win a $50 prize. Joe's request was for the subject to buy some raffle tickets at 25 cents apiece: "Any would help, the more the better." The major finding of the study concerns the number of tickets subjects purchased from Joe under the two conditions. Without question, Joe was more successful in selling his raffle tickets to the subjects who had received his earlier favor. Apparently feeling that they owed him something, these subjects bought twice as many tickets as the subjects who had not been given the prior favor. . . .

Think of the implications. People we might ordinarily dislike — unsavory or unwelcome sales operators, disagreeable acquaintances, representatives of strange or unpopular organizations — can greatly increase the chance that we will do what they wish merely by providing us with a small favor prior to their requests. Let's take an example that, by now, many of us have encountered. The Hare Krishna Society is an Eastern religious sect with centuries-old roots traceable to the Indian city of Calcutta. Its spectacular modern-day story occurred in the 1970s when it experienced a remarkable growth, not only in followers, but also in wealth and property. The economic growth was funded through a variety of activities, the principal and still most visible of which is society members' requests for donations from passersby in public places. During the early history of the group in this country, the solicitation for contributions was attempted in a fashion memorable for anyone who saw it. Groups of Krishna devotees — often with shaved heads, and wearing ill-fitting robes, leg wrappings, beads, and bells —

would canvass a city street, chanting and bobbing in unison while begging for funds.

Although highly effective as an attention-getting technique, this practice did not work especially well for fund raising. The average American considered the Krishnas weird, to say the least, and was reluctant to provide money to support them. It quickly became clear to the society that it had a considerable public-relations problem. The people being asked for contributions did not like the way the members looked, dressed, or acted. Had the society been an ordinary commercial organization, the solution would have been simple — change the things the public does not like. . . .

The Krishnas' resolution was brilliant. They switched to a fund-raising tactic that made it unnecessary for their targets to have positive feelings toward the fund-raisers. They began to employ a donation-request procedure that engaged the rule for reciprocation, which, as demonstrated by the Regan study, was strong enough to overcome dislike for the requester. The new strategy still involved the solicitation of contributions in public places with much pedestrian traffic (airports are a favorite), but, before a donation was requested, the target person was given a "gift" — a book (usually the *Bhagavad Gita*), the *Back to Godhead* magazine of the society, or, in the most cost-effective version, a flower. The unsuspecting passersby who suddenly found flowers pressed into their hands or pinned to their jackets were under no circumstances allowed to give them back even if they asserted that they did not want them "No, it is our gift to you," said the solicitor, refusing to take it back. Only after the Krishna member had thus brought the force of the reciprocation rule to bear on the situation was the target asked to provide a contribution to the society. This benefactor-before-beggar strategy has been wildly successful for the Hare Krishna Society, producing large-scale economic gains and funding, the ownership of temples, businesses, houses, and property in 321 centers in the United States and abroad. . . .

It is a testament to the societal value of reciprocation that even those of us who know what the Krishnas are up to have chosen to avoid them or to deflect their flowers rather than to withstand the force of their gift giving directly by taking the flower and walking away with it. The reciprocation rule that empowers their tactic is too strong — and socially beneficial — for us to want to challenge head-on. . . .

The reciprocity rule governs many situations of a purely interpersonal nature where neither money nor commercial exchange is at issue. Perhaps my favorite illustration of the enormous force available from the reciprocation weapon of influence comes from such a situation. The European scientist Eibl-Eibesfeldt (1975) provides the account of a German soldier during World War I whose job was to capture enemy soldiers for interrogation. Because of the nature of the trench warfare at that time, it was extremely difficult for armies to cross the no-man's-land between opposing front lines, but it was not so difficult for a single soldier to crawl across and slip into an enemy trench position. The armies of the Great War had experts who regularly did so to capture enemy soldiers, who would then be brought back for questioning. The German expert had often successfully completed such missions in the past and was sent on another. Once again, he skillfully negotiated the area between fronts and surprised a lone enemy soldier in his trench. The unsuspecting soldier, who had been eating at the time, was easily disarmed. The frightened captive, with only a piece of bread in his hand, then performed what may have been the most important act of his life. He gave his enemy some of the bread. So affected was the German by this gift that he could not complete his mission. He turned from his benefactor and recrossed the no-man's-land empty-handed to face the wrath of his superiors. . . .

The ability of uninvited gifts to produce feelings of obligation is recognized by a variety of organizations besides the Krishnas. How many times has each of us received small gifts through the mail — personalized address labels, greeting cards, key rings — from charitable agencies that ask for funds in an accompanying note? I have received five in just the past year, two from disabled veterans' groups and the others from missionary schools and hospitals. In each case, there was a common thread in the accompanying message. The goods that were enclosed were to be considered a gift from the organization; and money I wished to send should not be regarded as payment but rather as a return offering. As the letter from one of the missionary programs stated, the packet of greeting cards I had been sent was not to be directly paid for but was designed "to encourage your [my] kindness." If we look past the obvious tax advantage, we can see why it would be beneficial for the organization to have the cards viewed as a gift instead of merchandise: There is a strong cultural pressure to reciprocate a gift, even an unwanted one; but there is no such pressure to purchase an unwanted commercial product. . . .

There is yet another feature of the reciprocity rule that allows it to be exploited for profit. Paradoxically, although the rule developed to promote equal exchanges between partners, it can be used to bring about decidedly unequal results. The rule demands that one sort of action be reciprocated with a similar sort of action. A favor is to be met with another favor; it is not to be met with neglect and certainly not with attack; however, considerable flexibility is allowed. A small initial favor can produce a sense of obligation to agree to a substantially larger return favor. Since, as we have already seen, the rule allows one person to choose the nature of the indebting first favor *and* the nature of the debt-canceling return favor, we could easily be manipulated into an unfair exchange by those who might wish to exploit the rule.

Once again, we turn to the Regan experiment for evidence. Remember in that study, Joe gave one group of subjects a bottle of Coca-Cola as an initiating gift and later asked all subjects to buy some of his raffle tickets at 25 cents apiece. What I have so far neglected to mention is that the study was done in the late 1960s, when the price of a Coke was a dime. On the average, subjects who had been given a 10-cent drink bought two of Joe's raffle tickets, although some bought as many as seven. Even if we look just at the average, though, we can tell that Joe made quite a deal. A 500 percent return on investment is respectable indeed! . . .

. . . A person who violates the reciprocity rule by accepting without attempting to return the good acts of others is disliked by the social group. The exception, of course, occurs when a person is prevented from repayment by reasons of circumstance or ability. For the most part, however, there is a genuine distaste for an individual who fails to conform to the dictates of the reciprocity rule. Moocher and welsher are unsavory labels to be scrupulously shunned. So undesirable are they that people will sometimes agree to an unequal exchange in order to dodge them. . . .

I was walking down the street when I was approached by an 11 or 12-year old boy. He introduced himself and said he was selling tickets to the annual Boy Scouts Circus to be held on the upcoming Saturday night. He asked if I wished to buy any tickets at $5 apiece. Since one of the last places I wanted to spend Saturday evening was with the Boy Scouts, I declined. "Well," he said, "if you don't want to buy any tickets, how about buying some of our big chocolate bars? They're only $1 each." I bought a couple and, right away, realized that something noteworthy had happened. I knew that to be the case because (a) I do not like chocolate bars; (b) I do like dollars; (c) I was standing there with two of his chocolate bars; and (d) he was walking away with two of my dollars.

To try to understand precisely what had happened, I went to my office and called a meeting of my research assistants. In discussing the situation, we began to see how the reciprocity rule was implicated in my compliance with the request to buy the candy bars. The general rule says that a person who acts in a certain way toward us is entitled to a similar return action. We have already seen that one consequence of the rule is an obligation to repay favors we have received. Another consequence of the rule, however, is an obligation to make a concession to someone who has made a concession to us. As my research group thought about it, we realized that was exactly the position the Boys Scout had put me in. His request that I purchase some $1 chocolate bars had been put in the form of a concession on his part; it was presented as a retreat from his request that I buy some $5 tickets. If I were to live up to the dictates of the reciprocation rule, there had to be a concession on my part. As we have seen, there was such a concession: I changed from noncompliant to compliant when he moved from a larger to a smaller request, even though I was not really interested in *either* of the things he offered. . . .

The reciprocation rule brings about mutual concession in two ways. The first is obvious; it pressures the recipient of an already-made concession to respond in kind. The second, while not so obvious, is pivotally important. Because of a recipient's obligation to reciprocate, people are freed to make the *initial* concession and, thereby, to begin the beneficial process of exchange. After all, if there were no social obligation to reciprocate a concession, who would want to make the first sacrifice? To do so would be to risk giving up something and getting nothing back. However, with the rule in effect, we can feel safe making the first sacrifice to our partner, who is obligated to offer a return sacrifice.

. . . Posing as representatives of the "County Youth Counseling Program," [Cialdini and research assistants] approached college students walking on campus and asked if they would be willing to chaperon a group of juvenile delinquents on a day trip to the zoo. This idea of being responsible for a group of juvenile delinquents of unspecified age for hours in a public place without pay was hardly an inviting one for these students. As we expected, the great majority (83 percent) refused. Yet we obtained very different results from a similar sample of college students who were asked the very same question with one difference. Before we invited them to serve as unpaid chaperons on the zoo trip, we asked them for an even larger favor — to spend two hours per week as counselors to juvenile delinquents for a minimum of two years. It was only after they refused this extreme request, as all did, that we made the small, zoo-trip request. By presenting the zoo trip as a retreat from our initial request, our success rate increased dramatically. Three times as many of the students approached in this manner volunteered to serve as zoo chaperons (Cialdini, Vincent, Lewis, Catalan, Wheeler, & Darby, 1975). . . .

It seems that certain of the most successful television producers, such as Grant Tinker and Garry Marshall, are masters of this art in their negotiations with network censors. In a candid interview with *TV Guide* writer Dick Russell (1978), both admitted to "deliberately inserting lines into scripts that a censor's sure to ax" so that they could then retreat to the lines they really wanted to include. Marshall appears especially active in this regard. Consider, for example, the following excerpt from Russell's article:

But Marshall . . . not only admits his tricks . . . he seems to revel in them. On one episode of his [then] top-rated "Laverne and Shirley" series, for example, he says, "We had a situation where Squiggy's in a rush to get out of his apartment and meet some girls upstairs. He says: 'Will you hurry up before I lose my lust?' But in the script we put something even stronger, knowing the censors would cut it. They did; so we asked innocently, well, how about 'lose my lust?' 'That's good,' they said. Sometimes you gotta go at 'em backward."

On the "Happy Days" series, the biggest censorship fight was over the word *virgin*. That time, says Marshall, "I knew we'd have trouble, so we put the word in seven times, hoping they'd cut six and keep one. It worked. We used the same pattern again with the word *pregnant*." . . .

Let's . . . say that I wish to borrow $5 from you. By beginning with a request for $10, I really can't lose. If you agree to it, I will have received from you twice the amount I would have settled for. If, on the other hand, you turn down my initial request, I can retreat to the $5 favor that I desired from the outset and, through the action of the reciprocity and contrast principles, greatly enhance my likelihood of success. Either way, I benefit; it's a case of heads I win, tails you lose. . . .

. . . The desirable side effects of making concessions during an interaction with other people are nicely shown in studies of the way people bargain with each other. One experiment, conducted by social psychologists at UCLA, offers an especially apt demonstration (Benton, Kelley, & Liebling, 1972). A subject in that study faced a "negotiation opponent" and was told to bargain with the opponent concerning how to divide between themselves a certain amount of money provided by the experimenters. The subject was also informed that if no mutual agreement could be reached after a certain period of bargaining, no one would get any money. Unknown to the subject, the opponent was really an experimental assistant who had been previously instructed to bargain with the subject in one of three ways. With some of the subjects, the opponent made an extreme first demand, assigning virtually all of the money to himself and stubbornly persisted in that demand throughout the negotiations. With another group of subjects, the opponent began with a demand that was moderately favorable to himself; he, too, steadfastly refused to move from that position during the negotiations. With a third group, the opponent began with the extreme demand and then gradually retreated to the more moderate one during the course of the bargaining.

. . . [C]ompared to the two other approaches, the strategy of starting with an extreme demand and then retreating to the more moderate one produced the most money for the person using it. . . .                            ■

## Notes

*1. Opening Offers and the Negotiation Dance.*   Howard Raiffa offers the following observations of how his students acted in a negotiation simulation in which the buyer's reservation price was $550 and the seller's reservation price was $300:

(a) A "typical" pattern of offers and counteroffers was: seller opens with an offer of $700; buyer responds with $250; seller then offers $500; buyer offers $300; seller offers $450, buyer responds with $400; parties agree on contract price of $425.

(b) If the midpoint between the buyer's and seller's initial offers is within the bargaining zone, that midpoint is the most likely final contract price. However, "if the midpoint falls outside this zone, then it's hard to predict where the final contract will fall. . . . The reason is that the concessions will have to be lopsided, and it's hard to predict the consequences." Howard Raiffa, The Art and Science of Negotiation 47-49 (1982).

**2. The Number and Size of Concessions.**   How many rounds of offers and counteroffers is typical, and how large are the differences between the initial and final offers and counteroffers likely to be? Attorney V. Hale Starr claims that the majority of lawyers expect that the value of a lawsuit is 20-50 percent lower than the initial settlement demand, and that juror-qualified survey respondents believed that plaintiffs' lawyers expected to receive 30-55 percent less than their initial demand. Starr also claims that experienced negotiators expect a negotiation to include three to seven rounds of offers and counteroffers, with more than five rounds constituting a "difficult" negotiation. V. Hale Starr, The Simple Math of Negotiating, 22 Trial Law. 5, 7-8 (Jan-Feb. 1999). Of course, expectations about the number of rounds of offers and counteroffers will depend a great deal on the context of the negotiation, especially the time that negotiators set aside for the negotiations. Starr says that when a dispute resolution negotiation is scheduled for a full day, negotiators usually expect four rounds of offers and counteroffers; two before lunch, two after. Id. at 8.

**3. The Reciprocity Norm and Reservation Prices.**   Because the reciprocity norm is so ingrained in the negotiation process, expectations of reciprocal concessions can often make an initial offer or demand a signal of the negotiator's reservation price. That is, an opponent is likely to interpret a buyer's initial offer as a signal that her reservation price is substantially higher than the amount offered and a seller's initial demand as a signal that his reservation price is substantially lower than that demand. As one experienced litigator counsels, "Do not start the negotiations with a number that reflects where you expect to be at the end. . . . If a negotiator does make this error, he is actually misleading his counterparts, who have every reason to believe that continued negotiations and discussions of the issues could lead to movement." Normal J. Watkins, Negotiating the Complex Case, 41 For the Defense 36, 38, 53 (July 1999). Refusing to engage in the negotiation dance of reciprocal concessions could cause an opponent to believe not only that the negotiator is not dealing fairly but also that the negotiator is demanding a final deal that is far superior to his actual reservation price, whether or not this is the case.

*4. Nonmonetary Reciprocity.*  The reciprocity norm operates in a variety of ways, not merely when negotiators are haggling over price. Consider the following advice, given by a mergers and acquisitions expert about negotiating contract terms:

> . . . [A]ssume that the seller has objected to provisions in paragraphs 2, 3, 6 and 7. Paragraph 2 deals with an issue that seriously concerns you, as purchaser's counsel; but the points raised with respect to paragraphs 3, 6 and 7 are not significant and can be yielded. In that situation, you might very well approach opposing counsel as follows (although obviously not so briskly):
>
> "With respect to the point in 3, I'll give you that one. . . . Now on the issue in 6, I'm not inclined to argue about that. . . . With respect to the point in 7, I still think the provision is fair but if it really bothers you we can change it as you suggested. . . . Now, about that question in number 2. . . ."
>
> If you handle the matter in this fashion, there may be an understandable predisposition on the part of your adversary to be cooperative on paragraph 2, especially if you can drum up some reasonable support for your position. On the other hand, if you had kicked off the negotiating session by saying, "Now, on number 2, I have a lot of trouble . . . ," the other lawyer doesn't know whether you are going to have the same sort of problems on every one of his points, and he will probably be less inclined to go along with you.

James Freund, Anatomy of a Merger: Strategies and Techniques for Negotiating Corporate Acquisitions 30 (1975).

*5. Anchoring Effects and Reciprocity.*  In one study of settlement negotiation behavior, described in more detail in Chapter 3, the experimenters instructed their subjects to assume the role of a plaintiff in a lawsuit. The subjects were given information about a contested claim they had against an automobile dealership for selling them what they considered to be a defective car. Subjects were informed that if the case proceeded to trial there was an approximately equal chance that they would recover $24,000 (the price of the car) or that they would recover $0. They were then asked whether or not they would accept a final settlement offer of $12,000.

Half of the subjects were told that the defendant initially offered to settle for $10,000, and then increased its final offer to $12,000. The other half of the subjects were told that the defendant initially offered $2,000, and then increased its final offer to $12,000. Although both subject groups were faced with the same choice — $12,000 or trial — those who had originally been offered only $2,000 were nearly twice as likely to accept the $12,000 final offer.

To explain these results, the authors suggested that the initial offers anchored the subjects' expectations concerning settlement. When the defendant increased its offer to $12,000 this appeared to be a far greater concession to the subjects who were originally offered $2,000 than to the subjects who were originally offered $10,000. See Russell Korobkin & Chris Guthrie, Opening Offers and Out of Court Settlement: A Little Moderation Might Not Go a Long Way, 10 Ohio St. J. Disp. Res. 1 (1994). These results also might indicate the power of the reciprocity norm. Perhaps subjects who received a large concession from the defendant felt obligated to reciprocate by making a significant concession of their own, whereas subjects who received a small concession from the defendant did not on average feel obligated to make as large of a return concession.

*6. Boulwarism.*   In the post-World War II period, the General Electric Company was known for using a strategy in labor negotiations, conceived of by one of its vice presidents, Lemuel Boulware, of making an initial offer to employees that the company believed was fair to both sides, underscoring the inherent fairness of the proposal, and then refusing to reassess its position. In recognition of this controversial approach, the negotiation tactic of refusing to revisit an initial offer is often referred to as "Boulwarism." See NLRB v. General Electric Co., 418 F.2d 736, 740 (2d Cir. 1969).

In legal negotiation situations, Boulwarism might appear to be a risky strategy. But it bears remembering that Boulwarism is the dominant negotiating strategy employed in most consumer transactions. When was the last time that the supermarket was willing to bargain with you over the price of the produce? In fact, Lemuel Boulware developed his negotiating strategy by analogizing bargaining with employees to the methods General Electric used when it priced and marketed its products to consumers. See Note, Boulwareism: Legality and Effect, 76 Harv. L. Rev. 807, 807-810 (1963).

There is a complicated set of social norms that defines when fairness demands reciprocity in bargaining and when it does not. When there is a disagreement over whether or not reciprocity is required for a negotiation to be considered fair, bargaining can break down. Consider the following situation:

Dear Miss Manners:

We sell antiques, with the prices plainly marked on them. Our policy is to show the prices are fair and firm — and yet people keep trying to haggle with us, asking "What is the best you can do?" or "What would you really take?" after we have told them the price. Once we had an Italian customer who said, "What is your final word?" and I said, "It's 'arrivederci.' " "What is a gracious way of telling people that their attempts at lowering the prices are not appropriate without making customers lose face?

Gentle Reader:

What your customers need is proof that the policy applies to everyone and is not simply a bargaining strategy you are using on them. Assuming that you think a "Fixed Prices" sign slightly crude for your type of business, Miss Manners suggests you find an oddly framed, dusty old sign saying this in French or Italian. The words are similar enough for anyone who speaks English to understand them, and yet you can seem to be displaying it as a curiosity. The customers will forget to lose face because they'll feel flattered at the assumption that they read French or Italian.

Judith Martin, Miss Manners' Guide to Excruciatingly Correct Behavior 424 (1982).

## B. CONVENTION

By relying on the reciprocity norm, negotiators often divide a cooperative surplus by staking out initial positions and then engaging in a series of concessions and reciprocal concessions until the process converges on a single deal point. Another method of relying on social conventions to divide a cooperative surplus is to base the deal point on what is normal or conventional — that is, what agreements have been reached in other similar negotiating situations. Convention carries with it a strong sense of reasonableness, such that an agreement reached on terms that are normal is one likely to be viewed as fair to both parties.

Convention can also provide a justification for the negotiator who makes concessions up to a point but then stops. Imagine a seller who reduces his initial demand of $20 to $19, then to $18, then to $17. Unless the seller is able to convince the buyer that $17 is her reservation price (i.e., successfully exercises power), why should the buyer not assume that the seller will make more concessions, given that she has already made three? Thomas Schelling observes that the negotiator "has to have a reason for standing firmly on a position; and along the continuum of qualitatively undifferentiable positions one finds no rationale." Thomas Schelling, The Strategy of Conflict 70 (1960). Consistency with what is perceived as normal can provide the necessary qualitative differentiation between one position and a range of others.

The challenge of reaching agreement based on the principle of convention is that the appropriate "reference transaction" from which to judge what is conventional is often contested. A customer and a merchant might be able to agree that they will seal a mutually profitable agreement by both agreeing to accept the normal price of the goods in question. But translating agreement on this general proposition to agreement on a specific price may prove difficult. Is the "normal price" what the customer paid for the same items last year? Is it last year's price plus an adjustment for inflation? Is it what a different customer paid yesterday? Is it what yet another customer is likely to offer today? Is it the merchant's cost plus a reasonable profit? What constitutes normalcy and therefore substantive fairness depends in part on social convention and in part on negotiator skill in framing the debate.

Three excerpts follow. The first uses an experimental methodology to try to unveil what types of reference transactions most people intuitively feel are normal. The second advises negotiators on how to use the notion of convention to reach agreement. The third demonstrates a possible result of attempting to stray from convention by using power.

## ■ Daniel Kahneman, Jack L. Knetsch & Richard H. Thaler, Fairness as a Constraint on Profit Seeking: Entitlements in the Market*

**76 Am. Econ. Rev.** 728, 729-737 (1986)

... The present research uses household surveys of public opinions to infer rules of fairness for conduct in the market from evaluations of particular actions by hypothetical firms. ...

A central concept in analyzing the fairness of actions in which a firm sets the terms of future exchanges is the *reference transaction,* a relevant precedent that is characterized by a reference price or wage, and by a positive reference profit to the firm. The treatment is restricted to cases in which the fairness of the reference transaction is not itself in question.

The main findings of this research can be summarized by a principle of *dual entitlement,* which governs community standards of fairness: Transactors have an entitlement to the terms of the reference transaction and firms are entitled to their reference profit. A firm is not allowed to increase its profits by arbitrarily violating the entitlement of its transactors to the reference price, rent or wage. When the reference profit of a firm is threatened, however, it may set new terms that protect its profit at transactor's expense.

Market prices, posted prices, and the history of previous transactions between a firm and a transactor can serve as reference transactions.

*Copyright © 1986 by the American Economic Association. Reprinted with permission.

When there is a history of similar transactions between firm and trans-actor, the most recent price, wage, or rent will be adopted for reference unless the terms of the previous transaction were explicitly temporary. For new transactions, prevailing competitive prices or wages provide the natural reference. The role of prior history in wage transactions is illustrated by the following pair of questions:

Question 2A. A small photocopying shop has one employee who has worked in the shop for six months and earns $9 per hour. Business continues to be satisfactory, but a factory in the area has closed and unemployment has increased. Other small shops have now hired reli-able workers at $7 an hour to perform jobs similar to those done by the photocopy shop employee. The owner of the photocopying shop reduces the employees wage to $7.
(N = 98) Acceptable 17% Unfair 83%

Question 2B. A small photocopying shop has one employee . . . [as in Question 2A] . . . The current employee leaves, and the owner decides to pay a replacement $7 an hour.
(N = 125) Acceptable 73% Unfair 27%

The current wage of an employee serves as reference for evaluating the fairness of future adjustments of that employees wage — but not necessarily for evaluating the fairness of the wage paid to a replace-ment. The new worker does not have an entitlement to the former worker's wage rate. As the following question shows, the entitlement of an employee to a reference wage does not carry over to a new labor transaction, even with the same employer:

Question 3. A house painter employs two assistants and pays them $9 per hour. The painter decides to quit house painting and go into the business of providing landscape services, where the going wage is lower. He reduces the workers' wages to $7 per hour for the landscaping work.
(N = 94) Acceptable 63% Unfair 37%

Note that the same reduction in wages that is judged acceptable by most respondents in Question 3 was judged unfair by 83 percent of the respondents to Question 2A.

Parallel results were obtained in questions concerning residential tenancy. As in the case of wages, many respondents apply different rules to a new tenant and to a tenant renewing a lease. A rent increase that is judged fair for a new lease may be unfair for a renewal. However, the circumstances under which the rules of fairness require landlords to bear such opportunity costs are narrowly defined. Few respondents consider it unfair for the landlord to sell the accommodation to another landlord who intends to raise the rents of sitting tenants, and even fewer believe that a landlord should make price concessions in selling an accommodation to its occupant.

The relevant reference transaction is not always unique. Disagreements about fairness are most likely to arise when alternative reference transactions can be invoked, each leading to a different assessment of the participants' outcomes. Agreement on general principles of fairness therefore does not preclude disputes about specific cases. When competitors change their price or wage, for example, the current terms set by the firm and the new terms set by competitors define alternative reference transactions. Some people will consider it unfair for a firm not to raise its wages when competitors are increasing theirs. On the other hand, price increases that are not justified by increasing costs are judged less objectionable when competitors have led the way.

It should perhaps be emphasized that the reference transaction provides a basis for fairness judgments because it is normal, not necessarily because it is just. Psychological studies of adaptation suggest that any stable state of affairs tends to become accepted eventually, at least in the sense that alternatives to it no longer readily come to mind. Terms of exchange that are initially seen as unfair may in time acquire the status of a reference transaction. . . .

## II.   CODING OF OUTCOMES

. . . In the present framework, the outcomes to the firm and to its transactors are defined as gains and losses in relation to the reference transaction. The transactor's outcome is simply the difference between the new terms set by the firm and the reference price, rent, or wage. The outcome to the firm is evaluated with respect to the reference profit, and incorporates the effect of exogenous shocks (for example, changes in wholesale prices) which alter the profit of the firm on a transaction at the reference terms. . . .

The issue of how to define relevant outcomes takes a similar form in studies of individuals' preferences and of judgments of fairness. In both domains, a descriptive analysis of people's judgments and choices involves rules of *naive accounting* that diverge in major ways from the standards of rationality assumed in economic analysis. People commonly evaluate outcomes as gains or losses relative to a neutral reference point rather than as endstates (Kahneman and Amos Tversky, 1979). . . .

The entitlements of firms and transactors induce similar asymmetries between gains and losses in fairness judgments. An action by a firm is more likely to be judged unfair if it causes a loss to its transactor than if it cancels or reduces a possible gain. Similarly, an action by a firm is more likely to be judged unfair if it achieves a gain to the firm than if it averts a loss. Different standards are applied to actions that are elicited by the threat of losses or by an opportunity to improve on a positive reference profit — a psychologically important distinction which is usually not represented in economic analysis.

Judgments of fairness are also susceptible to framing effects, in which form appears to overwhelm substance. One of these framing effects will be recognized as the money illusion, illustrated in the following questions:

Question 4A. A company is making a small profit. It is located in a community experiencing a recession with substantial unemployment but no inflation. There are many workers anxious to work at the company. The company decides to decrease wages and salaries 7% this year.
(N = 125) Acceptable 38% Unfair 62%

Question 4B. . . . with substantial unemployment and inflation of 12%. . . . The company decides to increase salaries only 5% this year.
(N = 129) Acceptable 78% Unfair 22%

Although the real income change is approximately the same in the two problems, the judgments of fairness are strikingly different. A wage cut is coded as a loss and consequently judged unfair. A nominal raise which does not compensate for inflation is more acceptable because it is coded as a gain to the employee, relative to the reference wage.

Analysis of individual choice suggest that the disutility associated with an outcome that is coded as a loss may be greater than the disutility of the same objective outcome when coded as the elimination of a gain. Thus, there may be less resistance to the cancellation of a discount or bonus than to an equivalent price increase or wage cut. As illustrated by the following questions, the same rule applies as well to fairness judgments.

Question 5A. A shortage has developed for a popular model of automobile, and customers must now wait two months for delivery. A dealer has been selling these cars at list price. Now the dealer prices this model at $200 above list price.
(N = 130) Acceptable 29% Unfair 71%

Question 5B. . . . A dealer has been selling these cars at a discount of $200 below list price. Now the dealer sells this model only at list price.
(N = 123) Acceptable 58% Unfair 42%

. . .

## III.   Occasions for Pricing Decisions

This section examines the rules of fairness that apply to three classes of occasions in which a firm may reconsider the terms that it sets for exchanges. (i) *Profit reductions*, for example, by rising costs or decreased demand for the product of the firm. (ii) *Profit increases*, for example, by efficiency gains or reduced costs. (iii) *Increases in market power*, for example, by temporary excess demand for goods, accommodations, or jobs.

### A.   PROTECTING PROFIT

. . . By large majorities, respondents endorsed the fairness of passing on increases in wholesale costs, in operating costs, and in the costs associated with a rental accommodation. The following two questions illustrate the range of situations to which this rule was found to apply.

Question 7. Suppose that, due to a transportation mixup, there is a local shortage of lettuce and the wholesale price has increased. A local grocer has bought the usual quantity of lettuce at a price that is 30 cents per head higher than normal. The grocer raises the price of lettuce to customers by 30 cents per head.

(N = 101) Acceptable 79% Unfair 21%

Question 8. A landlord owns and rents out a single small house to a tenant who is living on a fixed income. A higher rent would mean the tenant would have to move. Other small rental houses are available. The landlord's costs have increased substantially over the past year and the landlord raises the rent to cover the cost increases when the tenant's lease is due for renewal.

(N = 151) Acceptable 75% Unfair 25%

. . .

A firm is only allowed to protect itself at the transactor's expense against losses that pertain directly to the transaction at hand. Thus, it is unfair for a landlord to raise the rent on an accommodation to make up for the loss of another source of income. On the other hand, 62 percent of the respondents considered it acceptable for a landlord to charge a higher rent for apartments in one of two otherwise identical buildings, because a more costly foundation had been required in the construction of that building. . . .

### B.   THE ALLOCATION OF GAINS

The data of the preceding section could be interpreted as evidence for a cost-plus rule of fair pricing, in which the supplier is expected to act as a broker in passing on marked-up costs (Okun). A critical test of this possible rule arises when the suppliers costs diminish: A strict cost-plus rule would require prices to come down accordingly. . . .

The conclusion that the rules of fairness permit the seller to keep part or all of any cost reduction was confirmed . . . in the present study.

Question 11A. A small factory produces tables and sells all that it can make at $200 each. Because of changes in the price of materials, the cost of making each table has recently decreased by $40. The factory reduces its price for the tables by $20.

(N = 102) Acceptable 79% Unfair 21%

Question 11B. . . . the cost of making each table has recently decreased by $20. The factory does not change its price for the tables.

(N = 100) Acceptable 53% Unfair 47%

. . . In conjunction with the results of the previous section, the findings support a dual-entitlement view: the rules of fairness permit a firm not to share in the losses that it imposes on its transactors, without imposing on it an unequivocal duty to share its gains with them.

### C. EXPLOITATION OF INCREASED MARKET POWER

The market power of a firm reflects the advantage to the transactor of the exchange which the firm offers, compared to the transactor's second-best alternative. For example, a blizzard increases the surplus associated with the purchase of a snow shovel at the regular price, compared to the alternatives of buying elsewhere or doing without a shovel. The respondents consider it unfair for the hardware store to capture any part of the increased surplus, because such an action would violate the customers entitlement to the reference price. Similarly, it is unfair for a firm to exploit an excess in the supply of labor to cut wages (Question 2A), because this would violate the entitlement of employees to their reference wage.

As shown by the following routine example, the opposition to exploitation of shortages is not restricted to such extreme circumstances:

Question 12. A severe shortage of Red Delicious apples has developed in a community and none of the grocery stores or produce markets has any of this type of apple on their shelves. Other varieties of apples are plentiful in all of the stores. One grocer receives a single shipment of Red Delicious apples at the regular wholesale cost and raises the retail price of these Red Delicious apples by 25% over the regular price.

(N = 102) Acceptable 37% Unfair 63%

Raising prices in response to a shortage is unfair even when close substitutes are readily available. A similar aversion to price rationing held as well for luxury items. For example, a majority of respondents thought it unfair for a popular restaurant to impose a $5 surcharge for Saturday night reservations.

. . . A monopolist might attempt to increase profits by charging different customers as much as they are willing to pay. In conventional theory, the constraints that prevent a monopolist from using perfect price discrimination to capture all the consumers' surplus are asymmetric information and difficulties in preventing resale. The survey results suggest the addition of a further restraint: some forms of price discrimination are outrageous.

Question 14. A landlord rents out a small house. When the lease is due for renewal, the landlord learns that the tenant has taken a job very close to the house and is therefore unlikely to move. The landlord raises the rent $40 per month more than he was planning to do.
(N = 157) Acceptable 9% Unfair 91%

The near unanimity of responses to this and similar questions indicates that an action that deliberately exploits the special dependence of a particular individual is exceptionally offensive.

The introduction of an explicit auction to allocate scarce goods or jobs would also enable the firm to gain at the expense of its transactors, and is consequently judged unfair.

Question 15. A store has been sold out of the popular Cabbage Patch dolls for a month. A week before Christmas a single doll is discovered in a storeroom. The managers know that many customers would like to buy the doll. They announce over the stores public address system that the doll will be sold by auction to the customer who offers to pay the most.
(N = 101) Acceptable 26% Unfair 74%

. . .

## IV.  ENFORCEMENT

Several considerations may deter a firm from violating community standards of fairness. First, a history or reputation of unfair dealing may induce potential transactors to take their business elsewhere, because of the element of trust that is present in many transactions. Second, transactors may avoid exchanges with offending firms at some cost to themselves, even when trust is not an issue. Finally, the individuals who make decisions on behalf of firms may have a preference for acting fairly. . . .

A willingness to punish unfairness was . . . expressed in the telephone surveys. For example, 68 percent of respondents said they would switch their patronage to a drugstore five minutes further away if the one closer to them raised its prices when a competitor was temporarily forced to close; and, in a separate sample, 69 percent indicated they would switch if the more convenient store discriminated against its older workers.

. . . [E]xperimental studies often produce fair behavior even in the absence of enforcement. . . .

Question 17A. If the service is satisfactory, how much of a tip do you think most people leave after ordering a meal costing $10 in a restaurant that they visit frequently?
            (N = 122) Mean response = $1.28

Question 17B. . . . in a restaurant on a trip to another city that they do not expect to visit again?
            (N = 124) Mean response = $1.27

The respondents evidently do not treat the possibility of enforcement as a significant factor in the control of tipping. Their opinion is consistent with the widely observed adherence to a 15 percent tipping rule even by one-time customers who pay and tip by credit card, and have little reason to fear embarrassing retaliation by an irate server. . . .                                                                          ■

## ■ Roger Fisher, William Ury & Bruce Patton, Getting to Yes*

82-91 (2d ed. 1991)

. . . Suppose you have entered into a fixed-price construction contract for your house that calls for reinforced concrete foundations but fails to specify how deep they should be. The contractor suggests two feet. You think five feet is closer to the usual depth for your type of house.

Now suppose the contractor says: "I went along with you on steel girders for the roof. It's your turn to go along with me on shallower foundations." No owner in his right mind would yield. Rather than horse-trade, you would insist on deciding the issue in terms of objective safety standards. "Look, maybe I'm wrong. Maybe two feet is enough. What I want are foundations strong and deep enough to hold up the building safely. Does the government have standard specifications for these soil conditions? How deep are the foundations of other buildings in this area? What is the earthquake risk here? Where do you suggest we look for standards to resolve this question?"

It is no easier to build a good contract than it is to build strong foundations. If relying on objective standards applies so clearly to a negotiation between the house owner and a contractor, why not to business deals, collective bargaining, legal settlements, and international negotiations? Why not insist that a negotiated price, for example, be based on some standard such as market value, replacement cost, depreciated book value, or competitive prices, instead of whatever the seller demands? . . .

The more you bring standards of fairness, efficiency, or scientific merit to bear on your particular problem, the more likely you are to produce a final package that is wise and fair. The more you and the other side refer to precedent and community practice, the greater your chance of benefiting from past experience. And an agreement consistent with precedent is less vulnerable to attack. If a lease contains standard terms or if a sales contract conforms to practice in the industry, there is less risk that either negotiator will feel that he was harshly treated or will later try to repudiate the agreement. . . .

Approaching agreement through discussion of objective criteria also reduces the number of commitments that each side must make and then unmake as they move toward agreement. In positional bargaining, negotiators spend much of the time defending their position and attacking the other side's. People using objective criteria tend to use time more efficiently talking about possible standards and solutions. . . .

*Fair standards.* You will usually find more than one objective criterion available as a basis for agreement. Suppose, for example, your car is demolished and you file a claim with an insurance company. In your discussion with the adjuster, you might take into account such measure of the car's value as (1) the original cost of the car less depreciation; (2) what the car could have been sold for; (3) the standard "blue book" value for a car of that year and model; (4) what it would cost to replace that car with a comparable one; and (5) what a court might award as the value of the car. . . .

*Frame each issue as a joint search for objective criteria.* f you are negotiating to buy a house, you might start off by saying: "Look, you want a high price and I want a low one. Let's figure out what a *fair* price would be. What objective standards might be most relevant?" You and the other side may have conflicting interests, but the two of you now have a shared goal: to determine a fair price. You might be suggesting one or more criteria yourself — the cost of the house adjusted for depreciation and inflation, recent sale prices of similar houses in the neighborhood, or an independent appraisal — and then invite the seller's suggestions. . . .

*Never yield to pressure.* Consider once again the example of negotiating with the contractor. What if he offers to hire your brother-in-law on the condition that you give in on the depth of the foundations? You would probably answer, "A job for my brother-in-law has nothing to do with whether the house will be safely supported on a foundation of that depth." What if the contractor then threatens to charge you a higher price? You would answer the same way: "We'll settle that question on the merits too. Let's see what other contractors charge for this kind of work," or "Bring me your cost figures and we'll work out a fair profit margin." If the contractor replies, "Come on, you trust me, don't you?" you would respond: "Trust is an entirely separate matter. The issue is how deep the foundations have to be to make the house safe."

Pressure can take many forms: a bribe, a threat, a manipulative appeal to trust, or a simple refusal to budge. In all these cases, the principled response is the same: invite them to state their reasoning, suggest objective criteria you think apply, and refuse to budge except on this basis. Never yield to pressure, only to principle.                    ∎

## ∎ Steven Lubet, Notes on the Bedouin Horse Trade or "Why Won't the Market Clear, Daddy?"*
### 74 Tex. L. Rev. 1039, 1039, 1041-1142, 1053 (1996)

. . . Petra is Jordan's fabled "rose-red city" — half as old as Time. The Nabateans, who built Petra during biblical times, located their capital in an almost impregnable mountain stronghold. Even today, it is possible to enter Petra only by passing through the Bab es-Siq, a narrow gorge over a mile long and never more than a few meters wide.

What meant security to the ancient Nabateans is now a two-kilometer impediment to tourism. To make access easier, not to mention more romantic, the route of the Bab es-Siq was for many years plied by hundreds of horses-for-hire. For seven Jordanian Dinars (abbreviated as 7 JD, equal to about U.S. $10.00), a bedouin guide would take you into the site on horseback and meet you later to take you out again. The standard price was fixed, and tickets for the horses were sold at the entry gate.

Tourists could also walk into the site and negotiate for a one-way horse on the way out. The return-only transactions were conducted on a cash basis — no tickets, no fixed prices. . . . As nightfall approaches and the ranks of tourists thin, guides should become increasingly willing to bargain for rides out of the site. This did not turn out to be the case. Indeed, the fee for a horse was surprisingly nonnegotiable, sharply contrary to what would appear to be the sellers' rational best interest. . . .

As tourists stop arriving and start thinking about going back to their hotels, the horses begin to congregate in the theater plaza. Some of the guides are there to collect return tickets, but most are available for cash hiring. I know this because virtually all of the guides solicit virtually all of the tourists, offering, "Horse? Horse?" The scene is chaotic; there is nothing approaching a queue.

This is a market that should clear. Foot-sore tourists should be interested in riding, rather than walking, back through the Siq. The bedouin guides should be interested in minimizing their down time. At the right price, many tourists should find riding preferable to walking. For the guides, working should be preferable to standing around. Horse time, after all, is a wasting asset. It cannot be banked or saved for another day. Every "siq-unit" that a horse is unengaged is a unit that is lost forever. . . .

But here is how it really worked. The first price quoted for a return siq was invariably 7 JD — exactly the same as for a round trip. No matter how resolutely I bargained, the price never fell below 4 JD (six bucks). On each of our three days at Petra we were very nearly the last tourists to leave in the afternoon. By the time we got to the theater corral, the horses outnumbered the remaining pedestrians by at least two or three to one. Still, the price never dropped below four Dinars.

So we walked. Four of us. Three times. The potential siqs went unsold because we could not arrive at an agreeable price. (My goal was 2 JD although, in theory, a guide should have been willing to accept 1 JD or even less. I promised my impatient children, however, that I would have settled, and cleared my personal market, at three.) The result was clearly suboptimal. My family walked instead of riding; the horses idled instead of working. . . . So I asked my children why they thought the Bedouins refused my offers. "Because you didn't offer enough money, Daddy, and they thought that you didn't respect them." But they still should have preferred the money to just standing around not working. "No, Daddy, they would rather stand around than take less than they thought they were worth." From a common sense perspective, the answer is painfully obvious. Pride. They were desert horsemen, after all, and they probably were not thrilled about chauffeuring tourists in the first place. There was an amount of money that made the work worthwhile, and they just were not interested in anything less, efficiency be damned. . . .

Efficiency takes us only so far. Equilibrium trumps optimality. Without wisdom, we walk.                                                        ∎

## Notes

*1. The Relevance of "Market Price."*   Negotiators often contend that the "market price" of the subject of the negotiation should be the basis for an agreement. Such an argument can be powerful for two different reasons, and it is useful to understanding the negotiation process to recognize the difference.

When there is an active market for the subject of the negotiation, the market price can be a natural point of agreement because it is simultaneously the reservation price of both parties. If a buyer and seller are negotiating a sale of an ear of corn in the center of a busy farmer's market, they will probably reach an agreement — if at all — at the market price. The buyer will not pay more than this, because he can buy at this price by turning to the next seller. The seller will not accept less than this, because he can sell at this price by turning to the next buyer. In this case, the bargaining zone between buyer and seller contains only a single point. There is no cooperative surplus to divide; the negotiator's sole task is to locate that single point of possible agreement. Referencing the market price helps accomplish this goal.

When there is not an active market for the subject of the negotiation, or when buyer and seller are locked into a bilateral monopoly situation, referencing the "market price" serves another purpose entirely. In this situation, the market price is relevant because it reflects convention and thus is likely to be seen as fair to both parties. For example, when a plaintiff and defendant are attempting to negotiate a settlement, one or both might reference the settlement amounts in similar lawsuits. These amounts do not necessarily relate to either party's reservation price, because neither is able to settle for that price in the open market — the plaintiff must reach agreement if at all with this defendant, and vice versa. But the market price might be a deal point at which both parties feel they have achieved an agreement that is both beneficial (relative to pursuing their BATNAs) and equitable.

*2. Other Focal Points.*   The market price of an item, or the price charged in other reference transactions that seem appropriate, are appealing deal points because both parties are likely to think that they did not bend to the other party's will or use of power tactics. Negotiators often achieve this same goal by choosing as deal points other prominent values, or "focal points" — locations in the bargaining zone to which attention is naturally drawn.

J. Keith Murnighan demonstrates the power of prominence by asking people what they think the selling price of two cars will be if the dealer advertises them for $10,650 and $2,650 respectively. The vast majority of respondents predict the first car will sell for $10,000, and that the second car will sell for either $2,000 or $2,500. He concludes from this and related anecdotes:

> Sometimes bargaining outcomes are obvious, even before the bargaining begins. The bargainers themselves may not realize this. They're too busy trying to analyze the situation and find an advantage they can exploit. But outside observers can often see it and afterward, with the benefits of hindsight, the bargainers themselves may see it, too.
>
> The moral . . . is that prominence is a very important factor in bargaining. It underlies many negotiations, it can have a potent effect on the outcome of a negotiation. . . .
>
> Prominence is not a singular concept: It's fuzzy and can come in any of several forms (first, tallest, etc.). But it does make sense. We recognize it immediately when we think of it. It pays to pay attention to it in negotiations.
>
> The presence of a prominent solution is one of the most basic aspects of the structure of a bargaining game, whether the game is silent and without contact or more normal. Thus, *the structure of the game itself sometimes dictates the final outcome.* Even when it doesn't, prominence can limit the range of possible outcomes. When a prominent solution exists, it will be the most likely outcome. Thus, when you recognize the presence of prominent solutions and, more generally, the driving forces provided by the underlying structure of a bargaining game, you should work within that structure to your best advantage.

J. Keith Murnighan, Bargaining Games 45-46 (1992).

**3. The Power of Reference Points Revisited.** The study by Kahneman et al. shows that reference points play a significant role in judgments of fairness. For example, giving employees less than their reference wage in a noninflationary environment is considered unfair, but denying employees a raise above their reference wage in an inflationary environment is not judged unfair, even when the two results are economically identical. This finding bears a close relationship to the findings presented in Chapter 3 that individuals often place a higher value on maintaining what they perceive to be the status quo in the face of a "loss" from that position than they place on capturing a "gain" from that position.

**4. Are Appeals to Objective Criteria Really Objective?** When Fisher et al. counsel negotiators to search for objective criteria as a means of identifying a deal point, they suggest that such an approach is an alternative to either negotiator satisfying his desire to capture as much of the cooperative surplus as possible. James J. White has called this position "naive," claiming that "[m]ost of the time [objective criteria] will do no more than give the superficial appearance of reasonableness and honesty to one party's position." James J. White, Essay Review: The Pros and Cons of Getting to Yes, 34 J. Legal Educ. 115, 117 (1984). There is probably some truth to both positions. That is, sometimes appeals to convention are made in an effort to manipulate, and sometimes they are made in an effort to reach agreement in a cooperative way that does not result in "winners" and "losers."

*5. Another Perspective on Setting Aspirations.*   Chapter 2 raised the question of how negotiators should determine their prebargaining aspiration levels. One suggested approach was that negotiators use their prediction of the opponent's reservation point as their aspiration. In other words, set as your goal the opponent's minimum acceptable set of terms. Richard Shell recommends instead that negotiators use conventions (albeit conventions that favor them as much as possible) as the basis for aspirations:

> Once you have thought about what an optimistic, challenging goal would look like, spend a few minutes permitting realism to dampen your expectations. *Optimistic goals are effective only if they are feasible; that is, only if you believe in them and they can be justified according to some standard or norm.* . . . [N]egotiation positions must usually be supported by some standard, benchmark, or precedent, or they lose their credibility. No amount of mental goal setting will make your five-year-old car worth more than a brand-new version of the same model. . . .
>
> But do not let your ideas of what is appropriate or realistic take over completely. Simply note the reasons you come up with that explain why your optimistic goal may not be possible and look for the next highest *defendable* target. Your old car may not be worth the same as a new one, but you should be able to find a used-car guide that reports the "average" price for your model. With that foundation, you can justify asking for a premium over that standard based on the tip-top condition of your vehicle.

G. Richard Shell, Bargaining for Advantage 32-33 (1999).

---

## C.  NORMS OF DISTRIBUTIVE JUSTICE

Another way negotiators search for an answer to the elusive question of what deal point would be fair is by referring to norms of distributive justice. As is the case with convention, determining to reach agreement on the basis of "justice" does not solve the problem, but rather only begs the question of what justice principle the negotiators will rely upon and how they will apply that principle to the transaction or dispute at hand. Two justice norms are most frequently invoked in legal negotiation: equality (or parity), and equity (or contribution). "Equality" refers to identical distributions of benefits. "Equity" can be defined as a distribution of benefits according to the contribution or merit of the parties. A third justice norm, "need," prevalent in negotiations generally but less so in the legal arena, implies a distribution of benefits according to the differing individual needs of the parties.

The equality norm is undoubtedly quite powerful. Suppose Barton is bargaining with Chloe over a pear that Chloe owns. Barton's reservation price is $2 because he can buy a pear from another seller for that amount. Chloe's reservation price is $1 because she can sell her pear to another buyer for that amount. Given these facts, it would be reasonable to predict that Barton and Chloe would agree on a price of $1.50, thus equally dividing the cooperative surplus created by their agreement. The problem, of course, is that in real life neither negotiator is likely to know the other's reservation price with certainty. Dividing the cooperative surplus equally is impractical if Chloe cannot verify Barton's reservation price and Barton cannot verify Chloe's. If Barton's true reservation price is $2.50 — perhaps because he finds Chloe's pear more attractive than the ones offered by other sellers for $2 — the equality principle suggests he is entitled to a price of $1.75. If Barton claimed his reservation price was $2, Chloe would not know whether the claim was true or false.

Because reservation prices are usually unverifiable, negotiators often reach agreement by "splitting the difference" between two *offers*, rather than two reservation prices. For example, if Chloe advertises her pears for $2.25, Barton might offer $1.25, and Chloe might suggest that they split the difference and conclude the transaction for $1.75. This solution to the distribution problem appears to satisfy the equality norm (each party gets half of the difference between their offers) and the reciprocity norm (one party agrees to compromise if the other will reciprocate). Notice, however, that applying the equality norm in this manner favors the party that makes an offer most distant from his reservation price, and thus encourages extreme offers and demands.

Experimental evidence demonstrates that individuals are more likely to offer and to accept unequal distributions if they perceive the inequality as resulting from relevant differences between the parties — that is, inequality is acceptable if equity is served. In the "ultimatum game" and the "dictator game," proposers tend to offer a smaller and more unequal share of the stakes to responders, and responders (in the ultimatum game) are more likely to accept such unequal treatment, if the proposers "earn" their role in the game by scoring higher on a quiz compared to if the roles are assigned randomly. Elizabeth Hoffman et al., Preferences, Property Rights, and Anonymity in Bargaining Games, 7 Games & Econ. Behav. 346, 370 (1994).

In a slightly different experiment involving actual bargaining, player 1 was given the right to receive $12 and leave player 2 with nothing if the two could not reach agreement on how to divide $14. All of the dyads in the study agreed on a division of the $14 that left the subject with the player 1 role with less than $12 — thus, some degree of equality appeared to be important even to subjects who could have fared better by opting for the most unequal result. Just as interesting, however, was the finding that subjects with the player 1 role bargained for a larger share of the $14 if they earned their role by beating the other subject in a game than if they received their role by winning a coin flip. Thus, the subjects deviated further from strict equality when one party appeared more deserving of compensation than the other. Elizabeth Hoffman & Matthew L. Spitzer, Entitlements, Rights, and Fairness: An Experimental Examination of Subjects' Concepts of Distributive Justice, 14 J. Legal Stud. 259 (1985).

In actual two-party negotiation situations involving the division of an existing cooperative surplus, applying the equity principal is conceptually difficult. Suppose again that Chloe's reservation price for selling her pear is $1, and Barton's reservation price for purchasing it is $2. If it cost Chloe $1 to grow the pear, she could plausibly claim that the equity norm suggests the price should be $2, or at least some amount more than $1.50. Barton could just as plausibly argue that although Chloe expended resources to create the pear, she has no more of an equitable claim to the cooperative surplus that the two can create — the $1 between $1 and $2 — than he does. After all, the surplus is a consequence of both parties agreeing to a deal; if both parties do not consent to an agreement, neither will be able to capture any of the cooperative surplus. From Barton's perspective, then, the negotiating parties have the same equitable claim to the cooperative surplus, which means that an equal division and an equitable division are one and the same.

## Notes

*1. Fairness Norms and Relationships.*   Experimental evidence demonstrates that individuals' preferences for equal allocations often depend on their relationship with the other party. In one study, for example, decision makers were asked to divide a sum of money between themselves and another person, with the sum being determined by how well the two subjects performed a task. Subjects were more likely to divide the money equally (rather than equitably based on task performance) when they knew the other person prior to the experiment. William Austin, Friendship and Fairness: Effects of Type of Relationship and Task Performance on Choice of Distribution Rules, 6

Pers. & Soc. Psychol. Bull. 402 (1980). Other studies have found when an individual finds money in the presence of others, people believe that she is more likely to share it equally (and also that an equal division is fair) if the individual is a friend of the others rather than an acquaintance, and if the individual is an acquaintance with the others rather than a stranger. McLean Parks et al., Distributing Adventitious Outcomes: Social Norms, Egocentric Martyrs, and the Effects of Future Relationships, 67 Org. Behav. & Human Decision Proc. 181 (1996); Janice Nadler, Distributing Adventitious Resources: The Effects of Relationship and Grouping, 12 Soc. Justice Res. 133 (1999).

In a different type of study, subjects preferred that a reward be distributed equally between themselves and another subject rather than unequally *in their favor* if they had a positive relationship with the other person. If subjects had a negative relationship with the other subject, however, or no relationship at all, they preferred an unequal distribution in their favor to an equal distribution. See George F. Loewenstein et al., Social Utility and Decision Making in Interpersonal Contexts, 57 J. Pers. & Soc. Psychol. 426, 432-433 (1989). In a recent dictator game experiment, the researchers found that proposers offered responders less money on average if the experimenter shielded the two players' identities from each other as compared to if the players could see and/or speak to each other during the experiment. Iris Bohnet & Bruno S. Frey, The Sound of Silence in Prisoner's Dilemma and Dictator Games, 38 J. Econ. Behav. & Org. 43, 49 (1999).

If negotiators with positive relationships favor distributions according to the equality principle, it seems plausible that negotiators with positive relationships will have a far easier time concluding mutually beneficial transactions than negotiators without a prior positive relationship who might disagree on the appropriate principle of division as well as on the application of that principle. This prediction is supported by the results from an ultimatum game experiment in which the researchers compared the behavior of friends and of strangers. Proposers offered responders a larger share of the stake when the two were friends than when they were strangers, and responders were willing to accept a lower percentage of the stake when they were friends than when they were strangers. Jeffrey T. Polzer et al., The Effects of Relationship and Justification in an Interdependent Allocation Task, 2 Group Decision & Negotiation 135 (1993). These two findings together suggests that friends are likely to have a much easier time agreeing on a particular deal point in a negotiation than are strangers.

*2. Does Where You Stand Depend on Where You Sit?*   Another factor that appears to influence the likelihood that individuals will favor equal versus equitable allocations of resources is which principle would materially benefit them. The experiment by Austin described in the previous note also found that subjects were more likely to propose an equal allocation if the other subject did better than they did at the task, whereas they were more likely to propose an equitable allocation if they performed better at the task. William Austin, Friendship and Fairness: Effects of Type of Relationship and Task Performance on Choice of Distribution Rules, 6 Pers. & Soc. Psychol. Bull. 402 (1980). Jerald Greenberg and Ronald Cohen theorize that preferences among justice norms depend on individuals' relationships to each other, and that bargainers participating in an arms-length negotiation have an essentially antagonistic relationship that should cause each to advocate for a justice norm most beneficial to themselves (friends, however, might be expected to favor an equality norm). Jerald Greenberg & Ronald L. Cohen, Why Justice? Normative and Instrumental Interpretations, in Equity and Justice in Social Behavior 437, 446-447 (Greenberg & Cohen eds. 1982).

Other experiments, however, have also found that in some contexts the precise opposite is true. That is, individuals who contributed the majority of an asset's value (who would thus benefit from an equitable allocation method) favored equal allocations and those who contributed the smaller share favored equitable allocations. This is sometimes referred to as the "politeness" approach. See, e.g., Thomas Schwinger, Just Allocations of Good: Decisions Among Three Principles, in Justice and Social Interaction: Experimental and Theoretical Contributions from Psychological Research 95, 107 (Gerold Mikula ed. 1980). Some research suggests that individuals are more likely to follow the requirements of "politeness" if the activity that produces the value is one that is conducted more cooperatively between the parties rather than more individually. Id. at 111-112.

***3. The Incentive Effects of Distributive Justice Norms.*** When parties are negotiating to establish an ongoing cooperative relationship, the choice of a justice norm might affect the effort that the parties subsequently provide, and thus the value of the cooperative relationship. Assume, for example, that Barton and Chloe are considering establishing a business together that would produce and sell pear juice. Chloe would grow the pears in her orchard, and Barton would press the pears into juice and market the juice to retailers. The fundamental issue for negotiation is how Barton and Chloe will divide the profits from their operation, and they have agreed to rely on a justice norm to resolve the problem.

The success of the venture may depend on which norm they select, because the different norms will give Barton and Chloe different incentives to work hard. They might rely on the "equality" norm and agree to divide the profits 50/50 between them. Knowing that half of the value of their labor will go to the other partner, however, gives each an incentive to provide less effort to the venture. Chloe might not spend extra hours clearing land, planting new pear trees, and carefully pruning the trees, because half of the additional profits that would be created would go to Barton. Barton might not spend extra hours aggressively selling the pear juice for the same reason. If the parties relied on the "need" norm — perhaps by agreeing that Barton would receive 95 percent of the profits because he is the poorer of the two — Chloe would lack an incentive to work hard on the project. In contrast, the parties would both have optimal incentives to be productive if the "equity" principal was chosen and each profited according to the value of their contribution, perhaps measured in terms of hours worked.

Consequently, if the value of an asset depends on future effort, and if economic efficiency is a primary goal of the negotiating parties (rather than, for example, the ongoing relationship between the parties), the equity norm will be more desirable. Notice, however, that if the parties are negotiating only to divide an existing asset, these incentive considerations are not relevant because the value of the asset does not depend on future productive activity.

*4. Combining Fair Division with Integration.* In most of our examples, two negotiators are in a buyer-seller relationship — i.e., if they reach agreement, one will transfer money to the other in return for goods or services or a release from legal liability. With this type of relationship in mind, we can view integrative bargaining as an activity separate from dividing the cooperative surplus. Through integrative bargaining, the parties identify the optimal package of goods or services transferred from the buyer to the seller. For example, if a car buyer values an extended warranty at a monetary amount that is greater than what it will cost the dealer to provide it, the agreement should be for the car and a warranty. If the dealer's cost of providing the warranty is greater than the value the warranty would create for the buyer, the agreement should be for the car only. The price of the optimal package, in contrast, is a distributive bargaining issue, and norms of fair division can be used by negotiators as bargaining implements when the buyer and dealer haggle over the final price. When negotiators rely on fairness norms solely in an attempt to divide an amount of money — that is, to settle on a price — they are engaging in a purely distributive negotiation that, at that point, has no integrative potential.

In negotiation settings in which the parties must divide a shared set of entitlements — such as a divorcing couple who must divide their property, a group of heirs who must divide an estate in probate, or business partners winding up and disbanding a joint venture — the relationship between integrative bargaining and fair division is more complicated. In this setting, when what is being divided is not money, the method of division can affect the integrative potential of the bargain. Thus, negotiators who want to create as much joint value as possible and to divide the cooperative surplus fairly should take into account the integrative effect of various methods of fair division.

To understand the problem, consider the following simple example: Ward, a deceased father, wills a valuable antique grandfather clock to his sons Wally and Beaver. Assume that the brothers agree that the clock should be divided equally, either because they can agree on that justice principle, or because it is consistent with convention due to the fact that a court likely would rule the two are legally entitled to equal shares. One way they might divide the clock is to saw it down the middle. This would satisfy the brothers' desire for an equal division, but it would be very inefficient. Each brother would be left with an item of little or no value, and both would obviously have been better off if one kept the clock and made a side payment to the other. It is, of course, unlikely that the brothers would actually cut the clock in half, but they might well allocate the clock based on a coin flip. This could plausibly be viewed as an equal division of sorts: each brother receives an equal 50 percent chance at winning the clock. But this method could also fail to take advantage of the full integrative potential of the agreement, because there would be a 50 percent chance that the brother who valued the clock less would end up with it.

Wally and Beaver might use a number of possible strategies to try to structure an agreement that maximizes the joint value of their inheritance (by making sure goods are allocated to the brother who values them most) and divides that total amount of value equally. These methods can be divided into two categories: methods that require cash side payments from one party to the other and methods that do not.

Approaches that make use of cash side payments require the parties to reveal the monetary value that they individually place on the subject of the negotiation — here, the grandfather clock. Suppose that the clock would be worth $500 to Beaver and $400 to Wally. One approach that would divide the inheritance efficiently and arguably equally, is sometimes called the "naive method." Using this approach, Wally and Beaver would each state their monetary values for the clock, and the brother who places the highest value on the clock keeps it and pays half of that amount to the other. In our example, Beaver would keep the clock and pay Wally $250. Alternatively, the parties could use what we might call the "auction" method of allocation. Both brothers would bid for the clock in cash. The brother making the high bid would purchase the clock, and the money would then be split between the two. Using the auction method, Beaver would "buy" the clock with a bid of just over $400, so he would keep the clock and pay Wally approximately $200.

Both of these approaches result in an efficient allocation of the clock

— that is, the full integrative potential of the bargain is fulfilled. Because Beaver values the clock $100 more than does Wally, by making sure Beaver keeps the clock the brothers create $100 of joint value that would be lost if Wally were to keep the clock. But there are two important differences in the approaches. The more obvious difference is that the $100 of surplus is divided differently. Under the auction method, Beaver captures all of the cooperative surplus. Under the naive method, Wally and Beaver split the surplus $50/$50.

The other important difference is that the two methods provide different incentives for misrepresentation. Under the naive method, the amount of the side payment is based on Beaver's stated valuation. Therefore, if Beaver knows Wally's valuation is only $400, he has an incentive to claim that his valuation is lower than $500 so that he will get the clock but owe a smaller side payment to Wally. Under the auction method, the side payment is effectively based on Wally's valuation, because he will collect half of his highest bid. If Wally knows Beaver's valuation is $500, he has an incentive to bid almost to $500 for the clock to maximize his income. If neither party has any inkling of the value the other places on the clock, however, they will probably be truthful in stating their valuations under either method. Under the naive method, Beaver would not want to claim a valuation of much less than $500, because the result could be that Wally would end up with the clock even though he values it less than does Beaver. Under the auction method, Wally would not want to bid much, if any, over $400, because he might end up buying the clock for more than he values it.

A more complicated procedure, known as the Steinhaus Fair-Share procedure, effectively splits the difference between the distributive results of the naive and auction methods. According to the Steinhaus method, fairness requires that each brother receive one-half the value of the clock to him, and any additional surplus value should be divided equally between the two. The method is applied as follows: We begin by determining each brother's "fair share," which is one-half of the value he places on the clock. Thus, Wally's "fair share" is $200, and Beaver's is $250. We then award the clock to the party who values it most — in this case Beaver. Since Beaver values the clock at $500 and his fair share is only $250, Beaver now has $250 more than his fair share, while Wally (who has nothing at the moment) has $200 less than his fair share. Wally and Beaver combined now have $50 more than their fair shares ($250 − $200). This amount is divided equally ($25 each), so that Wally's *adjusted* fair share is $225, while Beaver's is $275. At this point, Beaver has $225 more than his adjusted fair share, and Wally has $225 less than his adjusted fair share. Beaver gives Wally $225, and the equal division, Steinhaus style, is achieved. For a more complete description of the Steinhaus method, see Howard Raiffa, The Art and Science of Negotiation 288-289 (1982). Because under this approach the side payment is based in part on Beaver's valuation and in part on Wally's, Beaver will have an incentive to understate his valuation and Wally will have an incentive to overstate his, assuming that the brothers have a good estimation of the value each other places on the clock.

One obvious shortcoming of any of these methods is that they assume Beaver and Wally have enough cash available that whomever turns out to value the clock more can make a side payment to the other. If multiple goods are to be allocated, it is possible to allocate goods based on norms of fairness and efficiency concerns (a) without the use of side payments if some of the goods are divisible or (b) with minimal side payments if the goods are not divisible. Consider the following application of the "adjusted winner approach," proposed by Steven Brams and Alan Taylor. See Steven J. Brams & Alan D. Taylor, Fair Division: From Cake-Cutting to Dispute Resolution 68-75 (1996).

Suppose that Ward has willed Wally and Beaver a desk and a set of books in addition to the grandfather clock. Under the adjusted winner approach, Wally and Beaver would each allocate a fixed number of points (let's say 100) among the three items based on how much they value the items relative to each other. Assume the brothers assign their points as follows:

|  | Clock | Desk | Book Set | Total |
|---|---|---|---|---|
| **Beaver** | 55 | 35 | 10 | 100 |
| **Wally** | 30 | 50 | 20 | 100 |

First, each keeps the items for which he has a higher relative value than his brother, so Beaver keeps the clock, and Wally keeps the desk and the book set. The next step is to equalize the brothers' point totals while creating the least amount of inefficiency possible. Because Wally has the desk and the books, he has 70 points. Beaver, with only the clock, has only 55 points. In order to equalize the point totals, Wally has to give up points and Beaver has to gain points. The least harm to efficiency is done by requiring Wally to give Beaver a portion of the item that Wally has where the two brothers' valuations are closest — here, the book set (because Wally values the books only a little more than Beaver but he values the desk a lot more than Beaver, it is less inefficient for Wally to give Beaver some of the book set than some of the desk). If Wally gives Beaver one-half of the book set, Wally will lose ten points (giving him 60) and Beaver will gain five points (giving him 60), thus equalizing the point totals. Some harm was done to efficiency by transferring books from Wally to Beaver, since points were lost in the process due to the fact that Beaver values the books less than Wally does. But the harm to efficiency was minimal, and in return the parties achieved an equal distribution of goods.

Three drawbacks to this approach should be noted. First, equality is only achieved without a monetary side payment because the book set is divisible. If Ward had left a cardigan sweater instead of the book set, achieving equality by cutting the sweater in half would not have been very practical. Equality would have required a side payment based on the value of the sweater to the two, using either the naive, auction, or Steinhaus methods of division (or some other method).

Second, the distribution of goods is only optimally efficient assuming that Wally and Beaver have the same amount of money and place the same value on everything else in life. Perhaps Beaver has a sentimental attachment to all of his father's possessions. Although he values the clock more than the desk or the books, he has a high absolute value for all three items. Perhaps Wally considers material possessions a nuisance and cares little about any of the items. Of the items, he likes the desk best, but he really doesn't care much about even that. In this scenario, it is probably most efficient for Beaver to keep all three items and make side payments to Wally for each based on the naive, auction, or Steinhaus method.

Third, as with the other strategies, both brothers have an incentive to misrepresent their valuations if they can estimate the other brother's valuations. For example, if Beaver knows Wally will allocate 50 points to the desk and 20 to the books, he can move four of his points from the clock to the desk, and thus be entitled to a larger share of the books to equalize the brothers' resulting point totals.

## DISCUSSION QUESTIONS AND PROBLEMS

*1. The Opening Offer.*   You represent Lion Corp., which wants to acquire one of its competitors, Mouse Inc. Your client believes that the acquisition would greatly increase profits. It estimates the present value of those profits will be approximately $2 million. The board of directors of Mouse Inc. appears interested in being acquired, but there is another suitor. Your client's president has heard rumors from colleagues that Tiger Company has made a firm offer of $800,000 to acquire Mouse Inc. He is relatively certain that Tiger has made an offer, but he can't be sure whether this precise figure is accurate. Last year Lion Corp. acquired another competitor, Rat Inc. (just slightly larger than Mouse Inc.), for $1.2 million. The value of Mouse Inc.'s shares on the stock exchange at today's price is $700,000. An investment bank, retained by Mouse Inc., has valued its assets at $1.4 million.

(a) You are on your way to negotiate a potential purchase of Mouse Inc. on behalf of your client. You have promised to bring an offer. How much will you offer? How did you determine this amount? How do you predict the bargaining process will proceed after your opening offer is made?

(b) In this situation, would you prefer not to make the opening offer, and instead ask Mouse Inc. to state an asking price? Why or why not? What are the costs and benefits of making the first offer versus allowing the other negotiator to make it?

*2. Relationships and Distributive Bargaining.* What does the experimental evidence about the role of the relationship between players in dictator and related games suggest about the effect of the relationship between negotiators in real world bargaining? Is it an advantage, or a disadvantage, or neither, to have a preexisting personal or business relationship with a negotiating opponent? Would you be willing to settle for less when negotiating against someone with whom you had a prior relationship? If so, why?

*3. Boulwarism.* Most analysts believe that Boulwarism will usually not be a successful negotiation strategy. Why do you think this is? Are there situations in which you think Boulwarism would be more effective than in others?

*4. Bedouins and Reservation Prices.* Lubet assumes that as darkness approached in Petra, the Bedouin horse guides' reservation prices for a ride out of the Siq were less than four dinars, but that they refused to accept less than four dinars for a ride because they believed a lower amount was unfair. Might Lubet's assumption be wrong? That is, could it be possible that the guides' reservation prices were four dinars, and that they refused to accept less because they were better off pursuing their BATNAs, not because their pride would be hurt if they accepted a lower amount?

*5. Unfair Price or Unfair Treatment?* Assuming that a particular Bedouin horse guide's reservation price for a ride out of the Siq late in the evening was two dinars, do you think his refusal to accept anything less than four dinars was due to a belief that any amount less than four dinars would be an unfair price for his service, or to a belief that Lubet was treating him unfairly by attempting to use power tactics to capture the cooperative surplus? Notice that Lubet's children failed to distinguish between these two possibilities by hypothesizing first that the guides thought Lubet didn't *respect* them and second that they would rather do nothing than accept less than they were *worth*. To better understand this distinction, ask yourself this question: if Lubet had had only three dinars with him that evening and could therefore not offer more than that, and Lubet was able to prove to the horse guide that this was the case, would the guide have given Lubet a ride for three dinars?

*6. Verifying BATNAs and Reservation Prices.* Suppose that Chloe (seller) and Barton (buyer) agree in principle that they will enter into an agreement at the midpoint of the bargaining zone, thus splitting equally the cooperative surplus to be gained from their transaction. Chloe claims that her reservation price is $1. Barton claims that his reservation price is $2. Barton agrees to pay $1.50 if he can verify Chloe's reservation price. Can this be done? Is it easier for Chloe to prove what her BATNA is than to prove her reservation price? If so, should verification of Chloe's BATNA satisfy Barton?

*7. Fairness as Means or Ends?* There is little doubt that negotiators often rely on fairness norms as a tactic to reach agreement. Thus, we can understand negotiators' fairness-type arguments as a means to the end of reaching agreement. Should fairness be an end in itself? That is, should negotiators be concerned about whether deals are fair to both parties, or should they only be concerned with achieving an agreement that is as favorable as possible to them or their client? In legal settings, does a lawyer who is concerned with reaching agreements that are fair to both sides run afoul of his ethical duty to zealously represent his client?

# PART III

# THE NEGOTIATOR

Part II of this book analyzed the negotiating process from a structural perspective, focusing on the issues that make all negotiations similar. In any negotiation situation, negotiators (often unknowingly) attempt to identify and estimate the bargaining zone, expand the bargaining zone to enlarge the potential cooperative surplus of an agreement, capture a large portion of the cooperative surplus, and/or rely on social norms to reach a deal point and thus conclude a mutually profitable transaction.

This structural view of negotiation describes much of what transpires at the bargaining table, but it is incomplete because it fails to account for the effects of the personal characteristics of and choices made by negotiators that differ from person to person. This part considers how, within the basic institutional structure of negotiation, the personalities and choices of negotiators can affect bargaining outcomes.

Like Part II, this part attempts to create analytical categories that you can use to help organize and understand the complicated dynamics of negotiation. Unlike Part II, which offered a single framework with which to understand the structure of negotiation, this part presents different structures in each chapter.

Chapter 7, The Negotiator's Dilemma, considers the implications for bargaining of one of the most fundamental strategic choices negotiators must make: whether or not to freely and forthrightly share relevant information with the opposing negotiator. This chapter categorizes negotiators on the basis of whether they honestly reveal relevant information that only they possess or whether they conceal such private information.

Chapter 8, Conflict Style, considers two typologies of conflict styles — one that categorizes negotiators as either "cooperative" or "competitive" and the other that describes negotiators based on the degree to which they are "empathetic" and "assertive" — and considers the extent to which negotiation can be better understood by identifying negotiators accordingly.

Chapter 9, Group Membership, categorizes negotiators by sex and cultural background (primarily "eastern" or "western") in order to examine whether these identities affect the negotiation process either directly, through the different outlooks that members of different groups bring with them to the bargaining table, or indirectly, as a result of stereotypes held by potential negotiating opponents.

# Chapter 7

# The Negotiator's Dilemma

To excel in all of the fundamental aspects of negotiation described in Part II, negotiators must adopt radically contradictory approaches to interacting with their opponents. In order to be certain that they will identify a bargaining zone if one does exist, and therefore be sure to take advantage of any possibility of a mutually beneficial agreement, negotiators need to be open and forthright about their BATNAs and reservation prices. In order to engage in optimal integrative bargaining, expanding the bargaining zone as wide as possible and creating the maximum amount of cooperative surplus, negotiators must be open and forthright about their interests and preferences. From these perspectives, it seems critical that negotiators adopt the approach of "revealing" private information — that is, information that they have about themselves or the negotiation that their opponent lacks.

In stark contrast, for negotiators to capture the maximum amount of that cooperative surplus for themselves, they need to be secretive and even misleading about their BATNAs, reservation prices, interests, and preferences. They must convince their opponent that their reservation price is higher than it actually is, that commitments they have no intention of keeping are credible, that they are more patient than they actually are, and that they believe the agreements they propose are fair to both parties even if they do not. From this perspective, it seems equally critical that negotiators adopt the approach of "concealing" their private information.

Of course, concealing and revealing are inconsistent negotiation strategies. The decision as to which to choose — whether to negotiate in the brightness of openness or the shadows of nondisclosure and sleight of hand — is sometimes called the "negotiator's dilemma." This chapter explores this dilemma in greater detail.

## A.  THE PRISONER'S DILEMMA AS METAPHOR

In game theory, there is a paradox called the "prisoner's dilemma," named for the story often used to illustrate the paradox. The facts of the story vary somewhat across descriptions, but the basics go something like this:

Two co-conspirators in a crime are arrested by the police and put in separate rooms for interrogation, where each prisoner receives the following information. The police have enough evidence to convict him and his comrade of criminal conspiracy, for which each faces a sentence of one year in prison. If the police obtain evidence that he and/or his comrade actually committed the crime, the implicated prisoner(s) will face a five-year sentence. If the prisoner provides a statement that implicates his co-conspirator in the commission of the crime, however, the district attorney will agree to a one-year reduction of his sentence. His comrade, the police represent, is receiving the same offer simultaneously.

These facts create two options for each prisoner: each can "cooperate" with his comrade by remaining silent or "defect" from his comrade by providing a statement. This creates four possible results. If both prisoners cooperate — refuse to provide statements — the police will convict both of conspiracy and each will receive a one-year sentence. If both prisoners defect, each will receive a four-year sentence (five years minus one year for ratting out the other). If prisoner #1 defects and prisoner #2 cooperates, prisoner #2 will be sentenced to five years — this is known as the "sucker's payoff" — while prisoner #1 will go free. If prisoner #2 defects and prisoner #1 cooperates, prisoner #2 will go free while prisoner #1 receives the five-year sucker's payoff.

The four possible outcomes and their associated payoffs can be arrayed on the following diagram (in years, with prisoner #1's payoffs listed first):

|  |  | **Prisoner #2** | |
|---|---|---|---|
|  |  | *Cooperate* | *Defect* |
|  | *Cooperate* | 1, 1 | 5, 0 |
| **Prisoner #1** | *Defect* | 0, 5 | 4, 4 |

The paradox is that each prisoner can maximize his individual payoff (that is, minimize his sentence) by defecting, but the prisoners are both better off if both cooperate than if both defect. If prisoner #2 defects, prisoner #1 is better off defecting as well, because he will therefore avoid the sucker's payoff and be sentenced to four years instead of five years. If prisoner #2 cooperates, on the other hand, prisoner #1 is still better off defecting, because he will then go free rather than being sentenced to one year. In game theory jargon, defection is a "dominant" strategy for prisoner #1. He is better off employing that strategy than he would otherwise be *no matter what* strategy prisoner #2 chooses. The same is true, of course, for prisoner #2. Consequently, both will rationally choose to defect, and both will be sentenced to four years, when they could each have escaped with only a one-year sentence if only they had both cooperated. The prisoners could solve their dilemma if they could enter into an enforceable contract in which both promise to cooperate by keeping silent. This is impossible, however, because the police won't permit them to communicate before making their decisions.

What if both prisoners thought it likely that after they were released from jail they would commit another crime, get caught, and find themselves in exactly the same position, and this was likely to happen again, and again, and again? In other words, would the results of the prisoner's dilemma be different if the prisoners knew that their reputations as cooperators or defectors might follow them into the future for an indeterminate period of time? Robert Axelrod explored this question by holding a tournament, in which he invited experts from a range of academic fields to submit computer programs of strategies for playing a multiround prisoner's dilemma. Axelrod then had the programs play against each other. Some of his findings are discussed in the following excerpt.

## ■ Robert Axelrod, The Evolution of Cooperation*
27-47 (1984)

Since the Prisoner's Dilemma is so common in everything from personal relations to international relations, it would be useful to know how best to act when in this type of setting. . . . [T]here is no one best strategy to use. What is best depends in part on what the other player is likely to be doing. Further, what the other is likely to be doing may well depend on what the player expects you to do. . . .

. . . I invited professional game theorists to send in entries to . . . a computer tournament. It was structured as a round robin, meaning that each entry was paired with each other entry. As announced in the rules of the tournament, each entry was also paired with its own twin and with RANDOM, a program that randomly cooperates and defects with equal probability. Each game consisted of exactly two hundred moves. The payoff matrix . . . awarded both players 3 points for mutual

---

*From The Evolution of Cooperation by Robert Axelrod. Copyright © 1984 by Robert Axelrod. Reprinted by permission of Basic Books, a member of Perseus Books, L.L.C.

cooperation, and 1 point for mutual defection. If one player defected while the other player cooperated, the defecting player received 5 points and the cooperating player received 0 points. . . .

TIT FOR TAT, submitted by Professor Anatol Rapoport of the University of Toronto, won the tournament. This was the simplest of all submitted programs and it turned out to be the best.

TIT FOR TAT, of course, starts with a cooperative choice, and thereafter does what the other player did on the previous move. This decision rule is probably the most widely known and most discussed rule for playing the Prisoner's Dilemma. It is easily understood and easily programmed. It is known to elicit a good degree of cooperation when played with humans. As an entry in a computer tournament, it has the desirable properties that it is not very exploitable and that it does well with its own twin. It has the disadvantage that it is too generous with the RANDOM rule, which was known by the participants to be entered in the tournament. . . .

Surprisingly, there is a single property which distinguishes the relatively high-scoring entries from the relatively low-scoring entries. This is the property of being *nice*, which is to say never being the first to defect. (For the sake of analyzing this tournament, the definition of a nice rule will be relaxed to include rules which will not be the first to defect before the last few moves, say before move 199.)

Each of the eight top-ranking entries (or rules) is nice. None of the other entries is. There is even a substantial gap in the score between the nice entries and the others. The nice entries received tournament averages between 472 and 504, while the best of the entries that were not nice received only 401 points. Thus, not being the first to defect, at least until virtually the end of the game, was a property which, all by itself, separated the more successful rules from the less successful rules in this Computer Prisoner's Dilemma Tournament.

Each of the nice rules got about 600 points with each of the other seven nice rules and with its own twin. This is because when two nice rules play, they are sure to cooperate with each other until virtually the end of the game. Actually the minor variations in end-game tactics did not account for much variation in the scores.

Since the nice rules all got within a few points of 600 with each other, the thing that distinguished the relative rankings among the nice rules was their scores with the rules which are not nice. . . .

. . . DOWNING [ ] is a particularly interesting rule. . . . The idea is that if the other player does not seem responsive to what DOWNING is doing, DOWNING will try to get away with whatever it can by defecting. On the other hand, if the other player does seem responsive, DOWNING will cooperate. To judge the other's responsiveness, DOWNING estimates the probability that the other player cooperates after it (DOWNING) cooperates, and also the probability that the other player cooperates after DOWNING defects. For each move, it updates its estimate of these two conditional probabilities and then selects the choice which will maximize its own long-term payoff under the assumption that it has correctly modeled the other player. If the two conditional probabilities have similar values, DOWNING determines that it pays to defect, since the other player seems to be doing the same thing whether DOWNING cooperates or not. Conversely, if the other player tends to cooperate after a cooperation but not after a defection by DOWNING, then the other player seems responsive, and DOWNING will calculate that the best thing to do with a responsive player is to cooperate. Under certain circumstances, DOWNING will even determine that the best strategy is to alternate cooperation and defection.

At the start of a game, DOWNING does not know the values of these conditional probabilities for the other players. It assumes that they are both .5, but gives no weight to this estimate when information actually does come in during the play of the game.

This is a fairly sophisticated decision rule, but its implementation does have one flaw. By initially assuming that the other player is unresponsive, DOWNING is doomed to defect on the first two moves. These first two defections led many other rules to punish DOWNING, so things usually got off to a bad start. . . . TIT FOR TAT . . . reacted in such a way that DOWNING learned to expect that defection does not pay but that cooperation does. All of the other nice rules went downhill with DOWNING.

The nice rules did well in the tournament largely because they did so well with each other, and because there were enough of them to raise substantially each other's average score. As long as the other player did not defect, each of the nice rules was certain to continue cooperating until virtually the end of the game. But what happened if there was a defection? Different rules responded quite differently, and their response was important in determining their overall success. A key concept in this regard is the forgiveness of a decision rule. *Forgiveness* of a rule can be informally described as its propensity to cooperate in the moves after the other player has defected.

Of all the nice rules, the one that scored lowest was also the one that was least forgiving. This is FRIEDMAN, a totally unforgiving rule that employs permanent retaliation. It is never the first to defect, but once the other defects even once, FRIEDMAN defects from then on. In contrast, the winner, TIT FOR TAT, is unforgiving for one move, but thereafter is totally forgiving of that defection. After one punishment, it lets bygones be bygones.

One of the main reasons why the rules that are not nice did not do well in the tournament is that most of the rules in the tournament were not very forgiving. A concrete illustration will help. Consider the case of JOSS, a sneaky rule that tries to get away with an occasional defection. This decision rule is a variation of TIT FOR TAT. Like TIT FOR TAT, it always defects immediately after the other player defects. But instead of always cooperating after the other player cooperates, 10 percent of the time it defects after the other player cooperates. Thus it tries to sneak in an occasional exploitation of the other player.

This decision rule seems like a fairly small variation of TIT FOR TAT, but in fact its overall performance was much worse, and it is interesting to see exactly why. . . . At first both players cooperated, but on the sixth move, JOSS selected one of its probabilistic defections. On the next move JOSS cooperated again, but TIT FOR TAT defected in response to JOSS's previous defection. Then JOSS defected in response to TIT FOR TAT's defection. In effect, the single defection of JOSS on the sixth move created an echo back and forth between JOSS and TIT FOR TAT. This echo resulted in JOSS defecting on all the subsequent even numbered moves and TIT FOR TAT defecting on all the subsequent odd numbered moves. . . .

A major lesson of this tournament is the importance of minimizing echo effects in an environment of mutual power. When a single defection can set off a long string of recriminations and counterrecriminations, both sides suffer. A sophisticated analysis of choice must go at least three levels deep to take account of these echo effects. The first level of analysis is the direct effect of a choice. This is easy, since a defection always earns more than a cooperation. The second level considers the indirect effects, taking into account that the other side may or may not punish a defection. This much of the analysis was certainly appreciated by many of the entrants. But the third level goes deeper and takes into account the fact that in responding to the defections of the other side, one may be repeating or even amplifying one's own previous exploitative choice. Thus a single defection may be successful when analyzed for its direct effects, and perhaps even when its secondary effects are taken into account. But the real costs may be in the tertiary effects when one's own isolated defections turn into unending mutual recriminations. Without their realizing it, many of these rules actually wound up punishing themselves. With the other player serving as a mechanism to delay the self-punishment by a few moves, this aspect of self-punishment was not picked up by many of the decision rules.

Despite the fact that none of the attempts at more or less sophisticated decision rules was an improvement on TIT FOR TAT, it was easy to find several rules that would have performed substantially better than TIT FOR TAT in the environment of the tournament. The existence of these rules should serve as a warning against the facile belief that an eye for an eye is necessarily the best strategy. There are at least three rules that would have won the tournament if submitted.

[One] defects only if the other player defected on the previous two moves. It is a more forgiving version of TIT FOR TAT in that it does not punish isolated defections. The excellent performance of this TIT FOR TWO TATS rule highlights the fact that a common error of the contestants was to expect that gains could be made from being relatively less forgiving than TIT FOR TAT, whereas in fact there were big gains to be made from being even more forgiving. The implication of this finding is striking, since it suggests that even expert strategists do not give sufficient weight to the importance of forgiveness.

. . . If DOWNING had started with initial assumptions that the other players would be responsive rather than unresponsive, it too would have won and won by a large margin. . . . DOWNING's initial assumptions about the other players were pessimistic. It turned out that optimism about their responsiveness would not only have been more accurate but would also have led to more successful performance. It would have resulted in first place rather than tenth place.

These results from supplementary rules reinforce a theme from the analysis of the tournament entries themselves: the entries were too competitive for their own good. In the first place, many of them defected early in the game without provocation, a characteristic which was very costly in the long run. In the second place, the optimal amount of forgiveness was considerably greater than displayed by any of the entries (except possibly DOWNING). And in the third place, the entry that was most different from the others, DOWNING, floundered on its own misplaced pessimism regarding the initial responsiveness of the others. . . .

The effectiveness of a particular strategy depends not only on its own characteristics, but also on the nature of the other strategies with which it must interact. For this reason, the results of a single tournament are not definitive. Therefore, a second round of the tournament was conducted. . . .

TIT FOR TAT was the simplest program submitted in the first round, and it won the first round. It was the simplest submission in the second round, and it won the second round. Even though all the entrants to the second round knew that TIT FOR TAT had won the first round, no one was able to design an entry that did any better. . . .

As in the first round, it paid to be nice. Being the first to defect was usually quite costly. More than half of the entries were nice, so obviously most of the contestants got the message from the first round that it did not pay to be the first to defect.

In the second round, there was once again a substantial correlation between whether a rule was nice and how well it did. Of the top fifteen rules, all but one were nice (and that one ranked eighth). Of the bottom fifteen rules, all but one were not nice. The overall correlation between whether a rule was nice and its tournament score was a substantial .58.

A property that distinguishes well among the nice rules themselves is how promptly and how reliably they responded to a challenge by the other player. A rule can be called retaliatory if it immediately defects after an "uncalled for" defection from the other. Exactly what is meant by "uncalled for" is not precisely determined. The point, however, is that unless a strategy is incited to an immediate response by a challenge from the other player, the other player may simply take more and more frequent advantage of such an easygoing strategy.

There were a number of rules in the second round of the tournament that deliberately used controlled numbers of defections to see what they could get away with. To a large extent, what determined the actual rankings of the nice rules was how well they were able to cope with these challengers. The two challengers that were especially important in this regard I shall call TESTER and TRANQUILIZER.

TESTER was submitted by David Gladstein and came in forty-sixth in the tournament. It is designed to look for softies, but is prepared to back off if the other player shows it won't be exploited. The rule is unusual in that it defects on the very first move in order to test the other's response. If the other player ever defects, it apologizes by co-operating and playing tit-for-tat for the rest of the game. Otherwise, it cooperates on the second and third moves but defects every other move after that. TESTER did a good job of exploiting several supplementary rules that would have done quite well in the environment of the first round of the tournament. For example, TIT FOR TWO TATS defects only after the other player defects on the preceding two moves. But TESTER never does defect twice in a row. So TIT FOR TWO TATS always cooperates with TESTER, and gets badly exploited for its generosity. Notice that TESTER itself did not do particularly well in the tournament. It did, however, provide low scores for some of the more easygoing rules. . . .

TRANQUILIZER illustrates a more subtle way of taking advantage of many rules, and hence a more subtle challenge. It first seeks to establish a mutually rewarding relationship with the other player, and only then does it cautiously try to see if it will be allowed to get away with something. TRANQUILIZER was submitted by Craig Feathers and came in twenty-seventh in the tournament. The rule normally cooperates but is ready to defect if the other player defects too often. Thus the rule tends to cooperate for the first dozen or two dozen moves if the other player is cooperating. Only then does it throw in an unprovoked defection. By waiting until a pattern of mutual cooperation has been developed, it hopes to lull the other side into being forgiving of occasional defections. If the other player continues to cooperate, then defections become more frequent. But as long as TRANQUILIZER is maintaining an average payoff of at least 2.25

points per move, it does not defect twice in succession, and it does not defect more than one-quarter of the time. It tries to avoid pressing its luck too far.

What it takes to do well with challenging rules like TESTER and TRANQUILIZER is to be ready to retaliate after an "uncalled for" defection from the other. So while it pays to be nice, it also pays to be retaliatory. TIT FOR TAT combines these desirable properties. It is nice, forgiving, and retaliatory. It is never the first to defect; it forgives an isolated defection after a single response; but it is always incited by a defection no matter how good the interaction has been so far. . . .

What seems to have happened is an interesting interaction between people who drew one lesson and people who drew another from the first round. Lesson One was: "Be nice and forgiving." Lesson Two was more exploitative: "If others are going to be nice and forgiving, it pays to try to take advantage of them." The people who drew Lesson One suffered in the second round from those who drew Lesson Two. Rules like TRANQUILIZER and TESTER were effective at exploiting rules which were too easygoing. But the people who drew Lesson Two did not themselves do very well either. The reason is that in trying to exploit other rules, they often eventually got punished enough to make the whole game less rewarding for *both* players than pure mutual cooperation would have been. For example, TRANQUILIZER and TESTER themselves achieved only twenty-seventh and forty-sixth place, respectively. Each surpassed TIT FOR TAT's score with fewer than one-third of the rules. None of the other entries that tried to apply the exploitative conclusion of Lesson Two ranked near the top either. . . .                                                                   ■

## Notes

*1. The Dilemma with a Finite Number of Rounds.*   It should be clear that in a single-round prisoner's dilemma game, both prisoners should defect if they wish to minimize their individual sentences because each is better off defecting regardless of whether the other cooperates or defects. Game theorists argue that mutual defection is also the dominant strategy in a multiround version of the game, so long as the number of rounds the game will be played is known at the outset. The reasoning is as follows: in the last round, both players will defect, just as they would if the game had only a single round. At this point, a reputation for being cooperative won't be of any further use. Because the players know that both will defect in the last round no matter what, both will defect in the second-to-last round. Cooperating in this round and developing a reputation as a cooperator won't be useful, because both players know they will each defect in the next (and final) round. Because the players know that both will defect in the second-to-last round, both will defect in the third-to-last round, and so on. See R. Duncan Luce & Howard Raiffa, Games and Decisions: Introduction and Critical Survey 97-102 (1957). What assumptions does this analysis make about the players of the game? Do you think these assumptions are accurate?

   **2. *The Generalizability of Axelrod's Results.*** Axelrod's results are often cited for the proposition that TIT FOR TAT is the optimal strategy in a multiround prisoner's dilemma game where the number of rounds is unknown. This overstates Axelrod's more modest conclusions. Axelrod is careful to point out that the optimal strategy depends on what strategy others are playing. TIT FOR TAT was the best overall strategy given the broad range of strategies that were represented in *his* tournament. In a world in which other players are on average either more or less "nice" than the strategies entered in his competition, TIT FOR TAT might not be the optimal strategy.

   To see this, consider a simple example. Assume a tournament in which one player plays TIT FOR TAT and all other players play an "ALL D" strategy — that is, "defect every time." In this tournament, TIT FOR TAT would finish last because it would receive the sucker's payoff in round one, and a defect/defect payoff in each subsequent round, while all the other players would receive the defect/defect payoff in every round.

   **3. *Does the Name of the Game Matter?*** Social psychologists often argue that individuals' behavior depends not only on the objective payoffs that their choices will create, but also their perceptions about what type of behavior is expected. This may be as true of the prisoner's dilemma as it is in less stylized interactions. Lee Ross and Andrew Ward asked student subjects who were identified by others who knew them as "cooperative" or "competitive" in disposition to play a seven-round game with the payoff structure of the prisoner's dilemma game. For some of the subjects, the game was called the "community game," for others it was called the "Wall Street game." The experimenters found that subjects were nearly twice as likely to cooperate when playing the "community game" than when playing the "Wall Street game," and that individuals' reputations as cooperators or competitors did not affect their strategies significantly. Lee Ross & Andrew Ward, Psychological Barriers to Dispute Resolution, 27 Advances Experimental Soc. Psychol. 255 (1995).

# B.  COPING WITH THE NEGOTIATOR'S DILEMMA

The prisoner's dilemma can be a useful metaphor for considering approaches to negotiation. First, replace the "prisoners" in the prisoner's dilemma with "negotiators." Second, define "cooperation" to mean being open, transparent, and candid about one's interests, alternatives, and preferences — that is, choosing to "reveal." Third, define "defection" to mean being closed, secretive, and deceitful — that is, choosing to "conceal."

■ **Gerald B. Wetlaufer, The Ethics of Lying in Negotiation**[*]

**76 Iowa L. Rev.** 1219, 1226-1230 (1990)

[One category] of lies . . . is comprised of those "distributive" lies by which the liar seeks to capture an advantage over the other party. These include, among others, the lies — like those involving one's reservation price — that Professor White has identified as the measure of a negotiator's effectiveness. To illustrate the effect of these lies, let us assume that Mr. Seller is negotiating to sell a factory and that his reservation price is $900,000. Below that price, he is better off keeping the plant. After an extensive search, he has identified one, and only one, prospective purchaser. Her name is Ms. Buyer. Mr. Seller has estimated that her reservation price, the price above which she will not buy, is $1,200,000. Though he has no way of knowing for sure, you and I know that this estimate is exactly right. Mr. Seller's objective is to sell at the highest possible price, even if it means lying. In the course of several hours of bargaining, Mr. Seller has, through an outright lie about a competing bid, persuaded Ms. Buyer that he will not sell the property for anything less than $1,100,000, a figure that is $200,000 above his actual reservation price. The bargaining continues and eventually they split the difference between Mr. Seller's *perceived* reservation price ($1,100,000) and Ms. Buyer's *actual* reservation price ($1,200,000). With a price of $1,150,000, Ms. Buyer is happy because she believes she has captured exactly half of the available surplus. Mr. Seller is ecstatic, believing (correctly) that he has captured $250,000 of the $300,000 surplus and that his "winning margin" of $200,000 is attributable solely to his skills as a liar. Other distributive lies, such as lies about the mileage of a used car, may operate in slightly different ways,

*Gerald B. Wetlaufer, The Ethics of Lying in Negotiations, 75 Iowa L. Rev. 1219, 1272–1273 (1990) (reprinted with permission).

sometimes by altering the other party's assessment of its own reservation price. What these lies all have in common is that, if they are successful, the liar becomes richer in the degree to which the victim becomes poorer. . . .

Integrative bargaining has several characteristics that bear upon the problem of lying in negotiations. First, opportunities for integrative bargaining are not always present. . . . Second, even when there are integrative opportunities to expand the pie, the pie will almost always, eventually, need to be divided. That division will be an occasion for distributive, win-lose bargaining. What complicates matters is that, while lying may be the watchword in distributive bargaining, full and truthful disclosure is the key to identifying and exploiting opportunities for integrative bargaining. Thus certain kinds of lies, told to secure distributive (pie-splitting) advantages, may make it impossible for the parties to discover and exploit the integrative (pie-expanding) opportunities that may be available. For example, lies about our interest or priorities can *simultaneously* win the liar a larger share of the pie *and* blind both parties to those avenues by which the pie might have been expanded. In this way, a successful distributive lie may injure both the liar and his victim by causing them to reach an agreement that is less productive of *total* profit than might, but for the lie, have been the case.

Lying in negotiations may also cause injuries that are more general and far-reaching than the immediate effects upon the parties to the negotiation. Lies that are discovered may, for instance, cause persons other than the liar to engage in defensive lying either later in that same negotiation or in *other* negotiations. Such lies can diminish the level of trust and increase the frequency with which additional lies are told. . . .

In the end, lying in negotiations can produce a wide range of possible effects. While the distribution of these effects is anything but symmetrical, they include both costs and benefits. Two things, though, are clear. The most important is that we cannot say as a general matter that honesty is the best policy for individual negotiators to pursue if by "best" we mean most effective or most profitable. In those bargaining situations which are at least in part distributive, a category which includes virtually all negotiations, lying is a coherent and often effective strategy. In those same circumstances, a policy of never lying may place a negotiator at a systematic and sometimes overwhelming disadvantage.

The second point is that one who lies in negotiations is in a position to capture almost all of the benefits of lying while suffering only a small portion of the costs and that, in the language of the economists, this state of affairs will lead, almost automatically, to an overproduction of lies.  ■

# ▪ David A. Lax & James K. Sebenius, The Manager as Negotiator*

35-38 (1986)

## STONE VERSUS WARD

Mr. Stone, representing MicroCable Inc., and Mayor Ward, representing the town council of a town we will call Clayton, are negotiating three issues: the price the town residents would have to pay for their subscriptions, the date by which the system would be fully operational (the completion date), and the number of cable channels to be offered.

The Mayor places greatest weight on a speedy completion date, in part because of his upcoming reelection campaign. Within the range of feasible prices and numbers of channels, he cares approximately the same about the price, which he would like to minimize, and the number of channels, which he would like to maximize. The cable company gives greatest weight to price and the least weight to the number of channels. MicroCable would of course like the highest price and the slowest completion, but perhaps surprisingly, Stone estimates that, though providing more channels involves additional costs, it would ultimately pay off handsomely because he will be able to sell more pay TV subscriptions. Neither party is certain about the other's beliefs and preferences. If both were to reveal their preferences to a third party and to ask her to construct a jointly desirable agreement, the agreement might well specify the maximum number of channels, a high price, and a relatively fast completion.

In preparing for the negotiation, Mayor Ward recalls the experience of a colleague who had negotiated with a different cable firm.

His colleague had publicly expressed a strong interest in a quick completion time — which he ultimately obtained but only after being unmercifully squeezed on price. Mayor Ward fears that Stone would respond opportunistically to a similar announcement, insisting that fast completion would be very costly for him but that perhaps he could arrange it only in return for very high prices and few channels. Such an agreement would be barely acceptable to the Mayor and the town, but would, the Mayor guesses, be quite desirable for Stone. In other words, Mayor Ward fears that if he attempts to jointly create value by sharing information about his preferences, Stone will attempt to claim the value by being misleading about his preferences. Thus, the Mayor elects to be a bit cagey and plans to downplay his interests in comple-

---

*Reprinted and abridged with the permission of The Free Press, a division of Simon & Schuster, Inc., from The Manager as Negotiator: Bargaining for Cooperation and Competitive Gain by David A. Lax and James K. Sebenius. Copyright © 1986 by David A. Lax and James K. Sebenius.

tion and the number of channels. He also plans to exaggerate his interest in a low price, with the hope of ultimately making a seemingly big concession on that issue in return for a big gain on completion and channels.

Stone has similar inclinations. If he lets the Mayor know that he is much more concerned with price than with speed of completion and that he actually wants more channels, he reasons, he will have given up all his bargaining chips. Mayor Ward would, he guesses, initially offer a moderately high price but only in return for an unbearably early completion date. And, he fears that the Mayor would use the town's political process to make it difficult to be dislodged from his offer. Thus, Stone is also afraid that if he attempts to create value by sharing information about his preferences, the Mayor will attempt to claim that value by being opportunistic about his and may also try to make a binding commitment to his preferred position. So, Stone also chooses to be cagey, but plans to let the Mayor and the town know, early on, that a moderate completion time and a moderate number of channels are barely possible and are very costly to him. He has an assistant prepare slides detailing the costs, but not the revenue forecasts, of additional channels. The assistant also prepares financial analyses that are intended to show that he will need high prices to recoup the cost of even such moderate concessions. Ultimately, he hopes to concede a little on the completion date for a modest price increase, and to appear magnanimous in making a final concession of the maximum number of channels for a last major price increase. . . .

As the formal negotiation starts, Mayor Ward and Stone begin to thrust and parry. The Mayor stresses the importance the city places on keeping the price down. He also mentions that speedy completion and a large number of channels would be preferred by Clayton's residents. Stone responds sympathetically but explains the high cost of even normal completion times and of the number of channels in a basic system. Adding channels to the system and accelerating construction of the system faster than its "normal rate" are sufficiently costly that a cable franchise would be virtually unprofitable. He presents financial analyses showing the costs both of more channels and of "accelerated" completion dates.

Unable to counter directly, Mayor Ward alludes to (not yet formally received) strong offers by other cable operators. Stone parries by mentioning another town that eagerly seeks the superior MicroCable system, but says that he would of course rather do business in Clayton. They move beyond this minor impasse by concentrating on the price, in which both sides have expressed strong interest. They bargain hard. The Mayor claims that neither the town council nor the citizenry could approve a franchise with anything more than a moderate price, unless the services were extraordinary. Stone then cites still more of his financial analyses. Each searches for a favorable wedge. After arguing about different definitions of "fair and reasonable profit" and "fair return on investment," they compromise by agreeing on the price reached in a negotiation between a neighboring town and one of MicroCable's competitors. The Mayor never realizes that Stone could be more flexible on completion dates and does not arrange as early a date as he might have gotten for the price. And, ironically, Stone's careful financial presentation about the costs of adding channels makes it difficult for him to offer the town the maximum number of channels without losing face. The bargaining is tense, but they ultimately settle at a compromise on each issue: a moderate price, a moderate completion date, and about half the maximum number of channels.

Both men leave feeling good about the outcome. As Stone says to his assistant, "We didn't get everything we wanted but we gave as good as we got." Before the town council's vote on the franchise agreement, the Mayor describes the negotiation as a success: "If both sides complain a bit about the agreement, then you know it must be a good deal." The town council approves the proposal unanimously.

In the negotiations, each of the parties was afraid that his attempt to create value by sharing information would be exploited by the other's claiming tactics. Each chose to attempt to mislead or claim a bit, in self-protection. And, relative to what was possible, they ended up with an inferior solution. They left joint gains on the table. Both would have preferred the maximum number of channels and both would have preferred a higher price in return for earlier completion. A pity, but not uncommon.                                                    ▪

## Notes

*1. Questions and Answers in Negotiation.*   The negotiator's dilemma is quite prevalent in almost all bargaining situations. Good negotiators spend much of their time at the bargaining table asking the other negotiator questions about facts to which only the latter has access, the latter's interpretation of those facts, and the latter's valuation of an agreement and his other alternatives. For example, a plaintiff and a defendant are likely to ask each other how confident they are that they will prevail at trial if settlement negotiations fail. The answer each receives will help him to estimate the other's reservation price and, if the answer is supported with facts and reasoned argument, it also might affect his own reservation price. If each cooperates by truthfully revealing he is only 50 percent confident of winning, perhaps the negotiators will find that there is a bargaining zone in which a mutually profitable settlement can be reached. If each defects by misrepresenting his beliefs by saying he is 90 percent confident of prevailing, the negotiators might determine that there is no bargaining zone, and that trial is the only possible result. If the plaintiff cooperates and the defendant defects, the defendant might claim an inflated level of confidence that places his apparent reservation price at the same point as the plaintiff's reservation price, thus allowing the defendant to capture all of the cooperative surplus.

**2. Evidence of the Problem.** The "Stone versus Ward" hypothetical scenario presented by Lax and Sebenius demonstrates why it is intuitively appealing for negotiators to consider misrepresenting and obfuscating their preferences in an effort to claim a larger share of the cooperative surplus. There is also data that shows (a) negotiators often use this tactic and (b) it can pay off. In one study, Kathleen O'Connor and Peter Carnevale had subjects negotiate an agreement between a union and management that covered five employment issues. The subjects received points based on how they resolved each issue. In the scenario, the two sides had conflicting interests on four of the issues, although differences presented in the intensity of preferences made integrative bargaining possible. The two sides had identical interests on the fifth issue. Kathleen M. O'Connor & Peter J. Carnevale, A Nasty but Effective Negotiation Strategy: Misrepresentation of a Common-Value Issue, 23 Personality & Soc. Psychol. Bull. 504, 507 (1997). Twenty-eight percent of subjects engaged in misrepresentation concerning the issue in which the two sides had identical preferences, either by lying about their preferences or failing to correct a statement made by the other party demonstrating an incorrect belief that their interests conflicted. On average, the subjects who misrepresented earned higher scores than those who did not, and 23 of the 25 misrepresenters earned a higher score than their opponent. Id. at 509-511.

**3. The Prisoner's Dilemma Analogy.** There are two possible ways to analogize the negotiator's dilemma to the prisoner's dilemma. First, one can think of each contact between negotiators as a round of play. Because most negotiations have a number of contacts before a deal is reached or impasse is declared, the negotiators can be viewed as participating in a multiround prisoner's dilemma game with an unknown number of rounds even if they will never again see each other after this transaction. If a negotiator defects at the first contact, he might gain an advantage, but this benefit must be weighed against the possibility that his behavior will cause the other negotiator to defect at future contact points. Second, one can think of each negotiation as a single round of play. Viewed this way, the game becomes multiround, and reputations matter, if either the negotiators may meet again in another transaction, or if a negotiator's reputation is likely to be communicated to other members of the community who the negotiator will meet in future circumstances. Which is the better way to think about the negotiator's dilemma? What are the implications of the answer to this question for the negotiator's strategic choices?

*4. A Litigation Example.*   Consider the following description of litigation as prisoner's dilemma:

> . . . Able and Baker dispute the proper division of $100 according to some legal standard. . . . Each party holds information not known by the other side. Some of this information is favorable and some of it is unfavorable. Before the judge decides the case, there is a one-stage simultaneous disclosure process in which each party hands to the judge and the opposing party a sealed envelope containing information. Only two moves are possible, and neither player can know in advance what the other will do. One move is cooperation: a player voluntarily (and at no cost to the other side) discloses to the other side and to the judge all material information in her possession. The second option, defection, involves the adversarial use of the disclosure process to hide unfavorable information. As a consequence, the other side must spend $15 to force disclosure of some but not all of the information withheld. After the envelope exchange and the "purchase" of some of the withheld information, the judge resolves the dispute based on the information disclosed.
>
> With the payoff structure indicated by the following matrix, this game poses a prisoner's dilemma. If both players cooperate, there are no discovery expenses for either side and we will assume the judge awards $50 to Able and $50 to Baker. If both players defect, each must spend $15 to pry out some but not all of the unfavorable information possessed by the other side. Although the judge lacks complete information, we assume that she divides the $100 in the same ratio; the net recovery to the parties is now $35 to Able and $35 to Baker. The third scenario, in which one player defects while the other cooperates, provides the defector with a higher payoff ($70) and hurts the "sucker" in two ways. First, because the cooperating player has disclosed all of its unfavorable information while the defecting party has only disclosed some of the information unfavorable to it, the judge awards the sucker a gross recovery of only $30. Second, the sucker has spent $15 to get less than all of the information unfavorable to the other side before the judge (without which his recovery would be even lower). Thus, the sucker's net recovery is only $15.
>
> In this litigation game, Able's best response to whatever strategy Baker chooses is to defect. . . . The same, of course, is true for Baker. Defect-Defect, therefore, is a "dominant strategy equilibrium," even though this result guarantees each party only $35, rather than the $50 produced by a strategy of mutual cooperation. . . .

Ronald J. Gilson & Robert H. Mnookin, Disputing Through Agents: Cooperation and Conflict Between Lawyers in Litigation, 94 Colum. L. Rev. 509, 514-515 (1994).

## DISCUSSION QUESTIONS AND PROBLEMS

*1. Is the Analogy Apt?*   In the prisoner's dilemma, if the game lasts only one round, defection is clearly the dominant strategy. Is the same true in the negotiator's dilemma? Suppose you are negotiating a single transaction with a party whom you know you will never see again. Are there any reasons, save personal ethical principles, for you to be forthright and candid about your interests and preferences? That is, are there any situations in which cooperation can actually be the dominant strategy in a single-round negotiator's dilemma?

*2. Avoiding the Dilemma Through Contract or Law.*   Recall that an important feature of the prisoner's dilemma is that the two prisoners cannot speak to each other, so they cannot enter into a contract in which each promises to cooperate. If they could do so, entering into the contract and cooperating would be the best strategy for each, because each would know the alternative is mutual defection. Negotiators, of course, can communicate. Do you think negotiators can avoid the dilemma, then, by contracting to behave cooperatively? How would you draft such a contract? Have the rules of civil procedure provided the regulatory equivalent of such a contract in litigation bargaining situations by specifying rules of discovery and giving judges the power to sanction lawyers who violate them?

*3. Applying Axelrod's Findings.*   Professor Axelrod's computer tournament suggests that "nice" strategies are desirable in prisoner's dilemma games in the long run, so long as they respond adequately to attempts to take advantage of them. Do you think this is a valid conclusion concerning the negotiator's dilemma?

*4.* One stylized feature of Axelrod's competition is that defection and cooperation are directly observable. Is this true of legal negotiation situations? That is, if one negotiator defects, how likely is it that this will be observed by the other, such that the other can respond appropriately? Are some types of defection more likely to be discovered and exposed than others? If some types of defections, or all defections in some types of situations, are undiscoverable, is there any justification for cooperating in those circumstances?

*5. Having It Both Ways.*   Can a negotiator cooperate and defect simultaneously? Professor Wetlaufer downplays the conflict created by the negotiator's dilemma with the following reasoning:

> . . . [T]he argument for openness and truthtelling is not an argument for openness and truthtelling with respect to everything, but instead, is limited

to information useful in identifying and exploiting opportunities for integrative bargaining. Thus, an opportunity for integrative bargaining will present an occasion for a certain amount of truthtelling with respect to one's relative interest in various issues (or one's projections about the future or aversion to risk) without also presenting even a weak argument for truthtelling with respect to one's reservation price.

Gerald B. Wetlaufer, The Limits of Integrative Bargaining 185 Geo. L.J. 369, 390-391 (1996).

Is it really possible for a negotiator to act in such a way that he never misses out on discovering a bargaining zone or expanding it to its maximum potential through integrative bargaining, but at the same time he never leaves himself vulnerable to the other party's attempts to garner the cooperative surplus? How would you walk this fine line in an actual negotiation setting?

**6. *Analogies to the Negotiation Process.*** One student of labor relations, in describing the negotiation process, remarks that "[t]he name of this game is poker, not chess." William McCarthy, The Role of Power and Principle in Getting to Yes, 1 Negotiation J. 59, 64 (1985). Do you agree with this characterization? Why or why not? To what extent does your answer depend on how you approach the negotiator's dilemma?

**7. *An Example from Family Law.*** Husband and Wife have two children, ages 9 and 12. Husband decides he has fallen out of love with Wife and moves out of the family home. One year later, he files for divorce. At a settlement hearing, Wife's lawyer explains that Wife has an interest in receiving enough alimony and child support to allow her to work not at all or only part time until the children finish high school, but her primary interest is in obtaining custody of the children. Husband has no interest in custody of the children. Nevertheless, Husband's lawyer angrily exclaims that custody is also Husband's primary interest, and that he intends to take the fight for custody all the way to the U.S. Supreme Court, if need be. After several hours of angry exchanges, the parties agree to a settlement under which Wife receives custody of the children but no alimony and minimal child support.

Did Wife's lawyer fail to protect her client's interests? Did Husband's lawyer behave improperly? What would you have done differently if you had been Wife's lawyer or Husband's lawyer?

**8. *What Game Are We Playing?*** Recall the evidence above that subjects exhibited more cooperative behavior in a prisoner's dilemma game when they were told they were playing the "community game" than when they were told they were playing the "Wall Street game." Do you think legal negotiators believe that in some types of negotiations "defection" is expected and in other types "cooperation" is expected, and thus behave accordingly? What types of negotiations carry with them the expectation of cooperation or defection? Is there any way for a negotiator to change the expectation of interaction in order to promote cooperation?

## Chapter 8

# Conflict Style

In Part II, we viewed negotiators as monolithic and unitary individuals who pursued the goals of estimating, expanding, and dividing a bargaining zone. This approach is useful for understanding the fundamental structure of the negotiation process, but it is obviously incomplete because it fails to take into account how differences in the way individual negotiators approach and deal with conflict can affect the process and bargaining outcomes. In this chapter, we relax the assumption that negotiators are monolithic in approach and explore the effects that differences in negotiator style can have on negotiation processes and outcomes.

Few commentators would disagree with the proposition that interpersonal dynamics affect negotiations. It is substantially more difficult to identify the specific elements of style that matter. This chapter employs two very different conceptual frameworks. Section A focuses on a landmark study, now two decades old, that categorizes negotiators on the basis of whether they employ cooperative or noncooperative tactics in bargaining. From this perspective, the fundamental distinction between negotiators is whether they are "cooperators" or "competitors." Section B categorizes negotiators based on the extent to which they use different communication skills. From this perspective, important implications flow from whether a negotiator is skilled at "asserting" his needs, "empathizing" with the adversary's needs, both, or neither.

As you read this chapter, think about what elements of a negotiator's personality or personal style you think have the most important impact on negotiation dynamics and outcomes. Have the authors of either of the main articles identified the traits that are most relevant, or is there another way of thinking about the issue of negotiator style that would be more fruitful?

# A.  COOPERATION VERSUS COMPETITION

## ■ Gerald R. Williams, Legal Negotiation and Settlement*

15-42 (1983)

... In the Phoenix version of the survey questionnaire, which is reported here, attorneys were asked to think of their most recently completed case or transaction, to briefly describe the matter, to think of the attorney representing the other party in the matter, and to describe that attorney according to 137 characteristics listed in the questionnaire. When they had completed the descriptive ratings, they were asked to rate the negotiating effectiveness of the attorney they had described. This rating scale was divided into three categories: ineffective, average and effective. . . .

... The results indicate that legal negotiation proceeds quite consistently within the parameters of two basic approaches. Both approaches are described in considerable detail by the analysis, providing exceptionally powerful insights into the nature of bargaining processes generally and the behavior of individual negotiators in particular. The pattern identified in a majority of the negotiators (65%) is best described as a cooperative approach to negotiation, while the second pattern (identified in 24% of attorneys) represents a competitive approach. . . .

The highest-rated characteristics of effective/cooperative negotiators fall into six informal clusters. The first cluster describes, in order of importance, their motivational objectives:

### Cluster One

Conducting self ethically
Maximizing settlement for client
Getting a fair settlement
Meeting client's needs
Avoiding litigation
Maintaining or establishing a good personal relationship with opponent

It is surprising to find the predominant concern is with *ethical conduct*. This theme recurs among cooperative negotiators at all levels of effectiveness. The second concern is with *maximizing settlement for the client*, but this must be interpreted in light of item number 3, concern for *getting a fair settlement*. Attorneys of this type feel constrained in

---

*Reprinted from Legal Negotiation and Settlement by Gerald R. Williams. Copyright © 1983 by West Publishing Co. Reprinted with permission of West Group.

their conduct by a standard of fairness and ethical dealing. They want to know their clients' needs and, if possible, meet those needs without the necessity of litigation. They are also concerned with maintaining a good personal relationship with the opposing attorney.

Their strategy for meeting these goals is straightforward, as reflected in the following descriptors:

### Cluster Two

Accurately estimated the value of the case
Knew the needs of the client
Took a realistic opening position
Probed opponent's position
Knew the needs of opponent's client
Willing to share information
Forthright
Trustful
Willing to move from original position
Objective
Fair-minded
Reasonable
Logical (not emotional)
Did not use threats

### Cluster Three

Courteous
Personable
Friendly
Tactful
Sincere

### Cluster Four

Organizing
Wise
Careful
Facilitating
Cooperative

The third cluster relates to personableness: effective/cooperative negotiators are seen as friendly, personable, courteous, and tactful. However, some degree of caution is called for in interpreting these words. A person unfamiliar with legal negotiation is likely to picture a "soft" negotiator who is, as a consequence of personableness, a pushover. This cannot be a correct interpretation, because the adjectives describe effective negotiators at work in the legal context. A richer sense of meaning will develop as additional adjective clusters are considered.

Effective/cooperative attorneys are also seen as fair, objective, reasonable, logical, and willing to move from their established positions. Interpretation of these adjectives is aided by the other cluster two descriptors, which indicate these attorneys take realistic opening positions, support their position with facts, and are forthright.

While these traits are quite general, there are a number of descriptors that are focused on negotiating situations. For example, cooperative effectives seek to facilitate agreement, they avoid use of threats, they accurately estimate the value of cases they are working on, they are sensitive to the needs of their clients, and they are willing to share information with their opponent. It appears from these items that their strategy is to approach negotiation in an objective, fair, trustworthy way, and to seek agreement by the open exchange of information. They are apparently as concerned with getting a settlement that is fair to both sides as they are with maximizing the outcome for their own client. . . .

The differences in approach between cooperative and competitive attorneys is most quickly illustrated by comparing motivational objectives. In order of their importance, competitive/effectives have as their goals:

### Cluster One

Maximizing settlement for client
Obtaining profitable fee for self
Outdoing or outmaneuvering the opponent

Obviously, the goal of getting a maximum settlement value for the client means something different to a competitor than to a cooperate. To competitors, the goal includes a reward to self both in monetary terms and in satisfaction from outdoing an opponent. The difference in view between these two types becomes more apparent from examining other competitor traits. They are seen as:

### Cluster Two

Tough
Dominant
Forceful
Aggressive
Attacking

### Cluster Three

Ambitious
Egotist
Arrogant
Clever

*Cluster Four*

Made a high opening demand
Took unrealistic opening position
Used take-it-or-leave-it approach
Rigid
Disinterested in needs of opponent's client
Did not consider opponent's needs
Unconcerned about how opponent would look to his client
Willing to stretch the facts
Knew the needs of own client
Careful about timing and sequence of actions
Revealed information gradually
Used threats
Obstructed
Uncooperative

In contrast to the friendly, trustworthy approach of cooperative effectives, effective/competitives are seen as dominating, competitive, forceful, tough, arrogant, and uncooperative. They make high opening demands, they use threats, they are willing to stretch the facts in favor of their clients' positions, they stick to their positions, and they are parsimonious with information about the case. They are concerned not only with maximizing the outcome for their client but they appear to take a gamesmanship approach to negotiation, having a principle objective of outdoing or outmaneuvering their opponent. Thus, rather than seeking an outcome that is "fair" to both sides, they want to outdo the other side; to score a clear victory. . . .

Competitive/effectives are careful about the timing and sequence of their actions which underscores the gamesmanship element of competitive negotiating behavior. This reflects a high level of interest in tactical or strategic considerations, suggesting that they orchestrate the case for best effect. One effective/competitive attorney laughed when his cooperative opponent said the objective of negotiation was to accomplish a just outcome. He said, "This is a poker game, and you do your best to put the best front on your case and you try to make the other fellow think that his weaknesses are bigger than he really ought to consider them." Another attorney reported that the insurance defense attorney opposing him "could have appraised the case more on injury to the plaintiff rather than on difficulty of plaintiff in putting on a good case at trial." These comments show the unbridgeable gap in perceptions and attitudes between cooperative and competitive attorneys. Cooperatives feel that cases should be evaluated objectively, on their merits, and that both sides should seek to find the most fair outcome. Competitive attorneys view their work as a game in which they seek to outwit and out-perform the other side. . . .

Both types of effective negotiators are ranked as highly experienced. . . .

More importantly, both types are seen as ethical, trustworthy and honest, thus dispelling any doubt about the ethical commitments of effective/competitives. . . .

Both effective types are seen as thoroughly prepared on the facts and the law of the case. They are also described as legally astute. . . .

The ineffective/cooperative does not have the skills or attitudes of an effective/cooperative, such as being perceptive, or convincing, or having the reasonableness cluster (realistic, rational, and analytical). Nor is he creative, self-controlled, versatile, objective, organizing, or legally astute. The ineffective is apparently unsure of himself or of the value of his case (conservative, staller, cautious, deliberate). He is torn between being gentle, obliging, patient, moderate, and forgiving, on the one hand, and demanding, "masculine", and argumentative on the other, and tends to be something of an idealist. The idealism may account for lack of versatility, adaptability, creativity, and wisdom. . . .

Competitive/ineffective attorneys are characterized by negative traits, and can be generally described as irritating. . . .

Somehow, competitive/effective legal negotiators are able to apply their expertise without being seen as greedy or conniving, but rather as reasonable and realistic. Again, these comparisons seem to point to the quality of the legal work being performed, including the expertise with which an attorney has investigated the facts of his case, studied and understood the legal rules applicable to it, taken a realistic position with respect to the value of the case, and presented his position in ways that other attorneys accept as being rational, fair, and persuasive (convincing). It may follow that an attorney in this posture has little cause to be argumentative, quarrelsome, rude, and hostile, since he is prepared to effectively go forward on the merits of his position rather than to seek advantage by being personally offensive to the opposing attorney, or by stalling, bluffing, or quarreling. . . .

. . . [O]ne wonders whether one approach or the other is more effective. The answer provided by our Phoenix data is that there is no difference in degree of effectiveness attributed to effective/cooperatives and effective/competitives. They received comparably high ratings for effectiveness. It does not appear, therefore, that either approach has the edge when it comes to obtaining the highest (as compared to greatest number) of effectiveness ratings. On the other hand, there are a substantially greater number of effective attorneys of the cooperative type than of the competitive type.

# Notes

*1. Negotiating Style versus Negotiating Goals.*   What Williams identifies as cooperative and competitive negotiation styles are often confused with the willingness of a negotiator to pursue the negotiating goals of integrative bargaining (expanding the bargaining zone) and distributive bargaining (dividing the cooperative surplus), respectively. It is important to realize that cooperative and competitive styles do not map exactly onto integrative and distributive bargaining goals. All negotiators must face up to the task of distribution. Williams' results suggest that "competitive" negotiators are those who address the need to distribute with power tactics, whereas "cooperative" negotiators are those who are more likely to conduct distributive bargaining on the basis of fairness norms. Williams' subjects described as competitive such traits as "dominating," "forceful," "rigid," "uses threats," and "unrealistic opening positions" — all characteristics consistent with attempting to use power. In contrast, they described as cooperative such traits as "trustworthy," "fair," "sincere," "fair minded," and "does not use threats" — all consistent with using norms of fair division.

Cooperative negotiators might be more likely to engage in integrative bargaining than competitive negotiators, however. "Willing to share information" and "probes opponent's position" are described as characteristics of the former style, whereas "reveals information gradually" is described as a characteristic of the latter style. On the other hand, being too cooperative might cause a negotiator to not engage in integrative bargaining, but rather to be satisfied with dividing equally or equitably the cooperative surplus that results from a negotiated agreement without thinking creatively about how to enlarge that surplus.

*2. Updated Statistics.*   In 1999, Andrea Kupfer Schneider surveyed lawyers in Chicago and Milwaukee with a survey instrument similar to the one used by Gerald Williams more than 20 years earlier. Schneider asked her respondents to describe the last lawyer-negotiator that they had negotiated against as employing a "problem-solving" or "adversarial" style — roughly but not precisely (as the preceding note suggests) corresponding to Williams' use of the terms "cooperative" and "competitive" — and to rate that negotiator's effectiveness. She found that negotiators rated 54 percent of their peers whom they identified as "problem-solving" as "effective," — similar to Williams' finding that 59 percent of "cooperative" negotiators were effective. However, Schneider's subjects rated only 9 percent of the negotiators that they identified as "adversarial" as being effective, far lower than Williams' finding that 25 percent of "competitive" negotiators were effective. Andrea Kupfer Schneider Perceptions, Reputation and Reality: An Empirical Study of Negotiation Styles, 6 Disp. Res. Mag. 24 (Summer 2000).

*3. Is Negotiator Style Consistent?* To what extent is the style with which a negotiator approaches a bargaining situation based on the peculiar characteristics of that situation, such as the stakes or the identity of the opponent, and to what extent do negotiators adopt the same stylistic approach regardless of context? Although it is undoubtedly true that context matters to negotiators to a certain extent, some research indirectly hints that negotiators are likely to rely on a preferred style across a range of contexts. In one study, for example, experimenters asked college student subjects to describe actual conflict situations involving peers and conflict situations involving parents, and also to assess hypothetical conflict situations. Using an expansive set of conflict resolution style categories, the experimenters found that although different subjects used different styles, individual subjects tended to use and prefer the same style regardless of whom the conflict was with, and regardless of whether the conflict was actual or hypothetical. The experimenters concluded that their "results suggest that the best predictor of style of a given interpersonal conflict is that individual's style either in another situation or with another person." Robert J. Sternberg & Diane M. Dobson, Resolving Interpersonal Conflicts: An Analysis of Stylistic Consistency, 52 J. Pers. & Soc. Psychol. 794, 810 (1987).

## B.  EMPATHY VERSUS ASSERTIVENESS

■ **Robert H. Mnookin, Scott R. Peppet & Andrew S. Tulumello, The Tension Between Empathy and Assertiveness***

**12 Negotiation J.** 217, 219-225 (1996)

. . . [This article] deals with an interpersonal aspect of negotiation: how should a negotiator approach his or her dealings with another? We propose that negotiation behavior can be conceptualized along two dimensions — *assertiveness* and *empathy*. . . .

### EMPATHY

For purposes of negotiation, we define empathy as the process of demonstrating an accurate, nonjudgmental understanding of the other side's needs, interests, and positions. There are two components to this definition. The first involves a skill psychologists call *perspective-taking* —

trying to see the world through the other negotiator's eyes. The second is the nonjudgmental *expression* of the other person's viewpoint in a way that is open to correction. . . .

The benefits of empathy relate to the integrative and distributive aspects of bargaining. Consider first the potential benefits of understanding (but not yet demonstrating) the other side's viewpoint. Skilled negotiators often can "see through" another person's statements to find hidden interests or feelings, even when they are inchoate in the other's mind. Perspective-taking thus facilitates value-creation by enabling a negotiator to craft arguments, proposals, or trade-offs that reflect another's interests and that may create the basis for trade.

Perspective-taking also facilitates distributive moves. To the extent we understand another negotiator, we will better predict their goals, expectations, and strategic choices. This enables good perspective-takers to gain a strategic advantage — analogous, perhaps, to playing a game of chess with advance knowledge of the other side's moves. It may also mean that good perspective-takers will more easily see through bluffing or other gambits based on artifice. Research confirms that negotiators with higher perspective-taking ability negotiate agreements of higher value than those with lower perspective-taking ability. . . .

### ASSERTIVENESS

By assertiveness, we mean the ability to express and advocate for one's own needs, interests, and positions. The underlying skills include identifying one's own interests, speaking (making arguments, explaining), and even listening. . . .

We can relate the benefits of assertiveness to the integrative and distributive aspects of bargaining. It is well established that assertion confers distributive benefits — assertive negotiators tend to get more of what they want. Less well understood is the role assertion plays in value-creation. Assertiveness contributes to value-creation because it is through direct expression of each side's interests that joint gains may be discovered. Assertion may be relatively easy in commercial negotiations between strangers, but can be more difficult where conflict arises in the context of a long-term relationship. If one or both parties fails to assert their interests, both may suffer because value may be left on the table. . . .

### NEGOTIATION STYLES: COMPETING, ACCOMMODATING, AND AVOIDING

Our claim that empathy and assertiveness represent different dimensions can be illuminated by considering three common negotiation "styles." . . .

COMPETING

A competitive style consists of substantial assertion but little empathy. A competitor wants to experience "winning" and enjoys feeling purposeful and in control. Competitive negotiators exude eagerness, enthusiasm, and impatience. Because conflict does not make them feel uncomfortable, they enjoy being partisans. Competitive negotiators typically seek to control the agenda and frame the issues. They can stake out an ambitious position and stick to it, and they fight back in the face of bullying or intimidation.

The advantages of this style flow directly from this characterization. Competitors are not afraid to articulate and push for their point of view. With respect to distributive bargaining, they fight hard to get the biggest slice of any pie.

But this tendency also has disadvantages. Competitive negotiators risk provoking the other side and incur a high risk of escalation or stalemate. In addition, because competitive negotiators are often not good listeners, they have difficulty developing collaborative relationships that allow both sides to explore value-creating opportunities. They may also pay a high price in their relationships, as others, perceiving them as arrogant, untrustworthy, or controlling, avoid them. We have found that competitors can be surprised by the resentment they engender, as they see their behavior as simply part of the negotiation game. . . .

ACCOMMODATING

Accommodating consists of substantial empathy but little assertion. An accommodator prizes good relationships and wants to feel liked. Accommodators exude concern, compassion, and understanding. Concerned that conflict will disrupt relationships, they negotiate in "smoothing" ways to resolve differences quickly. Accommodators typically listen well and are quick to second-guess their own interests.

This style has straightforward advantages. Negotiators concerned with good relationships on balance probably do have better relationships, or at least fewer relationships marked by open conflict. Because they listen well, others may see them as trustworthy. Similarly, they are adept at creating a less stressful atmosphere for the negotiation.

One disadvantage of this tendency is that it can be exploited. Hard bargainers may extract concessions by implicitly or explicitly threatening to disrupt or terminate the relationship. Another disadvantage may be that accommodators pay insufficient attention to the substance of the dispute because they are unduly concerned about disturbing a relationship. Accommodators, therefore, can feel frustrated dealing with both substantive and interpersonal issues.

AVOIDING

An avoiding style consists of low levels of empathy and assertiveness. Avoiders believe that conflict is unproductive, and they feel uncomfortable with explicit, especially emotional, disagreement. When faced with conflict, avoiders disengage. They tend not to seek control of the agenda or to frame the issues. Rather, they deflect efforts to focus on solutions, appearing detached, unenthusiastic, or uninterested. . . .

The greatest disadvantage of this tendency is that avoiders miss opportunities to use conflict to solve problems. Avoiders often disengage without knowing whether obscured interests might make joint gains possible — they rarely have the experience of walking away from an apparent conflict feeling better off. Even when they do negotiate, avoiders leave value on the table because they refrain from asserting their own interests or flushing out the other side's. Avoiders fare poorly in the distributive aspects of bargaining.

Like competitors, avoiders also have a difficult time sustaining strong working relationships. Others see them as apathetic or indifferent. . . .

Each of these problematic interactions highlights the importance of being able to both empathize and assert as needed in a given negotiation. If both negotiators can skillfully empathize and assert, the pair can work toward a beneficial solution that exploits the opportunities for value-creation and manages distributive issues.                        ■

## Notes

*The Thomas-Kilmann Instrument.*   The "competing," "avoiding" and "accommodating" style categories used by Mnookin et al. are borrowed from the Thomas-Kilmann Conflict Mode Instrument. The Thomas-Kilmann instrument assesses the propensity of subjects to exhibit five different styles of behavior in conflict situations (not necessarily limited to negotiation) by giving subjects 30 pairs of statements and asking them to choose which of each pair best describes their approach to conflict. In addition to "competing," "avoiding," and "accommodating," the instrument identifies the styles of "compromising" and "collaborating." Kenneth W. Thomas & Ralph H. Kilmann, Thomas-Kilmann Conflict Mode Instrument (1974).

Kenneth Thomas, one of the designers of the Thomas-Kilmann instrument, has elsewhere described the differences between these five categories of conflict orientation. Similar to the approach of Mnookin et al., Thomas describes the different categories in terms of the extent to which the negotiator focuses on satisfying her own desires and the extent to which she focuses on satisfying the desires of the opponent.

According to Thomas, collaborating and accommodating orientations evidence a strong desire to meet the needs of the opponent, a compromising orientation demonstrates a moderate desire to meet the needs of the opponent, and competing and avoiding orientations reflect a lack of concern for satisfying the opponent. Collaborating and competing orientations, and to a lesser degree a compromising orientation, demonstrate a desire to satisfy the negotiator's own interest, while accommodating and avoiding orientations evidence a relative lack of desire on this dimension. See Kenneth Thomas, Conflict and Conflict Management, in Handbook of Industrial and Organizational Psychology, 889, 900-902 (Marvin D. Dunnette ed. 1976).

## DISCUSSION QUESTIONS AND PROBLEMS

*1. Evaluating Negotiating Styles.*   Think back to your last negotiating experience, either in class or in real life. First, classify your opponent's style as either "cooperative" or "competitive." What characteristics did he or she exhibit that caused you to place him or her in the category that you did? Second, evaluate whether that opponent was "effective" or "ineffective" in the negotiation. What made him or her effective or ineffective? Third, evaluate the relationship between your opponent's dominant style and his or her effectiveness. Was his or her effectiveness a consequence of the style employed, or independent of the style?

*2. Style and Situation.*   Williams claims that negotiating effectiveness is generally independent of whether a negotiator uses a competitive or a cooperative style, but that one style might be more or less effective in different situations. In what circumstances do you think a cooperative style likely would be more effective than a competitive one? In what circumstances do you think a competitive style likely would be more effective than a cooperative one? In what situations do you think empathy might be more important than assertiveness, or vice versa?

*3. Personal Style and Context.*   In a study of preferred approaches to conflict resolution, Robert Sternberg and Lawrence Soriano asked subjects to rank the desirability of seven negotiation "styles" in scenarios that presented conflict between family members, conflict between organizations, and conflict between nations. The "styles" they asked their subjects about (i.e., physical action, economic action, accept the situation, enlist third party assistance, etc.) were defined quite differently than the way that Williams or Mnookin et al. define negotiating style. But one of their findings has implications for the studies highlighted in this chapter: Sternberg and Soriano found that subjects' conflict style preferences were highly correlated across the different conflict contexts. Robert J. Sternberg & Lawrence J. Soriano, Styles of Conflict Resolution, 47 J. Pers. & Soc. Psychol. 115, 118-119 (1984). Do you think that you personally employ the same conflict resolution styles regardless of the negotiation context, or does your style vary depending on context? Do you think the same is true for those against whom you have negotiated?

**4. Empathy and Assertiveness: What Is Your Style?**   Mnookin et al. describe three common negotiating styles: competing, accommodating, and avoiding, based on the degree of both empathy and assertiveness demonstrated by the negotiator. Which of these three common styles do you think best describes how you approach bargaining situations? What are the advantages of your style? What are the disadvantages? What can you do in future bargaining situations to alter your approach in a way that minimizes the disadvantages of your dominant style?

**5. A Clash of Styles.**   When negotiators with different conflict styles oppose each other in bargaining situations, the interaction of the two styles can have a significant effect on bargaining dynamics. What type of dynamics would you expect to observe in the following situations?:

(a) A "competing" negotiator opposes an "accommodating" negotiator.
(b) A "competing" negotiator opposes an "avoiding" negotiator.
(c) An "accommodating" negotiator opposes an "avoiding" negotiator.
(d) Two "competing" negotiators oppose one another.
(e) Two "accommodating" negotiators oppose one another.
(f) Two "avoiding" negotiators oppose one another.

**6. The Negotiator's Dilemma Revisited.**   Do you think the way in which a negotiator copes with the negotiator's dilemma, described in Chapter 7, is correlated with his or her negotiation style or styles? To use Williams' framework, do you think a "cooperative" and a "competitive" negotiator would be likely to respond differently to the negotiator's dilemma? Using the terminology of Mnookin et al., do you think negotiators who fit into the "competing," "accommodating," and "avoiding" categories would be likely to respond differently to the negotiator's dilemma?

# Chapter 9

# Group Membership

Just as a negotiator's conflict style and basic strategic choices can be relevant to the negotiation process, so too can background and group membership, such as gender and culture-specific norms of interaction. This chapter examines the extent to which gender and culture can affect the negotiation process.

Generalizing based on cultural background and gender, however, can be extremely dangerous, for obvious reasons. The variance in negotiating behavior between individuals within a group will often be far greater than the variance between groups, and stereotypes are likely to be misleading in individual cases. For example, some research has indicated that women tend to be less comfortable using power tactics in negotiation, are more open, and are more concerned with preserving relationships. See, e.g., Melvin J. Kimmel et al., Effects of Trust, Aspiration and Gender on Negotiating Tactics, 38 J. Pers. & Soc. Psychol. 9 (1980). But a negotiator (male or female) who first sits down to bargain with a woman assuming that she has these traits will often find that his or her results would have been better if he or she had begun the bargaining without any stereotypes in mind. In addition to the problem that stereotypes can be misleading, studying them also carries the risk of unconsciously and unintentionally reinforcing them.

Keeping in mind these cautions about discussing generalizations based on group membership, inquiring into how gender and cultural background might bear on the negotiating process is justifiable for two reasons. First, some generalizations may be accurate, on average, even given wide variation among members of a particular group. Second — and perhaps more importantly — even if the stereotypes have little or no validity, if a significant number of negotiators assume them to be true, this could affect the way that those negotiators bargain with members of particular groups.

## A.  GENDER

The gender of the bargaining parties can be relevant to the study of
negotiation for two distinct reasons. First, it is conceivable that men
and women, on average, tend to adopt different negotiating tactics or
interpersonal styles. Second, it is conceivable that, men and women,
on average, achieve different negotiation outcomes. It is theoretically
possible that either one of these possibilities could be true while the
other is not. For example, men and women could approach bargaining
situations in identical ways but achieve differential outcomes. On the
other hand, men and women might approach bargaining from very
different perspectives, but the differences might not have a noticeable
impact on bargaining outcomes achieved. The following excerpt by
Charles Craver and David Barnes adopts this latter view. The authors
hypothesize certain gender differences in negotiating approaches —
some rooted in considerable empirical research on gender differences
generally, others that appear to be founded more on anecdote — but
question whether those differences in approach lead to differences in
bargaining outcomes.

■ **Charles B. Craver & David W. Barnes, Gender, Risk
Taking, and Negotiation Performance***

5 Mich. J. Gender & L. 299, 309-321 (1999)

... Many people believe that men and women behave in stereotypically different ways when they interact. Various traits are attributed to
males, with other characteristics being attributed to females. While
some of these gender-based differences may reflect real — i.e., empirically demonstrated — behavioral traits, others are merely perceived
differences that have no scientifically established bases. Nonetheless,
whether these differences are real or imagined, they may influence the
way in which men and women interact when they negotiate, because
the participants expect these factors to affect their dealings.

Men are thought to be rational and logical, while women are considered emotional and intuitive. Men are expected to emphasize objective fact, while women focus more on relationships. As a result, men
are considered more likely to define issues in abstract terms and to
resolve them through the application of reasoning based on justice and
rights. Men are thought more likely to rely on theoretical legal principles than are women.

Men are expected to be dominant and authoritative, while women are viewed as passive and submissive. Research shows when the sexes interact, men tend to speak for longer periods of time and to interrupt more frequently than women. Men usually exert more control over the subjects being discussed; they employ more direct language, while women tend to exhibit tentative and deferential speech patterns. During conversations, women tend to adopt physical alignments that are cohesive and supportive of other group members, and they are inclined to make more eye contact than their male cohorts. The masculine tendency to dominate male-female interactions could provide men with an inherent advantage during negotiations, by enabling them to control the agenda and direct the substantive discussions. When Hanisch and Carnevale studied the mediative styles of male and female subjects, they found that men were more confident of their ability to influence the parties. Female mediators sent fewer verbal signals to the parties, and they evidenced a greater desire to obtain the approval of the disputing parties.

Professor Gilligan has suggested that perceived gender differences may be attributed to the fact that American women have historically felt less powerful than men. This phenomenon has often caused women to be less confident regarding their ability to influence others and more concerned with the manner in which others view their performance. Perceived power imbalances may also explain why women tend to be more apprehensive before impending negotiations than men. . . .

When men and women encounter competition, they may behave differently. Various scholars have suggested that "women are more likely [than men] to avoid competitive situations, less likely to acknowledge competitive wishes, and not likely to do as well [as men] in competition."[48] Many women are apprehensive regarding the negative consequences they associate with competitive achievement. "Again and again women report the feeling that a successful woman alienates herself from both women and men."[49] Gender-based differences in competitive behavior may be attributable to different acculturation processes for boys and girls. . . .

In competitive settings, males are generally expected to behave more aggressively than females. Boys usually receive parental approval for aggressive and competitive tendencies, while girls are encouraged to be passive and dependent. During interpersonal transactions, men

---

48. Irene P. Stiver, Work Inhibitions in Women 2, Paper published by the Stone Center for Developmental Services and Studies, Work in Progress Series, at 5 (1983); Carol Gilligan, In a Different Voice 41 (1982); Deborah L. Rhode, Missing Questions: Feminist Perspectives on Legal Education, 45 Stan. L. Rev. 1547, 1550-51 (1993).

49. Stiver, supra note 48, at 6; see also Gilligan, supra note 48, at 14-15.

are more likely to employ "highly intense language" to persuade others, and they tend to be more effective when using this approach. Women, on the other hand, are more likely to use less intense language during persuasive encounters, and they are inclined to be more effective behaving in this manner. During conversations, men tend to downplay their doubts, while women are likely to downplay their certainty, enabling male speakers to exude a greater degree of confidence in what they are saying. Females tend to employ language containing more disclaimers (e.g., "you know," "it seems to me") than males, which may be perceived by their listeners as indications of reduced confidence levels. Women are more likely than men to use more indirect language during conversations, which may be perceived as a sign of uncertainty, while men tend to make more direct statements, which enhances the appearance of male assertiveness. When women eschew traditionally feminine conduct and behave in a stereotypically masculine fashion, they are usually not rewarded. They are instead criticized for deviating from conventional male-female role expectations.

Men in the Legal Negotiating class have occasionally indicated that they are particularly uncomfortable when female opponents obtain extremely beneficial results from them. A few have even indicated that they would prefer the consequences associated with nonsettlements to the possible embarrassment of "losing" to female opponents. While male students almost never apologize for their successes, a number of female class members indicate discomfort with their achievements and apologize to opponents whom they have out-performed. Even female students tend to be more critical of women who attain exceptional bargaining results than they are of male classmates who achieve equally advantageous negotiation terms.

When men negotiate, they generally endeavor to maximize their own side's return, while women are inclined to emphasize the maintenance of relationships. This phenomenon may explain why women tend to employ more accommodating strategies than men when resolving conflicts. One scholar writes, "Women seem more likely to prefer less adversarial methods of resolving disputes that do not harm the other side — relying on methods of problem solving and reconciliation rather than aggressive posturing. . . ." This more accommodating style may be especially beneficial when long-term relationships are involved, because of its capacity to enhance business relationships over prolonged periods.

When men and women negotiate, they often have different expectations regarding the results they would prefer to achieve. Men tend to expect "equitable" bargaining distributions, while women tend to believe in "equal" exchanges. These predispositional differences may induce female negotiators to accept equal negotiating results despite their possession of superior relative bargaining strength, while male bargainers seek equitable exchanges that reflect relevant power imbalances. Their egalitarian propensity could disadvantage women who hesitate to use favorable power imbalances to obtain more beneficial results for their sides. This factor would be particularly important with respect to bargaining interactions that are primarily distributional in nature, such as those involving monetary exchanges. . . .

Empirical evidence indicates that women are not as effective when employing deceptive tactics as their male cohorts. Studies have shown that men are more comfortable in situations in which they are expected to dissemble, and they find it easier to behave in a Machiavellian manner. Women are inclined to be more trusting than men, and they tend to be less forgiving of deceitful behavior than their male cohorts. These factors should further benefit male negotiators, because individuals involved in legal negotiations are usually endeavoring to mislead their opponents. . . .

Despite the various factors that would support the theory that more competitive male negotiators should achieve more beneficial results than female negotiators, empirical studies involving competitive interactions do not consistently substantiate this supposition. Psychologists attempting to measure male-female differences during competitive encounters have most frequently employed variations on the "Prisoner's Dilemma" exercise. . . .

If the stereotypical belief that men are more competitive than women is correct, one might reasonably expect men to behave more competitively when they participate in the Prisoner's Dilemma game. Men would be more likely to establish higher aspiration levels and would endeavor to take advantage of the perceived feminine tendency to be more accommodating. Various Prisoner's Dilemma studies have, however, discerned few or no gender differences. In one compilation of numerous Prisoner's Dilemma studies, many of the cited studies found no statistically significant gender differences with respect to competitive tendencies; of those experiments that did discern different behavior, some found males to be more competitive, and some found females to be more competitive.[87] Almost identical findings were obtained with respect to cooperative behavior. Most studies discovered no difference based upon participant gender, while others obtained mixed results.[88] . . .

Another factor that may explain the lack of gender differences is the impact of educational attainment. "When individuals are trained

87. Eleanor Emmons Maccoby & Carol Nagy Jacklin, The Psychology of Sex Differences 228, 251-53 & tbls. 7.2 and 7.3 (1974) (summarizing results of Prisoner's Dilemma studies).

88. Malcolm J. Grant & Vello Sermat, Status and Sex of Other as Determinants of Behavior in a Mixed-Motive Game, 12 J. Personality & Soc. Psychology 151, 156 (1969).

to perform a specific role, gender communication-behavior differences disappear. . . ." Highly educated professionals exhibit a similar trend, with women adopting more masculine styles of communication. These findings would suggest that if professionals are trained in mediation or negotiation skills, gender-based communication differences would be minimized. This would not, however, guarantee that male and female subjects would be viewed identically even when they behaved similarly. Male-female stereotypes could still cause some observers to perceive women participants as less controlling and less influential than male participants, even in circumstances in which the women were objectively exhibiting dominant behavior.

One might reasonably expect gender-based communication stereotypes to place women at a disadvantage when facing legal negotiation exercises in the classroom. They would be likely to be perceived as less dominant and less forceful, and they would be expected to be less logical and more emotional. Nonetheless, two significant factors counterbalance these stereotypes. First, the advanced education possessed by law students and the specific training received in a legal negotiation course would minimize gender-based communication differentials. Second, the female negotiators may benefit from the established fact that women are typically more sensitive to nonverbal messages than their male cohorts. Since a significant amount of critical communication during interpersonal transactions is nonverbal, the enhanced ability of female negotiators to decode such signals could offset any disadvantage associated with latent stereotyping.

## ■ Carol Gilligan, In a Different Voice: Psychological Theory and Women's Development*

25-32 (1982)

The dilemma that . . . eleven-year-olds [Jake and Amy] were asked to resolve was one in the series devised by Kohlberg to measure moral development in adolescence by presenting a conflict between moral norms and exploring the logic of its resolution. In this particular dilemma, a man named Heinz considers whether or not to steal a drug which he cannot afford to buy in order to save the life of his wife. In the standard format of Kohlberg's interviewing procedure, the description of the dilemma itself — Heinz's predicament, the wife's disease, the druggist's refusal to lower his price — is followed by the question, "Should Heinz steal the drug?" The reasons for and against stealing

*Reprinted by permission of the publisher from In a Different Voice by Carol Gilligan, pp. 25–26, 27–28, 28–29, 32. Cambridge, Mass.: Harvard University Press. Copyright © 1982, 1993 by Carol Gilligan.

are then explored through a series of questions that vary and extend the parameters of the dilemma in a way designed to reveal the underlying structure of moral thought.

Jake, at eleven, is clear from the outset that Heinz should steal the drug. Constructing the dilemma, as Kohlberg did, as a conflict between the values of property and life, he discerns the logical priority of life and uses that logic to justify his choice:

> For one thing, a human life is worth more than money, and if the druggist only makes $1,000, he is still going to live, but if Heinz doesn't steal the drug, his wife is going to die. (*Why is life worth more than money?*) Because the druggist can get a thousand dollars later from rich people with cancer, but Heinz can't get his wife again. (*Why not?*) Because people are all different and so you couldn't get Heinz's wife again.

Asked whether Heinz should steal the drug if he does not love his wife, Jake replies that he should, saying that not only is there "a difference between hating and killing," but also, if Heinz were caught, "the judge would probably think it was the right thing to do." Asked about the fact that, in stealing, Heinz would be breaking the law, he says that "the laws have mistakes, and you can't go writing up a law for everything that you can imagine." . . .

Fascinated by the power of logic, this eleven-year-old boy locates truth in math, which, he says, is "the only thing that is totally logical." Considering the moral dilemma to be "sort of like a math problem with humans," he sets it up as an equation and proceeds to work out the solution. Since his solution is rationally derived, he assumes that anyone following reason would arrive at the same conclusion and thus that a judge would also consider stealing to be the right thing for Heinz to do. . . .

In contrast, Amy's response to the dilemma conveys a very different impression, [according to Kohlberg] an image of development stunted by a failure of logic, an inability to think for herself. Asked if Heinz should steal the drug, she replies in a way that seems evasive and unsure:

> Well, I don't think so. I think there might be other ways besides stealing it, like if he could borrow the money or make a loan or something, but he really shouldn't steal the drug — but his wife shouldn't die either.

Asked why he should not steal the drug, she considers neither property nor law but rather the effect that theft could have on the relationship between Heinz and his wife:

> If he stole the drug, he might save his wife then, but if he did, he might have to go to jail, and then his wife might get sicker again, and he couldn't

get more of the drug, and it might not be good. So, they should really just
talk it out and find some other way to make the money.

Seeing in the dilemma not a math problem with humans but a narrative of relationships that extends over time, Amy envisions the wife's
continuing need for her husband and the husband's continuing concern for his wife and seeks to respond to the druggist's need in a way
that would sustain rather than sever connection. Just as she ties the
wife's survival to the preservation of relationships, so she considers the
value of the wife's life in a context of relationships, saying that it would
be wrong to let her die because, "if she died, it hurts a lot of people
and it hurts her." Since Amy's moral judgment is grounded in the belief
that, "if somebody has something that would keep somebody alive, then
it's not right not to give it to them," she considers the problem in the
dilemma to arise not from the druggist's assertion of rights but from
his failure of response.

Just as Jake is confident the judge would agree that stealing is the
right thing for Heinz to do, so Amy is confident that, "if Heinz and
the druggist had talked it out long enough, they could reach something
besides stealing." As he considers the law to "have mistakes," so she
sees this drama as a mistake, believing that "the world should just share
things more and then people wouldn't have to steal." Both children
thus recognize the need for agreement but see it as mediated in different ways — he impersonally through systems of logic and law, she
personally through communication in relationship. Just as he relies on
the conventions of logic to deduce the solution to this dilemma, assuming these conventions to be shared, so she relies on a process of
communication, assuming connection and believing that her voice will
be heard. Yet while his assumptions about agreement are confirmed
by the convergence in logic between his answers and the questions
posed, her assumptions are belied by the failure of communication,
the interviewer's inability to understand her response. . . .

In this way, these two eleven-year-old children, both highly intelligent and perceptive about life, though in different ways, display different modes of moral understanding, different ways of thinking about
conflict and choice. In resolving Heinz's dilemma, Jake relies on theft
to avoid confrontation and turns to the law to mediate the dispute.
Transposing a hierarchy of power into a hierarchy of values, he defuses
a potentially explosive conflict between people by casting it as an im-
personal conflict of claims. In this way, he abstracts the moral problem
from the interpersonal situation, finding in the logic of fairness an
objective way to decide who will win the dispute. But this hierarchical
ordering, with its imagery of winning and losing and the potential for
violence which it contains, gives way in Amy's construction of the dilemma to a network of connection, a web of relationships that is sus-

tained by a process of communication. With this shift, the moral problem changes from one of unfair domination, the imposition of property over life, to one of unnecessary exclusion, the failure of the druggist to respond to the wife. ∎

## Notes

*1. Gender and Conflict Style.* As Craver and Barnes point out, one common stereotype of gender differences is that men are more concerned with winning and women are more concerned with maintaining relationships. Some studies (but not all) provide support for this stereotype. In one study, the experimenters compared the responses of undergraduate students to the Thomas-Kilmann Conflict Mode Instrument (described in Chapter 8). They found that male subjects were significantly more likely than female subjects to use the "competing" style when dealing with conflict, while female subjects were significantly more likely to use the "cooperating" style. Cynthia Berryman-Fink & Claire C. Brunner, The Effects of Sex of Source and Target on Interpersonal Conflict Management Styles, 53 S. Speech Comm. J. 38, 43-44 (1985).

The same researchers also investigated how conflict behavior was affected by whether the *other* party to the conflict was a male or female. When responding to the questions in the Thomas-Kilmann Conflict Mode Instrument, some subjects were asked to think of the question in the context of a relationship with a member of the same sex or a member of the opposite sex. Respondents were significantly more likely to adopt an accommodating conflict style when engaged in conflict with a female than with a male, regardless of the respondent's gender. Id. If Robert Mnookin et al. are correct that an accommodating conflict style signals high empathy (see Mnookin et al. in Chapter 8) one might cautiously hypothesize that negotiators are somewhat more empathetic toward women than to men.

*2. Gender and Fair Division.* Related to the stereotype that women care more about relationships than do men is the stereotype that women are more altruistic. There is some experimental evidence that suggests women might place more value than do men on treating a negotiating opponent fairly. In one dictator game experiment (see Chapter 6), women proposers allocated more than twice as much of the stakes to an anonymous responder than did men. Catherine Eckel & Philip Grossman, Are Women Less Selfish Than Men?: Evidence from Dictator Experiments, 108 Econ. J. 726 (1998). (It should be noted, however, that other researchers have found no difference between the way men and women play the dictator game.)

In a similar but slightly different context, Rachel Croson and Nancy Buchan report similar findings. Experimental subjects played a "trust game," in which the "proposer" could send some, all, or none of $10 to the "responder"; the amount sent was then *tripled* by the experimenter, and the responder could then return some, all, or none of the existing amount back to the proposer. Thus, the responders are effectively dictators regarding how to divide the portion of the $10 given to them. Female responders (American, Chinese, Japanese, and Korean) returned a significantly larger portion of the money to the proposer than did male responders. Rachel Croson & Nancy Buchan, Gender and Culture: International Experimental Evidence from Trust Games, 89 Am. Econ. Rev. 386 (1999).

*3. Propensity to Punish.*    If it is true that women are more likely than men to behave altruistically, women might also be more likely to avoid selfish trading partners. In one experiment in which players chose whether to split a small stake with another subject who had been a generous proposer in an earlier dictator game or a larger stake with a subject who had been a selfish proposer in an earlier dictator game, Catherine Eckel and Philip Grossman found women were more likely than men to choose the former (thus rewarding another player for being "fair" at a cost to themselves), although the difference disappeared as the stake became larger. Catherine Eckel & Philip Grossman, The Relative Price of Fairness: Gender Differences in a Punishment Game, 30 J. Econ. Behav. & Org. 143 (1996).

*4. Cooperation and BATNAs.*    If women generally place a higher value on good relationships than men, this could benefit men in cross-gender negotiations. This is especially true when reaching agreement would satisfy preferences to build and maintain relationships and, in contrast, the parties' BATNAs are to labor individually, without building and maintaining other relationships. This possibility is illustrated by an anecdote provided by Carol Rose, in the context of presenting a theory of why men in American society have more material resources than women:

> . . . [T]wo people, Sam and Louise, have access to a common field, and they decide to cooperate by restraining their cows, so that the grasses can regenerate. Suppose that they are collectively better off by some amount, which I will call "X." Their now-renewable grassy field has a capitalized value of X dollars more than it would have been if their respective Bossies and Sadies had just munched and tramped away until all the grass died out. That X amount is the surplus of their positive-sum, win-win deal.
>
> But another question lurks here: how are Sam and Louise going to split that X gain? Sam and Louise have entered a positive sum game from their big decision to cooperate, but after that, they face a zero sum game about

splitting gains made from cooperation. What Sam gets of X is at Louise's expense, and vice versa.

Suppose Louise has a greater taste for cooperation than Sam does. This characterization should make their bargaining develop along predictable lines, but those lines will not be to Louise's advantage. First, while it is predictable that she will indeed be better off when she and Sam decide to cooperate, it is also predictable that she will not be as much better off as Sam is. She will find herself getting less than Sam because of her greater taste for cooperation.

Louise has to offer Sam more incentives for him to cooperate, or even to notice that cooperation might be a good idea. He was not terribly interested in cooperating in the first place, so he will not cooperate at all unless he receives a disproportionate amount of the gain. Conversely, Louise is more interested in a cooperative relationship, more quickly sees its necessity, or feels more responsible for it; for those reasons, she is likely to agree to the deal even though, in a sense, she has to pay a somewhat higher price for it. In sum, Sam has a bargaining advantage, because of his relative indifference or even hostility to cooperation.

Carol Rose, Bargaining and Gender, 18 Harv. J. L. & Pub. Poly. 547 (1995).

Rose's hypothetical can be placed in the context of the negotiating process as follows: Sam and Louise both have BATNAs of tending their own cows without any cooperation. To Sam, who does not mind "going it alone" (or perhaps even prefers doing so), agreement is only preferable to pursuing his BATNA to the extent that agreement will result in more grass being produced. To Louise, who values cooperation and relationships, agreement is far more desirable than pursuing her BATNA because pursuing her BATNA means not only less grass, but also isolation. Because Sam has a more desirable BATNA (and thus a higher reservation price) than does Louise, it is likely that Sam will be able to bargain for more of the increased grass production than Louise, although this will not necessarily be the case. This likelihood will be increased if Sam knows that Louise values cooperation in its own right — or correctly assumes that she does because of her gender — and thus suspects that Louise has a relatively low reservation price.

Rose's hypothetical, though nicely illustrative of a particular asymmetry in bargaining power that can disadvantage women, might be idiosyncratic. Valuing cooperation might in some circumstances be an advantage in bargaining rather than a disadvantage. Suppose, for example, that Sam and Louise jointly own a field, but that they could increase grass production by dividing their ownership rights, building a fence down the middle, and operating independent cattle operations. In this hypothetical, cooperation and relationship building would be best served by not reaching agreement (i.e., dividing the field) rather than by reaching agreement. If Louise places a great deal of value on relationships, she might have to be offered a large amount of extra grass before she would believe that reaching agreement would be superior to pursuing her BATNA of continuing to work jointly with Sam. In this version of the hypothetical, Louise's high reservation price suggests she would be more likely than Sam to capture more than a 50/50 share of increased grass production.

**5. Integrative Bargaining Ability.** In the "Heinz dilemma," described by Carol Gilligan, Jake responded to the question of whether Heinz should steal the drug by ranking Heinz's and the druggist's relative claims to the drug. Amy, in contrast, did not respond directly to the question, which would have required compromising the interests of either Heinz or the druggist. Instead, she attempted to identify solutions that would not leave either unable to satisfy their desires. In analyzing and generalizing from these responses, Gilligan asserted that women are more likely than men to attempt to find solutions to problems that satisfy everyone. Carol Gilligan, In a Different Voice: Psychological Theory and Women's Development 62-63 (1982).

From one perspective, Amy failed to answer the question posed. From another, she demonstrated an ability to think creatively about solutions that might be better than either of the two that were suggested to her (i.e., Heinz steals the drug or Heinz's wife dies). If Gilligan's efforts to generalize the responses of Jake and Amy are valid, women might on balance enjoy a greater ability to find integrative solutions to negotiating problems — to search beyond the positions of the parties (i.e., the druggist wants to charge for the drug, Heinz wants the drug for free because he has no money) to their interests and find ways to satisfy those interests that are not zero-sum in nature.

Along similar lines, Amy's response could be classified as more empathetic than Jake's response. Amy attempted to take into account the underlying needs of both Heinz and the druggist. Jake, on the other hand, seems to care relatively little about either, instead focusing on the identification of a nonarbitrary rule to cleanly resolve the problem. To the extent that empathy is necessary for identifying mutually advantageous bargains and finding ways to expand bargaining zones, as Robert Mnookin et al. contend (see Chapter 8), negotiators with Amy's characteristics might attain more desirable bargaining outcomes.

**6. Gender Stereotypes Concerning Patience in Bargaining.** In a study of the role of race and gender in negotiations over new cars, Ian Ayres found that Chicago car dealerships offered women far higher prices than they offered men. In fact, after a number of offers and counteroffers, Ayres found that "final offers" made to white females provided the dealerships with three times as much profit as those made to white males. Ian Ayres, Fair Driving: Gender and Race Discrimination in New Car Bargaining, 104 Harv. L. Rev. 817 (1991). Ayres' careful statistical analysis suggested that women (and African-Americans as well) were charged more not because dealers disliked dealing with them or believed that selling to them would be more costly than selling to men, but because the dealers estimated that women would be willing to pay more than men. Ayres noted that this seems counterintuitive, because white males are wealthier on average than white females or African-Americans, and thus would be likely to have more money to spend on a car. But he argued that women might be willing to pay more for a car from a particular dealership than men nonetheless for the following reason (among others):

> ... [R]evenue-based statistical discrimination might be based on an inference by dealers that some consumer groups are averse to the process of bargaining. If black or female consumers are more likely than white males to make bargaining concessions, revenue-based disparate treatment may ensue: profit-maximizing dealers would exploit such differences by charging more to members of those groups that tend to dislike bargaining. The process of negotiation at a given dealership is in a sense a consumer's "intra-dealership" search for the best price. If dealers believe that blacks and women have a greater aversion to bargaining (and thus experience higher "intra-dealership" search costs) than white males, dealers might believe they could generate additional revenues by making higher offers to blacks and women. A higher consumer aversion to bargaining is analogous to a higher bargaining cost. Inferences about different bargaining costs (including different aversions to bargaining), like inferences about different search costs, can analogously lead dealers to treat groups of consumers differently. . . .

Ian Ayres, Fair Driving: Gender and Race Discrimination in New Car Bargaining, 104 Harv. L. Rev. 817, 850 (1991).

In the excerpt at the beginning of this section, Charles Craver and David Barnes note that research on gender characteristics has often found that women tend to be more uncomfortable than men in highly competitive situations. If this is in fact true, it could follow that women would tend to be less patient in distributive negotiating settings — that is, would endure a relatively higher cost of bargaining and thus be willing to accept a lesser share of the cooperative surplus in order to conclude negotiations more quickly. As the Ayres study suggests, if such a gender bias is perceived — whether or not it actually exists — both male and female negotiators might attempt to rely on it by making less generous offers to women negotiators and more reluctant concessions.

*7. Gender Stereotypes and Lawyer-Negotiators.* In a later section of the article excerpted above, Craver and Barnes compared the performance of male and female students on scored negotiation simulations (that counted towards the students' course grades) in Craver's negotiation courses at George Washington University over an 11-year period during the 1980s and 1990s. The authors found no statistical difference in the results of male and female students who took the course for a letter grade. The women scored higher than the men in 6 of the 11 years, the men scored higher in the other five. Charles B. Craver & David W. Barnes, Gender, Risk Taking and Negotiating Performance, 5 Mich. J. Gender & L. 299, 339-341 (1999). The results are subject to various plausible explanations. It may be that differences between male and female negotiators are diminishing over time. It may be that there are few differences between male and female negotiators who share similar professional training. Or it may be that there are differences in style between male and female negotiators but that neither style is more likely to lead to negotiating success, defined as obtaining the best possible agreement for the negotiator's client.

In another study, researchers compared the responses of under-graduate and law students to the Thomas-Kilmann Conflict Mode In-strument. They found that the female law students' answers were significantly more competitive and significantly less accommodating than the female undergraduate students' answers, while there were no significant differences between the responses of male undergraduates and law students. The responses of the male and female law students were similar. Based on these results, the researchers hypothesized that "law school socialization serves to make women, as a group, more as-sertive." Steven Hartwell et al., Women Negotiating: Assertiveness and Relatedness, in Constructing and Reconstructing Gender 53, 56 (Linda A.M. Perry et al. eds. 1992).

Taken together, these studies suggest that gender-based differences in negotiating styles may be less pronounced among lawyer-negotiators than others.

## B.  CULTURE

There is no doubt that how a negotiator behaves in bargaining situa-tions depends *in part* on the culture in which she has been socialized. The problems with studying the role of culture in negotiation, however, are the same problems that plague the study of gender. There is a great deal of variation among individual negotiators with the same cultural background. Consequently, unless there are quite significant differ-ences between cultures, it is extraordinarily difficult to determine whether any observed differences between two negotiators from differ-ent cultures are due to cultural differences or personal differences.

Thus, while there are certainly real differences between the cultures of Belgium and the Netherlands, for example, or even between the cultures of California and Oregon, it is difficult to identify if and how those differences translate into systematic differences in negotiating behavior. And even if those differences between cultures do lead to systematic differences in negotiating behavior, individual variation will often be far more important for understanding the conduct of any particular negotiation than cultural variation.

Despite these difficulties, studying the role of culture in negotiation is arguably still a useful endeavor for two reasons. The more obvious of these is that an understanding of cultural differences can usefully inform a negotiator's approach to bargaining with someone from a different culture, especially if he keeps in mind that culture is not a perfect predictor of any particular negotiating behavior. Less obvious is that in a world full of cultural stereotypes, another negotiator's stereotypes of your culture will often affect how she bargains with you, so it is important to understand what stereotypes are widespread even if they are only marginally true or even completely false. Jeffrey Rubin and Frank Sander illustrate this point with the following thought experiment:

> Now imagine that you have begun to negotiate with someone from another culture, who at some point in the proceedings simply insists that he or she can go no further, and is prepared to conclude without an agreement if necessary; in effect, says this individual, his BATNA has been reached, and he can do just as well by walking away from the table. How should you interpret such an assertion? If you share the general cluster of stereotypes described by [our] students, your interpretation will probably depend on the other person's culture or nationality. Thus, if the other negotiator is British, and (among other things) you regard the British as "fair" you may interpret this person's refusal to concede further as an honest statement of principle. The same behavior issuing from a Central American, however (someone you suspect of being "stubborn in arguments"), may lead you to suspect your counterpart of being stubborn and perhaps deceitful. Wouldn't you therefore be more likely to strike an agreement with a British than a Central American negotiator — despite the fact that each has behaved in the identical way?

Jeffrey Z. Rubin & Frank E.A. Sander, Culture, Negotiation, and the Eye of the Beholder, 7 Negotiation J. 249, 251-252 (1991).

The observations of cultural differences that seem to be the most consistent across studies — and therefore that are the most likely to accurately reflect true cultural variation and result in widely held stereotypes — are those between negotiators from "western" and "eastern" cultures. The former category is usually exemplified by the United

States, Canada, Great Britain, and Western Europe, while the latter category is often, but not exclusively, exemplified by Japan and China. The oft-observed cultural differences can be viewed as reflecting the western focus on the individual, solving problems, and material progress, and the eastern emphasis on the collective good and preserving social structures.

Raymond Cohen calls the western approach a "low-context, problem-solving model" that views "people as part of the problem, not the solution," believes "each problem can be solved discretely," and defines goals in terms of "material, not psychic, satisfactions." In contrast, he describes the eastern approach as based on a "nonverbal, implicit, high-context style of communications," that "declines to view the immediate issue in isolation; lays particular stress on long-term and affective aspects of the relationship between the parties; is preoccupied with considerations of symbolism, status, and face; and draws on highly developed communication strategies for evading confrontation." Raymond Cohen, Negotiating Across Culture 153-155 (1991). The western approach is implicit in the description of the negotiation process provided in Part II of this book. That part organizes the activity of negotiation into discrete problems that demand resolution in an analytically rigorous manner, and it implicitly views relationships as instrumentally important in creating an atmosphere conducive to problem solving, but relatively unimportant in their own right.

Cohen's description of the differences between eastern and western cultures that affect negotiation can be viewed as both differences in values or preferences and differences in negotiating style. In other words, the differences, as he identifies them, are relevant both to the procedure and substance of negotiation. This dichotomy can be helpful in determining how cultural differences can actually affect negotiating outcomes. To the extent culture affects values or preferences, culture can have an effect on the negotiators' reservation prices and thus bargaining zones. To the extent that culture affects negotiating behaviors, culture can determine in part whether and how negotiators are able to identify integrative agreements, exercise power, defer to social norms, set aspirations, or cope with the "negotiator's dilemma."

In the following excerpt, Jeanne Brett creates a conceptual structure for thinking specifically about the types of cultural variation that can have an important systematic effect on negotiating behavior by identifying three critical cultural dichotomies: an individualist versus a collectivist view of the individual's role in society; an egalitarian versus a hierarchical social structure; and a high-context versus a low-context style of communication.

# ■ Jeanne M. Brett, Culture and Negotiation*
## 35 Intl. J. Psychol. 97, 99-102 (2000)

### CULTURE

Culture is the unique character of a social group. It encompasses the values and norms shared by members of that group. It is the economic, social, political, and religious institutions that direct and control current group members and socialize new members (Lytle, Brett, Barsness, Tinsley, & Janssens, 1995). All of these elements of culture can affect social interactions like negotiations. Cultural values direct group members' attention to what is more and less important. Cultural norms define what is appropriate and inappropriate behaviour. Cultural values and norms provide the philosophy underlying the society's institutions. At the same time cultural institutions preserve cultural values and norms, give them authority, and provide a context for social interaction.

There are many different cultural values, norms, and institutions. Not all relate to negotiation. However, many do because they provide a basis for interpreting situations (this is a negotiation, therefore I behave) and a basis for interpreting the behaviours of others (he or she threatened me, therefore I should . . . ) (Fiske & Taylor, 1991). Cultural values that our research indicates are relevant to norms and strategies for negotiation include individualism versus collectivism, egalitarianism versus hierarchy, and direct versus indirect communications. Other values, no doubt, are also relevant.

*Individualism versus Collectivism.* Individualism versus collectivism refers to the extent to which a society treats individuals as autonomous, or as embedded in their social groups (Schwartz, 1994). In individualistic cultures, norms and institutions promote the autonomy of the individual. Individual accomplishments are rewarded and revered by economic and social institutions, and legal institutions protect individual rights. In collectivist cultures, norms and institutions promote interdependence of individuals through emphasis on social obligations. Sacrifice of personal needs for the greater good is rewarded and legal institutions place the greater good of the collective above the rights of the individual. Political and economic institutions reward classes of people as opposed to individuals.

The way a society treats people affects the way people self-construe and the way they act toward and interact with each other. People in all cultures distinguish between in-groups, of which they are members, and out-groups, of which they are not (Turner, 1987). In collectivist cultures self-identity is interdependent with in-group membership, but in individualistic cultures self-identity consists of attributes that are independent of in-group membership (Marcus & Kitayama, 1991). Perhaps because collectivists identify more strongly with their in-groups, they are said to be more attuned to the needs of others than individualists (Schweder & Bourne, 1982) and to make stronger in-group/out-group distinctions than individualists (Gudykunst et al., 1992).

Individualism versus collectivism, according to Schwartz (1994, p. 140), reflects cultures' basic preferences and priorities for "some goals rather than others." Goals are motivating; they direct behaviour and sustain effort (Locke & Latham, 1990). We have found that individualists, because of their strong self-interests, set high personal goals in negotiation (Brett & Okumura, 1998). We think these goals motivate individualists to reject acceptable, but suboptimal, agreements and to continue to search among alternative possible agreements for one that best meets the individualists' self-interests.

Because of their identification with in-groups, collectivists' goals should be aligned with their in-groups' goals. If the other negotiator is an in-group member, goal alignment should generate cooperative behaviour in negotiations, whereby parties search together for a mutually satisfying agreement. However, if the other negotiator is an out-group member, as is likely in any inter-cultural negotiation, goals are unlikely to be aligned and competitive behaviour may ensue. In Prisoners' Dilemma games negotiators with individualistic motivational orientations do not change their behaviour depending upon with whom they are interacting (Kelley & Stahelski, 1970). However, in some recent multiparty negotiation research, some individualists changed to a cooperative strategy, perhaps because they were confronted with the possibility of an impasse (Weingart & Brett, 1998), suggesting that individualists may be pragmatic. Negotiators with cooperative motivational orientations vary their behavior, depending on the orientation of the other negotiator (Kelley & Stahelski, 1970). They cooperate when they are dealing with other cooperative negotiators, but in dyads will compete when dealing with negotiators with individualist or competitive orientations.

The distinction between individualistic and competitive behaviour is important. The individualist goes his own way regardless of the behaviour of the other, but may be affected by the structure of the situation. The competitor, like the cooperator, is sensitive to the needs of others, and the competitor seeks to maximize the difference between his own and other's outcomes (Messick & McClintock, 1968). This is a very different orientation from the individualist, who essentially is unconcerned with how well or how poorly the negotiation is going for the other party, so long as it is going well for himself.

*Egalitarianism versus Hierarchy.* Egalitarianism versus hierarchy refers to the extent to which a culture's social structure is flat (egalitarian) versus differentiated into ranks (hierarchical) (Schwartz, 1994). In hierarchical cultures, social status implies social power. Social superiors are granted power and privilege. Social inferiors are obligated to defer to social superiors and comply with their requests. However, social superiors also have an obligation to look out for the needs of social inferiors (Leung, 1997). No such obligation exists in egalitarian societies, where social boundaries are permeable and superior social status may be short-lived.

Conflict within hierarchical cultures poses a threat to the social structure, since the norm in such a culture is not to challenge the directives of high status members. Thus, conflict between members of different social ranks is likely to be less frequent in hierarchical than egalitarian cultures (Leung, 1997). Conflict between members of the same social rank is more likely to be handled by deference to a superior than by direct confrontation between social equals (Leung, 1997). So, hierarchy reduces conflict by providing norms for interaction, primarily by channeling conflict that does break out to superiors. The decision by the high status third party reinforces his/her authority without necessarily conferring differentiated status on the contestants as would be the case in a negotiation in which one party won and the other lost.

Conflict within egalitarian cultures also poses a threat to the social structure, but the egalitarian nature of the culture empowers conflicting members to resolve the conflict themselves. Egalitarian cultures support direct, face-to-face negotiations, mediation or facilitation by a peer, and group decision making, to resolve conflict. An agreement between two disputing parties may not distribute resources equally. One party may claim more and the other less. Yet, differentiated status associated with successful claiming in one negotiation may not translate into permanent changes in social status. There are two reasons for this. First, there are few avenues in egalitarian societies for precedent setting. Second, social status is only stable until the next negotiation.

Thus, one implication for negotiations of the cultural value, egalitarianism versus hierarchy, is the way conflict is handled in a culture. A second implication is the view of power in negotiations.

Negotiators from egalitarian and hierarchical societies have rather different views of the bases of power in negotiations (Brett & Okumura, 1998). Consistent with the transitory notion of social structure that is characteristic of egalitarian societies, power in negotiations in egalitarian cultures tends to be evaluated with respect to the situation under negotiation and the alternatives if no agreement can be reached. Every negotiator has a BATNA (best alternative to negotiated agreement). BATNAs are not fixed. If, in analyzing the alternatives, the negotiator is dissatisfied with her BATNA, she may invest in action to improve her BATNA by seeking another alternative. In transactional negotiations, parties' BATNAs are frequently unrelated. The buyer has an alternative seller with whom to negotiate and the seller has an alternative buyer with whom to negotiate. However, in dispute resolution negotiations one party may be able to impose its BATNA on the other. For example, in a dispute over the terms of a contract, the defendant may not simply be able to walk away from a negotiation that has reached an impasse, but will have to defend himself in court, which is the claimant's BATNA. . . .

In hierarchical societies interpersonal relationships are vertical. In almost all social relationships a difference in status exists based on age, sex, education, organization, or position in the organization (Graham, Johnston, & Kamins, 1998). Social status confers social power and knowledge of status dictates how people will interact. In within-culture negotiations, when parties' social status is known, there may be little need to negotiate the relative distribution of resources. However, when relative status is in doubt, negotiators must somehow determine each party's relative status, and thus the distribution of resources. Research on transactional negotiations shows that negotiators from hierarchical cultures are more likely than negotiators from egalitarian cultures to endorse as normative and to use all types of power in negotiation: status, BATNA and persuasion (Adair et al., 1998a; Brett et al., 1998).

*High- versus Low-context Communication.* High- versus low-context communication refers to the degree to which within-culture communications are indirect versus direct (Hall, 1976; Ting-Toomey, 1988). In high-context cultures little information is in the message itself. Instead, the context of the communication stimulates pre-existing knowledge in the receiver. In high-context cultures meaning is inferred rather than directly interpreted from the communication. In low-context cultures information is contained in explicit messages, and meaning is conveyed without nuance and is context free. Communication in low-context cultures is action oriented and solution minded. The implications of the information are laid out in further detailed communications.

Information is the central factor affecting the degree to which negotiated agreements are integrative. Differences between parties in priorities and interests provide one source of integrative potential. Compatibility with respect to issues provides another. If parties are going to realize integrative potential, they must learn about the other party's interests, preferences, and priorities. Negotiation research has shown that integrative agreements may result from information sharing about preferences and priorities (Olekalns, Smith, & Walsh, 1996; Pruitt, 1981; Weingart et al., 1990), or from heuristic trial-and-error search (Pruitt & Lewis, 1975; Tutzauer & Roloff, 1988). Information sharing about preferences and priorities is a direct information sharing approach. Questions are asked and answered in a give-and-take fashion as both sides slowly develop an understanding of what issues are mutually beneficial, what issues are more important to one side than the other, and what issues are purely distributive.

Heuristic trial-and-error search is an indirect information sharing approach. It occurs in negotiations when parties trade proposals back and forth across the bargaining table. When one party rejects the other's proposal, and offers its own, the first party may infer what was wrong with the proposal from the way the second party changed it in making its own proposal. Multi-issue proposals provide a great deal of indirect information about preferences and priorities because the integrative trade-offs are contained within the proposal. Our research shows that negotiators from low-context cultures who share information directly are as capable of negotiating integrative agreements as negotiators from high-context cultures who share information indirectly (Brett & Okumura, 1998).

The cultural value for high- versus low-context communication may also be related to the willingness of parties in conflict to confront and negotiate directly versus to avoid confrontation and conceal ill feelings, or to confront indirectly by involving third parties (Leung, 1997; Tinsley, 1997; Ting-Toomey, 1988). . . . In research comparing Hong Kong Chinese and US intra-cultural negotiators, we placed parties in a simulated, face-to-face dispute resolution setting, perhaps an uncomfortable setting for the Hong Kong Chinese (Tinsley & Brett, 1998). We found that during the 45-minute negotiation, the Hong Kong Chinese negotiators resolved fewer issues and were more likely to involve a third party than were the US negotiators (Tinsley & Brett, 1998).

## MODEL OF CULTURE AND NEGOTIATION

When people from two different cultural groups negotiate, each brings to the table his or her way of thinking about the issues to be negotiated and the process of negotiation. Some of that thinking is affected by the negotiator's cultural group membership and the ways in which issues are typically assessed and negotiations carried out within that cultural group. . . .

Cultural values may result in preferences on issues that are quite distinct. For example, negotiators from cultures that value tradition may be less enthusiastic about economic development that threatens to change valued ways of life, than negotiators from cultures that value change and development. The same values that generate cultural differences in preferences may also act as cultural blinders. Members of one culture expect preferences to be compatible, and cannot understand the rationality of the other party, whose views on the same issue are at odds with their own. It is generally always unwise in negotiation to label the other party as irrational. Such labeling encourages persuasion to get the other party to adopt the first's view of the situation, rather than the search for trade-offs that are the foundation of integrative agreements. There is opportunity in differences. . . .

Cultural values and norms also may affect negotiators' strategic negotiation processes. For example, negotiators from cultures where direct, explicit communications are preferred may share information by stating and reciprocating preferences and priorities, by commenting on similarities and differences, and by giving direct feedback. Negotiators from cultures where the norm is to communicate indirectly and infer meaning may share information by making multi-issue proposals and inferring priorities from subtle changes in proposals. In our research contrasting US and Japanese negotiators, we found that the Japanese were using a relatively large number of proposals, compared to the US negotiators, and the US negotiators were using a whole array of direct communications relatively more frequently than the Japanese (Adair et al., 1998c).

. . . [W]hen the strategies negotiators bring to the table clash, the negotiation process is likely to be less efficient, and agreements are likely to be suboptimal. We found, for example, that Japanese intra-cultural negotiators, using indirect communications, and US intra-cultural negotiators using direct communications, reached similarly efficient agreements. However, when Japanese expatriate managers negotiated with US managers, agreements were suboptimal. Japanese inter-cultural negotiators understood the US negotiators' priorities, because the US negotiators were sharing information directly. The US negotiators did not understand the Japanese negotiators' priorities, even though the inter-cultural Japanese negotiators shut down their culture's normative indirect approach to information sharing and tried to adapt to the US strategy of direct information sharing (Adair et al., 1998c; Brett & Okumura, 1998).                                         ∎

---

The following two excerpts focus on specific cultural differences between American negotiators and negotiators from certain foreign countries. As you read the authors' observations, consider to what extent the identified differences fall into Brett's categories of individualism versus collectivism, egalitarianism versus hierarchy, and high-context versus low-context communication, and to what extent other categories might be usefully added to her list. Consider also the extent to which the observations reflect differences in values and preferences and the extent to which they represent differences in approaches to the negotiation process.

# ■ Jeswald W. Salacuse, Making Deals in Strange Places: A Beginner's Guide to International Business Negotiations*

**4 Negotiation J.** 5, 5-6, 9-12 (1988)

. . .

## []   PROBLEMS OF IDEOLOGY

Whether they are Republicans or Democrats, American business negotiators generally share a common ideology, but in the international arena business negotiators normally encounter — and must be prepared to deal with — ideologies vastly different from their own. Three areas of ideological difference often faced by U.S. negotiators are private investment, profit, and individual rights.

Americans tend to view private investment as a positive good, a force to create wealth, jobs, useful products and income; however, many foreign countries look at it more circumspectly. For them, foreign investment has its benefits and its costs, and they seek to maximize the benefits and minimize the costs though governmental regulation. The subject of profit is also viewed differently. For Americans, profit results from growth and is good because it can be reinvested to yield further benefits; however, in some countries the profit one party gains is seen as value taken away from someone else. Similarly, Americans tend to stress the rights of the individual, but other nations emphasize the rights of the group.

The existence of a conflict in ideologies often requires the negotiator to find ways of wrapping proposals in ideological packages that are acceptable to the other party, and to find neutral means of communicating with negotiators on the other side.

## []   CULTURAL DIFFERENCES

International business transactions not only cross political and ideological boundaries, they also cross cultures. As a powerful factor shaping thought, communication, and behavior, culture conditions the negotiating process in some very fundamental ways. Negotiators from different cultures may have quite distinct approaches to negotiations, and their styles of negotiating may be markedly different. Numerous books and articles have stressed the differences in negotiating styles of such diverse cultural groups as the Japanese, the Soviets, the Chinese, (e.g., Pye, 1982); and the Americans (e.g., Graham and Herherger, 1983). While this literature is useful, some works are overly anecdotal and tend to create cultural stereotypes.

---

*Copyright © 1988 by Kluwer Academic/Plenum Publisher. Reprinted with permission.

Persons of different cultures often speak different languages, a factor that certainly complicates the negotiating process, requiring interpreters and translators or forcing one side to negotiate in a foreign language. But communicating with another culture is not just a matter of learning the other side's vocabulary; it also requires all understanding of its values, perceptions, and philosophies. Different cultures operate on the basis of different unspoken assumptions, and each may interpret the same phenomenon in very different ways.

For example, it is possible for negotiators from different cultures to interpret the very purpose of their negotiation differently. For most Americans, the purpose of negotiations, first and foremost, is to arrive at a signed contract between the parties. Americans view a signed contract as a definitive set of rights and obligations that strictly binds the two sides, an attitude succinctly summed up in the declaration that "a deal is a deal."

Japanese and Chinese, on the other hand, view the signed contract in a very different light. For them, the "deal" being negotiated is not the contract, but the relationship between the parties. Although the written contract expresses that relationship, the essence of the deal is the relationship, and it is understood that the relationship may be subject to reasonable changes over time. For the American, signing a contract is "closing a deal"; for the Japanese, signing the contract might more appropriately be called "opening a relationship."

Since the Japanese and the American view the end product of negotiations differently, perhaps one can say that, from an intercultural perspective, "a deal is not always a deal." The consequences of this difference in perception is important. For example, if a Japanese joint-venture partner seeks to modify the terms of the contract because of a change in business conditions, the American participant may view these efforts as an outrageous attempt to renege on a deal. The Japanese participants, on the other hand, may consider the American reaction to be unreasonable rigidity and a refusal to allow the contract to conform to the underlying relationship.

A reflection of this dichotomy is also found in differing approaches to writing a contract. Generally, Americans prefer very detailed contracts that attempt to foresee and anticipate all possible circumstances, no matter how unlikely. Why? Because the "deal" is the contract itself, and one must go to the contract to determine how to handle a new circumstance that may arise.

Other cultures, such as China, prefer a contract in the form of general principles, rather than detailed rules. Why? Because the essence of the deal is the relationship of trust that exists between the parties. If unexpected circumstances arise, the parties should look to their relationship, not the written contract, to solve the problem.

So in some cases, the American drive at the negotiating table to foresee all possible contingencies may be seen by another culture as evidence of mistrust in the stability of the underlying relationship.

Related to this issue is the question of whether negotiating a business deal is an *inductive* or a *deductive* process. Does it start from agreement on general principles and then proceed to specific items, or does it begin with agreements on specifics (e.g., price, delivery date, product quality), the sum total of which becomes the contract?

One observer (Pye, 1982, p. 95) believes that the Chinese prefer to begin with agreement on general principles, while Americans seek first to agree on specifics. For Americans, negotiating a deal is basically making a whole series of compromises and tradeoffs on a long list of particulars. For Chinese, the essence is to agree on basic general principles which will guide and indeed determine the negotiation process afterwards.

A further difference in negotiating style is the dichotomy between the "building-down approach," where the negotiator begins by presenting the maximum deal if the other side accepts all the stated conditions, and the "building-up approach," where one side starts by proposing a minimal deal that can be broadened and increased as the other party accepts further conditions. According to many observers, Americans tend to favor the building-down approach, while the Japanese prefer the building-up style of negotiating a contact.

The purpose of any negotiation is not merely to reach an agreement, but to reach an agreement that will regulate the parties' behavior. For the Westerner, this necessary element raises the question of contract enforcement, of creating mechanisms to impose the agreement on one of the parties who at some later time may refuse to respect its provisions.

For Westerners, enforcement means the use of the courts, compulsory arbitration, and, ultimately, state power in some form. Many countries in Asia resist this tendency. China, for example, has opposed the use of Western courts and even international arbitration, preferring instead to resort to friendly negotiations, conciliation, and mediation in the event of a dispute.

As many authors have pointed out, culture also influences the organization of the negotiators. Here, the American approach to organization is sometimes characterized as "John Wayne" style of negotiations: one person has all the authority and plunges ahead to do the job, and to do the job as quickly as possible (Graham and Herberger, 1983, p. 162). Other cultures, [e.g., the Japanese culture and the culture of the former Soviet Union], stress team negotiations and collective decision making. Indeed, it may not be fully apparent who has the authority to bind the side.

. . . In any international business negotiation, it is therefore important for each side to determine how the other side is organized, who has the authority, and how decisions on each side are made.

The various methods of organization, the varying degrees of authority given to the negotiators, and the differing needs to foster mutual trust and to build relationships all may significantly affect the pace of the negotiation process. Americans are often accused of wanting to go too fast in negotiations, of pushing to close the deal in the quickest time possible. On the other hand, one of the commonest complaints from American negotiators about any given international business negotiation — with virtually any foreign enterprise — is that the negotiations are proceeding too slowly. Rarely does one hear an American complain that negotiations are going too quickly.                    ■

■ **Michele J. Gelfand & Sophia Christakopoulou, Culture and Negotiator Cognition: Judgment Accuracy and Negotiation Processes in Individualistic and Collectivistic Cultures***

**79 Org. Behav. & Hum. Decision Proc.** 248 (1999)

The current research examines aspects of negotiator cognition across cultural contexts. The general proposition advanced in this paper is that judgment biases in negotiation are perpetuated by cultural values and ideals, and therefore, certain judgment biases will be more prevalent in certain cultural contexts. We considered the possibility that fixed pie error, a judgment bias in which negotiators fail to accurately understand their counterparts' interests (Pruitt & Lewis, 1975; Thompson & Hastie, 1990), would be more prevalent at the end of negotiations in the United States, an individualistic culture, as compared to Greece, a collectivistic culture.

To preface the following discussion, since cultural ideals and values in individualistic cultures emphasize separating from others and promoting one's own internal attributes (Markus & Kitayama, 1991; Triandis, 1989), we expected that negotiators' cognitions in these cultures would be directed to their own interests during negotiations, which would inhibit an accurate understanding of their counterparts' interests, and would enhance fixed pie judgments at the end of negotiations. By contrast, since cultural ideals and values in collectivist cultures emphasize maintaining relatedness and fitting in with relevant others, we expected that negotiators' cognitions in these cultures would be directed to the needs of others during negotiations, which would enhance an accurate understanding of their counterparts' interests, and reduce fixed pie judgments at the end of negotiations. Additionally, as will be described below, we expected that these cultural ideals and values would also be manifested in negotiator processes (i.e., offers and behavioral strategies) during the negotiation. . . .

. . . [O]ne goal of the cognitive tradition is to identify faulty assumptions that negotiators have during negotiation situations (Bazerman & Carroll, 1987; Pruitt & Carnevale, 1993; Thompson, 1990). Perhaps the most pervasive of errors identified is the fixed pie error, which is the judgment that one's own interests are diametrically opposed to one's opponent (i.e., that parties have opposite preferences on each issue), and that the issues that are most important to oneself are also the most important to one's opponents (i.e., that parties have the same priorities on each issue). In other words, negotiators often assume that their counterparts place the same value on the issues as they do (Bazerman & Neale, 1983). However, many real-world negotiations involve issues on which there are differences in priorities, thus creating the potential for mutually beneficial outcomes for both parties (Thompson & Hastie, 1990). To the extent that negotiators fail to realize that their counterparts' interests and priorities differ from their own, this is considered to be a judgment bias.

Despite the fact that many negotiation situations involve differences in priorities, research has consistently shown that negotiators fail to recognize this because they make inaccurate judgments of the other party's interests. . . .

### CULTURE AND JUDGMENT BIASES IN NEGOTIATION

. . . [W]e postulated that negotiator cognitions and behaviors in individualistic cultures will be focused on the promotion of personal needs and interests, whereas negotiator cognitions and behaviors in collectivistic cultures will be focused on maintaining relatedness and attending to the interests of others with whom the negotiator is interacting.

More specifically, we expected that (while negotiators in all cultures may assume similarity in their priorities at the beginning of negotiations due to naive realism[1]; i.e., fixed pie judgments may be universal at the beginning of negotiations), because of differing cultural values and ideals, fixed pie judgments would be more *pronounced* at the end

---

1. Naive Realism refers to the tendency to assume that others share one's attitudes or ways of viewing the world (Ross & Ward, 1996).

of negotiations in individualistic cultures than in collectivistic cultures. Implicit in this argument is the notion that in individualistic cultures, cultural ideals of attending to one's own internal attributes, such as one's interests and priorities in negotiations, inhibit an accurate understanding of others' interests during negotiations, and perpetuate fixed pie judgments. However, in collectivistic cultures, in which there is more of an emphasis on assessing the needs and interests of others in relationships, the tendency to have inaccurate judgments of another's interests at the end of negotiation should be attenuated.

This general proposition was investigated through a comparison of negotiators in the United States, a highly individualistic culture (Hofstede, 1980, 1991; Triandis, 1995), and negotiators in Greece, a highly collectivistic culture (Georgas et al., 1997; Hofstede, 1980, 1991; Triandis & Vassiliou, 1972; Vassiliou & Vassiliou, 1973). Hofstede (1980, 1991), for example, found that the United States was the most individualistic culture out of his sample of 39 countries, receiving a score of 91. By comparison, Greece was much more collectivistic, receiving a score of 35 (the average being 51). Recent research by Georgas et al. (1997) also supports these findings. Based on the previous discussion, the following prediction was made:

HYPOTHESIS 1. Culture will affect judgment accuracy (accurate judgments of others' priorities in negotiation). Negotiators in Greece will gain more knowledge about their opponents' priorities in negotiations, as compared to negotiators in the United States.

In addition, we reasoned that the same psychological processes which underlie the predicted differential understanding of an opponent's interests in individualistic and collectivistic cultures (namely attending to one's own interests and needs versus maintaining relatedness and understanding the interests of others, respectively) would also be apparent in behaviors which are exhibited throughout the negotiation. Specifically, we expected that cultural ideals in individualistic cultures, which emphasize promoting one's own goals and achieving one's desires, would be reflected in the amount of value claimed for oneself throughout the negotiation.

HYPOTHESIS 2. Negotiators in the United States will claim more value for themselves throughout the negotiation when making offers, as compared to negotiators in Greece.

In essence, while previous research has demonstrated that in the United States high first offers and overbidding are commonly used to signal high aspirations (i.e., wherein demands are far above goals and limits; Lewicki, Litterer, Minton, & Saunders, 1994), we did not expect this "door-in-the-face" technique to be utilized as much by negotiators in Greece, given that claiming value to oneself would likely interfere with maintaining relatedness in interactions.

Finally, consistent with the culture theory presented, we expected that negotiators in individualistic cultures would be more likely to promote themselves, and therefore, would make more self-enhancing statements during negotiations (i.e., those which place the self above others), as compared to negotiators from collectivistic cultures.

> HYPOTHESIS 3. Negotiators in the United States will be more likely to engage in more behaviors to promote the self (e.g., use of threats, warnings, comparisons, and putdowns), as compared to negotiators in Greece.

In sum, based on differing values and ideals which are cultivated in individualistic and collectivistic cultures, we expected to find cultural differences in negotiators' judgment accuracy, offers, and behaviors in negotiations.

[The researchers had American and Greek university students negotiate with each other over e-mail. The students were asked to try to negotiate the terms of a joint venture agreement between two hypothetical companies that would need to hire employees. The students were given three issues to negotiate: (1) Work Schedule (how many Saturdays employees would be expected to work), (2) Layoff Procedures (if layoffs are necessary, how much notice should employees be given), and (3) Vacation Time. American negotiators and Greek negotiators could each earn up to 280 "points" depending on the precise terms negotiated, but the point possibilities provided indicated a different set of preferences and priorities among the three issues for the Greeks and the Americans. The researchers asked the students to estimate their opponent's payoff schedule both before and after negotiations, and monitored the students' e-mail correspondence to assess the size of offers made, the amount of information shared, and the frequency with which the subjects used threats as a tactic.

The researchers found the following results:

- Before negotiations, there was no difference in the level of understanding Greek and American students had about their counterpart's negotiating priorities. After negotiations, however, the Greek students had significantly more accurate assessments of the American's priorities than vice versa. There was no difference, however, in the degree to which the two groups revealed information during the negotiations.

- The American students made significantly more one-sided (i.e. beneficial to the offeror) first offers and average offers than the Greek students.
- The American students made more self-enhancing statements during the negotiation than the Greek students.
- The American students believed that they had the same amount of concern for the Greek negotiators as the Greeks did for them. The Greek students believed that they had more concern for the Americans than the Americans did for them.]

## DISCUSSION

. . . [J]udgment accuracy, offers, and behaviors among U.S. participants reflected an orientation toward attending to their own needs and interests. U.S. participants claimed more value to themselves throughout the negotiation, learned less about the priorities of their counterparts, and engaged in behaviors to enhance their own status in comparison to their Greek counterparts. In contrast, the behavior of the Greek participants reflected an orientation toward attending to the needs and interests of their counterparts, as evidenced in their greater judgment accuracy of their counterparts' interests, their offers, and their behaviors during the negotiation. At the same time, even though Greeks and Americans achieved similar objective outcomes, Greeks were less satisfied with the negotiation, and this was associated with the degree to which their American counterparts understood their interests. While this study only involved a one-shot negotiation, such subjective evaluations are likely to have important consequences in real-world negotiations, where there is a likelihood of continuous interaction. Indeed, given that satisfaction has been related to withdrawal behavior (Hulin, 1991), it is quite possible that satisfaction may be linked to other important variables in negotiations, such as implementation of agreements, choice to continue with the same negotiation partner, etc.

The more general implication of this research is that the assumptions underlying the dominant paradigm in negotiation need to be explicated and examined for universality (cf. Gray, 1994). In our view, it is likely that there are both universal and culture-specific aspects of negotiation processes. For instance, this study illustrated that American and Greek negotiators did not vary on fixed pie judgments at the beginning of negotiations, which suggests that the tendency to assume similarity in priorities at the onset of negotiations may be a universal phenomenon, perhaps stemming from naive realism. However, this bias was also greatly reduced among negotiators from Greece, as compared to the United States, suggesting that cultural processes are involved in the perpetuation of such biases. In other words, our analysis suggests that the larger cultural context in which negotiators are embedded plays an important role in directing negotiators' cognitions, restricting attention to particular aspects of the self and the environment, and rendering certain judgments more susceptible to error. Indeed, when the promotion of another's interests is paramount, as is typically found in collectivistic cultures, fixed pie biases can be greatly attenuated. These biases, on the other hand, can be perpetuated in cultures in which self-interest is paramount. Put this way, it is not surprising that the literature on fixed pie biases has been largely developed in the United States, a culture in which assumptions of self-interest, economic transactions, and competition are pervasive (Gray, 1994). Yet, as the current theory and data suggest, these assumptions may not be as appropriate in other cultures.  ▮

## Notes

*1. The "East-West" Cultural Divide.*  Many scholars agree that whether a culture is "eastern" or "western" is highly predictive of how it rates on the three dichotomies identified by Brett. Brett warns that the east-west distinction is an oversimplification and that there are cultural variations within geographical regions, but she concludes nonetheless that "sources agree that there is a major cultural divide between east and west, with the west's profile generally being individualism, egalitarianism, and low-context communication, and the east's profile being collectivism, hierarchy, and high-context communication." Jeanne M. Brett, Culture and Negotiation, 35 Intl. J. Psychol. 97, 103 (2000). Numerous specific cultural comparisons reach this conclusion as well. See, e.g., Bee Chen Goh, Sino-Western Negotiating Styles, 7 Canterbury L. Rev. 82 (1998) (identifying China as a collectivist and high-context communication culture).

*2. Culture and Social Norms of Division.*  One way to view Brett's discussion of egalitarian versus hierarchical societies is that negotiators from the latter type of culture are more likely than negotiators from the former type to agree on the relevant social norm to rely on when dividing a cooperative surplus — at least when the negotiators occupy different positions in the status hierarchy. Brett observes that in hierarchical societies, "when parties' social status is known, there may be little need to negotiate the relative distribution of resources." In other words, both negotiators are likely to agree that the cooperative surplus created rightly belongs to the party with the higher social status. In egalitarian societies, in contrast, no one is considered entitled by social position to the fruits of cooperation. The appropriate division depends entirely on the situation, which is likely to give rise to disputes about which elements of the situation are most relevant, and thus who is entitled to the greater share of the surplus. Notice that the types of social norms that negotiators rely on that are described in Chapter 6 — reciprocity, convention, and justice — are those relevant in an egalitarian type of culture. In a hierarchical culture, "social status" would need to be added to that list.

   **3. Problems of Cross-Cultural Negotiations Generally.**   Understanding that cultural differences can affect negotiating behavior can help students of negotiation to predict differences in intracultural negotiations conducted by members of two very different cultures. More importantly, however, an understanding of cultural differences can help negotiators foresee the pitfalls of cross-cultural negotiations. One potential problem is that if two negotiators have different cultural values that underlie preferences, they might make incorrect assumptions about the other party's interests, BATNA, and reservation price, thus assuming there is a bargaining zone when there is not or failing to identify a bargaining zone that does exist. This potential pitfall seems to cry out for more explicit, direct communication between negotiators with different cultural backgrounds, but this "solution" reflects a western bias toward what Brett calls "low-context" negotiation, which may be anathema to many eastern negotiators.

   **4. The Context of Communication and Integrative Bargaining.**   Whether a culture is noted for high-context or low-context communication can have a significant effect on integrative bargaining techniques. Recall from Chapter 4 that integrative bargaining requires a sophisticated and nuanced understanding of the other negotiator's needs. In a low-context culture, like the United States, such an understanding is most often acquired by the negotiators making direct assertions and asking each other direct and probing questions. In high-context cultures, this direct approach is disfavored — negotiators are more likely to rely on more indirect cues. As Brett's example of U.S. and Japanese negotiators illustrates, neither approach is necessarily more effective when negotiations are intracultural, but when a negotiator from a high-context culture bargains with one from a low-context culture, the low-context negotiator is likely to have considerable difficulty developing the necessary understanding of the opponent's interests.

   **5. Speed and Efficiency.**   Salacuse's observation that Americans usually want to conclude negotiations as quickly as possible with a minimal amount of socializing or extraneous conversation is a widely noted cultural feature. One author describes as tenets of the American negotiating style that "[e]ffective use of time (efficiency) on substantive tasks is valued over ceremony and social amenities" and that "for the U.S. negotiator, negotiation is a business not a social activity." Paul R. Kimmel, Cultural Perspectives on International Negotiations, 50 J. Soc. Issues 179, 180-181 (1994). These observations probably reflect both that the United States is an individualistic culture, in which negotiators are primarily concerned with satisfying their own needs (and the needs of opponents are important in order to help identify integrative solutions but not for their own sake), and also a low-context communication culture, in which the norm of direct communication reduces the need to develop a personal relationship in order to facilitate mutual understanding.

*6. The Subculture of Lawyers.* One problem with relying on cultural generalities is that there are often subcultures that differ significantly in many respects from the larger general culture. As Salacuse describes, it is accepted lore that American negotiators are oriented toward establishing a specific set of contract terms while Chinese and Japanese negotiators are oriented toward establishing a more general relationship with the other party. But an international survey later conducted by the same author found that whether the negotiator's primary goal was a relationship or a contract depended far more on whether the negotiator was a lawyer than on his or her nationality. In that study, slightly more than half of U.S. and Japanese subjects said they were primarily interested in establishing contracts rather than relationships, and only slightly fewer Chinese respondents said they focused primarily on contract. However, 71 percent of lawyer subjects across cultures said that they were primarily interested in establishing contracts, a far higher percentage than any other occupational group. Jeswald W. Salacuse, Ten Ways That Culture Affects Negotiating Style: Some Survey Results, 14 Negotiation J. 221, 225-226 (1998).

This and other strong correlations between occupational group membership and beliefs about negotiation caused the author to conclude that "the survey suggests that professional and occupational culture may be as important as national culture in shaping a person's negotiating style and attitudes toward the negotiation process. . . . [S]cholars and practitioners need to take into account professional culture, as well as national culture in their studies and analysis of the impact of culture on negotiating." Id. at 238. This advice is particularly important for lawyer-negotiators, who are extremely likely to find that their opponents in cross-cultural bargaining situations are also lawyers.

*7. Collectivism versus Individualism and Integrative versus Distributive Outlooks.* Gelfand and Christakopoulou found that negotiators from a collectivist society (Greece) were more likely to learn about their opponent's interests during the course of negotiation than negotiators from an individualistic society (the United States). This suggests that negotiators from collectivistic countries might be more oriented toward integrative bargaining than negotiators from individualistic cultures. This hypothesis also found support in Salacuse's international survey. That survey found that 100 percent and 82 percent respectively of subjects from Japan and China — both considered collectivistic cultures — viewed negotiation as a process in which both sides can gain rather than a process in which one side wins and the other side loses. Only 71 percent of American negotiators and 59 percent of British negotiators similarly viewed negotiation as a "win-win" rather than a "win-lose" process. Jeswald W. Salacuse, Ten Ways That Culture Affects Negotiating Style: Some Survey Results, 14 Negotiation J. 221, 227-228 (1998).

## DISCUSSION QUESTIONS AND PROBLEMS

*1. Behavioral Studies and Personal Experience.*   The materials on gender in this chapter suggest that there may be some differences in conflict and negotiating behavior among men and women on average. From your personal experience, what gender differences, if any, do you think exist? Do you think that any gender differences on average in the general population also exist among law students? What about among practicing attorneys with substantial negotiation experience?

*2. The Impact of Gender Differences.*   If men and women do negotiate differently, on average, in the ways suggested in the excerpts and notes in this section, what consequences would you expect these differences to have on bargaining outcomes when men negotiate against men, when women negotiate against women, and when men negotiate against women?

*3. The Gender of the Opponent.*   Do you negotiate differently in any way if the opposing negotiator is a man or a woman? How so? Do you think that relating differently to male and female negotiators can improve your negotiation outcomes? Why or why not?

*4. Process and Outcomes.*   Think back to your last negotiating experience, either in class or in the real world. To what extent did your approach reflect typically "western" views of how negotiations should be conducted? If you and your opponent in that negotiation were from cultures with a more typically "eastern" orientation to negotiation, how do you think the bargaining process would have been different? Do you think those differences would have led to a different agreement?

*5. Cross-Cultural Negotiation Strategies.*   Imagine that you, as an American negotiator, must attempt to negotiate an agreement to buy parts necessary for your client's manufacturing process from a supplier whose culture is notable for being collectivist, hierarchical, and favoring a high-context approach to communication. How would you approach the negotiation differently than you would a negotiation over the same subject matter with another American negotiator as your opponent?

6. *Culture and the Importance of Self-Esteem.* In a study of the determinants of subjective well-being, or "life satisfaction," among student subjects from 31 nations, Ed Diener and Marissa Diener found that the correlation between "satisfaction with self" and life satisfaction was higher among subjects from nations rated as "individualistic" (i.e., the U.S. and Western Europe) than nations rated as "collectivistic." Ed Diener & Marissa Diener, Cross-Cultural Correlates of Life Satisfaction and Self-Esteem, 68 J. Pers. & Soc. Psychol. 653, 656 (1995). Assuming that negotiators are likely to tailor their approach to negotiation in a way that enhances their life satisfaction, the Diener & Diener study raises the question of what negotiating styles are most conducive to building self-esteem. What styles do you think are most likely to have this effect? Do you think such styles are prevalent among the "western" negotiators with whom you have come into contact?

7. *Negotiation Tactics and Stereotypes About You.* What stereotypes do you think people have about people from your culture or particular subgroups of your culture with which you are identified by others? Are there ways that you should adjust your negotiating behavior in light of these stereotypes others might have of you? Would you be better off trying to disprove the validity of these stereotypes to your negotiating opponents or taking advantage of the stereotypes?

8. *Are Stereotypes Useful?* Any differences that might exist between negotiators from different cultures or negotiators of different genders are going to be average differences, and will certainly be misleading in many or most circumstances. Given this fact, is it useful to study such group characteristics? Is it dangerous to do so?

# PART IV

# ADDITIONAL PARTIES

In order to focus attention first on the fundamental institutional structure of negotiation and then on issues concerning negotiator characteristics and choice, we have implicitly assumed to this point that negotiations involve only two parties. Some examples have assumed that two principal parties negotiate against each other. Other examples have involved two lawyers negotiating against one another on behalf of clients, but these examples implicitly assumed that lawyers representing clients would negotiate exactly as the clients themselves would negotiate on their own behalf.

Although the dynamics of many types of simple personal negotiations are adequately captured with the two-party model of negotiation, that model is insufficient to fully understand the complexities of most negotiating situations in which lawyers find themselves. A fundamental feature of most legal negotiations is that the lawyers negotiate not on their own behalf but as agents acting on the behalf of principal parties. Many transactions, complex litigation matters, and regulatory matters involve more than two principal parties, and thus require multilateral negotiations. Finally, as lawyers have become more sophisticated and creative in their thinking about how to resolve disputes, the process of mediation, which brings a neutral third-party into the negotiation process, has become a common tool of lawyer-negotiators. This part examines how and to what extent the involvement of more than two parties affects the negotiation process.

Inserting agents, such as lawyers, between principal parties in the negotiation process can have substantial benefits for the parties but also has costs and carries risk. Lawyers need to have a sophisticated understanding of the benefits and the costs, both in order to advise clients on whether representation in a negotiating situation is warranted, and in order to maximize the benefits of agency while minimizing its costs when it is so indicated. Chapter 10, The Principal-Agent Relationship, considers these issues.

Chapter 11, Multilateral Negotiations, considers how a negotiator's imperatives are different in a multilateral bargaining situation than in a bilateral situation. Although the structure of negotiation does not change as the context changes to involve more principal parties, the possibility of coalitions between some but not all of the parties, the increased uncertainty about what constitutes a fair division of the cooperative surplus, and greater communication challenges that arise as more participants sit at the bargaining table increase the number and complexity of issues for the negotiator to consider.

The presence of a neutral mediator or other facilitator at the bargaining table creates new opportunities for the negotiators to achieve their strategic goals. Chapter 12, The Use of Mediation in Negotiation, considers these opportunities, as well as the choices that negotiators must make about what type of mediation to select.

# Chapter 10

# The Principal-Agent Relationship

One extremely important characteristic of negotiations involving lawyers is that when lawyers negotiate they do so on behalf of a client. No understanding of legal negotiation can be complete without considering the implications of the relationship between the principal (in legal situations, the client) and agent (the lawyer) on the process.

When a principal engages an agent to negotiate on his behalf, he creates a relationship that has both benefits and costs. While many lawyers (and other types of professionals who act as negotiating agents) usually assume that the benefits outweigh the costs, this is not always the case — sometimes, all things considered, a principal would be well advised to negotiate on his own behalf. Even when the benefits of agency are substantial, a good agent will be aware of the potential costs of the arrangement and take whatever steps are possible to minimize these costs. This chapter addresses the range of benefits that principals can obtain by hiring an agent to represent them in negotiations and the problems that the insertion of agents between principals can create.

## A. THE BENEFITS OF LAWYER-AGENTS

Principal parties to negotiations, both in litigation and transactional settings, commonly retain lawyers to negotiate on their behalf. Given this observation, it is not surprising that lawyer-agents often have the potential to help their clients achieve better results in negotiation than those clients would be likely to achieve negotiating on their own behalf. This section surveys and then examines in depth some of the primary potential benefits to clients of conducting negotiations through agents.

**Technical expertise.**   Principals often retain a lawyer to negotiate because the latter possesses superior substantive knowledge that will aid in the negotiation process. In dispute resolution situations, determining whether the principal's BATNA is litigating or walking away from the dispute requires an analysis of the legal merits of the litigants' claims, which a lawyer is usually best situated to provide. Predictions concerning the outcome of potential litigation usually are central to the calculation of the principal's reservation price. Again, a lawyer's substantive knowledge of the law and skills in applying the law to the particular dispute are often critically important. A transactional lawyer's substantive knowledge of the law can also be important in making sure that the principal is fully informed of the legal implications of proposed transactions and specific terms. This can help insure that the principal will avoid transactions that are inferior to his BATNA. A transactional lawyer's experience in dealing with particular types of transactions also can make her uniquely suited to exploiting the integrative potential of deals.

**Negotiation expertise.**   Although nearly everyone negotiates on a regular basis, for most lawyers negotiation is a substantial part of their livelihood. This experience has the potential to make lawyers better able to achieve the principal's goals through bargaining than the principal himself. This point deserves an important qualification, however. Experience alone, without feedback or careful attention to the lessons learned is not likely to improve an agent's ability in the art of negotiation. Thus, while lawyers are often skilled in negotiation, they often are not. Depending on the principal's background, there are some situations in which principals are probably best advised to negotiate on their own behalf, perhaps in conjunction with consulting a lawyer for assistance in planning a negotiation strategy when legal analysis is an important input to that strategy.

**Signaling.**   When a client retains a lawyer to represent him in a transaction, he sends a variety of signals to the other negotiator that are different than the ones he would send if he were to negotiate on his own. This is especially true in contexts in which principals are usually represented by an attorney. Depending on the exact context, the use of a lawyer-agent might signal that the principal is particularly serious about reaching an agreement (because hiring the agent is costly), willing to litigate if need be (because the lawyer is skilled in that area), well-prepared (because lawyers are presumed to be substantive experts in their fields), and unlikely to yield to power tactics (because lawyers have reputations for zealously protecting their principals' interests). It is common folklore that insurance companies offer more generous settlements to plaintiffs who are represented by counsel than those who are not. Presumably this is because they assume a lawyer is more likely to know the true value of a case and less likely to be intimidated by the insurance company than the average personal injury plaintiff.

**Dispassionate observation.**   In many situations, even principals who are skilled in the relevant substantive analysis and the negotiation process are well-served by retaining an agent who does not have a personal stake in the outcome of the negotiation. When negotiators are emotionally involved in the process, they are often less than objective in comparing the value of an agreement to their alternatives, as well as in identifying opportunities to improve the quality of agreements through integrative bargaining. Either an antagonistic relationship or a friendly relationship with the opposing party can cause a principal to fail to use power or social norms to his maximum advantage. An agent can often conduct a more dispassionate analysis, leading to more rational negotiating decisions.

**Access.**   In some situations, particular types of agents will have access that principals lack. Such access might be necessary for negotiation even to be possible, such as when a well-connected lawyer is able to arrange a meeting between an artist and a gallery owner. In this type of situation, the agent's personal connections or reputation provide value to the principal. Alternatively, the agent's access might improve the principal's BATNA, thus creating negotiating power. For example, hiring a lawyer-agent licensed to practice in the local courts gives the principal the option of litigation should negotiations fail.

**Strategic advantage.**   Negotiating through an agent can often give a principal a variety of strategic advantages in the negotiation process. For example, a negotiator might be better able to make credible commitments not to accept an agreement that appears to exceed his reservation price if his settlement authority is limited by a principal who is not present during the bargaining. Consider, for example, the strength of the negotiating position of a plaintiff's lawyer who says "I appreciate your offer of $75,000 to settle the case, but my client is adamant about not accepting anything less than $80,000." An agent might also be able to retreat from a commitment or offer an apology for past behavior when this would be difficult for a principal to do without "losing face."

**Cost effectiveness.**   Although we normally think of lawyers as highly compensated professionals, principals will often find retaining a lawyer as a negotiation agent to be cost effective. For corporations, for example, paying a lawyer to handle a complicated negotiation might prove cheaper in the long run than leaving the task to senior management who will have to neglect other duties and opportunities in order to give the negotiation the necessary attention. Also, when a lawyer is experienced in negotiating a certain type of transaction, he is likely to be able to identify and deal with the relevant issues more quickly and efficiently than a principal who has less experience with that type of transaction, even if the principal is as skillful a negotiator as is the lawyer.

## ■ Ronald J. Gilson & Robert H. Mnookin, Disputing Through Agents: Cooperation and Conflict Between Lawyers in Litigation*

**94 Colum. L. Rev.** 509, 522-530, 533-535, 539-546 (1994)

### A.   THE PRE-LITIGATION GAME: CHOOSING LAWYERS

Assume that both clients must litigate through a lawyer (an assumption that, for a change, is descriptively accurate). Further suppose that there exists a class of sole practitioners who have reputations for cooperation which assure that, once retained, they will conduct the litigation in a cooperative fashion. Three final assumptions define our "pre-litigation game." First, clients disclose their choice of lawyer — and thus, whether they have chosen a cooperative lawyer — prior to the beginning of the litigation game. Second, if one client chooses a cooperative lawyer and her opponent does not, the client choosing a cooperative lawyer can change her mind without cost before the litigation game begins. Third, after the litigation game begins, clients cannot change lawyers.

Under these assumptions, disputing through lawyers provides an escape from the prisoner's dilemma. As we have defined the pre-litigation game, each client's dominant strategy is to choose a cooperative lawyer because the choice of a cooperative lawyer binds each client to a cooperative strategy. If client A chooses a cooperative lawyer and client B also chooses a cooperative lawyer, both clients receive the higher cooperative payoff. Alternatively, if client B does not choose a cooperative lawyer, client A is no worse off having initially chosen to cooperate. In that event, client A replaces her cooperative lawyer with a gladiator and is in the same position as if she had chosen a gladiator in the first instance. Thus, her dominant strategy is to choose a cooperative lawyer and to switch if her opponent does not adopt a parallel strategy. Of course, client B confronts the same choices and has the

---

*This article originally appeared at 94 Colum. L. Rev. 509 (1994). Reprinted by permission.

same dominant strategy. The result is a cooperative equilibrium because the introduction of lawyers has transformed the prisoner's dilemma payoff structure into a game in which the only choices are mutual cooperation or mutual defection. Mutual cooperation obviously has the higher payoff for each party. . . .

In the pre-litigation game, we first required clients to disclose their choice of lawyer before the game began. In real litigation, plaintiffs must typically disclose their choice of lawyer at the outset of litigation: the lawyer's name is, quite literally, the first thing that appears on the complaint. Similarly, the defendant must have a lawyer to respond to the complaint, and even to request an extension of the time in which to file an answer to the complaint. Again, this discloses the identity of the lawyer chosen.

We next assumed that a plaintiff choosing a cooperative lawyer could costlessly switch to a gladiator upon learning that her opponent had chosen a gladiator. In the real world, there are costs in switching lawyers, but these costs are likely to be low at the outset. A client will have expended little on her lawyer by the time the identity of her opponent's lawyer is revealed. Thus, for practical purposes, the game's assumption of a costless opportunity to switch lawyers on the disclosure of opposing counsel is roughly consistent with real litigation patterns.

The third assumption — that clients cannot change lawyers during the litigation game — is more problematic. At first glance, the assumption seems patently false; a client may discharge counsel at any time. On closer examination, the presence of substantial switching costs may provide a reasonable proxy for a prohibition against discharging cooperative counsel once the litigation is well underway. As litigation proceeds, a lawyer expends substantial time becoming familiar with the law and especially the facts of the case. The client pays for the lawyer's acquisition of this knowledge. The client's investment in the lawyer's knowledge is relationship-specific in the extreme; that is, it is of no value to the client if the lawyer is fired. Thus, the price of firing the lawyer is the cost of bringing another lawyer up to speed in the litigation. While not a prohibition on changing lawyers, switching costs impose a substantial penalty on defection. Indeed, the longer the litigation continues, the more switching will cost. . . .

## B. A REPUTATION MARKET FOR COOPERATIVE LAWYERS

. . . Lawyers would be willing to invest in achieving a reputation for cooperation because they would receive a return on that investment by virtue of the premium fees clients would be willing to pay. . . . Noncooperative behavior would forfeit the lawyer's investment in a cooperative reputation. Thus, so long as the lawyer's possible loss of investment in reputation exceeds the size of the bribe an opportunistic client would be willing to pay, cooperative lawyers will not be suborned and a market for cooperative lawyers should be available.

However, establishing that clients would demand demonstrably cooperative lawyers and that lawyers would want to supply that service is not sufficient to assure that the market operates. The key word in the previous sentence is "demonstrably." The linchpin of this model is that the lawyer's cooperative or noncooperative behavior be observable. What makes the client's commitment credible is that her lawyer will lose his investment in reputation if he behaves noncooperatively. But this penalty cannot be imposed if the noncooperative behavior cannot be observed. Thus, the structure fails if an erstwhile cooperative lawyer can behave noncooperatively and get away with it.

For this purpose it is critical to follow David Kreps and return to the distinction between observable and verifiable misconduct noted earlier. That misconduct be observable requires only that the party suffering the affront know with confidence that it occurred. For misconduct to be verifiable, in contrast, the party suffering the affront must be able to demonstrate to an enforcement agency, such as a court, that the misconduct occurred. The difference is important. Verification requires formal proof of misconduct sufficient to meet judicial thresholds. It is commonplace that misconduct which is observable — known to the participants — nonetheless may not be verifiable either because there is no extrinsic proof and the misbehaving party can simply deny the allegations, because the cost of verifying the misconduct is too high, or because the difficulty of defining misconduct limits the legal standard to extreme cases.

In our case, noncooperative conduct by one client's lawyer may not be verifiable, but may nonetheless be readily observable by the lawyer on the other side. . . . The lawyer can then pass on to the client the fact of noncooperative conduct — the reputation violation — following which both lawyer and client can impose the penalty of lost reputation on the misbehaving lawyer by distributing the information to the legal community. . . .

[One] problem with using sole practitioners to allow clients to precommit to cooperate [is that a]n individual practitioner can represent only a limited number of clients in ongoing litigation. . . . [T]he larger and more complex the matter, the greater the percentage of a lawyer's practice it represents, and the more intimidating is a client's threat to change counsel unless the lawyer breaches his reputation. Because the opposing client would anticipate the risk of defection, in this situation the pre-litigation game might not allow for a cooperative result. . . .

1. How the Law Firm Might Bond Cooperation When an Individual Lawyer Cannot. — Because a firm may provide a larger repository of

reputational capital — at a minimum composed of the aggregate reputational capital of its component lawyers — using a law firm instead
of a sole practitioner has the potential to mitigate the problem of collusion between opposing counsel. In effect, the firm pledges its reputation behind the cooperative commitment of each of its lawyers.
Defection by any single lawyer in any single case may damage the entire
firm's reputation for cooperation. The size of the penalty imposed on
the firm for noncooperation in any single case may therefore be larger
than the penalty that can be imposed against a sole practitioner for a
similar defection. In this way, the difficulties of detection discussed
earlier are balanced by an increase in the penalty if the misconduct is
observed. . . .

   . . . [C]lient preferences may deconstruct the law firm, thereby re-
versing the increased investment in reputation that supported any single lawyer's commitment to cooperation. The catch phrase for large
clients has become that they "hire lawyers, not law firms." Their goal
is to maintain competition among firms for their work by avoiding what
Oliver Williamson refers to as the "fundamental transformation" — the
shift from market conditions characterized by many competing suppliers to market conditions characterized by one supplier with a substantial advantage over potential competitors as a result of a
relationship specific investment following the supplier's initial selection. A cost to this strategy is the law firm's decreased ability to bond
cooperation. Shifting the search for reputation back to the individual
from the firm potentially offsets the increase in the size of the reputational capital achieved by moving from individual to firm representation. If it is only the individual lawyer's reputation upon which the
client relies, then the aggregate of the reputational capital of the lawyers in the firms does not bond the conduct of the individual lawyers. . . .

### A.   Understanding the Contentiousness of
Commercial Litigation

. . .

1. The Changing Payoff Structure in Litigation. — Two conclusions
about the character of large commercial litigation have emerged in
recent years, one empirical and relating to its frequency, the second
subjective and relating to its conduct. Recent studies have documented
a dramatic increase in the amount of commercial litigation after
1970. . . .
   Over the same period, commercial litigators attested to the increasingly uncivil conduct of civil litigation. The phenomenon of discovery
abuse was the most obvious manifestation. . . .

To be sure, most lawyers do not identify themselves as bombers or gladiators. Rather, they describe their personal strategy as flexible, either cooperator or gladiator, depending on how the other side plays. In effect, the picture is of a population of tit-for-tat lawyers: each cooperates until the other side defects and then retaliates. . . .

The puzzle, then, is to explain what generates all the litigation conflict. If litigators generally claim that they always cooperate unless the other side defects, who is left to defect first? The problem is that the effectiveness of the tit-for-tat strategy depends on a particular characteristic of the environment in which the game is played. As typically stated (and as was the case in Axelrod's tournament), the tit-for-tat strategy assumes that each player has perfect information about the other player's actions. That is, each player knows with certainty whether the other player has cooperated or defected. In contrast, when one player may mistake the character of the other player's actions, tit-for-tat leads not to cooperation, but to continuing gladiatorial defection. Suppose one player misinterprets her opponent's action as defection when her opponent actually meant to cooperate. Tit-for-tat dictates following the opponent's move on all moves after the first. Thus, cooperation ends after the misinterpretation. One player defects, mistakenly thinking her opponent had done so, and her opponent then follows suit, the mistake "echoing" back and forth as the players simply repeat the initial mistake.

Thus, the information structure of the litigation game can explain the presence of significant conflict in litigation even though most lawyers claim to play tit-for-tat. Litigation is quite "noisy." Clearly identifying whether the other side has cooperated or defected in a competitive environment where cooperation is defined as being not too conflictual, is often quite difficult. For example, not all objections to discovery requests are defections. . . .

The same problem also hinders the maintenance of reputations. For a reputation market to work, defections by cooperative lawyers must be observable. However, both aspects of noise we have considered — a mixed environment of cooperative and noncooperative litigation, and the difficulty of evaluating whether a particular action by an opponent is cooperative when the standard for cooperation is being not too competitive — makes observation of defection more difficult.

### B.   UNDERSTANDING THE PRESENCE OF COOPERATION IN FAMILY LAW PRACTICE

. . .

. . . Family law practice tends to be both localized and specialized. A divorcing husband and wife usually hire attorneys in the same legal community. Increasingly, some lawyers have tended to specialize in family practice, especially in metropolitan areas. Typically, over a period of time, these local specialists repeatedly deal with one another. Through this repeated exposure lawyers can develop and sustain their reputations. . . .

Interviews with California family law specialists suggest that a reputational market does exist; that some lawyers cultivate reputations as cooperative problem-solvers, while others are viewed as more adversarial, both by themselves and others; and that, as suggested by our prelitigation game, there is a substantial amount of self-selection both by clients and attorneys. The small sample size and the informal methodology of our survey mean that one should view our conclusions only as suggestive, but the anecdotal evidence we have gathered seems consistent with our framework. . . .

Not surprisingly, the interviews suggested that cooperative problem-solvers much preferred dealing with lawyers who shared their orientation. A great deal of sorting and self-selection appears to occur based on reputation. Lawyers who saw themselves as cooperative said they would describe their problem-solving orientation during initial meetings with clients. They reported that their clients often were seeking lawyers with a particular orientation. Several cooperative lawyers reported that they regularly turned away clients who sought highly adversarial representation. As one stated, "If a client is hell bent upon hiring an advocate to disembowel the adverse party, I direct them elsewhere." . . .

A final feature of matrimonial practice may also facilitate cooperation. Unlike a commercial litigator, a family law specialist is usually not unduly dependent upon a single client for his or her livelihood. This should make it easier for a cooperative problem-solver to resist client pressure to defect after the case is underway.

We do not mean for our analysis of family law practice to suggest that matrimonial practice is exclusively or even predominantly cooperative. Instead, we use matrimonial practice to illustrate that reputational markets presently exist that permit clients to commit to cooperative strategies in circumstances in which the clients themselves might have great difficulty doing so. . . . ■

## ■ Ronald J. Gilson, Value Creation by Business Lawyers: Legal Skills and Asset Pricing*

94 Yale L.J. 239, 253, 255, 258-272, 280-282 (1984)

. . . When markets fall short of perfection, incentives exist for private innovations that improve market performance. As long as the costs of innovation are less than the resulting gains, private innovation to

*Reprinted by permission of The Yale Law Journal Company and William S. Hein Company from The Yale Law Journal, Vol. 94, pp. 239–313.

reduce the extent of market failure creates value. It is in precisely this fashion that opportunity exists for business lawyers to create value. . . .

I suggest that the tie between legal skills and transaction value is the business lawyer's ability to create a transactional structure which reduces transaction costs and therefore results in more accurate asset pricing. . . . My hypothesis about what business lawyers really do — their potential to create value — is simply this: Lawyers function as transaction cost engineers, devising efficient mechanisms which bridge the gap between [a] hypothetical world of perfect markets and the less-than-perfect reality of effecting transactions in this world. . . .

[Professor Gilson uses the example of an acquisition agreement to illustrate his hypothesis of how business lawyers create value.] A skeletal outline of the form of a typical agreement provides a representative picture.

*Description of the Transaction.* The initial, and usually most straight-forward, portion of the agreement provides an overall description of the transaction. The parties are identified, the structure of the trans-action — for example, a purchase of stock or assets, or some triangular variation — is described, and details concerning such matters as the timing and location of the closing of the transaction are set forth.

*Price and Terms of Payment.* The next portion of the agreement typi-cally focuses on the price to be paid and the medium and timing of payment. The text is most straightforward when the medium of pay-ment is cash and the entire amount is to be paid on closing. But where the transaction contemplates other than immediate payment of the entire purchase price, the document inevitably becomes a great deal more complicated. . . .

*Representations and Warranties.* The next major portion of the agree-ment consists of representations and warranties made by the seller and, typically to a much lesser extent, by the buyer. These provisions consist of a series of detailed statements of fact concerning the relevant busi-ness. . . .

*Covenants and Conditions.* The two final steps in our survey of the major portions of a typical acquisition agreement result from the fact that many acquisition transactions contemplate a significant gap be-tween the date on which the acquisition agreement is signed and the date on which the transaction is closed. . . . This [is accounted for] by two complementary techniques: covenants governing the operation of the business during the gap period, and conditions which, if not sat-isfied, relieve a party of its obligation to complete the transaction. Typ-ically these two techniques combine with the representations and warranties to operate as a unit, providing a hierarchy of obligations and the potential for a hierarchy of remedies if one or more of the other party's obligations are not met. . . .

Imagine a negotiation between the presidents of a buyer and seller concerning the price at which the transaction will take place. Imagine further that the negotiations have progressed to the point where agreement has been reached on an abstract, but nonetheless important, pricing principle, that the appropriate way to value the seller's business is $1 in purchase price for each $1 in annual sales. . . . Even after agreement on a valuation principle, the parties will agree on price only if they share the same expectations about the seller's future sales. The problem, of course, is that they will not. The negotiating dance that results is familiar to practitioners.

Now suppose that the buyer's president, having done his homework, believes that there is a 50% chance the seller will do $10 million in sales next year and a 50% chance that it will do only $5 million. The expected value of the alternatives is $7.5 million which the buyer's president offers as the purchase price which the agreed-upon valuation principle dictates. The president of the seller, not surprisingly, has different expectations. He is much more optimistic about the probabilities associated with next year's sales. His homework suggests an 85% chance of $10 million in sales and only a 15% chance of sales as low as $5 million. These figures yield an expected value, and a purchase price under the agreed valuation principle, of $9.25 million. The result is inaccurate pricing at best and, because of the resulting conflict over the purchase price, at worst no transaction at all if the parties are unable to resolve their differences.

It is important to emphasize at this point that the problem which "kills" our hypothetical deal is not distributional conflict—disagreement over sharing the gains from the transaction. The distributional principle in the form of a valuation formula has already been approved. Rather, the problem is [that the] parties simply have different expectations concerning the future performance of the business. If this problem could be solved, a deal could be made. Tautologically, the value of the transaction would be increased. And if my hypothesis about what business lawyers do is correct, a particularly inviting opportunity then exists for value creation by a business lawyer. The lawyer can increase the value of the transaction if he can devise a transactional structure that creates homogeneous expectations.

As my hypothesis predicts, there is a familiar remedy, commonly called an "earnout" or "contingent price" deal. . . . It is intended, as a prominent practitioner has put it, to "bridge the negotiating gap between a seller who thinks his business is worth more than its historical earnings justify and a purchaser who hails from Missouri." The solution that business lawyers resort to for this problem is one that economists refer to as state-contingent contracting. Its central insight is that the difference in expectations between the parties as to the probabilities assigned to the occurrence of future events will ultimately disappear as time transforms a prediction of next year's sales into historical fact. If determination of the purchase price can be delayed until next year's sales are known with certainty, the deal can be made. . . . The solution, therefore, is to formulate the purchase price as an initial payment, here $7.5 million, to be followed by an additional payment at the close of the next fiscal year equal, in this case, to $1 for each $1 of sales in excess of $7.5 million. The problem of non-homogeneous expectations is avoided by making the failure irrelevant. . . .

Where the parties . . . have different time horizons, each has an incentive to maximize value in the period relevant to it, even at the expense of a decrease in value in the period relevant to the other party. This conflict reduces the value of the transaction.

Consider first what behavior we would expect during the earnout's one-year measuring period if the seller's original management were allowed to run the company for that time. From the seller's perspective, the earnout formula reduces to one year the relevant period over which asset value is to be determined; at the end of that year the seller's shareholders will receive whatever payment is due under the earnout formula. At least for them, the asset will cease to exist. To the seller's shareholders, therefore, the asset is worth only what it can earn for them in a year's time. Their goal is to maximize value over that short period. The buyer, in contrast, is concerned with the value of the business over a much longer period: the entire time it expects to operate the seller's business. Accordingly, the buyer's behavior will differ substantially from that which would be dictated by the seller's short-term orientation.

Returning to the terms of the hypothetical earnout formula — an additional $1 in purchase price for each $1 in sales over $7.5 million — the seller would maximize sales during the one-year measuring period. For example, prices might be cut and advertising expenditures substantially increased, even if these actions meant that the company actually suffered a loss. In contrast, the buyer, which would ultimately bear the loss because it continues to own the company after the one year period, has a very different interest. And the conflict is not merely the result of a poorly specified earnout formula. Stating the formula in terms of profits rather than sales, thus eliminating the seller's incentive to maximize sales at the expense of the buyer's long term interest in earnings, would be a possible improvement. But even then the different time horizons would create an incentive for the seller's management to behave opportunistically. Short-term profits could be maximized by eliminating research and development expenditures, cutting maintenance, and, in general, deferring expenses to later periods.

This failure of the common-time-horizon assumption reduces the value of the transaction. So long as the buyer anticipates that the seller's management will behave opportunistically — which hardly requires a crystal ball — it will reduce its offer accordingly. The business lawyer then has the opportunity to create value by devising a transaction structure that constrains the seller's ability to maximize the value of the business over a period different from that relevant to the buyer. The typical earnout agreement responds to precisely this challenge.

Stated most generally, a complete earnout formula is a complicated state-contingent contract that, by carefully specifying in advance the impact on the purchase price of all events that might occur during the earnout period, substantially reduces the incentives and opportunity for the parties to behave strategically. For example, the perverse incentives growing out of a formula specifying either earnings or sales as a sole measure of performance might be reduced by a measure that combines them: e.g., a $1 increase in purchase price for each $1 increase in sales provided that profits remain above a specified percentage of sales. Similarly, where the earnout period is greater than one year, incentives to manipulate the year in which particular events occur can be minimized by provisions which specify whether shortfalls or overages in one year carry forward or backward to other years.

A thoroughly specified earnout formula is extraordinarily complex and, in any event, cannot entirely eliminate the potential for strategic behavior. To be fully effective, a formula would have to specify not only the complete production function for the business, but all possible exogenous events that might occur during the earnout period and the impact of such events on the formula. Neither, of course, is possible. . . . That transaction costs are, at some level, irreducible hardly diminishes the value of efforts to keep costs at that level. It is value creation of the sort that reflects what I understand clients to mean by the comment that a particular lawyer has good "judgment," to know when the game is not worth the candle. . . .

The portion of the acquisition agreement dealing with representations and warranties — commonly the longest part of a typical acquisition agreement and the portion that usually requires the most time for a lawyer to negotiate — has its primary purpose to remedy conditions of asymmetrical information in the least-cost manner.

. . . First, as a simple result of its prior operation of the business, the seller will already have large amounts of information concerning the business that the buyer does not have, but would like to acquire. Second, there usually will be information that neither party has, but that one or both would like and which one or the other can acquire more cheaply. The question is then how both of these situations are dealt with in the acquisition agreement so as to reduce the informational differences between the parties at the lowest possible cost.

At first, one might wonder why any cooperative effort is necessary. Assuming that the seller did not affirmatively block the buyer's efforts to acquire the information the buyer wanted (and the seller already had), nothing would prevent the buyer from independently acquiring the desired information. Similarly, assuming both parties had the opportunity to acquire the desired new information, nothing would prevent both parties from independently acquiring it.

Actually, however, it is in the seller's best interest to make the information that the seller already has available to the buyer as cheaply as possible. Suppose the seller refused to assist the buyer in securing a particular piece of information that the seller already had. If the information could have either a positive or negative value on the buyer's evaluation of the worth of the business, a rational buyer would infer from the seller's refusal to cooperate that the information must be unfavorable. Thus, the seller has little incentive to withhold the information. Indeed, the same result would follow even if the information in question would not alter the buyer's estimate of the value of the business, but only increase the certainty with which that estimate was held. Once we have established that the seller wants the buyer to have the information, the only issue that remains is which party can produce it most cheaply. The total price the buyer will pay for the business is the sum of the amount to be paid to the seller and the transaction costs incurred by the buyer in effecting the transaction. To the extent that the buyer's information costs are reduced, there simply is more left over for division between the buyer and seller.

Precisely the same analysis holds for information that neither party has yet acquired. The seller could refuse to cooperate with the buyer in its acquisition. To do so, however, would merely increase the information costs associated with the transaction to the detriment of both parties. . . .

This analysis, it seems to me, accounts for the quite detailed picture of the seller's business that the standard set of representations and warranties presents. Among other facts, the identity, location and condition of the assets of the business are described; the nature and extent of liabilities are specified; and the character of employee relationships — from senior management to production employees — is described. This is information that the buyer wants and the seller already has; provision by the seller minimizes its acquisition costs to the benefit of both parties. . . .

Problems of information cost do not end when the information is acquired. Even if cooperative negotiation between the buyer and seller minimizes the costs of reducing the informational asymmetry confronting the buyer, another information-cost dilemma remains: How can the buyer determine whether the information it has received is accurate? After all, the seller, who has probably provided most of the information, has a clear incentive to mislead the buyer into overvaluing the business.

. . . If, before a transaction, a buyer can neither itself determine the quality of the seller's product nor evaluate the accuracy of the seller's representations about product quality, the buyer has no alternative but to treat the seller's product as being of low quality, regardless of the seller's protestations. To avoid this problem, a high quality seller has a substantial incentive to demonstrate to a buyer that its representations about the quality of its product are accurate and can be relied upon. And because it is in the seller's interest to keep all information costs at a minimum, there is also an incentive to accomplish this verification in the most economical fashion.

Verification techniques, then, are critical means of reducing total information costs. Like efforts to reduce acquisition costs, verification techniques can be implemented both by the parties themselves and through the efforts of third parties. . . .

. . . [T]he insight is simply to devise what Oliver Williamson has called a "hostage" strategy, i.e., an artificial second period in which misrepresentations in the first period — the acquisition transaction — are penalized. If any of the seller's information turns out to be inaccurate, the seller will be required to compensate the buyer; in effect, the seller posts a bond that it has provided accurate information. This technique has the advantage of being quite economical: Beyond the negotiating cost involved in agreeing to make the buyer whole, there is no cost to the seller unless the information proves inaccurate. . . . ∎

## Notes

*1. Experimental Evidence.*    Gilson and Mnookin advance two related hypotheses. First, they suggest that lawyers can help to solve the negotiator's dilemma by promising in advance to "cooperate" rather than "defect" in negotiations and making that promise credible by pledging as collateral their reputations as cooperators. Second, they hypothesize that if lawyers can make credible commitments to cooperate, clients will choose to hire "cooperators," so long as they can switch to "defectors" if their opponent hires a "defector." Using law students as subjects, Croson and Mnookin tested the second hypothesis experimentally, and their results support the theory.

Subjects were asked to select an agent to represent them in a tenround prisoner's dilemma game, and the subjects won money based on the scores their agent was able to obtain against agents chosen by other subjects. There were three agents from which to choose, and the strategy that each agent employed was known to the subjects. "Agent A" would cooperate in every round of the prisoner's dilemma game. "Agent B" would defect in every round. "Agent C" would play whatever sequence of moves the subject specified in advance. When subjects

were told that they could not change their agents based on what type
of agent their adversary selected, 33 out of 40 subjects selected either
Agent B or Agent C. When subjects were told that they would have the
opportunity to change agents before the game began after both players
selected an agent, however, 35 out of 46 subjects chose Agent A — the
cooperator. Rachel Croson & Robert H. Mnookin, Does Disputing
Through Agents Enhance Cooperation? Experimental Evidence, 26 J.
Legal Stud. 331, 335-342 (1997).

   *2. Principal-Agent Communication and Integrative Bargaining.* Both
the Gilson and Mnookin article on litigation and the Gilson article on
transactional contracts demonstrate reasons that lawyer-agents can
make negotiations more integrative than they might otherwise be. An
implicit prerequisite to lawyer-agents being able to enlarge the cooperative surplus to be shared between the principals is that the agents
have a thorough understanding of their principal's interests and the
interests of the opposing principal as well. Such an understanding begins with the agent taking pains to understand his client's interests (not
merely the client's positions) and what his client knows about the opponent's interests, often as a result of asking a lengthy set of probing
questions and follow-up questions.

   Mnookin, Peppet, and Tulumello claim that many lawyers fail to
communicate thoroughly with their clients because lawyers believe that
asking too many questions about their client's interests makes them
look foolish and uninformed, or that lawyers believe such questions
are unnecessary because they know what their client's interests are,
having practiced in a particular area for many years. These authors
also believe that lawyers routinely fail to question their clients about
the opponent's interests because they assume that the client does not
know or care about the opponent's interests or because such questions
might suggest disloyalty. Robert H. Mnookin et al., Beyond Winning:
Negotiating to Create Value in Deals and Disputes 179-182 (2000). In
fact, effective integrative bargaining requires the lawyer to pursue both
lines of inquiry prior to negotiating with the opponent, as well as to
attempt to learn more about the opponent's interests directly during
early bargaining sessions.

## B.  THE PRINCIPAL-AGENT TENSION

Understanding the effects that representation by an agent can have on
the dynamics of a negotiation requires careful consideration of problems created by agency in addition to its benefits. Each of the following
costs of agency can affect the tactics used in negotiation and the payoffs

of potential negotiation outcomes in ways that disadvantage the agent's principal.

**Different preferences.**   Effective negotiation requires a thorough knowledge of one's own preferences and values. Agents are likely to have different preferences and values than their principals. While a good agent will try to understand his client's values and attempt to satisfy them through the negotiation process, he is unlikely to ever know his client as well as his client knows himself. Consider a lawyer who is negotiating the purchase of components from a seller for a manufacturer client. The client instructs the lawyer that he needs the components delivered as soon as possible, and that another supplier stands ready to deliver them immediately. The lawyer conveys this to the seller, and the seller responds that he can provide the components for 10 percent less than the competition but cannot make delivery for one week. Is this an offer that is inferior or superior to the BATNA of purchasing from the alternative supplier? If the lawyer owned his client's company, he might be willing to sacrifice the week for a 10 percent savings, but does his client share the same preference? It might be possible for the lawyer to consult with the client on this question, but in other circumstances such consultation might be difficult, and the time and inconvenience involved might reduce the benefit to the client of negotiating through an agent.

**Different interests.**   Principals and agents often have conflicting interests, which can cause a principal who negotiates through an agent to achieve a less advantageous outcome. A faithful agent sets aside his own interests and seeks to fulfill only the interests of his principal, but it would be naive to think that all agents are completely faithful or even that they could completely divorce their analysis and behavior from their own interests even when they make their best effort to do so.

Consider first the different financial interests of an attorney and her client that arise from different attorney compensation structures. Assume that the lawyer is compensated with an hourly fee. In this case, the lawyer's financial interest is best served by extending negotiations, whereas the client's financial interest is served by concluding them as expeditiously as possible. In litigation, it is in the hourly fee lawyer's personal interest not to settle at all, so he can charge the client for the numerous hours required to prepare for and stage a trial.

In many types of litigation matters, it is typical for a plaintiff's lawyer to be paid on a contingent fee basis, under which the lawyer collects a certain percentage of any settlement or judgment the plaintiff receives. In this situation, the attorney will often have an interest to settle the matter quickly for a relatively modest amount of money, since this enables him to earn a large percentage of his maximum possible payoff with little effort. For example, an attorney might prefer a $50,000 settlement offer from the defendant obtained with little effort to a $60,000 settlement or a $60,000 trial verdict obtained after hundreds of hours spent preparing for litigation and/or actually litigating the case. The quick settlement will provide the lawyer with a much higher effective hourly wage. In contrast, the plaintiff client is likely to prefer the larger settlement or trial verdict that would result from additional work by his lawyer. On the other hand, because contingent fee lawyers get paid only when litigation is employed or at least threatened, such lawyers will sometimes have an interest in encouraging litigation even if the time and emotional toll suggests that the potential plaintiff would be better off not bringing suit.

Differences in interests go beyond financial concerns. A lawyer might have an interest in gaining a certain type of experience or developing a certain type of reputation. Seeking a trial, avoiding a trial, negotiating unnecessarily aggressively, ingratiating himself with the opponent, or demanding that a contract account for every conceivable contingency no matter how remote might further his personal agenda, but these behaviors will not necessarily best serve the needs of his client.

Another way that an agent can pursue his own interests at the expense of his principal's interests is by shirking his duties. Whereas the principal's interests will be furthered by the agent's hard and careful work, the agent might prefer to exercise less than the maximum amount of care and effort possible in the situation. The opportunity for an agent to shirk depends upon the ability of the principal to monitor the quality of the agent's performance. If an agent is caught shirking, the principal might refuse to pay him, might refuse to hire him for future projects, and might report his shirking to other principals, thus harming the agent's reputation. Unfortunately, the quality of legal work is difficult for most clients to monitor effectively. Even an excellent lawyer can lose a case if the facts and law favor the other party, and even a well-drafted contract can fail to protect against all possible contingencies that might arise in the future. Thus, unless a client is a lawyer herself — and even sometimes if she is — it will be difficult for her to detect all but the most overt shirking.

**Different personalities.** Because lawyer-agents are usually more emotionally detached from negotiating situations than their clients can be, they can sometimes maintain a demeanor that promotes successful negotiation in situations where a client would not. On the other hand, lawyers enjoy an unfortunate reputation in many circles as being contentious, aggressive, and argumentative — traits not generally conducive to discovering opportunities for mutually beneficial trade. There is little doubt that this stereotype is often false, but where it is true the lawyer's personality can impede successful negotiation.

**Expense.**   Although the costs of retaining an agent are often well spent, negotiating through an agent usually entails higher out-of-pocket costs than a principal would face if he were to negotiate on his own behalf. Ironically, to the extent that a principal takes steps to mitigate the problems of different preferences and different interests, he is likely to exacerbate the expense problem. If the principal painstakingly and thoroughly shares his preferences and valuations with his agent, he can reduce the problems caused by the agent and principal having different preferences. If the principal carefully monitors the actions of his agent, he can perhaps avoid the worst excesses of a faithless agent who places his own interests before his client's. But either of these actions requires time and money, reducing the cost-effectiveness of the agency relationship.

## ■ Evans v. Jeff D.

**475 U.S.** 717, 106 S. Ct. 1531 (1986)

JUSTICE STEVENS delivered the opinion of the Court.

### I

The petitioners are the Governor and other public officials of the State of Idaho responsible for the education and treatment of children who suffer from emotional and mental handicaps. Respondents are a class of such children who have been or will be placed in petitioners' care. . . .

In March 1983, one week before trial, petitioners presented respondents with a new settlement proposal. As respondents themselves characterize it, the proposal "offered virtually all of the injunctive relief [they] had sought in their complaint." Brief for Respondents 5. See App. 89. . . . As was true of the earlier partial settlement, however, petitioners' offer included a provision for a waiver by respondents of any claim to fees or costs. Originally, this waiver was unacceptable to the Idaho Legal Aid Society, which had instructed Johnson to reject any settlement offer conditioned upon a waiver of fees, but Johnson ultimately determined that his ethical obligation to his clients mandated acceptance of the proposal. The parties conditioned the waiver on approval by the District Court.

After the stipulation was signed, Johnson filed a written motion requesting the District Court to approve the settlement "except for the provision on costs and attorney's fees," and to allow respondents to

present a bill of costs and fees for consideration by the court. App. 87.
At the oral argument on that motion, Johnson contended that petitioners' offer had exploited his ethical duty to his clients — that he
was "forced," by an offer giving his clients "the best result [they] could
have gotten in this court or any other court," to waive his attorney's
fees. The District Court, however, evaluated the waiver in the context
of the entire settlement and rejected the ethical underpinnings of Johnson's argument. Explaining that although petitioners were "not willing
to concede that they were obligated to [make the changes in their
practices required by the stipulation], . . . they were willing to do them
as long as their costs were outlined and they didn't face additional
costs," it concluded that "it doesn't violate any ethical considerations
for an attorney to give up his attorney fees in the interest of getting a
better bargain for his client[s]." Id., at 93. Accordingly, the District
Court approved the settlement and denied the motion to submit a costs
bill. . . .

## II

. . . Although respondents contend that Johnson, as counsel for the
class, was faced with an "ethical dilemma" when petitioners offered him
relief greater than that which he could reasonably have expected to
obtain for his clients at trial (if only he would stipulate to a waiver of
the statutory fee award), and although we recognize Johnson's conflicting interests between pursuing relief for the class and a fee for the
Idaho Legal Aid Society, we do not believe that the "dilemma" was an
"ethical" one in the sense that Johnson had to choose between conflicting duties under the prevailing norms of professional conduct.[14]
Plainly, Johnson had no ethical obligation to seek a statutory fee award.
His ethical duty was to serve his clients loyally and competently. Since
the proposal to settle the merits was more favorable than the probable
outcome of the trial, Johnson's decision to recommend acceptance was
consistent with the highest standards of our profession. The District
Court, therefore, correctly concluded that approval of the settlement
involved no breach of ethics in this case. . . .

---

14. Generally speaking, a lawyer is under an ethical obligation to exercise independent professional judgment on behalf of his client; he must not allow his own interests,
financial or otherwise, to influence his professional advice. ABA, Model Code of Professional Responsibility EC 5-1, 5-2 (as amended 1980); ABA, Model Rules of Professional Conduct 1.7(b), 2.1 (as amended 1984). Accordingly, it is argued that an attorney
is required to evaluate a settlement offer on the basis of his client's interest, without
considering his own interest in obtaining a fee; upon recommending settlement, he
must abide by the client's decision whether or not to accept the offer, see Model Code
of Professional Responsibility EC 7-7 to EC 7-9; Model Rules of Professional Conduct
1.2(a).

## III

The text of the Fees Act provides no support for the proposition that Congress intended to ban all fee waivers offered in connection with substantial relief on the merits. On the contrary, the language of the Act, as well as its legislative history, indicates that Congress bestowed on the "prevailing party" (generally plaintiffs) a statutory eligibility for a discretionary award of attorney's fees in specified civil rights actions. It did not prevent the party from waiving this eligibility any more than it legislated against assignment of this right to an attorney, such as effectively occurred here. Instead, Congress enacted the fee-shifting provision as "an integral part of the remedies necessary to obtain" compliance with civil rights laws, S. Rep. No. 94-1011, p. 5 (1976), U.S. Code Cong. & Admin. News 1976, p. 5912, to further the same general purpose — promotion of respect for civil rights — that led it to provide damages and injunctive relief. The statute and its legislative history nowhere suggest that Congress intended to forbid all waivers of attorney's fees — even those insisted upon by a civil rights plaintiff in exchange for some other relief to which he is indisputably not entitled — any more than it intended to bar a concession on damages to secure broader injunctive relief. Thus, while it is undoubtedly true that Congress expected fee shifting to attract competent counsel to represent citizens deprived of their civil rights, it neither bestowed fee awards upon attorneys nor rendered them nonwaivable or nonnegotiable; instead, it added them to the arsenal of remedies available to combat violations of civil rights, a goal not invariably inconsistent with conditioning settlement on the merits on a waiver of statutory attorney's fees. . . .

Most defendants are unlikely to settle unless the cost of the predicted judgment, discounted by its probability, plus the transaction costs of further litigation, are greater than the cost of the settlement package. If fee waivers cannot be negotiated, the settlement package must either contain an attorney's fee component of potentially large and typically uncertain magnitude, or else the parties must agree to have the fee fixed by the court. Although either of these alternatives may well be acceptable in many cases, there surely is a significant number in which neither alternative will be as satisfactory as a decision to try the entire case. . . .

JUSTICE BRENNAN, with whom JUSTICE MARSHALL and JUSTICE BLACKMUN join, dissenting. . . .

It seems obvious that allowing defendants in civil rights cases to condition settlement of the merits on a waiver of statutory attorney's fees will diminish lawyers' expectations of receiving fees and decrease the willingness of lawyers to accept civil rights cases. Even the Court ac-

knowledges "the possibility that decisions by individual clients to bargain away fee awards may, in the aggregate and in the long run,
diminish lawyers' expectations of statutory fees in civil rights cases."
Ante, at 1544, n. 34. The Court tells us, however, that "[c]omment on
this issue" is "premature at this juncture" because there is not yet supporting "documentation." Ibid. The Court then goes on anyway to observe that "as a practical matter the likelihood of this circumstance
arising is remote." Ibid.

I must say that I find the Court's assertions somewhat difficult to
understand. . . . [N]umerous courts and commentators have recognized that permitting fee waivers creates disincentives for lawyers to
take civil rights cases and thus makes it more difficult for civil rights
plaintiffs to obtain legal assistance.

. . . [I]t does not require a sociological study to see that permitting
fee waivers will make it more difficult for civil rights plaintiffs to obtain
legal assistance. It requires only common sense. Assume that a civil
rights defendant makes a settlement offer that includes a demand for
waiver of statutory attorney's fees. The decision whether to accept or
reject the offer is the plaintiff's alone, and the lawyer must abide by
the plaintiff's decision. See, e.g., ABA, Model Rules of Professional
Conduct 1.2(a) (1984); ABA, Model Code of Professional Responsibility EC 7-7 to EC 7-9 (1982). As a formal matter, of course, the statutory
fee belongs to the plaintiff, ante, at 1539, and n. 19, and thus technically the decision to waive entails a sacrifice only by the plaintiff. As a
practical matter, however, waiver affects only the lawyer. Because "a
vast majority of the victims of civil rights violations" have no resources
to pay attorney's fees, H.R. Rep. 1, lawyers cannot hope to recover
fees from the plaintiff and must depend entirely on the Fees Act for
compensation. The plaintiff thus has no real stake in the statutory fee
and is unaffected by its waiver. See Lipscomb v. Wise, 643 F.2d 319,
320 (CA5 1981) (per curiam). Consequently, plaintiffs will readily
agree to waive fees if this will help them to obtain other relief they
desire. . . .                                                         ∎

## ∎ Russell Korobkin & Chris Guthrie, Psychology, Economics, and Settlement: A New Look at the Role of the Lawyer*

76 Tex. L. Rev. 77, 98-100, 129-136 (1997)

[The authors conducted an experiment in which subjects playing
the role of a plaintiff in a negligence lawsuit that followed an automobile accident were asked to choose between an out of court settle-

ment offer of $21,000 or a trial in which they had a roughly 50 percent chance of recovering $10,000 and a 50 percent chance of recovering $28,000. Half of the subjects (Group A) were told that they lost a $14,000 Toyota in the accident, while the other half (Group B) were told they lost a $24,000 BMW in the accident, although the car they were driving was irrelevant to their trial prospects. (The experiment is described in more detail at Chapter 3.) Practicing attorneys participated in the same experiment, except that they were asked to advise hypothetical clients on whether they should choose settlement or trial.]

Although Group A and B subjects faced the same choice from an expected financial value perspective, they might have perceived that choice differently if they evaluated the options from a pre-accident (rather than a post-accident) reference point. . . . The $21,000 settlement offer promised to leave them . . . better off than they were before the accident; that is, they could replace their lost automobile, if they so chose, and still have [money] remaining. Thus, settlement could be coded as a gain relative to the pre-accident reference point. The $19,000 expected value of a trial is superior to their pre-accident position . . . but with potential actual awards of $10,000 or $28,000, a trial could leave them better or worse off than they were prior to the accident.

[T]he $21,000 settlement offer, if accepted, would leave [Group B subjects] worse off than they were prior to the accident; that is, it would not enable them to replace the lost $24,000 automobile. . . . Consequently, these subjects could have coded settlement as a loss relative to the pre-accident reference point. Although the $19,000 expected value of a trial is inferior to settlement, a trial, with its possibility of a $28,000 award, provided the only chance of avoiding a result that could be perceived as a loss.

The wealth-maximizing choice for Toyota and BMW Drivers (and their lawyers) was to accept the settlement offer: for all subjects, the actual value of settlement was $2000 higher than the expected value of trial. Risk-seeking subjects in either group might have preferred trial. Nevertheless, because the BMW Drivers could code the settlement offer as a loss from their pre-accident position, while trial allowed for the possibility of avoiding such a loss, we hypothesized that more BMW Drivers than Toyota Drivers would opt for the risky option of trial.

Our results strongly support this hypothesis for litigants, but not for lawyers. Litigant subjects in both experimental groups favored settlement over trial, but that preference was much weaker for the BMW Drivers. . . .

By contrast, our experimental manipulation had virtually no effect on the lawyer subjects. Lawyers for the Toyota Drivers strongly favored the settlement offer. . . . Lawyers for BMW Drivers provided almost identical responses. . . . In other words, the litigants as a class appeared to take into account whether the settlement offer appeared to be a gain or loss from a pre-accident reference point, even when doing so caused them to reject the option that would maximize their expected financial return from litigation, while the lawyers apparently did not. . . .

. . . The critical question raised by our experimental results is whether lawyers and clients evaluate litigation options differently because they seek different ends or because they use different means in an effort to attain the same ends. If the latter is the case, lawyers may assume that clients fall prey to computational or representational errors that a lawyer can remedy, leading to settlement decisions that better serve the clients' interests; if the former is the case, lawyers should recognize that their influence on clients' decisionmaking could lead to settlements that do not maximize client utility and are thus inefficient, at least under a Pareto standard.

We think it nearly self-evident that a lawyer who knows his client is embarking on a course with a lower expected utility than an alternative course has an ethical obligation to take preventive action. On the other hand, when the client's expressed litigation desires maximize his expected utility, the lawyer should avoid any action that might convince the client to abandon his position. In other words, the lawyer should avoid substituting her utility function for her client's.

The cognitive error approach to counseling, then, requires the lawyer to assess whether an observed difference between the lawyer's and client's analysis of decision options is due to the client's cognitive error or is merely the manifestation of differences in utility functions. If the difference is due to cognitive error, the lawyer should attempt to change the client's outlook. If the difference is the result of different preference structures, the lawyer should scrupulously avoid any interference. Although the prescription is clear in theory, the following analysis of our experimental scenarios makes it clear that lawyers may find it quite difficult to make such judgments in individual cases. . . .

Under the [rational choice] view of decisionmaking in negotiation — the conventional view — some of the BMW Drivers in our Automobile Accident scenario erred by permitting the value of the lost vehicle to affect their comparison of the two options before them. . . .

If our BMW Driver subjects maximize utility by maximizing wealth, this characterization is accurate. In the language of an accountant, the BMW Drivers faced a thinly veiled "sunk-cost" problem. The value of the subject's destroyed automobile is a sunk cost: it is nonrecoverable and does not affect the expected value calculation of either decision choice. An accountant would no doubt advise the client that the BMW's value is irrelevant to the settlement-versus-trial decision. So would most economists. From this perspective, a subject's decision to settle or demand adjudication should not depend on the car destroyed in the accident. . . .

Individuals derive utility from a broad range of sources, and their preferences often may be situationally dependent rather than absolute. In the Automobile Accident scenario, for instance, some BMW Drivers might have had a strong desire for maintaining the status quo in their lives. The possibility of recovering enough money at trial to maintain a pre-accident level of consumption could conceivably be important enough to a BMW-driving litigant that he would maximize expected utility — although not expected dollar income — by engaging in risky behavior. Other subjects might have sought to satisfy a taste for status rather than a taste for transportation. BMW Drivers with such an outlook could have viewed trial as providing a fifty percent chance at maintaining a "BMW" level of status, whereas settlement, because it would leave them unable to replace the lost automobile, would result in a loss of status that would leave them no worse off (or only marginally worse off) than would an adverse trial verdict.

Given these possible explanations of their decisions, we cannot state with certainty that BMW Drivers who opted for trial made decisions that failed to maximize their expected utility, although such a conclusion is certainly one possibility. Thus, a lawyer representing a BMW Driver must recognize that his client's reluctance to accept the $21,000 settlement offer could be either a cognitive error (if the client seeks to maximize wealth) or a utility-maximizing choice (if the client prefers maintaining the status quo or maximizing status over maximizing dollar income). . . .

Lawyers, of course, are neither trained psychologists nor mind readers. As the previous discussion suggests, in a vast array of instances in which a client's expressed litigation preference deviates from expected value analysis, the lawyer will be unable to determine whether the deviation represents a different but stable set of preferences or a mistake. We believe that, in these cases, the lawyer should steer a middle course between indiscriminately attempting to influence client settlement decisions and indiscriminately avoiding such a role. The lawyer should engage the client in an interactive counseling process and may eventually want to volunteer advice, but such advice should be accompanied by an explicit description of the considerations underlying the advice and an explanation of the considerations that suggest the client might not want to alter his analysis despite the lawyer's urging. The lawyer who shies away from making recommendations altogether, or who makes them only when pressed, risks abetting client mistakes; the lawyer who makes recommendations without providing sufficient explanation risks persuading clients to abandon good decisions, in the sense that they maximize client utility, for bad ones.

Although the cognitive error approach is difficult to apply in individual cases, it offers lawyers a compass with which to navigate the murky waters of client counseling in the settlement context.    ■

## Notes

*1. Fee Structure and Type of Settlement.*    It is not only the case that the lawyer's fee structure (i.e., whether he is paid on an hourly or contingency basis) will affect his interest in settling the case. The fee structure will also affect his interest in the type of settlement negotiated. In a study of settlement behavior, Herbert Kritzer found that the difference in personal interests translates into differences in negotiating behavior in the following way:

> Contingent-fee lawyers have a strong reason to concentrate on dollars and cents: it is difficult to take a percentage of something else (e.g., a third of a house, or a third of an apology, or a third of a job). . . . Seventy-seven percent of the contingent-fee lawyers reported that their demands . . . were entirely monetary; this compares with entirely monetary demands and/or offers by 51 percent of hourly fee lawyers and 44 percent of lawyers retained on some basis other than hourly or contingent fees. . . . Clearly, having a stake in the outcome has some impact on the nature of the outcome that is sought.

Herbert M. Kritzer, Let's Make a Deal: Understanding the Negotiation Process in Ordinary Litigation 45 (1982).

*2. Controlling and Mitigating Agency Problems.*    The law provides a number of mechanisms in an effort to reduce the ability of an attorney to serve her own interests to the detriment of her client's interests. For example, in litigation, the rules of professional responsibility require that plaintiffs (rather than their lawyers) have the ultimate decision as to whether to accept a settlement offer. ABA, Model Rules of Professional Conduct Rule 1.2(a) (2001). Furthermore, a client always maintains the ability to discharge her attorney. Some rules also attempt to prevent an attorney from taking action that would tempt an opposing attorney to violate professional ethics rules. For example, following the Supreme Court's ruling in Evans v. Jeff D., supra, some bar associations issued opinions stating that it is unethical for an attorney to make a settlement proposal that is contingent upon the opposing lawyer waiving or limiting his right to a statutory award of fees. See Edward F. Sherman, From "Loser Pays" to Modified Offer of Judgment Rules: Reconciling Incentives to Settle with Access to Justice, 76 Tex. L. Rev. 1863, 1879 & n.93 (1998).

In the final analysis, however, it is exceedingly difficult for clients to control faithless lawyer-agents. Plaintiffs might have the ultimate legal authority to decide whether to accept a settlement, but if they view their lawyer as an expert, her advice might be difficult to ignore. And although clients can discharge their attorneys, doing so requires not only that the client be able to detect the lawyer's faithlessness, but also that she be willing to shoulder the start-up costs associated with a new attorney becoming familiar with the matter, and (in the case of a contingent fee lawyer) be prepared to pay the lawyer the fair market value of work already performed.

Lawyers and clients might be able to reduce the extent that their interests conflict by creatively structuring fee agreements in ways that differ from the usual hourly fee or fixed contingent fee method. For example, a sliding contingent fee, in which the lawyer receives a larger percentage of any settlement or judgment the further the case has progressed, might dampen the contingent fee lawyer's usual financial incentive to settle quickly. For a general discussion of principal-agent conflicts in litigation, see Geoffrey P. Miller, Some Agency Problems in Settlement, 16 J. Legal Stud. 189 (1987).

Other than structuring compensation to align the interests of principal and agent as much as possible, the other principle way to mitigate conflicts of interests is for principals to closely monitor their agents. In theory, close monitoring can ensure that the agent is not pursuing her own interests at the expense of the principal's or shirking her duties. In practice, however, monitoring is often impractical. Principals usually hire lawyers as agents because the principal lacks the lawyer's training and knowledge, making it impossible for the principal to determine whether or not the agent is faithfully serving him. Principals can and sometimes do hire other experts to monitor their agents — for example, many businesses have in-house counsel to supervise "outside" lawyers — but this is obviously costly and creates another set of agency problems: who monitors the expert hired to monitor the agent?

**3. Conflicts of Interest in Criminal Defense.** More than 90 percent of criminal prosecutions are resolved through negotiation — namely, "plea bargains." This seems curious in light of the evidence from prospect theory that people tend to be risk-seeking when facing the possibility of losses from a reference point (see Chapter 3). By entering into a plea bargain that sends him to jail, a criminal defendant chooses a certain loss of liberty over a chance of a greater loss of liberty (if a jury returns a guilty verdict at trial) coupled with a chance of avoiding any loss of liberty (if the jury returns a not guilty verdict).

The usual explanation for the high rate of plea bargains is that prosecutors must be offering deals that provide *much* less prison time than the expected value of a trial in order to overcome criminal defendants' presumed preference for risk in such a circumstance. Richard Birke argues that this is unlikely, because prosecutors are limited in just how favorable a deal they can offer defendants. He contends that prosecutors are constrained in their ability to "charge bargain" — that is, offer to replace the charged crime with a less serious offense — by "real offense" sentencing statutes that require the judge to determine the sentence to give to plea bargainers by reference to the "real" offense that they allegedly committed. Similarly, prosecutors are constrained in their ability to "sentence bargain" — that is, offer lower sentences in return for a guilty plea to the charged offense — by mandatory minimum sentencing laws. Richard Birke, Reconciling Loss Aversion and Guilty Pleas, 1999 Utah L. Rev. 205, 220-226 (1999).

Birke argues that the high rate of settlement in criminal prosecutions is due instead to defense attorneys pursuing their own interests at the expense of their clients' interests. Public defenders need to settle most of their cases to avoid being crushed by their heavy workloads. Most private criminal defense attorneys are either paid a flat fee for their representation, which gives them an incentive to dispose of cases quickly, or an inadequate court-determined hourly rate that they accept for the opportunity to network at the courthouse, not because they wish to work for that rate. In addition, their future business often depends on the good offices of prosecutors and judges who wish to see cases settled without trial. Consequently, Birke believes that criminal defense attorneys overstate the risks of trial and attempt to frame plea offers as "gains" relative to the maximum possible sentences rather than as "losses" relative to their current unincarcerated status, in an effort to make settlement more appealing to their clients than it would otherwise be. Id. at 238-245.

***4. Conflicts of Interest as a Strategic Advantage.***   Conflicts of interest between a principal and agent can work to the principal's disadvantage if the agent is faithless and pursues his personal goals. But when an agent is faithful to his principal, there are situations in which the existence of conflicts of interest can provide the principal with negotiating power. Gross and Syverud studied jury verdicts in California Superior Court. One of their findings was that plaintiffs were less likely to prevail in personal injury trials when the defendants made no settlement offer or settlement offers smaller than the plaintiffs' cost of litigating as compared to cases in which defendants made higher offers. The authors reasoned that because personal injury plaintiffs usually compensate their lawyers on a contingent fee basis and thus the lawyers bear the costs of litigating if the plaintiffs do not recover, plaintiffs have an incentive to go to trial with weak cases unless defendants offer settlements greater than the cost of litigating. This, in turn, enables plaintiffs to make credible commitments to try weak cases, even when doing so would have a lower expected value than dismissing their suits:

> A plaintiff in that situation can routinely instruct his lawyer to proceed to trial even if the expected outcome of the trial does not exceed the expected

trial costs, since the plaintiff (unlike the lawyer) has essentially nothing to lose. . . . This creates a bargaining advantage for the personal injury plaintiff, and his lawyer: both stand to gain in settlements because the lawyer can claim in negotiations that her client will insist on trial, regardless of cost, unless he receives a significant offer.

Samuel R. Gross & Kent D. Syverud, Getting to No: A Study of Settlement Negotiations and the Selection of Cases for Trial, 90 Mich. L. Rev. 319, 349 (1991).

**5. Attorney Ethics and the Public Interest.**  When the interests of a principal and an agent conflict, it is clear that the ethical agent acts in the best interests of his principal, not himself. See, e.g., ABA, Model Rules of Professional Conduct Rule 1.7(6) (2001). But what about when the interests of the lawyer-agent's principal conflict with the interests of third parties, the legal system, or society in general? The answer depends on whether one subscribes to the "libertarian" or "regulatory" view of lawyering. Supporters of the former view believe the lawyer's sole responsibility is to advance the interests of his client. Supporters of the latter view believe the lawyer must balance the responsibility to his client against another set of responsibilities to others affected by his client's actions. See William H. Simon, Ethical Discretion in Lawyering, 101 Harv. L. Rev. 1083, 1085-1090 (1988).

The Model Rules of Professional Responsibility offer only the following brief statements on this subject:

### ABA, MODEL RULES OF PROFESSIONAL CONDUCT (2001)

Rule 1.2

(A) A lawyer shall abide by a client's decisions concerning the objectives of representation, subject to paragraphs (c), (d) and (e), and shall consult with the client as to the means by which they are to be pursued. . . .

Comment

*Scope of Representation*

Both lawyer and client have authority and responsibility in the objectives and means of representation. The client has ultimate authority to determine the purposes to be served by legal representation, within the limits imposed by law and the lawyer's professional obligations. . . . In questions of means, the lawyer should assume responsibility for technical and legal tactical issues, but should defer to the client regarding such questions as the expense to be incurred and concern for third persons who might be adversely affected. . . .

**6. Agency Relationships and Organizations.**  Because this book focuses on legal negotiation, this section has focused its discussion of principal-agent conflicts on the attorney-client relationship. The problems caused by agency relationships (as well as the benefits such relationships can create), however, arise in other relevant contexts. The most obvious, perhaps, is that when business people participate in negotiations, they serve as agents for their firms (unless, of course, the business is a sole proprietorship). Any particular agent representing a firm is likely to have personal interests that conflict to some degree with the firm's interests generally, and she is likely to have different preferences and perceptions than the firm's managers or shareholders might have collectively, all of which might affect the negotiation. When a lawyer represents a firm in negotiations, he will usually report to a particular officer of the firm (i.e., the president or general counsel), or perhaps the firm's board of directors. In this situation, there are two agency relationships to consider. The important general point is that a careful analysis of any negotiating situation should take into account a broad range of principal-agent relationships, not merely issues raised by the lawyer-client relationship.

## DISCUSSION QUESTIONS AND PROBLEMS

*1. Why Lawyers as Transaction Cost Engineers?*  Gilson describes a number of ways that lawyers as agents can create value in the design of transactions — a process he calls "transaction cost engineering." The observation that value can be created through transaction cost engineering, however, does not in itself explain why agents are required for this task. Gilson's defense of using agents to structure corporate acquisitions seems to rest implicitly on the claim that transaction cost engineering is difficult and complex, and thus repeat players who are used to seeing similar transactions over and over will have a comparative advantage in optimally structuring such transactions relative to principals who are likely to be less familiar with particular types of transactions.

This still does not answer the question of whether lawyers are better suited to structure business transactions than other potential agents — management consultants, investment bankers, accountants, etc. After all, transaction cost engineering, as Gilson describes it, does not seem to be a peculiarly legal skill. Gilson bases his answer to this question on the observation that the legal knowledge of business lawyers is required to structure transactions to conform with various types of regulatory requirements:

Because the lawyer must play an important role in designing the structure of the transaction in order to assure the desired regulatory treatment, economies of scope should cause the nonregulatory aspects of transactional structuring to gravitate to the lawyer as well. Knowledge of alternative transactional forms and skill at translating the desired form into appropriate documents are as central to engineering transactions for the purpose of reducing transaction costs as for the purpose of reducing regulatory costs; indeed, if these purposes in one or another way conflict, facility at both tasks should result in more optimal trade-offs between them. Viewing the matter from this perspective, it would have been surprising if lawyers had not dominated the field.

Ronald J. Gilson, Value Creation by Business Lawyers: Legal Skills and Asset Pricing, 94 Yale L.J. 239, 297-298 (1984).

Do you agree with Gilson's explanation of why lawyers are well-suited to structure business transactions? If a sophisticated business executive asked why he should pay you as a business lawyer to negotiate an important deal for him, rather than hiring a different type of professional or conducting the negotiations for himself, how would you respond? If you were a business executive, would you be persuaded by that response?

**2. Agents and Power Tactics.**   Negotiating through an agent may allow a principal to use power tactics that would be less likely to succeed if he were to negotiate on his own behalf. Thomas Schelling highlights two possible structural advantages of negotiating through an agent:

> First, the agent may be given instructions that are difficult or impossible to change, such instructions (and their inflexibility) being visible to the opposite party. . . .
> Second, an "agent" may be brought in as a principal in his own right, with an incentive structure of his own that differs from his principal's. This device is involved in automobile insurance; the private citizen, in settling out of court, cannot threaten suit as effectively as the insurance company. . . .

Thomas C. Schelling, The Strategy of Conflict 29 (1960).

Why do you think Schelling believes that providing an agent with a narrow set of instructions or allowing an insurance company to bargain on behalf of one of its customers would create a strategic advantage?

**3. Can Conflicts of Interests Be a Benefit?**   Gilson and Mnookin's argument that lawyers can solve the prisoner's dilemma turns on its head the conventional wisdom that the existence of lawyer self-interest is bad for principals. After all, the value they claim lawyers can create stems from the assumption that lawyers will so value their reputations as cooperators that they will not succumb to a client's demand that they "defect." Might there be a dark side to what Gilson and Mnookin see as an advantage? Do you think, for example, that lawyers might be hesitant to use certain types of power tactics that could benefit their clients against other lawyers with whom they have repeated interactions? Would your concern for your reputation ever cause you to shy away from any tactics that might work to your client's advantage but adversely affect your reputation? If so, do you see this as problematic?

**4. The Reference Point Heuristic.**   Assume that Korobkin and Guthrie are correct when they theorize that the "BMW Driver" subjects were more likely to oppose settlement than their attorneys because some BMW Drivers viewed settlement as a "loss" from their pre-accident reference point while the lawyers were more likely to compare the expected value of settlement and trial. Assume also that principals in litigation are likely to rely on the advice of their more experienced lawyer-agents. Would the principals who relied on the lawyers' recommendations be better or worse off as a result?

**5. The Problem of Different Perspectives.**   The experiment by Korobkin and Guthrie raises broader questions about the principal-agent relationship. Agents will often view the world differently than their principals. Rules of professional ethics provide that principals, not their lawyer-agents, must decide whether or not to settle a lawsuit out of court. See Model Rule of Professional Responsibility Rule 1.2(a) (2001) ("[a] lawyer shall abide by a client's decision whether to accept an offer of settlement of a matter"). But this rule fails to fully address the problem. Many smaller decisions than whether or not to accept a fully formed offer of settlement are made in the course of negotiations, and it would be impractical and undesirable for an agent to consult his principal each step of the way, never exercising any independent judgment. For example, if in the course of bargaining a plaintiff's lawyer suggests his client might agree to a nondisclosure agreement if the defendant will increase his settlement offer, the defendant's lawyer might well reject this proposition without first conferring with his client. Perhaps more importantly, even when principals make negotiation decisions, they almost always expect their lawyers to advise them, and they are often swayed by their lawyer's recommendation.

How can a lawyer-agent minimize the costs of the unavoidable fact that she and her client will have somewhat different preferences and world views? Is Korobkin and Guthrie's "cognitive error approach" to client counseling an adequate response to this problem, or would you advocate a different approach?

**6. Can Lawyer-Agents Be More Objective Than Principals?**   Recall the article by George Loewenstein and colleagues in Chapter 3 that demonstrated how the "self-serving bias" can affect negotiators' reservation prices and, thus, negotiation outcomes. Do lawyer-agents have an advantage of being less likely to view their clients' opportunities and attributes through rose-colored glasses than do the clients? Loewenstein et al. have this to say:

> [A] potential shortcoming of our experiment is that subjects negotiated for themselves, whereas, in most high-stakes lawsuits, litigants hire agents to negotiate on their behalf. . . . There are two main reasons why agents might not exhibit the [self-serving] bias.
>
> First, agents typically participate in large numbers of cases providing ample opportunity for learning from experience; after failing to settle a large fraction of cases, they might learn to moderate their demands. This would require agents to learn the right lesson from repeated attempts to settle — namely, that their own demands are unrealistic — as opposed to attributing nonsettlement to the actions of the opposing party. In order to benefit from prior experience, the agents would also need to be able to persuade their less experienced principles to moderate their demands. Whether either of these conditions would be met is questionable.
>
> Second, it is possible that agents face incentives that discourage self-serving assessments of fairness. Incentives might moderate the bias if agents were particularly hurt by nonsettlement, which would be true if repeated nonsettlement caused them to lose business or if fee structures were designed to make nonsettlement unattractive.

George F. Loewenstein et al., Self-Serving Assessments of Fairness and Pretrial Bargaining, 22 J. Legal Stud. 135, 156-157 (1993).

What arguments can you make that the position or the self-interest of lawyer-agents might make them even more subject to the self-serving bias than their clients? On balance, would you expect lawyer-agents to view their clients' positions in a more or less self-serving way than the clients themselves?

*7. Constructing a Lawyer-Client Relationship with Fewer Conflicts of Interest.* In *Jeff D.*, the settlement offer made by the state was problematic for the plaintiffs because of an extreme conflict of interest between the class of principals (the children), who stood to benefit from injunctive relief but not from attorneys' fees and costs, and their attorney, who would benefit from a fee award. As the dissent points out, the problem is not limited to this case. All civil rights plaintiffs and their attorneys who rely on statutory fee awards to finance litigation are subject to a similar conflict of interest. Can you think of any ways in which civil rights attorneys might restructure their relationship with their clients to make themselves less vulnerable to such negotiating tactics by defendants? What new problems would be caused by such responses to the problem that surfaced in *Jeff D.*?

*8. Obligations to Client and Society.* You are an attorney representing a client who is suing a municipal police department for excessive use of force. Specifically, an officer used a choke hold on your client in a

situation in which he was unarmed and not resisting arrest. The use of
the choke hold was proper under department procedures because your
client was wanted for allegedly committing a violent crime. In the lawsuit, you are seeking both monetary compensation for your client and
an injunction prohibiting the department from using the choke hold
to subdue a suspect who is neither armed nor resisting arrest. The city
has offered a large monetary settlement if your client will agree to drop
the charges. The amount is more than you believe you are likely to
recover in court. Considering your client no longer lives in the city, an
injunction against future use of the choke hold would have no tangible
benefit to him. It would, however, benefit many other suspects. If you
accept the settlement, of course, the police will continue their objectionable practice.

Your client has said he will follow your advice as to whether he should
accept the settlement. What will you recommend? Does your choice
depend on whether you subscribe to the libertarian or regulatory view
of lawyering? Does Model Rule of Professional Conduct 1.2 provide
any relevant guidance?

*9. The Opponent's Principal-Agent Relationship.*    Most of this section
has focused on how a negotiation agent can provide value and how
the principal and agent can minimize conflicts of interests. In most
legal negotiations, however, the opposing principal will also be represented by an agent. How might you use this fact to your advantage at
the bargaining table?

## Chapter 11

# Multilateral Negotiations

When a negotiating situation includes more than two principals, additional complexities are introduced that do not exist in the prototypical bilateral bargaining encounter. The fundamentals of the negotiating process are the same: parties still must estimate the bargaining zone, find ways to expand the zone through integrative bargaining, and divide any cooperative surplus that agreement would create using power or fairness norms. More parties, however, means a more complicated negotiation process (how can negotiators go about exchanging information among multiple parties in a way that will enable them to locate or create a bargaining zone?) and additional strategic complexities.

Three issues stand out as requiring particular attention in multiple party, or "multilateral" bargaining situations. First, in multilateral situations two or more parties might form a coalition. The possibility of coalitions has strategic implications, because that possibility can affect the balance of power between the parties. Second, although which of many possible divisions of a cooperative surplus is most "fair" under the circumstances is often a contentious issue, the presence of multiple parties in a transaction makes the question of fair division even more complicated. Third, it is inherently more difficult logistically in multilateral negotiations than in bilateral negotiations to identify a deal point that exceeds the reservation points of all the parties, even when such a point (or a number of such points) does exist.

## A. COALITIONS AND NEGOTIATING POWER

### 1. The Problem of "Unstable" BATNAs

Suppose that three companies are negotiating to launch a joint venture called "the Outernet," which would create a new virtual information

329

network to compete with the World Wide Web. One of the three, software giant Alexis Technologies, would provide the majority of the computer programmers necessary to make the Outernet a viable information superhighway. The second company, Bartleby Inc., currently provides Internet service for five million American consumers. Its primary contribution to the venture would be the ability to provide, through its current customer base, a critical mass of customers for the new venture. The third partner, the media conglomerate Colossus Communication, would provide the Outernet's initial content by drawing on its newspapers, magazines, books, and movies. Initial estimates are that the Outernet project would produce $500 million in revenue.

The starting point for each party is no different than if this were a two-party bargaining situation: each must estimate its reservation price. If each party assumes its BATNA is to *not* build the Outernet and continue with business as usual, each might set its reservation price at the amount it would cost it to participate in the joint venture. Assume that participation would cost Alexis $30 million in salaries to programmers, so it sets its reservation price at $30 million. Bartleby can link its customers to the Outernet for virtually no out-of-pocket cost, but it will lose some of the revenue that it currently generates from those customers. Bartleby estimates this cost would be approximately $50 million, so it sets its reservation price at that amount. Colossus estimates it will cost it $20 million in actual costs and lost sales from other sources to make its content available on the Outernet, so it estimates its reservation price at $20 million.

Clearly, it would be socially efficient for the parties to reach agreement: by spending a combined $100 million, they can generate $500 million. And the revenues easily can be divided in such a way that participation would be advantageous for all three companies individually. But perhaps it is possible for two of the parties to form a coalition and proceed without the third. If so, it turns out that some or all of the parties' BATNAs might not be business as usual — their BATNAs might be to create a joint venture with *one* of the other parties. The possibility of forming such a coalition introduces a high degree of complexity into the parties' attempts to calculate their reservation prices and their efforts to divide the cooperative surplus that an agreement would produce.

Suppose that Alexis and Bartleby could construct the Outernet without Colossus, but content would suffer and thus they would expect revenues of only $425 million. Alternatively, Alexis and Colossus could construct the Outernet without Bartleby, but there would be fewer initial customers, so projected revenues would only be $350 million. Bartleby and Colossus could proceed without Alexis, but the technology would be far worse without Alexis' involvement, so expected revenues would be only $250 million. Suppose also that all three parties know all of these projections, or at least can come close to estimating them. How do these alternatives affect the parties' reservation prices? The answer is difficult to calculate, because it depends on what deal each could strike with a single coalition partner.

Consider the problem from Alexis' perspective. Alexis knows that Bartleby's best alternative to dealing with Alexis is to contract with Colossus and divide $250 million. Alexis could offer to contract with Bartleby, giving Bartleby $130 million (more than ½ of $250 million) and keeping $295 million for itself. But Alexis cannot count on Bartleby accepting such an offer because Colossus, not wanting to be left out, might offer Bartleby $150 million of the $250 million they could create together, thus wooing Bartleby away from Alexis. To Colossus, receiving $100 million ($250MM−$150MM) would be superior to being left out. Of course, if Colossus did try to entice Bartleby in this way, Alexis might try to woo Colossus by proposing a joint venture that would give Alexis $240 million and Colossus $110 million. At this point, Bartleby would not want to be left out, so it would have an incentive to offer Colossus, say, $120 million to restore their alliance, keeping only $130 million for itself, or to offer Alexis $245 million to restore their original alliance, which would also leave $130 million for itself. In theory, such machinations could go on and on, with no stable coalition emerging.

In a two-party negotiation setting, each negotiator's BATNA is an opportunity external, or removed, from the negotiating situation under consideration. In such a circumstance, it is usually easier for the parties to identify, or at least estimate, their BATNAs, and to use that information as a basis for estimating their reservation prices. When the best alternative to reaching a unanimous agreement for one or more parties in a multiparty situation is to form a coalition with some but not all of the other parties, and when other parties' best alternative is forming a different coalition, it often would be more difficult for a negotiator to know whether the coalition he envisions as his best alternative would be viable in light of the fact that other parties might simultaneously attempt to form coalitions that would make his envisioned coalition impossible.

## 2.  Power Dynamics: To Join or Not to Join the Coalition

Another complexity created by the possibility of coalitions in multilateral bargaining situations is that the situation creates a new possible intermediate outcome of negotiations in addition to the usual possibilities of reaching agreement or not reaching agreement. That is, there exists the possibility of an "intermediate coalition" in which some but not all of the relevant parties agree to cooperate. Each negotiator must determine whether its interests are best served by joining a coalition at this intermediate stage or "holding out" — that is, allowing other parties to form an intermediate coalition and then negotiating against that coalition. Which strategy is optimal will depend on several factors.

When it is possible for an intermediate coalition to act without agreement of the hold-out(s), being a hold-out entails two risks. First, a hold-out could be left out of the coalition altogether. In our hypothetical situation, Alexis and Bartleby could reach an intermediate coalition and then decide to exclude Colossus entirely, thus resulting in Colossus failing to capture any profit.

Second, if the coalition has an attractive BATNA, a hold-out might find itself with less bargaining power if it faces the consolidated power of the intermediate coalition than if it were negotiating with a group of nonaligned parties, or if it were part of the intermediate coalition. For example, Alexis and Bartleby might enter into a joint venture, which could then negotiate with Colossus for the latter's involvement in the Outernet project. At this point, the Alexis-Bartleby syndicate could earn $425 million on its own, while adding Colossus would increase revenues by $75 million (to $500 million total). The syndicate's reservation price would be $425 million, while Colossus' would be $20 million (its cost of participation). Facing the syndicate, Colossus would be able to negotiate for $75 million at most, and probably much less. It might have achieved a far better outcome if it had participated in an initial coalition with Alexis and Bartleby, rather than allowing those other two companies to form an intermediate coalition.

In some multilateral bargaining situations, one party can form an intermediate coalition with either (or any) of the other parties, but those other parties cannot form any intermediate coalitions with each other. In this situation, the party able to form the intermediate coalition has two or more good alternatives to reaching a multilateral agreement, while the other parties lack any desirable alternatives. This provides the party able to form the intermediate coalition a great deal of power. With skill, she can use the existence of her alternatives against the other parties, forcing them to bid against each other to avoid being left out of the coalition. Consider, for example, the bargaining power Alexis would have if it could partner with Bartleby and earn a combined $425 million or partner with Colossus and earn $350 million, but Bartleby and Colossus could not build the Outernet at all without Alexis' involvement.

Return now to our primary hypothetical. It seems likely that Colossus will want to enter into a trilateral agreement or form an intermediate coalition with either Alexis or Bartleby rather than allow Alexis and Bartleby to form an intermediate coalition that then negotiates against

Colossus. But it is important to recognize that this conclusion turns on the specific facts of the hypothetical: an Alexis-Bartleby intermediate coalition would have a very attractive BATNA to reaching an agreement with Colossus (recall that Alexis and Bartleby could build the Outernet on their own and share $425 million). In contrast, Colossus has a relatively undesirable BATNA of not participating in the project and gaining nothing as a result (although it would save the $20 million in costs it would contribute to the project as a party to an agreement).

Assume for a moment a slight change in the hypothetical facts: if the Alexis-Bartleby coalition constructs the Outernet without the participation of Colossus, Colossus' revenues would increase by $100 million because the competition between the Internet and the Outernet would cause both to purchase more content from Colossus and its subsidiaries. In this scenario, Colossus would have a strong BATNA, namely "free-riding" on the efforts of Alexis and Bartleby while saving the $20 million in costs associated with it joining the project. With such a strong BATNA, Colossus might find it strategically advantageous to allow Alexis and Bartleby to form an intermediate coalition and then determine whether that coalition would offer Colossus enough incentive to joint the project.

A somewhat different strategic calculus is required if a coalition cannot act without unanimous agreement of all relevant parties. Such a situation produces the possibility of a "hold-out" problem, because one uncooperative party can stymie the desires of a group. Of course, what is a hold-out *problem* for the group can be a strategic opportunity for the party that holds out.

Suppose that Factory has built a plant adjacent to a neighborhood where ten Neighbors reside, and the Neighbors have successfully won an injunction prohibiting Factory from emitting pollution, which can be enforced in court by any of the ten Neighbors. In truth, the Neighbors are only slightly bothered by the pollution, and each one would be happy to agree not to enforce the injunction if Factory would pay her $500 per year. On the other hand, not operating the plant would cause a huge loss of investment for Factory, such that it is willing to pay up to $100,000 per year to keep operations running. Not knowing the reservation prices of the ten Neighbors, Factory has offered them jointly $30,000 per year, but only if all will sign a pledge not to enforce the injunction. Suppose that you are one of the Neighbors. Would you want to be one of the first to sign the pledge, or would you prefer to be the lone hold-out after the other nine have agreed to sign?

The answer is probably that you would prefer to be the hold-out. Suppose that Neighbors one through nine have agreed to the offer, thus forming a coalition with Factory. They assume that if all ten Neighbors sign the pledge, each will receive $3,000 per year from Factory. As Neighbor ten, your status as the lone hold-out might create a substantial amount of bargaining power. You might threaten to refuse to sign the pledge unless you receive $10,000 dollars per year, leaving $20,000 for the other nine neighbors to divide. Your gambit may not succeed, but it stands a good chance. First, the other Neighbors don't know your reservation price precisely. You might convince them that your reservation price is $10,000 by claiming a sensitivity to pollution. Alternatively, you might convince them that your threat is credible because you believe each of them will certainly give up $1,000 to cinch the deal, and you are willing to risk losing your opportunity to collect a $3,000 even-share in return for the possibility that they will concede and grant you $10,000.

## B.  FAIR DIVISION

As discussed in Chapter 6, when two parties rely on fairness norms to divide a cooperative surplus that is created by reaching a negotiated agreement, they are apt to rely on the principle of equality (even distributions) or the principle of equity (distributions according to the value of their contributions).

Suppose that Alexis and Bartleby reach an agreement (Colossus does not participate) to build the Outernet. Dividing the $425 million dollars of revenue in two $212.5 million dollar shares would be consistent with the equality principle. If the parties could verify each other's reservation prices — $30 million for Alexis and $50 million for Bartleby — it also might be consistent with the equality principle to first return $30 million to Alexis and $50 million to Bartleby, and then to evenly divide the $345 million cooperative surplus created by the deal. This division might also be seen as satisfying the *equity* principle, on the grounds that the transaction created $345 million of surplus that neither party could have created on its own, and thus the contribution to the surplus of each is identical. The parties also might plausibly divide the $425 million by giving Alexis ⅜ and Bartleby ⅝. Although this would violate the equality principle, it could be viewed as consistent with the equity principle, since Bartleby invested ⅝ of the costs of the project.

Fair division becomes a more complicated problem if Alexis, Bartleby, and Colossus enter into a tripartite agreement to construct the Outernet, especially if they wish to follow the equity principle. The problem is a direct result of their unstable BATNAs. Colossus might point out that if it and Alexis worked together, they could jointly create $350 million. If Bartleby then joined the coalition, the three working together could create an additional $150 million. Thus, its equitable share should be ($\frac{1}{2}$ × $350MM) + ($\frac{1}{3}$ × $150MM) = $225MM, Alexis share should be the same, and Bartleby's should be only $\frac{1}{3}$ × $150MM = $50MM. Bartleby likely would complain about Colossus' perspective. It could propose thinking about the problem as follows: Alexis and Bartleby can create $425 million together, whereas Colossus' addition to the project would only allow the three-way coalition to add $75 million in revenues. Consequently, Bartleby and Alexis are each entitled to ($\frac{1}{2}$ × $425MM) + ($\frac{1}{3}$ × $75MM) = $237.5 million, while Colossus receives ($\frac{1}{3}$ × $75MM) = $25 million. Alexis might have a different perspective entirely. It might reason that the best Bartleby and Colossus could do without it is to create a $250 million project. Equity demands that it receive at least the additional $250 million that it creates by joining the coalition.

Of course, the parties could split the $500 million in equal shares of $167.33 million, but Alexis is likely to feel that equal shares are inequitable given the larger amount of value it appears to add to the project than either Bartleby or Colossus. How could they divide the revenue equitably in light of the different amounts of value each brings to the table and the variety of coalitions that any two of the parties could form if they did not reach a three-way agreement?

There is no "correct" answer to this complicated question, but one contender is the Shapley value solution. A brief description of this procedure follows. For a more detailed description and analysis, see Michael J. Meurer, Fair Division, 47 Buff. L. Rev. 937 (1999).

The Shapley value solution imagines all of the possible orders in which the parties could join a three-way coalition, and then calculates the average marginal value that each party would add to the project given those possible combinations. For example, one possible order in which the coalition could be formed is for Alexis to be the first party to commit, Bartleby to join with Alexis, and then Colossus to join the existing coalition. In this scenario, Alexis alone can create no revenue, so its marginal contribution to the project is $0. When Bartleby joins, the coalition can create $425 million, so Bartleby's marginal contribution is $425 million. When Colossus joins, the coalition can now create $500 million, so Colossus' marginal contribution is $75. This distribution would hardly seem equitable to Alexis, but in other hypothetical combinations Alexis will be the second or third party to join the coalition.

With three parties, there are six possible orders for forming a coalition. The Shapley value solution is found by calculating the marginal value added by each party in each possible order, adding each party's marginal contributions, dividing each party's total contribution by the sum of all three parties' total contribution (to find the percentage of the total revenue due to each party), and then multiplying each party's percentage by the total revenue to calculate the fair share of each.

In our particular hypothetical, the arithmetic is as follows:

| Coalition Order | Marginal Value of A | Marginal Value of B | Marginal Value of C |
|---|---|---|---|
| A + B + C | $0 | $425 | $75 |
| A + C + B | $0 | $150 | $350 |
| B + A + C | $425 | $0 | $75 |
| B + C + A | $250 | $0 | $250 |
| C + A + B | $350 | $150 | $0 |
| C + B + A | $250 | $250 | $0 |
| Total | $1275MM | + $975MM | + $750MM = $3000MM |
| Percentage | 42.5% | 32.5% | 25% |
| **Fair Share** | **$212.5MM** | **$162.5MM** | **$125MM** |

## C.  IDENTIFYING THE BARGAINING ZONE

In negotiations involving two parties, determining whether or not a bargaining zone exists can be difficult. Especially when multiple issues are being negotiated, skillful communication and acute attention to both parties' interests are necessary for negotiators to develop a package that is superior to the reservation points of both. As the number of parties to the negotiation expands, so does the challenge associated with ferreting out whether an agreement is possible that benefits all concerned. The following passage suggests one tactic that can help facilitate the search for a beneficial bargain: the "single negotiation text."

### ■ Donald G. Gifford, Legal Negotiation: Theory and Applications*

181-183 (1989)

. . . The *single negotiation text* is a problem-solving negotiation procedure of particular value in multiple party negotiations. In this process, one of the negotiating parties or their lawyers, or a neutral third party, drafts a proposed agreement and asks the other negotiators for their suggestions and criticisms. At this point, the other negotiators

---

*Reprinted from Legal Negotiation: Theory and Applications by Donald G. Gifford. Copyright © 1989 by West Publishing Co. Reprinted with permission of West Group.

are not requested to accept the proposal or to evaluate its over-all desirability. After receiving specific suggestions and criticisms from the other negotiators, the original author redrafts the proposal, taking into account the feedback she received and incorporating the other parties' suggestions. Then she submits the revised draft to the parties. The process of soliciting criticism and redrafting begins again, and may recur three or four times — or even twenty or thirty times.

No single negotiator usually perceives the *single negotiation text* as becoming a better document at every step of the process. It is more likely that a negotiator finds that one round of modifications to the text result in a substantial improvement for her client's interests — sometimes at the expense of other parties — but that the next set of changes benefit other parties, perhaps to her client's detriment. Because the negotiators all desire to reach agreement, however, they probably tolerate changes that modestly diminish their clients' level of satisfaction as the process moves along. Eventually the drafter believes that the current draft does the best possible job of addressing the parties' interests. Accordingly, she submits it to the parties for their possible acceptance.

The *single negotiation text*, of course, can be used even in two party negotiation. When multiple parties negotiate, however, some type of a focal point is required, and the *single negotiation text* is a desirable alternative.

Probably the most famous use of the *single negotiation text* occurred during the negotiation between President Sadat of Egypt and Prime Minister Begin of Israel at Camp David during 1978. Representatives of the United States, after listening to the Egyptian and Israeli delegations, prepared an initial *single negotiation text* which then went through twenty-three more drafts during the next thirteen days. At that point, the American facilitators believed that no further improvement was possible, and they recommended adoption of the text. Both Egypt and Israel agreed.

The use of the *single negotiation text*, however, is not limited to international diplomacy. Typically, committee chairpersons circulate a draft of a proposal or report to members of the committee and invite their feedback either prior to or during the next committee meeting. After receiving the comments of other committee members, the chair or committee staff makes revisions. For example, consider a state legislature driven to address the medical malpractice crisis by public outcry about dramatically increased medical malpractice premiums. Staff of the legislature's judiciary committee, working together with representatives of a state study commission who have been investigating the malpractice crisis, draft a comprehensive reform proposal. This initial draft legislation is widely circulated among key legislators, the governor's office, staff from other affected legislative committees, and representatives of various interest groups including physicians, hospitals, lawyers, insurance companies and consumer groups. As in other *single negotiation text* proceedings, changes are made as a result of feedback, and the process is repeated. In most instances in the political arena, it is not possible to achieve the support of all the affected interest groups; some end up opposing the legislation. Eventually, however, after many drafts and modifications, the proposal attracts support from enough of the key legislators and interest groups, whose suggestions are now incorporated into the draft legislation, to be enacted into law.

The *single negotiation text* process is most effective if the individual drafting the proposal, soliciting criticism and redrafting the agreement is a mediator or other third party. Under these circumstances, the initial proposal is likely to be an honest attempt to reconcile the conflicting parties' interests, and not a document drafted to manipulate the negotiating process. Moreover, when the initial proposal is drafted by a neutral mediator, the negotiators often feel more willing to offer honest criticisms and suggestions. It is understood by the participants that no one, not even the mediator hired to facilitate negotiation with techniques such as the *single negotiation text,* is committed to the initial draft.

The *single negotiation text* procedure does not require the negotiator to make any concessions until the final stage of the process when she is asked to accept the final version of the text. Instead, she is asked only for her input, suggestions and criticisms. With her reaction to each successive draft, this procedure allows the negotiator to communicate effectively her client's priorities and his level of resistance to acquiescence on particular issues. This is accomplished, however, without any image loss; the negotiator's response or lack of response to any particular provision of the *single negotiation text* does not communicate to the other negotiators that her bargaining resolve is being weakened or that their competitive bargaining tactics are working. . . .

The *single negotiation text* is only one problem-solving tactic particularly suited for multiple party negotiation. The complexity of multiple party negotiation means that competitive negotiating tactics such as extreme proposals, bluffing, and information concealment usually result in frustration and stalemate, at least in those negotiations in which the parties do not readily divide into two bargaining coalitions. The most important difference between multiple party and two party negotiation remains the increased use of various problem-solving tactics to determine whether there is a zone of agreement that satisfies the underlying interests of the many participants.                           ■

# Notes

*1. The Slippery Slope Between Bilateral and Multilateral Negotiations.* In this section we have assumed that bilateral and multilateral negotiations are dichotomous — negotiating situations can be identified as one or the other. The world is, in fact, much more complicated. In most bilateral negotiating situations, each negotiator represents more than one constituency: a head of state represents a variety of political interest groups, a corporation's lawyer speaks for management, labor, shareholders, creditors, etc. Thus, bilateral negotiations can often be viewed as negotiations between two coalitions. In some circumstances, members of such a coalition have the ability, if pressed, to split off from the remainder of their coalition and negotiate their own agreement with the other party to the (formerly) bilateral negotiation. When this is true, what appears to be a bilateral negotiation takes on many of the characteristics of a multilateral negotiation.

Consider, for example, a labor-management negotiation in which the labor union represents two types of employees. Group #1 employees have skills that are transferable to other employers. Thus, they are in high demand in the job market. Group #2 employees have skills specific to their employer and would therefore have trouble finding work elsewhere. Although labor-management negotiations appear to be classically bilateral in nature, the divergent interests between the two groups of employees make the negotiation potentially multilateral. If the union demands job security and management offers high salaries in lieu of job security, Group #1 employees (who have less need for job security) may decide to negotiate a separate agreement with management, splintering the labor coalition. For a more detailed example of this, see David A. Lax & James K. Sebenius, Thinking Coalitionally: Party Arithmetic, Process Opportunism, and Strategic Sequencing, in Negotiation Analysis 153, 158-159 (H. Peyton Young ed. 1991). Another way of thinking about this is to realize that, just as a multilateral negotiation can turn bilateral if the parties form intermediate coalitions, a bilateral negotiation can turn multilateral if one or more constituencies have the ability to create their own seat at the bargaining table.

*2. The Negotiator's Dilemma in Three Dimensions.* The single negotiating text (SNT) procedure recalls the problem of the negotiator's dilemma discussed earlier in the context of two-party bargaining. Should a negotiator criticize every aspect of the SNT that doesn't serve her interests, claim that the package described in the SNT is unacceptable even if the beneficial portions of the package outweigh the objectionable portions, and threaten to break off negotiations if the other parties don't accede to her demands in the next draft of the SNT? Or should a negotiator honestly disclose her range of interests, accept changes in the SNT that are contrary to her interests (so long as the SNT is superior to her reservation point overall) in order to accommodate the interests of the other parties, and work to find a way to serve the interests of everyone at the table?

The issue is more complex in multiple-party negotiations than in two-party negotiations, because when the negotiator decides whether to "cooperate" or "defect" (see Chapter 7 for a discussion of these terms), she must consider the likely strategies of not just one other negotiator, but many. It might pay in the short term — that is, ignoring reputational costs — to defect in a multiple-party negotiation if all the other parties cooperate. If there are many parties, the cooperators might have the ability and willingness to accommodate the demands of a single defector in order to reach agreement. But the more parties that defect, the more likely that the negotiator's defection will cause the parties to fail to produce an SNT satisfactory to all parties, and the chance for a beneficial agreement for all might be lost.

When determining how to cope with the negotiator's dilemma, a party to a multilateral negotiation must also consider coalition possibilities. If a subcoalition can act without the other parties, a single negotiator's attempt to defect and manipulate the SNT to his singular advantage is more likely to result in his exclusion from a coalition than if no action can be taken without the agreement of every party at the bargaining table.

## DISCUSSION QUESTIONS AND PROBLEMS

*1. Bilateral Versus Multilateral Negotiations.*   In your opinion, what is the single most important difference between bilateral and multilateral bargaining situations? In what ways does the difference that you identify make multilateral situations more (or less) complicated for the negotiator? What extra steps will you take, or what specific tactics will you use in multilateral situations to deal with this difference from the bilateral bargaining context?

*2. To Build or Not to Build a Coalition.*   Suppose that you are asked to try to arrange a deal among three companies to take advantage of a newly identified business opportunity (such as in the example used throughout much of this chapter of Alexis, Bartleby, and Colossus attempting to reach an agreement to build the Outernet). Would you advise that all three parties sit down at the outset and negotiate a multilateral agreement, or would you advise that two of the parties first form a coalition, which would then enter a bilateral negotiation with the third party? Why? If your answer would depend on the circumstances, describe what additional facts you would want to know, and how these facts would affect your advice.

**3. Identifying a Bargaining Zone.**   Using a "single negotiation text" is one approach to solving the problem of how to identify whether a bargaining zone exists when there are multiple parties to a negotiation. Can you think of other procedural tactics that might help to achieve this goal?

**4. Fairness in Multilateral Division.**   Reexamine the problem of Alexis, Bartleby, and Colossus building the Outernet from the perspective of a disinterested, neutral observer. Assume that all three companies agree to work together on the joint venture. In your opinion, what is the most "fair" division of the resulting $500 million? How did you reach your conclusion?

**5. A Multidefendant Lawsuit.**   Plaintiff has filed suit, naming X, Y, and Z as defendants. Plaintiff may choose to drop one, two, or all three defendants from the suit before trial. If a trial is held, attorneys' fees will cost all participating parties $10. Parties that are dismissed from the suit will not pay any attorneys' fees.

If Plaintiff chooses to go to trial against one or more of the defendants, the defendants will be found liable for the following amounts:

| Plaintiff Sues: | Verdict: |
|---|---|
| X alone | $35 |
| Y alone | $25 |
| Z alone | $16 |
| X & Y | $78 (split evenly between defendants unless they agree otherwise) |
| X & Z | $55 (split evenly between defendants unless they agree otherwise) |
| Y & Z | $52 (split evenly between defendants unless they agree otherwise) |
| X, Y, & Z | $82 (split evenly among defendants unless they agree otherwise) |

What negotiating advice would you give to each of the four litigants?

# Chapter 12

# The Use of Mediation in Negotiation

In law school texts and courses, the processes of negotiation, mediation, and arbitration are often grouped together under the label of "alternative dispute resolution" methods, and collectively contrasted with what is implicitly identified as the "standard" method of dispute resolution: adjudication by a court of law. It is true that negotiation, mediation, and arbitration are all "alternatives" to court adjudication, but the conventional grouping of this troika of dispute resolution techniques misleadingly suggests that conceptually the "alternative" methods are equally dissimilar to adjudication and equally similar to each other. In fact, adjudication and arbitration are conceptually very similar methods of dispute resolution, and these two processes are quite distinct from negotiation and mediation, which in turn are conceptually very closely related.

The most important distinction between the various conventional and alternative methods of dispute resolution is whether the terms of the dispute's resolution are arrived at through the consent of the interested parties or are imposed through a directive issued by an authoritative third party without a personal stake in the dispute. In negotiation, agreements are reached, if at all, by the consent of all principal parties, each of whom have presumably decided that the agreed-upon terms are more desirable than the outcome they could achieve by pursuing their BATNAs. In formal adjudication, in contrast, agreements are imposed on the parties by a court, which can call on the coercive power of the state to enforce its determinations. The voluntary consent of the parties to the court's directive is neither required nor requested.

Arbitration, like adjudication, resolves disputes through authoritative directive. An arbitrator (or a panel of arbitrators) hears arguments and evidence from the disputing parties and then renders a judgment. The arbitrator is not a public official, and she may follow different procedural and evidentiary rules than would judges, but the arbitrator otherwise acts like a judge. There is an element of party consent in arbitration, in that the parties must agree in advance to abide by the decision of the arbitrator (except when the parties enter into a distinct process known as "nonbinding arbitration," in which case the arbitrator's opinion is only advisory). This consent can be given either before there is any dispute to be resolved, such as when two parties enter into a contract to do business with one another and include an arbitration clause as one of the elements of their transaction, or after a dispute has arisen. Once consent is given to the arbitration process, however, the arbitrator determines the substantive terms of the dispute's resolution, and no further consent of the parties is required. The arbitrator's authoritative decision, like a judge's, is enforceable by the state's coercive power, subject to limited rights of appeal to the public courts.

A mediator, in stark contrast, lacks the authority enjoyed by judges and arbitrators to direct the parties to act according to her determination. The mediator can attempt to reason with, persuade, or cajole the disputing parties, but she cannot dictate any terms of a dispute's resolution, nor can she force the parties to reach any agreement at all. If the parties to a mediation are to reach an agreement, the consent to the substantive terms of that agreement must be given by the principal parties. In negotiation, the principal parties or their agents attempt to identify a deal desirable to all concerned. In mediation, the parties and their agents have the same goal, but they seek to achieve it with the assistance of a neutral third party. Mediation, then, is probably best understood as *facilitated negotiation*, rather than as a dispute resolution process that is distinct from negotiation. Like negotiation, mediation is fundamentally different from either adjudication or arbitration.

Mediation is usually thought of as a process to help parties resolve disputes — particularly disputes where lawsuits have been filed or threatened. It is important to keep in mind, however, that facilitated negotiation can also be employed in transactional settings where the parties are attempting to establish a relationship rather than resolve a dispute. Because the term "mediator" carries the connotation of a dispute context, the third-party neutral in a nondispute setting would most likely be called a "facilitator," "consultant," or "contract expert" rather than a "mediator," but the neutral in a transactional context can provide the same facilitative functions that a mediator can provide in a dispute context.

As is true of negotiation, there is no single template or "how-to" guide for mediation that is appropriate for all circumstances. However, many mediators employ some variation of the following basic approach: First, the mediator introduces herself and the parties and describes how she views her role in the mediation and the structure she intends to follow. Second, the parties (or their agents) are each given an opportunity to state their view of and position concerning the dispute. When the mediation concerns a litigation matter, the principal parties' lawyers will often present their assessment of the strength of their legal claims at this point. Third, the mediator and the parties will discuss possibilities for resolving the dispute or reaching some type of agreement. The mediator might ask the parties to make offers and counteroffers, or the mediator might recommend to the parties a particular deal or deals. Fourth, if an agreement acceptable to all parties appears possible, the mediator will attempt to close the deal. Negotiations involving a mediator can take place in a "joint session," in which the mediator holds discussions with all of the parties (or their agents) present, or in private "caucuses," in which the mediator meets alone with each party. Many mediations combine these methods, alternating between joint sessions and individual caucuses.

Because mediation is a method of negotiating, negotiators need to determine when mediation is an appropriate tool to use to assist bargaining. Involving a mediator in negotiations adds an additional cost to the process, so it is important to think critically about when the involvement of a mediator will be sufficiently beneficial to the negotiation process to justify that cost. To address this issue, Section A considers the different types of benefits that mediation can afford negotiators. A related issue for negotiators is, if the mediation is employed in a negotiating situation, what role should the parties ask the mediator to play in order to derive the maximum possible benefit from the process. To address this issue, Section B considers the range and appropriateness of different mediator styles.

## A.   THE POTENTIAL BENEFITS OF MEDIATION

As you learned in Part II, negotiators have a limited number of basic strategic goals: identify the bargaining zone, expand the bargaining zone (or create one when none exists), and divide the cooperative surplus by exercising negotiating power or invoking norms of fair division. In the following ways, a skilled mediator can potentially assist the negotiators in achieving these goals or, put somewhat differently, reduce the barriers that can prevent negotiators from achieving these goals.

### 1.   Facilitate Introspection and Analysis

In order to determine whether there is a bargaining zone such that an agreement will make both parties better off than they would be pursuing their BATNAs, negotiators must carefully determine their reservation prices. Of course, not all negotiators do this with sufficient attention to detail prior to entering negotiations. Many negotiators think only or primarily about their aspirations prior to bargaining, because this is often far more pleasant than facing up to the problems with their BATNA and, consequently, determining a rational reservation price.

A skilled mediator can focus the parties' attention on the factors relevant to their reservation prices by asking questions about the costs and benefits associated with not reaching an agreement. For example, the mediator might ask a party to estimate the total attorneys' fees he would have to pay if the dispute were litigated to verdict, as well as to take into account the emotional cost of litigation, the amount of time he would have to spend away from his job and family responsibilities, whether his relationship with the opposing party was important and the effect of litigation on that relationship, the risk of losing a trial verdict, etc. A good mediator will also encourage the parties to think carefully about the advantages of failing to reach a negotiated agreement, in addition to the disadvantages.

Just as careful introspection is needed for parties to determine their reservation prices, and thus to identify whether a bargaining zone exists, creating a large cooperative surplus through negotiation requires the parties to be introspective about their interests. A party who files a lawsuit intent on vanquishing his adversary might ask for a large monetary judgement but actually care more about an injunction against future acts than about compensation for past acts, or about repairing his reputation or his relationship with the opposing party. A skilled mediator can ask questions designed to force the negotiator to think carefully about the interests underlying his stated positions and to evaluate the value of different potential resolutions, all in an effort to permit the parties to create the negotiation package with the greatest joint value to the parties.

Integrative bargaining requires parties not only to be introspective about their own interests, but also empathetic toward and cognizant of the opponent's interests. Mediators can assist negotiators in taking the opponent's interests into account and constructing offers and counteroffers that meet both parties' needs.

## 2.  Facilitate Communication

In addition to introspection, identifying the bargaining zone and enlarging that zone through integrative bargaining requires negotiators to communicate critical information to their opponents. Mediators can facilitate this process by asking the parties questions in joint sessions designed to encourage them to clearly describe their interests, preferences, and desires to their opponents. For example, if a defendant thinks that a plaintiff cares only about money, but the plaintiff is just as interested in the defendant understanding and acknowledging the harm or inconvenience he has caused, a skilled mediator can elicit this information from the plaintiff, and potentially enable the parties to see that a settlement is possible when they previously thought a settlement would be impossible.

A skilled mediator can also help elicit information possessed by one party that is relevant to the other's reservation price, thus helping the parties to identify a bargaining zone. Whereas a plaintiff's claim that he is highly confident in prevailing at trial might not impress an equally confident defendant, the defendant might reassess his reservation price if the mediator can encourage the plaintiff to clearly elucidate his legal analysis or reveal facts that help his legal position. A mediator herself might also be able to help clarify to one party the other party's legal analysis or position.

In litigation (or potential litigation) situations, the relationship between the principal parties is sometimes so damaged that emotions can interfere with rational discussion, obscuring the possibility of reaching a mutually desirable settlement agreement. In an extreme case, the parties might find it difficult to even sit down together to begin the negotiation process — even with attorneys present. In this case, the presence of a neutral party might be necessary to make one or both parties comfortable enough to begin the negotiation process. Alternatively, the process might be advanced if the negotiation is conducted through a series of private caucuses, in which the mediator shuttles between the parties and the parties do not need to directly address each other.

In a less extreme case, the parties might be willing to meet with each other, but emotions might prevent the emergence of a fruitful dialogue. In that situation, the mediator might establish a basis for reaching a negotiated agreement by ensuring that each party has a full opportunity to be heard, and by ensuring that each party treats the other respectfully, or by separating the parties and conducting the negotiation partially or entirely through a series of private caucuses.

## 3. Evaluate Issues Relevant to the Parties' Reservation Prices

Litigating parties often have the same BATNA of going through the formal adjudication process but disagree about the likely outcome of that process (i.e., the value of their BATNA). The high costs and risks associated with litigation cause most parties to strongly prefer a negotiated settlement to a trial with the same expected value, but differences between the parties' estimates of the expected value of trial can often threaten to eliminate any possible bargaining zone. Mediators can often facilitate settlement by providing a neutral evaluation of the strengths and weaknesses of the parties' legal positions, or even the expected value of the parties' BATNA of submitting to formal adjudication (i.e., the litigation value of the dispute). If the parties have confidence in the mediator's judgment, the mediator's evaluation of the litigation value of a case can reduce or eliminate the difference between the parties' premediation assessments, thus greatly increasing the likelihood that the parties will identify a bargaining zone.

In some situations, a mediator might be no better qualified than the parties themselves or their lawyers to assess the litigation value of a dispute, but in other situations mediators might be able to provide more realistic estimates for a number of reasons:

First, as Chapter 3 discussed, the self-serving bias is likely to cause parties with a personal stake in the dispute to overestimate the strength of their position. It is not clear whether the client's lawyer is likely to be substantially less affected by this bias than the client herself. Lacking any personal interest in the dispute, a skilled mediator may be able to provide a more accurate assessment of the strength of the case.

Second, a mediator asked to evaluate the litigation value of a case can consider the best arguments offered by each side, just like a judge or jury would do if the case ever proceeded to court. A lawyer evaluating a case on behalf of his client has to attempt to imagine the best arguments of each party and rarely has the luxury that a mediator enjoys of being able to listen, with a clear mind, to the best arguments that each party can offer.

Third, if the mediation takes place before the discovery process is complete, or if the cost of discovery relative to the stakes of the case make complete and thorough pre-trial discovery by both sides impractical, a mediator might be able to offer an evaluation based on more complete evidence than either party can rely on. This will be true if one or both parties has access to some information to which the other side lacks access and does not wish to disclose that information to the other party for strategic reasons, but the parties agree to disclose in confidence all relevant information to the mediator for the purpose of the mediator evaluating the evidence. If exhaustive discovery has been completed in the dispute, of course, both parties might have access to all of the relevant factual information, thus reducing the mediator's comparative advantage in making evaluations.

Fourth, if the mediator is selected because of her experience handling a particular substantive type of dispute, as a lawyer, a judge, or a mediator, the mediator's substantive expertise might give her an advantage over the principals or their lawyers in predicting how a court would resolve the dispute.

Even if the mediator is in no better position than the parties or their attorneys to assess the litigation potential of a dispute, a respected mediator can provide a valuable second opinion to that developed by a negotiating party. As should have been evident in Chapter 2, estimating the litigation value of a dispute is a difficult and inexact science. A neutral opinion that deviates sharply from the negotiator's initial opinion could, at a minimum, cause the negotiator to reconsider her analysis. A neutral opinion can also help to resolve internal conflict within one of the negotiating camps, such as when a lawyer advises her client that the client's case is weak, but the client believes otherwise and demands that the lawyer maintain a high reservation price in negotiations.

A mediator's evaluation of the litigation value of a dispute can take a variety of different forms. At the most evaluative end of the spectrum, a mediator can predict how a court would rule on the merits of the dispute if the parties fail to settle out of court. For example, the mediator could tell the parties that she believes a judge would rule for the plaintiff and award $25,000 in damages.

Unlike a judge or arbitrator, however, a mediator providing a neutral evaluation of a case need not predict a specific outcome. The mediator can instead provide a probability assessment of possible outcomes. For example, the mediator might state that she believes there is a 75 percent chance that the plaintiff would prevail in court and recover $50,000, and a 25 percent chance that the defendant would prevail. Again, if the parties have confidence in the mediator's ability to predict the results of adjudication, the mediator's opinion can cause the parties to reassess their probability estimates and, consequently, their reservation prices.

Finally, rather than providing a global evaluation of the case, the mediator can provide more qualitative evaluations about particular aspects of the parties' cases. For example, in a negligence lawsuit, the mediator might advise the plaintiff that he is likely to prove duty and breach, but that his evidence of causation is weak. Alternatively, the mediator might advise the defendant that he stands a good chance of prevailing on liability, but should the jury find against him it would be likely to award very high compensatory and punitive damages.

When mediators provide evaluations to disputing parties, they most often evaluate the litigation value of a dispute. But a neutral party's evaluation of any issue relevant to the reservation price of one or both parties can conceivably help to facilitate a negotiated agreement. For example, if Alonzo is negotiating to buy Beauregard's business, Alonzo's reservation price will probably depend on the expected income that the business will generate in the future. If Alonzo estimates that the future income will be low, and Beauregard estimates it will be high, the difference in opinion can eliminate the possibility of an agreement being reached. The parties might benefit from calling in a neutral third party, perhaps one with accounting or finance skills, to provide a neutral evaluation of the business' earning potential.

## 4.  Filter Private Information

As Chapter 7 on the negotiator's dilemma emphasizes, negotiators have an incentive to withhold private information that could help the parties to reach a mutually beneficial agreement when they fear that their opponent will exploit that information to capture the cooperative surplus that an agreement would create. For example, if a plaintiff's reservation price for an out-of-court settlement is $10,000, she is unlikely to reveal this information to the defendant, for fear that the defendant will offer exactly $10,000 and refuse to pay one penny more to settle the case. Instead, the plaintiff is likely to try to convince the defendant that she has a much higher reservation price, perhaps by exaggerating her confidence in the strength of her case or making extremely high settlement demands. Of course, if the defendant similarly obfuscates his reservation price in an attempt to use power tactics to capture most or all of the cooperative surplus, the parties might fail to identify a bargaining zone even if one does exist.

A skillful mediator can reduce the likelihood that such strategic behavior by the parties will preclude a mutually beneficial settlement agreement by using private caucuses to obtain private information from the parties but only revealing portions of that information to the other party, and only under particular circumstances. Precisely how exactly a mediator can use private caucuses to reduce the pathologies of strategic bargaining behavior is complicated and not well understood.

It is important to realize that if the parties believe that the mediator will reveal everything that she learns from one negotiator in a private caucus to the other negotiator, neither negotiator will reveal any more information in a private caucus than she would in direct, unmediated negotiation with the other party. On the other hand, if the mediator pledges not to reveal any information learned in a private caucus, even indirectly, the parties might be forthcoming in front of the mediator, but the information cannot be used to help the parties to reach an agreement. The mediator could use information revealed by a party to advise that party, of course, but if the mediator is scrupulously maintaining the confidentiality of what she learned from the other party, the mediator's service as an advisor is not substantially different than the service that the party's lawyer could provide.

A mediator can use private caucuses to reduce strategic barriers to agreement, however, by collecting private information from the parties concerning their reservation prices, and then using that information to advise the parties whether there is a bargaining zone, and how much the parties need to concede from their stated positions in order to locate that bargaining zone. In this way, the mediator keeps the specific information provided by each party confidential, but implicitly reveals general aspects of the information in order to guide the parties toward the bargaining zone.

The mediator can use private information to guide the parties toward a mutually desirable agreement in a variety of ways, ranging from passive to active. After caucusing with both parties, a relatively passive mediator might inform one party that his latest offer is not going to be sufficient to close the deal, but encourage him that if he is somewhat more generous with his next proposal, the other party has some leeway to be more generous as well. Such gentle signaling might provide just enough impetus for the parties to then reach an agreement on their own. A more active mediator might use the same information to suggest a specific deal point that the mediator knows is superior to not reaching agreement for both parties, but shares the cooperative surplus between them.

In the hands of a skillful mediator, this approach can encourage the parties to be more forthcoming about their reservation prices than they would be speaking directly with their opponent, because they know that the opponent will not be able to use that information to exploit them. Ethical considerations require that the mediator obtain clear consent from the parties prior to beginning mediation as to what information the mediator plans to share with the opposing party. For a more detailed analysis of how mediators can use private information obtained in private caucuses to foster agreement, see Jennifer Gerarda Brown & Ian Ayres, Economic Rationales for Mediation, 80 Va. L. Rev. 323 (1994).

The mediator can also use private information about the negotiators' underlying interests in a similar way. Negotiators often hesitate to reveal their interests and preferences in negotiation, out of fear that the opponent will exploit this information by demanding extremely large concessions in return for satisfying the negotiator's most important needs. Of course, this impedes the ability of the negotiators to redefine the subject matter of the negotiation in a way that could maximize the joint value to the parties of reaching an agreement. By pledging not to reveal specific details provided by the parties, a good mediator can convince both parties to reveal to the mediator what is most important to them, and can then craft a settlement proposal that maximizes the joint value of an agreement to the parties while ensuring that neither party captures all of the cooperative surplus.

## 5.  Create Focal Points

Even when parties have enough information about the preferences and alternatives of each other to be confident that a bargaining zone exists, they can still have trouble reaching a negotiated agreement if they cannot agree on a particular deal point within that bargaining zone. Chapter 6 discussed a range of techniques negotiators use to converge on a single deal point within a range of possible deal points, including defaulting to terms that are conventional for similar types of agreements. A problem with this approach, however, is that in many negotiating situations more than one deal point can be plausibly identified as normal or conventional for the transaction in question. Mediators can help parties develop a shared conception of convention and thus help create a focal point for the parties to converge upon in two distinct ways.

First, when the negotiators agree conceptually on what deal point is conventional and thus fair under the circumstances, but cannot agree factually on what that point is, the mediator can provide a neutral evaluation. When a mediator evaluates the litigation value of a case, his evaluation can affect the reservation prices of one or both negotiators. But to the extent that the parties agree conceptually that the litigation value of the case is a fair settlement amount, a mediator's litigation evaluation also creates a focal point for an agreement. Similarly, if two parties agree that a fair sale price for a business is the expected income from the business for the next ten years but they have different predictions of what that amount will be, a mediator's neutral evaluation of likely future profits can serve as a reasonable proxy for a figure that cannot be known with precision but that the buyer has an incentive to minimize and the seller an incentive to exaggerate.

Second, a mediator's recommended settlement, so long as it is within the bargaining zone, can itself serve as an independent focal point that can justify both parties' agreement. Just as parties might agree that selling a commodity for its market price or settling a lawsuit for the expected value of the litigation is a reasonable basis for reaching agreement, they might also agree that the set of terms recommended by a neutral third party is a reasonable basis for reaching an agreement, even if the mediator does not determine that set of terms with reference to any particular objective standard. When a range of potential deal points exist that would make both negotiators better off than continuing their dispute, terms are sometimes agreed to solely because they represent a focal point. Terms that have no particular substantive justification can serve as such a focal point solely because the parties fix their attention on the mediator.

A mediator's settlement recommendation can encourage the parties to converge on that particular point for another reason as well. The mediator's recommendation can serve as a credible commitment point for a negotiator being pushed to make concessions, because accepting less than the mediator's recommendation can entail a loss of pride. Consider the following example: Defendant estimates that Plaintiff's reservation price for settling his lawsuit out of court is $5,000, and Plaintiff estimates that Defendant's reservation price is $30,000. Plaintiff threatens to go to court if Defendant will not agree to pay $25,000, but Defendant does not find this threat credible, because he knows that Plaintiff would be better off accepting a $10,000 or $15,000 settlement offer than going to trial. Defendant claims that he won't pay any more than $10,000, but Plaintiff does not find this claim credible either, because he surmises that Defendant would be better off paying $20,000 or $25,000 than going to trial. The parties are deadlocked, because each is trying to capture the majority of the cooperative surplus, and neither believes the other party's threats.

Now, imagine that the mediator states that she believes $13,000 would be a fair settlement, and she recommends that the parties agree to that amount. At this point, Defendant claims he will not pay more than that amount, and Plaintiff counters that he could never accept less. Arguably, these claims are more credible, because paying more or accepting less than what the mediator labels as fair would subject the party making a further concession to the loss of pride associated with being treated unfairly. If Plaintiff and Defendant believe these new commitments made by the other, they will identify $13,000 as the only possible deal point, and agree to settle for that amount.

## 6. Reduce Reactive Devaluation

As discussed in Chapter 3, proposed agreements can often look undesirable solely because they are advanced by the negotiator's opponent, regardless of the content of the proposal — this phenomenon is called "reactive devaluation." There are at least three plausible explanations for this phenomenon: (1) An opponent will only propose terms of an agreement if they are good for her. If the negotiator has a bad relationship with the opponent, the value of any agreement might be reduced if the opponent desires that agreement. (2) Although agreements can be desirable for both parties, nearly every negotiation has a distributive aspect. It is hard to escape the fear that if the opponent proposes an agreement, she might have private information that allows her to know the deal is not as desirable for the negotiator as it might appear on the surface. (3) Things that are out of reach often seem more desirable than things within reach. Once an opponent proposes an agreement, those terms are within reach, and thus lose their allure.

When a mediator proposes the terms of an agreement, all three of these reactive devaluation phenomena might be reduced. If a proposal does not originate with the negotiator's opponent, how desirable it is for the opponent is uncertain, at least initially, allowing each negotiator the opportunity to evaluate the proposal solely on its substantive merits. In addition, when the proposal originates with the mediator, the negotiator does not know if it will be acceptable to the opponent, and thus whether it is actually obtainable.

## 7.   Deter Extreme Distributive Tactics

Negotiators — and especially competitive negotiators — often take extreme positions in an effort to garner the lion's share of the cooperative surplus that an agreement will create. This tactic can be successful for a number of reasons. If a plaintiff makes and maintains an extremely high demand, for example, this can be a successful exercise of negotiation power if it convinces the defendant that the plaintiff has a very high reservation price. The same high demand might also help the plaintiff take advantage of the reciprocity norm or the convention of "splitting the difference" by making the midpoint between the plaintiff's and defendant's settlement proposals relatively high. Such hard bargaining tactics, of course, can potentially impede agreement by committing the negotiator to a demand that is outside of the bargaining zone, convincing the opponent that there is no bargaining zone, or causing the opponent to believe that he has been treated unfairly. At a minimum, hard bargaining can increase the amount of time and effort needed to reach agreement, thus increasing the costs of negotiating.

The mere presence of a neutral party might impede negotiators from adopting these types of hard bargaining tactics. Negotiators might be unwilling to risk appearing unreasonable in their demands or their bargaining approach in front of a mediator because they believe that appearing unreasonable will cost them the sympathy of the mediator in the present dispute or will harm their reputation with the mediator in the future. In addition, to the extent that a negotiator is uncomfortable with hard bargaining tactics, the presence of a neutral party might embarrass him into avoiding such tactics.

# Notes

*1. Benefits of Mediation Relative to Litigation.*   The mediation literature often emphasizes the benefits of mediation relative to the disputants' option of seeking formal adjudication of their dispute. For
example, it is often argued that party satisfaction with mediation is
often higher than it is with adjudication because the parties maintain
control over the outcome, and that parties are more likely to comply
with mediated agreements than with court imposed obligations. Our
primary concern here, however, is comparing the mediation process
to unmediated negotiation, so this section focuses on the potential
differences between these two approaches to dispute settlement. Since
the values of party control, voluntariness, and consent are served by
unmediated negotiation as well as by mediation, these "benefits" of
mediation are not emphasized here, although it is important to realize
that mediation, like unmediated negotiation, does have these features.

*2. Costs of Mediation.*   The benefits of mediation should be balanced against the additional transaction costs of mediation relative to
unmediated negotiation. In a recent study of 289 disputes across a
range of substantive areas mediated by four large mediation service
providers, Brett, Barsness, and Goldberg reported that the median cost
of mediation was $2,750, including the cost of the mediator's time (in
the study, mediations averaged one day in length) and the attorneys'
preparation and participation time (average = six hours). Jeanne M.
Brett et al., The Effectiveness of Mediation: An Independent Analysis
of Cases Handled by Four Major Service Providers, 12 Negotiation J.
259, 263-264 (1996). The cost of mediation, of course, will vary by the
type and complexity of the dispute. In addition, it is important to realize that some (but not all) of the costs of mediation will be incurred
if the parties choose to hold an unmediated negotiation session rather
than a mediated session.

*3. The Principal-Agent Problem in Mediation.*   Chapter 10 illustrated
that the use of a lawyer-agent by principal parties promises a range of
benefits but carries costs as well, including the possibility of conflicts
of interest between principal and agent. Like a lawyer-negotiator, a
mediator is an agent as well, but an agent for both principal parties
rather than for just one. This section described many of the potential
benefits of using an agent to help facilitate a negotiation, but there
are possible conflicts of interest inherent in this agency relationship as
well.

Perhaps foremost among them is that, while it is in the negotiators'
interest to reach agreement if and only if there is a bargaining zone
of mutually desirable deal points, the mediator will often have a per-

sonal interest in the parties reaching agreement whether or not agreement will leave them better off than failing to reach agreement. Since parties usually come to mediation hoping to reach agreement, and often believe that their time and money was well spent if agreement was reached but not if there is no agreement, a mediator's reputation and future business opportunities can depend on how often her mediations result in agreements. Consequently, it is not surprising that some mediators openly admit to twisting the parties' arms or "banging heads" in order to ensure an agreement is reached.

**4. The Transformative View of Mediation.**   This section's discussion implicitly assumes that the purpose of mediation is to help two or more parties involved in a dispute (or perhaps instead interested in forming a relationship) resolve a particular problem or set of problems in a way that is mutually agreeable. This view of mediation is typical, but it is not the only view. Some mediation advocates argue that the more important benefits that mediation can help achieve is to empower individuals with the knowledge that they can shape their own destiny and to teach them to recognize and have compassion for others. This broader view of mediation is often called the "transformative" view. Under the traditional view of mediation as a method of problem solving, the important question for principals or their lawyers is whether a mediator can bring to the table tools to help solve the problem at hand. Under the transformative view, the value of the mediation experience is not dependent on what the mediator can do to solve problems, but merely on the parties coming together in a forum that allows each the opportunity to be heard and forces each to hear the other. For the seminal work on the mediation process from the transformative perspective, see Robert A. Baruch Bush & Joseph P. Folger, The Promise of Mediation: Responding to Conflict Through Empowerment and Recognition (1994).

---

# B.  MEDIATOR STRATEGIES

Mediation is not a monolithic activity. Like negotiators, mediators make a number of fundamental strategic choices in how they approach their craft. This makes it imperative not only for negotiators to determine whether or not mediation would be appropriate in a particular circumstance, but also to determine what type of mediator would be best suited to the task or, alternatively, what style of mediation they would like to instruct the chosen mediator to follow. The following readings consider the fundamental strategic choices of mediators:

broad versus narrow mediation, facilitative versus evaluative mediation, and caucus versus noncaucus mediation.

# ■ Leonard L. Riskin, Understanding Mediators' Orientations, Strategies, and Techniques: A Grid for the Perplexed*

### 1 Harv. Negotiation L. Rev. 7 (1996)

. . . Nearly everyone would agree that mediation is a process in which an impartial third party helps others resolve a dispute or plan a transaction. Yet in real mediations, goals and methods vary so greatly that generalization becomes misleading. This is not simply because mediators practice differently according to the type of dispute or transaction; even within a particular field, one finds a wide range of practices. For example, in studying farm-credit mediation, I discerned two patterns of mediation, which I called "broad" and "narrow." These patterns differed so radically that they could both be called mediation only in the sense that noon meals at McDonald's and at Sardi's could both be called lunch. . . .

The system I propose describes mediations by reference to two related characteristics, each of which appears along a continuum. One continuum concerns the goals of the mediation. In other words, it measures the scope of the problem or problems that the mediation seeks to address or resolve. At one end of this continuum sit narrow problems, such as how much one party should pay the other. At the other end lie very broad problems, such as how to improve the conditions in a given community or industry. In the middle of this continuum are problems of intermediate breadth, such as how to address the interests of the parties or how to transform the parties involved in the dispute.

The second continuum concerns the mediator's activities. It measures the strategies and techniques that the mediator employs in attempting to address or resolve the problems that comprise the subject matter of the mediation. One end of this continuum contains strategies and techniques that facilitate the parties' negotiation; at the other end lie strategies and techniques intended to evaluate matters that are important to the mediation.

The following hypothetical, developed by Professor Charles Wiggins, will help illustrate the system of categorization that I propose.

## Computec

Golden State Savings & Loan NTC is the second largest savings and loan association in the state. Just over a year ago, it contracted with Computec, a computer consulting firm, to organize and computerize its data processing system and to operate that system for a period of ten years. Computec thus became responsible for all of the computer-related activities of the savings and loan, such as account management, loan processing, investment activity, and payroll. Golden State agreed to pay Computec a consulting and administration fee of over one million dollars per year for the term of the contract.

At the end of the first year of operation under this contract, Computec presented Golden State with a bill for approximately $30,000 in addition to the agreed-upon fee. This bill represented costs incurred by Computec staff in attending seminars and meetings related to the installation of computer technology in banks, and costs incurred while meeting with various outside consultants on aspects of the contract with Golden State. Upon receipt of this bill, Golden State wrote to Computec, advising Computec that because Golden State could find no express term in the contract requiring reimbursement for these charges, and because the bank had a strict policy against reimbursement for such expenses incurred by its own employees, it would not reimburse Computec staff for similar expenses. Computec responded quickly, informing Golden State that this type of charge was universally reimbursed by the purchaser of computer consulting services, and that it would continue to look to Golden State for reimbursement.

The conflict is generating angry feelings between these two businesses, who must work together closely for a number of years. Neither party can see any way of compromising on the costs already incurred by Computec, and of course Computec expects to be reimbursed for such charges in the future as well. Under applicable law, reasonable expenses directly related to the performance of a professional service contract are recoverable as an implied term of the contract if it is industry practice that they be so paid. It is unclear, however, whether the purchaser of these services must be aware of the industry practice at the time of contracting.[36]

### A.   THE PROBLEM-DEFINITION CONTINUUM: GOALS, ASSUMPTIONS, AND FOCUSES

. . .

In very narrow mediations, the primary goal is to settle the matter in dispute though an agreement that approximates the result that

36. Copyright 1985, 1996 Charles B. Wiggins. Reprinted with permission. All rights reserved.

would be produced by the likely alternative process, such as a trial, without the delay or expense of using that alternative process. The most important issue tends to be the likely outcome of litigation. "Level I" mediations, accordingly, focus on the strengths and weaknesses of each side's case.

In a "Level I" mediation of the Computec case, the goal would be to decide how much, if any, of the disputed $30,000 Golden State would pay to Computec. The parties would make this decision "in the shadow of the law." Discussions would center on the strengths and weaknesses of each side's case and on how the judge or jury would likely determine the relevant issues of fact and law.

### 2.    Level II: "Business" Interests

At this level, the mediation would attend to any of a number of issues that a court would probably not reach. The object would be to satisfy business interests. For example, it might be that Golden State is displeased with the overall fee structure or with the quality or quantity of Computec's performance under the contract, and the mediation might address these concerns. Recognizing their mutual interest in maintaining a good working relationship, in part because they are mutually dependent, the companies might make other adjustments to the contract. . . .

### 3.    Level III: Personal/Professional/Relational Issues

"Level III" mediations focus attention on more personal issues and interests. For example, during the development of the $30,000 dispute, each firm's executives might have developed animosities toward or felt insulted by executives from the other firm. This animosity might have produced great anxiety or a loss of self-esteem. On a purely instrumental level, such personal reactions can act as barriers to settlement. Although Fisher, Ury and Patton tell us to "separate the people from the problem,"[41] sometimes the people are the problem. Thus, mediation participants often must address the relational and emotional aspects of their interactions in order to pave the way for settlement of the narrower economic issues. In addition, addressing these relational problems may help the parties work together more effectively in carrying out their mediated agreement. . . .

#### B.    THE MEDIATOR'S ROLE: GOALS AND ASSUMPTIONS
#### ALONG THE FACILITATIVE-EVALUATIVE CONTINUUM

The second continuum describes the strategies and techniques that the mediator employs to achieve her goal of helping the parties address

41. See Roger Fisher et al., Getting to Yes (2d ed. 1991), supra note 21, at 17-39.

and resolve the problems at issue. At one end of this continuum are strategies and techniques that evaluate issues important to the dispute or transaction. At the extreme of this evaluative end of the continuum fall behaviors intended to direct some or all of the outcomes of the mediation. At the other end of the continuum are beliefs and behaviors that facilitate the parties' negotiation. At the extreme of this facilitative end is conduct intended simply to allow the parties to communicate with and understand one another.

The mediator who evaluates assumes that the participants want and need her to provide some guidance as to the appropriate grounds for settlement — based on law, industry practice or technology — and that she is qualified to give such guidance by virtue of her training, experience, and objectivity.

The mediator who facilitates assumes that the parties are intelligent, able to work with their counterparts, and capable of understanding their situations better than the mediator and, perhaps, better than their lawyers. Accordingly, the parties can develop better solutions than any the mediator might create. Thus, the facilitative mediator assumes that his principal mission is to clarify and to enhance communication between the parties in order to help them decide what to do.

To explain the facilitative-evaluative continuum more fully, I must demonstrate how it relates to the problem-definition continuum. . . .

### C.   THE FOUR ORIENTATIONS: STRATEGIES AND TECHNIQUES

#### 1.   *Evaluative-Narrow*

A principal strategy of the evaluative-narrow approach is to help the parties understand the strengths and weaknesses of their positions and the likely outcome of litigation or whatever other process they will use if they do not reach a resolution in mediation. But the evaluative-narrow mediator stresses her own education at least as much as that of the parties. Before the mediation starts, the evaluative-narrow mediator will study relevant documents, such as pleadings, depositions, reports, and mediation briefs. At the outset of the mediation, such a mediator typically will ask the parties to present their cases, which normally means arguing their positions, in a joint session. Subsequently, most mediation activities take place in private caucuses in which the mediator will gather additional information and deploy evaluative techniques, such as the following, which are listed below from the least to the most evaluative.

a. Assess the strengths and weaknesses of each side's case. — In the Computec case, an evaluative mediator might tell Computec's representatives that, even if a court were to interpret the law as they hoped, the firm would have trouble meeting its burden of establishing the existence of an industry custom that purchasers of such services normally pay the related travel expenses of their suppliers. The mediator would explain her reasoning, invoking her experience and knowledge.

b. Predict outcomes of court or other processes. — In Computec, the mediator might predict for Golden State the likely rulings on issues of law and fact, the likely outcome at trial and appeal, and the associated costs.

c. Propose position-based compromise agreements. — A mediator can make such proposals with varying degrees of directiveness. Some mediators might suggest resolution points so gently that they are barely evaluative — for instance, throwing out a figure at which she thinks the parties might be willing to settle, without suggesting that this corresponds to what would happen in court or is otherwise an appropriate settlement point. A slightly more directive proposal might be to ask Computec, "Would you accept $12,000?" or "What about $12,000?" A still more directive proposal would be to suggest that the case might settle within a certain range, say $10,000-$15,000. An even more directive move would be to say, "I think $12,000 would be a good offer."

d. Urge or push the parties to settle or to accept a particular settlement proposal or range. — In the Computec case, the mediator might tell Computec that she thinks Computec "should" accept a settlement offer of $12,000 because that would protect it against the risk and expense of litigation or because it is "right" or "fair" or "reasonable." If the mediator has any sort of "clout," she may threaten to use it. Or she may engage in "head-banging."

### 2. Facilitative-Narrow

The facilitative-narrow mediator shares the evaluative-narrow mediator's general strategy — to educate the parties about the strengths and weaknesses of their claims and the likely consequences of failing to settle. But he employs different techniques to carry out this strategy. He does not use his own assessments, predictions, or proposals. Nor does he apply pressure. He is less likely than the evaluative-narrow mediator to request or to study relevant documents. Instead, believing that the burden of decision-making should rest with the parties, the facilitative-narrow mediator might engage in any of the following activities.

a. Ask questions. — The mediator may ask questions — generally in private caucuses — to help the participants understand both sides' legal positions and the consequences of non-settlement. The questions ordinarily would concern the very issues about which the evaluative-narrow mediator makes statements — the strengths and weaknesses of each side's case and the likely consequences of non-settlement, as well as the costs of litigation (including expense, delay, and inconvenience).

b. Help the parties develop their own narrow proposals. — In the

Computec case, for instance, a facilitative-narrow mediator would help each party develop proposals as to how much of the $30,000 Golden State would pay.

c. Help the parties exchange proposals. — The mediator might present party proposals in private caucuses or encourage parties to make such proposals in a joint session. In either event, he would encourage participants to provide a rationale for each proposal that might help the other side accept it.

d. Help the parties evaluate proposals. — To do this, the mediator might ask questions that would help the parties weigh the costs and benefits of each proposal against the likely consequences of non-settlement.

The facilitative nature of this mediation approach might also produce a degree of education or transformation. The process itself, which encourages the parties to develop their own understandings and outcomes, might educate the parties, or "empower" them by helping them to develop a sense of their own ability to deal with the problems and choices in life. The parties also might acknowledge or empathize with each other's situation. However, in a narrowly-focused mediation, even a facilitative one, the subject matter normally produces fewer opportunities for such developments than does a facilitative-broad mediation.

### 3.   Evaluative-Broad

It is more difficult to describe the strategies and techniques of the evaluative-broad mediator. Mediations conducted with such an orientation vary tremendously in scope, often including many narrow, distributive issues, as the previous discussion of the problem-definition continuum illustrates. In addition, evaluative-broad mediators can be more-or-less evaluative, with the evaluative moves touching all or only some of the issues.

The evaluative-broad mediator's principal strategy is to learn about the circumstances and underlying interests of the parties and other affected individuals or groups, and then to use that knowledge to direct the parties toward an outcome that responds to such interests. To carry out this strategy, the evaluative-broad mediator will employ various techniques, including the following (listed from least to most evaluative).

a. Educate herself about underlying interests. — The evaluative-broad mediator seeks to understand the underlying legal and other distributive issues by studying pleadings, depositions, and other documents, as well as by allowing the parties (usually through their lawyers) to argue their cases during the mediation. Unlike the narrow mediator, however, the broad mediator emphasizes the parties' underlying interests rather than their positions, and seeks to uncover needs that typically are not revealed in documents. Pleadings in the Computec case, for instance, would not indicate that one of the causes of the dispute was Golden State's interest in protecting the sanctity of its internal policy against reimbursing convention travel expenses of its own employees, let alone that the policy was born when the CEO observed staff members, at a convention in Bermuda, frolicking instead of attending seminars.

For this sort of information, as well as other interests, the mediator must dig. To learn about the parties' underlying interests, the evaluative-broad mediator would be more likely than the narrow mediator to encourage or require the real parties (whether actual disputants or knowledgeable representatives of corporations or other organizations who possess settlement authority) to attend and participate in the mediation. For instance, the mediator might invite such individuals to make remarks after the lawyers present their opening statements, and she might interview such individuals extensively in private caucuses. She might explain that the goal of mediation can include addressing underlying interests, ask direct questions about interests, and seek such information indirectly by questioning the parties as to their plans, situations, and the like. Often, evaluative-broad mediators will speculate aloud about the parties' interests (generally in private caucuses) and seek confirmation of their statements.

Evaluative-broad mediators expect to construct proposed agreements. For that reason, they generally emphasize their own education over that of the parties. Accordingly, they typically will restrict or control direct communication between the parties; thus, for example, the evaluative-broad mediator would spend more time in private caucuses than in joint sessions.

b. Predict impact (on interests) of not settling. — After determining the parties' underlying interests and setting the scope of the problems to be addressed in the mediation, some evaluative-broad mediators would predict how failure to settle would impact important interests. In the Computec case, an evaluative-broad mediator might tell Golden State that unless it reaches an agreement that allows Computec executives to feel appreciated and effective, relations will sour and Computec might become less diligent, thereby impairing Golden State's ability to compete and to serve its customers.

An evaluative-broad mediator also might try to persuade the participants that her assessments are correct by providing objective criteria or additional data.

c. Develop and offer broad (interest-based) proposals. — An evaluative-broad mediator's goal is to develop a proposal that satisfies as many of the parties' interests, both narrow and broad, as feasible. Proposals in the Computec case, for example, might range from a payment scheme for Golden State (based on an allocation of costs), to a system for the submission and approval of travel and education expenses in future years, to the formation of a new joint venture.

d.  Urge parties to accept the mediator's or another proposal. — The evaluative-broad mediator (like the evaluative-narrow mediator) might present her proposal with varying degrees of force or intended impact. If the mediator has clout (the ability to bring pressure to bear on one or more of the parties), she might warn them or threaten to use it.

If the mediator has concluded that the goal of the mediation should include changing the people involved, she might take measures to effectuate that goal, such as appealing to shared values, lecturing, or applying pressure.

### 4.   Facilitative-Broad

The facilitative-broad mediator's principal strategy is to help the participants define the subject matter of the mediation in terms of underlying interests and to help them develop and choose their own solutions that respond to such interests. In addition, many facilitative-broad mediators will help participants find opportunities to educate or change themselves, their institutions, or their communities. To carry out such strategies, the facilitative-broad mediator may use techniques such as the following.

a.  Help parties understand underlying interests. — To accomplish this task, the facilitative-broad mediator will engage in many of the same activities as the evaluative-broad mediator, such as encouraging attendance and participation by the real parties, not just their lawyers, and explaining the importance of interests. Because he expects the parties to generate their own proposals, the facilitative-broad mediator emphasizes the need for the parties to educate themselves and each other more than the mediator. Thus, in contrast to the evaluative mediator, the facilitative-broad mediator will be inclined to use joint sessions more than private caucuses.

The facilitative-broad mediator also will help the parties define the scope of the problem to be addressed in the mediation, often encouraging them to explore underlying interests to the extent that they wish to do so. This behavior stands in sharp contrast to that of narrow mediators (even most facilitative-narrow mediators), who tend to accept the obvious problem presented, and that of evaluative-broad mediators, who often define the scope of the problem to be addressed themselves.

Many facilitative-broad mediators especially value mediation's potential for helping parties grow through an understanding of one another and of themselves. These mediators tend to offer the participants opportunities for positive change. One way to look at this is through Bush and Folger's concept of "transformation." In this view, by encouraging the parties to develop their own understandings, options, and proposals, the facilitative-broad mediator "empowers" them; by helping the parties to understand one another's situation, the facilitative-broad mediator provides them opportunities to give "recognition" to one another.

b. Help parties develop and propose broad, interest-based options for settlement. — The facilitative-broad mediator would keep the parties focused on the relevant interests and ask them to generate options that might respond to these interests. In the Computec case, the options may include various systems through which the already-incurred expenses could be allocated to the Golden State contract, methods for handling the same issue in the future (informally or by contract amendment), and opportunities to collaborate on other projects (an example of positive change). Next, he would encourage the parties to use these options — perhaps combining or modifying them — to develop and present their own interest-based proposals.

c. Help parties evaluate proposals. — The facilitative-broad mediator uses questions principally to help the parties evaluate the impact on various interests of proposals and of non-settlement. In Computec, for instance, a facilitative-broad mediator might ask the Computec representative how a specific settlement would affect the parties' working relationship and how it would alter Computec's ability to deliver appropriate services. . . .                                                        ■

## ■ Christopher W. Moore, The Caucus: Private Meetings That Promote Settlement

**16 Mediation Q.** 87, 87-91, 95-97 (1987)*

Mediators use a variety of procedures to assist people in conflict in reaching acceptable agreements. While no one technique guarantees settlement, there is a procedure — the caucus — that often is useful in breaking deadlocks. The caucus is a confidential, private meeting held by the mediator with individual parties or a brief private meeting of a negotiation team conducted during bargaining. In the caucus, the parties are physically separated from each other, and communication is intentionally restricted to increase the likelihood of a successful outcome to the negotiation. The caucus is usually of shorter duration than a formal recess in negotiations and is designed to handle specific emotional, procedural, or substantive blocks to negotiation. . . .

## Why Use a Caucus?

The premise for caucusing is that totally open and uninterrupted communications between parties in dispute are not always productive and that by modifying the communication structure, more areas of agreement can be identified. This premise directly contradicts the assumption that if the parties could only communicate with one another, their conflicts would resolve themselves.

Caucuses are initiated in response to events, external or internal to the negotiations, that block or hinder productive bargaining in joint session. External events may include changes in the legal, economic, or political climate, or actions taken by other parties (lawyers, the press, a party's constituents, custody evaluators, friends) that escalate the conflict or narrow the range of options for settlement. Internal events fall into three categories: (1) problems in interpersonal relationships between parties or within a team, (2) problems in the negotiation process, and (3) problems related to the substantive or content issues under discussion.

*Relationship Problems.* Relationship problems involve difficulties that arise in negotiations because of strong emotions, misperceptions, and poor communication. Caucuses can be used to respond to each of these problem areas.

*Emotional Problems.* Either the expression of strong emotions or their lack of expression can block agreement. Expression of strong feelings — anger, hurt, frustration — can on occasion be valuable. The issue is how and where feelings should be expressed.

Venting of feelings in joint session can be educational for both sides. It can demonstrate how strongly a party feels about an issue or how important a concession in a particular area will be. However, face-to-face expression of emotions can also damage relationships so that no agreement can be reached. Mediators must assess how much the party with strong emotions needs to say, how much the other party needs (or can stand) to hear, and then determine the appropriate format for the expression of feelings.

On occasion, it may be more productive to channel the venting of feelings into a caucus where it will not damage the negotiators' relationship than to encourage expression in joint session. Venting in private may provide negotiators with a cathartic release of tension and an opportunity to assess what needs to be said in joint session, and such expression may enable the intervenor to evaluate how best to facilitate an exchange of information about feelings.

When extremely strong emotions are deemed by the mediator to be a major stumbling block to further negotiations, he or she may discourage or prevent the parties from returning to joint session.

The mediator may initiate shuttle diplomacy by carrying messages between parties but never allow them to meet face-to-face until an agreement is reached. This procedure allows the parties to maintain communication but inhibits emotional exchanges that might result in impasse.

*Perceptual Problems.* The mediator may work with one or both parties in private session to improve their attitudes and perceptions of the other, design procedures to test the accuracy of perceptions, or plan activities that will change negative attitudes. When the mediator discovers information that may reinforce a negative view, the intervenor may occasionally suppress this data or steer the other party away from discovering it by using the caucus to bar information exchanges.

*Communications Problems.* Such problems are too numerous to catalogue. Mediator strategies regarding communications generally fall into two categories: (1) how to enhance the quality of communications, and (2) how to regulate the quantity of exchanges.

Caucuses are used to increase the quality of communication between parties by changing the form of information exchange. Variations in communications that may be considered in caucus include: direct or indirect communication, oral or written exchanges, varying who communicates (spokespeople, the whole team, or the mediator), and syntax, or how the messages are worded. The mediator may convey information gleaned from the caucus in several ways. He or she may act as a conduit, relaying the information exactly as it was presented; as a surrogate negotiator, presenting the logic or rationale of one negotiator to another; as a reshaper or reframer, recouching the argument of a negotiator into a form that will be better received by another; or as a clarifier, answering questions for another party (Kolb, 1983).

Caucuses are also used to regulate the quantity of communication. It is possible for parties to communicate too much and thus damage the possibility of settlement. Caucuses can be used to limit communication to only productive exchanges and filter out extraneous information or emotions.

*Procedural Problems. . . .*

Negotiators often fumble at the beginning of bargaining because they have an ill-thought-out negotiation plan or the procedure utilized is inappropriate to the situation. Mediators often work with negotiators to educate them about bargaining tasks, procedures, and techniques. This education often must be done in caucus to avoid embarrassing or disempowering a party, inadvertent disclosure of privileged information or the appearance of or bias on the part of the intervenor. . . .

When negotiators use different bargaining processes, they are often blocked from reaching settlement. Mediators in caucus can aid parties to shift from positional bargaining to interest-based bargaining or to make appropriate compromises if the parties refuse to move from the positional to the interest-based mode.

*Substantive Problems.*   Caucuses may also be needed to handle substantive problems. Examples of this type of problem include (1) too few or too many options on the table, (2) unacceptable alternatives, or (3) alternatives that are insufficiently developed or packaged in an unacceptable manner. Mediators can help parties develop and format substantive proposals that will be accepted.

Negotiators often are reluctant to make proposals in joint session. Reticence may be due to fear of premature commitment to a solution, lack of understanding of each other's needs, or confusion as to what to offer. Work in caucus with other team members or the mediator can assist negotiators in deciding what to offer, when to make a proposal, and how an option can be best presented to the other side. The mediator can often assist the party in proposing an option-generation process rather than a specific proposal that then can be used jointly by all parties to develop an acceptable solution. . . .

*Procedural Barriers to Settlement.*   Joint sessions often fail because parties are unable to develop or utilize an effective bargaining procedure. A caucus provides time for parties to devise new negotiation processes. . . .

*Shifting from an Emphasis on Positions to a Focus on Interests.*   Procedural deadlocks are [often] caused by the utilization of positional bargaining. This process, it will be recalled, is characterized by a party's adherence to positions or preferred solutions that meet his or her needs or interests but not necessarily those of other disputants.

Mediators and negotiators often use a caucus to move parties away from unacceptable positions and to help them develop proposals that will satisfy the interests of both sides. Mediators can begin the shift toward interest-based bargaining by discussing with a party what interests or needs are met by positions. The party is then asked to speculate about the needs of other disputants. The mediator then reframes the problem as a search for a solution that meets joint needs. The mediator may repeat the process with other parties as a means of coordinating activities.

*Substantive Barriers to Settlement.*   Substantive disagreements are perhaps the most frequent cause of an impasse. The reasons for parties' inability to concur on substance may be the result of inaccurate data, too little or too much information, an inability to generate options, the presence of unacceptable proposals, too many options, inappropriate linkage of issues, unacceptable trade-offs, an unrealistic appraisal of the viability of alternative means of settling the dispute outside of negotiation, and so forth.

Often, a mediator will start work on substantive impasses by asking the party with whom the caucus is being held to describe the substantive issues and barriers to settlement. By starting with the way that the party sees the situation, the mediator can promote rapport and build the belief that the needs are first and foremost in the mediator's mind.

It is crucial that the parties have a common understanding of the relevant data and similar methods of assessing this information. Misinformation, missing data, overly complex information, or diverse assessment procedures may cause unnecessary delays in reaching agreements.

Even if all necessary data is available and assessed in a similar way, the parties may still be reluctant to put forth any proposal. This may be because the disputants do not know how to generate options. They also may fear rejection, be afraid of giving away more information than is necessary for an agreement, feel that timing is wrong, or be using delay as a tactic to get more concessions from the other negotiator.

If a party does not know how to generate a proposal, the mediator may, through discussion, brainstorming, questioning, or procedural suggestions, assist the negotiator to develop a proposal. On the other hand, if the mediator determines that the party is reluctant to make a proposal because of fear of rejection or concern for giving away information, the intervenor may explore the fear or offer to test the proposal in caucus with the other side while claiming the option as the mediator's own idea.

If the party has a proposal but the timing of the offer is a problem, the mediator may discuss with the party standards or indicators for the timing of the offer or identify conditions or behaviors required from the other party that will induce movement. Frequently the mediator may have to work with both parties to develop a sequence of proposals in which each party makes an offer or concession in exchange for reciprocal benefits.

If a mediator discovers that one party is holding out for concessions or using delay as a tactic he may assess potential risks or benefits of intransigence with that party. Although a strategy of delay, a last-minute offer, or a proposal at the eleventh hour may work in some disputes, such proposals run the risk of being rejected because of psychological barriers created by the tactic or because there is too little time to evaluate or consider them.

If the substantive impasse is caused by the parties locking into mutually exclusive positions, the mediator may use several responses to loosen them up. The intervenor may refocus a party off of positions and onto the interests of both parties. The mediator may also look for principles, criteria, and standards independent of the disputing parties that might guide them in devising an acceptable solution. Criteria or principles might include an equitable exchange in dollars or goods, an agreement that is implementable, a settlement in which the parties have the resources to comply, or an agreement that will hold over time.

If a focus on interests, criteria, or standards fails to move an intransigent party, the mediator may discuss with the disputant the benefits and costs of maintaining a hard line. Frequently, parties take a hard line in negotiations without ever considering what their costs or options will be if negotiations fail. Negotiated settlements are highly dependent on the unavailability or unpredictability of alternative methods of settlement, such as court or administrative hearings. The recalcitrant disputant may need to reassess his or her position in light of other alternatives (Lax and Sebenius, 1985).

In some disputes, the issue may not be how to choose between two mutually exclusive options but how to select a solution from too many options or from several bad alternatives. In this rare event the mediator can revert to the previously mentioned procedure of exploring principles, criteria, or standards. Once criteria are identified, it often is easier to eliminate extraneous options and focus on the best ones. If it appears that the ultimate solution will have to be an arbitrary division of a resource, the intervenor can propose a mechanical means of reaching settlement, such as splitting the difference or using some random-choice procedures.

## Notes

*1. Evaluative Versus Directive Mediation.*   In Riskin's model of mediation styles, "evaluative" mediators actually engage in two types of activities that differentiate them from "facilitative" mediators: they assess the strength of the parties' cases, and they also propose settlement terms. The first of these activities is clearly evaluative in nature, but the second seems qualitatively different, having to do with how *directive* rather than how evaluative the mediator is.

Perhaps evaluative and directive mediation techniques complement each other, as the mediator's evaluation can be the first step in developing a proposal. It is possible, however, to conceive of a mediator who evaluates but does not propose, and likewise a mediator who proposes but does not evaluate. The former mediator might assess the strengths and weaknesses of the parties' cases and predict the likely outcome if the parties fail to settle out of court, but refrain from translating this assessment into a settlement proposal. The latter mediator might examine the parties' own views of the strengths and weaknesses of their legal positions, along with the parties' statements about their range of interests in the dispute, and craft a settlement proposal from that information without offering any judgments of her own about the parties' legal positions or interests.

*2. The Evaluation Controversy.* Nearly all mediators and mediation scholars agree that facilitation is an appropriate function of mediation. There is a split of expert opinion, however, as to whether it is desirable for mediators to evaluate the strength of negotiators' litigation positions. On one side of the debate, Kimberlee Kovach and Lela Love have argued:

> "Evaluative" mediation is an oxymoron. It jeopardizes neutrality because a mediator's assessment invariably favors one side over the other. Additionally, evaluative activities discourage understanding between and problem-solving by the parties. Instead, mediator evaluation tends to perpetuate or create an adversarial climate. Parties try to persuade the neutral of their positions, using confrontational and argumentative approaches.

Kimberlee K. Kovach & Lela P. Love, Evaluative Mediation Is an Oxymoron, 14 Alternatives to Litigation 31 (1996).

This argument suggests that mediator evaluations might have two different negative consequences. First, an evaluation that favors one party might alienate the other, causing him to lose confidence in the mediation process or trust in the neutrality of the mediator. Second, the mediator's evaluation of the litigation value of the case might suggest to the parties that mediation emphasizes the importance of legal entitlements rather than the interests of the parties, thus reducing the likelihood that the parties will engage in true integrative bargaining.

Other observers of the mediation process vociferously defend mediator evaluation, arguing that (1) differences in evaluation of the litigation value of a dispute often cause bargaining impasse, thus making mediator evaluation necessary to resolving the dispute, and (2) dispassionate evaluation does not imply any mediator bias and is not usually understood as doing so by negotiators. See, e.g., John Bickerman, Evaluative Mediator Responds, 14 Alternatives to Litigation 70 (1996).

*3. Evaluation and Settlement.* There are sound philosophical arguments both for and against evaluative mediation, but what effect does mediator evaluation have on the rate of settlement? One recent study (discussed also in Section A, Note 2 of this chapter) suggests that evaluative techniques might make postmediation settlement more likely. In the study of 289 disputes mediated by four major mediation services, Brett, Barsness, and Goldberg found that interest-based mediation without a mediator evaluation resulted in 60 percent of disputes settling during mediation and an additional 14 percent settling postmediation, for a total settlement rate of 74 percent. Interest-based mediation with the mediator providing an advisory opinion resulted in 61 percent of disputes settling during mediation (not statistically different than the 60 percent that settled without a mediator evaluation), but an additional 20 percent of disputes settling after mediation, for an overall settlement rate of 81 percent. Jeanne M. Brett et al., The Effectiveness of Mediation: An Independent Analysis of Cases Handled by Four Major Service Providers, 12 Negotiation J. 259, 261-262 (1996). These results seem consistent with the theoretical predictions that (1) some but not all disputes that fail to settle do so because the parties have different evaluations of the case's litigation value, and (2) a third-party opinion concerning the merits of the case can reduce the differences between the parties' evaluations, thus creating a bargaining zone in some but not all cases.

**4. Criticisms of Caucusing.**   Although caucusing is a common mediation tool, it is not without its critics. The central critique is that caucusing shifts power away from the parties to the mediator, because in a caucus mediation only the mediator has all of the information. Consequently, the mediator's perspective, rather than the parties' perspectives, can become the fundamental basis for any agreement. Mediator Gary Friedman, a critic of caucusing, describes the problem this way:

> By meeting individually with the parties, the mediator becomes more important to the success of the mediation — his or her point of view is likely to have a far greater impact on the disputants than if the three were working together. By extension, caucusing also gives the mediator more opportunities to manipulate the outcome, since each party depends only on what the mediator says to know what is acceptable to the other. In fact, without both parties in the room, the subjectivity of the mediator becomes the critical element, carrying much more weight than the parties' sense of fairness. If the mediator's sense of fairness happens to coincide with that of the parties, the damage is minimal. But if the mediator's sense of fairness conflicts with those of the other two . . . the parties may find themselves with a result they later regret.

Gary J. Friedman, A Guide to Divorce Mediation 281-282 (1993).

---

## DISCUSSION QUESTIONS AND PROBLEMS

*1. Mediation and Sophisticated Negotiators.*   Since mediators facilitate the negotiation process, it is easy to understand how a mediator could be of substantial benefit to negotiating parties who have little experience negotiating and little understanding of the dynamics of the negotiating process. But if principal parties are represented by lawyers who have studied and understand the negotiation process, and who have substantial negotiating experience, can mediation be valuable? If you found yourself in a professional negotiating situation where the other negotiator had also taken this negotiation course, would you consider hiring a mediator, or would the mediator seem unnecessary or superfluous?

**2. Evaluative Versus Facilitative Mediation.** Do the benefits to the negotiation process of a mediator's assessment of the litigation value of the case justify the possible drawbacks of evaluation? In what contexts would mediator evaluation be more or less desirable? If using a mediator, how would you decide whether to ask the mediator to evaluate the legal positions of the parties or to ask the mediator to limit herself to facilitation? Aside from assessing the strength of the parties' legal positions, are there other types of evaluation that a mediator might provide that could aid the negotiation process?

**3. Caucusing.** How do the advantages of holding private caucuses compare with the disadvantages? In what contexts do you think that caucusing would be most useful? Are there contexts in which caucuses would not be useful, or even contexts in which caucuses would be potentially damaging to the mediation?

**4. Substantive Expertise.** Mediation scholars disagree about how valuable it is for a mediator to have subject-matter expertise in the area of law at issue in a mediation. From the perspective of the negotiating parties, what are the advantages and disadvantages to selecting a mediator with substantive expertise in the subject of the mediation? Would your answer be any different if you were selecting a facilitator for a business transaction than if you were selecting a mediator to help resolve a litigation dispute? Would it matter whether the dispute concerned labor law, divorce law, or tort law?

**5. Mediator Pressure.** Theorists often criticize mediators who put pressure on the negotiating parties to accept certain settlement proposals on the grounds that such mediators interfere with the autonomy of the parties. Mediator David Matz contends, however, that mediator pressure can benefit negotiating parties:

> Parties come to a mediator because they are stuck. Going ahead with their dispute without mediation has become too painful, expensive, or difficult; and conversely, letting go of the dispute and ignoring it does not seem possible either. The parties are too invested in the dispute to let go or ignore it. Thus they are stuck, and come to the mediator to help them get unstuck.
>
> Mediators have many tools to help the parties to become unstuck, and one set of these techniques can properly be described as applying pressure

— pressure to get a party to see some things differently, to consider different choices. . . .

David E. Matz, Mediator Pressure and Party Autonomy: Are They Consistent with Each Other?, 10 Negotiation J. 359, 360 (1994).

As a lawyer-negotiator, would you ever want to retain a mediator with a reputation for pressuring parties to settle a dispute? In what circumstances might mediator pressure benefit you as a negotiator?

**6. Mediating an Employment Dispute.**   Patrick Porter worked for 15 years as a middle manager for a large corporation that manufactures and sells home appliances, Designs, Inc. Six months ago, shortly before Patrick turned 58 years old, Designs terminated Patrick. According to Designs, the company had to lay off 10 percent of its workforce due to an economic downturn that resulted in reduced sales for the company. Patrick's performance evaluations, while not terrible, had declined over the last few years, and he was therefore considered expendable.

Patrick argues that he consistently received "satisfactory" to "good" performance evaluations over the course of his tenure at Designs, and that the explanation offered by the company was merely a pretext for what was really blatant age discrimination on the company's part. Patrick claims that the layoffs were directed mostly at older workers, who tend to have higher salaries than younger workers. Patrick has filed an age discrimination lawsuit against the company. He has since found another job, but he claims that his new job pays him a salary of $20,000 a year less than he earned at Designs, and that the new job is not as challenging or as interesting as the previous one.

Patrick and the management of Designs Inc. have agreed to attempt to mediate the age discrimination claim before proceeding to litigation. In what ways, if any, do you think that mediation might help the parties to reach an out-of-court settlement that negotiation alone could not achieve? If you were advising the parties, what strategies and/or tactics would you recommend that they ask the mediator to employ? What strategies and/or tactics would you recommend that they ask the mediator not to employ?

# PART V

# THE LAW OF NEGOTIATION

To this point, we have analyzed negotiation as a purely private process with no oversight from the state. Implicit in the analysis has been the premise that negotiating behavior is constrained only by the limits of efficacy, and perhaps the negotiator's concern for his reputation in the community. Although negotiation is subject to fewer regulations than many types of private behavior, it is constrained, directed, and in some cases encouraged by a number of legal rules. This part considers several categories of relevant law.

The first category, the law of misrepresentation, distinguishes legally permissible secrecy, obfuscation, and even lying, from behavior that is egregious enough to subject the negotiator to legal sanctions. The precise legal boundaries are murky, but negotiators should be aware that some behavior that is commonly employed and possibly even expected in certain negotiation situations is of questionable legality and could conceivably lead to legal sanctions. Chapter 13, Misrepresentation, explores these imprecise boundaries.

The second and third categories, rules encouraging settlement and rules limiting settlement, apply specifically to dispute resolution negotiations in which a lawsuit (or threat thereof) converts a purely private matter into one that involves the state's dispute resolution apparatus. The former category includes rules of procedure, evidence, and substantive law that expand the bargaining zone between disputing parties, making an out-of-court agreement more likely. The latter category of rules establishes public oversight of settlement decisions in circumstances in which policy considerations arguably counsel against permitting the purely private resolution of disputes. Chapter 14, Rules Encouraging Litigation Settlement, and Chapter 15, Limitations on Settlement, examine these rules.

# Chapter 13

# Misrepresentation

Common experience suggests that negotiators consciously decide not to disclose information that they believe will hurt their bargaining position, and even act in ways intended to conceal such information, on a routine basis. Beyond this, negotiators often tell outright lies of various types in an effort to gain a bargaining advantage. Most negotiators assume such behavior is perfectly legal, if sometimes ethically problematic. In fact, there are legal limitations on the propensity of many negotiators to misrepresent. Although the doctrinal lines are not crystal clear, affirmative misrepresentations and knowing nondisclosure of certain information in the course of negotiations can, in some circumstances, be legally actionable as well as ethically questionable.

The legal status of negotiator misrepresentation is complex because it is governed by many different areas of substantive law: contract law, tort law, statutory law of unfair trade practices, and (for lawyer-negotiators) agency law and the law of professional responsibility. The following rules provide the broad parameters of the relevant legal regimes. The remainder of this section examines the legal and ethical status of misrepresentation in the negotiation in more detail.

## ■ Restatement (Second) of Torts
(1977)

### §525 Liability for Fraudulent Misrepresentation

One who fraudulently makes a misrepresentation of fact, opinion, intention or law for the purpose of inducing another to act or to refrain from action in reliance upon it, is subject to liability to the other in deceit for pecuniary loss caused to him by his justifiable reliance upon the misrepresentation.

## ◼ Restatement (Second) of Contracts

(1981)

### §164 WHEN A MISREPRESENTATION MAKES A CONTRACT VOIDABLE

(1) If a party's manifestation of assent is induced by either a fraudulent or a material misrepresentation by the other party upon which the recipient is justified in relying, the contract is voidable by the recipient. . . . ◼

## ◼ Restatement (Second) of Agency

(1958)

### §348 FRAUD AND DURESS

An agent who fraudulently makes representations, uses duress, or knowingly assists in the commission of tortious fraud or duress by his principal or by others is subject to liability in tort to the injured person although the fraud or duress occurs in a transaction on behalf of the principal. ◼

## ◼ ABA, Model Rules of Professional Conduct

(2001)

### RULE 4.1 — TRUTHFULNESS IN STATEMENTS TO OTHERS:

In the course of representing a client a lawyer shall not knowingly:

   (a) make a false statement of material fact or law to a third person; . . .

### COMMENT

*Misrepresentation*

[1] A lawyer is required to be truthful when dealing with others on a client's behalf, but generally has no affirmative duty to inform an opposing party of relevant facts. A misrepresentation can occur if the lawyer incorporates or affirms a statement of another person that the lawyer knows is false. Misrepresentations can also occur by failure to act.

*Statements of Fact*

[2] This Rule refers to statements of fact. Whether a particular statement should be regarded as one of fact can depend on the circum-

stances. Under generally accepted conventions in negotiation, certain types of statements ordinarily are not taken as statements of material fact. Estimates of price or value placed on the subject of a transaction and a party's intentions as to an acceptable settlement of a claim are in this category, and so is the existence of an undisclosed principal except where nondisclosure of the principal would constitute fraud. ■

## ■ ABA, Model Rules of Professional Conduct
(2001)

### RULE 8.4 — MISCONDUCT:

It is professional misconduct for a lawyer to: . . .
   (c) engage in conduct involving dishonesty, fraud, deceit or misrepresentation; . . .                                          ■

## A.   REPRESENTATIONS ABOUT THE NEGOTIATION'S SUBJECT MATTER

### ■ Vulcan Metals Co. Inc. v. Simmons Manufacturing Co., Inc.
248 F. 853 (2d Cir. 1918)

JUDGE LEARNED HAND delivered the Opinion of the Court.

The first question is of the misrepresentations touching the quality and powers of the patented machine. These were general commendations, or, in so far as they included any specific facts, were not disproved; e.g., that the cleaner would produce 18 inches of vacuum with 25 pounds water pressure. They raise, therefore, the question of law how far general "puffing" or "dealers' talk" can be the basis of an action for deceit.

The conceded exception in such cases has generally rested upon the distinction between "opinion" and "fact"; but that distinction has not escaped the criticism it deserves. An opinion is a fact, and it may be a very relevant fact; the expression of an opinion is the assertion of a belief, and any rule which condones the expression of a consciously false opinion condones a consciously false statement of fact. When the parties are so situated that the buyer may reasonably rely upon the expression of the seller's opinion, it is no excuse to give a false one. Bigler v. Flickinger, 55 Pa. 279. And so it makes much difference whether the parties stand "on an equality." For example, we should treat very differently the expressed opinion of a chemist to a layman about the properties of a composition from the same opinion between chemist and chemist, when the buyer had full opportunity to examine. The reason of the rule lies, we think, in this: There are some kinds of talk which no sensible man takes seriously, and if he does he suffers from his credulity. If we were all scrupulously honest, it would not be so; but, as it is, neither party usually believes what the seller says about his own opinions, and each knows it. Such statements, like the claims of campaign managers before election, are rather designed to allay the suspicion which would attend their absence than to be understood as having any relation to objective truth. It is quite true that they induce a compliant temper in the buyer, but it is by a much more subtle process than through the acceptance of his claims for his wares. . . .

In the case at bar, since the buyer was allowed full opportunity to examine the cleaner and to test it out, we put the parties upon an equality. It seems to us that general statements as to what the cleaner would do, even though consciously false, were not of a kind to be taken literally by the buyer. As between manufacturer and customer, it may not be so; but this was the case of taking over a business, after ample chance to investigate. Such a buyer, who the seller rightly expects will undertake an independent and adequate inquiry into the actual merits of what he gets, has no right to treat as material in his determination statements like these. The standard of honesty permitted by the rule may not be the best; but, as Holmes, J., says in Deming v. Darling, 148 Mass. 504, 20 N.E. 107, 2 L.R.A. 743, the chance that the higgling preparatory to a bargain may be afterwards translated into assurances of quality may perhaps be a set-off to the actual wrong allowed by the rule as it stands. We therefore think that the District Court was right in disregarding all these misrepresentations.

As respects the representation that the cleaners had never been put upon the market or offered for sale, the rule does not apply; nor can we agree that such representations could not have been material to Freeman's decision to accept the contract. The actual test of experience in their sale might well be of critical consequence in his decision to buy the business, and the jury would certainly have the right to accept his statement that his reliance upon these representations was determinative of his final decision. . . .                                    ■

## Notes

*1. The Fact-Opinion Distinction.*   It is often said that misrepresentations of fact are actionable but misrepresentations of opinion usually are not. As Judge Hand points out in *Vulcan Metals*, however, there is not necessarily a distinction between facts and opinions regarding the truthfulness of the utterance. Representations of facts and representations of opinions can be equally untruthful. See Restatement (Second) of Torts §530. If a negotiator says that she believes the sun sets in the east when in fact she believes that it sets in the west, she has told a lie. She might not have represented that the sun actually sets in the east, but she did falsely represent this to be her opinion.

The distinction in the law between misrepresentations of "fact" and "opinion" is more usefully understood as a proxy for whether the utterance is one upon which the law judges the recipient is justified in relying. See generally Restatement (Second) of Torts §525. Reliance on statements of fact is usually justified, whereas reliance on statements of opinion is usually not justified (although there are exceptions to this rule of thumb discussed in the following notes). For example, one court explained that a house seller's claim that the house was "well built" and "perfectly safe on the concrete, the roof and everything else of the construction" was not actionable as misrepresentation not because it was an opinion rather than a fact, but because "it is difficult to find these words, when reasonably considered, as capable of being understood by a man of average intelligence as a clear and definite representation of any particular fact." Milken v. French, 150 A. 28, 31-32 (Md. 1930). Another court found that a defendant bank's incorrect statement to its customer about the legal effect of a document was a nonactionable opinion because the customer had the ability to have the document reviewed by an attorney and was therefore not justified in relying on the bank's representation. Fina Supply, Inc. v. Abilene National Bank, 736 S.W.2d 537 (Tex. 1987).

*2. Trade Puffing.*   In negotiation settings from used car sales to litigation settlement discussions, sellers frequently boast about the high quality or value of what they have to sell in an effort to convince prospective buyers to pay more for it — that is, to raise buyers' reservation prices. General commendations of this sort are commonly referred to as "puffing" or "sales talk," and are not actionable misrepresentations even if the seller does not believe his own claims. The Restatement (Second) of Torts describes the intuition behind this rule: "It is common knowledge and may always be assumed that any seller will express a favorable opinion concerning what he has to sell; and when he praises it in general terms, without specific content or reference to facts, buyers are expected to and do understand that they are not entitled to rely literally upon the words." Restatement (Second) of Torts §542 cmt. e.

Royal Business Machines v. Lorraine Corp., 633 F.2d 34 (7th Cir. 1980), illustrates the general rule. In that case, the plaintiff purchased 128 copying machines from the defendant, who claimed his machines were "of good quality" and would "last a lifetime." When the machines began to experience problems, the plaintiff sued, claiming the sales-man was guilty of misrepresentation. The court rejected the cause of action on the ground that the statements were merely " '[p]uffing' to be expected in any sales transaction." Id. at 42. The same rule applies when the seller praises his wares by ascribing a high monetary value to them. For example, in Page Investment Co. v. Staley, 468 P.2d 589 (Ariz. 1970), the court dismissed a plaintiff's lawsuit claiming that de-fendant represented that his property was worth $7,500 per acre when it was only worth $4,000 per acre and defendant knew or should have known so, explaining that a claim of value is merely an opinion. Id. at 591.

*3. Future Value, Quality, or Prospects.*   Sellers also are apt to make claims during bargaining about the value that their wares will have in the future or the variety of uses to which the buyer will one day be able to put them. Statements about such future quality are generally treated like claims about current quality or value — that is, nonaction-able even if false because it is not reasonable to rely on such opinions. In Vaughn v. General Foods Corp., 797 F.2d 1403 (7th Cir. 1986), defendant General Foods was sued based on statements it made in efforts to sell "Burger Chef" restaurant franchises to the effect that the chain would remain viable and expand in the future, thus presumably increasing the value of the prospective buyers' investment in a fran-chise. The court held that the statements were nonactionable both because they constituted trade puffing and also because they con-cerned future events, despite the plaintiffs' allegation that General Foods did not believe the statements to be true at the time they were made and was already planning to sell the chain. Id. at 1411-1413.

Even more specific claims about the future quality or value of the subject of the negotiation have been held nonactionable because their future orientation identifies them as opinions that should not engen-der reliance. For example, over the years courts have held that sellers' statements concerning the income potential of a farm, Belka v. Allen, 74 A. 91, 93-94 (Vt. 1909), dividends that a stock would pay, Zeh v. Hotel Corp, 10 P.2d 190, 191 (Cal. Ct. App. 1932), how much rent could be charged for apartments, Pacesetter Homes v. Brodkin, 5 Cal. App. 3d 206 (1970), and how certain government approval for a proj-ect would be, Borba v. Thomas, 70 Cal. App. 3d 144 (1977), are merely opinions and cannot serve as the basis for a misrepresentation claim by a disappointed buyer.

*4. Specific, Present Characteristics.*   When sellers' claims about their wares concern specific, objective characteristics, and represent the pres-ent state of the world rather than a future state, courts have been far more likely to find false statements to be actionable "facts" rather than nonactionable "opinions." The distinction is illustrated by Horner v.

Wagy, 146 P.2d 92 (Or. 1944), in which the buyer of a business sued
the seller over the seller's claims that the business took in $450-$600
per week in revenue and was "very profitable." The court held that the
lack of specificity of the claim about profitability made it a nonactionable statement of opinion, id. at 99, but the specific statement concerning weekly revenues was a statement of fact that, if false, would be
an actionable misrepresentation. Id. at 97. In a more recent case, the
Seventh Circuit found that a claim by a home improvement store that
a specific list of products would be sufficient to build the house described in the customer's detailed plans could qualify as an actionable
misrepresentation, in contrast to a claim that the products were of
"good quality," which could not be actionable. Thacker v. Menard, 105
F.3d 382, 386 (7th Cir. 1997).

Most courts have ruled that the misrepresentation of a specific fact
is actionable even if the buyer easily could have discovered the truth
by conducting a prudent investigation of the negotiation's subject matter prior to the transaction. The Florida Supreme Court described the
intuition this way: "A person guilty of fraud should not be permitted
to use the law as his shield. Nor should the law encourage negligence.
However, when the choice is between the two — fraud and negligence
— negligence is less objectionable than fraud. . . . [T]he law should not
permit an inattentive person to suffer loss at the hands of a misrep-
resenter." Besett v. Basnett, 389 So. 2d 995, 998 (Fla. 1980).

**5. Actionable Opinions.**   Even statements of opinion that are normally nonactionable can be actionable when the opinion is based
implicitly on facts that the seller has superior access to or knowledge
of than the buyer. Again, the root inquiry is whether the buyer's reliance on the seller's claims is reasonable under the circumstances or
whether the buyer should conduct his own inquiry and reach his own
opinion. According to Restatement (Second) of Torts, "a statement of
opinion as to facts not disclosed and not otherwise known to the recipient may, if it is reasonable to do so, be interpreted by him as an
implied statement (a) that the facts known to the maker are not incompatible with his opinion; or (b) that he knows facts sufficient to
justify him in forming it. . . ." Restatement (Second) of Torts §539. In
Peterson v. Auvel, 275 Ore. 633 (Or. 1976), defendant real estate bro-
kers told customers that a signed earnest agreement was unenforcea-
ble. The court held that this representation was potentially actionable
because the defendants were acting "in a capacity which entitles the
recipient [of the information] to believe that [the defendants had] a
superior ability to reach an accurate opinion." Id. at 640.

A difficult question is what level of expertise or specialized access to
information must the seller have before the buyer is justified in relying
on the seller's statements rather than conducting his own investigation?

Recall that in *Vulcan Metals*, supra, Judge Hand held that the buyer could not rely on the seller's representations concerning the quality of his machine because, as a potential buyer of seller's business, the buyer had an adequate opportunity to conduct his own inquiry and reach his own opinion, and thus the two interacted "upon an equality." Id. at 857. But at the same time Judge Hand warned that the case would not necessarily have been decided the same way if the relationship between buyer and seller was one of manufacturer and customer or, if the product was a chemical compound, the relationship of chemist and layman. Id. at 856.

In *Vaughn*, supra, the court similarly noted that the plaintiffs were not justified in relying on the defendant's statements about the future because they had "an adequate opportunity" to make their own investigation into the future prospects of the franchise they were considering purchasing, despite the obvious fact that the seller had more information relevant to the franchises' future prospects than did the buyer. Id. at 412. One court observed that " '[s]uperior knowledge' in the context of fraudulent misrepresentation has become a term of art. It contemplates more than the possession by one party to a bargain of a greater acumen than is possessed by the other party. The concept has been applied primarily in situations where assumed knowledge possessed by the party expressing the fraudulent opinion is a motivation to the other to enter into the transaction, or where the defendant has held himself out as particularly knowledgeable." Pacesetter Homes v. Brodkin, 5 Cal. App. 3d 206, 212 (1970).

*6. Weight of Disclaimers.*   Defendants who have attempted to avoid liability by swathing overly optimistic statements in disclaimers have achieved mixed results. Whether a disclaimer can render reliance on the underlying claim unreasonable depends in part on the strength and clarity of the disclaimer. In In re Trump, 7 F.3d 357 (3d Cir. 1993), defendants claimed in their prospectus directed to potential investors that they believed income from their "Taj Mahal" casino could completely pay off all debt, both principle and interest, but repeatedly warned about the risk involved in the proposed investment. When the defendants filed for Chapter 11 bankruptcy and reorganization, disappointed investors brought suit, claiming misrepresentation in the prospectus. Unmoved, the court concluded that "due to the disclaimers and warnings the prospectus contains, no reasonable investor could believe anything but that the Taj Mahal bonds represented a rather risky, speculative investment. . . ." Id. at 369.

Compare this to an older opinion that considered a much weaker disclaimer: a seller of a land parcel claimed that the parcel contained "*about*" 60 acres of good bottom land, when in fact there were only 40 such acres. Jeffreys v. Weekly, 158 P. 522 (Or. 1916). Rejecting the defendant's claim that the word "about" suggested the claim was a mere opinion that did not justify reliance by the buyer, the court held that "whatever phraseology was employed by [the seller], [the buyer] was overreached and deceived in the transaction." Id. at 524.

Courts have also found that the extent to which the misrepresentation is a false statement of an objective fact rather than an overly optimistic opinion or prediction can affect the weight accorded to a disclaimer. In Shaw v. Digital Equipment, 82 F.3d 1194 (1st Cir. 1996), defendant corporation sought to attract capital through the sale of stock. In the sales prospectus, the defendant stated that "[t]he corporation believes that the remaining restructuring reserve of $443 million is adequate to cover presently planned restructuring actions." In fact, the corporation had already made plans to "accelerate" the restructuring efforts at an additional cost of $1.2 billion. Rejecting its claim that the statement was nonactionable because the prospectus "bespoke caution," the court held that even couching or cautionary language "cannot render misrepresentations of 'hard' fact non-actionable." Id. at 1213.

---

# B.  REPRESENTATIONS RELATED TO THE SPEAKER'S RESERVATION PRICE

## ■ Kabatchnick v. Hanover-Elm Building Corp.
### 103 N.E.2d 692 (Mass. 1952)

JUSTICE SPALDING delivered the Opinion of the Court.

In this action of tort for deceit the material averments of the declaration are as follows: The plaintiff, who was engaged in selling novelties, toys, and games at retail, occupied as a tenant under a written lease the first floor and basement of certain premises on Bromfield Street, Boston. The annual rental reserved in the lease was $4,500. The lease was dated January 15, 1945, and ran to March 1, 1947. Upon acquiring title to the premises in November, 1946, the defendants represented to the plaintiff "that they had a bona fide offer from one Melvin Levine for the leasing of the said premises to him at the rate of $10,000 per year and that unless the plaintiff met that offer and signed a lease for twelve (12) years at $10,000 per year the defendants would evict the plaintiff at the end of his lease on March 1, 1947." Believing these representations and in reliance upon them the plaintiff on December 6, 1946, entered into a written lease with the defendant Hanover-Elm Building Corporation for the term of twelve years from January 1, 1947, at an annual rental of $10,000 payable in monthly installments of $833.33. At the time that this lease was executed the defendants demanded as a condition to its execution that the plaintiff pay the sum of $833.33 beginning with the month of December, 1946. The plaintiff complied with this demand and has thereafter paid this amount monthly. "In truth and in fact the representations made by the defendants to the plaintiff . . . [concerning the offer purporting to have been made by Melvin Levine] were false and known by the defendants to be false and were made by them with the intent that the plaintiff rely thereon and execute the said lease and make the aforesaid payments." These facts were recently discovered by the plaintiff and "if he had known of the true facts he would not have executed the said lease." "The rental value of the said premises," it is alleged, "was not worth $10,000 per year for twelve (12) years, but was worth only $4,500 per year; all to . . . [the plaintiff's] great damage."

The case comes here on the plaintiff's appeal from an order sustaining the defendants' demurrer. The demurrer included several grounds, the first of which and the one on which it was sustained was that the declaration does not state a case.

In Commonwealth v. Quinn, 222 Mass. 504, the defendants were tried on an indictment charging them with larceny by means of false pretenses. At the trial, as proof of a false pretense, evidence was admitted, subject to the defendants' exception, to show that one of the defendants, Fuchs, had stated to Bullard (the victim of the alleged larceny) that he (Fuchs) had been offered $42,000 for certain property which was to be transferred to Bullard in exchange for certain real and personal property owned by the latter. In sustaining the exception this court said, "In civil actions the rule of the common law long has been recognized that mere statements of the vendor concerning either real or personal property, where there is no warranty as to its value or the price which he has given or has been offered for it, are to be treated as 'seller's talk'; that the rule of caveat emptor applies, and therefore they are not actionable even if the statements are false and intended to deceive. This rule has been affirmed in many decisions of this court and long has been understood to be the law of the Commonwealth. We know of no case in which this court has come to a contrary conclusion. We think it plain that, if such statements are not the ground of civil liability, with stronger reason they cannot be held to constitute a criminal offence" (pages 512-513).

The rule just quoted finds support in a long line of decisions. . . . If they are to be followed the demurrer was rightly sustained, for the defendants' statement as to the amount of rent that another had offered to pay must under these decisions be treated as "seller's talk." . . .

Most, if not all, courts hold that there are certain types of statements upon which a purchaser is not justified in placing reliance. Thus a statement that an article is made of the finest material obtainable, that a particular automobile is the most economical car on the market, or that a certain investment is sound and will yield a handsome profit, and similar claims are generally understood to be matters of opinion and if reliance is placed on them and they turn out otherwise the law does not afford a remedy. . . .

But the statement in the case at bar was not of that class. The defendants represented to the plaintiff that they had received a bona fide offer from Levine to take a lease of the premises at an annual rental of $ 10,000. This was more than a statement of opinion; it was a representation of an existing fact. Why, on principle, should one making such a representation be immune from liability if it was false, provided the other elements required by the law of deceit are present? . . .

The time has come, we think, to depart from the rule stated in Commonwealth v. Quinn, in so far as it affords no remedy for representations of the sort here involved. Not only is it opposed to the weight of authority but it is difficult to justify on principles of ethics and justice. Moreover, several exceptions have been engrafted upon the rule whereby liability is imposed in situations that do not differ materially from those falling within it. One of these exceptions is that if the vendor in selling real estate falsely states the amount of rent he is receiving the representation is actionable. Brown v. Castles, 11 Cush. 348, 350. Exchange Realty Co. v. Bines, 302 Mass. 93, 97. The reason given for the exception in Brown v. Castles is that the amount of the rent lies "in the private knowledge of the landlord and tenant" (page 350). But similar reasons can be urged with respect to representations concerning the purchase price or an offer from a third person. . . .

It follows, therefore, that the demurrer ought not to have been sustained on the first ground.    ■

## Notes

*1. Lying About Competing Offers.* As *Kabatchnick* explains, the historical rule was that sellers' claims about the existence of competing offers constitute puffing, or as the *Kabatchnick* court calls it, "seller's talk." Chancellor Kent's Commentaries reported that, so long as the seller did not have superior knowledge or expertise, "the cases have gone so far as to hold, that if the seller should even falsely affirm, that a particular sum had been bid by others for the property, by which means the purchaser was induced to buy, and was deceived as to the value, no relief was to be afforded; for the buyer should have informed himself from proper sources of the value. . . ." 2 Kent Com. 3d 485-486 (1827). The rule is based on the reasoning that a competing offer is only relevant because it suggests the value of the subject of the negotiation. In the usual case, with due diligence a buyer can evaluate the value of property or goods for himself, and therefore may not reasonably rely on the seller's statements on that issue. See, e.g., Saunders v. Hatterman, 24 N.C. 32, 34 (1841).

Cases from the latter half of the twentieth century, consistent with *Kabatchnick*, have usually reasoned that, as the seller has more information about alternative offers than the prospective buyer, it is reasonable for the prospective buyer to rely on the veracity of the very factual claims made by sellers about the existence of other firm offers. In Beavers v. Lamplighters Realty, a real estate agent told a prospective house buyer that another party was willing to pay the asking price for the house and would deliver a check later that day. The plaintiff immediately bought the house for $250 more than the asking price and sued the real estate agent when he discovered that there was no other buyer. In a ruling for the plaintiff, the court took an expansive view on when a buyer's reliance on a seller's statements is justified: "A prospective buyer has a right to rely on the veracity of the seller (or his agent) without investigation. The risk of harm in this state lies with the wrongdoer rather than his victim. . . . this right of reliance must be protected even if the representations be so extravagant that sensible, cautious people would not have believed them. . . ." Beavers v. Lamplighters Realty, 556 P.2d 1328, 1331 (1976). Courts are less likely to find claims about fictitious competing buyers actionable if they are vague and nonspecific. In Ravosa v. Zais, 661 N.E.2d 111 (Mass. Ct. App. 1996), for example, the court found nonactionable the seller's claim that he had "a buyer waiting in the wings" for his property. Id. at 116.

Although most reported cases consider false claims of other offers by sellers, some courts have also found the same strictures applicable to buyers. In Kansas Municipal Gas Agency v. Vesta Energy, Kansas Municipal's agent falsely represented in negotiations with a potential supplier, Vesta, that his client had a deal with another supplier at a lower price. In response, Vesta lowered its offer price. Finding for the supplier, the court called the claim "more than puffing or so-called trade talk. It is a motivational fact-related lie." Kansas Municipal Gas Agency v. Vesta Energy, 840 F. Supp. 814, 825-826 (D. Kan. 1993).

**2. Lying About Reservation Prices.**   Although some courts have found negotiators' false statements about the existence of alternatives to be actionable, it is highly unlikely that a negotiator's false statement about his reservation price would be found actionable. In one case dealing with a typical situation of a consumer bargaining with an insurance company claims adjuster over coverage for an injury, the adjuster represented that $900 was "all he could pay" to settle the claim. The consumer accepted the settlement offer, but later brought suit alleging, among other things, that this statement was fraudulent. The court dismissed the charge, holding that the statement was of the type "frequently made by parties during negotiation [and] simply does not amount to fraud." Morta v. Korean Insurance Corp., 840 F.2d 1452, 1456 (9th Cir. 1988). Even when parties are negotiating under a contract that requires them to bargain in "good faith," courts have found that negotiators have no duty to reveal their reservation price. PSI Energy v. Exxon Coal, 17 F.3d 969, 973 (7th Cir. 1994). The cases are consistent with the ABA, Model Rules of Professional Responsibility Rule 4.1, which proscribes lawyers from making false statements of fact or law, but asserts that a party's intentions as to an acceptable settlement of a claim are not considered a material fact. ABA, Model Rules of Professional Conduct Rule 4.1 cmt. 2 (2001).

*3. Should Reservation Prices Be Treated Differently?* Is it appropriate that the law permits negotiators to blatantly lie about their reservation prices when other types of lies are prohibited? Alan Strudler presents two arguments for why perhaps it is:

> ... [1] Ordinarily, it is not possible to prove that someone lied about her reservation price, because facts concerning reservation prices are only thoughts inside a person's head. Although there is no reason to doubt that there are objective facts about a person's thoughts and that such behavior provides some evidence about those facts, it is rarely feasible to obtain evidence sufficient to prove that a negotiator held a particular reservation price at the time of her negotiation. Even if a person reduces her attitudes toward her reservation price to written form, or otherwise communicates these attitudes to a third party in such a way as to create comparatively reliable external evidence, that action may not suffice as proof about her reservation price, because, in her own mind, she may have changed her reservation price once the negotiation commenced. Any attempt nonetheless to establish facts about a person's reservation price would be expensive because it would trigger court costs, legal fees, evidence gathering costs, and the like. Of course, the anticipated benefit of a law against fraud is a lower incidence of lying, as prospective liars would be deterred by the threat of being caught. As we have seen, however, catching those liars is no sure thing. . . .
>
> [2] Loss that derives from misrepresentation in negotiation is in allocational efficiency — misrepresentations about goods may cause a person to buy something that she does not really want. It is not obvious, however, that lies about reservation prices can have that effect. If someone buys something after being lied to about a reservation price, she gets what she wants at a price she finds acceptable, even if she would have preferred a better price. Because the parties to a negotiation thus get what they want, goods end up in the hands of those who value them most, and no allocational inefficiency occurs. Thus, from an economic point of view, it is hard to see why one would bother discouraging lies about reservation prices.

Alan Strudler, Incommensurable Goods, Rightful Lies, and the Wrongness of Fraud, 146 U. Pa. L. Rev. 1529, 1540-1541 (1998).

## C. NONDISCLOSURE

### ■ Swinton v. Whitinsville Savings Bank

42 N.E.2d 808 (Mass. 1942)

JUSTICE QUA delivered the Opinion of the Court.

The declaration alleges that on or about September 12, 1938, the defendant sold the plaintiff a house in Newton to be occupied by the plaintiff and his family as a dwelling; that at the time of the sale the house 'was infested with termites, an insect that is most dangerous and destructive to buildings'; that the defendant knew the house was so infested; that the plaintiff could not readily observe this condition upon inspection; that 'knowing the internal destruction that these insects were creating in said house', the defendant falsely and fraudulently concealed from the plaintiff its true condition; that the plaintiff at the time of his purchase had no knowledge of the termites, exercised due care thereafter, and learned of them about August 30, 1940; and that, because of the destruction that was being done and the dangerous condition that was being created by the termites, the plaintiff was put to great expense for repairs and for the installation of termite control in order to prevent the loss and destruction of said house.

There is no allegation of any false statement or representation, or of the uttering of a half truth which may be tantamount to a falsehood. There is no intimation that the defendant by any means prevented the plaintiff from acquiring information as to the condition of the house. There is nothing to show any fiduciary relation between the parties, or that the plaintiff stood in a position of confidence toward or dependence upon the defendant. So far as appears the parties made a business deal at arm's length. The charge is concealment and nothing more; and it is concealment in the simple sense of mere failure to reveal, with nothing to show any peculiar duty to speak. The characterization of the concealment as false and fraudulent of course adds nothing in the absence of further allegations of fact. Province Securities Corp. v. Maryland Casualty Co., 269 Mass. 75, 92, 168 S.E. 252.

If this defendant is liable on this declaration every seller is liable who fails to disclose any nonapparent defect known to him in the subject of the sale which materially reduces its value and which the buyer fails to discover. Similarly it would seem that every buyer would be liable who fails to disclose any nonapparent virtue known to him in the subject of the purchase which materially enhances its value and of which the seller is ignorant. See Goodwin v. Agassiz, 283 Mass. 358, 186 N.E. 659. The law has not yet, we believe, reached the point of imposing upon the frailties of human nature a standard so idealistic as

this. That the particular case here stated by the plaintiff possesses a
certain appeal to the moral sense is scarcely to be denied. Probably the
reason is to be found in the facts that the infestation of buildings by
termites has not been common in Massachusetts and constitutes a concealed risk against which buyers are off their guard. But the law cannot
provide special rules for termites and can hardly attempt to determine
liability according to the varying probabilities of the existence and discovery of different possible defects in the subjects of trade. The rule
of nonliability for bare nondisclosure has been stated and followed by
this court. . . .                                                                ■

## ■ Weintraub v. Krobatsch

### 317 A.2d 68 (N.J. 1974)

JUSTICE JACOBS delivered the Opinion of the Court. . . .

Mrs. Weintraub owned and occupied a six-year-old Englishtown
home which she placed in the hands of a real estate broker (The Ser-
afin Agency, Inc.) for sale. The Krobatsches were interested in purchasing the home, examined it while it was illuminated and found it
suitable. On June 30, 1971 Mrs. Weintraub, as seller, and the Krobatsches, as purchasers, entered into a contract for the sale of the
property for $42,500. The contract provided that the purchasers had
inspected the property and were fully satisfied with its physical condition, that no representations had been made and that no responsibility was assumed by the seller as to the present or future condition of
the premises. A deposit of $4,250 was sent by the purchasers to the
broker to be held in escrow pending the closing of the transaction.
The purchasers requested that the seller have the house fumigated
and that was done. A fire after the signing of the contract caused damage but the purchasers indicated readiness that there be adjustment at
closing.

During the evening of August 25, 1971, prior to closing, the purchasers entered the house, then unoccupied, and as they turned the
lights on they were, as described in their petition for certification,
"astonished to see roaches literally running in all directions, up the
walls, drapes, etc." On the following day their attorney wrote a letter
to Mrs. Weintraub, care of her New York law firm, advising that on the
previous day "it was discovered that the house is infested with vermin
despite the fact that an exterminator has only recently serviced the
house" and asserting that "the presence of vermin in such great quantities, particularly after the exterminator was done, rendered the house
as unfit for human habitation at this time and therefore, the contract
is rescinded." . . .

Mrs. Weintraub rejected the rescission by the purchasers and filed an action. . . . At the argument on the motions it was evident that the purchasers were claiming fraudulent concealment or nondisclosure by the seller as the basis for their rescission. Thus at one point their attorney said: "Your honor, I would point out, and it is in my clients' affidavit, every time that they inspected this house prior to this time every light in the place was illuminated. Now, these insects are nocturnal by nature and that is not a point I think I have to prove through someone. I think Webster's dictionary is sufficient. By keeping the lights on it keeps them out of sight. These sellers had to know they had this problem. You could not live in a house this infested without knowing about it." . . .

[Weintraub] contends . . . that even if she were fully aware she would have been under no duty to speak and that consequently no complaint by the purchasers may legally be grounded on her silence. She relies primarily on cases such as Swinton v. Whitinsville Sav. Bank, 311 Mass. 677, 42 N.E.2d 808, 141 A.L.R. 965 (1942). . . .

[*Swinton*] was written several decades ago and we are far from certain that it represents views held by the current members of the Massachusetts court. . . . In any event we are certain that it does not represent our sense of justice or fair dealing and it has understandably been rejected in persuasive opinions elsewhere. . . .

In Obde v. Schlemeyer, 56 Wash. 2d 449, 353 P.2d 672, the defendants sold an apartment house to the plaintiff. The house was termite infested but that fact was not disclosed by the sellers to the purchasers who later sued for damages alleging fraudulent concealment. The sellers contended that they were under no obligation whatever to speak out and they relied heavily on the decision of the Massachusetts court in *Swinton* (311 Mass. 677, 42 N.E.2d 808, 141 A.L.R. 965). The Supreme Court of Washington flatly rejected their contention, holding that though the parties had dealt at arms length the sellers were under "a duty to inform the plaintiffs of the termite condition" of which they were fully aware. . . .

In Loghry v. Capel, the plaintiffs purchased a duplex from the defendants. They examined the house briefly on two occasions and signed a document stating that they accepted the property in its "present condition." 132 N.W.2d at 419. They made no inquiry about the subsoil and were not told that the house had been constructed on filled ground. They filed an action for damages charging that the sellers had fraudulently failed to disclose that the duplex was constructed on improperly compacted filled ground. The jury found in their favor and the verdict was sustained on appeal in an opinion which pointed out that "fraud may consist of concealment of a material fact." 132 N.W.2d at 419. The purchasers' stipulation that they accepted the property in its present condition could not be invoked to bar their claim. See Wolford v. Freeman, 150 Neb. 537, 35 N.W.2d 98 (1948), where the court pointed out that the purchase of property "as is" does not bar rescission grounded on fraudulent conduct of the seller. 35 N.W.2d at 103.

In Simmons v. Evans, supra, the defendants owned a home which was serviced by a local water company. The company supplied water during the daytime but not at night. The defendants sold their home to the plaintiffs but made no mention of the limitation on the water service. The plaintiffs filed an action to rescind their purchase but the lower court dismissed it on the ground that the defendants had not made any written or verbal representations and the plaintiffs had "inspected the property, knew the source of the water supply, and could have made specific inquiry of these defendants or ascertained from other sources the true situation and, therefore, are estopped." 206 S.W.2d at 296. The dismissal was reversed on appeal in an opinion which took note of the general rule that "one may be guilty of fraud by his silence, as where it is expressly incumbent upon him to speak concerning material matters that are entirely within his own knowledge." 206 S.W.2d at 296. With respect to the plaintiffs' failure to ascertain the water situation before their purchase the court stated that the plaintiffs were surely not required "to make a night inspection in order to ascertain whether the water situation with reference to this residence was different from what it was during the day." 206 S.W.2d at 297. . . .

. . . [T]he purchasers here were entitled to withstand the seller's motion for summary judgment. They should have been permitted to proceed with their efforts to establish by testimony that they were equitably entitled to rescind because the house was extensively infested in the manner described by them, the seller was well aware of the infestation, and the seller deliberately concealed or failed to disclose the condition because of the likelihood that it would defeat the transaction. The seller may of course defend factually as well as legally and since the matter is primarily equitable in nature the factual as well as legal disputes will be for the trial judge alone. . . .

If the trial judge finds such deliberate concealment or nondisclosure of the latent infestation not observable by the purchasers on their inspection, he will still be called upon to determine whether, in the light of the full presentation before him, the concealment or nondisclosure was of such significant nature as to justify rescission. Minor conditions which ordinary sellers and purchasers would reasonably disregard as of little or no materiality in the transaction would clearly not call for judicial intervention. . . .

Our courts have come a long way since the days when the judicial emphasis was on formal rules and ancient precedents rather than on modern concepts of justice and fair dealing. . . .  ■

# Notes

*1. When Nondisclosure Constitutes Misrepresentation.* It is clear that nondisclosure is treated as misrepresentation when the nondisclosing party actively conceals a material fact from a negotiating opponent or tells a partial truth that implies a falsehood. Duquesne Light Co. v. Westinghouse Electric Corp., 66 F.3d 604 (3d Cir. 1995); Erie Insurance Co. v. Insurance Commissioner of Maryland, 579 A.2d 771 (Md. 1990). When a negotiator is merely silent as to the existence of a material fact that, if known, would weaken his bargaining position, however, there is no bright-line rule that can reliably divide actionable from nonactionable nondisclosure. The black-letter law provides that nondisclosure is not actionable except in specific circumstances, but the specific circumstances are quite open ended. Disclosure of material facts is required when the negotiator has a fiduciary-type relationship of trust with the opponent, or when disclosure is necessary to prevent a previous statement from being false (for example, when a lawyer acquires new information inconsistent with a previous assertion), but also in the apparently broad set of circumstances in which standards of fair dealing require disclosure. See Restatement (Second) of Contracts §161; Restatement (Second) of Torts §551; Nathan M. Crystal, The Lawyer's Duty to Disclose Material Facts in Contract or Settlement Negotiations, 87 Ky. L.J. 1055, 1076-1083 (1998).

*2. A Theoretical Perspective.* In an important article, Anthony Kronman has argued that disclosure of material facts should be required when the information was obtained casually but not when it was obtained as the result of deliberate effort. Kronman's intuition is that deliberately acquired information must be privileged in order to provide an incentive for parties to invest in searching for information that is economically valuable. Negotiators are not likely to spend time and money searching for information that affects the value of the subject of the negotiation if they must turn over the information to their negotiating opponents. On the other hand, requiring negotiators to disclose information that is acquired casually — i.e., without deliberate search — provides no disincentive to the production of valuable information. Requiring disclosure of such information is efficient because it saves the noninformed party the potentially high costs of searching for the information, while costing the knowledgeable party little or nothing (other than losing a bargaining advantage). Anthony Kronman, Mistake, Disclosure, and the Law of Contracts, 7 J. Legal Stud. 1 (1978).

Kronman's conceptual division between casually and deliberately acquired information can explain many — although certainly not all —

judicial decisions in non-disclosure cases. For example, in Baskin v. Collins, 806 S.W.2d 3 (Ark. 1991), the court held that the seller of a piece of land with buried gas tanks had no duty to disclose that a federal law regulating such tanks had recently been enacted because knowledge of the law was deliberately acquired information. Id. at 5. In Malon Oil Co. v. BEA, 965 P.2d 105 (Colo. 1998), the court found that the buyer of mining rights had no duty to disclose that there were coal deposits under the seller's property, as such information is almost always developed deliberately. Id. at 111-112. In contrast, in Mohr v. Commonwealth, 653 N.E.2d 1104, 1114-1115 (Mass. 1995), the court held an adoption agency responsible for disclosing that a child offered for adoption was mentally retarded (presumably such information is casually available to the agency).

**3. Unilateral Mistake.** In some situations, it might be prudent for a negotiator to disclose information about the subject matter of the negotiation that prejudices his position even if his failure to do so would not constitute misrepresentation. Under contract law, a contract can be rescinded if one party is mistaken as to a basic assumption that has a material effect on the transaction if the other party knows of the mistake and the first party does not bear the risk of such a mistake. Restatement (Second) of Contracts §153. A party is considered to bear the risk of a mistake if he agrees to bear the risk or if he enters the agreement knowing that his knowledge is incomplete or uncertain. Restatement (Second) of Contracts §154.

In Spaulding v. Zimmerman, 116 N.W.2d 704 (Minn. 1962), the plaintiff had settled a lawsuit arising out of an automobile accident for a relatively small amount of money based on his knowledge of the in-juries he had suffered in the accident. The defendant's physician had examined the plaintiff prior to settlement and found a very dangerous aneurysm that might have been caused by the accident. The plaintiff did not know about the aneurysm, and the defendant knew that the plaintiff lacked this information. The Minnesota Supreme Court found that the defendant was not guilty of fraud or bad faith for fail-ing to disclose the information, but still held that a lower court acted within its discretion when it vacated the original settlement agreement on the grounds that the defendant knew the plaintiff lacked the crit-ical information when it agreed to settle the case. Id. at 709-710. In Stare v. Tate, 21 Cal. App. 3d 432 (1971), a wife in a divorce pro-ceeding proposed a settlement agreement based on a mistake to her disadvantage in how she valued the property — a mistake that was pointed out by the husband immediately after the settlement agree-ment was finalized. The court upheld the wife's claim for rescission of the settlement. Id. at 440.

# D. SANCTIONS FOR MISREPRESENTATION

## ■ Cresswell v. Sullivan & Cromwell

**668 F. Supp.** 166 (S.D.N.Y. 1987)

JUDGE SWEET delivered the Opinion of the Court. . . .

[Plaintiffs originally brought suit against Prudential Bache in connection with a financial transaction. In preparation for a possible trial, the parties conducted discovery.] In January 1985, plaintiffs in this action entered into agreements with Prudential-Bache which resolved all their claims for approximately $1,600,000. Following execution of those agreements, this court entered a judgment and order dismissing plaintiffs' claims with prejudice on February 1, 1985.

. . . [P]laintiffs now contend that during the pendency of the prior actions, Prudential-Bache and [its attorneys] Sullivan & Cromwell intentionally withheld production of documents which purportedly fell within the ambit of a document request served in December 1983. . . .

The plaintiffs in this case are seeking damages for an alleged fraud committed upon them in the earlier actions, which they contend induced them to settle their claims for less than they otherwise would have been able to obtain. The issue raised on this motion is whether an action such as this is governed by Rule 60(b) of the Federal Rules of Civil Procedure. Rule 60(b) specifies the procedure for obtaining relief from a judgment when fraud or other misconduct has allegedly been committed in connection with obtaining the judgment. Under that Rule:

> The court may relieve a party or his legal representative from a final judgment, order, or proceeding for the following reasons: . . . (3) fraud (whether heretofore denominated intrinsic or extrinsic), misrepresentation, or other misconduct of an adverse party. . . . The motion shall be made within a reasonable time, and . . . not more than one year after the judgment, order, or proceeding was entered or taken. . . . This rule does not limit the power of a court to entertain an independent action to relieve a party from a judgment, order, or proceeding, . . . or to set aside a judgment for fraud upon the court.

The Rule thus sets forth an express mechanism for a party seeking relief from a judgment. If plaintiffs' action fell under Rule 60, plaintiffs would essentially be suing for rescission and presumably would be required to tender back their part of the settlement to return to the status quo and possibly face preclusion from suing for damages. The plaintiffs here, however, are not seeking "relief" from a "judgment" within the terms of Rule 60(b). Instead, they seek to affirm the judgment of settlement, and sue for additional damages caused only by the fraud involving the failure to produce certain documents. Of course, in trying such a case, the merits of the prior actions will be relevant, but the issue will be different: whether the settlement value of the cases would have been higher absent the fraud, and if so, by how much.

Defendants contend that Rule 60(b) is the exclusive remedy for a party claiming to have been defrauded into agreeing to a settlement leading to entry of a judgment or final order in a federal lawsuit. . . .

The proper avenue of redress for a party seeking relief from a judgment claiming fraud as grounds for relief is under Fed. R. Civ. P. 60(b)(3). . . .

. . . [N]othing in the language of Rule 60(b) supports the defendants' contention that it precludes an action for fraud in connection with a settlement. Rule 60(b) denotes instances when a court "may relieve a party . . . from a judgment," but it does not purport to cover damages actions for fraud that seek to affirm or ratify a judgment rather than seek relief from a judgment. Its focus is on a specific remedy — obtaining relief from a judgment — not on all available remedies for fraud.

Neither party disputes that under New York law, a second action for damages rather than for rescission of the judgment or settlement may be brought when a *state court* judgment or settlement is allegedly procured by fraud. . . . This result arises from the common law rule that a defrauded party can elect between rescission on the one hand and ratification and suit for damages on the other. . . .

In Slotkin v. Citizens Casualty Co., 614 F.2d 301 (2d Cir.), *cert. denied*, 449 U.S. 981, 66 L. Ed. 2d 243, 101 S. Ct. 395 (1980), the Second Circuit noted that New York law is "clear that one who has been induced by fraudulent misrepresentation to settle a claim may recover damages without rescinding the settlement." Id. at 312 (citing cases). . . .

If all that will result from a misrepresentation is a new trial, then the party making it has everything to gain and nothing to lose. The plaintiffs would be placed at a disadvantage by a new trial; the defendants would not. If anything, defendants would benefit by having a preview of plaintiffs' case. . . .

According to the defendants, a reasonable reading of Rule 60(b) would limit the plaintiffs to a suit to reopen the judgment to put plaintiffs and defendants back in the position they were in prior to settlement. . . .

If this were the rule, few plaintiffs would choose to enforce their claims of fraud in connection with a settlement, no matter how valid their cause of action. A plaintiff who must give up any benefit he has gained and risk receiving nothing in return will be reluctant to enforce his rights as a victim of fraud. Of course, he may ultimately gain more than he received in settlement the first time, either by going to trial this time around or settling for more, allowing negotiation to set a value on the second alleged instance of fraud. But this chance of receiving more does not justify the deterrent effect of requiring a plaintiff to give up the settlement he received for one claim of fraud to sue for further acts of fraud.                                                      ■

## Notes

*1. Range of Remedies.* Misrepresentation can give rise to both contract and tort causes of action. Under contract law, a negotiator's fraudulent or material misrepresentation that induces his opponent to enter into a transaction makes the resulting transaction voidable by the victimized party. Restatement (Second) of Contracts §164. Effectively, then, contract law provides the remedy of rescission of the transaction. As *Cresswell* describes, the Federal Rules of Civil Procedure provide an equivalent remedy when a misrepresentation of material fact induces a settlement, which, after all, is a particular type of contract. Fed. R. Civ. P. 60. Under tort law, a fraudulent misrepresentation gives rise to an action for damages caused by the reliance on the misrepresentation. Restatement (Second) of Torts §525. When a lawyer makes a fraudulent misrepresentation, he can be held personally liable for damages. See Slotkin v. Citizens Casualty Co., 614 F.2d 301, 314-315 (2d Cir. 1980). In addition to common law remedies, a range of federal and state statutes that prohibit unfair or deceptive acts or practices provide enhanced remedies for different kinds of fraudulent behavior by sellers directed at consumer and business buyers. See, e.g., The Federal Trade Commission Act, 15 U.S.C.A. §45(a)(1) (West 1997); Wis. Stat. §100.18 (2000); Cal. Bus. & Prof. Code §17200 et seq. (West 2000); Haw. Rev. Stat. §480-2 et seq. (2000); 815 Ill. Comp. Stat. §505/1 et seq. (West 2000). For a more detailed discussion of relevant statutes, see G. Richard Shell, Substituting Ethical Standards for Common Law Rules in Commercial Cases: An Emerging Statutory Trend, 82 Nw. U.L. Rev. 1198 (1988).

Lawyers who misrepresent in negotiations are subject to professional discipline as well, although reported cases in which lawyers have been sanctioned on this basis are rare. In one notable example, however, the court upheld a six-month suspension of an attorney who, representing a patient in negotiations with a hospital over the patient's bill, failed to disclose the existence of an insurance company that might have been legally liable for the patient's injuries, although he knew that the hospital was unaware of the insurer or its potential liability. State ex rel. Nebraska State Bar Assn. v. Addison, 412 N.W.2d 855

(Neb. 1987). There are important distinctions between the standards for professional discipline and for tort and contract actions. A lawyer is subject to professional discipline for misrepresentation only if the misrepresentation is "knowing[]." See ABA, Model Rules of Professional Conduct Rule 4.1 (2001); Brown v. Genesee County, 872 F.2d 169 (6th Cir. 1989). On the other hand, while contract and tort suits require actual reliance and damages on the part of the harmed party, such consequences are not required for professional discipline.

*2. Necessity of Intent to Misrepresent.* Even nonintentional misrepresentations can give rise to legal sanctions. The contract remedy of rescission is available for misrepresentations — regardless of scienter — as long as they are material and induce reliance. Tort law distinguishes between fraudulent, negligent, and innocent misrepresentations. See Restatement (Second) of Torts §§526, 552, 552C (1977). Although the extent of damages that are recoverable depends to some degree on scienter, the victim of a misrepresentation can recover at least the damages directly caused by the misrepresentation regardless of the level of scienter. See Restatement (Second) of Torts §§549, 552, 552C (1977).

# E.  MISREPRESENTING THE OBJECTIVE: "BAD FAITH" NEGOTIATION

When parties negotiate, we usually assume that their goal and their desire is to reach an agreement. This is not always the case however. Parties may negotiate with no intention of reaching an agreement in an attempt to delay the other party from taking an undesirable action (i.e., pursuing its BATNA) or to gain information that can later be used to the detriment of the other party. Parties might also negotiate in hopes that the opponent will expend resources in reliance on a potential agreement that will be useful only if an agreement is reached, thus making them vulnerable to exploitation.

Because the norm that negotiators genuinely hope to reach an agreement is so entrenched, it can be said that a negotiator who bargains with no desire at all to reach an agreement implicitly misrepresents his intentions. The law has struggled with the question of whether such behavior can ever be legally actionable conduct. Most often the debate is grounded doctrinally in the question of whether there exists a duty of good faith in precontractual negotiations and, if so, what is the extent of that duty.

■ **Venture Associates Corp. v. Zenith Data Systems Corp.**

96 F.3d 275 (7th Cir. 1996)

CHIEF JUDGE POSNER delivered the Opinion of the Court. . . .

One of the most difficult areas of contract law concerns the enforceability of letters of intent and other preliminary agreements, and in particular the subset of such agreements that consists of agreements to negotiate toward a final contract. See Steven J. Burton & Eric G. Andersen, *Contractual Good Faith: Formation, Performance, Breach, Enforcement* §§8.4-8.5 (1995); 1 E. Allan Farnsworth, *Farnsworth on Contracts* §§3.8a-3.8c, 3.26b-3.26c, pp. 186-207, 328-352 (1990); 1 *Corbin on Contracts* §§2.8-2.9, pp. 131-162 (Joseph M. Perillo ed., rev. ed. 1993). When if ever are such agreements enforceable as contracts? If they are enforceable, how is a breach to be determined? Is "breach" even the right word? Or is the proper rubric "bad faith"? Could the duty of good faith negotiation that a letter of intent creates be a tort duty rather than a contract duty, even though created by a contract? And can the victim of bad faith ever get more than his reliance damages? These questions lurk on or just beneath the surface of the principal appeal, which is from a judgment by the district court, after a bench trial, finding that the defendant had not acted in bad faith and was not liable for any damages to the plaintiff. . . .

The defendant, Zenith Data Systems Corporation (ZDS), owned Heath Company. . . . ZDS hired an investment banker to find someone who would buy Heath at a price, then estimated at $11 million, at which ZDS would lose no more than $6 million on the sale, the loss being calculated with reference to the net asset value shown for Heath on the books of ZDS. One of the prospects that the investment banker found was the plaintiff, Venture Associates Corporation. Apparently the investment banker did not conduct a credit check of Venture. Instead he relied on a representation by Venture that its most recent acquisitions had been of companies with revenues of $55 and $97 million.

On May 31, 1991, Venture sent a letter to the investment banker, for forwarding to ZDS, proposing to form a new company to acquire Heath for $5 million in cash, a $4 million promissory note, and $2 million in preferred stock of the new company — a total of $11 million, the price ZDS was seeking. The letter stated that it was "merely a letter of intent subject to the execution by Seller and Buyer of a definitive Purchase Agreement (except for the following paragraph of this letter, which shall be binding . . . ) [and] does not constitute a binding obligation on either of us." The following paragraph stated that "this letter is intended to evidence the preliminary understandings which we have reached regarding the proposed transaction and our mutual intent to negotiate in good faith to enter into a definitive Purchase Agreement, and [ZDS] hereby agrees that, pending execution of a definitive Purchase Agreement and as long as the parties thereto continue to negotiate in good faith," ZDS shall not "solicit, entertain, or encourage" other offers for Heath or "engage in any transaction not in the ordinary course of business which adversely affects" Heath's value.

The letter invited ZDS to sign it. ZDS refused, but did write Venture on June 11 stating that "we are willing to begin negotiations with Venture Associates for the acquisition of the Heath Business based in principle on the terms and conditions outlined in" Venture's May 31 letter. The next day, Venture wrote ZDS accepting the proposal in the June 11 letter.

Let us pause here and ask what if any enforceable obligations were created by this correspondence. The use of the words "in principle" showed that ZDS had *not* agreed to any of the terms in Venture's offer. . . .

. . . [I]nterpreting Illinois law, we have held that agreements to negotiate toward the formation of a contract are themselves enforceable as contracts if the parties intended to be legally bound. . . .

. . . The process of negotiating multimillion dollar transactions, like the performance of a complex commercial contract, often is costly and time-consuming. The parties may want assurance that their investments in time and money and effort will not be wiped out by the other party's footdragging or change of heart or taking advantage of a vulnerable position created by the negotiation. Feldman v. Allegheny Int'l, Inc., 850 F.2d 1217, 1221 (7th Cir. 1988); Runnemede Owners, Inc. v. Crest Mortgage Corp., 861 F.2d 1053, 1056 (7th Cir. 1988). Suppose the prospective buyer spends $100,000 on research, planning, and consultants during the negotiation, money that will have bought nothing of value if the negotiation falls through, while the seller has spent nothing and at the end of the negotiation demands an extra $50,000, threatening to cancel the deal unless the buyer consents. This would be an extortionate demand, and, as it is profoundly unclear whether it would be independently tortious, E. Allan Farnsworth, "Precontractual Liability and Preliminary Agreements: Fair Dealing and Failed Negotiations," 87 Colum. L. Rev. 217, 221-22 (1987), parties to a negotiation would want a contractual remedy. But they might prefer to create one in the form of a deposit or drop fee (what in publishing is called a "kill fee"), rather than rely on a vague duty to bargain in good faith. That is one reason why the notion of a legally enforceable duty to negotiate in good faith toward the formation of a contract rests on somewhat shaky foundations, though some contracts do create such a duty, see, e.g., PSI Energy, Inc. v. Exxon Coal USA, Inc., 17 F.3d 969, 972 (7th Cir. 1994), which shows that some business people want it. Anyway we have crossed these bridges, for the time being anyway. . . .

After Venture's confirmatory letter of June 12, the parties negotiated for six months. At the end of that time, with no sale contract signed, ZDS broke off the negotiations on the ground that Venture was refusing to furnish third-party guaranties of its post-closing financial obligations (namely to pay the $4 million promissory note and to honor the terms of the preferred stock) and agree to certain post-closing price adjustments. . . .

Venture argues that since the letter of intent — its May 31 letter, which ZDS accepted in principle — made no reference to third-party guaranties or contract-price adjustments, ZDS exhibited bad faith by insisting on these terms to the point of impasse. This argument overlooks the difference between an agreement to negotiate a contract and the contract to be thrashed out in those negotiations. The agreement to negotiate does not contain the terms of the final agreement. Otherwise it would *be* the final agreement. A preliminary agreement might contain closed terms (terms as to which a final agreement had been reached) as well as open terms, and thus be preliminary solely by virtue of having some open terms. 1 Farnsworth, *supra*, §3.8a, pp. 187-88. The parties would be bound by the closed terms. There were no such terms here.

Venture has another argument — that ZDS decided to pull out after the negotiations began because Heath's fortunes began to improve, and to this end imposed new conditions that it knew Venture would not accept. There is a fair amount of evidence that Heath's fortunes were improving, but only a bit of evidence, which the district judge was entitled to find outweighed by contrary evidence, that this improvement made ZDS reconsider its decision to sell the company. Since ZDS had not agreed on the sale price, it remained free to demand a higher price in order to reflect the market value of the company at the time of actual sale. Feldman v. Allegheny Int'l, Inc., supra, 850 F.2d at 1223. Self-interest is not bad faith. *Id.* Not having locked itself into the $11 million price, ZDS was free to demand as high a price as it thought the market would bear, provided that it was not trying to scuttle the deal, Chase v. Consolidated Foods Corp., 744 F.2d 566, 571 (7th Cir. 1984), or to take advantage of costs sunk by Venture in the negotiating process. The qualification is vital. If the market value of Heath rose, say, to $25 million, ZDS would not be acting in bad faith to demand that amount from Venture even if it knew that Venture would not go so high. ZDS would be acting in bad faith only if its purpose in charging more than Venture would pay was to induce Venture to back out of the deal. The analogy to constructive discharge in employment law, or, for theology buffs, the Catholic doctrine of double effect, should be apparent.   ■

# Notes

*1. Duty of Good Faith in Negotiation.*   Although the Uniform Commercial Code creates a duty of good faith in the performance of contracts, there is no general duty of good faith in the conduct of precontractual negotiations. Historically, negotiators could not even opt to be governed by a good faith requirement, on the ground that an agreement to negotiate in good faith would be too indefinite for enforcement. See G. Richard Shell, Opportunism and Trust in the Negotiation of Commercial Contracts: Toward a New Cause of Action, 44 Vand. L. Rev. 221, 243 (1991). Modern courts, however, have ruled that negotiators may contract for such an obligation. This can be done by formally and explicitly contracting for a good faith requirement, see PSI Energy Inc. v. Exxon Corp., 17 F.3d 969 (7th Cir. 1994), or, as *Venture Associates* demonstrates, through actions by both parties that imply such an agreement. See also Channel Home Centers v. Grossman, 795 F.2d 291 (3d Cir. 1986) (finding an implied contract to negotiate in good faith when parties agreed to a letter of intent to lease a commercial property).

*2. Scope of the Duty.*   When parties agree to negotiate in good faith, the scope of that obligation is determined by the parties' expectations, see, e.g., A/S Apothekernes Laboratorium for Specialpraeparater v. I.M.C. Chemical Group, Inc., 873 F.2d 155, 159 (7th Cir. 1989), making it difficult to describe the substantive parameters of the obligation. The task is made more difficult by the fact that, as a practical matter, violations of a contractually created duty to negotiate in good faith are rarely found by courts. A few general parameters can be inferred, however, from judicial decisions. A party does not breach the duty to negotiate in good faith by walking away from the negotiation table, negotiating in a completely self-interested manner, or holding steadfast on any particular term. See, e.g., id.; Feldman v. Allegheny International, 850 F.2d 1217, 1221 (7th Cir. 1988); PSI Energy, Inc., v. Exxon Coal USA, 17 F.3d 969, 973-975 (7th Cir. 1994). A party risks violating the duty, however, by opportunistically insisting on provisions contrary to those included in a preliminary agreement, see, e.g., A/S Apothekernes Laboratorium for Specialpraeparater, 873 F.2d at 158, or by negotiating with the purpose of delay rather than reaching an agreement. See, e.g., MCI Communications v. AT&T, 708 F.2d 1081, 1159 (7th Cir. 1982).

*3. Promissory Estoppel.*   Even without an agreement to negotiate in good faith, negotiators are protected from some opportunistic behavior by the doctrine of promissory estoppel. The promissory estoppel doctrine has been used to hold a negotiator liable for failing to fulfill a promise made during precontractual negotiations that is justifiably relied upon by the other party. The leading case is Hoffman v. Red Owl Stores, Inc., 133 N.W.2d 267 (Wis. 1965). Hoffman and Red Owl were engaged in ongoing negotiations over Hoffman operating a Red Owl grocery store franchise. Red Owl assured Hoffman that a franchise could be obtained for $18,000. On Red Owl's advice, Hoffman took a number of steps to prepare himself to operate a Red Owl store, such as selling his bakery and buying and operating a small grocery store for the experience. Eventually, Red Owl informed Hoffman that significantly more money than $18,000 would be necessary to obtain a franchise. Hoffman sued, and the Wisconsin Supreme Court ruled in his behalf, concluding that "injustice would result here if plaintiffs were not granted some relief because of the failure of defendants to keep their promises which induced plaintiffs to act to their detriment." Id. at 274-275.

*4. Quasi-Contract.*   If a negotiator convinces his opponent to perform a portion of what the opponent's duties would be under a contract before the contract is formed, the negotiator can be held liable for the value of the services rendered under the doctrine of quasi-contract. In Earhart v. William Low Co., 600 P.2d 1344 (Cal. 1979), a landowner and a contractor agreed that, subject to the landowner receiving financing, the contractor would build a trailer park. Before financing was obtained, the contractor began clearing the land at the landowner's request. When the financing fell through and the contract never finalized, the California Supreme Court found the landowner liable for the work performed by the contractor. Id. at 1348.

*5. Statutory Duties of Good Faith.*   Although a legal requirement that parties negotiate in good faith usually exists only if the parties contract for such a duty, some statutes impose a duty of good faith negotiation in particular situations. A prime example is the National Labor Relations Act (NLRA), which requires good faith negotiation of collective bargaining agreements. 29 U.S.C. §158(d) (parties must "meet at reasonable times and confer in good faith with respect to wages, hours, and other terms and conditions of employment, or the negotiation of an agreement . . ."). While the NLRA does not require negotiators to concede terms or conditions of employment, the good faith requirement imposes an obligation on the parties to continue to negotiate until an agreement is reached. See N. Peter Lareau, 2 National Labor Relations Act: Law and Practice §12.01[1] (2d ed. 2000); 29 U.S.C.A. §158(d).

The substantive requirements of "good faith" remain illusive in this context. "The test is whether the 'totality of the employer's conduct . . . manifests a mindset at odds with reaching an agreement.' " (Leroy S. Merrifield et al., Labor Relations Law 579 (9th ed., 1994) (quoting Bethea Baptist Home, 310 N.L.R.B. No. 28 (1993)). Hard bargaining by itself is not unlawful, see, e.g., Dierks Forests Inc., 148 N.L.R.B. 923 (1964), and at some point in the bargaining an employer may make a firm and final offer. Merrifield, supra, at 579. But the parties must negotiate with "an open and fair mind and sincerely endeavor to overcome obstacles or difficulties existing between the employer and the employees.... [M]ere pretend bargaining will not suffice, neither must the mind be hermetically sealed against the thought of entering into an agreement." Lareau, supra, §12.01[1].

# F.   THE ETHICS OF MISREPRESENTATION

The preceding sections of this chapter describe the legal consequences of engaging in misrepresentation and related behavior in the negotiation context. What is legal and what is ethical, however, are not necessarily the same, and professionals who engage in negotiation should not engage in conduct that they personally believe is inappropriate, even if such conduct is not proscribed by the law. The following four excerpts offer perspectives on the ethical implications of misrepresentation in negotiation. As you read them, consider what differences in values and assumptions underlie the authors' differing evaluations of the act of misrepresentation, and try to determine which of the four, if any, are most consistent with your personal view of ethical negotiating behavior.

■ **James J. White, Machiavelli and the Bar: Ethical Limitations on Lying in Negotiation***
**1980 Am. B. Found. Res. J.** 926-930

. . .

. . . Like the poker player, a negotiator hopes that his opponent will overestimate the value of his hand. Like the poker player, in a variety of ways he must facilitate his opponent's inaccurate assessment. The critical difference between those who are successful negotiators and those who are not lies in this capacity both to mislead and not to be misled.

Some experienced negotiators will deny the accuracy of this assertion, but they will be wrong. I submit that a careful examination of the behavior of even the most forthright, honest, and trustworthy negotiators will show them actively engaged in misleading their opponents about their true positions. That is true of both the plaintiff and the defendant in a lawsuit. It is true of both labor and management in a collective bargaining agreement. It is true as well of both the buyer and the seller in a wide variety of sales transactions. To conceal one's true position, to mislead an opponent about one's true settling point, is the essence of negotiation. . . .

Pious and generalized assertions that the negotiator must be "honest" or that the lawyer must use "candor" are not helpful. They are at too high a level of generality, and they fail to appreciate the fact that truth and truthful behavior at one time in one set of circumstances with one set of negotiators may be untruthful in another circumstance with other negotiators.

The definition of truth is in part a function of the substance of the negotiation. Because of the policies that lie behind the securities and exchange laws and the demands that Congress has made that information be provided to those who buy and sell, one suspects that lawyers engaged in SEC work have a higher standard of truthfulness than do those whose agreements and negotiations will not affect public buying and selling of assets. Conversely, where the thing to be bought and sold is in fact a lawsuit in which two professional traders conclude the deal, truth means something else. Here truth and candor call for a smaller amount of disclosure, permit greater distortion, and allow the other professional to suffer from his own ignorance and sloth in a way that would not be acceptable in the SEC case. . . .

Apart from the kinds of differences in truthfulness and candor which arise from the subject matter of the negotiation, one suspects that there are other differences attributable to regional and ethnic differences among negotiators. Although I have only anecdotal data to support this idea, it seems plausible that one's expectation concerning truth and candor might be different in a small, homogeneous community from what it would be in a large, heterogeneous community of lawyers. For one thing, all of the lawyers in the small and homogeneous community will share a common ethnic and environmental background. Each will have been subjected to the same kind of training about what kinds of lies are appropriate and what are not appropriate. ∎

## ∎ Charles B. Craver, Negotiation Ethics: How to Be Deceptive Without Being Dishonest/How to Be Assertive Without Being Offensive*

### 38 S. Tex. L. Rev. 713, 714-718, 724-728 (1997)

Most attorneys feel some degree of professional discomfort when they negotiate with other lawyers. If they hope to achieve beneficial

*Copyright © 1997 South Texas Law Review, Inc. Reprinted with permission.

results for their clients, they must convince their opponents that those parties must offer more generous terms than they must actually offer if agreements are to be generated. To accomplish this objective, lawyers usually employ some deceptive tactics. Take for example two parties bargaining over the purchase/sale of a small business. The Seller is willing to accept $500,000, while the Buyer is willing to pay $575,000. The Seller's attorney initially indicates that the Seller must obtain $600,000, with the Buyer's lawyer suggesting that the Buyer cannot go above $450,000. Once these preliminary offers have been exchanged, the parties are pleased with the successful way in which they have begun their discussions. Yet both have begun with position statements designed to mislead the other side. Have they behaved unethically? Are they obliged to disclose their true bargaining needs and intentions to preserve their professional reputations? May they never reject offers they know their clients will accept? . . .

I frequently surprise law students and practitioners by telling them that while I have rarely participated in legal negotiations in which both participants did not use some misstatements to further client interests, I have encountered few dishonest lawyers. I suggest that the fundamental question is not whether legal negotiators may use misrepresentations to further client interests, but when and about what they may permissibly dissemble. Many negotiators initially find it difficult to accept the notion that disingenuous "puffing" and deliberate mendacity do not always constitute reprehensible conduct. . . .

Did the Buyer and Seller representatives mentioned above commit ethical violations when they disingenuously said that the Seller had to obtain $600,000 — while willing to accept $500,000 — and that the Buyer could not go above $450,000 — while willing to pay $575,000? Some lawyers attempt to circumvent this moral dilemma by formulating opening positions that do not directly misstate their actual intentions. For example, the Buyer may indicate that he or she "doesn't wish to pay more than $450,000" or the Seller may say that he or she "would not be inclined to accept less than $600,000." While these preliminary statements may be technically true, the italicized verbal leaks ("wish to" or "inclined to") would inform attentive opponents that these speakers do not really mean what they appear to be communicating. The Seller does not care whether the Buyer wishes to pay more than $450,000, but only whether he or she will do so, just as the Buyer does not care whether the Seller is inclined to accept less than $600,000. If these were true limitations, the speakers would be likely to use more definitive language containing no undermining modifiers, such as "I cannot go above or below X." As a result of these speaker efforts to maintain their personal integrity, careful listeners should easily discern the disingenuous nature of the statements being made by them. The use of these devices to "truthfully" deceive opponents would thus be unavailing. . . .

Although the ABA Model Rules unambiguously proscribe all lawyer prevarication, they reasonably, but confusingly, exclude mere "puffing" and dissembling regarding one's true minimum objectives. These important exceptions appropriately recognize that disingenuous behavior is indigenous to most legal negotiations and could not realistically be prevented due to the nonpublic nature of bargaining interactions. . . .

When I discuss negotiating ethics with legal practitioners, I often ask if lawyers are obliged to disclose information to correct erroneous factual or legal assumptions made by opposing counsel. Most respondents perceive no duty to correct legal or factual misunderstandings generated solely by the carelessness of opposing attorneys. Respondents only hesitate when opponent misperceptions may have resulted from misinterpretations of seemingly honest statements made by them. For example, when a plaintiff attorney embellishes the pain being experienced by a client with a severely sprained ankle, the defense lawyer may indicate how painful broken ankles can be. If the plaintiff representative has said nothing to create this false impression, should he or she be obliged to correct the obvious defense counsel error? Although a respectable minority of respondents believe that an affirmative duty to correct the misperception may exist here — due to the fact plaintiff embellishments may have inadvertently contributed to the misunderstanding — most respondents feel no such obligation. So long as they have not directly generated the erroneous belief, it is not their duty to correct it. They could not, however, include their opponent's misunderstanding in their own statements, since this would cause them to improperly articulate knowing misrepresentations of material fact.

When opponent misperceptions concern legal doctrines, almost no respondents perceive a duty to correct those misconceptions. They indicate that each side is obliged to conduct its own legal research. If opposing counsel make incorrect assumptions or carelessly fail to locate applicable statutes or cases, those advocates do not have the right to expect their adversaries to provide them with legal assistance. The more knowledgeable advocates may even continue to rely on precedents supporting their own claims, so long as they do not distort those decisions or the opinions supporting the other side's positions. . . .

When lawyers are asked if negotiators may overtly misrepresent legal or factual matters, most immediately reply in the negative. Many lawyers cite Model Rule 4.1 and suggest that this prohibition covers all intentional misrepresentations. While attorneys are correct with respect to deliberate misstatements by negotiators concerning material legal doctrines, they are not entirely correct with respect to factual issues. Almost all negotiators expect opponents to engage in "puffing" and "embellishment." Advocates who hope to obtain $50,000 settlements may initially insist upon $150,000 or even $200,000. They may also embellish the pain experienced by their client, so long as their exaggerations do not transcend the bounds of expected propriety. Individuals involved in a corporate buy out may initially over- or under-value the real property, the building and equipment, the inventory, the accounts receivable, the patent rights and trademarks, and the goodwill of the pertinent firm. . . .

A frequently debated area concerns representations about one's authorized limits. Many attorneys refuse to answer "unfair" questions concerning their authorized limits because these inquiries pertain to confidential attorney-client communications. If negotiators decide to respond to these queries, must they do so honestly? Some lawyers believe that truthful responses are required, since they concern material facts. Other practitioners assert that responses about client authorizations merely reflect client valuations and settlement intentions and are thus excluded from the scope of Rule 4.1 by the drafter's Comment. For this reason, these practitioners think that attorneys may distort these matters.

Negotiators who know they cannot avoid the impact of questions concerning their authorized limits by labeling them "unfair" and who find it difficult to provide knowingly false responses can employ an alternative approach. If the plaintiff lawyer who is demanding $120,000 asks the defendant attorney who is presently offering $85,000 whether he or she is authorized to provide $100,000, the recipient may treat the $100,000 figure as a new plaintiff proposal. That individual can reply that the $100,000 sum suggested by plaintiff counsel is more realistic but still exorbitant. The plaintiff attorney may become preoccupied with the need to clarify the fact that he or she did not intend to suggest any reduction in his or her outstanding $120,000 demand. That person would probably forego further attempts to ascertain the authorized limits possessed by the defendant attorney!                ■

## ■ Gerald B. Wetlaufer, The Ethics of Lying in Negotiations

**75 Iowa L. Rev.** 1219, 1272-1273 (1990)*

Effectiveness in negotiations is central to the business of lawyering and a willingness to lie is central to one's effectiveness in negotiations. Within a wide range of circumstances, well-told lies are highly effective. Moreover, the temptation to lie is great not just because lies are effective, but also because the world in which most of us live is one that honors instrumental effectiveness above all other things. Most lawyers are paid not for their virtues but for the results they produce. Our

*Gerald B. Wetlaufer, The Ethics of Lying in Negotiations, 75 Iowa L. Rev. 1219, 1272-1273 (1990) (reprinted with permission).

clients, our partners and employees, and our families are all counting on us to deliver the goods. Accordingly, and regrettably, lying is not the province of a few "unethical lawyers" who operate on the margins of the profession. It is a permanent feature of advocacy and thus of almost the entire province of law.

Our discomfort with that fact has, I believe, led us to create and embrace a discourse on the ethics of lying that is uncritical, self-justificatory and largely unpersuasive. Our motives in this seem reasonably clear. Put simply, we seek the best of both worlds. On the one hand, we would capture as much of the available surplus as we can. In doing so, we enrich our clients and ourselves. Further, we gain for ourselves a reputation for personal power and instrumental effectiveness. And we earn the right to say we can never be conned. At the same time, on the other hand, we assert our claims to a reputation for integrity and personal virtue, to the high status of a profession, and to the legitimacy of the system within which we live and work. Even Gorgias, for all his powers of rhetoric, could not convincingly assert both of these claims. Nor can we.

Somehow we must stop kidding ourselves about these matters. We must grant a place to ethics, first in our discourse and then in our actions. There are, I think, several concrete steps that might be taken. First, we might acknowledge that we have a personal stake in the existing discourse concerning the relationship between effectiveness and ethics. As a result of that personal stake, we have shown a strong disposition in favor not just of self-justification but also of the conclusion that there are no hard choices to be made, no price to be paid in the name of ethics. Second, we might admit that, in a wide range of circumstances, lying works. Third, we might become more critical of our self-serving claims about what is not a lie and about what lies are ethically permissible. This involves acknowledging, for instance, that many lies are ethically impermissible even though they effectively serve our interests and those of our clients — and even though they are not forbidden either by law or by our codes of professional self-regulation. It also involves giving up our claim that all our lies are justified by the rules of the game or by our duties to our clients. It entails accepting the proposition that ethics and integrity are things for which a price may have to be paid. Fourth, we might clearly define winning in a way that leaves room for ethics. It might, for instance, be understood not as "getting as much as we can" but as "winning as much as possible without engaging in unacceptable behavior" and "unacceptable behavior" might then be understood to exclude not just those things that are stupid or illegal but also those other things that are unethical. And finally, we might give up our claim that this is all too hard, that we have no choice in these matters and that we are not responsible for the choices we make and the harm we inflict upon others. . . .  ■

## ■ Reed Elizabeth Loder, Moral Truthseeking and the Virtuous Negotiator*

8 Geo. J. Legal Ethics 45, 69-76 (1994)

Statements believed false, made with intent to deceive, may be prevalent in negotiation. A clear instance of a lie follows. A lawyer negotiating a possible purchase of the client's business property states false factual information to the lawyer-opponent about the positive financial condition of the client's business, where the lawyer speaking knows the information is false and pivotal to a purchase and sale contract. The intent to deceive here serves the primary intent to extract more money from the prospective purchaser. . . .

What of a more controversial case of deception through words that hits closer to home? A favorite in the literature is an example like the following. A lawyer confers with a client prior to a negotiation session. The client-plaintiff tells the lawyer she will accept $15,000 to settle her civil property damage suit. During bargaining, the opponent's lawyer offers $17,000 in settlement. Believing a still higher figure is possible, the plaintiff's lawyer responds, "My client will not accept less than $20,000."

A favorite strategy of commentators is to deny that this statement is a lie at all, i.e., a statement, believed false, made with intent to deceive. Several arguments underlie this strategy. None is satisfactory. One argument is that the plaintiff's lawyer has no intent to deceive, thus not satisfying part of the definition of deception. The opponent's lawyer does not expect this type of statement to be truthful, and the lawyer making the statement knows that the other lawyer will not believe him. That lawyer does not intend to deceive the listener, and an essential ingredient of lying is lacking, the argument concludes.

This argument on intent is fallacious. It confuses overall intent to deceive with the likelihood of success at deception in a particular case. Indeed, the defendant's lawyer may be savvy and well aware that lawyers often misstate their clients' bottom lines (or upper limits). The opponent, therefore, may not believe this particular statement, or even the next. At some point, however, the opponent has to make some assessment about the other lawyer's actual bottom line authority. The particular statements, although not literally believed, confuse the opponent about that settlement threshold. Indeed, the very point of the bottom line statement is to instill such confusion. Otherwise the statement has no apparent function. Thus the overall intent to deceive is present, although the attorney realizes that success at a particular deception may be harder to achieve in this setting. . . .

Another telling obstacle to justifying this conduct may be that non-deceptive alternatives are readily available. Indeed, alternatives to making assertions about specific settlement authority seem preferable from a strategic as well as an ethical perspective. If the point is to persuade the opponent that an offer is too low, a well supported opinion about a minimum fair figure may go as far or farther than an assertion about bottom line. Instead of saying, "my client won't accept less than $20,000," the lawyer might have said, "I would advise my client that the case justifies $20,000," or simply, "the case appears worth $20,000," followed by reasons supporting those high-end assessments. These statements reflect the lawyer's considered opinion and are truthful even if they are at the upper end of the lawyer's actual estimations of a reasonable settlement range. The statements are not damaging because the opponent can present counter-arguments supporting a chiseled-down settlement figure.

These statements do convey some important information about the client's willingness to settle for a certain amount, because the opponent understands that the lawyer's opinion of a case's worth generally influences the client's expectations. The lawyer is not saying untruthfully that she or the client will refuse to consider lower proposals. Rather, she is challenging the opponent to support such proposals with reasons not adequately considered or weighed in the thinking she already has presented. Thus her statements about case-worth can pave the way for a mutually beneficial and truthful exchange about the support for various bargaining positions. This openness to exchange is not an admission of weakness but a mutual recognition that most good legal decisions are not fixed stars, but involve justified selections from a limited array of possibilities. . . .                                    ■

## DISCUSSION QUESTIONS AND PROBLEMS

*1. Problems.* Consider whether the following statements (or lack thereof) constitute actionable misrepresentations. If there is an actionable misrepresentation, consider whether the speaker could adjust the content of the statement to avoid the legal or ethical problem.

(a) Lawyer, representing Owner in the sale of a 50-year-old house, tells Buyer that "this house is in top condition," knowing that the chimney needs repairs and that cracks are beginning to form in the plaster in some portions of the walls. What if Lawyer instead says, "you won't find a nice older house like this in better condition for this low of a price," knowing that there is a very similar house down the street in better condition being offered for a lower price.

(b) Lawyer, representing Defendant in a lawsuit, tells the opposing lawyer "my client refuses to pay a penny over $40,000 to settle this lawsuit," after having had a conversation with Defendant in which Defendant told Lawyer that she would be willing to pay as much as $50,000 to settle.

(c) Lawyer, representing Plaintiff, who has been slightly injured in an automobile accident, tells the opposing lawyer "if we cannot agree on a reasonable settlement this month, I will file a lawsuit against your client," knowing that Plaintiff has decided that he does not wish to go to the financial and emotional expense of initiating a lawsuit should negotiations fail.

(d) Lawyer, representing Plaintiff, who has been involved in an automobile accident, tells the opposing lawyer that Plaintiff has seen a number of medical specialists since the accident and "will definitely need surgery," knowing that Plaintiff is experiencing no pain and has been given a clean bill of health by the specialist. Would it matter if Lawyer instead says that Plaintiff "may need to have surgery"?

(e) After being given a clean bill of health by the specialist, Plaintiff tells opposing counsel that he will require back surgery for the injuries suffered in the collision. Opposing counsel offers a $20,000 settlement to Plaintiff's attorney, Lawyer, stating "this amount seems fair given the strong possibility that Plaintiff will require surgery." Lawyer knows about the specialist's diagnosis and the statement Plaintiff made to the opposing lawyer but accepts the settlement offer without disclosing the true facts.

(f) Lawyer, representing Defendant in an employment discrimination case, tells the opposing lawyer, "I have thoroughly researched the case law and I believe your client has, at best, a 10 percent chance of surviving a summary judgment motion." In fact, Lawyer has concluded that the odds of his client prevailing in such a motion are approximately 50/50.

(g) Lawyer, a solo practitioner with a small office and library, representing Defendant in an employment discrimination case, tells the opposing lawyer, who works at a large downtown law firm with vast resources, "I have thoroughly researched the law in our jurisdiction, and there are no reported cases that support your position." Lawyer knows that, while most of the reported cases support Defendant's position, one case in the jurisdiction clearly supports Plaintiff's position. Would it change your analysis if Lawyer worked at a large downtown law firm and the opposing lawyer were a solo practitioner?

(h) Lawyer represents a corporate raider who wishes to acquire Company Q from Owner and, unbeknownst to Owner, plans to immediately sell off Q's assets. Lawyer tells Owner that it is critical that part of the deal be that Owner agrees to work for Q for one year after the sale to help the new management transition into the company.

Lawyer knows that his client has no interest in Owner's services, and he makes this demand only so he can later "give it up" in return for a price concession.

2. *BATNAs and Reservation Prices.*   Is it sensible for the law to treat lies about the existences of alternative buyers and sellers (effectively, lies about BATNAs) differently than lies about reservation prices? Consider whether the arguments presented by Professor Strudler in Section B, Note 3 concerning why the law should not prohibit lies about reservation prices apply equally well to lies about BATNAs.

3. *Law and Ethics.*   Should some negotiator misrepresentations be legally actionable, or would the law do better to establish a clear rule of "caveat emptor" — thus putting negotiators on notice that they could not rely on the veracity of any statements made by their opponents — and leave questions about the propriety of lying to the realm of ethics?

4. *Should Buyers and Sellers Be Treated Differently?*   The Roman philosopher Cicero told the story of a merchant from Alexandria who brought corn to Rhodes when Rhodes was suffering from famine. The merchant knew, and the Rhodesians did not, that other merchants were on their way with large quantities of grains. See Michael H. Rubin, The Ethics of Negotiation: Are There Any?, 56 La. L. Rev. 447 (1995). Should the merchant have revealed this information in the course of bargaining over the corn?

In Laidlaw v. Organ, 15 U.S. (2 Wheat.) 178 (1817), Organ learned that the Treaty of Ghent had been signed, ending the war of 1812 and accordingly the British blockade of American ports, which would no doubt cause the price of tobacco in New Orleans to rise. Before news of the treaty became widely known, Organ negotiated an agreement to buy tobacco from Laidlaw for a relatively low price. Prior to consummating the deal, Laidlaw asked Organ if the latter had any information relevant to the tobacco's value, to which Organ said nothing. Should Organ have told Laidlaw about the peace treaty? Were his ethical duties any different than the Alexandrian corn merchant?

5. *Ethical Principles.*   What accounts for the different positions taken by White and Craver on one hand and Wetlaufer and Roder on the other concerning the ethics of lying in negotiations? Who has the most sound view of the ethics of lying? What is your view of the issue, and how does it differ from those of the authors?

6. *The Difference Between Law and Ethics.*   Does ethics require more of negotiators than does the law, or do legal requirements mirror ethical requirements? Should law and ethics merge, or is there a justification for holding negotiators to lower standards (or higher standards) under the law than ethics requires?

**7. *Lying Versus Subtle Attempts at Deception.*** Consider two potential automobile purchasers bargaining with an automobile dealer over a car that has a sticker price of $10,000, both of whom have a reservation price of $9,000. Buyer 1 tells the dealer: "I like the car, but I am unwilling to pay more than $7,000 for it." When the dealer offers to reduce the price to $9,000, buyer 1 responds: "I can't possibly afford to pay any more than $8,000." Buyer 2 tells the dealer: "I like the car. I'll give you $7,000 for it." When the dealer offers to reduce the price to $9,000, Buyer 2 responds: "That's more than I want to pay. I'll give you $8,000."

Geoffrey Peters argues that the buyer's strategies are equally deceptive, because the intent of both is to falsely convince the dealer that their reservation prices are lower than they actually are. Peters claims that the two approaches should be viewed as equally objectionable or unobjectionable, although under the dominant social conventions the lies told by Buyer 1 are considered more objectionable than the technically true statements made by Buyer 2. Geoffrey Peters, The Use of Lies in Negotiation, 48 Ohio St. L.J. 1, 26-29 (1987). Do you agree with Peters, or do you think there is an ethical difference between the two approaches?

**8. *Fair Warning of Deception.*** Suppose that two sophisticated parties signed the following agreement before entering into negotiations over a proposed transaction:

> Both parties and their lawyers understand that in negotiation either side may tell lies about a wide range of facts or opinions in an effort to gain a strategic advantage. Both parties agree that such behavior is an expected part of the process, and that each party assumes the risk that the other will lie or mislead him or her during negotiations. Neither lawyer will be subject to professional discipline as a result of the lack of veracity of statements made during negotiations, and, to the extent permitted by law, no statement made during negotiations will serve as a basis to void or rescind any agreement subsequently reached between the parties.

Would this agreement eliminate ethical concerns over subsequent lies the negotiators might tell each other? If the signatories are lawyers, would signing such an agreement protect them from subsequent charges that they violated the rules of professional ethics?

**9. *What Did Venture Associates Gain?*** In *Venture Associates*, supra, the court held that Zenith was free to demand from Venture Associates a higher price than it initially sought notwithstanding its agreement to negotiate in good faith. Given this holding, what did Venture Associates actually gain by forming an agreement to negotiate in good faith? Did the preliminary agreement limit Zenith's strategic alternatives in the subsequent negotiations at all?

*10. Protecting Your Clients from Opportunism.* In what type of negotiating situations would you find a preliminary agreement to negotiate in good faith valuable to a client? What are the general characteristics of these situations that would make such an agreement valuable? How would you propose drafting such a preliminary agreement that would protect your client but would be acceptable to the opposing party?

*11. What Did Red Owl Do Wrong?* Even when parties contract to negotiate in good faith, courts generally find that they are not required to accept any particular terms. Given this, why did the court in Hoffman v. Red Owl Stores — a case in which there was not even a preliminary agreement to negotiate in good faith — find that Hoffman had a right to rely on the amount of investment Red Owl initially stated would be sufficient? If the parties had never reached an agreement because they failed to agree on a location for Hoffman's Red Owl franchise, would Hoffman have had a cause of action? If not, what is it about the particular term at issue in the case — the amount of initial investment — that caused the court to rule that Red Owl could not seek to modify that term?

# Chapter 14

# Rules Encouraging Litigation Settlement

As mentioned earlier, the vast majority of disputes that result in lawsuits are settled out of court rather than through formal adjudication. On one level it is easy to explain why most lawsuits settle: there is usually a bargaining zone between the litigants' reservation prices in which settlement can make both better off ex ante than they would be if they invoked formal adjudication. The dominant reasons for this are obvious. The costs, uncertainty, and delay associated with litigation usually cause plaintiffs to set their reservation prices below and defendants their reservation prices above the parties' estimates of the expected value of a court-determined outcome.

There is something more to the explanation of litigation settlement, however, than this story about private incentives of the litigants suggests. Legal rules can, and in some cases do, promote settlement by making out-of-court agreement more desirable to one or both negotiating parties than it otherwise might be. This chapter investigates three types of procedural rules that facilitate the litigation negotiation process: rules that shift the burden of legal fees and court costs to the losing party, rules that permit judges to require litigants to participate in settlement conferences and other nonadjudicatory dispute resolution procedures, and rules that limit the admissibility of evidence of settlement negotiations at subsequent trials.

## A.  FEE SHIFTING AND "OFFER OF SETTLEMENT" RULES

The rules by which the legal system allocates litigation costs can affect the reservation prices of parties to settlement negotiations, and thus indirectly affect the likelihood that disputes will settle out of court. In the United States, subject to some particular statutory exceptions, each litigant bears his own legal fees, regardless of the litigation outcome. This is known as the "American rule." An alternative rule under which the losing party must pay the legal fees of the prevailing party — often known as the "English rule" due to its use in Great Britain and much of Europe — could affect the likelihood of settlement.

The "loser pays" approach of the English rule can create an unintentional distributive benefit for defendants when the litigants' dispute concerns damages rather than liability. Assume, for example, that a plaintiff seeks $1 million in damages and the defendant admits liability but believes he owes the plaintiff only $10,000. Under a strict application of the "loser pays" approach, a $10,000 jury verdict for the plaintiff would seem to require the defendant to pay the plaintiff's legal fees, although it would appear unreasonable to call the defendant the "loser" in such a case. Arguably, the consequence of such an application of the English rule would be that plaintiffs would have very little incentive to settle cases in which damages are low but liability is clear unless a defendant offered a settlement vastly larger than the expected value of trial. Put another way, the English rule would seem to shift both the plaintiff's and the defendant's reservation prices higher than they would be under the American rule, giving defendants a relative power advantage.

One way to implement the "loser pays" concept without redistributing bargaining leverage from defendants to plaintiffs would be to determine which party "prevails" in court on the basis of whether the judgment for the plaintiff, if any, is more or less than the defendant offered in pre-trial settlement negotiations. This approach, often termed an "offer of judgment" rule, is partially embodied in Federal Rule of Civil Procedure 68 (although, importantly, this rule pertains only to court costs, *not* attorneys' fees, and works only against plaintiffs). Under the rule, a plaintiff who rejects a defendant's specific settlement offer (made at least ten days before trial) and recovers less than the offered amount is liable for the defendant's court costs and fees incurred after the date of the offer. Fed. R. Civ. P. 68.

Some of the implications of "loser pays" and "offer of judgment" rules are considered in the following excerpt.

# ■ Edward F. Sherman, From "Loser Pays" to Modified Offer of Judgment Rules: Reconciling Incentives to Settle with Access to Justice*

**76 Tex. L. Rev.** 1863, 1863-1877 (1998)

. . .

Perhaps the strongest historical justification for the American rule is centered in the American faith in liberal access to the courts for righting wrongs. If a wronged party is deterred from filing and prosecuting a suit by the risk that he will have to pay the opposing party's attorneys' fees if the suit is unsuccessful, there is a concern that many wrongs could go unremedied in our society. That rationale is essentially pro-litigation, indeed pro-plaintiff, in the sense that it reflects a view that access to the courts by claimants should not be discouraged by the threat of substantial, potential penalties for losing. . . . Since plaintiffs are generally more risk averse than defendants, a "loser pays" rule impacts disproportionately on plaintiffs' access to the courts. . . .

. . . [A] large number of statutes have been passed since the 1930s to allow recovery of attorneys' fees by a prevailing party despite the American rule. Most of these statutes apply only to prevailing plaintiffs. The justification for such fee shifting has been based on providing an incentive for parties to vindicate their rights under the particular statute (for example, the Civil Rights Act) and to make them whole by not diminishing their damage award through a requirement that they pay their own attorneys. Thus the "access to the courts" concern underlies the departure from the American rule in most attorney's fee shifting statutes, serving as an exception that actually reinforces the pro-plaintiff rationale of the American rule.

## II.  ATTACK ON THE AMERICAN RULE GIVES WAY TO MODIFIED OFFER OF JUDGMENT PROPOSALS

Although the American rule remains a bedrock of American jurisprudence, it has increasingly come under attack in recent years. In the early 1980s, Florida passed a "loser pays" rule that shifted legal fees to the losing party in medical malpractice suits as part of "malpractice reforms" sought by doctors and insurance companies. . . . The "tort reform" and "competitiveness" movements of the 1980s and 1990s, particularly supported by business interests, mounted a new attack on the American rule, calling for state legislatures and Congress to replace it with the English "loser pays" rule. . . .

One of the major planks of the Contract with America was the "loser pays" rule. Early in its first hundred days, the 104th Congress intro-

*Copyright © 1998 by the Texas Law Review Association. Reprinted with permission.

duced the Common Sense Legal Reforms Act of 1995 which required the application of the "loser pays" rule in actions arising under state law but brought in federal courts under diversity jurisdiction. The proposed rule was modified by provisions that attorneys' fees recovered by the winning party could not exceed those of the losing party, and that the court could limit awards under special circumstances. Along the way, however, resistance to the "loser pays" rule arose, and its advocates shifted to an offer of judgment procedure as an acceptable substitute. A bill was introduced to replace the "loser pays" provision in the Common Sense Legal Reforms Act with a provision that allowed any party to make an offer of judgment to an opposing party. If this offer of judgment were refused, and the ultimate judgment were not more favorable than the original offer, the offeree would have to pay the offeror's costs, including its attorneys' fees up to an amount equal to the offeree's attorneys' fees. [This proposed legislation was never enacted.]

Th[e] legislative history highlights the nexus between "loser pays" and expanded offer of judgment rules. Both accomplish the shifting of attorneys' fees — under the "loser pays" rule automatically to the winner, while under the offer of judgment rule to an offeree who refused his opponent's offer to settle and did not do better at trial. Both deter parties' willingness to prosecute a suit by threatening to shift the successful party's attorneys' fees. The offer of judgment rule, however, requires an additional step — a party must first make an offer of judgment to settle for a certain sum as a prerequisite to being allowed to invoke the fee shifting provisions. Offer of judgment thus has an added settlement potential because, in order to invoke it, a party must be prepared to settle if his offer is accepted. Because fee shifting will only occur if the offeree does not do better in the final judgment than in the offer, the offeror has an incentive to make an offer that will be better than what he expects the judgment might be. The offer of judgment rule is thus less directly punitive than the "loser pays" rule, and the manner in which it creates incentives is more complex. It is also more susceptible to fine-tuning, although the drafting job to create the desired incentive structure and to factor for competing policies is enormously complicated.

### III.   INCENTIVES UNDER FEE SHIFTING STRUCTURES

. . .

#### A.   "LOSER PAYS" RULE

There has been much debate in the law and economics literature over the effect of fee shifting rules on settlement. Richard A. Posner and Steven Shavell have concluded that fee shifting of the English "loser pays" type would decrease the likelihood of settlement. They viewed parties as pursuing litigation because they are overly optimistic about their chances at trial, which causes them to discount the amount of attorneys' fees they will have to pay, and thus makes settlement less attractive. . . . John C. Hause also argued that fee shifting rules raise the stakes, creating an incentive to spend more at trial and, by increasing the projected costs, a heightened expectation of benefits from settlement. Keith N. Hylton differentiated between a "filing effect" and a "settlement effect." He concluded that "[d]efendants who can credibly commit to large litigation expenses are less likely to be sued under the British than under the American rule," while "[t]he incentive to litigate rather than to settle a dispute is greater under the British than under the American rule."[40] . . .

. . . The legal and political debate over the "loser pays" rule, on the other hand, generally takes as a given that fee shifting has a significant impact on settlement incentives. The debate has increasingly focused not on whether the rule creates incentives, but whether the incentives are so powerful as to deter legitimate access to the courts. A premise of the Contract with America "loser pays" incentive was that the rule would deter the filing of a significant number of cases, particularly in areas in which businesses are most prone to suit — torts, products liability, civil rights, and employment. The much lower litigation rates in Britain have been cited as proof that the "loser pays" rule deters litigation (or "frivolous" litigation, depending on how the argument is made). But there are marked cultural, political, and social differences in Britain that arguably make resorting to the courts as a remedy for injuries or grievances less attractive or necessary — ranging from a wider administrative compensation system to the absence of the contingent fees that foster private suits in the U.S. . . .

### B.   OFFER OF JUDGMENT

The offer of judgment device was included in Rule 68 when the Federal Rules of Civil Procedure were adopted in 1938. It was new to federal procedure, being borrowed from the practice of a few states. Today twenty-nine states and the District of Columbia have rules similar in language and effect to Rule 68.

Rule 68 provides that any party defending a claim may make a settlement offer to the plaintiff. If the plaintiff rejects the offer and does not receive a more favorable judgment at trial, he must pay the defen-

---

40. Keith N. Hylton, Fee Shifting and Predictability of Law, 71 Chi.-Kent L. Rev. 427, 444-445 (1995).

dant's court costs and fees incurred after the date of the offer. The final judgment must result from an actual trial and not by way of settlement or voluntary dismissal. . . .

1. Limitations Reducing Its Usefulness — Two factors have particularly limited parties' resort to Rule 68: only defendants may use it, and only court costs, and not attorneys' fees, are shifted. The Judicial Conference of the United States proposed in 1983 and 1984 to amend the rule because it "has rarely been invoked and has been considered largely ineffective as a means of achieving its goals."[67] The amendments would have made the rule available to both parties, allowed an offer to be made up to thirty days before trial, and required that the offer remain open for thirty days. A party who refused an offer and did not obtain a more favorable judgment would have to pay the costs and expenses (including reasonable attorneys' fees) incurred by the offeror after making the offer. The rigor of the fee shifting would be lessened by allowing a reduction to the extent that the fees shifted were found by the court to be excessive or unjustified, and by prohibiting fee shifting if the offer was found to have been made in bad faith. These proposals were never adopted by the Rules Advisory Committee.

Although proposals for changes in Rule 68 have primarily focused on expanding it to apply to offers by plaintiffs and recovery of attorneys' fees, a number of proposals have also tinkered with the basic terms of what triggers cost shifting. One of the more interesting proposals came from the local rule experimentation fostered by the Civil Justice Reform Act of 1990 (CJRA). For example, the CJRA-generated plan adopted in 1993 by the United States District Court for the Eastern District of Texas provides that "a party may make a written offer of judgment" and "if the offer of judgment is not accepted and the final judgment in the case is of more benefit to the party who made the offer by 10%, then the party who rejected the offer must pay the litigation costs incurred after the offer was rejected." "Litigation costs" is defined to include "those costs which are directly related to preparing the case for trial and actual trial expenses, including but not limited to reasonable attorneys' fees, deposition costs and fees for expert witnesses." If the plaintiff recovers either more than the offer or nothing at trial, or if the defendant's offer is not realistic or in good faith, the cost shifting sanctions do not apply. Chief Judge Robert M. Parker reported that in the rule's first two years, hundreds of parties made offers of judgment, generally resulting in settlement at a subsequently negotiated figure. No sanctions had to be granted under the rule for failure of the offeree to have obtained a judgment less than 10% better than the offer. There is a question, however, as to whether such a local

---

67. Preliminary Draft of Proposed Amendments to the Federal Rules of Civil Procedure, 98 F.R.D. 337, 363 (1983).

federal rule is inconsistent with Rule 68, and similar modification of Rule 68 has not been followed in other local rules.    ■

## Notes

*1. Would a "Loser Pays" Rule Encourage Settlement?* As Sherman briefly describes, scholars have advanced competing hypotheses as to whether a "loser pays" rule would actually increase the rate of settlement. Much depends, it seems, on assumptions concerning what factors would otherwise impede or encourage settlement. If both Plaintiff and Defendant have the same prediction of the likelihood of Plaintiff prevailing in court, and if both parties are risk neutral, the English rule should lead to neither more nor fewer settlements than the American rule. If both litigants are risk averse, the English rule should encourage settlement because Plaintiff will demand less and Defendant will offer more than would be the case under the American rule because of each party's desire to avoid the risk of having to pay both side's legal fees. If the litigants are risk neutral and highly confident about their chances of prevailing (i.e., Plaintiff believes his chance of prevailing is greater than Defendant believes), the English rule should discourage settlement because the parties will believe that a trial will mean that the other party will likely have to pay their legal fees. If Defendant is risk neutral and Plaintiff is risk averse, the English rule could cause Plaintiff never to file suit in the first place.

*2. Contracting for Alternative Fee Shifting Rules.* Although the American rule is prevalent in the United States, parties are not precluded from agreeing to litigate under the English rule if they so desire. Put in different words, there is no reason to think that the American rule is anything other than a "default rule" that parties can replace via contract.

John Donohue observes that if trials are primarily the consequence of both parties being optimistic about their likelihood of prevailing in court, we should expect to see many litigants contract for the English rule, because both parties would think it likely that such a contract would result in the other party paying his legal fees. John J. Donohue III, Opting for the British Rule, or If Posner and Shavell Can't Remember the Coase Theorem, Who Will?, 104 Harv. L. Rev. 1093 (1991). Donohue's insight can be understood as identifying an opportunity for integrative bargaining by taking advantage of the litigants' difference in predictions about a future action (here, the decision that a judge or jury will render). Donohue's insight can also be viewed from the opposite direction. That is, when statutes provide for the English rule (as some do), litigants can contract to abide by the American rule if they believe such a rule would be advantageous — for example, if both parties are very risk averse and not excessively optimistic. Trading partners sometimes contract to litigate under the English rule if a dispute arises in the future, but there are few, if any, known instances of litigants contracting to change fee allocation rules after a dispute has arisen. The reasons why remain somewhat of a mystery.

3. *The Scope of Rule 68.* As Sherman notes, Rule 68 has had little influence because it governs only court costs, which are usually a small percentage of litigation costs, and not attorneys' fees. In Marek v. Chesny, 473 U.S. 1 (1985), the Supreme Court determined, however, that when a plaintiff litigates under a statute that entitles him to costs *including* attorneys' fees if he prevails, and the defendant makes a Rule 68 offer of settlement, the plaintiff is entitled to recover his statutory attorneys' fees only if the court judgment is larger than the settlement offer. Id. at 9. In other words, the "costs" put at issue by a Rule 68 offer of settlement include attorneys' fees if a substantive statute specifically enumerates attorneys' fees as a recoverable litigation cost. In such cases, then — which include many civil rights actions — Rule 68 can have a significant effect on a plaintiff's trial recovery and, thus, on the defendant's decision as to whether to make a significant settlement offer and the plaintiff's subsequent decision as to whether to accept such an offer.

4. *Costs Incurred After an Offer of Settlement.* Another issue addressed by the Supreme Court in *Marek* is what happens when a defendant's settlement offer is larger than the plaintiff's recovery plus relevant fees and costs incurred *prior to the offer* but less than the plaintiff's recovery plus fees and costs incurred *through the conclusion of litigation.* In that case, the plaintiffs brought suit against defendant police officers under a civil rights statute that permitted them to recover attorneys' fees and costs. Defendants made a $100,000 offer of settlement, including attorneys' fees and costs, which plaintiffs refused. At the subsequent trial, plaintiffs won a verdict of $60,000 plus costs and fees. Because their fees and costs were far in excess of $40,000, the plaintiffs claimed that their judgment was in excess of the defendants' offer, and therefore Rule 68 did not preclude them from recovering those costs and fees. Defendants claimed that, because at the time of their offer of settlement plaintiffs' fees and costs totaled only $32,000, the plaintiffs' recovery at trial for purposes of Rule 68 analysis was only $92,000 — less than the defendants' offer. The Court sided with the defendants, holding that post-offer costs should not be included in the Rule 68 calculus. *Marek*, supra, at 7.

5. *Comparing Monetary Settlement Offers to Court Judgments.* Another difficult interpretive question raised by offer of settlement rules is

whether a plaintiff's verdict that is somewhat less in dollar terms than the defendant's offer of settlement can be considered more favorable than the offer because it includes the intangible benefits that come with the defendant being labeled a wrongdoer by the court. In Jolly v. Coughlin, 1999 WL 20895 (S.D.N.Y. 1999), the plaintiff prisoner sued three prison guards for violations of his civil rights. The defendants made a Rule 68 settlement offer of $30,360, which the plaintiff declined. When the plaintiff won a jury verdict of $30,000, the defendants claimed the plaintiff was liable for their costs under Rule 68. The plaintiff, in turn, argued that the trial verdict was more favorable than the settlement offer, because the settlement offer did not include an admission of wrongdoing, whereas the trial verdict established that the defendants had violated the plaintiff's constitutional rights. The court held that tangible, nonmonetary relief such as an injunction could be properly compared to a defendant's monetary offer of settlement, but the personal value of "vindication" achieved through adjudication should not be taken into account under Rule 68 because a plaintiff could then always claim that his trial verdict was more favorable than any offer of settlement that did not include an admission of liability. Id. at 8-9.

***6. Alternative Mechanisms to Increase the Likelihood of Settlement.***  Offer of settlement rules such as Fed. R. Civ. P. 68 and fee shifting proposals such as the English rule are two mechanisms that have the potential, at least under some circumstances, of encouraging litigants to make more reasonable settlement offers and thus to keep more litigation matters out of court. Gertner and Miller suggest a different institutional mechanism for encouraging litigants to make reasonable settlement offers. In what they term a "settlement escrow," the plaintiff would make a settlement demand and the defendant a settlement offer to an escrow agent, who could be either the clerk of the court or a private party. If the offers "cross" — that is, if the plaintiff's demand is lower than the defendant's offer — the court would impose a settlement at the midpoint between those two values. If the offers do not cross, no agreement would be imposed, and the parties' proposals would remain secret.

The authors claim that plaintiffs and defendants hesitate to make reasonable settlement demands and offers because they fear that doing so will signal to their opponent that they believe their case is weak, which in turn can cause the opponent to believe his case is stronger than he previously thought. Because "escrowed" settlement proposals would remain secret unless they crossed, the Gertner and Miller proposal would dampen the normal incentives of plaintiffs to make unreasonably high demands and defendants to make unreasonably low offers, which often impose costs of delay on both parties and sometimes result in no settlement being reached even when a positive bargaining zone exists. Robert H. Gertner & Geoffrey P. Miller, Settlement Escrows, 24 J. Legal Stud. 87 (1995).

# B. JUDICIAL SETTLEMENT CONFERENCES

The volume of litigation relative to the availability of judges and other resources of the adjudicatory system means that interminable delays in the legal system can be prevented only if an extremely high percentage of lawsuits settle out of court. Judges have responded to this reality by promoting the settlement of cases on their dockets. In so doing, they rely both on specific federal and state rules that empower them to order parties to participate in settlement conferences, as well as the tradition of the courts' "inherent authority" to manage their dockets.

## ■ Federal Rules of Civil Procedure

(West 2000)

RULE 16. PRETRIAL CONFERENCES; SCHEDULING;
MANAGEMENT

(a) Pretrial Conferences; Objectives. In any action, the court may in its discretion direct the attorneys for the parties and any unrepresented parties to appear before it for a conference or conferences before trial for such purposes as . . .

(5) facilitating the settlement of the case. . . .

(c) Subjects for Consideration at Pretrial Conferences. At any conference under this rule consideration may be given, and the court may take appropriate action, with respect to . . .

(9) settlement and the use of special procedures to assist in resolving the dispute when authorized by statute or local rule. . . .

At least one of the attorneys for each party participating in any conference before trial shall have authority to enter into stipulations and to make admissions regarding all matters that the participants may reasonably anticipate may be discussed. If appropriate, the court may require that a party or its representatives be present or reasonably available by telephone in order to consider possible settlement of the dispute. . . .

(f) Sanctions. If a party or party's attorney fails to obey a scheduling or pretrial order, or if no appearance is made on behalf of a party at a scheduling or pretrial conference, or if a party or party's attorney is substantially unprepared to participate in the conference, or if a party or party's attorney fails to participate in good faith, the judge, upon motion or the judge's own initiative, may make such orders with regard thereto as are just, and among others any of the orders provided in Rule 37(b)(2)(B), (C), (D). In lieu of or in addition to any other sanction, the judge shall require the party or the attorney representing the party or both to pay the reasonable expenses incurred because of any noncompliance with this rule, including attorney's fees, unless the judge finds that the noncompliance was substantially justified or that other circumstances make an award of expenses unjust.                               ■

## ■ In re Novak

**932 F.2d** 1397 (11th Cir. 1991)

TJOFLAT, CHIEF JUDGE: . . .

The facts underlying this dispute are relatively simple. The appellant, Roger Novak, is a senior claim analyst for Continental Casualty Company (CNA). Novak resides in Naperville, Illinois and is employed at CNA's home office in Chicago.

In May 1989, Vickie Roberts filed a legal malpractice suit against David Hammock and his law firm in the United States District Court for the Southern District of Georgia; jurisdiction was based on diversity of citizenship. The defendants were insured by CNA. Under the terms of the policy, CNA hired local counsel, Clay Ratterree, to defend the suit on the defendant's behalf. CNA supervised Ratterree's performance from its Atlanta branch office. Ratterree, although authorized to enter into settlement negotiations, had no power to settle the case without CNA's express approval.

The trial of the case was scheduled for Monday, November 13, 1989 in Savannah, Georgia. On Thursday, November 8, the district judge conducted a pretrial conference; the following day he met with counsel for a settlement conference. At this conference, Ratterree, pursuant to CNA's instructions, offered the plaintiff $150,000 to settle the case. Plaintiff's counsel rejected the offer, stating that his client needed more money. Ratterree, in response, said that he had to take the matter up with CNA in Atlanta. At this point, the district court instructed Ratterree to find out who in CNA had full settlement authority for the case. Ratterree contacted the case manager in Atlanta, who told him that Novak had the last word on settlement for the case, and Ratterree gave this information to the district court. The court then issued an order directing Novak to appear before it in Savannah on November 13 for a settlement conference. . . .

. . . [T]o decide whether the order directed at Novak was transparently invalid, we must determine whether such an order is arguably within the scope of the district court's power to facilitate settlement discussions, pursuant to Fed. R. Civ. P. 16. We begin, in subpart A, with a brief explanation of how the Federal Rules of Civil Procedure envision the operation of pretrial settlement conferences; we also discuss the means Rule 16 gives the district courts to conduct these conferences. Then, we examine, in subpart B, the inherent powers district courts possess to overcome certain obstacles, not explicitly mentioned in the Federal Rules of Civil Procedure, that frustrate the goals of settlement conferences.

### A.

As originally drafted, Rule 16 focused on "the use of the pretrial conference as a means to familiarize the litigants and the court with the issues actually involved in a lawsuit so that the parties [could] accurately appraise their cases and substantially reduce the danger of surprise at trial." 6A C. Wright, A. Miller & M. Kane, Federal Practice and Procedure §1522, at 218 (2d ed. 1990) [hereinafter Federal Practice and Procedure]; *see also Clark v. Pennsylvania R.R.*, 328 F.2d 591, 594 (2nd Cir.) ("One of the prime objectives [of Rule 16] is to do away with the old sporting theory of justice and substitute a more enlightened policy of putting the cards on the table, so to speak, and keeping surprise tactics down to a minimum."), *cert. denied,* 377 U.S. 1006, 84 S. Ct. 1943, 12 L. Ed. 2d 1054 (1964). This rule fit perfectly with the entire system created by the Federal Rules of Civil Procedure, the goal of which was to "secure the just, speedy, and inexpensive determination of every action." Fed. R. Civ. P. 1. In a system with simplified notice pleading, *see* Fed. R. Civ. P. 8, unlimited joinder, *see* Fed. R. Civ. P. 13, 14, 18-24, and broad discovery, *see* Fed. R. Civ. P. 26-37, pretrial conferences were essential because they afforded courts and litigants opportunities to sharpen disputes and, thus, to expedite the determination of the merits of each case.

The value of pretrial conferences has not diminished since the adoption of Rule 16 in 1937. Federal civil litigation, however, has changed significantly; increasingly, the focus of pretrial procedures is to resolve, rather than simply sharpen, disputes. To reflect these changes, the rule was "extensively rewritten and expanded [in 1983] to meet the challenges of modern litigation" by "more accurate[ly] reflect[ing] . . . actual practice." Fed. R. Civ. P. 16 advisory committee's notes. The advisory committee recognized "that it ha[d] become commonplace to discuss settlement at pretrial conferences." *Id.* Accordingly, Congress amended Rule 16 to provide that "[i]n any action, the court may in its discretion direct the attorneys for the parties and any unrepresented parties to appear before it for a conference or conferences before trial for such purposes as . . . facilitating the settlement of the case." Fed. R. Civ. P. 16(a); *see also id.* 16(c)(7); 6A Federal Practice and Procedure §1522, at 225-26 (1983 amendments to Rule 16 officially recognized that "settlement is a legitimate objective that should be fostered during the pretrial conference").

Settlement conferences are valuable tools for district courts. First, they provide neutral forums to foster settlement, which, in turn, "eases crowded court dockets and results in savings to the litigants and the judicial system." Fed. R. Civ. P. 16 advisory committee's notes. . . .

The success of pretrial settlement conferences depends primarily upon the preparedness of the participants. If the participants are unprepared, these conferences, rather than assisting in the resolution and management of the case, are simply cathartic exercises — the parties divulge their general feelings about the case, but neither party shares sharp analysis concerning its merit or provides the court with any reliable information for planning purposes. When participants are fully prepared, however, pretrial settlement conferences may be extremely productive. Prepared litigants are able to discuss the merits of the case cogently and negotiate settlement terms intelligently; furthermore, courts can rely upon these litigants' representations to manage their dockets.

Given the important interests district courts have invested in pretrial settlement conferences, the prospect of unprepared litigants frustrating these conferences is particularly troubling. "At a time when the federal courts [and judges] — which are a scarce dispute resolution resource, indeed — are straining under the pressure of an ever-increasing caseload," *Pelletier v. Zweifel*, 921 F.2d 1465, 1522 (11th Cir. 1991) (discussing Fed. R. Civ. P. 11), we simply cannot permit litigants to waste the courts' assets, not to mention those of their adversaries, in this manner. Since, however, the Federal Rules of Civil Procedure provide for open and extensive discovery prior to trial, *see Hickman v. Taylor*, 329 U.S. 495, 507, 67 S. Ct. 385, 392, 91 L. Ed. 451 (1947) ("Mutual knowledge of all the relevant facts gathered by both parties is essential to proper litigation. To that end, [the Federal Rules of Civil Procedure provide that] either party may compel the other to disgorge whatever facts he has in his possession."), individuals participating in pretrial settlement conferences are *expected* to come to these conferences fully prepared. Indeed, Rule 16 specifically empowers district courts to direct unrepresented parties or the attorneys for parties to appear before them to facilitate settlement discussions and to sanction these individuals if they come "substantially unprepared to participate in the conference." Fed. R. Civ. P. 16(f). Thus, parties or their attorneys must evaluate discovered facts and intelligently analyze legal issues before the start of pretrial conferences. Furthermore, parties and their attorneys must discuss settlement options thoroughly prior to these conferences to ensure that settlement discussions are meaningful — in other words, participants in pretrial settlement conferences must be prepared and authorized to negotiate and commit to settlement terms at that time. *See G. Heileman Brewing Co. v. Joseph Oat Corp.*, 871 F.2d 648, 653 (7th Cir. 1989) (en banc). The model for pretrial settlement conferences, then, as envisioned by the Federal Rules of Civil Procedure, presumes that fully prepared individuals, having taken advantage of the extensive discovery provided by the rules and then evaluated their cases, will participate in such conferences; if these individuals (unrepresented parties or parties' attorneys) actually are unprepared, Rule 16 authorizes the court to sanction them.

## B.

Sometimes, however, these pretrial conference participants, through no fault of their own, are not fully prepared to discuss settlement. This usually occurs in two situations: (1) when a represented party refuses to give full settlement authority to his attorney, who appears on behalf of the party at the pretrial conference, and (2) when a nonparty insurer in charge of the litigation for one of the parties refuses to give full settlement authority to either that party or his attorney. In those situations, a pretrial conference participant's ability to discuss settlement is impaired, and the value of the conference may be limited. The district courts, though, have no statutory or regulatory power to overcome such an impediment to fruitful settlement conferences; Rule 16 does not explicitly authorize them to issue orders directed at represented parties or nonparty insurers. Therefore, we must look to the inherent power of the district courts in order to determine whether they can issue orders and levy sanctions to remove, or diminish, these obstacles. We begin with a brief explanation of the scope of a district court's inherent power. Then we discuss its application to the situations described above.

### 1.

"Inherent power" describes "the control necessarily vested in courts to manage their own affairs so as to achieve the orderly and expeditious disposition of cases." *Link v. Wabash R.R.*, 370 U.S. 626, 630-31, 82 S. Ct. 1386, 1389, 8 L. Ed. 2d 734 (1962); *see also Jones v. Graham*, 709 F.2d 1457, 1458 (11th Cir. 1983) (per curiam). Such powers are "essential to the administration of justice." *Young v. United States ex rel. Vuitton et Fils S.A.*, 481 U.S. 787, 795, 107 S. Ct. 2124, 2131, 95 L. Ed. 2d 740 (1987) (quoting *Michaelson v. United States ex rel. Chicago, St. P., M. & O. Ry.*, 266 U.S. 42, 65-66, 45 S. Ct. 18, 19-20, 69 L. Ed. 162 (1924)). As the Supreme Court noted in *United States v. Hudson*, 11

U.S. (7 Cranch) 32, 34, 3 L. Ed. 259 (1812): "Certain implied powers must necessarily result to our courts of justice, from the nature of their institution . . . because they are necessary to the exercise of all others."

"Because inherent powers are shielded from direct democratic controls, they must be exercised with restraint and discretion." *Roadway Express, Inc. v. Piper,* 447 U.S. 752, 764, 100 S. Ct. 2455, 2463, 65 L. Ed. 2d 488 (1980). Recognition and application of such power is "grounded first and foremost upon necessity." *United States v. Providence Journal Co.,* 485 U.S. 693, 701, 108 S. Ct. 1502, 1508, 99 L. Ed. 2d 785 (1988) (dismissing certiorari) (discussing federal courts' inherent power to initiate criminal contempt proceedings). Thus, a federal court may only invoke its inherent power when *necessary* to protect its ability to function. This includes more than "the power to impose silence, respect and decorum, in [its] presence, and submission to [its] lawful mandates," *Anderson v. Dunn,* 19 U.S. (6 Wheat.) 204, 227, 5 L. Ed. 242 (1821); it also encompasses the power to issue orders necessary to facilitate activity authorized by statute or rule.

2.

We now address the district courts' inherent power to overcome the obstacles, which we mention above, to productive Rule 16 settlement conferences. The first obstacle arises when a party refuses to give his attorney, who appears in his behalf at a settlement conference, full authority to settle the case — i.e., full authority to negotiate terms and to commit the party to a particular position. In that situation, the attorney's ability to participate meaningfully in the settlement conference on the party's behalf is limited. In effect, such an attorney serves simply as a courier, relaying offers and counter-offers between his client and the opposing attorneys; the party acts as his own lawyer for settlement purposes. While such a process, which could continue for weeks or months, might be acceptable to the parties (and, indeed, they are free to arrange it on their own time), it is unacceptable for litigants to waste the court's valuable time and to jeopardize its interests in this manner.

The district courts' power, pursuant to Rule 16, to sanction attorneys substantially unprepared to participate in pretrial conferences is of little help in removing this obstacle. Attorneys in this situation are unprepared because of their *clients'* actions, not their own inaction. Coercive measures against the attorneys, then, are unlikely to achieve the desired results because the parties may have little interest in protecting their attorneys from sanctions. Thus, to ensure that the goals of Rule 16 are not frustrated, it is necessary for a district court to be able to order any party, who, by retaining full settlement authority, effectively has decided to represent himself for settlement purposes,

to produce an individual at the pretrial conference substantially prepared to discuss settlement options; this individual may be the party
himself. To enforce such an order, the court may rely on its power to
adjudge defiant parties in civil contempt and impose sanctions — ranging from fines to the striking of pleadings — on them. Therefore, we
conclude that the power to direct parties to produce individuals with
full settlement authority at pretrial settlement conferences is inherent
in the district courts. *See G. Heileman Brewing Co.,* 871 F.2d at 648; 6A
Federal Practice and Procedure §1525.1, at 254.

The second obstacle outlined above, and the one involved in the
present case, arises when a nonparty insurer controls the litigation and
does not give full settlement authority to either its named party insured
or that party's attorney. Once again, this obstacle may prevent the individuals participating in the pretrial conference from fully discussing
settlement options; this, in turn, frustrates Rule 16's goals. As with the
first obstacle discussed above, Rule 16 does not explicitly provide the
district courts with the power to remove this obstacle; Rule 16 makes
no mention of nonparties or insurers. The district court in the present
case, faced with such a situation, concluded that it had the inherent
power to direct an employee of the nonparty insurer to attend the
settlement conference. We, however, conclude that it is not necessary
for a trial judge to issue such an order to guarantee that settlement
discussions are fruitful; thus, the district courts do not have the inherent power to issue such orders. . . .

Because these nonparty insurers have a real stake in the litigation,
however, the district courts may rely on their power to order named
parties to produce individuals with full settlement authority at pretrial
conferences . . . to coerce cooperation from nonparty insurers. When
an insurer controls a party's litigation, this party, if ordered to produce
such an individual, must turn to his insurer to comply with the order
and avoid sanctions; the insurer either must provide the necessary individual or confer full settlement authority on the party or his attorney.
The insurer, of course, has a strong incentive to prevent the imposition
of civil contempt sanctions that would harm its interests. Thus, the
effect of directing an order to the named party (the insured) would
be to coerce action by the nonparty insurer controlling the
litigation. . . .                                                                              ■

## Notes

*1. Rule 16 Authority.* When the Federal Rules of Civil Procedure
were adopted in 1938, facilitating settlement was not a goal of Rule 16.
In fact, an original member of the Advisory Committee for the Federal
Rules wrote that "compelled settlement negotiations are dangerous as

bringing into question the impartiality of the tribunal." Charles E. Clark, To an Understanding Use of Pre-Trial, 29 F.R.D. 454, 456 (1962). The rule was amended in 1983 and again in 1993, however, and it now provides judges with explicit authority to mandate settlement conferences. Although Rule 16 does not permit judges to coerce the parties to settle, it provides a set of tools that judges can use to actively promote settlement.

**2. Who Must Attend a Settlement Conference?**   Following the adoption of the 1983 amendments to Rule 16, there was debate about whether the explicit language of section (a) permitting a court to require the presence of an attorney or an *unrepresented* party at a settlement conference prohibited courts from requiring the presence of other individuals. In Heileman Brewing Co. v. Joseph Oat Corp., 871 F. 2d 648 (7th Cir. 1989), the Seventh Circuit sitting *en banc* held — over five dissents — that the court's inherent authority to manage its case load was not limited by Rule 16, and the court therefore had the discretion to order the presence of a represented party at a settlement conference even though Rule 16 provided no such authority — at least when the burden to the party was not out of proportion to the potential benefits from settlement. Id. at 656-657. Although *Novak* ultimately held that the court could not require the presence of a nonparty at a settlement conference, the decision seems consistent with *Heileman* in that it finds that the limiting factor is the extent of the courts' inherent authority rather than the language of Rule 16.

As revised in 1993, Rule 16 now gives explicit permission to courts to require a represented party to be available by telephone if needed. Fed. R. Civ. P. 16(a)(9). Citing *Heileman,* however, the advisory committee notes to the revised rule state that this provision "is not intended to limit the reasonable exercise of the court's inherent powers" or authority under other statutes that may concern settlement. Fed. R. Civ. P. 16 (Advisory Committee Notes on 1993 Amendments).

**3. Authority to Settle.**   The more important issue at stake in both *Novak* and *Heileman* is whether a judge may order a party to send to a settlement conference a representative with full authority to enter into a settlement. The Seventh Circuit *en banc* majority duly noted that a court could not "coerce" a party into settling but found it unobjectionable for a court to order the presence of a representative with authority to settle should acceptable terms be proposed. *Heileman,* 871 F.2d at 653. Citing *Heileman,* the Eleventh Circuit agreed in *Novak.* In re Novak, 932 F.2d at 1406 n.18.

Dissenting in *Heileman,* Judge Easterbrook noted a practical problem with requiring settlement conference participants to have full authority. Easterbrook complained that the court's requirement was unduly burdensome if not outright impossible in that case, because the plaintiff's demand was so large that if the defendant had wished to agree to it a majority vote of its board of directors would have been required. *Heileman,* 871 F.2d at 665. Apparently responding to this observation, the 1993 advisory committee notes to the Rule 16 revisions state that when no single individual has settlement authority, "the most that should be expected is access to a person who would have a major role in submitting a recommendation to the body or board with ultimate decision-making responsibility." Fed. R. Civ. P. 16 (Advisory Committee Note on 1993 Amendments). At least one court has dealt with this problem by ordering a party to submit the settlement proposal to the body with ultimate authority to accept or reject it. See Local 715, United Rubber, Cork, Linoleum & Plastic Workers of Am. v. Michelin Am. Small Tire, 840 F. Supp. 595, 597 (N.D. Ind. 1993) (requiring union representative to submit settlement proposal to the union membership).

*4. The Judicial Role in Settling Criminal Cases.* Unlike civil settlement negotiations, in which courts can and do participate in settlement conferences and even suggest potential settlement agreements, courts in criminal matters are expressly forbidden from taking part in plea negotiations. Federal Rule of Criminal Procedure 11 governs negotiated pleas. Rule 11(e)(1) provides that the attorney for the government and the attorney for the defendant may "engage in discussions with a view toward reaching an agreement" by which the defendant will plead guilty or no contest to an offense in return for the government dismissing other charges, recommending a particular sentence, or agreeing not to oppose the defendant's request for a particular sentence. The rule provides, however, that "[t]he court shall not participate in any such discussions." Id.

## ■ Nick v. Morgan's Foods, Inc.

**99 F. Supp. 2d** 1056 (E.D. Mo. 2000)

SIPPEL, DISTRICT JUDGE. . . .

In contravention of this Court's Order referring this matter to Alternative Dispute Resolution (ADR), Morgan's Foods failed to submit the required mediation memorandum and failed to send a corporate representative with authority to settle the case to the mediation. Not surprisingly, the mediator was unable to mediate a settlement. After being called upon to explain why it ignored the Court's Order regarding ADR, counsel for Morgan's Foods admitted that his client — on his advice — made a calculated decision to disregard some of the provisions of the ADR Referral Order. Based on Morgan's Foods' failure to comply with key provisions of the ADR Referral Order, the Court concluded that Morgan's Foods failed to participate in mediation in good faith and entered sanctions accordingly. Morgan's Foods now asks the Court to reconsider the imposition of sanctions. Because the Court remains convinced that Morgan's Foods and its counsel did not participate in good faith in the ADR process, its motion for reconsideration will be denied. . . .

### BACKGROUND

Gee Gee Nick filed this lawsuit against Morgan's Foods alleging sexual harassment and retaliation in violation of Title VII of the Civil Rights Act of 1964, 42 U.S.C. §2000e et seq. . . . The matter was set for referral to ADR on August 1, 1999. The parties were to complete the ADR process and report back to the Court the results of the mediation. . . .

The August 2, 1999 Order of Referral required the ADR process to be conducted in compliance with E.D. Mo. L.R. 6.01-6.05. The Order of Referral also specifically required: . . .

(4) ***Duty to Attend and Participate:*** All parties, counsel of record, and corporate representatives or claims professionals **having authority to settle claims** shall attend all mediation conferences and **participate in good faith.** Early neutral evaluation conferences shall be attended by all counsel of record. . . .

Prior to the mediation, counsel for Morgan's Foods indicated to Nick's counsel, but not the Court, that he did not feel that the mediation would be fruitful. . . .

Morgan's Foods did not provide the memorandum to the neutral as was required by the Court's Order. Morgan's Foods also failed to have a representative attend the conference who had authority to settle. Morgan's Foods' corporate representative who attended the conference did not have any independent knowledge of the case, nor did she have authority to reconsider Morgan's Foods' position regarding settlement. The limit of Morgan's Foods' regional manager's authority was $500. Negotiation of any settlement amount above $500 had to be handled by Morgan's Foods' general counsel, who was not present at the ADR conference.

Not surprisingly, the ADR conference did not result in a settlement. Nick made an offer of settlement which was rejected without a counteroffer by Morgan's Foods. Nick made another offer to settle the case. Again, this offer was rejected without a counteroffer. The ADR conference was terminated shortly thereafter. . . .

### GOOD FAITH PARTICIPATION IN ADR DOES NOT REQUIRE SETTLEMENT

The Court understands that ADR conferences and settlement negotiations can fail to achieve the settlement of a case for many reasons. The Federal Rules of Civil Procedure, this court's local rules and the specific court order in this case referring the case to ADR do not mandate settlement. Good faith participation in ADR does not require settlement. In fact, an ADR conference conducted in good faith can be helpful even if settlement is not reached. On the other hand, the rules and orders governing ADR are designed to prevent abuse of the opponent, which can and does occur when one side does not participate in good faith. . . .

### GOOD FAITH PARTICIPATION IN ADR INCLUDES PROVIDING THE NEUTRAL WITH A MEDIATION MEMORANDUM

This Court's referral order required preparation of a memorandum seven days in advance of the ADR conference. The memorandum was required to contain:

a. A summary of the disputed facts;
b. A discussion of the party's position on liability and damages;
c. The name and general job title of the employee of the corporation who will attend and participate at the ADR conference. Failure to provide the information required in the memorandum undermines the ADR process. . . .

Morgan's Foods' calculated refusal to prepare a mediation memorandum was a direct violation of the Court's local rules and the Court's ADR Referral Order.

### GOOD FAITH PARTICIPATION IN ADR REQUIRES THE PARTICIPATION OF A CORPORATE REPRESENTATIVE WITH AUTHORITY TO SETTLE

Morgan's Foods also violated the Referral Order by failing to have an appropriate corporate representative attend the mediation.

The August 2, 1999 Referral Order specifically required attendance of a "corporate representative . . . having authority to settle claims." Presence of the corporate representative is the cornerstone of good faith participation. . . .

During the ADR conference, all parties have the opportunity to argue their respective positions. In the Court's experience, this is often the first time that parties, especially corporate representatives, hear about the difficulties they will face at trial. As a practical matter this may also be the first time that firmly held positions may be open to change. For ADR to work, the corporate representative must have the authority and discretion to change her opinion in light of the statements and arguments made by the neutral and opposing party.

## CONCLUSION

Morgan's Foods did not participate in good faith in the ADR process. The absence of good faith is evidenced not by the parties' failure to reach settlement, but by Morgan's Foods' failure to comply with the Court's August 2, 1999 Referral Order. Morgan's Foods' failure to participate in the ADR process in good faith would not be vindicated by a defendant's verdict at trial. Whether the parties participated in good faith in the ADR process is measured by their actual conduct at the mediation, not by the hypothetical result of a subsequent trial.

Morgan's Foods' lack of good faith participation in the ADR process was calculated to save Morgan's Foods a few hours of time in preparing the mediation memorandum and to save its general counsel the expense and inconvenience of a trip to attend the mediation. The consequence of Morgan's Foods' lack of good faith participation in the ADR process, however, was the wasted expense of time and energy of the Court, the neutral, Nick, and her court-appointed counsel. . . .

IT IS FURTHER ORDERED that Defendant Morgan's Foods shall pay $1,390.63 to counsel for plaintiff as sanctions in this matter. Defendant's counsel shall pay $1,390.62 to counsel for plaintiff as sanctions in this matter. That amount includes $1,045.00 in attorney's fees for preparing and attending the mediation in this case, the $506.25 fee paid to the neutral for the cost of the ADR conference, and $1,230.00 in attorney's fees for preparing and arguing the motion for sanctions regarding Morgan's Foods' participation in the mediation.

IT IS FURTHER ORDERED that Defendant Morgan's Foods shall pay $30.00 to Plaintiff Gee Gee Nick for the costs she incurred in attending the mediation of this case. Defendant's counsel shall also pay $30.00 to Plaintiff Gee Gee Nick for the costs she incurred in attending the mediation of this case.

IT IS FURTHER ORDERED that Defendant Morgan's Foods shall pay $1,500.00 to the Clerk of the United States District Court, Eastern District of Missouri as sanctions in this matter. That amount reflects the savings realized by Morgan's Foods' by virtue of its failure to prepare the required mediation memorandum and its decision not to send Morgan's Foods' general counsel to attend the ADR conference. Defendant Morgan's Foods and its counsel shall each pay $1,250.00 to the Clerk of the United States District Court, Eastern District of Missouri as a sanction for vexatiously increasing the costs of this litigation by filing a frivolous Motion for Reconsideration which further demonstrated the lack of good faith in Morgan's Foods conduct in this case.                                                                       ■

## Notes

*1. "Good Faith" Participation in Settlement-Related Activities.*   Fed. R. Civ. P. 16(f) requires parties to participate in judicial settlement conferences in "good faith." As the *Nick* case suggests, many courts also require by local rule good faith participation in other court-sponsored methods of encouraging settlement, such as mediation or nonbinding arbitration. In addition, judges often order the parties to participate in such activities in good faith even in the absence of textual authority. Relatively little case law attempts to define what exactly is required by an order to participate in settlement activities in good faith, or whether the courts' inherent authority permits such an order.

Edward Sherman recommends that instead of "good faith," courts should require of parties both a minimum amount of written preparation for court-ordered alternative dispute resolution proceedings and a minimum quality of oral participation in such proceedings:

> A reasonable order would be that the parties provide a position paper in advance of the ADR proceeding which would include a plain and concise statement of: (1) the legal and factual issues in dispute, (2) the party's position on those issues, (3) the relief sought (including a particularized itemization of all elements of damage claimed), and (4) any offers and counter-offers previously made. This is a shortened list of the kinds of items that are routinely required by federal courts in proposed pretrial orders under the authority of the Rule 16 pretrial conference rule. . . .
>
> Although exchange of position papers and objective information often provides an alternative to mandating a specific level of participation in ADR, there can still be a need for a minimal level of oral participation by the parties if the process is to have a genuine hope of success. It is not easy to fashion a term to describe what that minimal level should be because the necessary degree of participation varies with the type of ADR process involved. For want of a better term, I have adopted the language used by some courts that require the parties to participate "in a meaningful manner." Although hardly a model of certainty and precision, a "minimal meaningful participation" standard avoids the subjectivity of "good faith participation" by suggesting that the degree of participation required to be "meaningful" is related to the goal of the ADR procedure. Since the methodology and objectives of ADR processes vary a good deal, the "minimal meaningful participation" standard allows flexibility of participation depending on the particular process involved in each case.

Edward F. Sherman, Court-Mandated Alternative Dispute Resolution: What Form of Participation Should be Required? 46 SMU L. Rev. 2079, 2095-2096 (1993).

*2. Coercion.* Although no rules give judges the authority to attempt to force parties to settle out of court, and although judicial opinions are usually careful to mention that judges lack the authority to coerce settlements, there is no doubt that judges sometimes put pressure on a party either generally to reach a settlement or more specifically to accept a particular settlement offer made at a settlement conference. Because under Rule 16 the judge that presides over a settlement conference also presides over the litigation if settlement efforts fail, parties might understandably fear the practical consequences of ignoring a judge's settlement advice. Although judges may be disqualified from presiding over a case if they demonstrate partiality at a settlement conference, disqualification is quite rare. In Fong v. American Airlines, Inc., 431 F. Supp. 1334 (N.D. Cal. 1977), the defendant moved to have the judge disqualified on the grounds that he expressed outrage at a settlement conference over the defendant's conduct toward the plaintiff. Denying the motion, the reviewing court explained:

> The challenged statements were made in the course of a Status and Settlement Conference. They reflected the Court's reaction and opinion. If comments made by a court in the course of pretrial proceedings, based on matters disclosed by the case file at that time were regarded as extrajudicial, the court's ability to promote the settlement of civil litigation would be crippled. Judicial intervention in the settlement process, even if not universally favored or practiced, is an absolute necessity in the federal judicial system, burdened as it is by a staggering and ever growing case load. Without that intervention, and the resultant volume of pretrial settlements, the federal courts would be hopelessly congested with little chance for civil litigants who must have a trial to get one, at least within a reasonable time. Conversely, that intervention frequently helps to avoid the expense of litigation, thereby serving the purpose of the Federal Rules of Civil Procedure "to secure, the just, speedy, and inexpensive determination of every action." Rule 1, Fed. R. Civ. Pro.
>
> Intervention may, of course, take many different forms depending on the personality, style and experience of the individual judge. It may, among others, take the form of an expression by the judge of his reaction to the allegations, admissions and denials contained in the pleadings and his evaluation of each party's prospects of success in the litigation. To subject judges to the risk of disqualification on the basis of statements of this kind would jeopardize their effectiveness as catalysts in the settlement process.

Fong v. American Airlines, Inc., 431 F. Supp. 1334, 1338-1339 (N.D. Cal. 1977).

When a court successfully pressures a party into accepting a settlement offer, the judge's actions are essentially unreviewable, because the settlement results in the dismissal of the underlying lawsuit. See, e.g., Thomas A. Tozar, The Heileman Power: Well-Honed Tool or Blunt Instrument?, 66 Ind. L.J. 977, 993 (1991).

## C. INADMISSIBILITY OF SETTLEMENT NEGOTIATIONS

As the discussion in Chapter 7 of the negotiator's dilemma suggests, negotiators must be wary of revealing information in negotiations because the opponent can use that information to better estimate the negotiator's reservation price and employ tactics designed to capture most or all of the cooperative surplus that a deal would produce. In litigation settlement negotiations, the negotiator's dilemma is even more severe because information revealed by the negotiator could improve the opponent's reservation price by improving his litigation prospects. For example, information revealed by a defendant in a civil lawsuit during settlement negotiations could often be used to strengthen the plaintiff's claim of liability, which would increase the plaintiff's reservation price. Federal Rules of Evidence 408, along with similar rules in most states, mitigates this problem by excluding from use in litigation evidence of statements, conduct, or offers or acceptance of offers made in settlement negotiations if introduced for the purpose of proving liability for or invalidity of the claim or its amount.

Rule 408, adopted in 1975, expanded on the protection offered by the common law against the use at trial of some statements made during compromise discussions. Under the common law, evidence that a party made a settlement offer was inadmissible in a judicial proceeding, but statements of fact made during the negotiation were not so privileged, unless presented in the hypothetical. For example, to protect against an admission made during settlement talks being introduced as evidence, a party would have to preface a statement as "made for the sake of discussion only." This requirement hindered free communication during settlement talks, as parties had to be exceedingly careful about how they phrased their statements, and it forced courts to make difficult (and often arbitrary) distinctions between statements that were and were not made hypothetically. See 2 John W. Strong, et al., McCormick on Evidence §226 at 185 (5th ed. 1999).

Rule 408 expands on the common law rule of exclusion but, as the following cases and notes indicate, fine distinctions remain between what statements are and are not admissible in court proceedings. The two most contested issues are (1) when a statement is used to prove or disprove "the claim or its amount" (in which case the statement is inadmissible) rather than for "another purpose" (in which case the statement is admissible), and (2) when the parties are sufficiently adversarial such that it can be said that the "claim . . . [is] disputed."

## ■ Federal Rules of Evidence

(West 2000)

RULE 408.   COMPROMISE AND OFFERS TO COMPROMISE

Evidence of (1) furnishing or offering or promising to furnish, or (2) accepting or offering or promising to accept, a valuable consideration in compromising or attempting to compromise a claim which was disputed as to either validity or amount, is not admissible to prove liability for or invalidity of the claim or its amount. Evidence of conduct or statements made in compromise negotiations is likewise not admissible. This rule does not require the exclusion of any evidence otherwise discoverable merely because it is presented in the course of compromise negotiations. This rule also does not require exclusion when the evidence is offered for another purpose, such as proving bias or prejudice of a witness, negativing a contention of undue delay, or proving an effort to obstruct a criminal investigation or prosecution.                                                                                   ■

## ■ Thomas v. Resort Health Related Facility

**539 F. Supp.** 630 (E.D.N.Y. 1982)

JUDGE NEAHER delivered the Opinion of the Court. . . .

[Plaintiff, a black male originally from Granada, sued his former employer after being suspended from work, alleging discrimination based on race, sex, and national origin. The defendant sought partial summary judgment, alleging that its offer during litigation to reinstate the plaintiff to his job without prejudice to his pending claims for back pay — which the plaintiff declined — precluded the plaintiff's claim for lost wages after that date because Title VII provides back pay is unavailable when a reasonably diligent person could have avoided the loss.]

The foregoing facts raise two main questions which must be resolved before defendants' motions can be decided. First, does Rule 408, F. R. Evid., preclude defendants from submitting evidence as to the reinstatement offers on the motion for summary judgment? If evidence of the offers is excluded, defendants' various motions relating to the offers must be denied. But if evidence of the offers is admissible, the legal effect upon plaintiff's back pay claim must then be addressed, the second issue.

Evidence of the reinstatement offers and of plaintiff's rejection is admissible for the following reasons. First, there is no genuine issue that the reinstatement offers were not made to compromise the claim for back pay, which puts the proffered evidence outside the scope of the first sentence of the Rule. Although defendants made their initial offer at the same meeting at which they discussed settlement of the entire case with plaintiff and his attorney, the offer could not reasonably be viewed as one to settle the back pay claim, since plaintiff's acceptance of its terms was without prejudice to his demand for back pay. Thus, the fact issue whether or not settlement negotiations had reached an impasse is not material.

For this same reason, evidence as to the offer and its rejection falls within the admissible scope of Rule 408's third sentence, and does not suffer the exclusionary effect of the Rule's second sentence. Regardless of when the offer was made, there is no question that legally it was unrelated to the discussions about settling the lawsuit including the back pay claim, although plaintiff's counsel may not have realized it.

Plaintiff's counsel urges that all the discussions on February 24 were "without prejudice." But to deny legal effect to an unconditional offer of reinstatement and preclude a defendant-employer from attempting to reduce a potential back pay award by an amount "earnable with reasonable diligence" from itself, because counsel for the offeree plaintiff insisted that all the discussions were "without prejudice," would grant the plaintiff too much control over the litigation, and subject employers to unnecessarily burdensome claims for back pay. In providing that a Title VII back pay award "shall be reduced by amounts earnable with reasonable diligence," Congress undoubtedly sought to achieve two desirable economic goals, to prevent a "double recovery" by a discriminatee of both back pay and income from employment the plaintiff would otherwise not have obtained, and with respect to discriminatees who did not seek other jobs, to discourage unjustified idleness and thus minimize the consequent detriment to the defendant and the economy. Significantly, Congress did not expressly exclude the alleged discriminating employer from the class of persons from whom a plaintiff might reasonably be required to seek employment.

Even if the evidence as to the offers and rejection could be considered within Rule 408, it would be admissible under the Rule's last sentence because "offered for another purpose" than the one proscribed by Rule 408. Defendant is not seeking to use its offer and plaintiff's rejection of it as an admission by either party as to the "invalidity" of the back pay claim, or its "amount," which is the chief evidentiary purpose on which Rule 408 focuses. Defendants' purpose is to show that back pay otherwise recoverable after the date of its offer should not be allowed because the loss of back pay during that period is not attributable to defendants' discrimination. Accordingly, the evidence as to the reinstatement offers is ruled admissible and not barred by Rule 408. ■

## ■ Affiliated Manufacturers, Inc. v. Aluminum Co. of America
56 F.3d 521 (3d Cir. 1995)

RESTANI, JUDGE.

. . . [Defendant] Alcoa filed a motion *in limine* on November 5, 1993, and a supplemental submission dated November 23, 1993, seeking to exclude portions of a total of fifteen items from admission at trial, including excerpts from correspondence between [plaintiff] AMI and Alcoa, Alcoa internal memoranda and deposition testimony. The district court granted this motion with respect to thirteen of the fifteen items, by memorandum order dated December 23, 1993. . . .

The dispute between AMI and Alcoa arose from a contract for design and fabrication of an automated greenline handling system ("the system"). . . . During the construction of the system, AMI submitted to Alcoa invoices for work not included in the contract. Upon receipt, Alcoa processed the invoices for payment. The parties disagree concerning one unpaid invoice for hardware costs (four screen printers) totaling $280,000, and another unpaid invoice for $208,130 in software costs. These two invoices were submitted by AMI at the end of the project, on April 5, 1990, to the attention of Thomas Pollak ("Pollak"), Alcoa's procurement manager.

Pollak consulted with Alcoa employees Earle Lockwood ("Lockwood") and Phil Kasprzyk ("Kasprzyk") concerning the invoices, because both were closely involved with the project. In memoranda, Lockwood and Kasprzyk each evaluated one of the two invoices from AMI. At a meeting between Pollak, Lockwood and AMI's president, Beson Austin ("Austin"), on May 2, 1990, one topic of discussion was the issue of [the] unpaid invoices [ ].

[In 1991, AMI filed suit against Alcoa, seeking payment of the invoices. Granting Alcoa's motion *in limine*, the district court excluded from evidence portions of an Alcoa internal memorandum written by Kasprzyk dated May 1, 1990, stating that he believed AMI had a legitimate claim to some compensation; notes from the May 2, 1990 meeting containing mathematical calculations and impressions about a "settlement proposal"; deposition testimony in which Pollak stated that at the May 2 meeting Alcoa offered to pay AMI a portion of the amount of the invoices; a series of letters from Pollak to Austin written after the May 2 meeting proposing a "compromise" or "settlement"; letters from Austin to Pollack also written after the May 2 meeting discussing Alcoa's offers and explaining why he was declining them; and an Alcoa internal memorandum written by Lockwood discussing Alcoa's proposal. All of the memoranda and correspondence in question were prepared prior to the date that AMI filed suit against Alcoa.] . . .

AMI contends that the district court erred in its interpretation and application of Rule 408. AMI alleges that the court took an extreme view of the meaning of "settlement negotiations" as contemplated within the rule. AMI asserts that the district court incorrectly found that even an "apparent difference of opinion between the parties" could trigger an exclusion under the rule. . . . Further, AMI argues that the district court erred in its factual finding that a dispute existed between the parties. . . .

AMI argues that the case law clearly delineates distinctions as to what constitutes "a claim which was disputed," and characterizes the excluded documents at issue as merely evidencing discussions that had not yet reached the "dispute" stage for Rule 408 purposes. Thus, AMI maintains that Rule 408 is inapplicable here, arguing that the intended construction of Rule 408 is that there must be a threat or contemplation of litigation, that goes beyond conduct or statements made to resolve differences of opinion as to the validity or amount of a claim. AMI relies chiefly upon the holdings from other circuits to support its view that the district court misinterpreted the term "dispute" and misapplied the rule. Alcoa responds that AMI has mischaracterized these decisions, as well as the district court's reasoning, in its discussion of relevant precedent. . . .

In *Big O Tire* [Dealers, Inc. v. Goodyear Tire & Rubber Co., 561 F.2d 1365 (10th Cir. 1977)], a small tire manufacturer that had used the term "Big Foot" in its business was approached by Goodyear Tire, who wished to use the same term for a national ad campaign for a new product. 561 F.2d at 1368. Both parties participated in a series of discussions about how to proceed, and Goodyear sought assurance from Big O Tire that it would not object to such use. *Id.* In addition to phone conversations and meetings to discuss the issue further, correspondence indicated that Big O Tire requested that Goodyear conclude its ad campaign as soon as possible, and that Goodyear responded it would use the concept as long as it "continued to be a helpful advertising device." *Id.* The district court in *Big O Tire* determined that phone and letter communications between the parties prior to litigation concerning use of the trademark did not fall within the Rule 408 exclusion, as the calls and letters were merely "business communications." *See id.* at 1368, 1372-73. The Court of Appeals for the Tenth Circuit concluded that the district court did not commit manifest error in finding the disputed statements were business communications because the discussions at issue "had not crystallized to the point of threatened litigation." *Id.* at 1373.

To the extent *Big O Tire* establishes a strict standard for application of Rule 408, it was rejected by *Alpex* [Computer Corp. v. Nintendo Co., 770 F. Supp. 161 (S.D.N.Y. 1991)]. The plaintiff in *Alpex* held certain rights relating to a patent for video games and pursued a program to combat infringement by sending letters from counsel offering certain alleged infringers the opportunity to settle what plaintiff viewed as meritorious infringement claims. *Id.* at 162. In some instances these notices led to extended negotiations, licensing agreements and settlement without litigation, while in other instances litigation was pursued. *Id.* at 162-63. The *Alpex* court determined that certain license agreements reached in the absence of litigation fell within the purview of the Rule 408 exclusion. *Id.* at 165. In its analysis, the *Alpex* court examined various factors in addition to indicia of threat of litigation, that might call for application of the exclusion. *Id.* at 164-65.

We believe that AMI has oversimplified the *Big O Tire* and *Alpex* holdings. Regarding the issue of when a "dispute" between parties exists, the *Alpex* court acknowledged that litigation need not have commenced for Rule 408 to apply. 770 F. Supp. at 164; *see* North Am. Biologicals, Inc. v. Illinois Employers Ins., 931 F.2d 839, 841 (11th Cir. 1991) (finding letter written prior to suit excludable under Rule 408 as offer of settlement). . . . *Alpex* and other courts make clear that the Rule 408 exclusion applies where an actual dispute or a difference of opinion exists, rather than when discussions crystallize to the point of threatened litigation. *See Alpex,* 770 F. Supp. at 163; Dallis v. Aetna Life Ins. Co., 768 F.2d 1303, 1307 (11th Cir. 1985) (citing Weinstein's Evidence, supra, ¶408[01]) (affirming admission of testimony involving settlement of similar claim between party to action and third party, where no evidence that validity or amount of payment had been in dispute).

Accordingly, we hold that the district court's construction of Rule 408 did not constitute legal error. As a matter of interpretation, the meaning of "dispute" as employed in the rule includes both litigation and less formal stages of a dispute, and this meaning "is unchanged by the broader scope of Rule 408." Weinstein's Evidence, supra, ¶408[01] at 408-12. The district court properly interpreted the scope of the term "dispute" to include a clear difference of opinion between the parties here concerning payment of two invoices.

The facts of each case bear upon the trial court's exercise of discretion to apply the exclusion. *See Alpex,* 770 F. Supp. at 164-65; Bradbury v. Phillips Petroleum Co., 815 F.2d 1356, 1364 (10th Cir.1987) (holding if application of Rule 408 exclusion doubtful, better practice is to exclude evidence of compromise negotiations). Admittedly, it can be difficult to discern whether an "offer" was made to attempt to "compromise a claim." The existence of a disputed claim as well as the timing of the offer are relevant to making this determination. Pierce v. F. R. Tripler & Co., 955 F.2d 820, 827 (2d Cir. 1992). The district court here found that inherent in each of the documents presented for exclusion was the parties' disagreement or dispute as to the amount and the validity of the invoice presented for payment. *AMI I* at 6-14. . . .

. . . In his deposition Pollak stated that "[i]n preparation for [a May 2 settlement] meeting, I asked Phil Kasprzyk, an Alcoa engineer familiar with the project, his view of the disputed invoices." . . . That Kasprzyk's evaluation was written in order to prepare Pollak for a meeting to discuss a possible compromise necessarily demonstrates that at least as of May 1 there was a dispute. We cannot say that the district court erred in concluding that a dispute existed as of May 1 and that the documents at issue evidenced attempts to compromise the dispute. ■

## Notes

*1. Limitations on the Scope of Rule 408.*   As a careful reading of Rule 408 suggests and *Thomas* reinforces, the rule does not render all statements concerning the subject of litigation inadmissible in court. In addition to offers not made to induce a compromise, the rule does not prohibit the introduction of statements made for the purpose of impeachment, to contradict a contention of undue delay, or to prove obstruction in a criminal investigation or prosecution. Fed. R. Evid. 408.

Courts have often held that evidence settlement talks occurred are admissible for a range of purposes other than to prove that the defendant is or is not liable in the particular circumstance. In Breuer Electric Manufacturing Co. v. Toronado Systems of America, Inc., 687 F.2d 182 (7th Cir. 1982), the court permitted the plaintiff to introduce evidence of the content of settlement discussions that predated the filing of the lawsuit to rebut the defendants' assertion that they had not been aware of the issues until the lawsuit was filed. Id. at 185. In Bradbury v. Phillips Petroleum, 815 F.2d 1356 (10th Cir. 1987), the court ruled that to prove its claim that the defendant's activities were part of a pattern of "outrageous conduct" rather than an isolated incident, a plaintiff could introduce evidence that the defendant settled seven similar claims brought by other plaintiffs. Id. at 1364.

Further, Rule 408 does not preclude an opponent from using a statement made in settlement negotiations to focus his discovery efforts. Moreover, material communications or those revealed during negotiations which are otherwise discoverable cannot be immunized from discovery or admission at trial by introduction in a settlement conference. For example, in In re B.D. International Discount Corp., 701 F.2d 1071 (2d Cir. 1983), the court held that a defendant debtor's financial statements were admissible even though they had been divulged to the plaintiff creditors in settlement negotiations. Id. at 1075 n.5.

Additionally, while Rule 408 protects unaccepted offers of compromise, admissions with respect to independent facts that are made during the course of compromise negotiations may be received in evidence. See Megarry Bros., Inc. v. U.S. for Use of Midwestern Electric Construction, Inc., 404 F.2d 479 (8th Cir. 1968) (holding that offer to pay one-tenth of amount in dispute, which plaintiff claimed was an admission that defendant owed her for certain parts, was not an independent admission because the admission was ambiguous and formed an inseparable part of the efforts to compromise).

*2. At What Point in a Disagreement Does Rule 408 Become Applicable?* Courts are split over when Rule 408 begins to protect evidence of settlement negotiations from admissibility in court, and the contexts to which the rule applies. Consistent with *Affiliated Manufacturers*, some jurisdictions have held that the rule applies to negotiations over a prospective claim yet to be filed. See *Breuer*, at 182 (7th Cir. 1982); Bradbury v. Phillips Petroleum, 815 F.2d 1356 (10th Cir. 1987). Other jurisdictions, however, have held that the rule protects only claims that are the subject of litigation. See Cassino v. Reichhold Chemicals, 817 F.2d 1338 (9th Cir. 1987).

## DISCUSSION QUESTIONS AND PROBLEMS

*1. The Efficacy of the "English Rule."* If your only policy concern were to increase the rate of settlement, would you support a general shift in the law from the "American rule" (each litigant pays his own attorneys' fees) to the "English rule" (i.e., "loser pays")? Why or why not? If you believe the English rule would increase the rate of settlement on balance, are there other policy reasons that would cause you to hesitate supporting its implementation?

*2. Rule 68 and the Bargaining Zone.* Some scholars argue that the primary effect of Rule 68 "is not to encourage settlement but to benefit defendants and harm plaintiffs by shifting downward the relevant settlement range." Geoffrey P. Miller, An Economic Analysis of Rule 68, 15 J. Legal Stud. 93 (1986). The argument goes like this: A defendant will make a lower settlement offer under Rule 68 than he would otherwise, knowing the effect that the added impact of cost shifting will have on the plaintiff's decision. Plaintiff, for his part, will accept something less than he otherwise would, knowing the increased cost of not surpassing the offer at trial. Thus, the entire settlement range is shifted downward. The effect is even more pronounced if the plaintiff is risk averse (as many are) and the defendant is more risk prone (as is customary before trial begins). Is this analysis correct?

**3. Settlement Conference Authority.**   What are the benefits and costs to litigants of rules that permit judges to require the parties to participate in settlement conferences? On balance, do you think that judicially mandated settlement conferences are desirable?

**4. Participation Requirements.**   Assess the desirability to litigating parties of each of the following controversial requirements of settlement conference participants that courts have imposed:

  (a) The principal must attend the conference rather than merely sending his attorney.
  (b) The principal or the attorney must have full settlement authority.
  (c) The parties must negotiate in "good faith" at the settlement conference.

**5. Judicial Involvement in Settlement Conferences.**   It is one thing for a judge to order litigants to sit down together and discuss the possibility of settlement. It is quite another for the judge to evaluate the strength of the parties' cases, encourage parties to accept settlement offers, require parties to explain why they are rejecting a particular settlement proposal, or even to propose settlements. Is direct judicial involvement of this sort in settlement conferences appropriate? What is it about the nature of judicial involvement that might be helpful to the parties? What is it that might be unduly coercive?

**6. The Civil/Criminal Distinction.**   Is it sensible that judges be permitted to interject themselves into settlement discussions between civil litigants but not into settlement discussions between prosecutors and criminal defendants? What justifications do you think might underlie this distinction?

**7. Settlement Conferences and the Bargaining Zone.**   Judges evidently believe that mandatory settlement conferences can increase the rate of settlement — otherwise, presumably, they would not order such conferences. Drawing on your knowledge about the structure of negotiation, explain how you think mandatory settlement conferences can facilitate settlement. Can they actually help to create or expand a bargaining zone between two negotiating parties, or is their value limited to helping the parties see that a bargaining zone exists? If the latter, explain why parties participating in a mandatory settlement conference would be more likely than they otherwise would be to perceive the existence of a bargaining zone.

**8. The Scope of Rule 408.**   Assuming that the goal of Rule 408 is to help litigants to reach out-of-court settlements whenever a bargaining zone exists, does the *Thomas* decision, by reading narrowly the scope of Rule 408's exclusion of "statements" made in compromise negotiations, undermine the rule's purpose? After reading *Thomas*, are there statements that might help litigating parties identify a potential settlement that you would discourage a client from making due to fear that the statement would be used against him in court?

**9. An Apology Subsequent to an Incident.**   Last week, there was an eight-car collision on an interstate highway in which your client's car was first hit by another car and then struck a third car. Your client escaped injury, but the driver of the third car was injured and has been hospitalized since the accident. Your client wants to visit the driver of the third car in the hospital and apologize for striking her with his car. Will you encourage or discourage him from doing so? How does Rule 408 affect the advice you will give your client? Would your advice be different if the driver of the third car had already filed a lawsuit against your client?

# Chapter 15

# Limitations on Settlement

In most circumstances, the enforceability of settlement agreements is a matter of standard contract law. A plaintiff's agreement to give up a potentially meritorious claim serves as consideration for whatever concessions a defendant makes to settle the case. See Restatement (Second) of Contracts §74 (1981). A settlement can be attacked on the grounds of misrepresentation, of course, or other common law defenses such as mistake, duress, or unconscionability. Otherwise, in ordinary circumstances, courts do not evaluate the merits of a voluntary settlement — judicial involvement in the matter is terminated by a dismissal filed by the plaintiff.

Complete freedom to settle is limited by the law, however, in two different types of situations. First, in certain circumstances, settlement agreements are suspect, and thus subject to judicial oversight. Such judicial oversight can result from a paternalistic fear that imbalances in bargaining power might produce inequitable agreements or a concern that settlements might be mutually beneficial to the bargainers but prejudicial to third parties or to the public generally. Second, in lawsuits involving multiple defendants in which some defendants settle and others do not, a variety of contribution and set-off rules can affect the plaintiff's rights vis-à-vis the nonsettling defendants. In this type of situation, the law does not limit the plaintiff's ability to settle with a defendant, but the settlement imposes limitations on the plaintiff's ability to recover via adjudication from other defendants, and concerns about the effect of partial settlement on nonsettling defendants can lead to some restrictions on the types of settlements the law will permit.

## A.  JUDICIAL REVIEW OF SETTLEMENTS

### 1.  Power Imbalances

In some special categories of litigation, court approval of settlement agreements is required to guard against the ill effects of potential power imbalances between parties. Because there is often a power imbalance between divorcing spouses (and also because any settlement affects children who are not parties to the litigation), divorce settlement agreements must be approved by a court before they are binding on the parties. The precise standards for this approval vary subtly among jurisdictions, but the general principle is that courts have the equitable power to reject settlement agreements that are substantively unfair given the context of the negotiations. See, e.g., Drawdy v. Drawdy, 268 S.E.2d 30 (S.C. 1980) ("it is incumbent on the family court to satisfy itself that the agreement is a fair contractual end to the parties' marital claims"); see generally Sally Burnett Sharp, Fairness Standards and Separation Agreements: A Word of Caution on Contractual Freedom, 132 U. Pa. L. Rev. 1399 (1984).

Some jurisdictions permit courts to refuse to uphold negotiated divorce settlements only when some element of procedural unfairness in the negotiating process is demonstrated, such as fraud, duress, deceit, or coercion. See, e.g., Baker v. Baker, 394 So. 2d 465 (Fla. Ct. App. 1981). As the following case demonstrates, other jurisdictions permit judicial interference in private settlement agreements even in the absence of the indicia of procedural irregularities in the bargaining process and even when third parties are not affected by the agreement.

■ **Lewis v. Lewis**
  **603 P.2d** 650, 652-653 (Kan. Ct. App. 1979)

JUDGE ABBOTT delivered the Opinion of the Court.

This is an appeal from a judgment in a divorce action modifying an oral separation agreement. . . .

1. Donald Lewis contends the court erred in modifying the agreement made by the parties by awarding defendant future support payments. As we read the findings by the trial court, it did not award "future support payments" to Mrs. Lewis. Its adjustment of the parties' agreement is clearly intended to be a part of the property division, as evidenced by the trial court's letter of November 29, 1978, and the subsequent journal entry which recites:

[T]he Court . . . approves the division of the property previously made by the parties hereto and finds *to provide a fair settlement of the parties' property,* the settlement should include payment for a period of three years of $150.00 per month from the Plaintiff to Defendant *to divide the total property of the parties including Plaintiff's retirement income.* (Emphasis supplied.)

Thus, the question presented is whether the trial court erred in its modification of the parties' agreement. . . .

We do not quarrel with plaintiff's contention that a court is powerless to modify a valid, just and equitable separation agreement, except as to matters authorized by statute, unless the agreement provides for or the parties consent to such power. K.S.A. 60-1610(*e*) (now K.S.A. 1978 Supp. 60-1610[*e*]); Rasure v. Wright, 1 Kan. App. 2d 699, Syl. para. 3, 573 P.2d 1103 (1977), *rev. denied* 225 Kan. 845 (1978) . . . It is also clear that all separation agreements which are found to be fair, just and equitable by the trial court are merged into the divorce decree and become a judgment of the court. Fiske v. Fiske, 218 Kan. 132, Syl. para. 2, 542 P.2d 284 (1975). However, we do not agree that the trial court's modification of the parties' agreement here was contrary to the principles set out above.

In our opinion, the answer to plaintiff's contention is found in K.S.A. 60-1610(*e*), which provided in pertinent part: "If the parties have entered into a separation agreement *which the court finds to be valid, just and equitable,* it shall be incorporated in the decree." (Emphasis supplied.). . . . In Spaulding v. Spaulding, 221 Kan. 574, 577, 561 P.2d 420 (1977), the Court stated: "[I]n finding that an agreement is valid, just, and equitable, as required by the statute, the agreement must be carefully scrutinized." A necessary corollary of the trial court's duty to examine a separation agreement as to whether it is valid, just and equitable, is the power to modify such agreement prior to its incorporation into the decree. To hold otherwise would render meaningless the trial court's power to adjust the interests of the parties in a divorce proceeding. . . .

A finding that it is necessary to add to one party's share to make an agreement fair is tantamount to finding that an agreement is not just and equitable. In the present case, the trial court obviously gave considerable credence and weight to the parties' mutual intent manifested in their oral agreement, but felt that an adjustment in the nature of cash payments to Mrs. Lewis was necessitated to offset Mr. Lewis's retirement income and make the parties' property division equitable. Such payments may be ordered to effect a just and equitable property division. K.S.A. 60-1610(*c*). We hold that if a trial court finds that a separation agreement is not just and equitable as required by 60-1610(*e*), it is free either to reject or make reasonable adjustments to the agreement as provided for by 60-1610(c), provided it does so before entering a final judgment that merges the separation agreement into a divorce decree.

Our review of the appropriate factors to be considered in making a division of property (Parish v. Parish, 220 Kan. 131, 133-34, 551 P.2d 792 [1976]) leads us to the conclusion that the trial court's addition of the cash payments to the parties' separation agreement was not an abuse of discretion. See Stayton v. Stayton, 211 Kan. 560, 562, 506 P.2d 1172 (1973).                                                                ■

## 2.   Principal-Agent Conflicts

Court approval is also required in some instances when one party is a fiduciary for others who are not directly involved in the litigation. Class action suits, in which named class members prosecute an action on behalf of many other similarly situated parties, are a prime example. To protect the rights of class members who do not actually have a seat at the bargaining table from potential self-dealing by named class members or the attorneys for the class, the Federal Rules of Civil Procedure require judicial approval of any proposed settlement. See Fed. R. Civ. P. 23(e); Officers for Justice v. Civil Service Commission, 688 F.2d 615 9th Cir. 1982); Weinberger v. Kendrick, 698 F.2d 61 (2d Cir. 1982). The same principle underlies the requirement of court approval of shareholder derivative suit settlements. See, e.g., Schlusselberg v. Colonial Management Associates, 389 F. Supp. 933 (D. Mass 1974).

### ■ Mars Steel Corp. v. Continental Illinois National Bank

834 F.2d 677, 678-684 (7th Cir. 1987)

JUDGE POSNER delivered the Opinion of the Court. . . .

Class actions differ from ordinary lawsuits in that the lawyers for the class, rather than the clients, have all the initiative and are close to being the real parties in interest. This fundamental departure from the traditional pattern in Anglo-American litigation generates a host of problems well illustrated by this appeal, which challenges the settlement in a class action.

In 1983, the Chicago law firm of Joyce and Kubasiak filed Tunney v. Continental Illinois National Bank in an Illinois state court. This was a class action on behalf of persons who had borrowed money from Continental at interest rates pegged to Continental's prime rate. The complaint alleged that since 1973 Continental had defrauded (and broken its contracts with) these borrowers by failing to adhere to its agreement to charge an interest rate pegged to the "prime rate," which the loan agreements defined as the rate the bank charges "for 90-day unsecured commercial loans to large corporate customers of the highest credit standing." The complaint alleged that throughout this period Continental had made loans to large corporate customers at rates well below the prime rate quoted to members of the class. In 1984 the state court judge certified the suit as a nationwide class action, appointed Joyce and Kubasiak to represent the class, and certified his certification for an interlocutory appeal. Because of the settlement negotiations described later in this opinion, the appeal was never taken; neither was notice to the class ever issued. Joyce and Kubasiak conducted little discovery, and did little other investigating, concerning the merits of the "prime rate" claim.

In 1985, Mars Steel Corporation, represented by Jerome Torshen, sued Continental in federal court in Chicago on behalf of a class defined identically to that in the *Tunney* suit. The only violation alleged in *Mars* was a violation of the RICO statute (Racketeer Influenced and Corrupt Organizations Act, 18 U.S.C. §§1961 et seq.), for a period beginning in 1973; treble damages were sought. Although *Mars* was filed after *Tunney*, Torshen, unlike Joyce and Kubasiak, pursued discovery on the merits. To comply with his document demands Continental developed a computer program that enabled it to discover which 90-day unsecured loans made between January 1980 and September 1982 might have been made below its prime rate. The computer search turned up 140 questionable loans, but further investigation showed that none of these was below prime within the meaning of the loan agreements with the members of the class. Some of the loans were for fewer than 90 days, some for more than 90 days; some were at fixed interest rates rather than rates pegged to the prime rate; some had not been made to corporate customers; some imposed compensating-balance requirements that had the effect of jacking up the real interest rate; and in some the interest rate was misstated because of clerical error. There is no suggestion that in making loans to large corporate customers for periods different from 90 days or at fixed interest rates rather than rates pegged to a fluctuating prime rate Continental was attempting to circumvent the terms of the loan agreements with the members of the class.

Discovery set the stage for settlement negotiations, which Continental conducted separately with Joyce and Kubasiak and with Torshen. Early in 1986 Joyce and Kubasiak offered a settlement whereby Continental would agree not to oppose a request for an attorney's fee of $2 million (later reduced to $1.25 million) and the class members would be given an opportunity to take out new loans from Continental at below-market rates. Continental refused the offer, and shortly afterward settled with Torshen. Under the terms of the settlement

Continental would not oppose Torshen's request for $305,000 in fees, while the members of the class, defined as all corporate borrowers from Continental since 1973 at rates tied to the prime rate, would be entitled to take out new loans from Continental of up to $100,000 for one year at an interest rate roughly one-half of one percent below the borrower's previous interest rate. If (a big if) interest rates had not changed, Continental would be giving a $500 interest credit to every member of the class who wanted to borrow and met the bank's standards of creditworthiness. If interest rates had risen, the class members would do better than this; if rates had fallen, they would do worse. Since there are 23,000 class members, the maximum value of the settlement to them if interest rates have not changed is $11.5 million. . . .

. . . [This] brings us to the second issue presented by the appeal, the fairness of the settlement. The fairness of a settlement of a legal dispute is like the adequacy of the consideration supporting a contractual promise: a matter best left to negotiation between the parties. A settlement is a contract, and normally the test for the fairness of a contract is strictly procedural: were the parties competent adults duly apprised of the basic facts relating to their transaction? The problem in the class-action setting, and the reason that judicial approval of the settlement of such an action is required, see Fed. R. Civ. P. 23(e), is that the negotiator on the plaintiffs' side, that is, the lawyer for the class, is potentially an unreliable agent of his principals. See, e.g., Dam, Class Actions: Efficiency, Compensation, Deterrence, and Conflict of Interest, 4 J. Legal Stud. 47 (1975); Rosenfield, An Empirical Test of Class-Action Settlement, 5 J. Legal Stud. 113 (1976). Ordinarily the named plaintiffs are nominees, indeed pawns, of the lawyer, and ordinarily the unnamed class members have individually too little at stake to spend time monitoring the lawyer — and their only coordination is through him. One solution, illustrated by the events narrated above, is competition by other lawyers to represent the class. It is only a partial solution, because a lawyer may be able to obtain a large fee not just by outbidding another class lawyer but, alternatively, by "selling out" the class, a danger discussed in In re General Motors Corp. Engine Interchange Litigation, 594 F.2d 1106, 1125 (7th Cir. 1979). Joyce and Kubasiak hints that Torshen sold out the class to Continental (which was eager to buy) in exchange for a $305,000 mess of potage. The danger of collusive settlements — vividly described many years ago by Justice Jackson in Cohen v. Beneficial Industrial Loan Corp., [*682] 337 U.S. 541, 549-50, 93 L. Ed. 1528, 69 S. Ct. 1221 (1949), and rendered much greater than in the ordinary litigation by the tenuousness of the control exerted by the client (principal) over the lawyer (agent) — makes it imperative that the district judge conduct a careful inquiry into the fairness of a settlement to the class members before allowing it to go into effect and extinguish, by the operation of res judicata, the claims of the class members who do not opt out of the settlement. . . .

A settlement is fair to the plaintiffs in a substantive sense (we examine the procedural fairness of the settlement later) if it gives them the expected value of their claim if it went to trial, net of the costs of trial (minus the costs of settlement, but we can disregard that detail). In re General Motors Corp. Engine Interchange Litigation, supra, 594 F.2d at 1132 n. 44. Suppose the claim of the class in this matter is worth $750 million, but the probability that the class would prevail if the case were tried is only one percent and if it did prevail it would have to pay a contingent fee of $10 million. Then assuming risk neutrality (meaning indifference between a sum certain and its uncertain equivalent — e.g. between $2 and a 10 percent chance of $20), the class would be better off settling for any amount greater than $7.4 million than taking its chances on a trial. And if the members of the class were risk averse they might consider themselves better off even if the settlement were much smaller.

Joyce and Kubasiak argues that a trial might result in a judgment for the class of anywhere from $750 million to $1.5 billion, but it has not established the realism of this projection and the judge was not required to take it at face value. Continental's computer study, though admittedly limited to only a portion of the complaint period, reveals no loans below Continental's prime rate. If the results of that study can be generalized to the rest of the complaint period, not only was there no fraud or breach of contract, there were no damages. Furthermore, although many "prime rate" cases have been brought against banks in recent years, none has resulted in a victory at trial for the plaintiffs and apparently none in a settlement significantly (if at all) more favorable to the plaintiffs than the *Mars* settlement. See, e.g., NCNB National Bank v. Tiller, 814 F.2d 931 (4th Cir. 1987); Haroco, Inc. v. American National Bank & Trust Co., 662 F. Supp. 590 (N.D. Ill. 1987); Kleiner v. First National Bank, 581 F. Supp 955 (N.D. Ga. 1984). As *Kleiner* notes, a prime rate is merely a bank's forecast of what it would charge its most creditworthy corporate customers for a 90-day unsecured loan. It is not an actual transaction price, because the computation of such a price — requiring, as it would, averaging interest rates across numerous loans made at different times on different terms (e.g., compensating balances) — would be infeasible. See id. at 958-60. Reasonable pretrial discovery conducted by Torshen brought to light no evidence that the forecasts that Continental used in deciding how much interest to charge members of the class were not good-faith estimates of what Continental would charge its most creditworthy customers for a 90-day unsecured loan.

Hence if this case went to trial (assuming it could surmount a summary judgment motion by the bank) the prospects for the plaintiffs would be very dim. In these circumstances a settlement possibly worth as much as $11.5 million to the plaintiffs (conceivably even more), net of attorneys' fees and other costs of suit and without the delay of litigation, seems generous — and certainly adequate, as the district judge found. True, the settlement extinguished the claims of the *Tunney* class; but almost no members of that class objected, for the excellent reason that the settlement gave the class more than it could realistically have hoped to obtain either by litigation or by separate settlement negotiations — given the underlying weakness of the claim, the lack of vigorous prosecution of *Tunney*, and Joyce and Kubasiak's preoccupation with attorneys' fees. The fact that *Mars* charged only a RICO violation would be relevant if the omission of other theories had caused Torshen to scale down his settlement demand; the settlement would not be fair if it yielded the plaintiffs less money than they could reasonably have hoped to obtain in the parallel state court suit, where other theories had been advanced. But the amount of the settlement negotiated by Torshen was reasonable not merely in relation to the RICO claim but in relation to any theory of Continental's liability, for any such theory depended on proof of violations of the prime-rate loan agreements, and it appears there were no such violations. . . .

Last, a variety of procedural rulings are challenged, including the district judge's refusal to hold an evidentiary hearing before giving preliminary approval to the settlement. These rulings are said to have had the cumulative effect of preventing Joyce and Kubasiak from conducting discovery of Continental's settlement negotiations with Torshen — discovery that Joyce and Kubasiak argues would have shown that the settlement lacked merit — and from introducing evidence that the settlement was disadvantageous to the class. However, the challenged rulings were within the district judge's broad discretion in managing a class action. Discovery of settlement negotiations in ongoing litigation is unusual because it would give a party information about an opponent's strategy, and it was not required in the circumstances of this case. Suppose Joyce and Kubasiak, allowed to discover the details of Continental's negotiations with Torshen, had found out that Continental had acknowledged certain weaknesses in its defense; Joyce and Kubasiak could have used that information to drive a harder bargain with Continental or, if settlement negotiations had broken down, to undermine Continental's defense at trial. Such discovery is proper only where the party seeking it lays a foundation by adducing from other sources evidence indicating that the settlement may be collusive, as in the *General Motors* case, where negotiations with one class counsel were carried out in violation of the district court's order. See 594 F.2d at 1126. There is no indication of such hanky-panky here. Nothing in the terms or timing or other circumstances of the *Mars* settlement — a settlement highly favorable to the class, as we have said — suggests that Torshen was selling out the class in an effort to beat Joyce and Kubasiak to the attorney's fee trough. Indeed, Torshen's fee seems modest in relation to the benefits to the class in a lawsuit so thin that probably it should never have been brought, while Joyce and Kubasiak's equity in requesting a discovery order is weak in light of its failure to pursue discovery in the state court proceeding. Cf. Weinberger v. Kendrick, supra, 698 F.2d at 79.

The temptation to convert a settlement hearing into a full trial on the merits must be resisted. Airline Stewards & Stewardesses Assn., Local 550 v. American Airlines, Inc., 573 F.2d 960, 963-64 (7th Cir. 1978) (per curiam). Yet that is essentially what Joyce and Kubasiak is seeking. It hopes to unearth evidence showing that, contrary to what the discovery conducted by Torshen revealed, Continental really did violate the prime-rate loan agreements. The time for that discovery was in 1983 when *Tunney* was filed. . . .

The settlement was fair, both substantively and procedurally, and the order of the district court affirming it is therefore

AFFIRMED.                                                                    ■

## 3.  Protecting the Public Interest

Various statutes require prospective judicial approval of settlement agreements in order to insure that settlements that affect the general public serve the public interest. The extent of the judicial role in assuring that settlements of antitrust lawsuits brought by the Department of Justice serve the public interest, as required by the Tunney Act, is considered in the following case.

## ■ United States v. Microsoft Corp.

**56 F.3d** 1448 (D.C. Cir. 1995)

JUDGE SILBERMAN delivered the Opinion of the Court. . . .

Section 16(e) of the Antitrust Procedures and Penalties Act, known as the Tunney Act, requires the district court to determine whether entry of an antitrust consent decree is "in the public interest." 15 U.S.C. §16(e) (1988). In this case, the district court refused to enter a proposed consent decree the Antitrust Division of the Department of Justice negotiated with Microsoft Corporation. We conclude that the proposed consent decree is in the public interest, and that the district court exceeded its authority in concluding to the contrary. We therefore reverse and remand with instructions to enter an order approving the decree. . . .

In July 1994, the Department filed a civil complaint under the Sherman Act, 15 U.S.C. §§1 and 2 (1988), charging Microsoft with unlawfully maintaining a monopoly of operating systems for IBM-compatible PCs and unreasonably restraining trade of the same through certain anticompetitive marketing practices. . . .

In a not uncommon technique, the Department of Justice filed a proposed consent decree along with its complaint, which embodied the Department's and Microsoft's settlement of the case. . . .

At the first substantive status conference on September 29, 1994, the district judge informed the parties that over the summer he had read a book about Microsoft — Hard Drive — because he "thought it would be a good idea maybe to know as much about Microsoft as probably they're going to know about me." Much of the ensuing discussion focused on accusations against Microsoft contained in the book. The district judge asked whether the government's lawyers had read the book and whether they had investigated the allegations made by its authors. In particular, the judge focused on the allegation that Microsoft engages in "vaporware," which he described in differing terms but ultimately defined as "the public announcement of a computer product before it is ready for market for the sole purpose of causing consumers not to purchase a competitor's product that has been developed and is either currently available for sale or momentarily about to enter the market." United States v. Microsoft Corp., 159 F.R.D. 318, 334 (D.D.C. 1995) ("Opinion"). . . .

On February 14, 1995, the district court issued an order denying the government's motion to approve the consent decree. The judge stated that he could not find the proposed decree to be in the public interest for four reasons:

First, the Government has declined to provide the Court with the information it needs to make a proper public interest determination. Second, the scope of the decree is too narrow. Third, the parties have been unable and unwilling adequately to address certain anticompetitive practices, which Microsoft states it will continue to employ in the future and with respect to which the decree is silent. Thus, the decree does not constitute an effective antitrust remedy. Fourth, the Court is not satisfied that the enforcement and compliance mechanisms in the decree are satisfactory. . . .

Both the government and Microsoft contend that the district judge vastly exceeded his authority under the Tunney Act, and that as a matter of law they are entitled to the court's entry of the consent decree. . . .

At the heart of this case, then, is the proper scope of the district court's inquiry into the "public interest." Is the district judge entitled to seize hold of the matter — the investigation into the putative defendant's business practices — and decide for himself the appropriate combined response of the executive and judicial branches to those practices? With respect to the specific allegations in the government's complaint, may the court interpose its own views of the appropriate remedy over those the government seeks as a part of its overall settlement? To be sure, Congress, in passing the Tunney Act, intended to prevent "judicial rubber stamping" of the Justice Department's proposed consent decree. H.R. Rep. No. 1463, supra, at 8, reprinted in 1974 U.S. Code Cong. & Admin. News at 6538. The Court was to "make an independent determination as to whether or not entry of a proposed consent decree [was] in the public interest." S. Rep. No. 298, supra, at 5. Yet, Congress did not purport to alter antitrust precedent applying the public interest in reviewing consent decrees. H.R. Rep. No. 1463, supra, at 11, reprinted in 1974 U.S. Code Cong. & Admin. News at 6539. The difficulty with that stated purpose is that there was virtually no useful precedent — certainly none in which an appellate court had approved a trial court's rejection of a consent decree as outside the public interest. Cf. Antitrust Procedures and Penalties Act: Hearings on S.782 and S.1088 Before the Subcomm. on Antitrust and Monopolies of the Senate Comm. on the Judiciary, 93d Cong., 1st Sess. 92 (1973) ("Senate Hearings") (Statement of Thomas E. Kauper, Assistant Attorney General, Antitrust Division, Dept. of Justice) ("[E]xcept in cases where a previous judicial mandate is involved and the consent decree fails to comply with that mandate, or where there is a showing of bad faith or malfeasance, the courts have allowed a wide range of prosecutorial discretion.").

Although the statute does not give specific guidance, it does speak in rather broad terms. In determining whether the decree is in the public interest, the district court is authorized to "consider":

(1) the competitive impact of such judgment, including termination of alleged violations, provisions for enforcement and modification, duration or relief sought, anticipated effects of alternative remedies actually considered, and any other considerations bearing upon the adequacy of such judgment;

(2) the impact of entry of such judgment upon the public generally and individuals alleging specific injury from the violations set forth in the complaint including consideration of the public benefit, if any, to be derived from a determination of the issues at trial.

15 U.S.C. § 16(e) (1988).

The government, cautioning us as to the constitutional difficulties that inhere in this statute, urges us to flatly reject the district judge's

efforts to reach beyond the complaint to evaluate claims that the government did not make and to inquire as to why they were not made.
We agree. Although the language of section 16(e) is not precise, we
think the government is correct in contending that section 16(e)(1)'s
reference to the alleged violations suggests that Congress did not
mean for a district judge to construct his own hypothetical case and
then evaluate the decree against that case. Moreover, in section
16(e)(2), the court is authorized to consider "the public benefit . . . of
the determination of the issues at trial." Putting aside the perplexing
question of how the district judge could insure a trial if the government did not wish one, "the issues" referred to must be those formulated in the complaint. Congress surely did not contemplate that the
district judge would, by reformulating the issues, effectively redraft the
complaint himself. We therefore dismiss the claim that the last line in
section 16(e)(1), the catchall clause allowing the district court to entertain "any other considerations bearing upon the adequacy of such
judgment," authorizes the wide-ranging inquiry the district court
wished to conduct in this case. That language recognizes, inter alia,
that a consent decree might well do unexpected harm to persons
other than those "alleging specific injury from the violations set forth
in the complaint." 15 U.S.C. §16(e)(2) (1988). And the district court
might ponder those sort of concerns in determining whether to enter
the judgment. . . .

When the government and a putative defendant present a proposed
consent decree to a district court for review under the Tunney Act, the
court can and should inquire, in the manner we have described, into
the purpose, meaning, and efficacy of the decree. If the decree is ambiguous, or the district judge can foresee difficulties in implementation, we would expect the court to insist that these matters be attended
to. And, certainly, if third parties contend that they would be positively
injured by the decree, a district judge might well hesitate before assuming that the decree is appropriate. But, when the government is
challenged for not bringing as extensive an action as it might, a district
judge must be careful not to exceed his or her constitutional role. A
decree, even entered as a pretrial settlement, is a judicial act, and
therefore the district judge is not obliged to accept one that, on its
face and even after government explanation, appears to make a mockery of judicial power. Short of that eventuality, the Tunney Act cannot
be interpreted as an authorization for a district judge to assume the
role of Attorney General.

Accordingly, the case is remanded with instructions to enter the proposed decree.                                                          ■

## B. SETTLEMENT IN MULTIPLE-DEFENDANT LITIGATION

In most jurisdictions, if a plaintiff wins a liability verdict against multiple defendants, liability among the defendants is joint and several but damages are apportioned amongst the defendants on the basis of comparative fault. What, then, is the effect on the plaintiff's recovery in court if she negotiates a settlement agreement with one (or more) defendants before securing a verdict against one (or more) nonsettling defendants?

Although rules vary across jurisdictions, two approaches predominate. Under the traditional approach, often called the "pro tanto" rule, nonsettling defendants receive a credit to be applied toward any liability judgment against them equal to the amount of money the plaintiff has received from a settling defendant. Thus, if Plaintiff sues defendants Hansel and Gretel and settles out of court with Gretel for $1 million before trial, Hansel's maximum liability will be Plaintiff's total damages minus $1 million. If a jury finds that Plaintiff suffered $5 million in damages and that Hansel and Gretel were each 50 percent at fault, Hansel will face a $4 million judgment. He may be able to then bring a contribution claim against Gretel for $1.5 million, but many jurisdictions would protect Gretel from such a claim so long as her settlement with Plaintiff was made in "good faith." If a jury finds that Plaintiff suffered only $1.1 million in damages, and that Hansel and Gretel were equally at fault, Plaintiff's recovery from Hansel would be limited to $100,000.

Under the pro tanto approach, then, Plaintiff's settlement with one of multiple defendants does not affect her total recovery (assuming that Plaintiff prevails in court), but it does affect the distribution of liability among the defendants. If the settling defendant negotiates a "good" deal (i.e., one that is less than her proportionate share of liability as subsequently determined by a jury), the nonsettling defendant pays more than his equitable share, assuming a contribution claim against the settling defendant is barred; if the settling defendant negotiates a "bad" deal (i.e., one that is more than her proportionate share of liability as subsequently determined by a jury), the nonsettling defendant pays less than his proportionate share.

Under the alternative approach, often called the "proportionate share" rule, Plaintiff's settlement with Gretel would reduce Hansel's liability to his proportionate share of any damage award based on his and Gretel's comparative fault. That is, if the jury decided that Hansel and Gretel were each 50 percent liable for Plaintiff's damages, Hansel would be liable for 50 percent of any damage award, whether that award was $1.1 million or $5 million. Under the proportionate share rule, the amount of Plaintiff's total recovery is dependent on the amount of her settlement with Gretel, whereas the extent of Hansel's liability is not affected by the settlement between Plaintiff and Gretel. The proportionate share rule has been adopted by the Supreme Court for cases arising under federal maritime law. See McDermott v. Am-Clyde, 511 U.S. 202 (1994). This proportionate share rule is also favored by recently enacted apportionment of liability provisions of the Restatement (Third) of Torts. Restatement (Third) of Torts: Apportionment of Liability §26 (proposed final draft 1999).

In order to enlist the assistance of a settling defendant in litigation against non-settling defendants, plaintiffs sometimes negotiate settlements that are contingent on the amount recovered from other defendants. That is, the higher the judgment won from the nonsettling defendants, the lower the settlement amount collected from the settling defendant. The legality of this type of agreement, known as a "Mary Carter" agreement after the case of Booth v. Mary Carter Paint Co., 202 So. 2d 8 (Fla. App. 1967), is considered in the following case.

■ **Elbaor v. Smith**

**845 S.W.2d** 240 (Tex. 1992)

JUSTICE RAUL A. GONZALEZ delivered the Opinion of the Court. . . .
. . . Dr. Syrquin had performed emergency surgery on Ms. Smith's ankle. Testimony at trial revealed that Dr. Syrquin, who was not an orthopedic specialist, committed malpractice by closing the ankle too soon after debriding it. Eight days after the surgery, Dr. Syrquin recommended transferring Ms. Smith to ACH where she came under the care of, among others, Dr. Elbaor, an orthopedic specialist. [Ms. Smith brought suit against Dr. Syrquin, ACH, Dr. Stephens, and Dr. Elbaor. Prior to trial, she entered into "Mary Carter" agreements with the first three, but not with Dr. Elbaor.]

During the trial, the settling defendants' attorneys, who sat at the table with Dr. Elbaor's attorneys, vigorously assisted Ms. Smith in pointing the finger of culpability at Dr. Elbaor. This created some odd conflicts of interest and some questionable representations of fact. For example, although Ms. Smith's own experts testified that Dr. Syrquin committed malpractice, her attorney stated during voir dire and in her opening statement that Dr. Syrquin's conduct was "heroic" and that Dr. Elbaor's negligence caused Ms. Smith's damages. And during her closing argument, Ms. Smith's attorney urged the jury to find that Dr. Syrquin had not caused Ms. Smith's damages. This is hardly the kind of statement expected from a plaintiff's lawyer regarding a named defendant. ACH and Drs. Syrquin and Stephens had remained defendants of record, but their attorneys asserted during voir dire that Ms. Smith's damages were "devastating," "astoundingly high," and "astronomical." Furthermore, on cross examination they elicited testimony from Ms. Smith favorable to her and requested recovery for pain and mental anguish. The settling defendants' attorneys also abandoned their pleadings on Ms. Smith's contributory negligence, argued that Ms. Smith should be awarded all of her alleged damages, and urged that Dr. Elbaor was 100 percent liable.

## A.

The term "Mary Carter agreement" has been defined in different ways by various courts and commentators. . . . Today we clarify what we mean by the term "Mary Carter agreement." A Mary Carter agreement exists when the settling defendant retains a financial stake in the plaintiff's recovery **and** remains a party at the trial of the case. This definition comports with both the present majority view and the original understanding of the term.

A Mary Carter agreement exists, under our definition, when the plaintiff enters into a settlement agreement with one defendant and goes to trial against the remaining defendant(s). The settling defendant, who remains a party, guarantees the plaintiff a minimum payment, which may be offset in whole or in part by an excess judgment recovered at trial. See General Motors Corp. v. Simmons, 558 S.W.2d 855, 858 (Tex. 1977), *overruled on other grounds by* Duncan v. Cessna Aircraft Co., 665 S.W.2d 414, 427 (Tex. 1984). This creates a tremendous incentive for the settling defendant to ensure that the plaintiff succeeds in obtaining a sizable recovery, and thus motivates the defendant to assist greatly in the plaintiff's presentation of the case (as occurred here). Indeed, Mary Carter agreements generally, but not always, contain a clause requiring the settling defendant to participate in the trial on the plaintiff's behalf.

Given this Mary Carter scenario, it is difficult to surmise how these agreements promote settlement. Although the agreements do secure the partial settlement of a lawsuit, they nevertheless nearly always ensure a trial against the non-settling defendant. Bedford School Dist. v. Caron Constr. Co., 367 A.2d 1051, 1054 (N.H. 1976) (agreement required plaintiff to prosecute claim against remaining defendant and plaintiff could not settle the claim for under $20,000 without the consent of the settling defendant); Lum v. Stinnett, 488 P.2d 347, 348 (Nev. 1971) (same). Mary Carter agreements frequently make litigation inevitable, because they grant the settling defendant veto power over any proposed settlement between the plaintiff and any remaining defendant. See Bass v. Phoenix Seadrill/78 Ltd., 749 F.2d 1154, 1156 (5th Cir. 1985) (Mary Carter agreement gave settling defendant veto power). Thus, "only a mechanical jurisprudence could characterize Mary Carter arrangements as promoting compromise and discouraging litigation — they plainly do just the opposite." Stein v. American Residential Mgmt., 781 S.W.2d 385, 389 (Tex. App.-Houston [14th Dist.] 1989), *writ denied per curiam*, 793 S.W.2d 1 (Tex. 1990).

In his concurring opinion in Scurlock Oil Co. v. Smithwick, 724 S.W.2d 1, 8 (Tex. 1986) (on motion for rehearing), Justice Spears pointed out that "Mary Carter agreements should be prohibited because they are inimical to the adversary system, and they do not promote settlement — their primary justification." The truth of this statement has been recognized by commentators and has been proven by the subsequent history regarding the use of Mary Carter agreements. . . .

The case before us reveals yet another jury trial and verdict distorted by a Mary Carter agreement. . . .

As a matter of public policy, this Court favors settlements, but we do not favor partial settlements that promote rather than discourage further litigation. And we do not favor settlement arrangements that skew the trial process, mislead the jury, promote unethical collusion among nominal adversaries, and create the likelihood that a less culpable defendant will be hit with the full judgment. The bottom line is that our public policy favoring fair trials outweighs our public policy favoring partial settlements.

This case typifies the kind of procedural and substantive damage Mary Carter agreements can inflict upon our adversarial system. Thus, we declare them void as violative of sound public policy. . . .   ■

## Notes

*The Validity of Mary Carter Agreements.* *Elbaor* notwithstanding, only a minority of jurisdictions have found Mary Carter agreements per se invalid. Some courts have observed that such agreements are beneficial because they enable plaintiffs to raise capital that allows them to prosecute cases they otherwise might not be able to afford to litigate. See, e.g., Bass v. Phoenix Seadrill, 749 F.2d 1154 (5th Cir. 1985). Others have noted that such agreements are consistent with a public policy of allowing plaintiffs to control their own cases. See, e.g., Hackman v. Dandamudi, 733 S.W.2d 452 (1986). Many courts have expressed concern about the consequences of the plaintiff's agreement with the settling defendant or defendants remaining secret, but most have addressed this concern by requiring disclosure of the agreement to the nonsettling parties and the jury or by making the existence of such an agreement a discoverable fact in litigation. See, e.g., General Motors v. Lahocki, 286 Md. 714 (1980); Pacific Indemnity Co. v. Thompson-Yeager, Inc., 260 N.W.2d 548 (Minn. 1977).

# DISCUSSION QUESTIONS AND PROBLEMS

*1. The Policy of Judicial Involvement in Settlement.* As a matter of policy, in what circumstances should court approval of settlement agreements be mandated? Given that settlement agreements, like other contracts, can always be contested on the common law grounds of misrepresentation, mistake, undue influence, duress, or unconscionability, is it ever desirable to require judicial approval, or are such requirements misplaced paternalism?

*2. Defining a "Fair" Settlement Agreement.* When courts have authority to approve settlement agreements, what substantive standard should judges use to determine whether the settlement is fair? In *Mars Steel Corp.,* Judge Posner suggests, in effect, that a settlement is fair if it falls within the bargaining zone that existed at the time of negotiations, when he asserts that "[a] settlement is fair to the plaintiffs in a substantive sense . . . if it gives them the expected value of their claim if it went to trial, net of the costs of trial. . . ." *Mars Steel Corp.,* supra. Is this a desirable substantive standard for courts to use?

If this is the appropriate substantive standard, a number of practical questions arise. Must the court assessing the fairness of the settlement essentially try the case on the merits in order to assess the expected value of a trial? Judge Posner ruled that such a "temptation" should be resisted. But how else could the court render an accurate determination of the expected value of a case? Further, while a court could in theory evaluate the expected value of trying a case, how could a judge ever divine the reservation price of the class, given that such a reservation price would embody unobservable factors such as subjective preferences for adjudication relative to settlement, relative risk aversion, and so on?

*3. The Impact of Judicial Involvement on Negotiation.* Building on your knowledge of the negotiation process, describe how you would expect bargaining to be different in circumstances in which judicial approval of settlements is required than in the more ordinary circumstance in which judicial approval is not necessary. How would the element of judicial approval affect the parties' BATNAs and reservation prices? How might it affect the likelihood that the parties will use power tactics, rely on fairness norms, or find integrative bargaining opportunities?

*4. Courts and the Protection of the Public Interest.* In United States v. Microsoft Corp., the D.C. Circuit recognized the importance of the judicial act of approving a consent decree in an antitrust prosecution and cautioned that a district court should not "rubber stamp" such decrees or allow the parties to make "a mockery" of the judicial process. At the same time, the court criticized the district judge for rejecting the parties' proposed consent decree on the grounds that the government's lawsuit was too narrow in scope, and it ordered the district judge to approve the decree. In light of the court's holding, does the judicial power to decline to enter antitrust consent decrees have any real teeth? Recall that the court noted that the government often files its antitrust claim at the same time as the proposed consent decree. If the government tailors its claim so that the concurrently filed consent decree is completely responsive to it, can the judiciary ever protect the public interest from a settlement that is insufficient in light of the full range of actual violations that the government believes the defendant committed?

As a related issue, is judicial approval of antitrust claims filed by the government necessary? Can the public interest be adequately protected by the Department of Justice, which presumably would not agree to the settlement of its claims if it believes settlement is not in the public interest?

**5. Multiple-Defendant Settlement Rules.**   How would you expect the pro tanto and proportionate share approaches to dealing with partial settlements in multiple-defendant litigation affect the reservation prices of plaintiffs and defendants? How do you think the two approaches would affect the likelihood of settlement between (a) the plaintiff and the first defendant, and (b) the plaintiff and the remaining defendant (after other defendants have settled)?

**6. Mary Carter Agreements and Subsequent Bargaining.**   In *Elbaor*, the court states that Mary Carter agreements "nearly always ensure a trial against the nonsettling defendant." Given your understanding of the negotiation process, do you agree with this empirical prediction? How would the fact that Dr. Syrquin, ACH, and Dr. Stephens settled with Smith affect the bargaining zone in subsequent settlement negotiations between Smith and Dr. Elbaor? If the three settling defendants have veto power over any potential settlement, how might this fact affect the bargaining zone in the Smith-Elbaor negotiations? Would it make a trial inevitable?

# TABLE OF CASES

*Principal cases reproduced or excerpted are noted by bold type.*

**469**

# COLLECTED REFERENCES

*Excerpted items are noted by bold type.*

Adamowicz, Viktor L., et al., "Experiments on the Difference Between Willingness to Pay and Willingness to Accept," 69 Land Econ. 416 (1993), 86

**Arrow, Kenneth, et al., eds., *Barriers to Conflict Resolution* (1995), 103,** 147, 184

Austin, William, "Friendship and Fairness: Effects of Type of Relationship and Task Performance on Choice of Distribution Rules," 6 Pers. & Soc. Psychol. Bull. 402 (1980), 211, 212

**Axelrod, Robert, *The Evolution of Cooperation* (1984), 225**

Ayres, Ian, "Fair Driving: Gender and Race Discrimination in New Car Bargaining," 104 Harv. L. Rev. 817 (1991), 268

Ayres, Ian, & Barry J. Nalebuff, "Common Knowledge as a Barrier to Negotiation," 44 UCLA L. Rev. 1631 (1997), 163


Bakow, Lawrence, & Michael Wheeler, *Environmental Dispute Resolution* (1984), 162

Bazerman, Max H., & Margaret A. Neale, *Negotiating Rationally* (1992), 93

———, "The Role of Fairness Considerations and Relationships in a Judgmental Perspective of Negotiation," in *Barriers to Conflict Resolution* (Kenneth Arrow, et al., eds., 1995), 147, 184

Berryman-Fink, Cynthia, & Claire C. Brunner, "The Effects of Sex of Source and Target on Interpersonal Conflict Management Styles," 53 S. Speech Comm. J. 38 (1985), 265

Bickerman, John, "Evaluative Mediator Responds," 14 Alternatives to Litigation 70 (1996), 371

Birke, Richard, "Reconciling Loss Aversion and Guilty Pleas," 1999 Utah L. Rev. 205 (1999), 322

Birke, Richard, & Craig R. Fox, "Psychological Principles in Negotiating Civil Settlements," 4 Harv. Negotiation L. Rev. 1 (1999), 100

Bohnet, Iris, & Bruno S. Frey, "The Sound of Silence in Prisoner's Dilemma and Dictator Games," 38 J. Econ. Behav. & Org. 43 (1999), 212

Brams, Steven, & Alan D. Taylor, *Fair Division: From Cake-Cutting to Dispute Resolution* (1996), 217

**Brett, Jeanne M., "Culture and Negotiation," 35 Intl. J. Psychol. 97 (2000), 273,** 287

Brett, Jeanne M., et al., "The Effectiveness of Mediation: An Independent Analysis of Cases Handled by Four Major Service Providers," 12 Negotiation J. 259 (1996), 355, 372

Brown, Jennifer Gerarda, "The Role of Hope in Negotiation," 44 UCLA L. Rev. 1661 (1997), 62

Brown, Jennifer Gerarda, & Ian Ayres, "Economic Rationales for Mediation," 80 Va. L. Rev. 323 (1994), 351

Bush, Robert A. Baruch, & Joseph P. Folger, *The Promise of Mediation: Responding to Conflict Through Empowerment and Recognition* (1994), 356


**Cialdini, Robert B.,** *Influence: Science and Practice* **(1993), 185**

Cohen, Raymond, *Negotiating Across Culture* (1991), 272

Cooter, Robert, et al., "Bargaining in the Shadow of the Law: A Testable Model of Strategic Behavior," 11 J. Legal Stud. 225 (1982), 176

**Craver, Charles B., "Negotiation Ethics: How to Be Deceptive Without Being Dishonest/How to Be Assertive Without Being Offensive," 38 Tex. L. Rev. 713 (1997), 406**

**Craver, Charles B., & David W. Barnes, "Gender, Risk Taking, and Negotiation Performance," 5 Mich. J. Gender & L. 299 (1999), 258,** 269

Croson, Rachel, & Nancy Buchan, "Gender and Culture: International Experimental Evidence from Trust Games," 89 Am. Econ. Rev. 386 (1999), 266

Crystal, Nathan M., "The Lawyer's Duty to Disclose Material Facts in Contract or Settlement Negotiations," 87 Ky. L.J. 1055 (1998), 394


Diener, Ed, & Marissa Diener, "Cross-Cultural Correlates of Life Satisfaction and Self-Esteem," 68 J. Pers. & Soc. Psychology 653 (1995), 291

Dunnette, Melvin D., ed., *Handbook of Industrial and Organizational Psychology* (1976), 254


Eckel, Catherine, & Philip Grossman, "Are Women Less Selfish Than Men?: Evidence from Dictator Experiments," 108 Econ. J. 726 (1998), 265

———, & ———, "The Relative Price of Fairness: Gender Differences in a Punishment Game," 30 J. Econ. Behav. & Org. 143 (1996), 266

Edwards, Harry, & James J. White, *The Lawyer as Negotiator* (1977), 52


Fehr, Ernst, & Simon Gachter, "Fairness and Retaliation: The Economics of Reciprocity," 14 J. Econ. Persp. 159 (2000), 183

**Fisher, Roger, William Ury, & Bruce Patton,** *Getting to Yes* **(2d ed. 1991), 25, 38, 134,** 141, **203,** 359

Fobia, Cynthia S., & Jay J. Christensen-Szalanski, "Ambiguity and Liability Negotiations: The Effects of the Negotiator's Role and the Sensitivity Zone," 54 Org. Behav. & Human Decision Proc. 277 (1993), 100, 101

Freund, James, *Anatomy of a Merger: Strategies and Techniques for Negotiating Corporate Acquisitions* (1975), 193

Friedman, Gary J., *A Guide to Divorce Mediation* (1993), 372

Gelfand, Michele J., & Sophia Christakopoulou, "Culture and Negotiator Cognition: Judgment Accuracy and Negotiation Processes in Individualistic and Collectivistic Cultures," 79 Org. Behav. & Hum. Decision Proc. 248 (1999), 282

Gifford, Donald G., *Legal Negotiation: Theory and Applications* (1989), 336

Gilligan, Carol, *In a Different Voice: Psychological Theory and Women's Development* (1982), 259, **262**, 268

Gilson, Ronald J., "Value Creation by Business Lawyers: Legal Skills and Asset Pricing," 94 Yale L.J. 239 (1984), 139, **303**, 325

Gilson, Ronald J., & Robert H. Mnookin, "Disputing Through Agents: Cooperation and Conflict Between Lawyers in Litigation," 94 Colum. L. Rev. 509 (1995), 239, **298**

Goh, Bee Chen, "Sino-Western Negotiating Styles," 7 Canterbury L. Rev. 82 (1998), 287

Grant, Malcolm J., & Vello Sermat, "Status and Sex of Other as Determinants of Behavior in a Mixed-Motive Game," 12 J. Personality & Soc. Psychology 151 (1969), 261

Greenberg, Jerald, & Ronald L. Cohen, "Why Justice? Normative and Instrumental Interpretations," in *Equity and Justice in Social Behavior* (Greenberg & Cohen, eds., 1982), 213

Gross, Samuel, & Kent Syverud, "Getting to No: A Study of Settlement Negotiations and the Selection of Cases for Trial," 90 Mich. L. Rev. 319 (1991), 179, 323

Guthrie, Chris, "Framing Frivolous Litigation: A Psychological Theory," 67 U. Chi. L. Rev. 163 (2000), 75


Halpern, Richard G., "Settlement Negotiations: Taking Control," 34 Trial 64 (Feb. 1998), 179

Hammack, Judd, & Gardner Mallard Brown Jr., *Waterfowl and Wetlands: Toward a Bioeconomic Analysis* (1974), 85

Hartman, Raymond S., et al., "Consumer Rationality and the Status Quo," 106 Q.J. Econ. 141 (1991), 85, 86

Hartwell, Steven, et al., "Women Negotiating: Assertiveness and Relatedness," in *Constructing and Reconstructing Gender* (Linda A.M. Perry, et al., eds., 1992), 270

Hastorf, Albert H., & Hadley Cantril, "They Saw a Game: A Case Study," 49 J. Abnormal & Soc. Psychology 129 (1954), 97

Hirshleifer, Jack, "Game-Theoretic Interpretations of Commitment," in *Evolution and the Capacity for Commitment* (Randolph M. Nesse, ed., 2001), 169

Hoffman, Elizabeth, et al., "Preferences, Property Rights, and Anonymity in Bargaining Games," 7 Games & Econ. Behav. 346 (1994), 210

Hoffman, Elizabeth & Matthew L. Spitzer, "Entitlements, Rights, and Fairness: An Experimental Examination of Subjects' Concepts of Distributive Justice," 14 J. Legal Stud. 259 (1985), 211


Kahneman, Daniel, & Amos Tversky, "Choices, Values, and Frames," 39 Am. Psychologist 341 (1984), 86

————, & ————, "Prospect Theory: An Analysis of Decision Under Risk," 47 Econometrica 263 (1979), 68

Kahneman, Daniel, & Dale T. Miller, "Norm Theory: Comparing Reality to Its Alternatives," 93 Psychology Rev. 136 (1986), 87

**Kahneman, Daniel, Jack L. Knetsch, & Richard H. Thaler, "Experimental Tests of the Endowment Effect and the Coase Theorem," 98 J. Pol. Econ. 1325 (1990), 76**

**————, ————, & ————, "Fairness as a Constraint on Profit Seeking: Entitlements in the Market," 76 Am. Econ. Rev. 728 (1986), 196**

Kimmel, Melvin J., et al., "Effects of Trust, Aspiration and Gender on Negotiating Tactics," 38 J. Pers. & Soc. Psychol. 9 (1980), 257

Kimmel, Paul R., "Cultural Perspectives on International Negotiations," 50 J. Soc. Issues 179 (1994), 288, 289

Knetsch, Jack L., & J.A. Sinden, "Willingness to Pay and Compensation Demanded: Experimental Evidence of an Unexpected Disparity in Measures of Value," 99 Q.J. Econ. 507 (1984), 85

**Korobkin, Russell, "Inertia and Preference in Contract Negotiation: The Psychological Power of Default Rules and Form Terms," 51 Vand. L. Rev. 1583 (1998), 81, 86, 163**

**————, "A Positive Theory of Legal Negotiation," 88 Geo. L.J. 1789 (2000), 21, 37, 157**

Korobkin, Russell, & Chris Guthrie, "Opening Offers and Out of Court Settlement: A Little Moderation Might Not Go a Long Way," 10 Ohio St. J. Disp. Res. 1 (1994), 93, 194

**————, & ————, "Psychological Barriers to Litigation Settlement: An Experimental Approach," 93 Mich. L. Rev. 107 (1994), 75, 88, 108**

**————, & ————, "Psychology, Economics, and Settlement: A New Look at the Role of the Lawyer," 76 Tex. L. Rev. 77 (1997), 316**

Kovach, Kimberlee K., & Lela P. Love, "Evaluative Mediation Is an Oxymoron," 14 Alternatives to Litigation 31 (1996), 371

Kramer, Roderick M., et al., "Self-Enhancement Biases and Negotiator Judgment: Effects of Self-Esteem and Mood," 56 Org. Behav. & Human Dec. Proc. 110 (1993), 100

Kritzer, Herbert M., *Let's Make a Deal: Understanding the Negotiation Process in Ordinary Litigation* (1982), 320

Kronman, Anthony, "Mistake, Disclosure, and the Law of Contracts," 7 J. Legal Stud. 1 (1978), 394

Langer, Ellen J., "The Illusion of Control," 32 J. Pers. & Soc. Psychol. 311 (1975), 100

Lareau, N. Peter, *2 National Labor Relations Act: Law and Practice* (2d ed. 2000), 404

**Lax, David, & James Sebenius, *The Manager as Negotiator* (1986), 111, 115, 123, 147, 235**

————, & ————, "Thinking Coalitionally: Party Arithmetic, Process Opportunism, and Strategic Sequencing," in *Negotiation Analysis* (H. Peyton Young, ed., 1991), 339

Locke, Edwin A, & Gary P. Latham, *A Theory of Goal Setting and Task Performance* (1990), 57

**Loder, Reed Elizabeth, "Moral Truthseeking and the Virtuous Negotiator," 8 Geo. J. Legal Ethics 45 (1994), 411**

Loewenstein, George F., et al., "Social Utility and Decision Making in Interpersonal Contexts," 57 J. Pers. & Soc. Psychol. 426 (1989), 212

**Loewenstein, George , Samuel Issacharoff, Colin Camerer, & Linda Babcock, "Self-Serving Assessments of Fairness and Pretrial Bargaining," 22 J. Legal Stud. 135 (1993), 95,** 102, 109, 327

**Lubet, Steven, "Notes on the Bedouin Horse Trade or 'Why Won't the Market Clear, Daddy?' " 74 Tex. L. Rev. 1039 (1996), 205**

Luce, R. Duncan, & Howard Raiffa, *Games and Decisions: Introduction and Critical Survey* (1957), 232

Maccoby, Eleanor Emmons, & Carol Nagy Jacklin, *The Psychology of Sex Differences* (1974), 261

Martin, Judith, *Miss Manners Guide to Excruciatingly Correct Behavior* (1982), 195

Matz, David E., "Mediator Pressure and Party Autonomy: Are They Consistent with Each Other?" 10 Negotiation J. 359 (1994), 374

McCarthy, William, "The Role of Power and Principle in Getting to Yes," 1 Negotiation J. 59 (1985), 241

**Menkel-Meadow, Carrie, "Toward Another View of Legal Negotiation: The Structure of Problem-Solving," 31 UCLA L. Rev. 754 (1984), 17**

Merrifield, Leroy S., et al., *Labor Relations Law* (9th ed. 1994), 405

Mikula, Gerold, ed., *Justice and Social Interaction: Experimental and Theoretical Contributions from Psychological Research* (1980), 213

Miller, Geoffrey P., "Some Agency Problems in Settlement," 16 J. Legal Stud. 189 (1987), 321

Mnookin, Robert H., et al., *Beyond Winning, Negotiating to Create Value in Deals and Disputes* (2000), 139

**Mnookin, Robert H., "Why Negotiations Fail: An Exploration of Barriers to the Resolution of Conflict," 8 Ohio St. J. Disp. Res. 235 (1993), 26**

**Mnookin, Robert H., Scott R. Peppet, & Andrew S. Tulumello, "The Tension Between Empathy and Assertiveness," 12 Negotiation J. 217 (1996), 250**

**Moore, Christopher W., "The Caucus: Private Meetings That Promote Settlement," 16 Mediation Q. 87 (1987), 365**

Murnighan, J. Keith, *Bargaining Games* (1992), 207, 208

Nadler, Janice, "Distributing Adventitious Resources: The Effects of Relationship and Grouping," 12 Soc. Justice Res. 133 (1999), 212

Nesse, Randolph M., ed., *Evolution and the Capacity for Commitment* (2001), 169

Note, "Boulwareism: Legality and Effect," 76 Harv. L. Rev. 807 (1963), 194

Ochs, Jack, & Alvin E. Roth, "An Experimental Study of Sequential Bargaining," 79 Am. Econ. Rev. 335 (1989), 183

O'Connor, Kathleen M., & Peter J. Carnevale, "A Nasty but Effective Negotiation Strategy: Misrepresentation of a Common-Value Issue," 23 Personality & Soc. Psychology Bull. 504 (1997), 238

Parks, McLean, et al., "Distributing Adventitious Outcomes: Social Norms, Egocentric Martyrs, and the Effects of Future Relationships," 67 Org. Behav. & Human Decision Proc. 181 (1996), 212

Perry, Linda A.M., et al., eds., *Constructing and Reconstructing Gender* (1992), 270

Peters, Geoffrey, "The Use of Lies in Negotiation," 48 Ohio St. L.J. 1 (1987), 415

Pinkley, Robin L., et al., "The Impact of Alternatives to Settlement in Dyadic Negotiation," 57 Org. Behav. & Human Decision Proc. 97 (1994), 153

Polzer, Jeffrey T., et al., "The Effects of Relationship and Justification in an Interdependent Allocation," 2 Group Decision & Negotiation 135 (1993), 212

Priest, George, & Benjamin Klein, "The Selection of Disputes for Litigation," 13 J. Legal Stud. 1 (1984), 101

**Rachlinski, Jeffrey J., "Gains, Losses, and the Psychology of Litigation," 70 S. Cal. L. Rev. 113 (1996), 69**

Raiffa, Howard, *The Art and Science of Negotiation* (1982), 184, 192

——, "Post-Settlement Settlements," 1 Negotiation J. 9 (1985), 141

**Restatement (Second) of Agency, Section 348 (1958), 378**

Restatement (Second) of Contracts, Section 153 (1981), 395

Restatement (Second) of Contracts, Section 154 (1981), 395

Restatement (Second) of Contracts, Section 161 (1981), 394

**Restatement (Second) of Contracts, Section 164 (1981), 378,** 398

**Restatement (Second) of Torts, Section 525 (1977), 377,** 381, 398

Restatement (Second) of Torts, Section 526 (1977), 399

Restatement (Second) of Torts, Section 539 (1977), 383

Restatement (Second) of Torts, Section 542, cmt. e (1977), 381

Restatement (Second) of Torts, Section 549 (1977), 399

Restatement (Second) of Torts, Section 551 (1977), 394

Restatement (Second) of Torts, Section 552 (1977), 399

Restatement (Second) of Torts, Section 552C (1977), 399

Rhode, Deborah L., "Missing Questions: Feminist Perspectives on Legal Education," 45 Stan. L. Rev. 1547 (1993), 259

**Riskin, Leonard L., "Understanding Mediators' Orientations, Strategies, and Techniques: A Grid for the Perplexed," 1 Harv. Negotiation L. Rev. 7 (1996), 357**

Rose, Carol, "Bargaining and Gender," 18 Harv. J.L. & Pub. Poly. 547 (1995), 266, 267

**Ross, Lee, "Reactive Devaluation in Negotiation and Conflict Resolution," in *Barriers to Conflict Resolution* (Kenneth J. Arrow, et al., eds., 1995), 103**

Ross, Lee, & Andrew Ward, "Psychological Barriers to Dispute Resolution," 27 Advances Experimental Soc. Psychol. 255 (1995), 232

Rubin, Jeffrey Z., & Frank E.A. Sander, "Culture, Negotiation, and the Eye of the Beholder," 7 Negotiation J. 249 (1991), 271

Rubin, Michael H., "The Ethics of Negotiation: Are There Any?" 56 La. L. Rev. 447 (1995), 414


Salacuse, Jeswald W., **"Making Deals in Strange Places: A Beginner's Guide to International Business Negotiations,"** 4 Negotiation J. 5 (1988), 279
———, "Ten Ways That Culture Affects Negotiating Style: Some Survey Results," 14 Negotiation J. 221 (1998), 289
Schelling, Thomas, *The Strategy of Conflict* (1960), **165,** 195, 325
Schneider, Andrea Kupfer, "Perceptions, Reputation and Reality: An Empirical Study of Negotiation Styles," 6 Disp. Res. Mag. 24 (Summer 2000), 249
Schwinger, Thomas, "Just Allocations of Good: Decisions Among Three Princi-ples," in *Justice and Social Interaction: Experimental and Theoretical Contributions from Psychological Research* (Gerold Mikula, ed., 1980), 213
Shell, G. Richard, *Bargaining for Advantage: Negotiation Strategies for Reasonable People* (1999), **58,** 209
———, "Opportunism and Trust in the Negotiation of Commercial Contracts: Toward a New Cause of Action," 44 Vand. L. Rev. 221 (1991), 403
———, "Substituting Ethical Standards for Common Law Rules in Commercial Cases: An Emerging Statutory Trend," 82 Nw. U.L. Rev. 1198 (1988), 398
Sherman, Edward F., "From 'Loser Pays' to Modified Offer of Judgment Rules: Reconciling Incentives to Settle with Access to Justice," 76 Tex. L. Rev. 1863 (1998), 320
Simon, William H., "Ethical Discretion in Lawyering," 101 Harv. L. Rev. 1083 (1988), 323
Starr, V. Hale, "The Simple Math of Negotiating," 22 Trial Law. 5 (Jan.-Feb. 1999), 192
Sternberg, Robert J., & Diane M. Dobson, "Resolving Interpersonal Conflicts: An Analysis of Stylistic Consistency," 52 Pers. & Soc. Psychol. 794 (1987), 250
Sternberg, Robert J., & Lawrence J. Soriano, "Styles of Conflict Resolution," 47 J. Pers. & Soc. Psychol. 115 (1984), 254
Stiver, Irene P., "Work Inhibitions in Women 2," Paper published by the Stone Center for Developmental Services and Studies, Work in Progress Series (1983), 259
Strudler, Alan, "Incommensurable Goods, Rightful Lies, and the Wrongness of Fraud," 146 U. Pa. L. Rev. 1529 (1998), 389


Thaler, Richard H., "Anomalies: The Ultimatum Game," 2 J. Econ. Persp. 195 (1988), 183
Thomas, Kenneth, "Conflict and Conflict Management," in *Handbook of Industrial and Organizational Psychology* (Melvin D. Dunnette, ed., 1976), 254
Thomas, Kenneth W., & Ralph H. Kilmann, *Thomas-Kilmann Conflict Mode Instru-ment* (1974), 253
Thompson, Leigh L., et al., "Some Like It Hot: The Case for the Emotional Ne-gotiator," in *Shared Cognition in Organizations: The Management of Knowledge* (1999), 180
Thomspon, Leigh, & Reid Hastie, "Social Perception in Negotiation," 47 Org. Beh. & Human Dec. Processes 98 (1990), 133

Tversky, Amos, & Daniel Kahneman, "Advances in Prospect Theory: Cumulative Representation of Uncertainty," 5 J. Risk & Uncertainty 297 (1992), 75

Ury, William, *Getting Past No: Negotiating Your Way From Confrontation to Cooperation* (1993), 171

van Dijk, Eric, & Daan van Knippenberg, "Buying and Selling Exchange Goods: Loss Aversion and the Endowment Effect," 17 J. Econ. Psych. 517 (1996), 85

Watkins, Normal J., "Negotiating the Complex Case," 41 For the Defense 36 (July 1999), 192

**Wetlaufer, Gerald B., "The Ethics of Lying in Negotiation," 76 Iowa L. Rev. 1219 (1990), 233, 409**

―――, **"The Limits of Integrative Bargaining," 85 Geo. L.J. 369 (1996), 121, 142, 241**

White, James J., "Essay Review: The Pros and Cons of Getting to Yes," 34 J. Legal Educ. 115 (1984), 208, 209

―――, **"Machiavelli and the Bar: Ethical Limitations on Lying in Negotiation," 1980 Am. Bar Found. Res. J. 926 (1980), 405**

**Williams, Gerald R., *Legal Negotiation and Settlement* (1983), 244**

# INDEX